IBM® Cognos® TM1
The Official Guide

Karsten Oehler
Jochen Gruenes
Christopher Ilacqua

New York   Chicago   San Francisco
Lisbon   London   Madrid   Mexico City
Milan   New Delhi   San Juan
Seoul   Singapore   Sydney   Toronto

The **McGraw·Hill** Companies

Cataloging-in-Publication Data is on file with the Library of Congress

McGraw-Hill books are available at special quantity discounts to use as premiums and sales promotions, or for use in corporate training programs. To contact a representative, please e-mail us at bulksales@mcgraw-hill.com.

IBM® Cognos® TM1: The Official Guide

1234567890   DOC DOC   1098765432

ISBN   978-0-07-176569-5
MHID   0-07-176569-7

Sponsoring Editor Wendy Rinaldi	**Technical Editor** David Corbett	**Production Supervisor** James Kussow
Editorial Supervisor Patty Mon	**Copy Editor** Margaret Berson	**Composition** Cenveo Publisher Services
Project Editor Madhu Bhardwaj	**Proofreader** Paul Tyler	**Illustration** Cenveo Publisher Services
Acquisitions Coordinator Joya Anthony	**Indexer** Jack Lewis	**Art Director, Cover** Jeff Weeks

The book is dedicated to the millions of business analysts world wide who are tirelessly seeking to improve their organizations' performance. We hope this book provides an additional tool and best practices to help you meet your goals.

About the Authors

Dr. Karsten Oehler is head of the Performance Management Client Technical Professionals (CTP) with IBM Deutschland GmbH, Frankfurt. Prior to joining IBM, he spent more than 15 years with several international companies (Hyperion, Oracle, SAP, and INFOR) as a product manager, marketing executive, and consultant for financial accounting and business intelligence software. He was project leader for many performance management implementations with large international companies.

He has published four books on IT systems for financial applications and OLAP, as well as 130 articles on software systems for managerial accounting. He earned his doctorate from the University of Frankfurt, Germany, with a thesis about modeling flexible costing based on a multidimensional accounting system.

He is a frequent speaker at conferences and seminars. He teaches at the European Business School in Östrich-Winkel, Germany, and at the Technische Universität Darmstadt, Germany.

Jochen Gruenes worked with Cognos TM1 for over ten years as a technical sales consultant. He started this role at Applix, where he was responsible for presales, consulting, and training in Germany, Austria, Switzerland, and Eastern Europe. He went along with Cognos TM1 through the acquisitions by Cognos and IBM. He led the German competence center for Cognos TM1 within the technical sales organization for IBM Deutschland GmbH until October 2011. He has conducted several projects and workshops on the enhanced uses of TM1. As a technical sales consultant Jochen has developed several solution prototypes to prove the power of Cognos TM1 in a departmental environment.

Dr. Christopher Ilacqua is an experienced Cognos TM1 practitioner with more than 20 years' experience working with TM1 as a customer, OEM Manager, and Director of Product Management and Marketing, helping global organizations who are seeking to improve their planning, forecasting, and analysis solutions. Currently Chris is an Adjunct Faculty Professor at New England College of Business and Finance, where he instructs undergraduate and graduate students in marketing, management, strategic planning, and leadership.

About the Technical Editor

David Corbett is a Senior Product Manager with IBM and has worked with TM1 as a product manager for eight years. He has been fortunate to work together with a passionate TM1 community to evolve this technology from a departmental budgeting solution to its current capacity to serve global enterprises with performance management solutions. David has 25 years of enterprise product experience, including product management positions at McCormack & Dodge, Elcom, and Workscape.

Contents at a Glance

Contents

Foreword

When the authors of this guide kindly asked me to write a foreword to this book, I saw a great opportunity to thank all those who over the years have used and supported TM1. When I decided to embark on this venture back in 1983, I thought the concepts and features of TM1 would be obvious to all and that its success would be fast and furious, almost explosive, and that my main concern was going to be fending off competitors who, along with users, would flock to the idea. Although I was right about what TM1 can do for users and organizations, to this day I marvel at how wrong I was about the speed with which it has been adopted. For this reason, I owe a great debt of gratitude to those few who shared my vision in the first years of the TM1 saga.

After much reflection, I have come to ascribe the hurdle that kept many users away—but fortunately also kept most competitors away—to the fact that TM1 uses a different data model. This model is fundamentally different from the relational database model, which nowadays is the foundation of most information processing. TM1's functional data model does not pretend to supplant the relational database model, but rather to complement it. It has a different paradigm that makes it easy for managers to do business modeling and analysis. Users are able to easily interact and experiment in the same way they do with spreadsheets. It is fundamental to the success of analytic solutions for users to be able to develop their own business models that incorporate their experience and knowledge of the business; models they can understand and trust and on the basis of which they can gain better and more accurate insights into the future, and make more profitable decisions.

Analytics and the Functional Model

Enterprises, like all living organisms, must be aware of and adapt to their environment in order to survive and thrive. Their behavior starts with a planning process that assesses the current business climate and attempts to predict its future evolution. This involves an understanding of the enterprise's markets and customers, the competition, government regulations, technology, the economy, and so on.

Once the plan, or intended course of action, is established, the enterprise proceeds to execute the plan. As it does so, it periodically compares its actual performance vis-à-vis the plan, and adjusts its behavior or the plan accordingly.

The process is effectively a feedback control loop—plan the work, work the plan, measure the results—as shown in the following illustration:

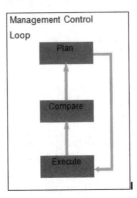

Efforts to automate these processes, mechanically or electronically, predate the invention of the modern computer. But thanks to the exponential growth of computer speed and capacity, as well as the much slower but still significant development of data management software, the automation of analytics now plays a central role in making management control loops more efficient and effective.

Analytics has two distinct, though tightly integrated, aspects: *retrospective* and *prospective*. Retrospective analytics looks at the past and compares actual results to plans and projections. Prospective analytics looks to the future and is the area where the modeling and interactive capabilities of TM1 and the functional model make the biggest difference. Prospective analytics is also the area of the most strategic importance to the enterprise.

The importance of analytics to the success of an enterprise is now generally considered vital. While the management control loop is the nervous system of the enterprise, analytics is its brain, and prospective analytics its frontal lobe. The speed, accuracy, and effectiveness of analytics can make the difference between success and failure. Effective analytics makes the enterprise smarter.

Other Requirements of the Functional Model

In addition to implementing the functional model, a functional database server must satisfy a number of qualitative requirements if it is going to succeed as a sound foundation for analytics.

- **Speed and scalability**   Functional servers must deliver close to real-time response. Users must be able to change assumptions and see the results immediately. Servers must be able to accommodate large models and use memory efficiently, particularly for sparse data. And servers must scale to large numbers of users doing updates or queries.

- **Simplicity**   Users must be able, on their own, to easily incorporate their domain experience and knowledge of the business into the models. Users must be able to understand and have confidence in how the model works. User understanding and confidence are key to success. Models should also be easy to document, cross-reference, and maintain.

- **Flexibility**   Models must be adaptable to changing business needs. The server should accept structural changes dynamically. Models need to grow organically within centers of knowledge, and then interconnect. Users should be able to have a private sandbox in which to experiment, and then synchronize with the public model. The modeling language must have rich built-in functions, and be expandable to express multiple business needs.

- **Openness**   Functional servers should interface easily with relational servers and provide facilities for import, export, and transparent drill-through. To further facilitate ad-hoc analyses, there should be an easy-to-use live interface to electronic spreadsheets. Servers should also interface to resources that manage metadata and security globally across multiple relational and functional servers.

These concepts continue to drive the innovation of IBM Cognos TM1 as we seek to solve the ever-expanding business requirements in the marketplace.

This book provides an excellent resource for people who have just started out on their journey with TM1, as well as providing excellent insights for long-time customers who are seeking to apply TM1 to new solutions. As I mentioned earlier, I am humbled by the speed at which TM1 has been adopted globally and I thank you all for your continued support of TM1, which continues to drive TM1's innovation. Also, I invite you to listen to an interview that is available (http://www.youtube.com/watch?v=VYt8cNv8lJw) that will continue our conversation on TM1.

All the Best,

Manny Perez

Acknowledgments

First of all, without Manny Perez's vision and ability to implement this unique solution, we could not have written this book. Thanks to Manny for his continuous ambition to improve multidimensional modeling.

We would like to thank our IBM Business Analytics colleagues in Germany and the United States. The business concepts described in the third part of the book in particular are the results of discussions with customers, partners, and colleagues. For these intensive discussions, we want to thank specifically Sonja Pressel and Michael Kurc from the IBM German sales organization (group performance management), Christoph Papenfuss from IBM BA international marketing (rolling forecast), Frank Hofmann from Staedler and Frank Hendricks from our partner Serwise (risk management), Christian Wagner from the German technical sales team (production), Jan-Philip Menke who joined the IBM German technical sales team some months ago (sales analysis), and Jens Schuette from the German IBM GBS organization (costing). From the U.S. offices, a special thanks to our product team members: Dave Corbett, our technical editor, who spent countless hours helping us refine our chapters, as well as Trevor MacPherson, Tom Baldwin, Clint Parker, and Rickard Rygin for their help with the latest capabilities in TM1 10.1 and extending Cognos TM1 with Business Insight.

To find an excellent publisher is not easy. Therefore we would like to thank Susan Visser from IBM, who found the best possible publisher.

A special thanks to the professional team of McGraw-Hill: Wendy Rinaldi, the editorial director, and Patty Mon, Joya Anthony, and Madhu Bhardwaj for outstanding support and for their patience with German authors who are deeply involved in consulting obligations and hence missed many deadlines.

And finally, thanks to our families: Eva-Maria, Annika, and Sarah Oehler; Pat, David, and Nora Ilacqua; and Sebastian, Julia, and Kirsten Grünes.

Preface

L et us say it enthusiastically: Cognos TM1 is fantastic. We can't stress this enough. After writing this book, we are even more convinced than before. Although all of the authors have worked with or are now working with IBM, we also have years of experience with other products, so we are qualified to assess the true value of Cognos TM1. All of the competitive tools have their strengths, but Cognos TM1 is unique in its approach to implementation. Cognos TM1's strength is a simple but ingenious concept: Store all multidimensional data in memory and let everything calculate on the fly using aggregation and the rules language. It is one of the concepts that can really change the way businesspeople work with computers. Cognos TM1 is very close to the way management accountants see the world.

It started 25 years ago with the revolutionary idea that forecasting, planning, and analysis constitute a cohesive process that cannot be separated, and this process is highly interactive: Calculation in memory was very limited because of limitations on memory itself. But to provide real-time results, in-memory calculation is the only possible way to create powerful simulations. The most interesting thing is that over the years, the concepts haven't changed. The rules language remains pretty much the same. But scalability and performance have been constantly improved to address bigger and more distributed challenges. Many functions have been added in the last 25 years, and the scope of Cognos TM1 has changed dramatically. But the core concepts are still at the heart of the solution. This is a good sign that the product has a sound basis.

Why We Wrote This Book

It is not surprising that in 25 years, best practices and fantastic ideas of how to use Cognos TM1 have evolved. For many business problems, excellent solutions already exist. We participated in this development process and learned from experienced people. But knowledge about Cognos has been like a patchwork. Only a few sites and communities exist, and most experience has been gained by intuition and trial and error. Every novice has to go the hard way and build solid knowledge from various more or less trustworthy sources. It often takes years to become an expert. We have felt this ourselves: to train our colleagues in the secrets of Cognos TM1 takes time and effort.

Our intention is to increase the speed of the diffusion of Cognos TM1 into the business world. For this, of course, marketing is necessary, but good and comprehensive knowledge is more important. So we want to provide everything that is necessary to work with Cognos TM1 effectively, or at least what we think is necessary to work with it.

The obvious question is: why hasn't there been a book about Cognos TM1 before now? Perhaps Cognos TM1 has been a tool for insiders. You definitely need critical mass for a book project. However, with Cognos TM1 becoming part of the IBM software family, the time is right: the first comprehensive book is now available.

Who This Book Is For

Who should read this book? Everybody who is interested in increasing their company's performance can profit from it. External and internal consultants in particular will find a broad range of solutions.

Do you already work with Cognos TM1? Do you want to improve your existing applications? You can find lots of practical tips and tricks for projects and your daily work in this book. If you are a consultant, you can find ideas to improve your service offerings. Are you an implementer or a so-called end user? Although we provide concrete implementation advice, our conceptual proposals help users to understand better what is possible with Cognos TM1. This facilitates the communication between the user and the developers.

Perhaps you plan to use Cognos TM1, or are you simply interested in the core concepts of Cognos TM1? You can see what is possible with a modern multidimensional solution.

This Book Will Help You...

Why should you read this book? We are convinced that you will find what you are searching for:

- A better understanding of how Cognos TM1 works internally
- Techniques for applying Cognos TM1 to the most difficult performance management problems
- A better understanding of the Cognos TM1 tools (including the new ones)
- A better understanding of how to model with Cognos TM1

Although this book has a limited academic orientation, we hope we provide a sufficient explanation of the business background that is necessary to implement the solutions.

We structured this book in three parts. The first part gives an introductory overview of Cognos TM1. What are the typical problems and how can Cognos TM1 address these? You can learn how other companies profited from using Cognos TM1. All tools available for use with Cognos TM1 are briefly introduced.

If you want to get a better understanding of how Cognos TM1 works and how to use the tools, a technical deep dive in the second part of the book provides the necessary insights. For performance optimization, a sound understanding of how Cognos TM1 works internally is necessary. All core concepts are explained in detail.

The last part of the book covers the business solutions. The business requirements drive everything. The best tool can't help if you don't understand the business background. We will provide the business background and small, easy-to-understand models. These techniques should help you to solve typical business challenges and can become the foundation of your own solution. We try to span a wide area to cover the intelligent usage of Cognos TM1.

PART

I

Introduction

Challenges to Meeting Enterprise Performance Management Requirements

The goal of this chapter is to highlight the increased demands on planning, analysis, and performance management processes in organizations. In today's highly volatile business environment, organizations demand more accurate plans, forecasts, and analysis to meet and exceed market demands. These demands range from increased market pressures, investment demands, profitability, strategy validation, and regulatory requirements for decision transparency. These increased demands require a fusion of planning and analysis capabilities at every level of decision making across an organization to create a more agile organization to meet these diverse requirements. Over time we have seen how markets respond to corporations that fail to meet stockholder expectation with decreased market capitalization. This chapter will focus on the effects of these forces on the following:

- Increased forecasting and budget cycles
- Rise of scenario analytics
- Heightened Enterprise Resource Planning (ERP) requirements
- Rising demands on data warehouses

Increased Forecasting and Budget Cycles

Let's start our review with causes of increased forecasting and budget cycles. There are a host of common problems that plague organizations. These problems include

- Long planning cycles
- Disconnected operational and financial plans
- Spreadsheet-based plans

- Lack of ownership and accountability
- Lack of control, transparency, and governance

Let's take a look at some of these key challenges in more detail.

Long Planning Cycles

The increased volatility and collection of data planning, budgeting, and forecasting cycles need to be in sync with business cycles in order to reflect current business assumptions. Before we begin, let's review a number of key definitions:

- **Strategic plan**   A disciplined effort to define fundamental decisions and actions that shape and guide an organization's future, addressing what the organization is, what it does, and why it does it

- **Budget/ annual operating plan**   Projection of revenues, expenses, and cash for a specified period of time (first year of SP). Identifies targets, at the line of business, functional, or cost center level

- **Forecast**   A period-by-period projection of either revenue or expense that considers actuals to date and any changes to market conditions

- **Modeling**   Process of developing models that characterize an organization, allowing it to evaluate the impact of decisions so as to fully understand the financial impact

- **Reporting**   Collection, analysis, summarization, and presentation of the financial performance of the business

Table 1-1 specifies the primary use, frequency, and key participants for each of these key terms.

Now that we have key terms defined, let's turn our attention to an example of a planning process. As noted in Figure 1-1, in this example the budgeting, planning, and forecasting processes typically require the collaboration of at least four management layers, which include corporate finance, business unit leaders, line of business leaders, and finally cost center managers. Each of these planning groups has different levels of data and analysis requirements to render an accurate plan for their areas of responsibility. This requires a highly coordinated process for the target definition through distribution, aggregations of plans, variance analysis, and revisions.

This process is further complicated by an increasing number of people in the planning process and pressure to recast assumptions based on changing business conditions. The notion of a quarterly plan no longer meets business requirements.

Disconnected Operational and Financial Plans

Companies that roll out plans from the top down in the organization will not only have a limited view but will also suffer from lack of commitment and buy-in from many or all levels, which will drive a disconnection between management and contributors. As noted in the simple case shown in Figure 1-2, disconnected planning processes will send inaccurate

Key Term	Primary Use	Frequency	Who Is Involved?
Strategic plan	Define vision, strengths, weaknesses, opportunities, and threat (SWOT), high-level corporate goals, and objectives and strategies for how to attain them	Horizon: 3 to 5 years, sometimes 10 Frequency: Once per year	• Corporate executives • Senior management • Strategy • Finance Department
Budget/annual operating plan	Financial guide for the current year: Control expenses, evaluate performance, and determine bonus compensation	Horizon: One year, across months, quarters, weeks Frequency: Once per year/Infrequently updated	• Corporate planning • Line of Business managers • Cost Center managers
Forecast	Provides the most current estimates for the balance of the year/horizon	Horizon: Balance of the year or rolling week, month, quarter, annual. Frequency: Refreshed often	• Corporate planning • Line of Business managers
Modeling	• What if analysis • Acquisition modeling • Scenario analysis • Define contingency plans	Ad hoc	• Corporate planning • Strategy • Sales/HR/IT
Reporting	• Comparison with actual • Cause and effect analysis	Horizon: Various Frequency: Monthly, Qtrly, Annual, Ad hoc	• Corporate planning • Reviewed at all levels

TABLE 1-1   Key Terms

demand signals across the organization. For example, a corporate planning process cannot be accurate without answers to the following questions:

- What are the pipeline revenue forecasts?
- What are the expense demand signals?
- What are the planned capital expenditures to drive both current and strategic plans?
- Based on pipeline projects, what are the demand signals for employee hiring?

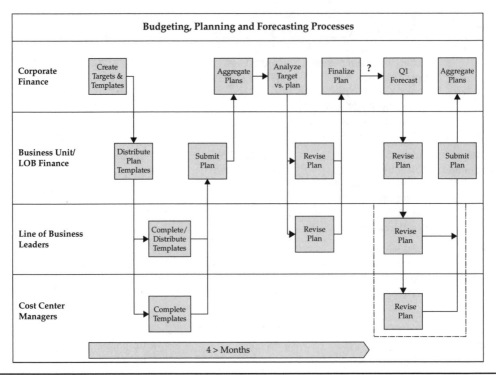

FIGURE 1-1   Planning cycle example

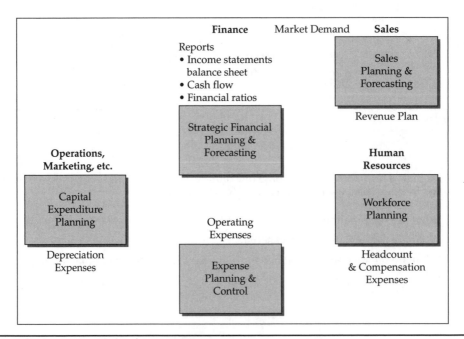

FIGURE 1-2   Disconnected planning processes

These simple questions highlight the interrelationship of cross-departmental planning processes and the critical importance of connecting these processes for better decision making.

Companies don't often have the complete picture of the impact of business drivers, the key metrics that steer their expenses and profits. These drivers, which are often interdependent and yet changeable given market realities, are buried in hundreds of spreadsheets and disparate databases spread throughout business functions. As a result, companies cannot command a single version of the truth and are hard pressed to produce reliable forecasts and plans, thus hindering growth and profitability.

If the annual planning process takes several months to complete—with time dedicated to reconciliation and reworking—it has long since been disconnected from the cycle that optimal performance requires. Similarly, by not forecasting frequently or as needed, a company cannot fully and expediently understand the demand for operating cash and thus make necessary reallocations of resources.

Companies should seek to avoid disconnected planning processes where divisional or departmental objectives, goals, and targets do not align with those of finance. Such fragmented processes create silos that do not take departmental interdependencies into account. Additionally, plans for revenue, expenses, and capital expenses are often insular. Roll-ups to the profit and loss, cash flow, and balance sheet projections can therefore be slow and error-prone. This fragmentation leads to tedious reconciliation and reworking that drain productivity and hinder crucial, timely analysis.

Spreadsheet-Based Plans

Many companies carry out planning with spreadsheets that supplement inflexible planning systems or have gone to pure spreadsheet solutions for their annual budget and planning processes, which creates inaccuracies and miscommunication. Although spreadsheets are an excellent personal productivity tool, they are inherently unable to offer the control, security, and structured collaboration approach that enterprises require. Worse still, the manual overhead required in using spreadsheets lengthens the planning process.

Not only are spreadsheets prone to data errors, but they also cannot handle the complex processes of business modeling, the aligning of data definitions, business assumptions, and financial and operations targets, and the complex business analytics required today, such as product or customer profitability. They also lack collaborative features such as workflow, metadata management, and version control for interdepartmental planning processes.

In a volatile business climate, there is often no time to schedule scarce IT resources or explain evolving requirements. Users with varying software backgrounds, such as marketers or facility managers, want the applications they touch frequently for all aspects of the planning cycle to be easy to use and change. They want a measure of control without having to become programmers themselves. Moreover, when they cannot share spreadsheets and files easily with team members, their work will become isolated.

Lack of Ownership and Accountability

Most planning processes start from a "top down" approach from finance that imposes goals and targets without proper input from all lines of business. Worst of all, these plans do not have current actual information to provide context for planning decision processes.

Without bidirectional value from all stakeholders in the planning process, which fosters a collaborative process between both upper and lower layers of management, ownership and accountability will be elusive.

Lack of Control, Transparency, and Governance

One major concern today as organizations seek to increase their planning cycles and expand their reach in organizations is lack of control, transparency, and governance. Planning and forecasting processes require a number of different source systems to create a baseline forecast for planners. For many companies, critical data, from internal financial and operational sources and from external systems such as vendors and benchmarks (external marketing reports), usually resides in numerous systems, in an array of dissimilar formats. In a typically ungoverned fashion, employees piece together data from the various systems and then analyze and report on it differently, which leads to conflicting data definitions and views of the company's performance. These errors are then compounded when used as a baseline for a planning process. Without a strategy to centrally define and manage the data that provides critical information to planning and forecasting, processes cannot accurately model cross–business-function activity, much less access the critical data. Moreover, resources are engaged in redundant, expensive work.

A second area of concern is transparency and governance surrounding the planning process itself. Unlike actual data, which requires a snapshot of the transaction at a point in time, plans and forecasts evolve and mature over time as assumptions and business requirements change. Creating an audit trail of some of the following key data points surrounding the planning submission is not only challenging but extremely time-consuming for the finance department. These questions include:

- How mature is the current plan?
- When was a plan submitted?
- Who changed or reworked specific areas, and when?
- Who approved the plan and when?
- What was the "soft" data or rationalization for key decisions?
- Are there certain submissions that need to be re-forecasted, or is a new planning process required?

Most organizations lose this key information during re-forecasting after an initial planning cycle and are required to start all over again, increasing the cycle time.

Rise of Scenario Analytics

Now let's turn our attention to increased business requirements for analysis. As mentioned earlier, given the rise of uncertainty and volatility in organizational assumptions and business models, there is an increased requirement for scenario analytics to manage this uncertainty. Scenario analytics is the ability to evaluate several outcomes of a potential strategy before making a final decision. Scenario analytics provides the ability to:

- Explore and test "what if" scenarios
- Reduce risk and create contingency plans

- Formulate growth strategies
- Best responses to economic change, a competitor move and marketing
- Profitability analysis to optimize price, channel, and marketing strategy

Let's take a look at each of these key areas in more detail.

Explore and Test "What If" Scenarios

As organizations struggle to meet the demands of a highly volatile business environment, the ability to explore and test "what if" scenarios becomes critical in order to validate strategy assumptions and tactics. Let's first define what is meant by "what if" scenarios. According to BusinessDictionary.com, a common definition of "what if" scenarios or "goal seeking" is the ability to test key quantitative assumptions and computations (underlying a decision, estimate, or project) by changing them systematically to assess their effect on the final outcome. According to Porter's Five Forces Model defined by Michael E. Porter of Harvard Business School in 1979, there are five main forces that drive not only an organization's strategy and tactics but also assumptions and decision making. These include the following:

1. The threat of the entry of new competitors
2. The intensity of competitive rivalry
3. The threat of substitute products or services
4. The bargaining power of customers
5. The bargaining power of suppliers

Each of these forces as noted in Figure 1-3 drives decision making across finance and operations.

These forces drive key questions that impact organizational performance. Some examples include:

- What if the economy slows?
- What if inflation rises?
- What if taxes increase or exchange rates change?
- What if supplier increases prices?
- What if a competitor makes an acquisition?
- What if governmental regulations change?
- What if ......?

These examples are only a small sample of business environmental changes that can impact the financial performance of a business and require an analysis process that allows individuals in each business department (Finance, Marketing, Production and Distribution, Customer Service, IT, Sales and Purchasing) to generate best- and worst-case scenarios.

Now let's turn our attention to an additional requirement of scenario analytics: risk management.

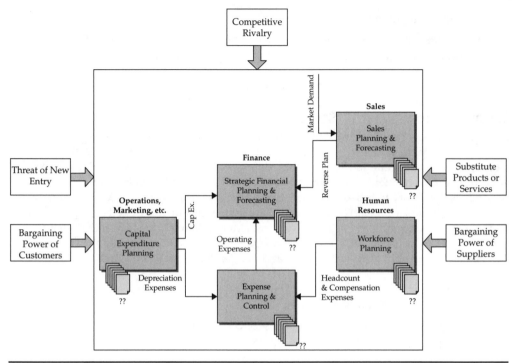

FIGURE 1-3   Forces driving what if scenarios

Reduce Risk and Create Contingency Plans

Finance executives are under increasing pressure from governments and business units to improve the quality and speed of risk reporting, insight, and decision making. They need to reduce risk exposures and losses, while anticipating the next big area of concern and opportunity. In order to fulfill this mandate, these areas require the ability to perform scenario analysis that synthesizes disparate data into an integrated, enterprise-wide view of risk across divisions, geographic locations, and risk classes. A common definition of risk management is systematic methods for estimating, assessing, and projecting risk associated with investments and business practices. These systematic methods frequently are founded on mathematical models known as drivers derived from historical data enhanced with statistical algorithms to provide an environment for testing outcomes. In areas like financial risk, models are expressed in logical relationships that enable simulation of scenarios and subsequent outcomes, including testing and consolidation of risk exposure.

Risk management has a heightened importance; the increasing complexity of products and correlation across asset classes has elevated the importance of risk analytics to an enterprise level. Four areas, in particular, have fostered evolution in these applications:

- Increased regulation
- Cross-border, cross-asset investment strategies

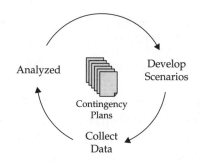

Figure 1-4   Reducing the risk process

- Interest-rate risk, long a primary factor in fixed-income analytics and valuations, once again painting a clear picture of its impact on credit markets
- Magnitude of risk, difficulty in valuation, and lack of transparency in over the counter (OTC) derivatives

Requirements for reducing risk and creating contingency plan as noted in Figure 1-4 include:

- **Collect Data**   Data collection is a critical component of the ability to create accurate scenarios and contingency plans. Data needs to be complete and accurate, and delivered in an automated way. Current business volatility is increasing the requirements for more frequent data updates to feed the ever-growing requirements of business models.
- **Analyze**   Analysis and definition of benchmarks to compare investment and/or financial performance against a designated standard that fits the firm's style. Variations from benchmarks provide insight into over- or under-performance, as well as risking exposure. This provides a proactive approach to identifying risk-to-reward trade-offs.
- **Develop Scenarios**   Scenario analysis enables the end user to test outcomes and estimate risk under various conditions. Scenarios can be derived from historical data and driver-based calculations or sophisticated statistical functions. The objective is to provide a test environment to garner insight into potential future outcomes and improve the firm's ability to manage risk.

Formulate Growth Strategies

An additional area that "what if" analysis supports is the ability to formulate growth strategies. Business growth goals are essential in any company's long-term planning process. Organizations pursue growth through mergers and acquisitions (inorganic growth), focused business development to drive sales (organic growth), or a combination of both. These strategies go beyond increasing local market share. They serve as a means to enter new markets and seek international growth. Whether a company seeks to evolve through organic or inorganic growth, an in-depth analysis and market research coupled with scenario analysis is required.

Let's start with the key areas of increased business development or organic growth. Organic growth can include the following scenarios that require quantitative validation:

- Increased market penetration, which includes strategies to sell more products to existing customers.
- Market development through selling current products to geographic regions.
- Evaluation of alternative channels, which involves having customers access your product in new ways. These can include online stores, new licensing terms, and so on.
- New product development for existing and new customers.
- Development of new products for new customers.

The second growth strategy is through acquisitions and mergers (see Figure 1-5). This approach can include the following:

- **Horizontal** This growth strategy would involve buying a competing business or businesses.
- **Backward** A backward integrative growth strategy would involve buying one of your suppliers as a way to better control your supply chain.
- **Forward** Acquisitions can also be focused on buying component companies that are part of your distribution chain, allowing better control over quality and costing of products.

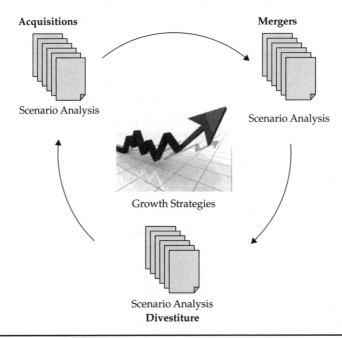

FIGURE 1-5 Formulating growth strategy process

Each of these strategies requires the definition of multiple scenarios that present best- and worst-case scenarios and their financial impact on an organization, which typically includes an impact analysis of the company's income, cash flow, and balance sheet statements.

Profitability Analysis

An additional key area that what if analysis supports is profitability analysis. As noted in a recent International Data Corporation (IDC) market forecast (March 2008), profitability management represents 20 percent of the total performance management software and services market and was named by customers as the single most important business capability in the recent BPM Partners survey. Profitability analysis is a relatively new cross-enterprise discipline that unlocks profit potential to drive performance. Once a reporting exercise driven by management and accounting, it is now being used to help all parts of a company gain the insight necessary to deploy limited resources in pursuit of the most profitable opportunities. Company departments and divisions, such as sales, marketing, operations, and engineering, can use profitability analysis to answer simple profit-focused questions in the context of their day-to-day strategic and tactical business decisions. Key questions include

- Who are my profitable customers?
- What are my profitable products or service lines?
- Which are my profitable sales channels?

Each of these questions involves a myriad of what if scenarios, as noted in Figure 1-6.

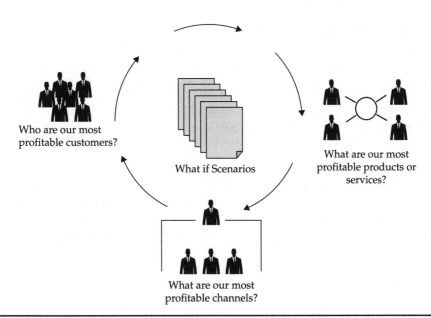

FIGURE 1-6   Profitability analysis process

With this evolution of profitability analysis, profitability itself has moved to the front lines of a business where employees are making "micro-optimization" business decisions. This transformational shift is compelling finance organizations to move beyond the complexity of costing to focus on an approach that helps their entire business. The requirement that finance become a better business partner underscores the importance of looking at profitability modeling and optimization through the eyes of the company (as opposed to looking at it through accounting and financial lenses only). Finance starts with a business decision that needs to be made and moves back through a number of activities and disciplines to get the source information needed to make the decisions.

Organizations are required to apply new business practices, tools, and automation to profitability analysis so that they can effectively:

- Assess the right profitability measures that optimize business performance.
- Move from a merely costing-oriented profitability reporting exercise to a forward-looking profitability modeling paradigm.
- Undertake profitability analysis for different dimensions of profitability (for example, customer, channel, product, and so on).
- Use statistical and advanced analytical techniques to predict profitability outcomes better and thereby work toward optimizing resource inputs.
- Tie profitability analysis to all other enterprise performance management processes such as planning, consolidation and control, strategy management, scorecarding, and more.

However, given the current economic times, there are a number of challenges preventing organizations from meeting these requirements.

Challenges with Profitability Analytics

Finance organizations have traditionally monitored profit, but in many organizations analysis is done using spreadsheet models, where it is difficult to handle the complex array of cost drivers that are required for effective profitability analysis and forecasting. In a study conducted by BPM Partners, profitability analysis and optimization was ranked as the top business capability requirement. One of the challenges to business analysts is that the data is not being captured, or if the data is captured, it is not available in a consumable structure for interaction with the analyst community within an organization. Additionally, this information may be spread across numerous applications within an organization without a centralized view of this information. The situation may be further exasperated by the collection of this information in a data warehouse that has denormalized the data to a point where it is no longer useful. For these reasons, profitability analysis is a manual process in most organizations where analysts rely on spreadsheets to gather transactional data from source systems into a cohesive view of information, providing a time-consuming and error-prone process.

Heightened ERP Requirements

Now let's turn our attention to the heightened Enterprise Resource Planning (ERP) requirements driven by increased business volatility and velocity of change. ERP systems have traditionally done an excellent job of capturing transactional information about a whole host of enterprise information that spans a host of departmental requirements, as noted in Figure 1-7.

An ERP solution set is a collection of loosely integrated prebuilt applications to meet the key requirements of Supply Chain Management (SCM), Finance Resource Management (FRM), Manufacturing Resource Planning (MRP), Customer Relationship Management (CRM), and Human Resource Management (HRM). Although organizations typically find it easy to accumulate data from their ERP system, it often remains unusable or unavailable to the decision makers who need it. Some of the barriers to better use of data include:

- **Cost**   Organizations often balk at the cost of strategic investments necessary to make data usable, such as master data management and tools for creating standardized reports, scorecards, and dashboards.

- **Ad hoc tools**   In the absence of automation, people create their own reporting and analysis tools, typically in Excel, which leads to various versions of the truth, different ways to interpret data, and lost productivity.

- **Static reports**   Reporting systems based on static reports are costly because they require report builders to continually create new customized report iterations in order to meet end users' evolving needs and preferences.

- **Silos of data**   In the absence of a structured way to use and analyze data, and without integration among data sources, employees get at best a limited view of their business, which severely limits their analytical and decision-making abilities.

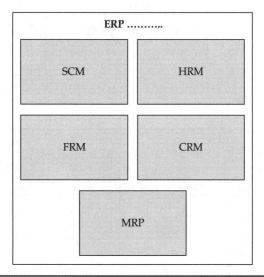

FIGURE 1-7   ERP applications

This problem is exasperated as global companies see growth through acquisitions and mergers where each acquired company has a different ERP system to integrate into the planning and analysis process, which requires a composite view of information across all business units, as noted in Figure 1-8.

To add to the complexity of different ERP systems with varying account structures and data definitions, organizations are knitting together a composite view of data between these systems with spreadsheets. These spreadsheet "shadow systems" shown in Figure 1-9 proliferate in organizations due to the inability of ERP systems to meet the broad range of planning and analysis requirements within an organization.

These spreadsheets play a valuable role within an organization by allowing individual users to combine disparate data sources to analyze, model, plan, and report. Unfortunately, although spreadsheets are an excellent individual personal productivity tool, their ability to create a collaborative planning and analysis environment that is governed by common data definition and business rules is problematic. Gaining a common view of information and translating that information into a fact-driven decision process that is actionable can be quite challenging. This has led to the implementation of a data warehouse strategy that is implemented to meet the needs of a specific ERP system and has its own challenges, which leads us to our next topic.

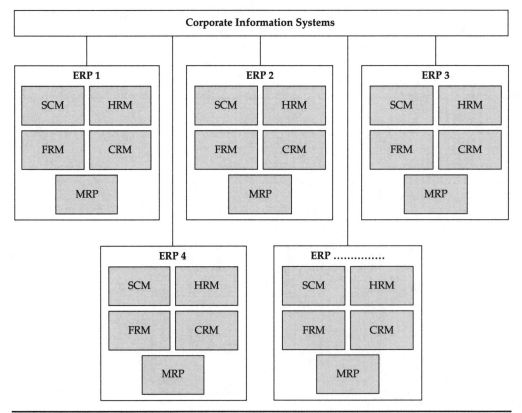

FIGURE 1-8 Heterogeneous ERP systems

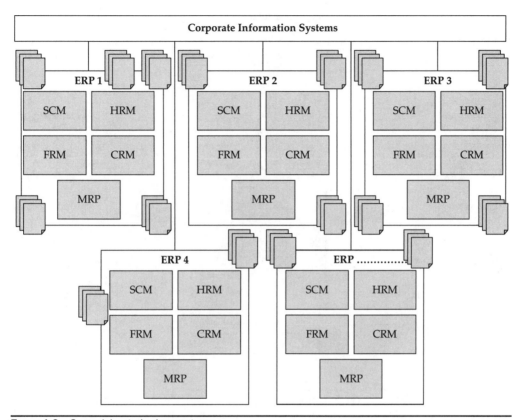

FIGURE 1-9   Spreadsheet shadow systems

Rising Demands on Data Warehouses

Data warehouse managers are under increased demands to meet the current business requirements. These range from the diversity of corporate systems through acquisitions and/or mergers, increased collection of internal data on customers and employees, as well as the increased demand to access and interact with this information in a way that business users can consume to drive analysis and planning processes with little or zero latency, as shown in Figure 1-10.

To solve the issue of data definition diversity within a single or multiple corporate ERP systems, the notion of a separate data store specifically designed for corporate reporting, analysis, and reporting has emerged in organizations. A *data warehouse* is a repository of data, which can provide most or all of the data and information requirements of an enterprise. This means that the data warehouse pulls data from all the production and other sources. Once the data is pulled onto an offline staging area, it is cleansed, transformed, and loaded in a sanitized, uniform, and well-organized manner so that you can run queries, reports, and all kind of analysis on the data.

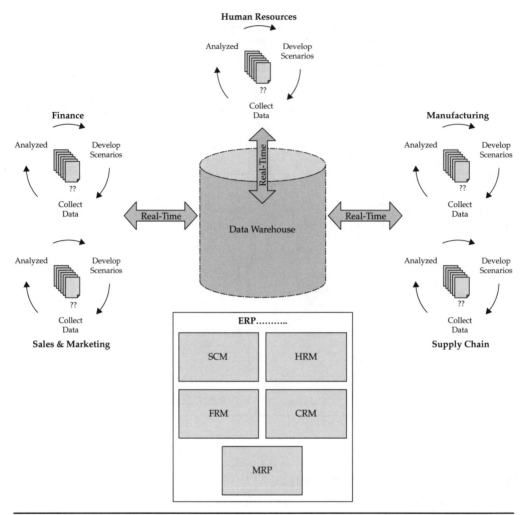

FIGURE 1-10 Increasing real-time demands on data warehouses

Data Warehouse Challenges

Data warehousing has traditionally focused on relational technology. While well suited to managing transactions and storing large amounts of data, relational databases are typically unable to handle ad hoc, highly responsive scenario querying for large user communities. In addition to providing limited flexibility to meet the requirements of business analysts, these systems are maintained by IT experts due to the complexity of the data storage, and they lack the process management required of business analysts. Online analytical processing (OLAP) technology, however, provides the scalability, performance, and analytic capabilities necessary to support sophisticated, calculation-intensive queries for large user populations. For these reasons, relational and OLAP technologies are often combined for maximum benefits. This has led to a two-tiered data warehouse strategy or a spoke-and-hub approach, as noted earlier in Figure 1-9, that incorporates data marts to service the specific requirements of the business analyst.

Two-Tiered Data Warehousing

The two-tiered approach to data warehousing consists of a data warehouse (see Figure 1-11), where data from multiple sources has been extracted, transformed, and cleansed, and one or more data marts, where subject-specific data is deployed to business users. To understand why companies have adopted the two-tiered model, it is useful to examine the historic

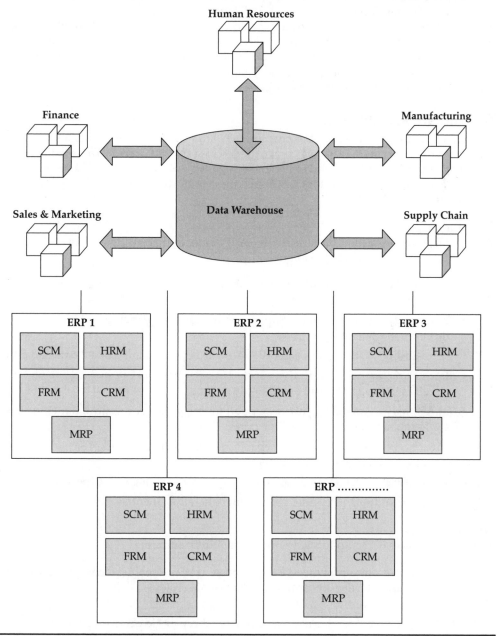

FIGURE 1-11   Two-tiered Data warehouse strategy

development of data warehousing. Bill Inmon is widely recognized as the father of the data warehouse. In his book *Effective Data Base Design* (Prentice-Hall 1981), Inmon defines a data warehouse as "a subject-oriented nonvolatile, and integrated, time-variant collection of data in support of management's decisions."

A *data mart* is a subset of the data resource, usually oriented to a specific purpose or major data subject that may be distributed to support business needs. The concept of a data mart can apply to any data whether it is operational data, evaluational data, spatial data, or metadata. Data marts provide a repository of a business organization's data implemented to answer very specific questions for a specific group of data consumers, such as organizational divisions of marketing, sales, operations, collections, and others. A data mart is one or a grouping of multidimensional cubes called a model that is specifically designed to facilitate a department's planning and analysis requirement.

Key Software Requirements

As we have discussed throughout this chapter, there are a number of key capabilities to meet the diverse requirements of planning and analysis across an organization. These requirements were first defined by Dr. E. F. Codd in 1993[1] and extended in 1995. These papers outlined 12/18 rules on the requirements for OLAPs, and these rules were categorized in four main groups that include the following:

Basic Features

The basic features of Dr. Codd's key software requirements are considered foundational to an OLAP solution and include the following:

- **Multidimensional conceptual view**   To support ad hoc slicing and dicing of data across business-defined dimensions.

- **Intuitive data manipulation**   Support of drag-and-drop manipulation of data as a direct action upon cell-level data.

- **Accessibility**   OLAP plays a middleware role between transactional data and client.

- **Batch extraction vs. interpretive**   Includes the support of internal staging of data as well as the ability to drill down to source data.

- **OLAP analysis models**   Provide support for categorical, exegetical, contemplative, and formulaic models.

- **Client/server architecture**   The separation of the data store and presentation layers to support the use of various clients.

- **Transparency**   The use of OLAP embedded in the existing user experience.

- **Multiuser support**   Provides concurrent data retrieval with security.

Special Features

The special features of Dr. Codd's key software requirements are

- **Treatment of non-normalized data**   Updated data in an OLAP environment should not be allowed to alter denormalized source data systems.

---

[1] E. F. Codd, S. B. Codd, and C. T. Salley. "Providing OLAP (Online Analytical Processing) to User-Analysts: An IT Mandate." (Codd and Date, Inc., 1993).

- **Storing OLAP results**   OLAP data results should be kept separate from source data systems.
- **Extraction of missing values**   An OLAP system should differentiate missing data from the value of zero.
- **Treatment of missing values**   All missing values should be ignored.

Reporting Features

The reporting features of Dr. Codd's key software requirements are

- **Flexible reporting**   Provides reporting capabilities that present information based on user requirements.
- **Uniform reporting performance**   As dimension and/or data volumes grow, reporting performance should remain responsive.
- **Automatic adjustment of physical level**   The OLAP environment should adapt its physical schema automatically to adapt to the attributes of the model, data volumes, and density.

Dimensional Control

The dimensional control aspects of Dr. Codd's key software requirements are

- **Generic dimensionality**   Data dimensions must be equivalent in structure and operational capabilities.
- **Unlimited dimensions and aggregation levels**
- **Unrestricted cross-dimensional operations**   Allow for calculations and data manipulations in any number of dimensions so as not to restrict the relationship between cells.

These requirements were further enhanced by Nigel Pendse who coined the term FASMI[2] (Fast Analysis of Shared Multi-dimensional Information), which condensed Codd's earlier 12/18 rules into five keywords and definitions that allow organizations to summarize and evaluate OLAP capabilities. Let's take a look at these attributes. The FASMI attributes include

- **Fast**   The ability to deliver user responses in five seconds or less.
- **Analysis**   The ability to handle a broad range of relevant business or statistical analysis across an organization.
- **Multidimensionality**   Must provide a multidimensional, conceptual data view and support multiple data hierarchies to meet an organization's actual business dimensions.
- **Information**   Must contain the data required by the user and offer effective analysis techniques to make this information meaningful to the user.

Each of these attributes is critical in meeting the solution requirements in each of the areas discussed in this chapter.

---

[2] Pendse, Nigel. "What is OLAP?" (*The BI Verdict*, 2005).

Summary

In summary, the goal of this chapter was to highlight the increased demands on planning and analysis processes in global organizations. In today's highly volatile business environment, organizations demand more accurate plans, forecasts, and analysis in order to meet and exceed market demands. For organizations, who seek to meet these challenges through a fusion of planning and analysis capabilities at every level of decision making across an organization to create a more agile organization, the market rewards are great. This chapter focused on the effects of these forces, such as the increase frequency of forecasting and budget cycles, the importance of scenario analytics, the heightened ERP requirements, and finally, the rising demands on data warehouses. Let's continue our conversation in Chapter 2, where we will discuss the promise of in-memory analytics and how IBM Cognos TM1 is specifically meeting these diverse requirements in global organizations similar to your own.

The Promise of In-Memory Analytics with IBM Cognos TM1

The goal of this chapter is to continue our conversation about the increased demands on planning and analysis processes in global organizations, and to share how Cognos TM1 has met and continues to meet the broadest planning and analysis requirements in the industry. Over 4,000 companies spanning all industries have come to depend on Cognos TM1 to help drive decisions across their organizations. This chapter will review today's highly volatile business environment and how leading organizations have met these challenges to drive increased performance with Cognos TM1. These demands range from increased market pressures, investment demands, and strategy validation to regulatory requirements for decision transparency. These increased demands require a fusion of planning and analysis capabilities at every level of decision making across an organization to create a more agile organization that can meet these diverse requirements. These requirements fall into four key areas:

- Enterprise planning
- Scenario analytics
- Extending your ERP solutions
- Extending data warehouse value

Let's start our discussion on some of the key attributes of Cognos TM1 that drive its broad use and adoption.

In-Memory Analytics with Cognos TM1

The rise of the importance of in-memory analytics is directly tied to the increase in volatility of the current business climate. In-memory analytics promises to provide business users with highly responsive ways to analyze data and create new information through planning and forecasting. Cognos TM1 provides the ability to calculate on demand key metrics facilitating scenario analysis, planning, and forecasting across an organization. Because of this, users can examine current business assumptions and test alternative business scenarios to meet business goals.

In-memory analytics has grown due to business requirements and advances in hardware and software technology, such as 64-bit operating systems, multicore processors, and improvements in processor speed. What was once relegated to the most cutting-edge technology has become standard technology for organizations seeking to optimize their decision processes. The improved price/performance ratio of in-memory analytic solutions, due to reduced hardware and software costs and superior performance in meeting business requirements, has driven broader adoption of these solutions in the enterprise.

As we will review in more detail in Chapter 3, Cognos TM1 takes a unique approach to in-memory analytics that elevates the in-memory approach by combining analysis and write-back to create an integrated planning and analysis solution to meet the broadest planning, forecasting, and analysis requirements. Cognos TM1 architecture from its earliest incarnations was in-memory based. In-memory–based systems provide the highest calculation performance and user interaction with reduced latency. This concept is at the core of all Cognos TM1–based solutions that are extended by rich clients to serve finance, line of business, and IT.

So the question arises as to how to evaluate key attributes of an OLAP solution to meet business user requirements. Fortunately, Edgar F. Codd and Nigel Pendse have provided guidance, as mentioned in Chapter 1. Let's take a look at Cognos TM1 first through the lens of Codd's 12/18 rules of OLAP. Cognos TM1 includes basic, special, supporting, and dimensional control features.

Basic Features

The basic features of Cognos TM1 include

- **Multidimensional conceptual view**   Cognos TM1 supports high-performance ad hoc slicing and dicing of data across unlimited business-defined dimensions.
- **Intuitive data manipulation**   Cognos TM1 supports drag-and-drop manipulation of data as well as unlimited nesting of dimensions on the row and column axis.
- **Accessibility**   Cognos TM1 is a high-performance in-memory OLAP server that supports a range of clients to meet the broadest requirements of planning and analysis.
- **Batch extraction vs. interpretive**   Cognos TM1 provides a highly interactive persistent data store as well as supporting drillthrough to source data.
- **OLAP analysis models**   Cognos TM1 provides support for a broad range of business models.
- **Client/server architecture**   Cognos TM1 supports both a client/server (two-stage) architecture as well as a web-based architecture (three-stage) for web deployment, which separates the data store and presentation layer to support the use of various clients.
- **Transparency**   Cognos TM1 is uniquely embedded in the existing user experience through both Microsoft Excel and the most popular browser-based clients.
- **Multiuser support**   Cognos TM1 provides concurrent data retrieval and writeback with role-based security.

Special Features

The special features of Cognos TM1 include

- **Treatment of non-normalized data**   Normalization of data refers to storage and organization of data that reduces redundancy. Cognos TM1 provides the ability to work with normalized and non-normalized data.

- **Storing OLAP results**   Cognos TM1 stores all metadata. OLAP data results should be kept separate from source data systems.

- **Extraction of missing values**   Cognos TM1 does not store missing data, creating very efficient data storage.

- **Treatment of missing values**   Cognos TM1 ignores missing values.

Reporting Features

The reporting features of Cognos TM1 include

- **Flexible reporting**   Cognos TM1 as a component of Cognos BI provides a broad range of reporting capabilities that presents information based on user requirements.

- **Uniform reporting performance**   Cognos TM1 provides consistent performance as models and users grow.

- **Automatic adjustment of physical level**   As a read/write OLAP program, Cognos TM1 is self-adjusting as attributes of the model, such as data volumes, user counts, and density, increase.

Dimensional Control Features

The dimensional control features of Cognos TM1 include

- **Generic dimensionality**   All Cognos TM1 dimensions are treated the same way, allowing for greater modeling flexibility.

- **Unlimited dimensions and aggregation levels**   Cognos TM1 supports virtually unlimited dimensions and aggregations.

- **Unrestricted cross-dimensional operations**   Cognos TM1 allows for calculations and data manipulations for any number of dimensions through its extensive rules language that provides not only cross-dimensional calculation but also cross-cube calculation.

Also, Cognos TM1 exceeds these attributes by support of three-tiered web architecture as mentioned earlier, as well as providing workflow, which is critical to a read/write application that spans thousands of users. Now let's turn our attention to how Cognos TM1 manifests itself in key solution areas to drive greater organizational performance.

Enterprise Planning

As noted in Chapter 1, there is increased pressure due to volatility and velocity of change in our current business environment. These increased demands included market pressures, investment demands, and strategy validation as well as regulatory requirements for decision transparency for stockholders. These demands are reducing the cycle time between forecasting and analysis, requiring a fusion of planning and analysis capabilities at every level of decision making within an organization.

Cognos TM1 is specifically designed to meet the broadest requirements of planning and forecasting within an organization. As noted in Figure 2-1, to meet evolving customer requirements, Cognos TM1 provides the ability to analyze key performance gaps and quickly move to model alternative scenarios and finally deploy those models in an application context through a rich set of web and desktop clients. We will expand on these key capabilities in Chapter 3.

Cognos TM1 provides a rich set of capabilities that allow organizations to reduce long planning cycles, disconnected operational and financial plans, reliance on spreadsheets, lack of ownership, and lack of accountability and control. Let's take a look at these areas a bit more closely. Cognos TM1 reduces long planning cycles in a number of key ways, which include

- Providing a centralized data store with consistent data definitions, reducing data errors.
- Automating the submission process through workflow, thereby reducing data collection.
- Using popular clients like Microsoft Excel by extending their capabilities with a centralized data model.

Contribute

- Familiar web and Excel deployment
- Rich workflow
- Enterprise in scope with application linkage
- Start small and expand enterprise wide
- Analysis embedded in contribution process

Model

- Centralized metadata, data and business rule definitions
- Owned by Department of Finance
- Support of planning best practices
  - Driver-based planning
  - Rolling forecasts

Analyze

- Explore performance gaps
- Validate corporate drivers
- Define "what if" scenarios
  - Organizational, product family, product/channel mix
  - Test confidence levels of what if scenarios
- Validate planning assumptions

FIGURE 2-1   Evolving customer requirements

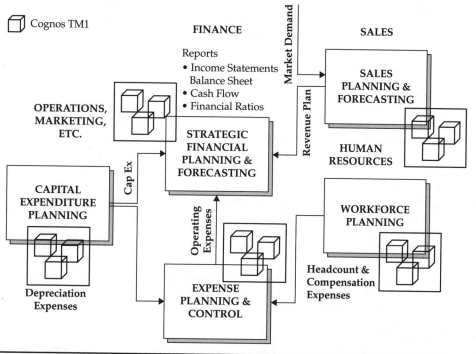

FIGURE 2-2   Cognos TM1 planning solutions

- Eliminating the control and versioning problem.
- Providing a standardized planning toolset that can be applied to both operational and financial planning, thereby creating a planning and analysis network across an organization (see Figure 2-2) that connects financial plans with operational realities, driving better decisions across an organization.

Now let's turn our attention to some key companies like First Command and Eraring Energy, who are using Cognos TM1 to meet and exceed their planning requirements.

First Command

Founded in 1958 with a mission to improve the financial well-being of America's professional military families, First Command Financial Services[1] today serves clients from all walks of life at all stages of life. A Registered Investment Adviser firm, First Command develops and delivers comprehensive financial plans to assist American families in their efforts to reduce debt, build wealth, and pursue their financial goals and dreams. First Command embraces time-tested financial principles, advocating a disciplined, long-term approach to saving and investing, supported by strategies to manage financial risk. And First Command supports

---

[1] IBM case study: From spreadsheets to streamlined planning: Business analytics at First Command. 12 Jan 2011. http://www-142.ibm.com | Software | Library.

their clients' pursuit of their goals with a wide range of investment, insurance, and banking products and services. Through a values-centered approach to financial planning and a "client-first" philosophy, First Command has for 50 years established lasting relationships with hundreds of thousands of client families. First Command is committed to helping clients plan confidently for the future and to accompanying them on their financial journey.

Business Challenges

The Finance Department at First Command had been using PowerPoint, spreadsheets, and multiple data sources to analyze and report on the company's financial performance. The manual process was plagued by a number of issues: It was time-consuming, prone to errors, had no audit trail, and left little time for analysis, planning, or forecasting. "We wanted to do more in-depth, bottom-up forecasting, but the spreadsheets and Access databases really weren't doing the trick," says Sunday Grace, Director of Financial Analytics at First Command. "We were managing multiple databases, multiple spreadsheets being e-mailed back and forth and no collaboration tools. So there were a lot of pain points when it came to using these tools for everything." As well, the system couldn't address some of the heavier reporting and analysis requirements that were being driven by changes in market conditions and the information requirements of the executive team. What the company needed was a single, dynamic platform to collect, consolidate, analyze, and report on financial data—and provide deeper insight into company performance, financial measurement, and more accurate predictability. A Cognos business analytics solution offered the answer.

Benefits Realized

Today all financial reporting and budgeting is done using TM1 and a SQL database. To get there, the consulting team built the processes to go in and update GL accounts and various modules such as fixed assets and accounts payable. As well, payroll data feeds are pulled in from an Oracle database. To help the department even further, the team built an approval process into the system to automate the workflow rather than depending on the manual steps that were done previously.

In addition to more efficient budgeting, reporting and analysis have become much easier with Cognos software. "We're developing more and more reports that are helping us," says Grace. "It's scaled back on the time that I have to spend writing reports. Because once you get these reports written, you can update them, they can be refreshed, and they're drillable. So I have more time for high-level analysis, which is where the value add for my time is." It's been a learning process: what kinds of reports to develop, how TM1 works, testing and integrating various calculations. The company handles "some pretty complicated revenue calculations because of our business," notes Grace. Here again, the tool has helped reduce the time spent on processing and compiling. She also adds that the software has been quite easy to understand and use, allowing her to go in and build things like cost allocation cubes for product profitability modeling and reporting. "I'm not a technical type of person. So for me to be able to go in and use the development side of TM1 is quite remarkable."

Version Control, Better Reporting   The department now has standardized reports and uses a SharePoint collaborative tool for distribution. So everyone accesses the same information in a consistent format. A secure reporting platform also ensures that users only see what they need to see. "We put all of our reports in SharePoint," says Grace. "And we have one version of each report. If we need to see a report, we don't have to worry about which iteration of the spreadsheet is out there. We don't have to be concerned about whether or not we have the latest version of the financials." Using Cognos, it is also much easier for department heads to go in and update their expenses by line item and drill through to the underlying data if further analysis is required. This provides increased accountability—with more detailed reporting, management can see who is accountable down to the transaction level, which helps them better manage their areas of the business. As well, the real-time information updates mean less of a burden on management, particularly at month-end when financials are reviewed by the CFO and require changes. The process is now much faster. "The GL group used to have to go in and update the database, then update the spreadsheets. It would take 30 to 40 minutes just for the database, followed by a ten-step process to get the financials up to date. Now we run a seven-minute process that goes in and updates all of our GL into a cube with the real-time data."

Compliance   Finally, while compliance and data governance are largely handled by another group in the organization, the Finance Department has been able to use the capabilities of the Cognos system to improve regulatory reporting. They are also able to conduct operational expense budgeting. "We've been able to use the hierarchies that are built within TM1 to create different types of reports," says Grace. "We're in the process right now of building our auditing and some of the regulatory reporting we need to do. We have to roll things up differently, depending on which company or which agency we're reporting to. So it's been very helpful to be able to go in and use these hierarchies, which we didn't have before."

In summary, in only three months' time, First Command Financial Services increased operational efficiency and decision making by

- Automating data collection to reduce the risk of manual errors
- Creating a central data repository for historical consolidated financials and current plans
- Reducing financial reporting cycle time
- Developing budget and forecast targets that are linked to all levels of the organization
- Ensuring collaborative planning between operating units and key contributors
- Migrating toward a rolling forecast
- Improving regulatory reporting

Eraring Energy

Eraring Energy[2] is a state-owned corporation that manages a diverse set of electricity-generating assets located throughout New South Wales, Australia. Eraring Energy's portfolio has a number of generators including a thermal power station, New South Wales' first wind farm, hydro sites, and pumped storage schemes. Eraring Energy has a combined generating capacity of over 3,000 megawatts (MW), including the Eraring Power Station at 2,640MW, which is Australia's largest.

---

[2] IBM case study: Eraring Energy adopts TM1 Web for collaborative budgeting and forecasting. 05 Oct 2010 http://www-142.ibm.com | Software | Library.

Business Challenges

Managing a diverse set of electricity-generating assets located throughout New South Wales, Eraring Energy not only needed to provide efficient energy sources, but it also needed to run their business operations much the same way: in a timely, accurate, and efficient manner.

With a generation portfolio consisting of ten power stations—86 percent of capacity being sourced from Eraring Power Station and the remainder consisting of smaller hydro and wind generation plants—Eraring Energy's employees range from shift workers, contractors, and day workers, right through to executives. With such a wide range of employment levels and pay structures, labor budgeting and forecasting had become complicated due to manual processing with a substantial amount of cost averaging.

According to Adela Murphy, Eraring Energy's Financial Systems Accountant, "The problem with running our labor budgeting manually meant that it was not only time-consuming but inaccurate and unreliable. We had a lot of cost averaging and it was difficult to identify where the variances were coming from."

Strategy

The primary requirement was to use Cognos TM1 to identify real labor costs by sourcing the variances accurately, with plans to decentralize the financial reporting at a later stage using Cognos TM1 Web.

In 2004 Eraring Energy decided to implement TM1 into their labor forecasting system, with assistance from IBM and its partner Cubewise. With implementation complete after only one month, TM1 saved the finance department at least two weeks in data entry and consolidation in quarterly labor forecasting.

Murphy commented, "With TM1 we can now pinpoint why the labor budget is out. Once we had streamlined the process, it improved our labor budget variance analysis." The next area of focus for Eraring Energy was to address the issue of accountability of the budgeting process. By deploying budget data entry and reporting via the web, Eraring Energy was able to decentralize their budget and forecasting system—responsibility and accountability immediately shifted from the finance department to the cost center managers. Murphy describes the Cognos TM1–based budgeting and forecasting system as "a revolution."

Following the initial success of Cognos TM1 in the finance department, Eraring Energy took the necessary next steps of web-enabling their budgeting, forecasting, and reporting system with the deployment of TM1 Web. By decentralizing the budgeting, forecasting, and reporting, both management and cost centers were given direct access to the monthly reporting, which gave cost center line managers greater control over their labor cost, and more importantly, it gave them total accountability for their own budgets. Managing the budget over the web saved two to three weeks in just consolidating and reconciling—now it is instantaneous.

"Decentralization and accountability of our budgeting and forecasting system was enabled by deploying Cognos TM1 Web. Our cost center line managers can now access, view, and manage their respective cost center reports. Budgeting time was substantially decreased and line managers now have the ability to retrieve their financial reports in an easy-to-use format and timely manner."

The main elements of Eraring Energy's budgeting and forecasting system involved labor costing and data analysis. Labor costing is a very large part of Eraring Energy's expenses, so accuracy was crucial. Using this, Eraring Energy is able to readily identify variances down to individual levels and breakdown by rate and hours; and manage headcount and annual, long service and other leave.

Benefits Realized

By implementing Cognos TM1 and TM1 Web, Eraring Energy transformed their complicated financial and labor reporting into a streamlined, web-enabled system providing accurate, timely analysis and accountability throughout the organization.

Labor information security was also an issue, so moving this information into TM1 allowed control of security down to an element level—a substantial improvement to the existing system.

The variance analysis process used to be heavily time-consuming. Once this reporting process was implemented, it eliminated discrepancies of figures, giving management more time to spend on labor strategy. Minimizing figure analysis was definitely a value add to the variance process.

Now, having such easy-to-use financial reports that can break down the information by employees, hours, labor rates, and so on, the finance department no longer has to do financial interpretation for the line managers. In the two years since the system was put in place, Eraring Energy now run their labor budgeting and forecasting four times per year as opposed to only once per year. All cost center line managers are monitoring their labor variances more closely now that the system is more accurate.

"We used to close off the account each month and then create, run, and distribute the reports via e-mail—all of which took 3–4 days. Now we can close off the month and reconcile, then notify the cost centers to log on and view their reports," continued Murphy.

Management now conducts monthly business review meetings with the financial reports as an integral part of these monthly reviews.

Each of these success stories highlights the role that Cognos TM1 provides in reducing long planning cycles, disconnected operational and financial plans, reliance on spreadsheets, lack of ownership, and lack of accountability and control.

Scenario Analytics

Now let's turn our attention to how Cognos TM1 meets increased business requirements for analysis. As mentioned earlier, given the rise of uncertainty and volatility in organizational assumptions and business models, there is an increased requirement for scenario analytics to manage this uncertainty. Cognos TM1 provides the ability to evaluate several outcomes of a potential strategy before making a final decision. These include the following:

- Explore and test "what if" scenarios
- Reduce risk and create contingency plans
- Formulate growth strategies
- Best responses to economic change, a competitor move and marketing
- Optimize price, channel, and marketing strategy for profitability

As noted in Figure 2-3, Cognos TM1 helps organizations meet the broad spectrum of analysis requirements in order to meet business requirements.

Executive	Casual Users	Business Analyst	Financial Analyst	Advanced Analyst
Analytical Reporting	**Trending**	**Scenario Analysis & Planning**		**Advanced Analysis**
Top-down view	Personal exploration	Model scenarios		Uncover patterns
Drillable reports	Compare and contrast	Reorganize, reshape		Statistical algorithms
Sort top and bottom	Rotate and nest	Compare scenarios		Mine data and text
Review then query	Work disconnected	Save versions		Predict outcomes
Market shifts	Sales trend analysis	Enterprise planning		Fraud prevention
Product ranking	Market analysis	Profitability analysis		Sentiment analysis

FIGURE 2-3 Analysis requirements

These requirements include analytical reporting, trending, scenario analysis, and advanced analytics. Cognos TM1 plays a critical role in providing scenario analysis to global organizations. Although Cognos TM1 key features will be covered in more depth in the following chapters, let's look at some key features that Cognos TM1 supports, which include

- A high-performance in-memory OLAP server that is specifically designed for high-performance ad hoc exploration of data.

- Support for calculation on demand that allows for instantaneous updates of data, metadata, and business rules allowing for reduced latency in analysis and modeling.

- Full support for writeback across all dimensions for testing of assumptions.

- Support for unlimited user-defined scenarios through personal sandboxes.

- A broad range of desktop clients as well as web-based clients to facilitate analytical reporting, trending, scenario analysis, and advanced analytics.

Each of these features plays a critical role in providing business users with the ability to test "what if" scenarios to reduce risk, formulate growth strategies, and optimize decisions to drive profitability across an organization. These features and best practices will be explored in the following chapters.

Now let's take a look at how Sun World and British Arab Commercial Bank are realizing benefits of Cognos TM1 to deliver scenario analytics.

PART I

Sun World

Sun World[3] was established in early 1976 as a packer and marketer of fresh fruits and vegetables. In the 1980s, consumption of fresh fruit and vegetables was on the rise and consumers were increasingly seeking better-tasting, more conveniently available produce. As the market changed, so did Sun World. The company exited the commodity fruit and vegetable business and became involved in the farming, packing, and marketing of an extensive collection of specialty-branded produce. Sun World initiated a series of relationships with various research and academic organizations around the world, setting out on its quest to improve the flavor, color, texture and overall quality of specific fruits and vegetables. Throughout the 1980s and early 1990s, the company introduced more mainstream-branded fresh produce items to the marketplace than any other agricultural company. Produce included the sweet red pepper (1983), the seedless watermelon (1988), a vine-ripened tomato with long shelf life (1990), and the Black Diamond brand plum (1992). Other notable products include the Superior Seedless, Midnight Beauty, Sable Seedless, and Scarlotta Seedless brand grapes, and the Amber Crest brand peach. Today, Sun World operates one of the world's leading fruit development programs, has over 15,000 acres of farming land, and manages the farming, packing, and marketing operations for all of its U.S.-grown products. The company has five international offices, located in Italy, Australia, Chile, Mexico, and South Africa. The company's licensing department manages an extensive international program for growers and marketers around the world with licensing proprietary products. The sales and marketing department boasts a team of experienced professionals who manage relationships with many of the world's leading supermarket retailers. Sun World has its eye on the future, and is focusing efforts on increasing availability of the Midnight Beauty brand grape, the Scarlotta Seedless brand grape, and the Black Diamond brand plum, in addition to developing new varieties specializing in early and late season. Sun World is privately owned by Black Diamond Capital Management, LLP, an investment company based in Greenwich, Connecticut.

Business Challenges

If you look at the world of commercial farming on the surface, it looks a lot like it always has. It conjures a sentimental image that resonates with most. But on a deeper level, the increasingly globalized nature of commercial farming industry today leaves little room for sentimentality when profits are at stake. That's why producers are increasingly looking to a new kind of harvest—the ability to extract insights from data—as the key to their future success.

Steve Greenwood, Director of Budgets and Reporting for Sun World International, has seen this shift firsthand. Greenwood and his team have a direct impact on what crops go into the ground and what Sun World ultimately brings to market. It's a decision where—in Sun World's case—rational analysis trumps sentimentality. You'd think, for example, that as the first company to develop seedless watermelons, Sun World's planners might hold a special place for them in their heart. But when a closer look at the numbers showed that the company was bringing more and more product to market just as prices were plunging, Sun World abruptly changed course, dramatically cutting acreage and shifting to a new breed of table grape that now produces *twice* as much profit on a quarter of the acreage.

---

[3] IBM case study: Sun World International: Harvesting business insights to maximize profitability. 18 Nov 2010. http://www-142.ibm.com | Software | Library.

Benefits Realized

Here are some of the benefits.

The Seeds of Smarter Planning   The lesson of this story isn't just that there are no sacred cows in commercial agriculture. Nor does it signal a change in the importance of supply and demand in determining profitability. Instead, it is more a reflection of how—in an industry where market globalization has increased risk and made profitability more elusive—timely and accurate decision support is more important than ever.

As Greenwood explains it, profitability in commercial agriculture is in large measure a function of a provider's ability to come to market with the right product at the right time. But it's not as easy as it sounds. While the rhythms of seasonality may be a basic part of life to the average consumer in the produce aisle, commercial growers see them as a sort of moving landscape from which evolve threats and opportunities. To be avoided, he says, are crops whose harvests come due when the market is crowded with abundant supplies and falling prices. "Our aim is to produce quality products when they're currently not available," says Greenwood. "It's about hitting the market window when nobody else can."

One key dimension of Sun World's targeting strategy is its world-class breeding center, located on a 180-acre experimental farm not far from the company's headquarters. A complement to Sun World's focus on specialty-branded (as opposed to commodity) produce, the center seeks to breed and patent crop varieties with targeted characteristics (such as red seedless grapes that harvest in September, which, as grapes go, is late on the calendar). That's where the second important dimension comes in. Greenwood explains: "Pursuing a proactive market targeting strategy requires accurate, granular, and up-to-date forecasts of what's going on in the market. That's how we find opportunity and catch our competitors flat-footed."

A New Culture Takes Root   Greenwood was at Sun World when the pieces of this capability began falling into place. The watershed moment was a change in management and a corresponding shift in the company's competitive strategy. Sun World's executives recognized that successfully competing on a global level required a more information-driven, decision-making culture. It also realized that for such a culture to take root, Sun World needed to fundamentally transform the way it managed key business data.

One holdover of its old way of doing business was a reliance on manually updated spreadsheet data, which, for the purpose of decision making, became stale the moment it was entered. What's more, beyond being inefficient and error-prone, this fragmented approach made it impossible to perform the analytical functions Sun World would need to execute intelligent market planning as well as the optimization of its everyday operations. Sun World put that building block into place when it worked with Applied Analytix Inc., an IBM Business Partner with vast experience transforming data into actionable insights. Applied Analytix implemented Cognos TM1 and redesigned Sun World's processes to take full advantage of its advanced functionality.

Sun World's 16,000 acres of farmland are clustered into four growing areas in the San Joaquin and Coachella Valleys of California, each of which is directed by a farm manager. Greenwood is on a first-name basis with all of them, the result of a close and ongoing working relationship. Once a month, they come to Bakersfield to sit down and go through the numbers, discussing budgets, costs, and productivity. That is, unless it's harvest time, when their 18-hour days make it more practical for Greenwood to make the drive to them.

The aim of these meetings is to take stock, identify trends, and figure out the best way forward. With Cognos TM1 helping Greenwood and the managers to glean insights and improve forecast accuracy and granularity, these sessions have become much more fruitful. Fed by Sun World's ERP system, the analytics solution can provide a granular breakdown of sales, costs, and profitability by product type, variety, region, and individual ranch. Part of what makes a solution such a valuable forward-looking tool is its ability to do "what if" analysis around parameters like water costs, fuel costs, and changes in consumer buying patterns, and to use these insights to optimize its planting mix.

Data-driven Insights Complement Intuition   Like most experienced farmers, Sun World's farm managers and their foremen have learned to trust their gut in determining which practices—in areas like irrigation and fertilizing—work best. Greenwood doesn't dispute the value of experience, but he sees the insights derived from Cognos TM1 as adding the level of precision needed to optimize everyday farming practices. Take irrigation as an example. Given the water shortages endemic to the region, high-efficiency drip irrigation methods are gaining in favor as an alternative to traditional surface irrigation. Because Sun World can compare the costs of both at a granular level, it has been able to make better judgments about where to apply drip irrigation, resulting in lower water usage and better nourished produce. In the growing of table grapes, the targeted use of drip irrigation has resulted in a 5 percent reduction in harvesting costs, a 20 percent reduction in fuel usage, and a 50 percent increase in yield over the past five years.

Harvest time produces a series of important decisions that impact the cost and efficiency of the harvest—and thus the bottom line. There was a time when Sun World executives and farm managers didn't see the productivity numbers until the harvest was done, when it was too late to do anything different. Today, farm managers out in the field during the harvest can use their cell phone or PDA to get an up-to-date view of productivity metrics at the level of individual ranches or work crews. "This means that if a manager finds something wrong with a particular ranch or crew, he can find out the root problem and address it proactively to maximize the overall productivity of the harvest—as it's happening, not after it's done," says Greenwood. "In the same way, we can flag superior practices among specific crews and try to promote them where it makes sense."

In addition to the vagaries of nature, Sun World's profitability also depends on its ability to negotiate the best prices with retailers in a fluctuating market. The ongoing consolidation of the grocery business has exacerbated this challenge. To ensure that the sales staff has the most up-to-the-minute price data as they negotiate with their customers around the world, Sun World displays them on the selling floor via a ticker display, drawn from a near-real-time feed from Cognos TM1. "This gives our salespeople the ability to continually understand market conditions," explains Greenwood. "A penny here, a penny there matters when you're shipping 11,000,000 boxes per year."

Now let's turn our attention to how British Arab Commercial Bank (BACB) uses Cognos TM1 to drive the value of scenario analytics in their organization.

British Arab Commercial Bank (BACB)

British Arab Commercial Bank[4] (BACB) is a London-based wholesale bank that specializes in providing trade and project finance for Arab markets. Building on a successful track

---

[4] IBM case study: British Arab Commercial Bank enhances insight across the entire business. 24 May 2011. http://www-142.ibm.com | Software | Library.

record in the Arab Mediterranean region, BACB's market coverage has expanded steadily in recent years, and it is also able to handle business throughout the Arabian Gulf. With 150 employees, the company has total assets of more than £3.3 billion, and achieved pre-tax profits of nearly £19 million in 2010.

Business Challenge

To operate effectively in a highly complex and competitive international arena such as trade and project finance, BACB needs rapid access to detailed management information on the financial and operational aspects of its business. The bank is also subject to regulation by the UK's Financial Services Authority (FSA) and other regulators, which require detailed reports on various aspects of its operations. As a result, business analytics has a vital role to play in BACB's success. However, creating an environment in which business analytics could embed itself into users' everyday routine was a major challenge for BACB.

Like most banks, BACB has numerous different business units that deal with specific operational aspects such as core banking, trade finance, derivatives, and so on. Over a number of years, each of these business units had implemented and developed its own separate IT systems, which meant that data was siloed in numerous different formats and repositories.

"Analysts in our finance team had to collect data from all these systems and compile it into complex spreadsheets to calculate even the basic daily, monthly, and annual figures," explains Crispian Denby, Chief Financial Officer at BACB. "There was increasing demand for better management information in other areas too, such as customer profitability analysis, and we knew that a spreadsheet-based process simply wouldn't be a practical option. We needed a real business analytics solution."

Therefore, in 2008, HUK-COBURG's managers decided to look for a future-proof BI system. The aim was to expand and facilitate controlling and management in three main areas. In sales, the objective was improved quality control, with flexible analysis functions to identify regional developments and new business potential, as well as more targeted planning of personnel and the distribution network. In the call center too, the emphasis was on more efficient allocation of labor and development of service quality. Finally, in the claims management area, the aim was to optimize the insurance network of garages in terms of customer satisfaction and quality.

Benefits Realized

Once the Microsoft SQL Server data warehouse had been implemented, the BACB team began creating analytic applications in Cognos TM1 to serve the needs of different groups of business users. The first application was built to handle traditional finance requirements such as daily, monthly, and annual accounting and cost center reporting. The application uses a number of OLAP cubes to provide insight into planned and actual expenditure. Detailed ledger balances are collected daily in their underlying currencies: movements from one day to the next are determined (balance sheet versus P&L), and results are translated into various reporting currencies automatically.

"From the general finance perspective, we have been delighted with Cognos TM1 since the very beginning," says Denby. "The creation and distribution of daily reports is completely automated through TM1 Web, so users can get hold of the latest figures as soon as they log on in the morning. Month-end reporting can be completed within two days of the monthly close, and the year-end is an absolute breeze now."

Although the bank's annual report has expanded from 42 pages in 2000 under UK GAAP to 91 pages under the more demanding requirements of IFRS, it can still be completed within a month of the bank's year-end.

Denby adds: "It's a very flexible solution. Changes to reporting requirements and the evolution of the business can normally be easily accommodated within the existing framework. As a result, the Finance department has been able to accommodate the increasing complexity of the bank's business without needing to add to headcount."

Faster, Richer Insight   Denby adds: "The solution provides a near-real-time view of the bank's finances, which means that senior managers can track developments in a volatile market on a day-by-day basis. As a result, we can respond more quickly to changing situations: we can spot opportunities as they arise, and react to emerging issues before they cause problems.

"Besides the increased timeliness of the information, Cognos TM1 gives us much richer insight into our financial position. Previously, analysts spent so long collecting and validating the data, there wasn't much time for deep analysis. Now, because the collection is mostly automated, we can gather more data and perform more sophisticated analyses in the same amount of time.

Customer Profitability   The bank's second project was an application to analyze customer profitability. High-quality online inquiry reports are available to customer-facing teams and senior managers, listing the income and costs related to each customer, as well as their current activity in terms of deals and transactions, all up to date to the most recent end-of-day.

"Customer profitability analysis was one of the key requirements for the solution, and it has been a major success," comments Denby. "The Cognos TM1 application provides a huge and rich source of data for our customer-facing teams and senior managers, helping them understand how to manage individual accounts more effectively to maximize both profitability and customer loyalty."

Reusing Existing Assets   Once these first two applications had been developed, the team began to consider the next steps. "We had learned a lot about Cognos TM1 development, and we knew we could reuse the same structures and techniques to create other analytic applications relatively easily," says Denby. "Our IT/Finance team quickly built an application to report on credit risk for each customer compared to acceptable limits. This flags high-risk customers and prompts us to take action to minimize our exposure as quickly as possible. We also built in e-mail alerts that are generated automatically by the system, which enable users to identify problems quickly rather than having to review detailed underlying reports."

Predicting Risk and Managing Liquidity   In response to new FSA guidelines on liquidity management, the BACB team has also created a Cognos TM1 application that uses Monte Carlo simulation to create forward projections of the bank's balance sheet up to 90 days in advance. This enables BACB to assess its current assets, liabilities, and commitments against what if scenarios, and make crucial decisions to maintain the required level of liquidity at all times.

"The Monte Carlo analysis gives us a way to gauge probable best and worst case scenarios, and helps us decide whether we need to mitigate risk by buying more debt securities or raising more deposits," explains Denby. "Cognos TM1 performs these complex calculations automatically, giving us the information we need to make good decisions, as well as facilitating compliance with FSA guidelines."

Improved Information Governance   Finally, the introduction of the Cognos TM1 solution has led to cultural change within BACB, dramatically improving the standard of information and process-related governance. Instead of individuals managing a mass of interdependent spreadsheets, which often led to formula errors and inconsistent data, the bank has now instituted a more disciplined governance framework. Changes to the Cognos solution are implemented in a development environment and then rigorously tested before they are released into production. The incidence of reporting errors has steadily reduced over time, and system availability has become much more reliable as a result of the implementation of these types of controls.

"Users like it because they can still use a familiar Microsoft Excel front-end to interact with the data, but behind the scenes, the analysis is much more structured and reliable," says Denby. "Instead of each user relying on their own spreadsheets, there is a single, reliable source of business intelligence that is accessible to all."

Adapting to a Changing Business Environment   The bank's operations have recently been impacted by events in the Arab markets in which it specializes. Access to flexible reporting and high-quality information has been key to enabling the bank to adapt to a rapidly evolving business and regulatory environment.

Denby concludes: "With Cognos TM1, we have more confidence in our management information, which leads to faster, more responsive decision-making and ultimately helps us maintain our leading position in the Arab trade and project finance market."

Extending Your ERP Solution

Now let's turn our attention to how Cognos TM1 helps ERP systems meet the heightened requirements driven by increased business volatility and velocity of change. ERP systems have traditionally done an excellent job of capturing transactional information about a host of enterprise information that spans a host of departmental requirements. Unfortunately, as noted in Chapter 1, ERP systems face a number of challenges with meeting the business requirements of planning and analysis that Cognos TM1 can help with. Let's outline these challenges in order of importance and how Cognos TM1 can help.

- **Reduction of silos of data**   Cognos TM1 provides a centralized data store that is specifically designed to meet high-performance planning and analysis business requirements. This provides a single set of data definitions as noted in Figure 2-4.

- **Support for ad hoc analysis**   As mentioned earlier, Cognos TM1 is specifically designed for data exploration and provides a "single version of the truth" that reduces errors data errors and lost productivity.

- **Reduced reliance on static reports**   Cognos TM1 reduces reliance on static reports by creating a highly interactive environment for business users to explore current organizational performance and create new plans and scenarios on demand. This reduces the requirement for static reports and creates a self-service model for information that is owned by the business user but managed to IT standards for governance.

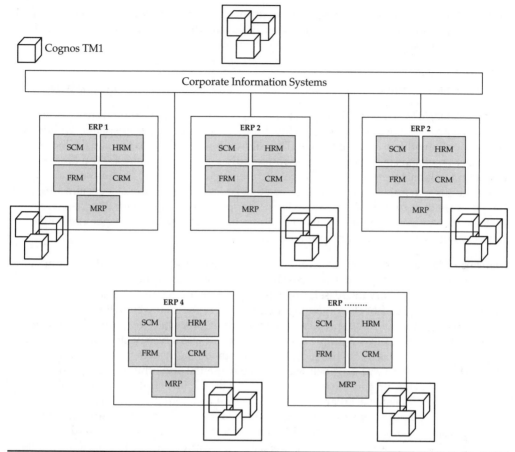

FIGURE 2-4   Extending an ERP system with Cognos TM1

- **Lower cost of ownership**   Cognos TM1 reduces the cost of strategic investments by creating a centralized data store that transforms data to information for a broad set of planning, analysis, reporting, scorecard, and dashboard requirements.

Now let's take a look at how Mitsubishi (SAP) and DHL (Oracle) have used Cognos TM1 to extend their ERP investment.

Mitsubishi

Mitsubishi Corporation's[5] European subsidiaries have found the recipe for success for profitable trading: This global trading company allocates its regional sales units as much responsibility as possible. At the lowest level, profit centers autonomously distribute goods

---

[5] IBM case study: Streamlined data and clear view of profits. 04 Mar 2011. http://www-142.ibm.com | Software | Library.

from product segments such as chemicals, machinery, and textiles. On the basis of specified targets, they draw up their own budget plans, which are then consolidated and checked several times a year in the European holding company.

Business Challenges
Mitsubishi faced a number of common business challenges in its global organizations.

Bottom-up Planning   Mitsubishi Corporation's decentralized organizational structure is based on a proven concept: Profit centers distributed throughout Europe plan their business independently within a specified scope. This allows the sales units to operate flexibly, target offerings to regional customers, and respond rapidly to customer requests. The downside is an elaborate planning process: The budget plans created in the profit centers—for example, for chemically generated food additives—need to be forwarded to the responsible areas. The plans are then consolidated, checked and, if applicable, aligned with the group's overall strategy. This takes place in the form of targets that are set by senior management for the individual product segments and profit centers.

Error-prone, Slow, and Elaborate   Due to its high complexity, the previous budget planning process, based on Excel spreadsheets, had become unviable, as Günther Bergdolt, Technical Manager at the subsidiary in Düsseldorf, explains: "Users in the profit centers created individual Excel spreadsheets containing their budget figures. However, there was no standardized format for these spreadsheets, which sometimes had to be consolidated and corrected manually—across multiple levels." This result was a highly labor-intensive and time-consuming process. Formatting problems also made the system prone to errors.

What's more, there was no quick way for departmental and other managers to obtain an overview of planning and business development and define strategic goals. Mitsubishi Corporation's European subsidiaries therefore needed a system that was capable of automating the planning process across the entire company. The main requirements were outlined in specifications from the subsidiary in London. "We needed a standardized system that was capable of centralizing data entry and capture and which could be accessed by all users in all European subsidiaries," explains Bergdolt. One key requirement was a workflow capable of controlling and accelerating the planning process across all departments. At the same time, the company was looking for a solution that would allow department managers to run individual queries such as target-performance comparisons—which called for the ability to rapidly process large volumes of budget and profit and loss figures from different sources.

Benefits Realized
With the implementation of Cognos TM1, Mitsubishi Corporation realized a number of business benefits.

Networked Across Countries   In September 2009, a project team led by Bergdolt was assigned the task of identifying the solution. An in-depth market assessment clearly showed that Cognos TM1 was the best fit for the requirements. The solution convinced the team not only on the basis of its workflow management functionalities, but also thanks to its integrated in-memory OLAP server, which allows data to be processed rapidly in the main memory. Another argument in favor of Cognos TM1 was the fact that the solution could be seamlessly integrated in the existing infrastructure—more specifically, the strategic, company-wide SAP ERP system and the Cognos 8 BI solution.

Over subsequent project steps, in November 2009 the precise requirements for the workflow were defined and a cross-country organizational structure, departments, and permissions were mapped in the Cognos TM1 multidimensional database. Following on from several workshops during which IBM consultants familiarized Mitsubishi employees with the functionalities of the new solution, the system went live in February 2010.

Automated, Fast, and Standardized   The workflow integrated in Cognos TM1 provides Mitsubishi planners with the technological foundations to map each individual level of the company's hierarchy and automate the planning process over all countries. Tasks and permissions are assigned to users throughout Europe. "At the lowest level, users enter budget figures for their respective region; at the next levels, plans are grouped according to permissions and then checked," explains Bergdolt. Access takes place online—all European offices are networked via a standard web interface.

Cognos TM1 is also integrated with Excel, allowing users to work with a familiar interface and standardized formats. "The entire planning process is now far faster, since all users are working with a central system and a clearly defined workflow. The fact that plans are now standardized and consolidated automatically has also helped to reduce the error rate," continues Bergdolt.

Cognos TM1 offers a convincing performance in the consolidation of budget plans as well as for individual queries. Budget figures and SAP data are loaded in the system and processed in main memory, which means that no access to the hard disk is required. "Cognos TM1 easily processes even large volumes of data in a short time. Performance is maintained at a high level, as is the access speed for individual analyses," states Bergdolt.

Target-performance comparisons can be easily carried out during operation. For example, a manager in the European subsidiary can see at a glance how much turnover was generated by chemicals in Germany last month. If turnover is above target, the figure for this product segment can be revised upwards. "This allows us to plan our business far more precisely, define strategic goals faster, and make more efficient use of resources," explains Bergdolt.

A Comprehensive Overview   The expanded reporting system also ensures the smooth distribution of information over all levels of the hierarchy for planning purposes. Cognos TM1 is the ideal complement for Cognos 8 BI, since budget figures from the TM1 database can be automatically exported and analyzed in reports. Cognos 8 BI also offers Bergdolt and his team the possibility of preconfiguring reports based on the requirements of different user groups. In addition to reducing the workload of the IT department, this benefits users by allowing them to query budget reports independently via web access before submitting them to their supervisor for checking.

For an additional overview, monthly reports keep department managers up to date depending on their permissions and area of responsibility. To support this feature, the latest performance figures are transferred from the SAP system to Cognos 8 BI. This provides a more precise overview of the development of individual product segments and regions.

Senior managers generally receive completed analyses only, in the form of summaries, graphics, and diagrams. "A senior manager is mainly interested in trends throughout Europe: How are our product segments performing in Europe? In which countries do we need to improve? The advanced visualization options offered by Cognos 8 are an added benefit.

Information can be displayed precisely in any required format," explains Bergdolt. This provides more reliable foundations for strategic decision making since managers have an overview of business developments at all times—from all of Europe to the lowest sales level.

Data Continues to Flow   The solution went live in February 2010, and around 70 users throughout Europe are now using the new system. "User satisfaction is apparent at many levels since the system has standardized and streamlined internal processes," explains Bergdolt. "As well as accelerating the planning process, we have also made significant improvements in reporting on a pan-European basis."

DHL Global

DHL Global Forwarding,[6] part of DHL Worldwide, remains the global market leader in both air and ocean freight. The company continues to provide a range of transportation and logistics services, including its strengthened U.S. Domestic Heavy Weight service, to meet customers' current and future logistic needs.

DHL is the global market leader of the international express and logistics industry, specializing in providing innovative and customized solutions from a single source. The company offers expertise in express, air, and ocean freight, overland transport, contract logistics solutions, and international mail services, combined with worldwide coverage and an in-depth understanding of local markets. DHL's international network links more than 220 countries and territories worldwide. Some 300,000 employees worldwide are dedicated to providing fast and reliable services that exceed customers' expectations. Founded in San Francisco in 1969, DHL is a Deutsche Post DHL brand, which is the world's leading provider of logistics services. The group generated revenues of more than 51 billion Euros (more than $72 billion) in 2010.

Business Challenges

DHL Global Forwarding needed to access its data in a quicker and more structured manner so that finance and operational managers could make better-informed budgetary decisions and do forecasting. Since it does business in an industry in which data is always changing, and running the most efficient operations depends on the most updated data, DHL must be agile. The need for reliable, accurate up-to-the-minute data is constant, and without it, finance directors are operating at a disadvantage.

"The biggest change from eight years ago is just how much emphasis we put into accessing information faster and faster," says Anand Saxena, Financial Reporting (FIRE) at DHL Global Forwarding. "The same reports that would come out on the tenth working day of the month now need to be available by the third or fourth working day."

A paramount concern for DHL was being able to access reliable data despite change. For example, over the past eight years, DHL has acquired five significantly sized companies, which resulted in major changes in the accounting system, among other areas. Despite that, it still has historical data in its system, and through all that change, some areas have been altered considerably, including accounting codes changing from 5 to 38 digits.

"We have retained all of our information and all its gory detail," Saxena adds. "So, if anybody still wants to know how much we spent on, say, warehouse employee salaries in Milwaukee, in Air Export in January 2002, they can go, in and dig right in to get it."

---

[6] IBM case study: DHL Global Forwarding stays on time with Cognos TM1 system. 25 Aug 2009. http://www-142 .ibm.com | Software | Library.

Another priority was security. Like thousands of other companies, DHL needs to pass quarterly security audits. As part of the audit, all the security facets of the applications at the DHL IT center are audited to make sure all pertinent regulations are followed. This entails a lengthy questionnaire disclosing who has access to the system, and how access is determined. Because Cognos TM1 is self-contained, DHL can implement security with the solution even at the cell level, which enables concurrent use without the threat of data getting overwritten by multiple users in the same application. This makes it very easy to manage access, and there is data integrity at all times. These features allow DHL's financial organization to focus on process improvements as much as possible, and as a result, its financial analytics have become more efficient.

Business Value

DHL evaluated numerous financial analytics solutions from several competing vendors before ultimately selecting Cognos TM1. The overall functionality, including the system's ability to provide highly intuitive analysis and reporting, and its comprehensive security and audit trails, was significantly better than any of the other products evaluated.

From an IT environment perspective, DHL operates on Microsoft Windows, and uses Oracle and IBM AS/400 for its accounting and business operations. DHL went live with the current version of Cognos TM1 in 2006, after it had completed its fifth acquisition. It took less than six weeks to provide a detailed and consolidated financial report of the acquisition—including accurate reporting of the key performance indicators (KPIs)—after data had been incorporated from the acquired company. According to Saxena, DHL has had such wide success and strong results that it will soon upgrade to the newest version of Cognos TM1.

While there are many new features and functionalities within each upgrade, DHL made special use of the TurboIntegrator function, which improved stability in importing data from files. The overarching goal, which the company continues to meet or exceed, is to provide decision makers with the most reliable, up-to-date budget information possible.

Benefits Realized

Approximately 55 licensed users across North America access Cognos TM1 practically every day for forecasting and budgeting data from the entire global organization. Everything from quarterly forecasts to annual budgets is being created within the Cognos TM1 environment. All users have their own templates that they can update directly from Cognos TM1 at their convenience, and the sales organization also uses data generated from reports. Nontechnical users are able to use the easy, intuitive solution with no snarls. The company's data from its accounting system in Prague is updated on an hourly basis so that finance can have a consolidated view of the company's performance. Because of the speed of Cognos TM1, 100,000 updated records are consolidated and available for view from the Cognos TM1 server in Arizona in as little as 90 seconds. DHL uses monthly reporting of the figures at all levels, down to the smallest reporting unit, which is considered a station. The organization can also use this data for measuring KPIs.

"Cognos TM1 fills a very particular role in the company and does it really well," Saxena adds. According to Saxena, the solution has also helped DHL avoid costly travel expenses that it used to incur when a dozen department heads met in one city for day-long budget sessions. In doing its 2009 fiscal year budget, DHL was able to accomplish the same goals by conference calls instead, because every stakeholder had access to the same data at the same time. What's more, as the slowing economy is forcing budget revisions, DHL is making these changes on the fly, and with great ease. The more streamlined approach to budgeting has enabled DHL to react faster to challenging business conditions.

"Cognos TM1 is flexible enough that it's very friendly in accepting data," Saxena says. "It's easy to change and it's easy to adapt it to changing conditions. You can change models 20 times if you need to, and do it rapidly."

DHL's use of Cognos TM1 is paving the way for users to have better experiences. Rather than running queries in the IBM AS/400 system, which has a DOS interface, users can look at the same data easily in Cognos TM1 and prepare their templates ahead of time, then just update them with the new numbers when needed. And as for administrative requirements, Cognos TM1 calls for almost no upkeep. Saxena reports that he spends roughly four hours per year on technical upkeep and administration, or approximately one hour each quarter. That very limited amount of maintenance enables Saxena and others to focus more on strategic analysis, reporting, and budgeting functions that can enhance the bottom line.

Saxena notes that every time DHL has made one of their five acquisitions, the company has decided to continue using the intuitive Cognos TM1 solution because of its superior analytical capabilities and ease of use, when compared with what other organizations were using prior to the acquisition. In one case, he notes, several people were doing tasks now handled by one person with Cognos TM1. "Cognos TM1 is a very versatile application— it's easy to test and it's easy to change and switch things around," Saxena adds. "It just makes business easier."

Extending Your Data Warehouse

As mentioned in Chapter 1, data warehouses are under increased demands to meet the current business requirements. These range from the diversity of corporate systems through acquisitions and/or mergers, increased collection of internal and external data on customers and employees, and increased demand to access and interact with this information in a way that business users can consume to drive analysis and planning processes with little or zero latency. Cognos TM1 not only meets Codd's 12/18 rules of OLAP but exceeds these requirements, as noted earlier in this chapter. Cognos TM1 has a long history in providing purpose-built data marts to meet the specific requirements of departments. These data marts, shown in Figure 2-5, allow businesses to organize data in a format that allows business users the ability to perform ad hoc queries, scenario analysis, and create new information through planning and forecasting. Cognos TM1 provides an extension of your data warehouse that is governed by data warehouse data and metadata definitions.

Now let's take a look at how Impregilo and Giant Tiger have extended their data warehouse strategy with Cognos TM1 to meet their business requirements for planning and analyses.

Impregilo

Listed on the Italian Stock Exchange, Impregilo[7] is a leading general contractor and one of the world's top-ranking construction groups, with a presence in over 29 countries. The Impregilo Group is an international specialist in major infrastructure projects and civil buildings of architectural prestige, such as the extension of the Panama Canal, the Thessaloniki subway, the Las Vegas tunnel, and hydroelectric plants in South Africa and Chile. Impregilo boasts

---

[7] IBM case study: Impregilo builds a powerful group-wide reporting solution: Gaining faster, more accurate budgets and forecasts with Cognos TM1. 01 Dec 2010. http://www-142.ibm.com | Software | Library.

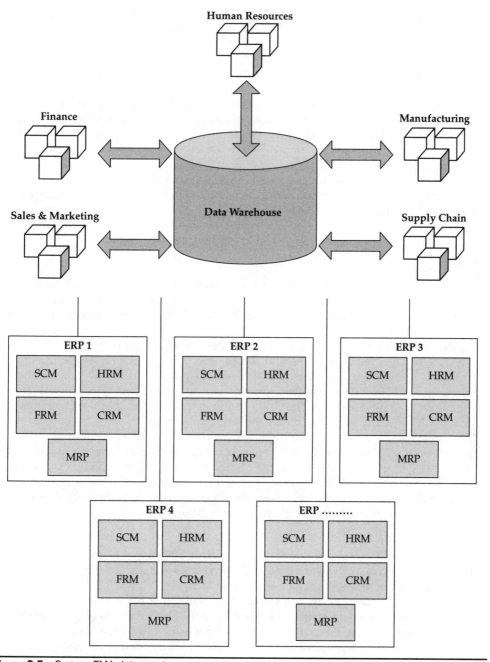

FIGURE 2-5   Cognos TM1 data marts

annual revenues of over 1 billion with net income at 52.6 million in the first half of 2010. A solid 75 percent of earnings are made up from the group's foreign sales.

Business Challenge

The Impregilo Group consists of around 120 different companies/project teams, each of which needs to manage large-scale, high-profile construction projects within set budgets and schedules. The challenge for Impregilo was to create an infrastructure that could collect a variety of information from this disparate set of companies, and enable users at corporate headquarters and within the subsidiaries to create detailed reports and perform budgeting and forecasting tasks. Furthermore, Impregilo wanted an easy-to-use system that could be quickly rolled out across the group.

Giovanni Manzini, IT Project Manager Accounting Consolidation and Reporting, comments: "With so many group companies and so many projects, we have to manage an enormous amount of data. We needed to find a way to collect all this information together in order to create, in as simple a manner as possible, a single repository for analysis and reporting."

Benefits Realized

Impregilo wanted to find a solution that it could roll out fast. The company evaluated a number of planning and reporting solutions before choosing Cognos TM1. Within a month the company had worked with Stratos, an IBM Business Partner, to complete the first phase of the implementation.

Manzini notes, "We had already spent five months creating a single central data repository using SAP NetWeaver Business Warehouse, which collects and structures all the financial information from our ERP system and other systems. Then we integrated this data warehouse with the Cognos TM1 solution in order to provide rapid access to powerful analytics. This took just one month to implement. The Cognos solution provides easy-to-use planning, budgeting, forecasting, reporting, and performance management.

"Our first goal was to make the planning and reporting department completely independent of the IT department—so that they could create their own reports and analyses without needing help from IT staff. We accomplished this in record time, and the department is now able to make its own budget plans. The need for technical skill used to be a barrier that prevented people from accessing the information they needed; but with Cognos TM1, information can flow throughout the company much more freely."

Eliminating Manual Workload Manzini adds: "For our second objective, the Director of the Budget Planning and Control department was very clear. He wanted to make changes in his department in order to avoid wasting time on the production of numbers. He wanted his team to concentrate on analysis, not data-collection.

"Now, the combination of Cognos TM1 and SAP NetWeaver BW provides a single central source of accurate data, so users can spend less time collecting and validating data, and have more time to focus on analyzing risks and opportunities for the Group. There was always a need to produce this information, but Cognos TM1 makes it much easier and much faster, which is a clear benefit for both the business as a whole and the individual users."

A Comprehensive Solution   Cognos TM1 has provided Impregilo with a comprehensive business analytics solution, capable of delivering everything from financial and operational modeling to performance management. Most importantly, Cognos TM1 is able to bring together data from the group's SAP system and other sources to provide a single version of the truth.

In addition to viewing information, Cognos TM1 also enables properly authorized users to add and edit data within the data warehouse. As an example, the budgeting and forecasting departments can use Cognos TM1 to create multiple versions of each budget to model different financial scenarios. When the analysis is complete, the final version of the budget can then be moved back manually into the SAP environment and used across the whole business.

Says Manzini, "We chose Cognos TM1 because it is very powerful and flexible, and the interface is simply excellent. The great thing is that you can use it to manipulate and analyze data in all sorts of different ways without having to develop any additional processes in the ERP system itself."

He concludes: "We currently have 20 users using the Cognos TM1 solution at headquarters, and we have begun the roll-out worldwide. The new users are happy with the solution because it makes it much easier for them to access the business information they need to make fast, accurate business decisions, without having to wait for help from technical specialists in the IT department. Our financial analysts, business managers, and executives are all able to use the solution to do their own real-time analytics, and we estimate that we will have 100 users by the end of the year."

Giant Tiger

Giant Tiger is a Canadian retail chain with more than 200 stores coast to coast. The company employs more than 7,000 people and has built an extensive network of franchise stores. Aiming to maintain a local presence even in smaller communities, Giant Tiger competes with both large out-of-town chains like Wal-Mart and Loblaw's, and smaller local stores.[8]

Business Challenge

Giant Tiger's planning processes were largely manual: data was extracted from the corporate financial system into a Microsoft Access database, and then processed into more than 200 separate spreadsheets, one for each of the company's stores. Collecting and validating the data took two or three weeks each quarter, and creating the spreadsheets and distributing them to the stores took an additional two days. "The process was slow and cumbersome even when everything ran smoothly," explains Foster. "But if something needed to be changed at a late stage, we had to manually update every one of the 200 files, which was really painful! More important, though, was the effect on the business. The lead time on the budgeting process made it difficult to react in an agile way to changing market situations: by the time the data was available, it was already several weeks old. Moreover, since each store was managing its own budget during the quarter and there was no easy way to join up the data, it was difficult to get a corporate or regional overview of operations."

---

[8] IBM case study: Giant Tiger bridges the gap in financial planning. 11 June 2011. http://www-01.ibm.com/ software/success/cssdb.nsf/CS/STRD-8JNMDB?OpenDocument&Site=default&cty=en_us

Benefits Realized

The Giant Tiger team began looking for a solution to these problems, and quickly selected Cognos TM1. "Cognos TM1 really ticked all the boxes for us," explains Foster. "It promised to be relatively quick and easy to implement." Working with IBM, the team implemented a planning and analysis solution that integrated the company's Teradata warehouse with Cognos TM1. This provided a closed-loop planning process that reduced planning cycles and increased analytics capability, as well as maximizing the value of Giant Tiger's Teradata investment. "We still have to import some data from other systems, but in the near future, everything will be in Teradata," says Foster. "The integration between the Cognos TM1 and Teradata is very stable and reliable—the close strategic relationship between IBM and Teradata is a big advantage here."

New Insight for Different User Groups   The new solution provides different groups of users with different levels of access, helping them find the information they need quickly and easily. Buyers can drill up and down through product hierarchies to understand sales trends in different categories and help them plan for the next six to nine months. Regional Support Managers (RSMs) can use store hierarchies to compare performance within and between regions. And individual store managers can submit actual data into the Cognos TM1 web interface on a daily basis, helping to track sales and costs against projections in real time. "The ability to do regional analysis easily is a major step forward," comments Foster. "Previously, there wasn't an easy way to group financial information for stores in different regions, so the RSMs had to look at each store's targets and results individually. Now, it's easy for them to compare stores and regions using hard numbers, which helps them to support their stores more effectively. Now, because the collection is mostly automated, we can gather more data and perform more sophisticated analyses in the same amount of time."

Faster Process, Greater Agility   With Cognos TM1, the quarterly budgeting process is largely automated and can be completed in three days—an 85 percent improvement on the previous lead time of three weeks. The solution also reduces workload for more than 220 users, who can each save approximately one hour per week by submitting data directly into the system via the web instead of using spreadsheets. "The time we save is put to good use: the planning team at corporate headquarters can now concentrate on actually analyzing the data instead of just putting the reports together," explains Foster. "Since the process can be completed so much faster, we are also now considering doing revisions on a monthly basis, which simply wouldn't have been possible with our old system. Above all, the new solution helps us give users access to budgeting and forecasting data in a more timely way, which helps us react to changing market conditions in a more agile way." As an example, Foster cites the effect of economic and political forces on Giant Tiger's planning processes: "The current political instability in the Middle East leads to rising oil prices, which leads to increased freight costs, which raises the price of cotton, which affects the pricing strategy for our clothing lines and therefore impacts our budgets and forecasts. Equally, recent layoffs in the automotive industry, which is a major part of Ontario's economy, mean that the average consumer in that region may have less money to spend—which again will have an effect on our sales performance. Previously, although we could identify these kinds of factors, our planning processes were too slow to react to them effectively. With Cognos TM1, we can be much more responsive, and ensure that our top-down corporate planning aligns better with what the stores can actually achieve."

Summary

In summary, the goal of this chapter was to continue our conversation about the increased demands on planning and analysis processes in global organizations and to share how Cognos TM1 has met and continues to meet the broadest planning and analysis requirements in the industry. Over 4,000 global companies spanning all industries have come to depend on Cognos TM1 to help drive decisions across their organizations. This chapter reviewed today's highly volatile business environment and gave examples of how leading organizations have met these challenges to drive increased performance with Cognos TM1. These demands ranged from increased forecasting and budget cycles, rise of scenario analytics, heightened ERP requirements, and rising demands on data warehouses. Cognos TM1 continues to play a critical role in an organization's ability to make informed decisions.

Now let's turn our attention in Chapter 3 to the incredible journey Cognos TM1 has made from a pioneer as a DOS-based in-memory analytics product to a 64-bit enterprise-scale OLAP product that over 4,000 companies rely on for daily decision making.

Evolution of IBM Cognos TM1

The goal of this chapter is to provide a historical perspective on the development and continued value that Cognos TM1 brings to global organizations. The simple yet powerful notion established by Manny Perez of a product that is simple to use, scalable, and flexible to meet the broadest challenges of planning and analysis has evolved over time as hardware and software have become more sophisticated and user requirements have expanded.

Cognos TM1 was initially created as a DOS-based personal productivity tool to respond to the forecasting and analysis requirements of the oil crisis in 1984. Exxon, the first customer of TM1, required a tool to help analyze and forecast the supply and demand of oil globally. Business users needed a highly flexible tool to instantly calculate changes in both data and business assumptions; in Exxon's case, between supply characteristics and demand signals globally. These requirements demanded a unique approach not offered by relational disk-based solutions that were currently available. Thus was born an in-memory OLAP database that allows users to interact with data and business rules as soon as the data is loaded in the OLAP structure. This approach reduced latency in data loading and precalculations while providing calculation on demand as data and business assumptions changed.

As noted in Table 3-1, Cognos TM1 has stood the test of time from an early DOS-based product to a core component of the Cognos 8 & 10 performance management platform, providing planning, budgeting, and forecasting solutions, profitability analysis, and scenario analytics to over 4,000 customers globally. Table 3-1 lists some key milestones in that journey.

Cognos TM1 has had a long history of OLAP firsts, which include a number of key highlights:

- First OLAP product to meet E. F. Codd's 12 rules of OLAP
- First in-memory OLAP engine
- First OLAP multicube architecture
- First OLAP multiserver
- First commercial OLAP databases linked to spreadsheets
- First spreadsheet add-in for multiuser OLAP database
- First OLAP vendor to provide an external API
- First client-server OLAP

Year	Innovation
1984	TM1 first release during 1984 oil crisis
1987	Sparsity Management
1990	Client/server product 1990; Lotus add-in
1992	Cube rules
1993	Windows: Excel add-in Perspectives
1995	Non-linear rules
1998	Stargate cache optimization Object-oriented development environment Multithreading multiprocessing Replication OLE DB for OLAP (ODBO)
1999	Web client TurboIntegrator 64-bit server
2000	Data-spreading capabilities Microsoft .NET support TM1 Perspectives Web Client
2005	SAP BW support for TurboIntegrator 256-dimension support
2008	Unicode-compliant Support for long strings Action buttons Websheets Active forms
2009	TM1 joins Cognos Platform Contributor client Support for Cognos Framework Manager Support for Cognos Connection Unified Cognos Security Sandbox Personal Scenarios
2010	Enhancements for parallel interaction Support for Cognos 10 Business Insight widget
2011	Performance Modeler Cognos Insight Operations Console

TABLE 3-1   Cognos TM1 Technical Innovation Timeline

TM1 Architecture

Let's examine these innovations in a bit more detail. To meet the broadest requirements of planning and analysis, TM1 architecture from its earliest incarnations was in-memory based. In-memory–based systems provide the highest calculation performance and user interaction with reduced latency. This concept is at the core of 32-bit and 64-bit TM1-based solutions that are extended by rich clients to serve finance, line of business, and IT. Figure 3-1 provides an overview of Cognos TM1 as a key component of the Cognos Performance Platform.

Cognos TM1 has a number of key advantages that have driven its adoption globally.

Compressed Data Storage and Data Explosion

The Cognos TM1 design uses a unique approach that differs from most OLAP products, which achieve response time requirements through precalculating consolidations and derived values. This approach often leads to "data explosion" with large data cubes that require complex calculation scripts to maintain each level of consolidation, as well as long waits.

To avoid this issue and reduce latency, Cognos TM1 stores only the lowest-level element values in the model extremely efficiently. For example, a 100MB input file from a relational database typically requires only 10MB in Cognos TM1. Based on this, large models can be put into memory and can be calculated quickly and efficiently on demand with little latency. This approach allows Cognos TM1 to support large models that would require several hundred gigabytes in precalculated OLAP products.

Sparsity Handling

In addition, data density can also be a challenge for OLAP products. For example, all products are not sold by all channels and regions. As the cube dimensionality grows, so does the scarcity or storage of zero data, which adds to the size of the cube. Cognos TM1 handles this issue by storing only non-zero data as well as supporting a multicube architecture, thereby reducing the cube size and creating more flexible cubes based on business requirements, not product requirements. This allows for highly efficient memory usage.

Multicube Architecture

Another important benefit of the multicube architecture as compared to single hypercube architecture is the ability to create and extend solutions as they evolve and are optimized for the data they represent. For example, an expense model and a sales revenue model can coexist in an application and feed a profit-and-loss statement cube to provide an analysis by each of these separate processes that are modeled differently. A distinct advantage of multicube architecture is the ability to reuse dimensions in multiple cubes, creating a single source for metadata management. So as a solution expands with new cubes to handle pricing, or as exchange rates are added, consistency between cubes is maintained. All of this enables Cognos TM1 applications to be more compact and maintainable and to evolve as your business requirements expand.

Enterprise Deployment and Scalability

Cognos TM1 provides a broad range of deployment options to meet both application requirements and global decentralized organizations. As noted in Figure 3-2, Cognos TM1

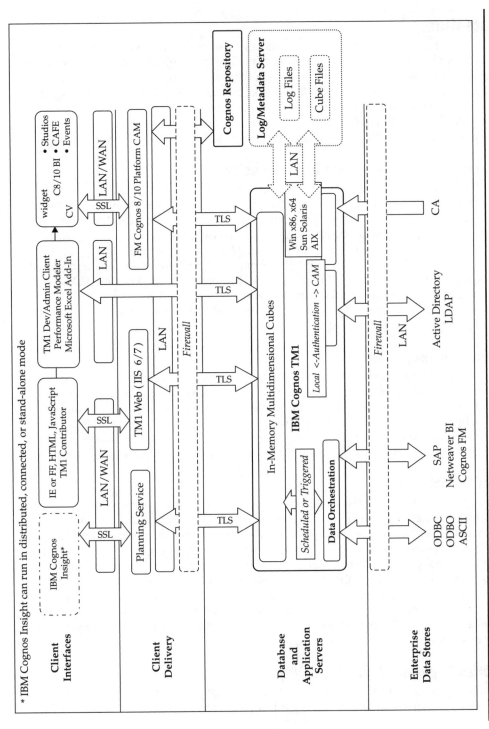

Figure 3-1 Cognos Performance Platform

IBM Cognos TM1 Deployment Options

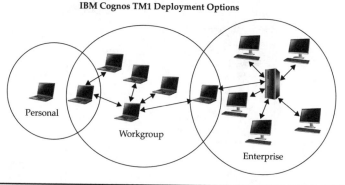

FIGURE 3-2   Cognos TM1 deployment options

can scale from a personal productivity process to a workgroup process and finally to an enterprise deployment that can take advantage of a centralized or distributed processing model, which takes the best of both deployment models, thus allowing for both offline and centralized planning and analysis.

Cognos TM1 provides unique deployment capabilities that in turn provide deployment options based on application, network, and finally hardware requirements to scale from one to one thousand users. Each of these deployments is based on the same development objects: dimensions, cubes, rules, applications, and processes. Let's take a look at these objects in a bit more detail.

Cognos TM1 Server

As mentioned earlier in this chapter, Cognos TM1 is a 64-bit in-memory OLAP database that provides on-demand calculations for a broad set of planning, forecasting, and analysis solutions. Let's now take a quick look at a number of key development objects. One of the hallmarks of a TM1-based solution is the simplicity of the development environment and objects. Cognos TM1 contains the following key objects, as shown in Figure 3-3:

- Dimensions
- Cubes
  - Rules
- Applications
- Processes
- Chores

Dimensions

Let's start our conversation with dimensions. A Cognos TM1 *dimension* is a listing of elements and their relationship to each other. As displayed in Figure 3-4, elements can be organized in endless consolidation methods to support the most complex business relationships. Cognos TM1 supports dimensions that are external to cube definition,

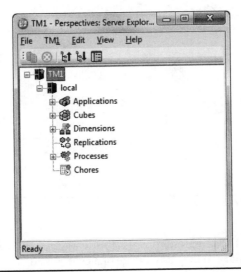

Figure 3-3 Cognos TM1 server objects

which allows for ease of metamaintenance across multiple cubes. Cognos TM1 dimensions are primarily used for defining the "what and how" you are measuring within a cube. For example, let's take a look at some common dimensions to consider for a profit and loss statement. In Figure 3-4 we can see a dimension called account2, which provides the "what" that is being measured. This includes the line items in a regional profit and loss

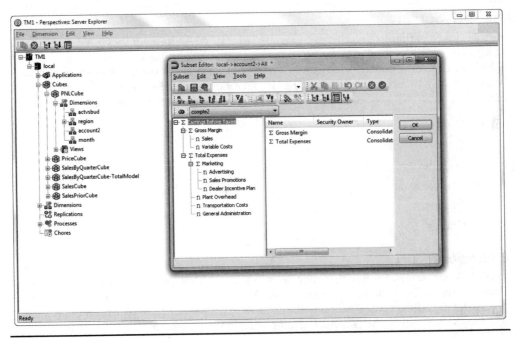

Figure 3-4 Cognos TM1 dimensions

statement with a number of consolidations that culminate in earnings before taxes. Also, a weight can be established in these consolidations, which can be either negative in the case of expenses or positive for sales.

Cognos TM1 aggregates data according to the child-parent relations explicitly defined within dimensions. This allows for advanced relationships like alternative hierarchies where a child element can have multiple parents, allowing for an unlimited number of rollups within a dimension. These relationships can be further enhanced with aliases to allow for simplification of element names from data sources while maintaining data consistency. Taking this example further, additional "how" dimensions include region, actvsbud, and month. Each of these dimensions provides context on "what" data will be stored and "how" it will be organized for analysis and planning.

Cubes

Now let's move on to Cognos TM1 cubes. Cognos TM1 cubes are made up of cells, which represent the intersection point of all distinct combinations of dimension elements. Although Cognos TM1 does not require specific types of dimensions to construct a cube, some common definitions are a time dimension and a measure dimension that contains the elements where data is stored. In Figure 3-5 we are using the Cognos TM1 Cube Viewer to examine the SalesCube, in which the measure dimension is account1 with the time dimension defined as month. This cube is further dimensioned as actvsbud, region, and month.

Once a cube is formed based on your business requirements, then advanced calculations are constructed, called Cognos TM1 rules.

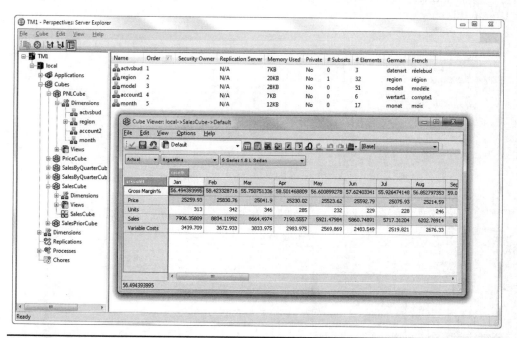

FIGURE 3-5 Cognos TM1 Cube Viewer

Cognos TM1 Rules

Rules in Cognos TM1 are a means of calculating results in a cube, which is a more powerful and flexible method than simple consolidation of a dimension. Rules can cross dimensions, refer to data in other cubes, and use metadata to limit the impact of calculations on the cube. Similar to consolidations, Cognos TM1 rules are calculated on demand. Unlike consolidations, sparsity cannot be determined in advance, which means that the results will be empty without additional information. For this purpose, feeders are used to identify which intersections need to have rules evaluated, and which can be skipped. Effective use of feeders is essential to making rules efficient and avoiding combinatorial explosion. The Cognos TM1 Rules Editor (see Figure 3-6) provides an easy way to create and modify rules.

This capability is augmented with a rules tracer that is available through the Cube Viewer to allow users to see how cells are calculated as well as provide an excellent debugging tool, shown in Figure 3-7.

Applications Folders

Application folders organize Cognos TM1 objects into logical groups and provide context for solution development. They can contain shortcuts to cubes, views, and Websheets. Each of these objects can be private or public depending on the scope of the application. In Figure 3-8, we have an application named Sales Forecasting that contains three views to support the input of a plan. The P&L and Sales Performance views provide actual information on sales by region combined with expenses. The Forecast Input view is primarily a data input vehicle for sales to commit forecasts.

Applications can be leveraged through our Microsoft Excel-based solution, as discussed later in this chapter.

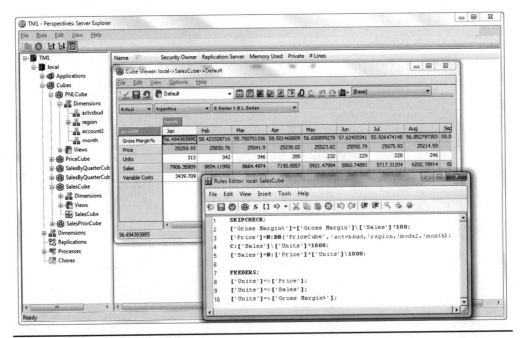

FIGURE 3-6 Cognos TM1 Rules Editor

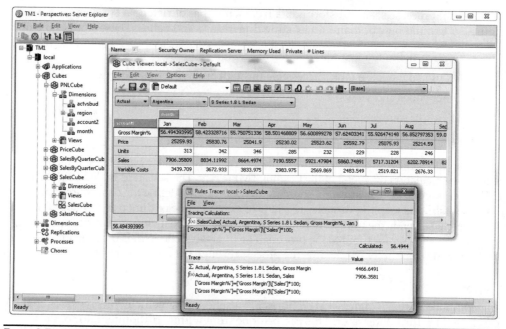

FIGURE 3-7   Cognos TM1 rules tracer

Processes

Cognos TM1 processes perform data and metadata maintenance such as importing data into a Cognos TM1 database, exporting data from a Cognos TM1 database, establishing dimensions, or moving data from one Cognos TM1 cube to another. Processes consist of TurboIntegrator "scripts" consisting of prescriptive programmatic logic, including Cognos TM1 functions for manipulating Cognos TM1 data structures. Once the TI process is designed, you can rerun it or schedule it to be used when importing data from a dynamic source. These processes can focus on either internal or external data sources.

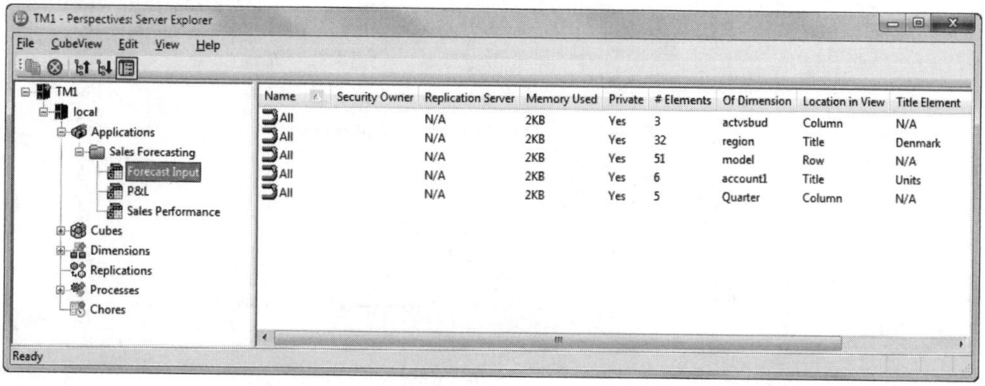

FIGURE 3-8   Sales Forecasting application

External processes can transform data from a number of rich data sources as shown in Figure 3-9 to build new or maintain existing dimensions and cubes. These sources include:

- Comma-delimited text files including ASCII files
- Relational database tables accessible through an ODBC data source
- Other cubes and views
- Microsoft Analysis Services
- Cognos packages

Processes can also be used to manage internal data that tends to be static, and thereby reduce the calculation overhead of the Cognos TM1 server. The key steps in defining a Cognos TM1 process are to identify the data source (Data Source tab), define the data source variables (Variables tab), and map the variables to a new or existing cube or dimension (Maps tab). The Advanced tab extends the transformation process, provides the inclusion of new parameters, and prompts the user for input to the process. The final tab (Schedule) is the schedule table, which provides the ability to schedule the process through the creation of a chore.

Chores

As mentioned earlier, Cognos TM1 Chores are a scheduling vehicle for processes that are created by TurboIntegrator. This can be done from within TurboIntegrator but also through the Chore definition process. The Cognos TM1 Chore definition process, as noted

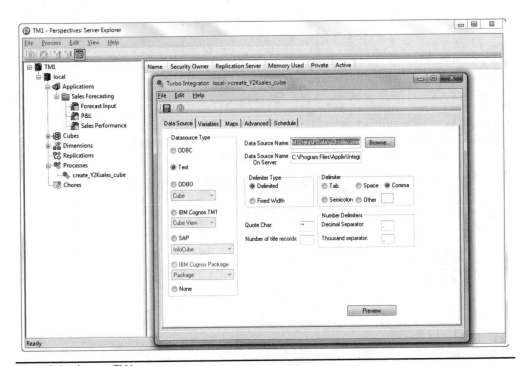

FIGURE 3-9   Cognos TM1 processes

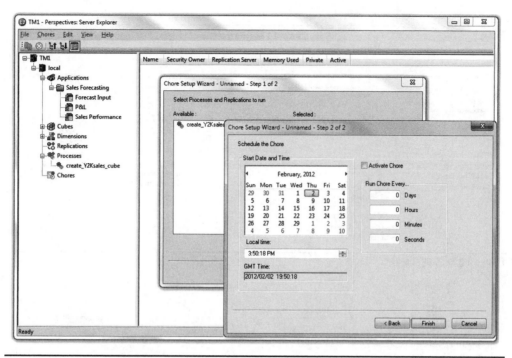

FIGURE 3-10 Cognos TM1 Chore Setup Wizard

in Figure 3-10, contains the identification of one or more processes and the scheduling of the start date and the frequency. This is particularly helpful for the batch scheduling of updates of multiple data sources, which require different time intervals for their update.

Cognos TM1 Clients

To complement Cognos TM1's high-performance server, there are a number of clients specifically created to serve a broad array of demands across an enterprise, as noted in Figure 3-11.

These clients can be categorized under Administration, Microsoft Excel-Based Solutions, Desktop Workspace, Managed Contribution, and finally Enterprise Portal. Let's begin our discussion from an administration perspective.

Cognos TM1 Administration

Cognos TM1 Administration is accomplished through a number of clients, which include Cognos TM1 Architect, Performance Modeler, and Cognos TM1 Operation Console.

Cognos TM1 Architect

Cognos TM1 Architect was specifically designed for users who seek to administer Cognos TM1–based solutions without requiring Microsoft Excel. Architect, noted in Figure 3-12,

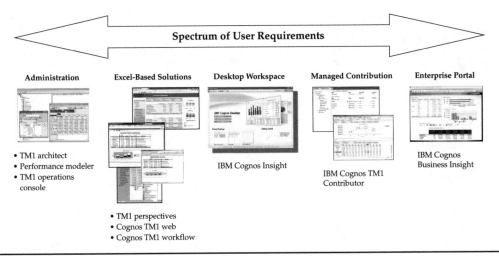

Figure 3-11 Cognos TM1 clients

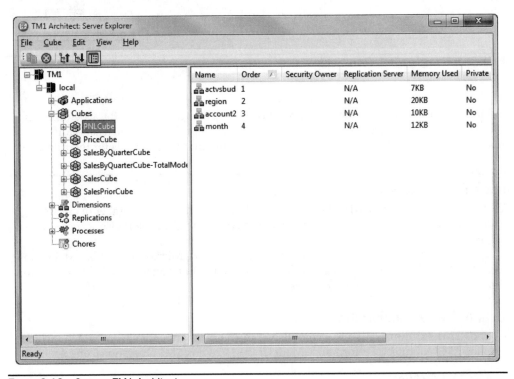

Figure 3-12 Cognos TM1 Architect

provides access to all core Cognos TM1 server-based objects for development and maintenance. Within Architect, users with proper security credentials can create or modify dimensions, cubes, rules, processes, and chores. They can also manage replication between servers as required based on your application requirements.

Cognos Performance Modeler

Cognos Performance Modeler, noted in Figure 3-13, extends Architect by providing a modern modeling environment specifically designed for the business user to ease the development and maintenance of Cognos TM1 solutions. Cognos Performance Modeler uses simple concepts of list, links, and cubes to generate rich Cognos TM1–based models. Performance Modeler uses a visual approach to Cognos TM1 modeling that generates complex dimension cubes and rules in a WYSIWYG environment that provides the ability to create and test business assumptions. This, combined with financial and time intelligence capabilities, accelerates the learning curve and development time of Cognos TM1–based solutions.

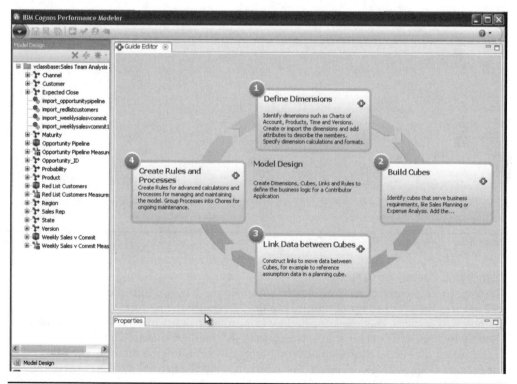

FIGURE 3-13   Cognos Performance Modeler

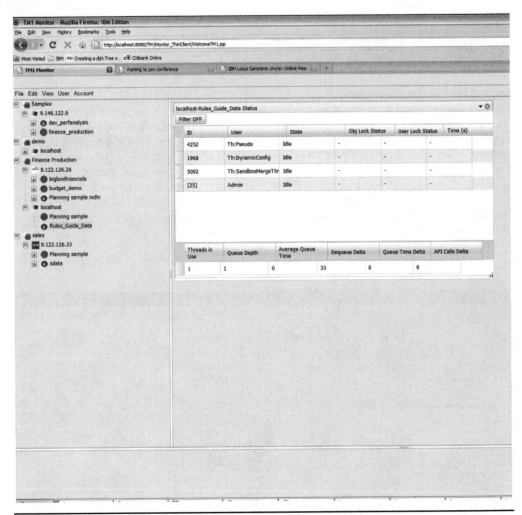

FIGURE 3-14   Cognos TM1 Operations Console

Cognos TM1 Operations Console

The Cognos TM1 Operations Console, shown in Figure 3-14, is a thin client administration tool specifically designed for IT administrators to monitor the performance of multiple Cognos TM1 servers. This console provides important insights into key operations of a server, which includes server status, sandboxes, and sandbox queries and threads.

Based on these operations, an administrator can shut down a server and restart it. For existing Cognos TM1 customers, this new console is the further development of the Cognos TM1 server utility known as Cognos TM1 Top.

Excel-Based Solutions

As mentioned earlier, Cognos TM1 has a rich set of clients that specifically extend Microsoft Excel-based solutions. These clients are part of the Cognos TM1 Perspectives family of clients.

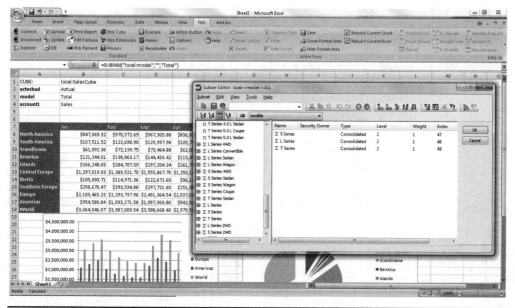

FIGURE 3-15   Cognos TM1 Perspectives

Cognos TM1 Perspectives

Cognos TM1 Perspectives is an Microsoft Excel add-in (see Figure 3-15) and is specifically designed to extend the capabilities of Excel by providing centralized data definition as well as complex modeling and writeback for planning and analysis-based applications. Cognos TM1 functions, available through Cognos TM1's Excel add-in, provide read/write connections to the Cognos TM1 database to integrate Cognos TM1 data with Excel's dynamic layout, formatting, charting, and logic functions to create powerful reports, analysis, and data entry forms. Perspectives for Excel can work locally or connect to a Cognos TM1 server to access information to produce multiuser systems solutions, all from within an Excel workbook.

Cognos TM1 Web

Cognos TM1 Web, displayed in Figure 3-16, extends the analytical power of Cognos TM1 Perspectives for Excel by allowing Cognos TM1 developers to publish their Excel-based solution to the web. Perspectives Web allows business users to view, analyze, edit, and chart your Cognos TM1 data in a controlled, locked-down web browser environment.

Cognos TM1 Web provides read, write, and what-if modeling capabilities from worksheets, or "Websheets," that support the functions and the formatting and graphic capabilities of Microsoft Excel on the web. Advanced personalization enables you to create and update your budgeting and modeling Websheets again, all based on the simple objects defined earlier.

Cognos TM1 Workflow

Cognos TM1 Workflow allows you to create and manage a workflow structure for your planning and budgeting activities from within Microsoft Excel.

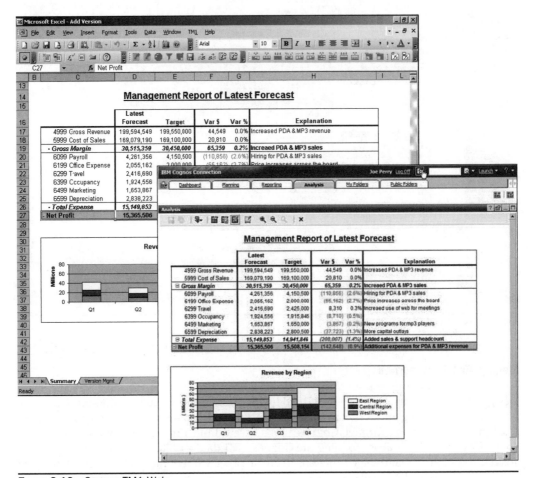

FIGURE 3-16   Cognos TM1 Web

Workflow, featured in Figure 3-17, is a critical component to many planning processes. Cognos TM1 Workflow provides control to the planning process by allowing plan managers to assign responsibility for portions of the plan, enabling contributors to submit their numbers, and empowering reviewers to accept or reject plans. With Cognos TM1 Workflow, organizations can view the status of the entire planning process, streamlining the work and reducing the errors typically encountered with dozens of loosely connected spreadsheets.

Desktop Workspace

Cognos Insight is the newest client of Cognos TM1, which fuses personal analysis with enterprise planning and analysis. Personal Insight, as shown in Figure 3-18, can be used as a personal productivity toolset as well as a rich planning client that provides additional context for planning submission based on analysis of local reports, Excel spreadsheets, and external information such as web links.

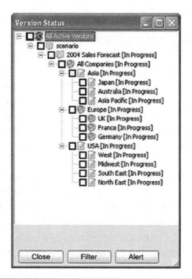

FIGURE 3-17   Cognos TM1 Workflow

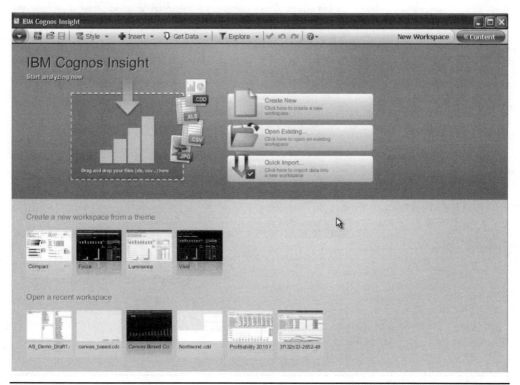

FIGURE 3-18   Cognos Insight

Managed Contribution

An additional client specifically designed to meet the needs of a managed planning and
forecasting process is Cognos TM1 Contributor. Cognos TM1 Contributor is an application
approach to planning and forecasting based on a thin client technology. This client allows
access to the same Cognos TM1 objects that the Excel client uses but creates a managed
collaboration process. Managed contribution users can enjoy the benefits of workflow,
pick-lists for executing driver based plans, and end-user personalization and charting
within their existing planning and analysis processes. The data scalability and analysis
capabilities of Cognos TM1 combined with the managed planning capabilities of Contributor
create a unique and unrivaled user experience in the industry. As shown in Figure 3-19,
Cognos TM1 Contributor is a deployment method within Cognos Performance Modeler,
which is a thin client that leverages the base Cognos TM1 server workflow dimension and
cube views and organizes these components in an application framework known as a
Contributor Application. The attributes are stored in XML and rendered through the
Contributor client. Cognos TM1 Contributor provides a consistent application look and
feel with Workflow, which launches the Contributor Grid that facilitates analysis and the
submission of a plan.

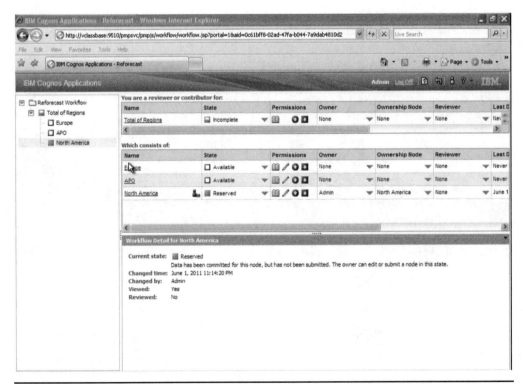

Figure 3-19   Cognos TM1 Contributor

Enterprise Portal

Cognos BI version 10 provides a rich portal for dashboard and scorecard creation. Cognos TM1 can be used to add scenario analysis, planning, and what-if analysis in the context enterprise dashboards through the Cognos TM1 widget.

Cognos Business Insight TM1 Widget

Business Insight provides an integrated business intelligence experience for business users as noted in Figure 3-20. This web-based tool allows you to use Cognos content to build sophisticated interactive dashboards that facilitate collaborative decision making.

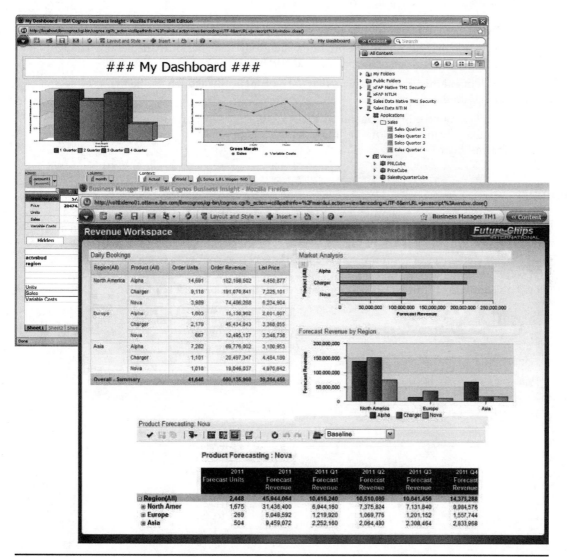

FIGURE 3-20   Business Insight with TM1 widget

These dashboards can include traditional business intelligence assets, along with Cognos Real Time Monitoring information, Cognos TM1 Websheets and Cube Views, as well as external data.

Features from Cognos Go! Dashboard and Cognos Viewer are now merged into one user interface. This brings information consumption, rather than viewing and opening folders, to the forefront of the experience. Cognos Viewer and Cognos Connection are still available and maintained in this release.

The intuitive user interface provides a breadth of capability in one place rather than a depth of capability in any one area. The user interface is visually attractive, easy to use, and interactive.

Key features include the following:

- Free-form layout of dashboard elements
- Interaction that allows you to sort, filter, and group data, perform calculations, change display types, customize the palette, and add comments
- On-demand menus and toolbars that are automatically activated when you select them with the mouse
- Seamless round-trip integration with Cognos Business Insight Advanced. This allows for more advanced exploration and enhancement options for the objects included on the dashboard.

Summary

In summary, this chapter has provided a historical perspective of the development and continued value Cognos TM1 brings to global organizations. Manny Perez set in motion a simple yet powerful notion of a product that is simple to use, scalable, and flexible to meet the broadest challenges of planning and analysis. This notion continues to evolve as hardware and software have become more sophisticated and user requirements have expanded. Now let's continue our discussion of Cognos TM1 in more detail in Chapter 4.

Develop and Manage Cognos TM1 Solutions

This part of the book is about how you can design and implement a solution that is based on Cognos TM1. A solution is built with the building blocks of a Cognos TM1 server. These building blocks are described in Part II: cubes, dimensions, and elements are described in Chapter 5, rules are described in Chapter 6, and TurboIntegrator is described in Chapter 7. We have tried to keep these chapters neutral from a business perspective to provide you a foundation that can be used in any kind of application. Part III of this book will focus on business requirements and how to solve these requirements with Cognos TM1. So this part of the book (Part II) is a prerequisite to Part III (Chapters 14 through 24).

A solution has to be accessed by user clients. We describe the usage of Cognos TM1 Perspectives and Cognos TM1 Perspectives for Web in Chapter 8. Chapter 9 is also about user clients. We will introduce some new user experiences with Performance Modeler and Cognos Insight.

Chapter 10 will go deep into the Cognos TM1 core and discuss how Cognos TM1 caches data and how it locks objects for parallel processing. Chapter 11 should show you how to work with huge amounts of data. Chapter 12 is about user scaling, or how to prevent or reduce "Object Locks," which are explained in Chapter 10. These three chapters deal with issues that could impact the design and development of a Cognos TM1 solution. We think that you should concentrate on the design of a solution in the first step. In the second step you can consider the operational issues. You may have to redesign your solution regarding the operational issues. For instance, because of the volume of the data, you have to partition the data, which means you may have to split cubes. In the last chapter of this part (Chapter 13), we will talk about how to set up the right hardware and how to keep your solution up and running.

But first we would like to introduce a logical architecture, which shows the interaction of the different components of a Cognos TM1 solution. This architecture is outlined as a "T," which stands for Cognos TM1 as an icon.

The T of Cognos TM1

To develop a Cognos TM1 solution, you need a deep understanding of the nature of Cognos TM1. In this chapter we start with the software components that could be involved in a Cognos TM1 solution. We separate the solution into components that are Cognos TM1-only components and components that can be added by the IBM Cognos Business Intelligence Platform. So you will see a small T (Cognos TM1 only) and a big T (Cognos BI included).

In Chapter 3 you already gained an insight into which components are part of Cognos TM1. Now we take a look at how these components work together. These concepts can be explained by the "T" of Cognos TM1. The T of Cognos TM1 is an icon for the logical architecture of a Cognos TM1 environment. We will develop this architecture step by step in the following sections. Let's start with the vertical bar of the small T.

The Cognos TM1 Server

The first component is the Cognos TM1 server, which is represented by a vertical bar. This is the core of a Cognos TM1 solution. The Cognos TM1 server manages information, which is shared by all involved users. The Cognos TM1 server is an instance of the Cognos TM1 OLAP engine and is often called the "database." It is possible to run multiple instances (Cognos TM1 servers) on one machine. A machine could be a physical or virtual computer. In Figure 4-1 you see only a single instance.

Generally when you develop a Cognos TM1 solution, you will start with the design of the multidimensional model. Cognos TM1 supports a multicube architecture. Multicubing is the ability to build an OLAP model with more than one cube and therefore is a main factor in developing a solution.

In Cognos TM1 you can create as many cubes as needed to fulfill the individual business requirements of various departments. All cubes can be linked to the data of another cube. This concept of Cognos TM1 was originally designed to enable departmental users (for instance, management accountants) to build Cognos TM1 models based on their individual business requirements. Cognos TM1 users should be able to "administer" the model without deep technical or IT know-how. Today Cognos TM1 is also used for cross-departmental solutions and for solutions outside the finance departments, and it is operated by the IT department in most cases. Even in these cases, it is important that departmental

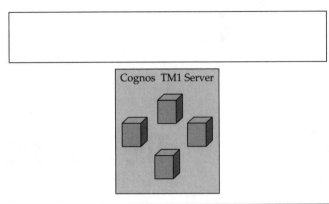

Cognos TM1 Server

FIGURE 4-1   The Cognos TM1 server

users are able to build Cognos TM1 models, because the departmental users can be involved in the development of an enterprise solution more deeply. This is one reason why Cognos TM1 solutions have a short development cycle and have a high acceptance by the departments. It is realistic for most requirements that a user with less IT know-how can develop a Cognos TM1 solution. However, there are exceptions: For instance, if you have to build very large models or build applications with a huge number of concurrent users, you need deeper technical know-how about Cognos TM1 to get Cognos TM1 running with sufficient performance.

Why does a multicube model help to fulfill the departmental requirements? From a departmental perspective, data consists of single values, whereas in an IT perspective, data is described as records. Each value has characteristics that describe what this value means. For instance, a management accountant would explain the figure 100,000 as the revenue, which was generated by region "A" in January of the year 2011 with the product "X." There are many more similarly structured figures that have different characteristics. Cognos TM1 handles this similarly structured data in the following way: A cube holds all figures that have the same number of characteristics.

However, the departmental user does not deal only with one type of figures; there are many different types of figures. For instance, there could be sales data, prices, currency rates, forecasts, project data, costs, and so on. Each of them could have a different set of characteristics. A user who designs the Cognos TM1 model can directly create corresponding cubes for each type. Each cube is built up by a certain set of dimensions. Dimensions represent the characteristics of a figure.

A dimension can be shared by multiple cubes if figures from different types have the same characteristics. In some cases figures are derived from other figures (with the same categories and/or different categories). For example: A set of figures represents the units that are sold by different regions. In the same context, related figures are needed: The revenue of each region could be derived from the units sold and the price. But price has different characteristics. In Cognos TM1 you can create a cube for each type. This could result in a sales cube and a price cube that are linked together by a calculation rule.

Now let us expand what we saw in Figure 4-1 in Figure 4-2.

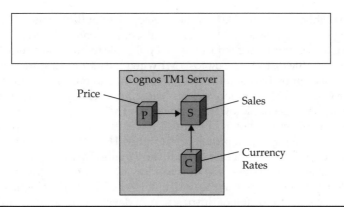

Figure 4-2   Multicube architecture

Figure 4-2 shows an additional cube that is also linked to the sales cube: This cube holds currency rates. These rates are used to convert the revenue in local currency to one or more target currencies. In Part III, which discusses business solutions, you will find some detailed examples that demonstrate the advantage of multicube architecture.

Cognos TM1 Clients

When you develop a Cognos TM1 solution, you need client software, to bring your ideas and designs into the Cognos TM1 server. These clients are represented by the horizontal bar of the T, which is added to the architecture in Figure 4-3.

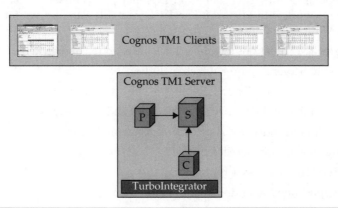

Figure 4-3   The small T

We want to highlight that this state of the development of the Cognos TM1 "T" as shown in the figures would be sufficient to have all components to build a Cognos TM1 solution. But some development clients are also applicable to business users. This capability can be traced back to the history of Cognos TM1 when the administrators, developer, and business users of a Cognos TM1 solution were constituted in one person. Generally a person who develops a Cognos TM1 solution is not a programmer. A Cognos TM1 developer is a business user who has a deeper knowledge of Cognos TM1.

So the simple architecture shown in Figure 4-3 is sufficient to be a complete Cognos TM1 solution. This is an important principle of Cognos TM1: No other system (server software, database, and so on) is necessary to make Cognos TM1 ready to use. But how can a user create dimensions and cubes, and how can the cubes be filled with figures? At this point we should have a closer look at the horizontal bar of the T. The Cognos TM1 software provides different clients for different purposes. As a developer of a Cognos TM1 solution, you should know which Cognos TM1 client has which capabilities in order to decide which user should use which client. So you have to ask questions like these:

- Which users require Excel as a front end?

- Which users require a browser as a front end?

- Does the user require a controlled interface experience for occasional data entry?

- Do the users consume only reports?

- Do the users need to have a simple form-based client to contribute data to a planning process?

- Do the users need a self-service analysis?

As you see, there are different requirements for the front end. In the role of a solution developer, you can decide among three Cognos TM1 clients:

- **Cognos TM1 Perspectives for Microsoft Excel (Excel add-in)**   This software is the most popular Cognos TM1 client for developers, power users, and business users who like to work with Microsoft Excel. Cognos TM1 Perspectives for Excel includes the following capabilities:

  - Cognos TM1 functions enabling data consumption and writeback through Excel

  - Access to Server Explorer, which includes

    - Performing Slice&Dice; pivoting of cube data for analysis

    - Definition and administration of cubes and dimensions

    - Definition and scheduling of TurboIntegrator processes

    - Administration of security

    - Replication and synchronization

    - Application folder document management

Cognos TM1 Perspectives for Excel includes all capabilities to administer a Cognos TM1 server and to develop and maintain the model. Even if these administration functions come with Cognos TM1 Perspectives, the user has to have adequate permission to use this client for development and administration. Actually a business user uses only the browsing functionality and the following features. Cognos TM1 Perspectives for Excel is integrated into Excel to provide interaction between Cognos TM1 servers and Excel worksheets. This integration is based on a library of Cognos TM1-specific Excel functions that can be used in Excel cell formulas. In the following illustration, you can see an example of the main Cognos TM1 function DBRW, which connects an Excel cell to a cell in a Cognos TM1 cube.

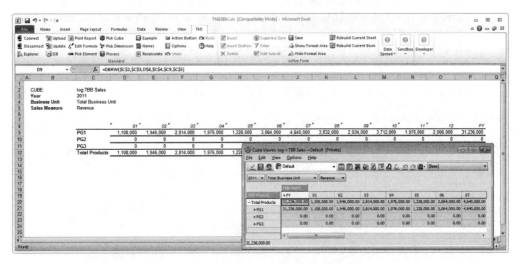

Another key feature of the Excel integration is the Active Form functionality. An Active Form is based on the Cognos TM1 Excel functions and provides the ability to create dynamic Excel reports. We just give you a glance into this feature in this chapter. Please refer to Chapter 8 for more details.

Excel Integration is the key feature that makes the Cognos TM1 Perspectives for Excel a business user tool. But these features are important for the developer, too. Excel reports are often part of a solution. They are provided as ready-to-use reports to users, or they are the source for Cognos TM1 Websheets when you develop a web-based solution. Cognos TM1 Websheets represent an Excel workbook transitioned to HTML and published for multiuser browser consumption. We will discuss Websheets as part of Cognos TM1 Perspectives Web later on. Designing an Excel report could be a part of the development. You will find more details in Chapter 8 regarding building solutions with Excel.

If you develop a solution that includes workflow functionality, you can enhance the Cognos TM1 Perspectives for Excel with the Cognos TM1 Perspectives Workflow (formerly Cognos TM1 Planning Manager). Using Cognos TM1 Perspectives Workflow, an administrator designs a multiuser application that walks users through their task-based assignments. Users open input templates and reports with context assignments, complete their work, and submit their tasks for approval up the workflow hierarchy. A developer can use existing Excel reports as input forms by attaching them to workflow tasks.

- **Cognos TM1 Architect**   The Cognos TM1 Architect is a tailored version of Cognos TM1 Perspectives for Excel. It has all the same capabilities except the integration into Excel (the Cognos TM1 Architect is the "stand-alone" version of the Server Explorer mentioned in the preceding description of Cognos TM1 Perspectives for Microsoft Excel). The purpose of this client is to administer a Cognos TM1 server without an installed version of Microsoft Excel. The Cognos TM1 Architect is commonly used by IT administrators. As a developer, you can use Cognos TM1 Architect if you develop a Cognos TM1 model and business logic only.

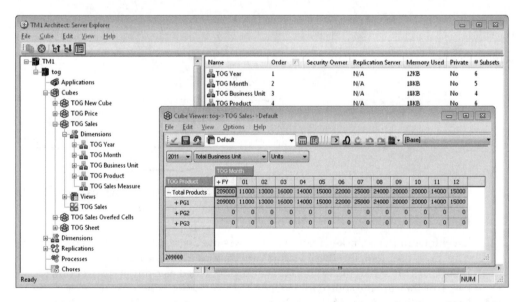

- **Cognos TM1 Performance Modeler**   The Cognos TM1 Performance Modeler is a new client for designing Cognos TM1 models and applications. This client addresses the needs of a model designer (business user or power user). For this purpose, the Cognos TM1 Performance Modeler provides a slightly different point of view to the model than the Cognos TM1 Perspectives/Architect. For instance, the Cognos TM1 Performance Modeler provides calculation rules on a dimension level, which are automatically translated in the background to Cognos TM1 Cube Rules statements. The first version of Cognos TM1 Performance Modeler does not cover all capabilities of Cognos TM1 Perspectives/Architect. So a model designer or administrator has to use Cognos TM1 Perspectives/Architect in addition.

The Cognos TM1 Performance Modeler needs additional software components on the server (Application Server). This additional software is not mentioned in the figures and illustrations because it is not relevant for a logical architecture

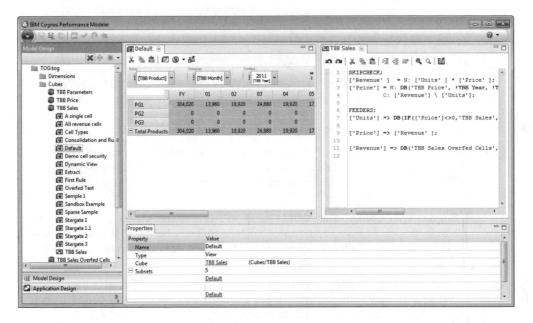

All client software mentioned in the preceding list is able to write back into Cognos TM1 cubes. This is also valid for the clients in the next list. The next clients are purely user front ends. That means that you cannot use these clients to develop the model. But as a developer, you have to use them to test your deliverables. Some of the clients in the next list allow the business user to create personal content. Users of these clients become the "developer" of their personal "solution":

- **Cognos TM1Web**   TM1 Web is a browser-based portal for housing Websheets and Web Cube views. Websheets are HTML versions of "published" Cognos TM1 Excel workbooks. Websheets are read/write-enabled and serve high-volume user

communities. Web Cube views are the HTML versions of Cube Viewer. We will
discuss Cognos TM1 Web in Chapter 8 in more detail.

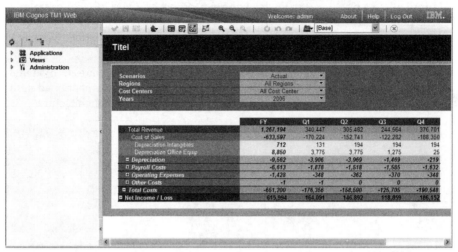

- **Cognos TM1 Contributor**   With Cognos TM1 Contributor you can assemble
  existing Cognos TM1 model components to create and deploy managed planning
  applications. The Cognos TM1 Contributor is not a single client but a bunch of
  clients for various purposes:

  - **Cognos TM1 Contributor Administration**   This client is used to develop and
    administer managed contribution applications. The Cognos TM1 Contributor
    Administration is obsolete since Cognos TM1 10.1, because it is included in the
    Cognos TM1 Performance Modeler.

  - **The Cognos Application Portal**   The Cognos Application Portal is the starting
    point for all users who contribute to a planning process. It is an overview of all
    contributions that are assigned to a user group.

- **Cognos TM1 Contributor Web Client**   Cognos TM1 Contributor Web Client
  consists of a predefined set of Web Cube Views and Websheets, rendered by the
  Cognos TM1 Perspectives Web Server engine. The business users do their input
  via Cube Viewers and/or Websheets. In this mode, Cube Viewers and Websheets
  are enhanced with functions to control the workflow.

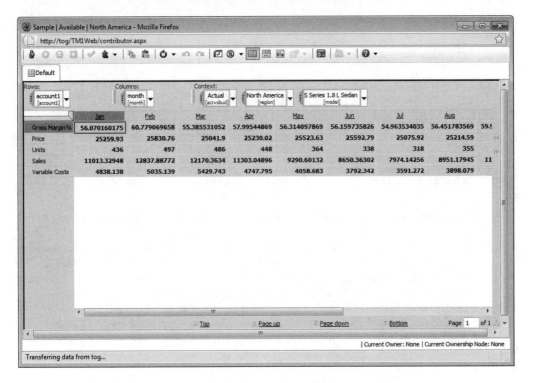

- **Cognos Insight Connected/ Cognos Insight Distributed**   These clients are based
  on the same software: Cognos Insight. Cognos Insight Connected and Cognos
  Insight Distributed are modes of Cognos Insight. Cognos Insight Connected is used

for online (connected) contributions. Cognos Insight Distributed is used for disconnected contributions. Please see the next section for further information.

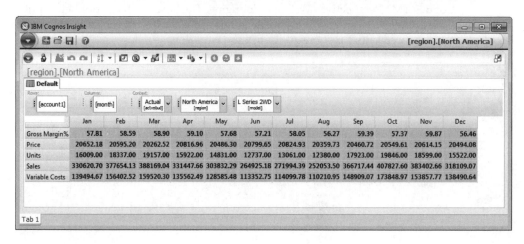

- **Cognos Insight**   Cognos Insight is a new Cognos TM1 client that can operate in a connected and a disconnected mode. These modes can be used for analysis but also as a part of a managed planning application (see the preceding section). If this client is disconnected from a Cognos TM1 server, Cognos Desktop uses a local built-in Cognos TM1 server. This server is hidden from the user. A business user can create cubes, dimensions. and business rules in his local Cognos TM1 instance. The business user becomes a "developer" of his personal analytical solution. The local solution can be published to a central application server to be shared with other business users. The look and feel of the Cognos Desktop is similar to Cognos

Business Insight. With Cognos Desktop the business user can create Dashboards using Cube Viewer, Images, Filters, and so on.

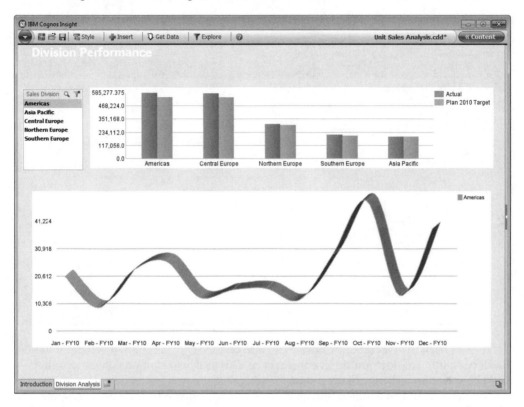

Now we are very close to finishing the discussion of the various clients that could be part of a Cognos TM1 solution. There is still one client left, which is an administrator tool:

- **Cognos TM1 Operations Console (formally Cognos TM1Top)**   The Cognos TM1 Operations Console is a web-based client that monitors a Cognos TM1 server. This client is used by administrators to ensure the operation of a Cognos TM1 server.

This console allows an administrator to monitor multiple Cognos TM1 servers on multiple machines, including the ability to start and stop them.

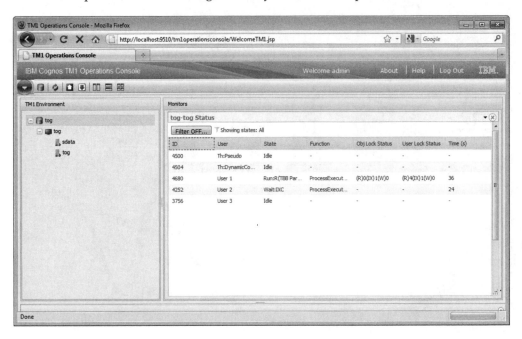

The Cognos TM1 Operations Console can also be used by a solution developer if the developer has to consider multiuser concurrency. This tool helps to find contentions that could be solved by a change of the model.

Now you should be familiar with all of the various clients. Which client is used in a Cognos TM1 solution could have an impact on the model. For instance, you are free to define your own control cubes like shadow cubes and shadow dimensions to solve a business requirement. Often these control cubes should be hidden to the business user. This is easy if your solution provides front ends via Excel or Websheets, because it is easy to hide information in sheets. Another example is a planning application with the requirement to contribute in multiple cubes. In this case, it takes more effort in designing the model because you have to consider the number of cubes. Each cube becomes one "input page" for the contributor, and this could be a conflict with the requirement of good usability. Now we have closed the loop back to the multicube architecture.

Data Sources

We assume that you know which tool can be used as a developer and you want to start to create a Cognos TM1 model now. At this point the Cognos TM1 server is "empty." But how can a user create dimensions and cubes, and how can the cubes be filled with figures? From a historical point of view, the intention of Cognos TM1 was to create the model and to input the figures via a client front end manually or by pushing the information from an Excel sheet to the Cognos TM1 server. But in present times it is not required to build the model by hand, but to import the model and the data from other data sources. For this purpose Cognos TM1 TurboIntegrator was added to the Cognos TM1 software. In Figure 4-4 we added the TurboIntegrator (TI) and external data sources. The TurboIntegrator is not additional software but an integrated part of the Cognos TM1 server. With the TurboIntegrator, the Cognos TM1 server is able to connect directly to various data sources. The data from those data sources can be used to build the model and import the data into cubes. The TurboIntegrator is able to do much more, but this will be discussed in detail in Chapter 7.

An important aspect in this context is shown in Figure 4-4. The different shades indicate that a cube can consist of data, which can be provided by different data sources (SQL databases via Open Database Connectivity (ODBC); files with data in separated fields, and direct input by a user; the OLAP database via OLE DB for OLAP (ODBO) is shown to complete the figure).

Please keep in mind that a cube, a dimension, a cell, and so on that was created by TurboIntegrator using external data sources, is not "connected" to these sources. A Cognos TM1 object is not aware of how it is built: Is it created manually or based on a data source? Cognos TM1 is fully independent of any data sources. Comparing this to some other OLAP software, we can say: A Cognos TM1 cube is not an OLAP view on a fact table[2]. (A fact table is the central table of a star schema in a relational database, which holds the measure values. A star schema is a group of tables that represent multidimensional information.) This statement is also valid for dimensions including elements and hierarchies. Although Cognos TM1 objects do not have to be based on an external data source, they *can* be created and/or populated by an extraction of an external data source. We are sure that you agree that this is a common case. Even if you use data from an external source to build and populate your Cognos TM1 model, you are still free to enhance the model or add data to Cognos TM1 manually.

Before leaving the topic of TurboIntegrator, we want to mention that it has roles beyond data import and export, such as programmatic intraserver data and metadata maintenance. Please refer to Chapter 7 for more details.

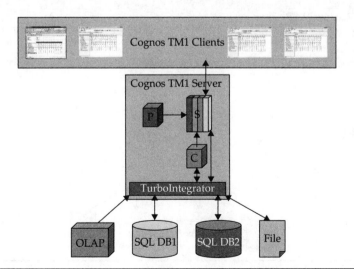

Figure 4-4   Sources for the model and the data

Now we have completed the description of the architecture that consists of Cognos TM1 components only (the small T). In the next section we are going to enhance the Cognos TM1 components by adding Cognos BI components (the big T).

Cognos BI Integration

A result of the Cognos acquisition was the integration of Cognos TM1 into the Cognos BI environment. In the next four figures you will see four different kinds of integration.

- **Integration of Cognos TM1 Web Clients**   Figure 4-5 shows the integration of the web clients into the Cognos Portal Cognos Connection. Cognos BI provides ready-to-use portlets for Cognos TM1 Websheets, Cognos TM1 Web Cube Viewers and Executive Viewer. In addition to the portlets, a user can use widgets for Cognos TM1 Websheets, Cognos TM1 Web Cube Viewer, and Cognos TM1 Contributor, which can be inserted into a Business Insight dashboard by drag and drop. Widgets have been available since Cognos 10.

- **Integration of Cognos TM1 as a data source**   The second way of integration is for the Cognos BI Connector to use Cognos TM1 as a data source (see Figure 4-6). By using this connector you can create a connection to a Cognos TM1 server. This connection is used in the Cognos Framework Manager. The Framework Manager is a modeler tool to define metadata and packages. In Cognos BI the data sources are encapsulated into packages. Packages hide technical information about a data source from departmental users. A package doesn't store the data but the information about the data and how Cognos BI can retrieve the data. Packages can contain information about data from different data sources. This enables the user to create

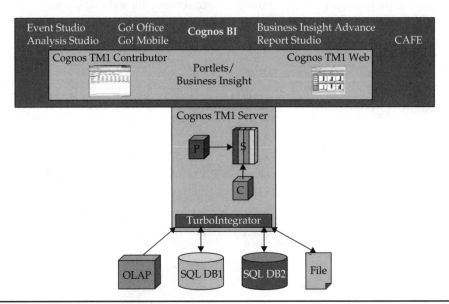

FIGURE 4-5   Integration of web clients

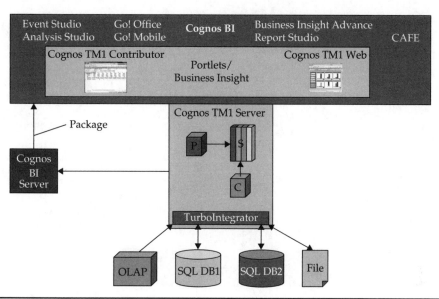

FIGURE **4-6**   Cognos TM1 as data source

reports that contain data from different data sources (for example, OLAP and
relational data). If a Cognos BI administrator creates a package to access Cognos TM1,
he just declares which Cognos TM1 cube should be accessible through the package.

- **Security integration**   If you like to use the first and/or second kind of integration,
  it is recommended also to use the integrated security. If you want to limit access to
  an object in Cognos TM1 (for example, a cube, a dimension element, and so on), you
  have to assign a group to an object with an access right (for example, group A has
  READ access to cube X). This is called *authorization*. Users are assigned to one or
  more groups and inherit the access right of their group(s). When a user wants to
  access a Cognos TM1 server, he has to log in first. This is called *authentication*. You
  can create users and groups manually. If you use the security integration of Cognos
  (CAM-Security), the authentication task is passed to Cognos BI. Cognos BI Groups
  can be imported to Cognos TM1 (see Figure 4-7). These groups can be assigned to
  Cognos TM1 objects. That means that the authorization is still a pure Cognos TM1
  authorization.

- **Integration of Cognos BI Packages**   The fourth way of integration has a different
  direction compared to the first three ways. This integration enables Cognos TM1 to
  use Cognos BI Packages as a data source (see Figure 4-8). This Cognos TM1
  capability is restricted to packages with multidimensional information only. These
  packages are called DMR packages. Packages with pure relational information
  cannot be used in Cognos TM1. This integration enables Cognos TM1 to access data
  sources other than files, ODBC sources, or ODBO sources. For example, you can
  access SAP BW via DMR packages. In this case you have to create a DMR package
  first. This package can be created with the Cognos Framework Manager. Cognos BI

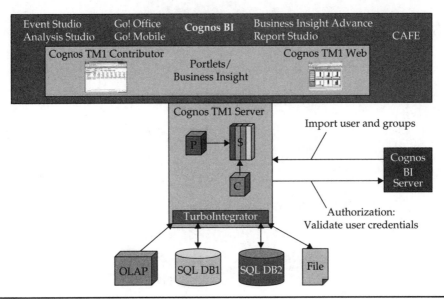

FIGURE 4-7 Security Integration

provides a SAP connector to connect to a SAP BW object (for example, SAP BW Query). After the package is created, you can access this package in TurboIntegrator. The package information is used to create and populate cubes and dimensions. The integration of DMR packages is available if additional software is installed on the Cognos TM1 Server machine. This software is called Cognos TM1 Package Connector.

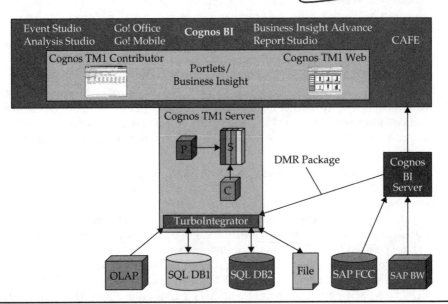

FIGURE 4-8 TM1 Package Connector

Summary

In this chapter we gave an overview of the architecture of Cognos TM1 components. We developed the Cognos TM1 T as an icon for this architecture. There are two versions of the T: The small T explains the interaction of the Cognos TM1-only components, and the big T explains the interaction between Cognos BI and Cognos TM1. We want to remind you again that the figures in this chapter describe a logical architecture. There are more components involved, but picturing them would make the figures confusing and cluttered. The missing components are not necessary in order to understand how the main components work together. Please keep in mind that Cognos TM1 was designed to be operated stand-alone (the small T), and remember the Cognos TM1 philosophy of being "disconnected" from other data sources, because this is one key factor of the flexibility of Cognos TM1.

In the next chapter we will explain the first building block you need to create the model. By doing this we will go into details of the vertical bar of the T.

PART II

Cognos TM1 Building Blocks: Cubes, Dimensions, Elements

In Chapter 4 we talked about the architecture of a Cognos TM1 environment and about the software tools you can use to develop a Cognos TM1 solution. Now we will have a look inside the Cognos TM1 Server. In this chapter we explain the building blocks of a Cognos TM1 solution and how they work together. First we will talk about the primary building blocks:

- Cubes
- Dimensions
- Elements
- Rules
- TurboIntegrator processes

These building blocks are used to develop the data model and the business logic, which is the foundation of a Cognos TM1 solution. Rules and TurboIntegrator processes will be discussed in separate chapters (6 and 7).

Later on we will discuss how a user can access and interact with the Cognos TM1 Server and its content. So we will take a closer look at some Cognos TM1 client capabilities. The user clients are the second part of a Cognos TM1 solution, which is important as the data model and the business logic.

Remember: The user client is the vertical bar of the T in Chapter 4.

Cognos TM1 provides an easy mechanism to create models for analysis, planning, and complex applications based on cubes. Cognos TM1 provides building blocks to design such models. The main building blocks are cubes, dimensions, and elements. In some other OLAP software, elements are called members. But let's use the word "elements" to underline some concepts of elements that are different from some member concepts. As mentioned in Chapter 4, cubes are not bound to any data source. Every Cognos TM1 object can be created based on a data source or manually with the Cognos TM1 administration tools.

In this chapter and the next two chapters (6 and 7), we take a look at the building block itself. For illustration we will construct the objects via the user client. At this point we like to refer to the Cognos TM1 documentation. The *Cognos TM1 User Guide* documentation explains how to use the dimension editor to create or modify the structure of a dimension and how to create a cube. This chapter does not intend to repeat the content of the Cognos TM1 documentation, but only to highlight what are the building blocks of Cognos TM1 and how they could be used to build a Cognos TM1 solution. In the next few chapters we choose some capabilities of Cognos TM1 to describe them in more detail. We think that these detailed descriptions will enable you to understand how Cognos TM1 works under the hood.

Cubes are the main building blocks. A cube is just a container of data (the business logic is established in dimension structures, cube rules, and TurboIntegrator processes). A cube consists of dimensions, and a cube can be built with 2 dimensions or up to 255 dimensions. If you want to build a cube, you need to have built the dimensions first. It is recommended to build cubes with few dimensions only, to keep the handling simple from a user perspective (and not for performance reasons).

Dimensions

A *dimension* is a container for elements. Elements are unique objects in the dimension. They are identified by their names or alias names. Each element has a type. You can create a C-element (Type: Consolidated), or an N-element (Type: Simple or Numeric), or an S-element (Type: String). With elements you can define trees (structures) in a dimension. We have used the word "tree" to highlight that Cognos TM1 does not work with explicit hierarchies. In other OLAP software, hierarchies are often separate objects. For example, multidimensional expressions, or MDX, uses hierarchies and levels in a query; thus, they are not part of the core data model. In Cognos TM1 you can define a hierarchy or tree by creating a parent-child relationship. In this case a parent element has always the type "Consolidated" (C-element) and the child element has always the type "Simple" (N-element): An S-element can be never used as a parent or child element. If you assign an N-element to another N-element, the parent element will automatically change its type to "Consolidated." This simple mechanism enables you to create unbalanced trees. That means you can define leaf elements on any level of a hierarchy (see Figure 5-1), which is a very important concept when it comes to typical business application that we introduce later.

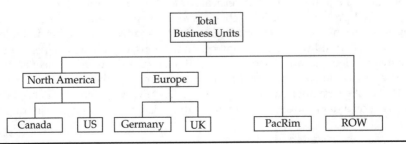

FIGURE 5-1   Unbalanced hierarchy

Another important note is to mention up front that in Cognos TM1, dimensions can be shared by multiple cubes. This is a differentiator from Essbase, streamlining maintenance.

Figure 5-1 shows an example of an unbalanced regional hierarchy. "Total Business Unit" has four children. Two of these children are also parents (C-elements). The other children are leaf elements (N-elements).

The S-element allows you to store text in a cube. This is commonly used to have comments in a cube that is designed for a planning application. S-elements are also very valuable if they are used as "drivers" for a calculated value in the cube.

A dimension can manage attributes for each element. This let you store some additional information for each element. There are three types of attributes:

- **Numeric**   A numeric attribute can hold figures, such as the number of inhabitants of a country.

- **Text**   A text attribute can hold text information, such as a description of the element.

- **Alias**   An alias attribute (often called "Alias") is a special attribute that holds an alternative name for the element. Because the name of an element identifies the element, aliases can be used as an identifier too. If you have multiple aliases per element, you are allowed to assign the same alias name to one element more than once. But it is not allowed to assign the same alias name to different elements.

Cognos TM1 also provides two special attributes that can be used optionally:

- **The attribute Format**   This attribute is a text attribute and holds a formatting expression. This expression is similar to an Excel format expression. It is used to format figures in the cube. It is best practice to assign this attribute to elements that describe the type or the kind of a value in the cube. Usually these elements are parts of a "measure dimension."

- **The attribute Picklist**   This attribute is a text attribute and holds an expression to provide a validation list for the cell value. If a cell is referenced by an element with a picklist, the cell will change to a drop-down list when you start to edit the value of the cell. From the drop-down list you can choose a value instead of typing the value. Picklist attributes can define valid values based on a static list, the contents of a named dimension, or the contents of a named dimension subset. The picklists are commonly used on S-elements.

Dimensions are not separated into different types in Cognos TM1. Cognos TM1 treats all dimensions the same to allow for unlimited flexibility in solution creation. Of course, Cognos TM1 dimensions can be used as time, measure, organizational dimension, and so on, but this is always seen from a business perspective, not enforced by technical means. Nevertheless, if you use Performance Modeler to design your model, you can assign a type to a dimension. Performance Modeler uses these types to generate element attributes and some business logic automatically. Although Cognos TM1 does not know dimension types, we are free to use dimensions as time or measure dimensions just by their content.

Third-party tools and Cognos BI use MDX to access Cognos TM1. The query language MDX expects the usage of levels and hierarchies. As we already mentioned, Cognos TM1 does not work with hierarchies based on levels. But to enable MDX as a query language, Cognos TM1 provides hierarchy levels by the configuration cube "}HierarchyProperties." With this cube, you can configure named hierarchy levels for each dimension. Please be aware that the best way to design a dimension if you intend to use MDX queries is to have only one balanced hierarchy per dimension.

Dimension elements are always accessed by a subset. A subset is a Cognos TM1 object that is linked to a dimension. You can find all subsets of a dimension in the Server Explorer. Each dimension node in the Explorer has the child "Subsets" if one or more subsets of the dimension exist. The "Subsets" node is the collection node of all subsets. You can find private and public subsets beneath this node. Private subsets are indicated by a small yellow key. They are visible to its creator only. Public subsets are visible to everyone. In the next two sections we will discuss static and dynamic subsets.

Static Subsets

A *static subset* is a simple list of element names. Keep this in mind and you will understand the behavior of the Subset Editor. The Subset Editor is a tool of the Cognos TM1 client to browse a dimension and to edit a subset.

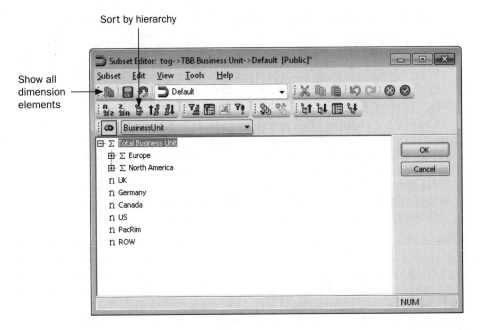

Sort by hierarchy

Show all dimension elements

The preceding illustration shows the Subset Editor browsing the dimension "TBB Business Unit." The example shows the common behavior of the Subset Editor, which is to display element by element. This is often confusing to the user because from a business perspective, the user expects to see the hierarchy of all business units. Remember, a Cognos TM1 dimension doesn't consist of hierarchies technically. But you can visualize the parent-child relations of Cognos TM1 dimension elements by sorting the elements. When you click the All button first and then the Hierarchy Sort button, as shown in the preceding illustration, you will get the result shown in the following illustration.

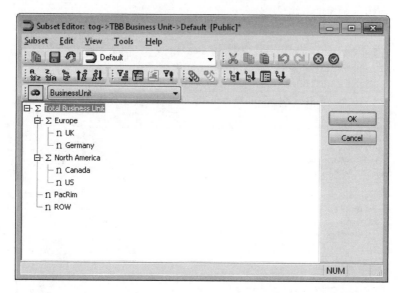

Another "confusing" behavior is shown in the following illustration. You will get this result when you sort all elements descending. The result is shown because Cognos TM1 sorts each element by name and indents an element if another element in the list above is a parent.

All elements between the element and the parent in the list have to be children of the same parent. For instance, change the sequence of the elements by dragging and dropping:

1. Move element "US" between "ROW" and "PacRim"; this will break display of the hierarchy.
2. Move element "Canada" between "North America" and "Germany"; this will indent "Canada" and show the parent-child relation.

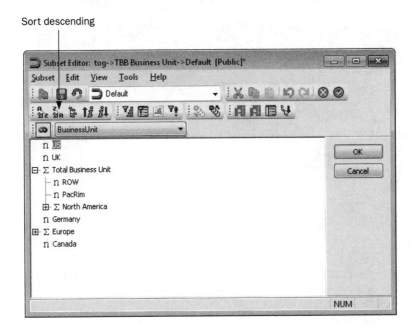

The result is shown in the following illustration, which demonstrates that a subset is only a list of elements and a hierarchy is only visible if the elements are sorted in proper order.

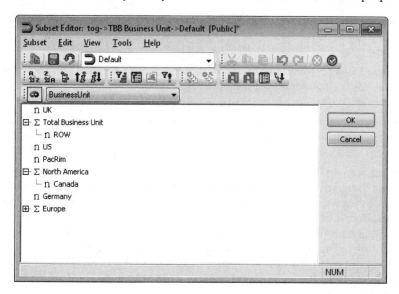

Another aspect of a subset is that you can have one element multiple times in a subset. So if you collapse "North America" in the subset shown in the preceding illustration, "Canada" will be removed from the List (subset). If you expand "North America" again, all children will be inserted into the list. Now you will see "US" twice, as shown in the following illustration.

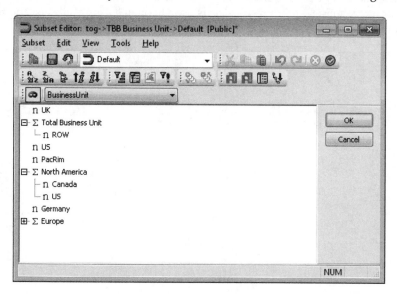

We mention these examples to make you comfortable with the behavior of subsets. Here are some further hints regarding subsets.

- **Working with cascading filters (apply one filter after another filter)** Each filter is applied to the current subset. If you apply a second filter, it will filter the result of the first filter.

- **Wildcard filter** The filter "Wildcard" filters on the element name shown in the Subset Editor. If you have turned on an alias name, it will filter alias names and not the element name.

- **You can add elements from the clipboard to the subset** Cognos TM1 will add valid elements to the subset only, even if you copy from any other source on your desktop (for example, from MS Excel, MS Word, a simple text file, and so on.)

- **You can turn on the property window of the Subset Editor** In the property window you will see element properties and attributes. If you select a single N-element, you will see the properties of the selection. If you select a single C-element, you will see the properties of the children of the selection. If you select multiple elements, you will see the properties of all selected elements. Be careful if you are working with a large dimension. If you select a parent element with a large number of children, the Subset Editor will retrieve all properties and attributes of all children. This could take a long time. We recommend turning off the property window if you work with large dimensions.

- **You can open multiple Subset Editors** You can copy or move elements from one subset to another subset via the clipboard (copy and paste) or per drag-and-drop gesture (the target subset must consist of at least one element); see the following illustration. For instance, if you have two Subset Editors open, one editor should be your target subset, and the other one is used to open existing subsets, and to filter and find elements that should be added to the target subset.

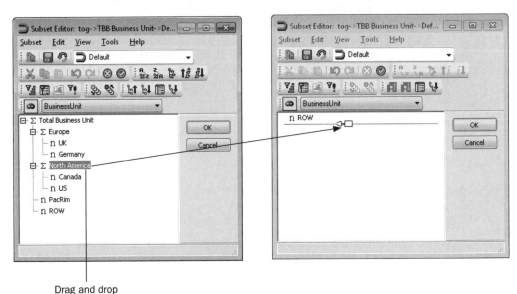

Drag and drop

Dynamic Subsets

Because a static subset stores the list of element names, they will not change automatically if the dimension has changed (exception: if you have deleted an element from the dimension, it will be removed from the subset). In some cases you will require that a subset changes automatically if you add a new element to the dimension. For that purpose, the dynamic subset was introduced. Instead of storing a list, a dynamic subset stores an expression. The expression describes how the list of elements is created. The syntax of such an expression is MDX syntax. To have a valid subset expression, the MDX statement has to return a "set." A set is a list of members (member = MDX name for element). There are two ways to create a dynamic subset:

- Open the Expression Window (View | Expression Window) and enter an MDX set expression.
- Record the expression.

You can also mix both methods: Record an expression first and modify this expression in the Expression Window. If you have the Expression Window visible while you record the expression, you can watch how the MDX is generated by the Subset Editor (see the following illustration). You can start and stop the recording with the menu items in the Tools menu.

A disabled OK button indicates the record mode.

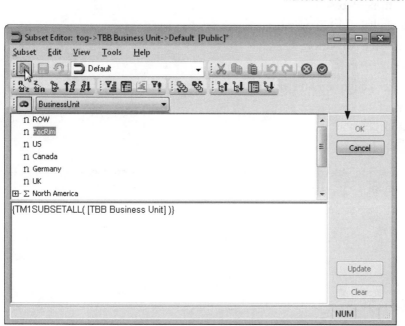

When you record an expression, you can use the filters and sort functions of the subset. As we mentioned in the last section, filters operate on the current elements that are displayed in the subset. For that reason, you should make sure that your recording starts with a well-defined set of elements. We recommend that you start your recording with the function "All" (see the preceding illustration). Clicking the All button will generate the TM1SUBSETALL statement. If you do not start with "All," the generated MDX statement will be based on the result of the TM1SubsetBasis() statement. What's the difference? If you save the subset, the list of elements that was displayed in the Subset Editor before you start the recording is stored together with the expression. This stored list is the "subset basis." If you start the recording with "All," this list is ignored and the expression will be based on all elements.

Here are some additional hints:

- Use the recording feature to get a base MDX expression that you can modify in the Expression Window.

- Use the Subset Editor to develop and test an MDX expression for active forms. (See Chapter 8; in an active form, the concept of using MDX expressions is enhanced by the ability to add a variable component to an MDX expression at run time. This is not possible with dynamic subsets, but you can perform this approach when defining the row dimension with active forms.)

- In an MDX expression you can access other cubes. To get a generated example, follow these steps:

  1. Tools | Record Expression.

  2. Click the All button.

  3. Tools | Filter.

  4. Select a cube and an element for each dimension.

  5. Select the Ascending sort.

  6. Click OK.

  7. Tools | Stop Recording.

The following illustration shows the result. The cube reference is marked in the illustration.

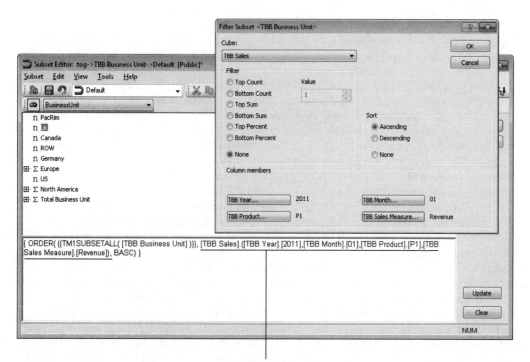

Reference to a cube

- The filter function can be used to generate ORDER and FILTER MDX statements.

- The MDX cube reference can be dynamic. You can remove some or all member (element) references (for example: [TBB Sales].([TBB Sales Measure] .[Revenue])). All missing references are implicitly replaced by default elements. The default element is evaluated by Cognos TM1 or can be set in the "} HierarchyProperties" cube. If you use such a dynamic subset in a view (see the section "Views" later in this chapter), the missing elements will be replaced by the current title elements. So the subset becomes double dynamic: dynamic by MDX and by selected title elements.

- The filter function can be used to filter by attributes. Here is an example:
  {FILTER({Cognos TM1SUBSETALL([TBB Business Unit])}, [TBB Business Unit].[Currency] = "EUR")}

  In the Expression Window you can change the "=" (equal sign) to "<>" (not equal) to get all Business Units with currency other than EUR.

- Use MDX to get the children of an element. Here is an example:
  `{[TBB Business Unit].[10100].children}`
- You cannot use "Filter by."

After you have defined a subset by filtering, selecting, hiding, moving elements, or recording an expression, you can save the subset with a name. A subset can be saved as private or public. A private subset is visible to its creator only. A public subset is visible to all users, but can be created only by an administrator. A subset is saved as a file (file name: *<subsetname>*.sub) in the data directory of the Cognos TM1 server. The subset files are organized in folders that have the following name pattern: *<dimensionname>*}subs. The folders of public subsets can be found in the data directory. The folders of private subsets can be found in a subdirectory that has the name of the user.

You can define a subset to be a default subset by naming the subset "Default." Unfortunately, the name of a default subset depends on the language of the Cognos TM1 client. For example, in an English environment you have to name the subset "Default." In a German environment you have to name it "Standard," which is the German translation of "default." The name of the default subset will be set by the Subset Editor if you check the option Default in the Save dialog. If you work in a multilanguage environment, you should create a default subset for each language. Cognos TM1 uses a default subset as a predefinition if you invoke the Subset Editor. In this case, Cognos TM1 is looking for a private default subset first. If no private default subset exists, Cognos TM1 will look for a public one. If no default subset is found, Cognos TM1 will show all elements sorted by element index. Default subsets are also used when you open a Cube Viewer. This is described in the section "Views" later in this chapter.

Finally we want to mention that the Subset Editor works in a different mode depending on how you invoke the editor: You can invoke the editor from the Server Explorer, from an Excel cell with a SUBNM formula, or from a Cube Viewer. Table 5-1 lists the different modes of the subset editor.

Mode	Description
Invoke Subset Editor from Server Explorer or Excel (SUBNM formula or TM1RPTROW formula)	• Rollup button is not available. • Filter by Extract is not available.
Invoke Subset Editor for title dimension from Cube Viewer	• Rollup button and Filter by Extract are available. • You are forced to select a single element. • The selected subset is used as a drop-down in the Cube Viewer.
Invoke Subset Editor for Row or Column Dimension from Cube Viewer	• Rollup button and Filter by Extract are available. • You are **not** forced to select a single element. • If you select an element of the subset and click OK, the selected element becomes the new subset, which is used in the Cube Viewer.

TABLE 5-1 Subset Editor Modes

Cubes

From a technical point of view, a cube is a container that holds the data and allocates the memory in RAM. A cube is defined by its dimensions. When you create a cube, you choose the dimensions you want to become a part of the cube. A dimension can be a building block of *multiple* cubes. This is the important concept of shared dimensions. A cube is a container for cells. You can compare this to an Excel sheet. In the terminology of a cube, the Excel sheet is a two-dimensional cube. The first dimension is "Column," which contains the elements "A", "B", "C", and so on. The second dimension is "Row," which contains the elements "1", "2", "3", and so on. Each cell in a sheet can be addressed by a coordinate: for example, the first upper-left cell has the address "A1." This is very similar to Cognos TM1. You can create a cube that looks like a sheet, as shown in the following illustration.

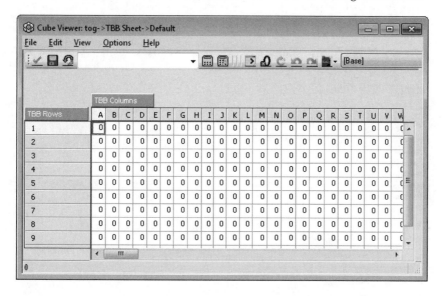

In this cube the upper-left cell has the address `['A','1']`. The expression we have used would be understood by Cognos TM1 rules, which are explained later in Chapter 6. In Cognos TM1 you will find different syntax of an address or a reference to a cell. Here are three examples:

- `DBRW("tog:TOG Sheet", "A","1")`

This syntax could be used in Excel as a Cognos TM1 worksheet formula:

- `DB('TBB Sheet','A','1')`

This syntax could be used as a reference in a Cognos TM1 rule (see Chapter 9).

- `CellGetN('TBB Sheet','A','1')`

This syntax could be used in a TurboIntegrator script (see Chapter 10).

Although the sample cube is very simple, the same mechanism of addressing a Cognos TM1 cell is used for cubes with many more dimensions. Each dimension of a cube contributes a single coordinate to the address of a cell. The coordinates are ordered by the sequence of the dimension. The sequence of a dimension is defined when a cube is created. This sequence cannot be changed regarding the mechanism of coordinates. You will find a feature in Cognos TM1 that allows you to change the sequence. But this sequence is used internally only to optimize the consumption of memory. This is an important method to improve performance on cubes containing a large amount of data. Be aware that the Cognos TM1 server needs to allocate additional memory to perform the reorganization. The additional memory could be the same amount that the cube already consumes. After you have reorganized the order, the original sequence is still valid for all functions that reference a cube cell. You can find an example in the following illustration.

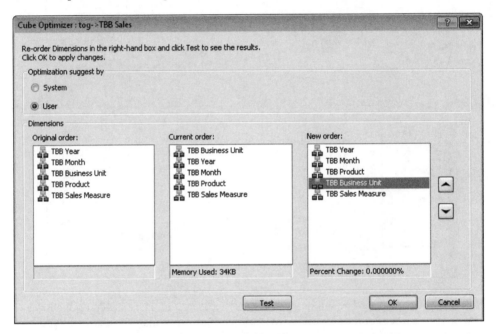

If you like to have large cubes with a large amount of data, it is recommended to keep an eye on the sequence of dimensions. But when you design your Cognos TM1 Model, you should choose the sequence from a business point of view. It is best practice to have a similar sequence across all cubes in your model. Here is a suggestion for the sequence of dimensions (this is not a suggestion for the names of the dimension, but the content and the meaning of the dimension):

- Versions/scenarios
- Years
- Periods

- Others…
- Organizations
- Organizations IC
- Positions
- Measures

That does not mean that all cubes should have the same dimension. But if dimensions are reused or different dimensions with similar content are used, they should have a similar sequence. If you want to optimize the consumption of the cube memory, you should consider the following rule:

> Order the smallest sparse dimension to the largest sparse dimension, followed by the smallest dense dimension to the largest dense dimension.

Here we like to reference the chapter "Creating Cubes" in the *Cognos TM1 Developer Guide* documentation. In this product documentation you will find more information about dense and sparse dimensions. Here is a quote from this guide that explains what a dense dimension is:

> As a first step toward ordering dimensions, divide the dimensions into two groups: sparse and dense dimensions. A dense dimension has a high percentage of values for its elements. You can estimate the density by answering this question: If one element in the dimension has a value, keeping the elements of the other dimensions constant, what is the probability that the other elements in the dimension have values?

> In real life it's too hard to identify which dimension is "dense" and which dimension is "sparse" because sparsity is an attribute of a cube and not of a dimension. You can find how many cells are populated in relation to how many cells a cube can hold hypothetically, but it's hard to say where you can find most of the populated cells (which elements are involved).

But even if there is no need to be careful about memory optimization, there is one restriction for a sequence of a dimension: If you want to store text in a cube (for example, a comment), you have to consider the sequence. This restriction is based on how Cognos TM1 evaluates the type of a cell. Just as dimensions contain different element types, cubes contain different cell types. Cognos TM1 knows the following cell types: N-cell, C-cell, and S-cell. Cognos TM1 evaluates the type of a cell by the element types of its coordinates. But a cell always has at least two coordinates, so Cognos TM1 uses the following conditions to evaluate the type of a cell:

- If one of the coordinates is a C-element, the cell is a C-cell.
- If the last coordinate is an S-element, the cell is an S-cell. This overrules C-cells.
- If all coordinates are N-elements, the cell is an N-cell.

The second condition leads to the restriction that you need an S-element in the last dimension of a cube. If you have an S-element in a dimension other than the last one, you will not be able to enter text into the cube. The best practice is to have S-elements like "Comment" in a "Measure" dimension, which should be the last one. (It is not necessary to name this dimension "Measure." Again, this is more the content of the dimension.) The "Measure" dimension is shown in the following illustration.

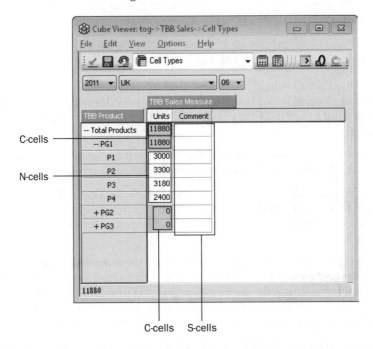

Typically users browse a cube by using a Cube Viewer. A Cube Viewer is based on the Cognos TM1 object "view," which is described in the next section, "Views."

Views

The Cube Viewer is a tool to browse a cube. But it is also a kind of editor to create and modify views. A view is the representation of a "slice" of a cube. What does "slice" mean? Because we like to browse a multidimensional space of data, it is a challenge to display this data on a two-dimensional screen. Imagine that Figure 5-2 shows the "TBB Sales" cube. Even in a 3D diagram, we have to reduce the cube from five dimensions to three dimensions to have a displayable figure. The dots in this figure should represent values in cube cells. The coordinate of a sample cell is displayed in the annotation. It is very hard to read the coordinate from the 3D diagram. Now we add a slice to the cube by spanning a pane along two of the dimensions and "fixing" one dimension to a single element. In Figure 5-2 the "fixed" dimension is "TBB Product," which is "set" to element "P4." Later on in this chapter we will talk about "Title" dimensions. These dimensions are the "fixed" dimensions of a "slice."

By moving and turning the slice, you can browse the data of a cube. This is known as the OLAP gesture "Slice&Dice," and it's exactly what you can do with the Cube Viewer. In Figure 5-3 we show another slice of the cube. You can compare this slice with the view

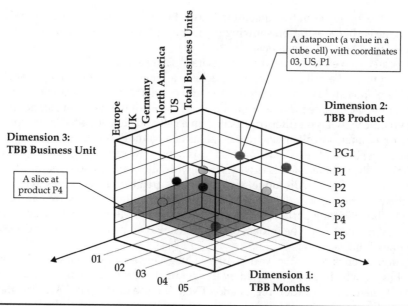

FIGURE 5-2   A slice of a cube

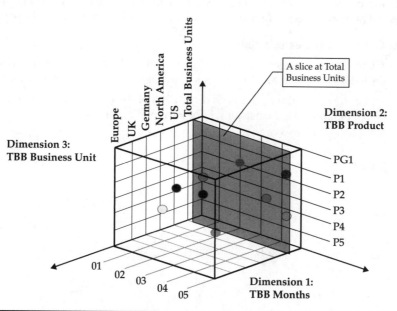

FIGURE 5-3   Another slice

shown in the Cube Viewer in the upcoming illustration of the Cube Viewer. Be aware that the view in the earlier illustration showing the Cube Optimizer works with five dimensions. So the view "fixes" three dimensions.

A view can be saved and reused by the users. As subsets are linked to a dimension, a view is linked to a cube. All cubes with views have a Views collection node in the Server Explorer. Here you can find the view objects. Similar to subsets, views can be static or dynamic, and you can save private or public views. Most of the views are static. You can create a dynamic view if you filter (right-click on a cell and choose Filter in the context menu) the row dimension elements by the values of a column. A filter (for example, the Top 5 Business Units) depends on data. For this reason, the view can change automatically if the data of the cube has changed. This is why views with filters are called dynamic. Dynamic objects are indicated by a small funnel symbol. Views are also saved to files that can be found in the data directory of the Cognos TM1 server. The view folders are named according to the following pattern: <*Cubename*>}vue. The folders of public views can be found in the data directory. The folders of private views can be found in a subdirectory that has the name of the user.

If you double-click on a cube, you invoke a Cube Viewer showing a view. This is the default behavior, which can be changed by the parameter `InSpreadsheetBrowser` in the Cognos TM1 client configuration file Cognos TM1p.ini (see the *Cognos TM1 Operations Guide* chapter "The Cognos TM1p.ini Client Configuration File"). When the Cube Viewer is opened in this way, the Cognos TM1 client will look for a default view. This is again similar to subsets. The Cognos TM1 client is looking for a view that is named "Default." But this is also language-dependent. For instance, in a German environment, it will look for a view named "Standard." The Cognos TM1 client will look for a private object first and then for a public object. If no view object is found, the Cube Viewer will perform the following steps:

1. The Cube Viewer creates a new view.

2. The Cube Viewer places the last two dimensions of the cube as row and column dimensions. The rest of the dimensions (if available) are placed as title dimensions.

3. The Cube Viewer evaluates for each dimension of the cube whether a default subset exists. If a default subset exists, it will be assigned to the view.

The names "row dimension," "column dimension," and "title dimension" are for describing where a dimension is placed in the view (see the following illustration).

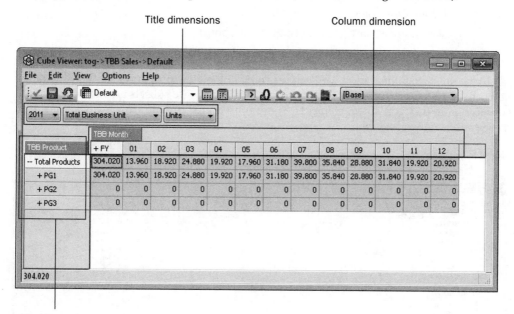

Now you can perform all OLAP gestures on the view:

- Slice and dice
- Stack dimensions on rows and/or columns
- Edit subsets
- Apply zero suppression to rows, columns, or both
- Filter rows by a column

If you are satisfied with your result, you can save the view and give it a name. The following information is stored with the view:

- The position of each dimension (title, row, or column)
- The assigned subset per dimension
- Zero Suppression option
- Automatic Recalculate option
- Format settings (Options | Format)
- Column width (Options | Columns Width)
- Width of the row dimensions

- Some properties, which are only valid for the Cube Viewer in Cognos TM1 Web, are stored in separate files (see Chapter 13):
  - Hidden dimension
  - Visibility of a chart (chart only, grid only, both)
  - Chart properties (for example, palette, 3D, titles)

In the following illustration, you can see some of the view properties. In this illustration you can see also three "private" subsets called "All." But these subsets are neither private subsets nor do they contain all elements. These subsets are "private" to view. That means these subsets only exist in the view and are stored with the view.

Show property window   These subsets are "private" to the view.

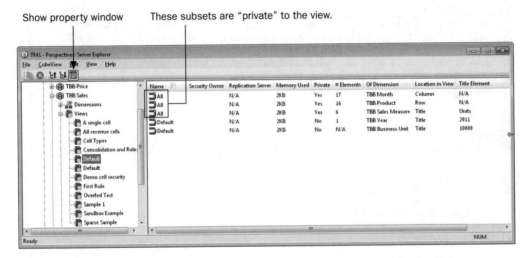

This might be a good point to take a deeper look at how to use subsets in a view. In the Cube Viewer you can identify which subset is used by an extension of the dimension name (you will find the dimension name on the selection button of the row or the column dimension and in the bubble text of a title dimension; see the following illustration). If you double-click on a title dimension or click once on the selection button, you will open the Subset Editor. As we mentioned in the section about subsets, two additional functions are available in the Subset Editor now: Filter by View and Rollup.

But there is also a different behavior of the Subset Editor if you open a subset of a title dimension or a subset of a row/column dimension.

- **Title dimensions**   When you accept your changes with the OK button, the Subset Editor will force you to select a single element. The Cube Viewer needs a selected element for each title dimension to retrieve data.

- **Row/Column dimensions**   When you accept your changes, it is an option to have one or multiple elements selected. But if you select elements, these elements will be the elements of a new subset that is applied to a dimension in the view.

The last point often leads to a subset that is not intended by the user because the user selects one or more elements by mistake, as shown in the following illustration. So keep this in mind when you work with the Subset Editor.

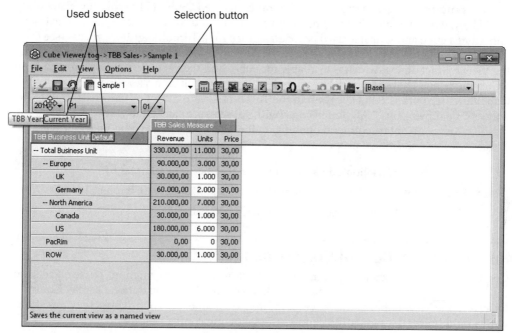

By using named subsets in a view, you can control how your views are updated automatically. A named subset can be used in several views. A modification of such a subset will have an impact on all views that use the subset. For instance, the subset "Default" of the dimension "TBB Business Unit" is changed. If you open the view "Sample 1," the changes are reflected (see the following illustration).

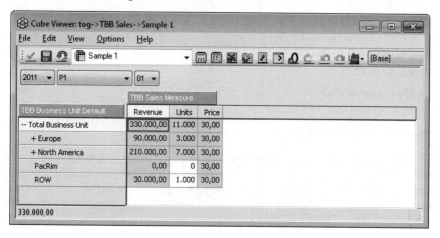

If you don't want the view to depend on a named subset, just edit the subset in the Cube Viewer without saving it in the Subset Editor. If the subset is not a named subset, it will be saved exclusively with the view. In the property window you will see this "private" subset as subset "All"; as in the earlier illustration labeled "Subset after moving elements").

Finally, we like to mention that there is a special kind of view, which is used to extract data from a cube and which is used as a data source for a TurboIntegrator process (see Chapter 10). These views are called *view extracts*. They are created when you save a view in the View Extract dialog, which is available for cubes and views (in Server Explorer: click on a Cube node and choose Cube | Export as Text Data, or click on a View node and choose CubeView | Export as Text Data) and in the TurboIntegrator Editor. A view extract does not know "Title dimensions." All dimensions (with subsets) are stacked to rows. That is the reason why we do not recommend opening a view extract with the Cube Viewer. A view extract has some additional properties:

- Suppressing consolidated values (for consolidation, see Chapter 6)
- Suppression rule calculated values (for rule calculation, see Chapter 6)
- Cell value filter (a filter operator and threshold values)

Cognos TM1 Inside: Control Objects and Security

Cognos TM1 also uses cubes and dimensions to store system information. These objects are called *control objects*. You will see these objects if you switch on the option Display Control Objects in the View menu of the Server Explorer. The name of a control object always starts with a right brace (}). Cognos TM1 knows the following control objects:

- Each object in Cognos TM1 is represented by an element in a control dimension (for example, Users | Dimension "}Clients"; Dimensions | Dimension "}Dimensions"; and so on). There is an exception for views, subsets, and private objects like private "Application Entries."
- Security objects
- Attribute objects
- Property objects (for example, cube properties used for replication or hierarchy properties used by MDX)
- Picklist cubes
- Drill assignment cubes
- Hold cubes
- Statistic objects (used by Performance Monitor)

These control objects are self-maintaining. For example, if you copy a TI process file (let's name it "abc.pro") into the database directory, Cognos TM1 will add the process to the Dimension "}processes" automatically when the server process is started. All objects exist in the memory of the Cognos TM1 server. Therefore Cognos TM1 creates the control objects on demand to reduce memory consumption. This mechanism has an impact on the behavior of Cognos TM1 regarding security. A Cognos TM1 security object is created only if it is needed. So if you do not assign security assignments to cubes, the Cube Security object does not exist. We will discuss more details in Chapter 13.

But let's take a glance at Cognos TM1 security and see how it treats dimension elements. Permissions on dimension elements are the most frequently used method of managing security in a Cognos TM1 solution. You can assign security rights to a dimension and/or a dimension element. Security rights on dimensions are not relevant to secure data. Instead, it is more common to secure elements. You can assign a security right to every single element. The right of an element doesn't depend on other elements like parent elements or children. With the right NONE, you can hide elements from users. For instance, imagine you are a user who is allowed to see values of the business unit "PacRIM" and of the whole company ("Total Business Units"). So the security for your security group on the elements "PacRIM" and "Total Business Units" is set to READ. The security of all other elements is set to NONE. Again, we will discuss security in Chapter 13.

Cognos TM1 Inside: Cube and Dimension Attributes

In this short section we want to mention that cubes and dimensions also can have attributes. This includes alias attributes, too. To access these attributes, follow these steps:

- Cube attributes

  Open a Cube Viewer: Edit | Edit Cube Attributes.

  A dialog opens where you can add new attributes and view and modify existing attributes. If you add an alias to the cube, you can access this cube by its alias name.

- Dimension attributes

  Select the node "Dimensions" in the Server Explorer: Dimensions | Edit Attributes.

  A dialog opens where you can add new attributes and view and modify existing attributes. If you add an alias to the dimension, you can access this dimension by its alias name.

There is no special function to access these attributes in Excel, TurboIntegrator, or rules. But you can use the access function to get the attribute values directly from the corresponding control cubes: }CubeAttributes and }DimensionAttributes.

Summary

In this chapter we have introduced the building blocks cubes, dimensions, and elements. These are the basic building blocks that define the "perspectives" of the user on the data in the Cognos TM1 solution. In the next chapter we take a look at rules that enhance cube data with business logic.

Building Business Logic: Rules

This chapter is about the calculation methods of Cognos TM1. These methods are the heart of Cognos TM1. This chapter will go deep into the core of Cognos TM1 and give you a foundation for understanding how Cognos TM1 works.

In a Cognos TM1 solution, the business logic is defined by calculations. There are two kinds of calculations, which are treated differently by Cognos TM1. The calculation differs according to consolidation and rules calculation. Why are there two different calculations? It's all about performance. Therefore you should know about the four performance factors of Cognos TM1, which are leveraged by Cognos TM1 when it calculates values. These performance factors are:

1. Everything is stored and executed in memory (Cognos TM1 is an in-memory OLAP engine).

2. Calculation (consolidation and rules calculation) is performed only on request.

3. Only requested cells and their dependents are calculated.

4. Cognos TM1 takes advantage of the sparsity of data when values are consolidated.

These four factors are the foundation of any calculation in Cognos TM1, and the last factor is the reason why Cognos TM1 calculation is separated into consolidation and rules calculation. Cognos TM1 can take advantage of the sparsity of data automatically only for consolidation. If rules are involved in the calculations, the developer of a Cognos TM1 solution has to tell Cognos TM1 how to work with sparse data. We will discuss this later in the chapter.

Before we focus on calculations we like to mention that you should care about performance when you deliver the final application. Performance is one of the most requested issues in user acceptance of an application. If you build an application with poor performance you should expect that the users will not use your solution because they won't accept it. But because Cognos TM1 has different performance factors, there is plenty of room to serve high performance. When you develop a Cognos TM1 solution you can start to define your business logic without taking care of the performance in the first step. In the second step you should check the performance of your solution. A performance check should be done by a user who is intent on using your solution. Why? The reason is that performance is not an absolute measure. A response time of 3 seconds might be experienced as good performance or as bad performance. The experience of the end user counts. If your solution has performed badly you have to improve it. Because this chapter is about calculation we want to discuss Cognos TM1 feeders. The feeders mechanism is a Cognos TM1 method to improve performance.

The Principles of Calculation

Let's take a closer look at the fourth performance factor and the principles of consolidation and rules calculations. To understand how Cognos TM1 calculates the rules, you have to understand how Cognos TM1 consolidates and takes advantage of sparsity. But overall, there is a golden rule in Cognos TM1 that you should always keep in mind: *Cognos TM1 calculates cell by cell.*

It's important to understand how Cognos TM1 takes advantage of the sparsity of data (see also Chapter 5). This is a very important mechanism of Cognos TM1 and it is bound to the principle of consolidation. As explained in Chapter 8, consolidations are defined in a natural way by parent-child relationships. At this point we want to introduce my model of understanding consolidation in Cognos TM1. (This model is just a simplification to help you understand consolidation in Cognos TM1. Please note that consolidation could be much more complex because of the multidimensional nature of a Cognos TM1 model.)

Understanding Consolidations

Imagine that you want to request a figure for "Total Business Unit" in the example in the following illustration. The hierarchy tree of the dimension elements is used to evaluate which leaf cells are needed to calculate "Total Business Unit" (because hierarchy trees can only be built by C elements and N elements, in this case leaf cells are always N cells). But Cognos TM1 doesn't care about all N cells. N cells are cells in a cube that are only referenced by an N element of each involved dimension. In the example in the following illustration, five dimensions are involved: TBB Year, TBB Product, TBB Sales Measure, TBB Month, and TBB Business Unit. All dimension elements in the example are N elements except "Total Business Unit," which is a C element. This simplifies the example because Cognos TM1 only has to look for leaf cells by investigating the dimension structure of "Business Unit." To find the leaf cells that are referenced by Business Unit N elements, Cognos TM1 gets all cells that are stored in RAM and are referenced by leaf elements where "Total Business Unit" is the ancestor. Here you encounter the Cognos TM1 sparsity algorithm. Cognos TM1 uses only relevant leaf cells, because Cognos TM1 can only "see" leaf cells that are stored in the memory of the cube. Cognos TM1 doesn't calculate the C cells, which represent the intermediate levels in the hierarchy. Keep in mind that this example simplifies the evaluation of leaf cells. But a more complex example (for example, if all elements of the requested cell are C elements) works on the same principle.

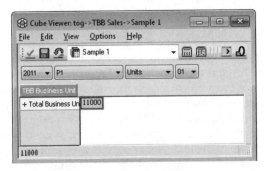

A single consolidated cell

The following illustration shows how to simulate the principle:

- **Step 1**.   Open the Subset Editor for the dimension "TBB Business Unit."
- **Step 2**.   Show all elements sorted by hierarchy.
- **Step 3**.   Remove all C elements between "Total Business Unit" and the leaf cells.
- **Step 4**.   Turn on "Suppress Zero" in the view.
- **Step 5**.   Recalculate the view.

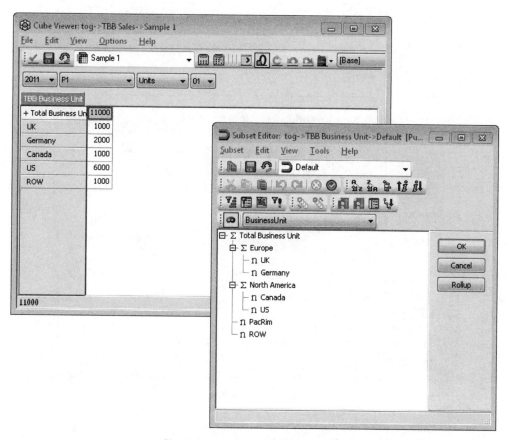

Simulation of the consolidation principle

This view simulates that Cognos TM1 ignores "Europe" and "North America" and doesn't "see" "PacRim" because there is no value for "PacRim" in memory. Again, keep in mind that Cognos TM1 does *not* check whether PacRim has a value or not. PacRim is simply ignored because no value exists. We can use "zero suppression" to simulate the principle of consolidation, because suppressing the zero figures is based on the same mechanism. If you use "Suppress Zero" on consolidated cells, Cognos TM1 uses the hierarchy tree of the dimensions to find out which part of the cube (=memory) is involved in the request, and checks whether there are values. If at least one cell exists, the consolidated cell is not suppressed.

Of course, the example in the preceding illustration is not a sparse one. But this is not the general case. In almost all OLAP models the cubes are sparse. So let's look at a sparse example: Product "P1" was only sold in "June" by the business unit "PacRim," as shown in the following illustration. If "Total Products" is requested, Cognos TM1 looks into the cube memory and "sees" only the 1000 that is referenced by "P1." So this shows what makes the difference in Cognos TM1: Instead of calculating "1000+0+0+0+0+...<some more zeros> ...+0+0+0+0+0+0+0+0=1000", Cognos TM1 just calculates "1000=1000." Needless to say, the first expression takes more time for calculation than the second one.

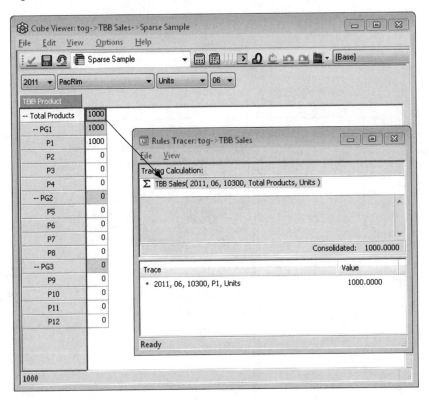

Trace of the consolidation

You can validate this example with your own model by following these steps:

- **Step 1.** Create a view on a cube with no rules attached, which is similar to the view shown in the preceding illustration. For this exercise, it is important that all Title Dimensions are set to an N element and only one dimension is used as Row-Dimension.

- **Step 2.** Right-click on the consolidated cell and execute the Rules Tracer. You should see that the intermediate levels of your hierarchy are ignored and only the leaf elements that have a value are displayed (see the Rules Tracer in the preceding illustration).

- **Step 3.** Now create a rule object that is attached to the cube: Select the cube node in the Server Explorer and choose Cube | Create Rule. Enter a rule statement that doesn't affect your sample view (especially do not use the skipcheck statement). (This example is version dependent and may require you to attach an empty rules object or one rule at least.) The syntax of rules will be discussed later in this chapter, in the section "Understanding Rules Calculation." Now you should see the rules object as a child of the cube object in the Server Explorer, as shown in the following illustration.

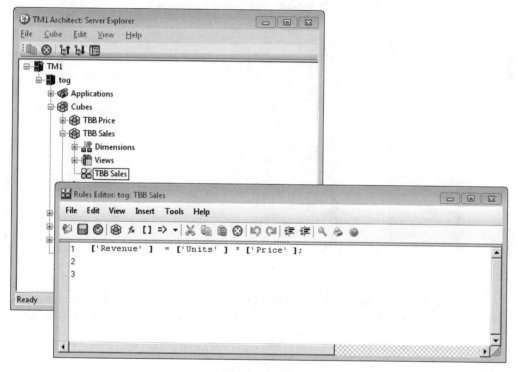

Adding a rule object

- **Step 4.** Repeat Step 1 and Step 2. You should see a result similar to that in the following illustration. This shows the calculation accounts for all leaf cells below "Total Products."

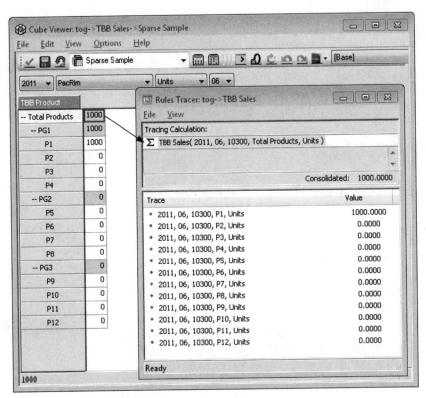

Consolidation mechanism has changed

What has happened? By attaching a rule to a cube (it doesn't matter what the rule is calculating), you switch off the fourth performance factor of Cognos TM1 mentioned in the beginning of this chapter. In spite of attaching rules to cubes, we are able to switch back to the sparsity algorithm of Cognos TM1. You will find more details in the section "Who's Afraid of Feeders?"

In some real models, the difference in calculation time between the two scenarios could be quite huge. This depends on the sparsity of a cube. You can check your model for sparsity with the following method:

- **Step 1**.   Count the number of leaf elements in each dimension of the cube. (You can use subsets to count: Create a subset by filtering Level 0, select the "Subsets"-Node in the Server Explorer tree, and turn on the Property Window; the number of subset elements is one of the properties of a subset; see the following illustration).

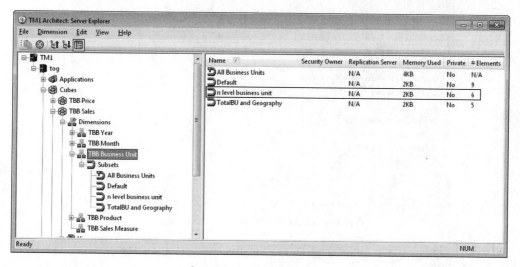

Counting element with subsets

- **Step 2**.   Multiply all numbers, and you will get the potential number of leaf cells in the cube. Example: 7 (years) ∗ 12 (months) ∗ 6 (business units) ∗ 12 (products) ∗ 1 (sales measure) = 6048.
- **Step 3**.   Turn on the Performance Monitor (select Cognos TM1 Server Node, Server | Start Performance Monitor).
- **Step 4**.   Show all control objects in Server Explorer (View | Display Control Objects).
- **Step 5**.   Create a view on the cube "}StatsByCube" as shown in the next illustration.

- **Step 6.**   Calculate the density ratio: 104/6048 = 1.7 percent.

Counting populated cells with statistics cube

This should give you some insight into consolidation in Cognos TM1.

Understanding Rules Calculation

A very important building block in Cognos TM1 is the feature of rules. A rule is used if an expression is needed, which cannot be defined as a consolidation, and if values of different cubes have to be linked.

Here are two examples:

```
Cost Ratio  = Cost / Sales * 100

Revenue     = Units * Price
```

A key concept with Cognos TM1 rules is that they work closely in conjunction with the principle of consolidation. That happens if at least one dimension of the cube consists of a C element. Make sure that you have understood the consolidation mechanism first. If you followed the last section, "Understanding Consolidations," we already added a rule statement to a cube. But let's start from the beginning. Assume that the cube "TBB Sales" holds the number of sold units for different products in different regions. Now we want to calculate the revenue. The revenue should be the number of sold units of a product multiplied by the price of this product. For this calculation, we use the three elements "Revenue," "Units," and "Price," and the rule should look like this:

```
Revenue= Units * Price
```

This sample calculation should be implemented in our "TBB Sales" cube now.
To create a rule, you can follow these steps:

- **Step 1.** Select the cube, which should be enhanced by rules, in the Server Explorer.
- **Step 2.** Create the rules object (Cube | Create Rule).
- **Step 3.** Enter a rule statement as shown in the following illustration:
  ```
  ['Revenue']= ['Units'] * ['Price'];
  ```

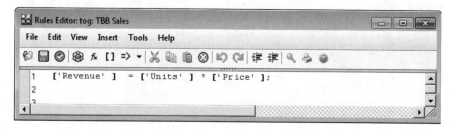

First rule

Now let us discuss the syntax of a rule statement, which calculates a value.

```
<A range of cells> = {N: | C: | S:} <Formula> ;
```

<A range of04 cells> is a placeholder for an expression that defines a set of cells. You define a range of cells by cutting down the whole cube. `<A range of cells>`, which defines the whole cube, is expressed as `[]`. With `['Revenue']`, you define a range of cells that are referenced by the element "Revenue." For a better understanding, you can visualize the meaning of `<A range of cells>` by creating a cube view:

- **Step 1.** Open a Cube Viewer for cube "TBB Sales."
- **Step 2.** Drag all dimensions into the rows of the Cube Viewer.
- **Step 3.** Make sure that all dimension subsets display all elements (see the next illustration).

All cells of the cube (this could be a huge number) should be listed in the view now. Of course, this only works with small cubes. With larger cubes you may get the "System Out of Memory" message, which is a notification that the view size has exceeded memory limits. This view is a visualization of [].

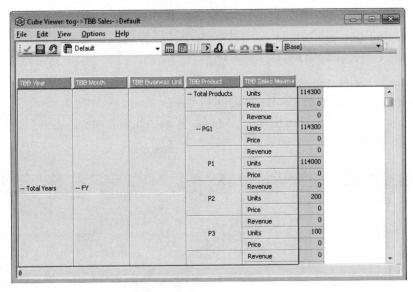

Visualization of a [] range

Now let us cut down the cube: Modify the subset of the dimension "Measures" so that only "Revenue" is visible. (See the following illustration.)

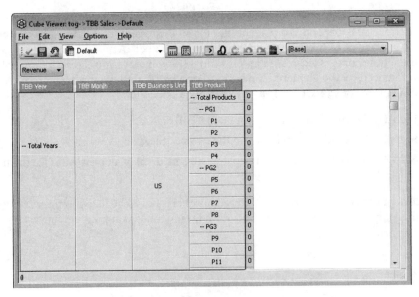

Visualization of ['Revenue'] range

This reflects the expression `['Revenue']`. Every additional element in the expression cuts down the cube further on. The smallest range you can define in the range-of-cells expression is one single cell. Like the coordinate of one cell, the range-of-cell expression contains one element of each dimension of the cube:

Example: `['2011','06','US','P1','Revenue']` can be visualized by the view in the following illustration.

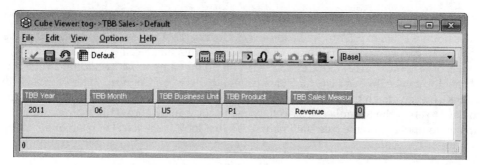

Visualization of `['2011','06','US','P1','Revenue']`

If you want to express a range that contains more than one element of a dimension, you can list these elements as a set in the following way:

```
[{'Q1','Q2','Q3','Q4'}, 'Revenue']
```

If the cube contains dimensions that have elements with the same name or alias, you have to add the dimension name of the element to make the reference unique.

```
['TBB Month':'01']
```

The dimension name has to be surrounded by quotes if the name contains blanks or other separators. Of course, the example is not needed because `'01'` is unique in the cube "TBB Sales." Also, you can use the set expression even if you reference only one element of a dimension. So the complete syntax of a range of all cells referenced by `'Revenue'` is `['TBB Sales Measure' :{'Revenue'}]`, which is optional in our example. So `['Revenue']` is an abbreviation of this expression.

Now let us go back to the syntax of a rule statement:

```
<A range of cells> = {N: | C: | S:} <Formula>;
```

The range-of-cell expression is the left-hand side of the rule statement. On the right-hand side of the equal sign, you will find at least one formula. In Cognos TM1 you can define different formulas for different cell types. If you want to define a formula for each cell type, the syntax of a rule statement looks like this:

```
<A range of cells> = N: <Formula for N-cells>;
                      C: <Formula for C-cells>;
                      S: <Formula for S-cells>;
```

If a rule statement doesn't have separate formulas for the different cell types, Cognos TM1 assumes that the formula calculates a value for N cells and C cells. To calculate a value for S cells, the "S:" in the rules statement is mandatory and the formula has to return a string value. A simple version of the rules syntax is this:

```
<Range of cells> = <Formula>;
```

Comparing Rules to Excel Formulas

At this point we like to refer to Microsoft Excel. Cognos TM1 rules can be compared to Excel formulas. In Excel you can enter either a value or formula into a cell (for example, 1000, =20000, or =SUM(A1..A10)). In Cognos TM1 you do the same thing by adding a rule statement to a cube. In this case, the major difference between Cognos TM1 and Excel is the fact that you can attach the same formula to a range of cells in Cognos TM1, while in Excel, you have to enter the formula cell by cell (or using copy and paste). This analogy should help you to understand the rule statement. Let's first look at the Excel version of our sample calculation: ['Revenue'] = ['Units']*['Price']. (See the following illustration.)

['Revenue'] = ['Units']*['Price'] as Excel formula

In Excel the revenue is calculated by a formula. The result is displayed in the cell where the formula was placed. The formula in our example consists of two cell references and the multiplication operator. If the Excel sheet is calculated, the references are used to get the unit and price values and perform the multiplication. Cognos TM1 uses the same mechanism to calculate rules. Like the "F2" in the Excel formula of cell E2, ['Units'] in the Cognos TM1 rule is a reference to a single cell.

Now this raises two questions. The first question is: Why is ['Units'] a reference to a single cell, although ['Revenue'] is a whole range of cells? The answer to the first question is simple: A [] expression on the left-hand side of the equal sign defines a range of cells, and on the right-hand side, it defines a reference to a cell. Therefore, if this expression is used on the right-hand side, sets of elements are not allowed.

The second question is: Which cell exactly is referenced with the expression ['Units']? The answer is: The exact reference of the cell is evaluated when the formula is calculated (the evaluation of the cell is explained in the next section). And that is very different from Excel. Excel stores the formula with the cell. Cognos TM1 stores the formula only in the rules object. If Cognos TM1 has to calculate the value of a cell, Cognos TM1 has to evaluate first, whether a rule is attached to the cell and which formula has to be calculated. This happens when the value of a cell is requested.

Following the Flow of Calculations

Now let's take a closer look at how Cognos TM1 calculates cells. To understand how Cognos TM1 evaluates the attached rule, we need an additional rule statement in our example (see the following illustration). The rule in this example is not correct from a business perspective. We will develop a correct rule later on.

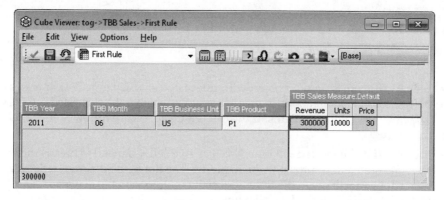

The second rule

If we take a look at the calculation mechanism, we have to do this for a single cell (here we remind you of the golden rule: Cognos TM1 calculates cell by cell). We will follow the calculation of the cell, which is referenced by the elements ['2011','06','US','P1', 'Revenue']. The corresponding view is shown in the following illustration.

Rule-calculated cells

As you see, the cell reference can be described with the rule expression. Cognos TM1 calculates a cell when the cell is requested. So a request could be initiated by a view (for example, our sample cell is requested by the view in the preceding illustration). A flow is started now. You can follow this flow in the 11 steps diagrammed in Figure 6-1.

Here is a detailed description of these steps:

- **Step 1.**   The value of a cell is requested.

- **Step 2.**   Cognos TM1 checks whether there is a rules object with rule statements. (This is not the check of whether the requested cell is calculated by a rule!) At this point the flow forks into two paths: If the cube has rules, please follow Step 3; if not, follow Step 6.

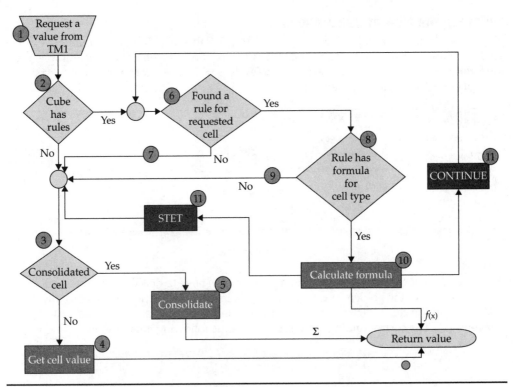

Figure 6-1   The calculation flow of Cognos TM1

- **Step 3.**   If there is no rules object with rule statements, Cognos TM1 operates in the default consolidation mode: Cognos TM1 checks whether the requested cell is a C cell. The flow forks into two paths: If the cell is a C cell, please follow Step 5; if not, follow Step 4.

- **Step 4.**   If the requested cell is an N cell or an S cell, Cognos TM1 reads the value from memory and returns it to the requester. The dot in the diagram reflects the green dot you will see in the Rules Tracer, if you trace a non-calculated leaf cell. At this point the flow ends. The following steps show other paths of the flow.

- **Step 5.**   This step is forked from Step 3. If the requested cell is a C cell, Cognos TM1 consolidates the value as described in the section "Understanding Consolidations." The result is returned to the requester. The sum symbol in the diagram reflects the blue sum symbol you will see in the Rules Tracer, if you trace a C cell. At this point the flow ends. The following steps show other paths of the flow.

- **Step 6.**   This is the forked path of Step 2. If a rules object with rules exists for the cube, Cognos TM1 starts a phase of looking for a formula that is attached to the requested cell. In this phase Cognos TM1 is just evaluating the left-hand side of one rule statement after another statement. Starting with the first statement in the rules object, Cognos TM1 checks whether the cell is in the range. If the cell is in the given range, Cognos TM1 finishes the phase of looking for a formula and goes on with processing the formula. You can imagine the process like this: Cognos TM1 is looking into the range of cells, and if the requested cell is found inside this range, Cognos TM1 "jumps over" the equal sign. Now the formula becomes visible and can be processed (this is described in Step 8). Keep in mind that once the process has "jumped over" the equal sign, Cognos TM1 will not go on with checking the ranges on the left-hand side (there is an exception, which is explained in Step 11). For that reason, a cell can have only one rule attached, although it could be inside more than one range defined in the rules object.

If the cell is not in the range, Cognos TM1 goes to the next statement to check the range. If no further statement exists, Cognos TM1 finishes the phase, with the result that the cell is not calculated by a formula, and forks the flow to Step 7.

- **Step 7**.   This step is forked from Step 6. If Cognos TM1 evaluates that the requested cell is not calculated by a formula, the flow goes on with Step 3.

- **Step 8**.   This step is forked from Step 6. If a formula was found for the requested cell, Cognos TM1 checks whether the rule statement contains a formula for the cell type of the requested cell. If there is no formula for the given cell type, the flow continues with Step 9. If the rule statement contains a formula for the given cell type, the flow continues with Step 10.

- **Step 9**.   This step is forked from Step 8. If the rule statement contains no formula for the cell type of the requested cell, the flow goes on with Step 3.

- **Step 10**.   This step is forked from Step 8. If the rule statement contains a formula for the cell type of the requested cell, Cognos TM1 processes the formula. The result is returned to the requester. The red function symbol in the diagram reflects the function symbol you will see in the Rules Tracer, if you trace a rule-based cell. At this point the flow ends. The following step shows two exceptions to the flow.

- **Step 11**.   This step describes two exceptions to the flow. If the processing of a formula returns not a value but a STET or a CONTINUE, the flow will jump to different steps in the flow:

  STET: If the formula returns STET, Cognos TM1 assumes that no rule is applied to the cell. The flow continues with Step 3. No further rule statement is checked.
  CONTINUE: If the formula returns CONTINUE, Cognos TM1 resumes to look for a formula. The flow continues with Step 6 and further rule statements could be checked, if there is another formula in the rules object that is attached to the requested cell.

This is the standard flow in Cognos TM1. With a parameter in the Cognos TM1 server configuration file (tm1s.cfg), you can change the behavior to a slightly different flow. If you set the parameter AllowSeparateNandCRules=T, Cognos TM1 will always continue with checking rule statements (Step 6). This allows you to replace a rule statement like

```
<range of cells> = N: <Formula for N-cells>;
            C: <Formula for C-cells>;
```

with two separate statements:

```
<range of cells> = N: <Formula for N-cells>;
<range of cells> = C: <Formula for C-cells>;
```

NOTE *The Performance Modeler uses the second version of the syntax if rules are generated from Links or Dimension rules.*

Understanding the Flow in an Example

We would like to use this flow with our example now (see the preceding two illustrations):

- The cell ['2011','06','US','P1','Revenue'] of cube TBB Sales is requested (Step 1).

- Cognos TM1 checks whether the cube has rules attached. The result of the check in our example is "Yes." (Step 2 and continue with Step 6.)

- Now Cognos TM1 "looks" into the rules object and goes to the first rule statement. Cognos TM1 just checks the left-hand side of the statement: ['Revenue']. Now Cognos TM1 evaluates whether ['2011','06','US','P1','Revenue'] is in the ['Revenue'] range. The answer is "Yes," and Cognos TM1 has found a formula for the cell (Step 6 and continue with Step 8).

- Cognos TM1 "jumps over" the equal sign and finds a formula. This formula is valid for N cells and C cells. ['2011','06','US','P1','Revenue'] is an N cell. So ['Units'] * ['Price'] is the attached formula of the requested cell (Step 8).

- Cognos TM1 knows the formula now and can calculate a value. The calculation is a multiplication of the values in two cells. Here we come back to the question: Which cells exactly are referenced by the expressions ['Units'] and ['Price']? The [] expression looks like a range, but it is a cell reference if it is used on the right-hand side of a rule statement. When Cognos TM1 calculates the formula, the processing is in the context of one single cell (remember the golden rule). Inside a formula, the [] expression is a relative cell reference to the cell that is in the context of the calculation (this can be compared to the relative cell reference in Excel). To resolve the relative reference into an absolute reference, Cognos TM1 extends the [] expression with the missing elements:

   ['Units'] becomes ['2011','06','US','P1','Units'] and ['Price'] becomes ['2011','06','US','P1','Price'] during the calculation. Cognos TM1 has obtained the references of the involved cells now. To calculate the revenue, Cognos TM1 needs the values of these cells. How is Cognos TM1 going to evaluate this condition? Cognos TM1 requests the value of ['2011','06','US','P1','Units'] and ['2011','06','US','P1','Price']. So we have to start a recursive flow for each cell (let's repeat this as two further examples):

   - The cell ['2011','06','US','P1','Units'] of cube "TBB Sales" is requested (Step 1).

   - Cognos TM1 checks whether the cube has rules attached. The result of the check in our example is "Yes" (Step 2 and continue with Step 6).

   - Now Cognos TM1 "looks" into the rules object and goes to the first rule statement. Cognos TM1 just checks the left-hand side of the statement: ['Revenue']. Now Cognos TM1 evaluates whether ['2011','06','US', 'P1','Units'] is in the ['Revenue'] range. The answer is "No" (Step 6).

- Cognos TM1 proceeds with the next rule statement. Cognos TM1 just checks the left-hand side of the statement: ['Price']. Now Cognos TM1 evaluates whether ['2011','06','US','P1','Units'] is in the ['Price'] range. The answer is "No" (Step 6). Because there is no further rule statement, Cognos TM1 cannot find a formula for the cell and continues with Step 9.

- Step 9 is just the fork to Step 3. Cognos TM1 checks the type of the cell. ['2011','06','US','P1','Units'] is an N cell. Cognos TM1 returns the value of the cell, which can be used in the calculation of the revenue (Step 4): 10000.

- Continue with the second cell: The cell ['2011','06','US','P1','Price'] of cube "TBB Sales" is requested (Step 1).

- Cognos TM1 checks whether the cube has rules attached. The result of the check in our example is "Yes." (Step 2 and continue with Step 6.)

- Now Cognos TM1 "looks" into the rules object and goes to the first rule statement. Cognos TM1 just checks the left-hand side of the statement: ['Revenue']. Now Cognos TM1 evaluates whether ['2011','06','US','P1','Price'] is in the ['Revenue'] range. The answer is "No" (Step 6).

- Cognos TM1 proceeds with the next rule statement. Cognos TM1 just checks the left-hand side of the statement: ['Price']. Now Cognos TM1 evaluates if ['2011','06','US','P1','Price'] is in the ['Price'] range. The answer is "Yes" and Cognos TM1 has found a formula for the cell. (Step 6 and continue with Step 8.)

- Cognos TM1 "jumps over" the equal sign and finds a formula. This formula is valid for N cells and C cells. ['2011','06','US','P1','Price'] is an N cell. So DB('TBB Price', !TBB Year, !TBB Month, !TBB Product, 'Price') is the applied formula of the requested cell (Step 8).

Now Cognos TM1 can calculate a value with the formula. The calculation is just the retrieving of a value. The DB function is another expression for a cell reference. Actually you can replace each [] expression on the right-hand side of the rule statement with an appropriate DB function. (You cannot replace the [] expression on the left-hand side, because it is not a cell reference but a range of cells.) Both represent an address of a single cell. The difference between both reference expressions is that the [] expression can only refer to cells of the current cube. The DB function can refer to cells of all cubes in the Cognos TM1 server.

Let's take a look at how the DB function works. The DB function contains the name of the cube and the coordinates of a cell as parameters. The coordinates have the same sequence as the dimensions of the cube in the first parameter. You can express the reference of our sample cell in the cube "TBB Sales" with the DB function: DB('TBB Sales', '2011','06','US','P1','Price')

Instead of a full reference with element names, you find a more flexible reference in our rule sample: The DB function is used with a placeholder. Each placeholder starts with an exclamation point (in Cognos TM1, this is called "Bang") followed by the name of a dimension. At the time of processing the formula, Cognos TM1 replaces the placeholder with the name of an element. Because we are in the context of the calculation of cell ['2011','06','US','P1','Price'], Cognos TM1 knows all the element names. In the rule, these element names of the context can be accessed by the Bang expression:

!TBB Year is replaced with '2011'
!TBB Month is replaced with '06'
!TBB Product is replaced with 'P1'

In our example Cognos TM1 calls the DB function with the substituted parameters:

```
DB('TBB Price', '2011', '06', 'P1', 'Price')
```

Please be aware that the rule statement allows Bang expressions of dimensions of the current cube only, because only the elements of the requested cell (and therefore only elements of the current cube) are known during the rule processing. This could lead to some confusion, if a DB function references a cell from a different cube that has a different dimension. (Our example is simple because "TBB Price" uses the same dimensions.) Imagine that we want to use another price cube:

"TBB Product Group 1 Price" with the dimensions TBB Product Group 1, TBB Year, TBB Month, and TBB Price Measure. This cube has one different dimension and the dimension sequence has changed. The dimension TBB Product Group 1 contains the C element PG1 and the N elements P1, P2, P3, P4. In the "TBB Sales" cube the DB function would look like this:

```
DB('TBB Product Group 1 Price', !TBB Product, !TBB Year, !TBB
Month, 'Price')
```

You have to use !TBB Product because !TBB Product Group 1 is not known in the TBB Sales cube! When Cognos TM1 processes the rule statement, it will substitute the element names: In the context of our sample cell ['2011','06' ,'US','P1','Price'], the DB function would be referenced to

```
DB('TBB Product Group 1 Price', 'P1', '2011', '06', 'Price')
```

which would be a valid reference. If the requested cell were ['2011','06', 'US','P12','Price'], the calculation would try to access

```
DB('TBB Product Group 1 Price', 'P1', '2011', '06', 'Price')
```

which does not exist. This will not throw an error but return zero instead. This is called the "silent error mode" of the DB function.

- Let's go back to the rule processing of the requested cell. Cognos TM1 calculates the function call of DB('TBB Price', '2011', '06', 'P1', 'Price'). This is again a request for a value of a single cell and we can repeat the Cognos TM1 calculation flow:

  - The cell ['2011','06','P1','Price'] of cube TBB Price is requested (Step 1).

  - Cognos TM1 checks whether the cube (TBB Price) has rules attached. The result of the check in our example is "No." (Step 2 and continue with Step 3.)

  - Cognos TM1 checks whether the requested cell is a C cell.
    ['2011','06','P1','Price'] is an N cell. (Step 3 and continue with Step 4.)

- Cognos TM1 retrieves the stored value from TBB Price: 30.

- Cognos TM1 has obtained both factors of the multiplication. The result is 10000*30=300000 as you can see in the preceding illustration. Just to remind you: This was Step 10 in the calculation flow.

Validating Calculation with the Rules Tracer

You can use the calculation flow that we've described to check all calculations in your Cognos TM1 model if you want to. This should help you to understand what happens in Cognos TM1 when a value is requested. To support this, you can also use the Rules Tracer for validation. Let's do this with our example:

- Right-click on the cell you want to trace. In the popup menu, choose Trace Calculation (see the following illustration):

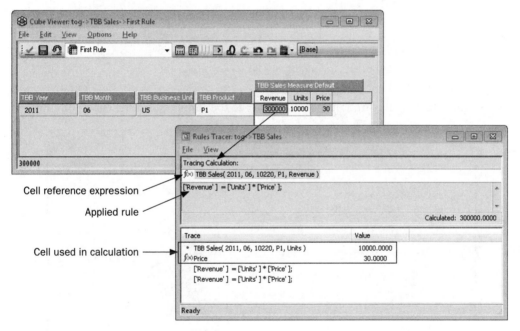

The trace of a rule-calculated cell

- The Rules Tracer shows the selected cell in the top pane. The leading symbol of the cell reference indicates that the cell is rule-based (steps in the calculation flow: 1 -> 2 -> 6 -> 8 -> 10). In the middle pane you can see the rule statement that is applied to the cell. In the bottom pane you can see all involved cells with their values, which are needed to process the calculation. Here you can follow the calculation path by double-clicking the cell you want to follow.

- The following illustration shows the path to the cell ['2011','06','US','P1', 'Units']. The cell is a simple cell that is stored in the cube memory. This cell is indicated by the green dot. You can compare this view with the following steps in our calculation flow: 1 -> 2 -> 3 -> 4.

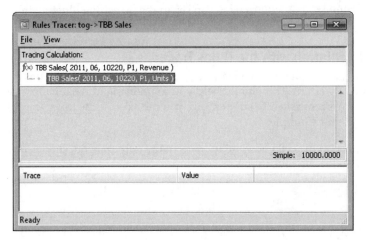

A trace to a stored cell

- The following illustration shows the trace to the simple cell in the cube TBB Price.

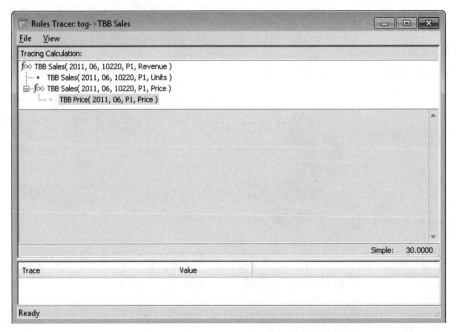

A trace to a stored cell in a linked cube

To complete this chapter about the rules calculation, we would like to share some thoughts with you:

- The formula `DB('TBB Price', !TBB Year, !TBB Month, !TBB Product, 'Price')` in our example could be replaced by `DB('TBB Price', !TBB Year, !TBB Month, !TBB Product, !TBB Sales Measure)` because each cell that is calculated by this rule is referenced by the element "Price" of the Dimension TBB Sales Measure. So for each case, `!TBB Sales Measure` will be replaced by `'Price'`. Both versions of the formula are valid. But using `DB('TBB Price', !TBB Year, !TBB Month, !TBB Product, 'Price')`, it is more clear what the rule is calculating at first glance.

- `<range of cells> = N: formula;`
  could be replaced by
  `<range of cells> = N: formula; C:STET;`
  But if `AllowSeparateNandCRules` is set to T, then
  `<range of cells> = N: formula;`
  could be replaced by
  `<range of cells> = N: formula; C:CONTINUE;`

- The sequence of rules statements inside the rule object doesn't matter in most cases. But there are some cases when you do have to care about the sequence:

  1. If two or more ranges intersect. For all cells that are not in the intersection of ranges, the sequence of the rules does not matter. All cells in an intersection are calculated by the rule that is found first.

  2. If a range is inside another range, the rule of the smaller range should come first. In general, you should sort the sequence of rules by the size of the ranges: small range to larger ranges.

  3. You can work around the behavior of cases 1 and 2 if you use the CONTINUE statement. With this statement you can reach ranges behind the current range.

- The Bang expression can be used everywhere in the formula expression, where you need the name of a dimension element of the requested cell.

Now you should understand the syntax and the flow of a rule-based calculation.

Cooperation of Consolidation and Rules

In this section we will take a look at how rules calculation works together with consolidation. In the previous sections of this chapter, we have just looked at calculation with leaf cells. Now we should look at our example on a consolidated level.

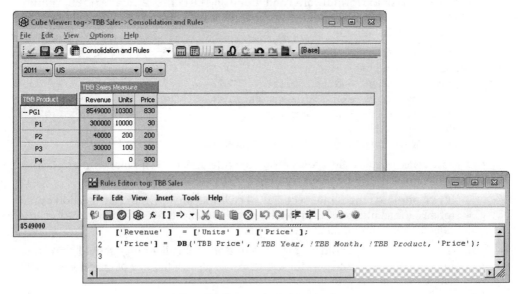

Consolidations and rule-based cells

As you can see in the preceding illustration, the element "PG1" in dimension "TBB Product" is a consolidation of the elements "P1," "P2," "P3," and "P4." Obviously the value of cell ['2011','06','US','PG1','Revenue'] is not consolidated but calculated by rule. You can validate this by using the flow diagram in Figure 9.1 or the Rules Tracer.

The calculation of this cell follows these steps in the flow: 1 -> 2 -> 6 -> 8 ->10. The applied formula of this cell performs a multiplication of ['2011','06','US','PG1','Units'] and ['2011','06','US','PG1','Price'] (10000 * 830 = 8300000). If you follow the flow of these factors, you will find that ['2011','06','US','PG1','Units'] is calculated by a consolidation and ['2011','06','US','PG1','Price'] is retrieved from the "TBB Price" cube. The cell ['2011','06','PG1','Price'] of the cube "TBB Price" is also a consolidated value, but the execution of this consolidation is performed in the memory of the "TBB Price" cube. This example shows that rules "overrule" consolidation.

Now we want to correct this calculation. First we change the rule statement of the range
['Revenue'] to change all cells on a consolidated level from rule-based cells to consolidated
cells, as shown in the following illustration:

Adding the N:

The solution in this case is to add the N: to the rule statement. Now we changed the
path of the calculation flow for all C cells from 1 -> 2 -> 6 -> 8 -> 10 to 1 -> 2 -> 6 ->8 -> 9 ->
3 -> 5. The result of the calculation is shown in the following illustration:

Correct calculation of revenue on the C level

The value of cell ['2011','06','US','PG1','Price'] in our example is not used in
the calculation any more. From a technical perspective, the calculation is correct. From a
business point of view, this value is not valid because it is senseless to consolidate prices of
different products. So we decide to calculate the price by a rule instead of a consolidation.
The price should be the revenue per unit. We change the rule statement of ['Price'] and
look at the result (see the next illustration). The retrieval of the prices is now applied to N
cells only. If you look at both statements, it seems that we have defined a circular reference
because ['Revenue'] is calculated by ['Price'] and ['Price'] is calculated by
['Revenue']. But it is not a circular reference in this case. Each of these calculations is
applied to different sets of cells. If ['Revenue'] is calculated by ['Price'], then the
['Price'] expression is always a reference to an N cell, which is retrieved from the cube

TBB Price. If ['Price'] is calculated by ['Revenue'], then the ['Revenue'] expression is always a reference to a C cell that is calculated by a consolidation.

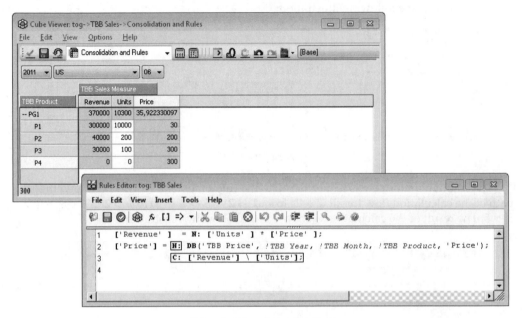

Enhancing the price calculation

Who's Afraid of Feeders?

As we discussed earlier in the section "Understanding Consolidations," there is an issue regarding the fourth factor in Cognos TM1 performance (this factor is about using the sparsity of data when values are consolidated). Cognos TM1 switches off the sparsity algorithm when using rules. We remind you that if the response time seems to be good, you shouldn't care about this algorithm, and you should provide the defined model to end users as is. But in many other models, this algorithm plays the main role in good performance. If your model runs into poor performance, you need to reactivate the sparsity algorithm of Cognos TM1. This can be done by placing the SKIPCHECK statement as the first statement in the rule object. When you add the SKIPCHECK statement, the consolidation of the element "Revenue" will fail (see the next illustration). What is the reason?

When consolidating the cell ['2011','06','US','PG1','Revenue'] in our example (Step 5 in the calculation flow), Cognos TM1 looks into the memory of the cube and grabs all stored cells that are needed for the consolidation. But in this case, there is no stored cell. The value of cell ['2011','06','US','P1','Revenue'] is not stored in the cube memory because the cell is calculated by a rule. The consolidation process cannot "see" this cell. Each calculated cell gets a value only when the cell is requested (that's the reason why we can see the value in the view, because the view itself requests the cell). The consolidation process does not request the cell, because the process does not know which cell has to be requested. The sparsity algorithm does not work with calculated N cells. That is the reason why Cognos TM1 switches off this algorithm for a cube by default if the cube has rules. After the algorithm is switched off, all cells are requested that are leafs of the consolidated cell. (An example is shown in the section "Understanding Consolidations.") That is the meaning of the statement SKIPCHECK. SKIPCHECK tells Cognos TM1 to skip the check of all N cells for values during a consolidation.

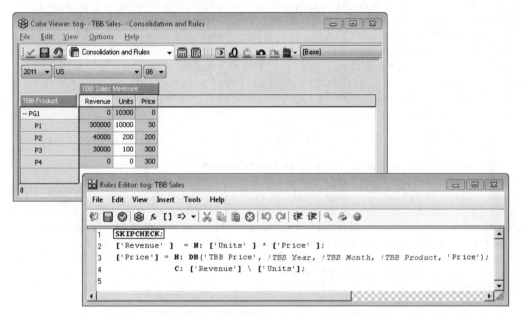

No consolidation of rule-calculated values

The question is how to use the sparsity algorithm with rule-calculated cells. An answer would be to store these calculated values in the cube memory so that the cells are visible to the consolidation process. But to store the calculated values, Cognos TM1 has to precalculate all values. That is not the intention of Cognos TM1. The solution of the problem is not to calculate and to store the value, but to make the calculated N cell visible to the consolidation process. This is done by creating a stored cell in the memory of the cube with no value but with a flag. This mechanism of Cognos TM1 is called "feeding" a cell. The flag inside this cell is called a "feeder flag." The statement that creates feeder flags is Feeders. A feeder flag consumes less memory than a stored value in the memory of the cube. If you want to create reasonable feeder flags, you should ask yourself which cells have to be flagged by a feeder to make sure that all relevant leaf cells are visible to a consolidation process. Your task is to find out which cell is rule-based and relevant for a consolidation. These cells are all leaf cells, which get a value that is not zero after calculation.

Let's take a look at our example. There are two ranges of cells that contains rule-calculated leaf cells:
```
['Revenue'] = N: ['Units'] * ['Price'];
```
and
```
['Price'] = N: DB('TBB Price', !TBB Year, !TBB Month, !TBB Product,
'Price');
```

Let's investigate the first rule statement. The question is which leaf cells of the range ['Revenue'] should be visible (and should allocate cube memory). The answer is all cells that get a non-zero value after calculating ['Units'] * ['Price']. To be more specific, we have to answer this question in this way: A ['Revenue'] cell has to be fed if the relative ['Units'] cell is not zero *and* the relative ['Price'] cell is not zero. So the criteria for a feeder flag could be found in another cell that holds a value. Please note that the rule-calculated ['Price'] cells could be used like stored cells if these cells are fed, because in this case the feeder flag is treated like a stored value. Unfortunately, the "and" in the statement leads to a complex "Conditional Feeder." We will discuss this later. To simplify the statement, we replace the "and" with an "or." Now we assume that the criteria for a feeder flag is given by a non-zero ['Units'] cell or a non-zero ['Price'] cell. With this in mind we can take a look at the feeders in Cognos TM1. Feeders are defined in a section in the rules object, which starts with the statement FEEDERS;. The syntax of the feeder statement is defined as follows:

```
<Range of leaf cells> => <cell reference> { , <cell reference> };
```

As within a rule statement, you find an expression on the left-hand side that defines a range in the same way: Here the [] expression is used again. But there is a difference. In the feeder statement the defined range is only checked against N and S cells. The "assignment" operator in a feeder statement is a "=>" to underline the "push" characteristic compared to the "get" characteristic of a rule statement. On the right-hand side of the feeder statement, you find a list of [] expressions or DB functions to define a cell reference. In most cases you will find only one cell reference. With this syntax, a feeder tells Cognos TM1 which cell should become visible by setting a feeder flag.

Figure 6-2 shows you a simple flow of how feeders are evaluated:

- **Step 1.** The first step stands for an event that triggers the evaluating process. As you know from the flow of calculating a cell, the evaluation is processed for a single cell. Whenever a cell becomes a stored cell in the memory of the cube, a trigger for the flow occurs. A cell becomes a stored cell in the memory when its value changes from zero to non-zero. (Changing a cell value from a non-zero value to another value does *not* trigger a feeder). This happens whenever

  1. A cube is loaded into memory (for example, at startup).

  2. The TurboIntegrator function CubeProcessFeeders(CubeName) is executed.

  3. A rules object is saved.

  4. A cell has changed from null because the user entered a value via a user front end (for example, entering a value in the Cube Viewer).

  5. A cell has changed from null via a TurboIntegrator process (for example, the CellPutN function).

  6. A null (and not fed) cell is fed (Feeders triggers feeders).

  There are two exceptions to these criteria:

  1. If the cell that has changed is an S cell. String cells always trigger a feeder when the value has changed, even if the cell already holds a value.

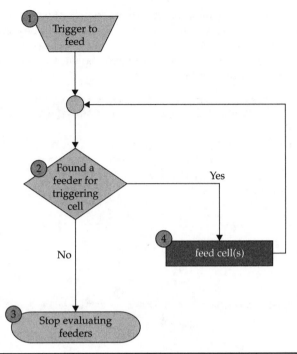

FIGURE 6-2 Flow of feeders

2. If the optional parameter ReevaluateConditionalFeeders is set to T and a cell which is referenced in the condition of a conditional feeder has changed, the conditional feeder is checked again. If the condition is true the target cell will be fed. (See the section "Conditional Feeders.")

When a cube is loaded or the feeders are processed by the CubeProcessFeeders (CubeName) function, each cell that is stored in the memory of the cube triggers the evaluation of feeder statements. This is the reason why feeders could increase the startup time of a Cognos TM1 server.

NOTE *With Cognos TM1 Version 9.5.1 and higher, you can set up the server config (tm1s.cfg) to save feeder "mappings" to disk. If this "Persistent Feeders" option is activated, the feeder processing step of server loading is bypassed, and instead the feeder cell mappings are loaded from a disk file. This will improve the server startup time.*

- **Step 2.** The left-hand side (the <range of cells> expression) of each feeder statement is checked.
- **Step 3.** If all feeder statements are checked for the triggering cell, the flow stops.
- **Step 4.** If the triggering cell is inside the range, a feeder flag is set to each cell that is referenced by an expression on the right-hand side.

Now let's add feeders to our example. We like to repeat that we have to feed all N cells in the range ['Revenue'] so that all C cells in the same range could be consolidated correctly. The criteria for a feeder flag in a ['Revenue'] cell is that a corresponding ['Units'] cell is not zero or a corresponding ['Price'] cell is not zero. So we add the first feeder statement to the rules object (see the following illustration).

Adding a feeder statement

When you save the rules object, Cognos TM1 triggers the evaluation of the feeders for all stored cells in the cube. In this case Cognos TM1 will set a feeder flag into all ['Revenue'] cells where the corresponding ['Units'] cell has a stored value. We call this "Units" feeds "Revenue." Now the consolidation of ['Revenue'] calculates the correct value (see the next). But do we need to feed "Revenue" from "Price"? The answer in this case is No. To understand why, assume that we feed "Revenue" from "Units" and "Price":

```
['Units' ] => ['Revenue' ];

['Price' ] => ['Revenue' ];
```

That results in the feeding of the following cells of our sample view (see the following illustration):

```
['2011','06','US','P1','Revenue']

['2011','06','US','P2','Revenue']
```

```
['2011','06','US','P3','Revenue']
```

```
['2011','06','US','P4','Revenue']
```

Well-fed cube

In our example, the feeder flag for "Revenue" for product "P4" is not necessary, because we feed rule-calculated cells that are zero after they are requested. This means that the consolidation process has to request four cells even if only one cell is needed. This is also known as *overfeeding*. Overfeeding could have a negative impact on performance, lead to unnecessary memory consumption, and slow down the loading of a cube. But again, this could be negligible in many Cognos TM1 models. Remember that performance is an impression of the user, and if the user "feels" that the performance is poor, your application will lose acceptance. So care should be taken not to overfeed, as it may impact performance.

If you are not sure if your model is "overfed," you can create an Auxiliary cube that counts "overfed" cells (see the section "Checking Overfeeding").

Unfortunately, we also run into potential overfeeding if we have only the feeder `['Units' ] => ['Revenue' ]`. This feeder could feed a `['Revenue']` cell even if "Price" is zero, and therefore a zero "Revenue" is fed. This overfeeding could be avoided by using a conditional feeder (see the section "Conditional Feeders"). But before you add a conditional feeder to your model, you should weigh whether this is necessary. On the one hand, the perception of performance could be acceptable even though some cells are overfed. On the other hand, maybe you can argue like this from a business point of view:

"`['Units' ] => ['Revenue' ]` does not lead in overfeeding because we do not have a product with no price or we do not give away any product." That means "Price" will never be zero.

Now let's discuss whether we have to feed the leaf cell in the `['Price']` range. As we have already explained, we need feeder flags to make relevant cells visible for consolidation. If this is the case, we do not have to define a feeder statement if C cells are calculated by a rule. If the requested cell in this range is a C cell, `['Price']` is calculated by `['Revenue' ]\ ['Units']`. No consolidation will be performed in the `['Price']` range. As you can see in the preceding illustration, Cognos TM1 calculates the "Price" for "PG1" correctly.

But there is another Cognos TM1 function that uses the same mechanism as consolidation: zero suppression. If you want to use zero suppression, you have to also feed leaf cells that are in the consolidation tree of a rule-calculated C cell.

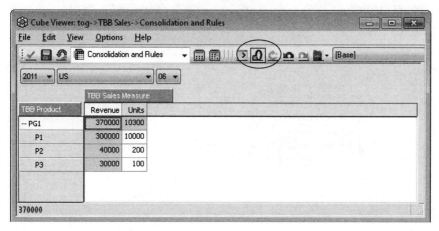

Missing prices when suppressing zeros

As you can see in the preceding illustration, all "Price" values are suppressed, although there are values for each "Price" cell. This can be solved by feeding the ['Price'] cells. The ['Price'] cells on the leaf level are calculated by a DB function that retrieves a corresponding value from the "TBB Price" cube. The question is, which cells can trigger feeders for these cells? The answer is the stored price value in the "TBB Price" cube. Now we have to add a feeder statement to the "TBB Price" cube (see the following illustration):

```
Rules Editor: tog: TBB Price
File  Edit  View  Insert  Tools  Help

1  SKIPCHECK;
2  |
3  FEEDERS;
4  [ ]  => DB('TBB Sales', !TBB Year, !TBB Month, 'Total Business Unit', !TBB Product, 'Price');
```

Feeding from a linked cube

As you can see in the following illustration, the zero suppression is working correctly if the "Price" cells are fed.

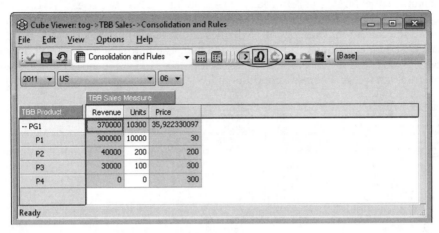

Well-fed cube

We want to point out that this behavior is also applied to S cells that are rule-calculated. Additionally, if you want to feed S cells, you need to add the FEEDSTRING statement as the first statement in the rules object of the cube that contains the S cells you want to feed. Otherwise, the feeder flag is not set to these cells.

Conditional Feeders

With conditional feeders, you can feed cells based on a condition. In our example, we need to express in a feeder statement that "Revenue" should be fed if "Units" is not zero and "Price" is not zero. The first condition is solved by the feeder itself because ['Units'] => ['Revenue'] defines that "Revenue" is fed if "Units" is not zero. But we want to extend the expression so that the feeder should be processed only if "Price" is also non-zero. Unfortunately, the Cognos TM1 feeder syntax doesn't allow surrounding the feeder statement with a condition. The feeder statement is always processed when the trigger condition occurs. The only option to prevent the setting of a feeder flag into a cell is to make the cell reference invalid. This can be done by manipulating the coordinates of the target cell. For that we have to substitute a DB function for a [] expression. As mentioned in the section "Understanding Rules Calculation," both expressions define a cell reference. So the statement ['Units'] => ['Revenue']; is equal to the statement ['Units'] => DB('TBB Sales', !TBB Year, !TBB Month, !TBB Business Unit, !TBB Product, 'Revenue');. Why do we have to substitute? The [] expression does not allow us to write code (in this case we need an IF statement to express a condition) inside the expression. Only string literals are allowed. The DB function allows other expressions than string literals as parameters.

Our objective is now to create an invalid cell reference. This is easy because if one of the parameters in the DB function is a nonexistent value, the DB function points to a nonexistent cell. For example, DB('TBB Sales', !TBB Year, !TBB Month, !TBB Business Unit,

!TBB Product, '') points to a nonexistent cell because '' is an invalid name for a dimension element. In most examples of conditional feeders, you find a DB function with a invalid cube name: DB('', !TBB Year, !TBB Month, !TBB Business Unit, !TBB Product, 'Revenue'). But in this case the cell reference would be always invalid. So we have to add the condition. The Cognos TM1 rules and feeder language provide a function that can be used for conditions. This is the IF function. The IF function has three parameters: IF(<condition>,<Value if condition is true>, <value if condition is false>). With this function we can express a conditional feeder (see the following illustration):

DB substitution in feeder statement

```
['Units'] => DB(IF(['Price']<>0,'TBB Sales',''), !TBB Year, !TBB Month,
!TBB Business Unit, !TBB Product, 'Revenue');
```

When the feeder is processed, Cognos TM1 has to evaluate the IF function first and then the DB function. If the "Price" is not zero, the IF function will pass "TBB Sales" to the DB function, which leads to a valid cell reference. If the "Price" is zero, the IF function will pass '', which makes this function invalid. As already mentioned, the DB function will not raise an error if an invalid parameter is passed. Cognos TM1 just cannot set a flag to an invalid cell reference.

Checking Overfeeding

We want to share with you a further exercise in rules and feeders. This example uses the described Cognos TM1 behavior to evaluate how many cells are overfed in a cube. The counter for overfed cells will be calculated in a new cube. This cube is called "TBB Sales Overfed Cells" in the example. The cube consists of the same dimension as the TBB Sales cube:

TBB Years, TBB Months, TBB Business Units, TBB Products, and TBB Sales Measures. All leaf cells should be calculated by the rule shown in the following illustration.

Rule to check overfeeding

This rule statement defines that all N cells for which the corresponding cell in the "TBB Sales" cube have a non-zero value get the value zero, and vice versa. In the "TBB Sales" cube, we add a feeder to feed the cells in "TBB Sales Overfed Cells" (see the following illustration).

Feeder to check overfeeding

But "Revenue" is rule-calculated, so why can we use this as a trigger for feeders? You can use rule-calculated cells if you fed these cells. As already mentioned, feeder flags trigger feeding. The feeder flag is treated like any other stored value. If the "TBB Sales" cube is well fed (not overfed), the feeder statement in our example feeds all cells in the "TBB Sales Overfed Cells" cube that are zero by the definition of the rule statement. In the following illustration, you can see that the consolidation is zero.

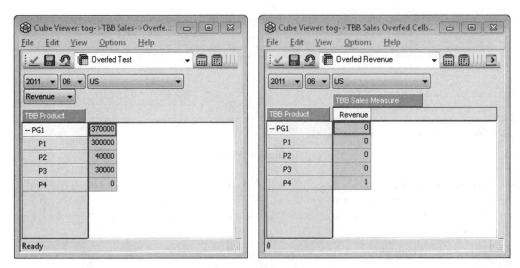

Analyze overfeeding (well-fed)

Why? The consolidation is zero because "P4" is not fed in the cube "TBB Sales Overfed Cells" if the "TBB Sales" cube is well fed. The consolidation process cannot "see" "P4." Now we force the overfeeding of the "TBB Sales" cube by adding an additional feeder as shown in the following illustration.

```
Rules Editor: tog: TBB Sales
File  Edit  View  Insert  Tools  Help

1   SKIPCHECK;
2   ['Revenue' ]  = N: ['Units' ] * ['Price' ];
3   ['Price'] = N: DB('TBB Price', !TBB Year, !TBB Month, !TBB Product, 'Price');
4              C: ['Revenue'] \ ['Units'];
5
6   FEEDERS;
7   ['Units'] => DB(IF(['Price']<>0,'TBB Sales',''), !TBB Year, !TBB Month, !TBB Business Unit, !TBB Product, 'Revenue');
8
9   ['Price'] => ['Revenue' ];
10
11  ['Revenue'] => DB('TBB Sales Overfed Cells', !TBB Year, !TBB Month, !TBB Business Unit, !TBB Product, !TBB Sales Measure);
12
```

Feeder to force overfeeding

You can see the result of the overfeeding in the "TBB Sales Overfed Cells" cube (see the following illustration).

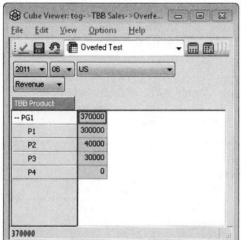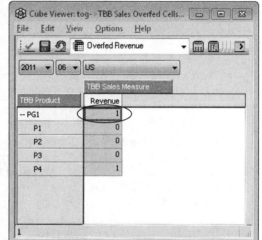

Analyze overfeeding: one cell is overfed.

"P4" in cube "TBB Sales Overfed Cells" is now fed triggered by the overfed cell in the cube "TBB Sales." Now the "1" can be "seen" by the consolidation.

Further Thoughts about Rules

In this section we will share with you some further thoughts about Rule and Feeders.

Using the DB Function

As we already mentioned, you can substitute a corresponding DB function for a [] expression in the right-hand side of a rule statement, because both expressions represent a reference to a single cell. In the following cases, you have to substitute for the [] expression:

- A [] expression allows only string literals as coordinates of a cell. If you want to calculate the coordinate dynamically, you cannot use a function inside the [] expression. An example for a dynamically calculated cell reference is rolling a value along a time period:

  ```
  ['revenue last period'] = N: [<dynamic element name of a period>,
  'revenue'];
  ```

  In this case the element name is not constant because the last period depends on the period of the calculated cell. You can calculate relative periods with Cognos TM1's index function (DIMIX) or with attributes. We recommend using attributes, which have to be added to the period dimension. Let's assume that we add the attribute "Last Period."

The function to calculate the last period of the current period is
`ATTRS('Period',!Period,'Last Period')`. `!Period` holds the current period
element when the requested cell is calculated. This function cannot be used inside
the [] expression. So we have to substitute the DB function for the [] expression:
`['revenue last period'] = N: DB(<Name of the current cube>, ...`
`some other coordinates..., ATTRS('Period',!Period,'Last Period'),`
`'revenue');`

- With a [] expression you can retrieve only numbers, although a [] expression on the right-hand side can refer to cells of any type. Cognos TM1 treats the referenced cell as a number. So if you want to calculate with a string value from an S cell, you have to express the cell reference by using the DB function. Example:

Assume that the measure dimension consists of two N elements ("Accepted Revenue," "Revenue") and an S element ("Status"). The "Accepted Revenue" should be the "Revenue" if the status is set to "Accepted":

`['Accepted Revenue'] = N: IF ( [ 'Status']`
`@= 'Accepted', ['value'],0);`
This rule will cause an error if you try to save the
rules object, as shown in the next illustration.

- In this case the `['Status']` is treated as a number. A number cannot be compared (`@=`) to a string. So we have to use the DB function:

`['Accepted Revenue'] = N: IF ( DB(<Name of the current cube>, ...`
`some other coordinates..., 'Status') @= 'Accepted', ['Revenue'],0);`

Lifetime of a Feeder Flag

Feeder flags are not deleted automatically. In most cases this is not a problem. It could be a
problem if the development of your feeders is still in progress. If the rules object is saved, all
feeders for all populated cells are executed. If you change feeder statements or delete them,
the old feeder flags still exist in the cube. So it might happen that you think your cube is
well fed and all consolidated values are correct. After you restart Cognos TM1, you may
realize that your cube is underfed. Feeder flags are only released if the Cognos TM1 server
is shut down or the cube is unloaded by the unloader. You can unload the cube by using the
TurboIntegrator function `CubeUnload(<Cubename>);` or by using the context menu: Cube |
Unload. If you use conditional feeders, the change of the condition from true to false will
also leave a flag artifact in the cube. The change of the condition will not delete a flag. This
leads into a slightly overfed calculation.

C Elements in Feeder Statements

Perhaps you have seen a feeder statement that uses the name of a C element on the left- or
the right-hand side of the statement. But such a statement does not feed from or to C cells.
Feeders are always triggered by leaf cells, and feeders can only feed leaf cells. Using C
elements is a shortcut. A C element in a feeder statement is always a shortcut to all N elements
below this element (down the whole hierarchy).

Check and Trace Feeders

You can check and trace feeders with functions that you can call from a cell context menu in the Cube Viewer. You can use "Trace Feeders" from populated leaf cells to find out which cells are fed by the selected cell, as shown in the following illustration.

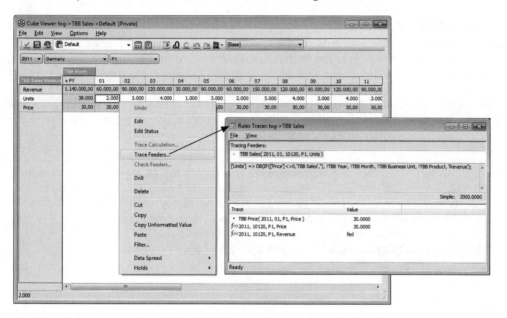

You can use "Check Feeders" to evaluate if the selected cell or the children of the cell are fed, as shown in the following illustration.

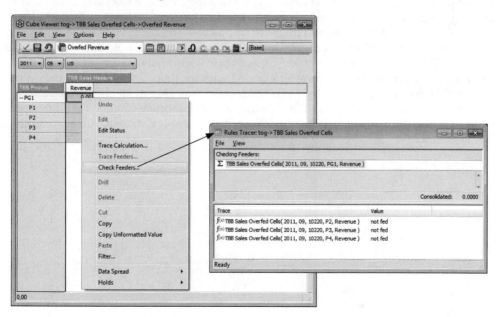

Feeding a Populated Cell

It may happen that you feed a cell that already holds a value or a feeder flag. Cognos TM1 ignores the feeding if the cell is already populated. So nothing is changed if you have multiple feeders on a single cell or the cell holds a value.

Persistent Feeders

As already mentioned, a feature is available in Cognos TM1 9.5.1 and higher, which allows the Cognos TM1 server to save the feeders to disk in a "<cubename>.feeders" file per cube. This feature improves the startup time of the Cognos TM1 server. Persistent feeders are activated if you set the configuration parameter `PersistentFeeders=T` in the tm1s.cfg file. If this option is activated, the Cognos TM1 server will load the feeders on startup from disk if the feeders file exists. If the feeders file of a cube doesn't exist on startup time, the feeders are calculated and written to a new feeders file.

NOTE *Because Cognos TM1 only adds new feeders and doesn't remove old feeders from memory, it could happen that invalid old feeders are also stored in the feeders files. For that reason it may be necessary to reorganize the feeders file. You can do this by removing the feeders files. This forces the re-creation of these files. In this case you can use the TI function* `DeleteAllPersistentFeeders()`. *(Please refer to the Cognos TM1 documentation:* Cognos TM1 Operations Guide, *Chapter 2, Section: Using Persistent Feeders.)*

Summary

From this chapter, you should have gained some insight into Cognos TM1 calculations. In the next chapter we will discuss TurboIntegrator processes. These processes can also be used to build business logic. The difference is that business logic built on calculations is "ad hoc." It will be performed every time data is retrieved from a Cognos TM1 server. Business logic built on TurboIntegrator processes is triggered by an event and could be more "batch" style.

Rules are an important and very powerful Cognos TM1 building block. In Part II of this book we will show you some examples where business requirements are implemented with rules. Furthermore, we recommend working with the *Rules Guide*, which is part of the Cognos TM1 documentation. In the *Rules Guide*, a Cognos TM1 model is built based on the requirements of a virtual "Fish Cake Factory." An appropriate Cognos TM1 database (in the directory "Rules_Guide_Data") is delivered as a sample database with every Cognos TM1 installation.

Cognos TM1 Building Blocks: TurboIntegrator

I n this chapter we will discuss the principles of TurboIntegrator and how you can use TurboIntegrator as a building block of your Cognos TM1 solution.

TurboIntegrator is often called the ETL (Extract, Transform, and Load) tool of Cognos TM1. But this is only half of the truth. TurboIntegrator is purely the script engine of Cognos TM1, with the following capabilities:

- TurboIntegrator is able to connect to external data sources and Cognos TM1 Cube and extract data.
- TurboIntegrator is able to transform data.
- TurboIntegrator is able to create and populate Cognos TM1 objects.

TurboIntegrator is actually not an ETL tool because

- Extracting data from a data source is just an option.
- TurboIntegrator is not a separate program (see Chapter 4).
- TurboIntegrator is able to manipulate only Cognos TM1 objects.

With these capabilities you can use TurboIntegrator for the following purposes:

- Automating Cognos TM1 models with TurboIntegrator
- Implementing business logic with TurboIntegrator processes
- Implementing workflow with TurboIntegrator processes
- Exporting data

Let's take a closer look at each of these points in the next sections.

Automating Cognos TM1 Models with TurboIntegrator

A TurboIntegrator process is purely a script that runs inside the Cognos TM1 server. Like other Cognos TM1 objects, a TurboIntegrator process is loaded into the memory of the Cognos TM1 server. With the script language of TurboIntegrator, you can automate almost all functions you can do manually in Cognos TM1 Architect or Perspectives. This includes creating Cognos TM1 objects like cubes or dimensions. The creation of an object can be done based on a data source, or you can create your model manually. Actually, in most cases, the Cognos TM1 model is created based on a data source.

We will now use such a scenario to explain the principles of TurboIntegrator. If you work with TurboIntegrator, you should keep in mind that you will always edit a TurboIntegrator process with a Cognos TM1 client, but the process is executed inside the TM1 server. The next sections describe the steps in setting up a script that will be generated by the TurboIntegrator Editor. This generated script has to be sent to the TM1 server to be executed. This happens when you save the TI process in the Cognos TM1 client. In the next sections we create a TurboIntegrator process step by step assuming that we are using a data source to manipulate the content of the Cognos TM1 server.

Data Source

In the first step we have to define the data source. In our example the data source is a text file (in this case, a .CSV file) as shown in the following illustration:

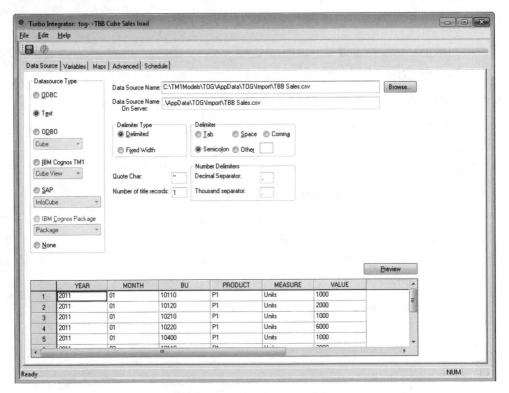

Data source in TurboIntegrator Editor

When you choose a data source, you should be aware that the Cognos TM1 server, which might be running on a different machine than the TurboIntegrator Editor, has to access the data source too. In this example, we choose a text file by clicking the Browse button. This button opens a file dialog. In this dialog you can choose a file that is accessible from your local machine only. To make sure that the Cognos TM1 server can access this file, you can choose a file that is stored on a "share" (a shared directory that can be accessed in the network). If you choose a share, the TurboIntegrator Editor will fill the field Data Source Name on the Data Source tab with the UNC (Unified Naming Convention) name of the path of the file. A UNC name has the following pattern:

```
\\<Server name or IP>\<share name\<path to file>
```

A UNC path is unique in a network and can be accessed from all machines in that network. TurboIntegrator will copy the path of the file for you from the field Data Source Name to the field Data Source Name On Server. If there is no UNC path available to share the source text file between the TurboIntegrator Editor and the Cognos TM1 server, you can copy and transfer the file to the server and change the path in the field Data Source Name On Server manually. Again, the path you enter here must be a valid path on the Cognos TM1 server machine. So if your path starts with C:, the source file is expected to be on the C drive of your server machine. You can also use a relative path to the file. The relative path will always start at the data directory of the Cognos TM1 server. The preceding illustration shows an example of a relative path, as follows:

```
\AppData\TOG\Import\TBB Sales.csv
```

Assuming that the data directory of the Cognos TM1 server is "C:\TM1Models\TOG," the TurboIntegrator process will try to open the file "C:\TM1Models\TOG\AppData\TOG\Import\TBB Sales.csv" when the process is executed. If this file doesn't exist, the process will throw an error. Actually you can work with two different files. The file that can be accessed by the server is used when the TurboIntegrator process is executed as the real data source. The file that can be accessed by the TurboIntegrator Editor on your local machine is just for reading the sample values of the first ten lines of the file to define the data variables and to map these variables to Cognos TM1 objects. This usage of two different data sources is only valid for the data source type text. An ODBC data source has to be configured on the Cognos TM1 server machine. If you browse for an ODBC data source in the TurboIntegrator Editor, the list of the available ODBC DSNs will be transferred from the server to the editor. You cannot choose an ODBC source that is configured on your local machine. The same mechanism is used if your data source type is a Cognos TM1 object or an RFC connection to a SAP BW System. We will discuss the data source type "TM1 Package Connector" later in this chapter.

The next steps in defining a TurboIntegrator process are common for all data source types except "TM1 Package Connector." These steps are based on the fact that the data source delivers records or lines that are separated in columns. In the preview table you can see these columns of the first ten records. After you have finished the definition of the data source, you have to set up the data variables.

Variables

The second step of the definition of the TurboIntegrator process is to set up variables. In the Variables tab, you can set up a data variable for each column of the data source. Cognos TM1 will suggest a name for each variable depending on the data source type. For a text data source, you can define a header record. This header record is used to preset the name for the variables. If you use an ODBC data source, the column names will be used for the names. If a name that is based on the data source does not match the TurboIntegrator script syntax (for example, blanks are not allowed in variable identifiers) or is a keyword (for example, YEAR and MONTH are function names, which cannot be used as variable identifiers), the suggested variable name will begin with the letter "v" followed by the column number. All names that are set by TurboIntegrator are suggestions only. You can change the name in the Variables tab. The following illustration shows an example.

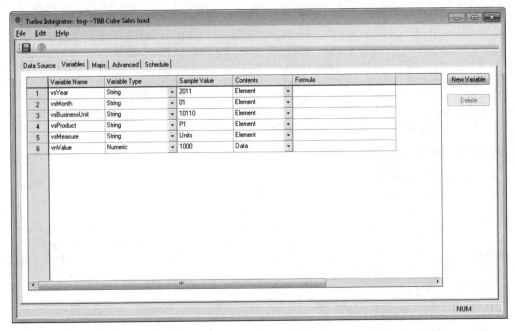

Variables in TurboIntegrator Editor

We recommend using a naming convention in all TurboIntegrator processes. In our example we use a prefix followed by a descriptive name. The prefix starts with a "v" to indicate that the variable is based on a data source, and a character that indicates the type of the variable value: "s" for strings, "n" for float numbers, "i" for integers. So if you enhance the script code later on by editing it manually, it is easier to identify which variable contains what. The variable is not linked to the data source by its name. It is up to you to give the variable a proper descriptive name. The variable is only linked to the data source by the position. The first variable is linked to the first column of the source, the second variable to the second column, and so on. In the Variables tab you define only the content of the variable. Table 7-1 gives a description of the fields in the Variables tab.

Field	Description
Variable Name	Enter a descriptive name for the variable, which represents a column in the data source. The name has to satisfy the TurboIntegrator syntax. You cannot use reserved names like YEAR, MONTH, and so on.
Variable Type	String or Numeric. The field is prepopulated by the TI Editor. The value is a suggestion that is evaluated based on the first ten records of the preview. The developer can change the value. When the TI process is executed, Cognos TM1 tries to convert the data source value into the type of the variable. If the conversion fails, Cognos TM1 will throw an error.
Sample Value	Just an example: the value of the first record of the previewed data.
Contents	This field defines which Cognos TM1 object should be manipulated by the value of the variable. The value of the content has an impact on which code is generated: A setting of "ignore" means that the variable will not exist/cannot be accessed in the script.
Formula	This field is empty for the variables that are linked to a data source column. You can add some additional variables. The field contains a button for each added variable. The button invokes a small editor to assign a formula to the variable. The value of additional variables has to be calculated and is treated as a value of a virtual column of the data source.

TABLE 7-1   Fields in the Variables tab

Mapping

The third step is to define which content will result in which Cognos TM1 object. This can be set up in the Maps tab. You can access the Maps tab if the content of at least one variable is not set to "ignore." In the Maps tab you assign the content of the variables to a TM1 object. Depending on what content you have assigned, some additional tabs will be enabled:

- **Cube**   The tab for Cube is always enabled.
- **Dimensions**   The content of one or more variables is set to "Element."
- **Data**   The content of *two* or more variables is set to "Data."
- **Consolidations**   The content of one or more variables is set to "Consolidation."
- **Attributes**   The content of one or more variables is set to "Attribute."

In the additional tabs you can define how the Cognos TM1 objects are manipulated by the data.

The following two illustrations show how we map the variables of our sample data source. In the Cube mapping we used an existing cube that is updated. If you use an existing cube, the number of data variables that have the content "Element" must match the number of dimensions of the cube. In our example we have assigned each dimension of the cube to a variable. We have used two different actions: "As Is" and "Update." With these definitions,

The TurboIntegrator Editor generates code that will update the dimensions "TBB Years" and "TBB Months" and load the data into the existing cube "TBB sales."

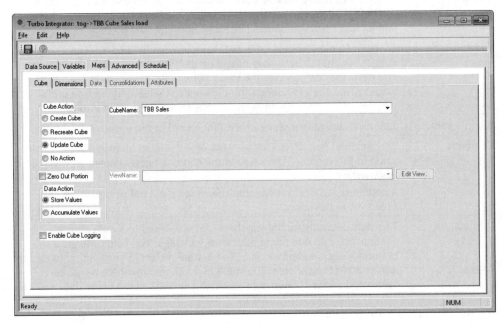

Mapping a cube in TurboIntegrator Editor

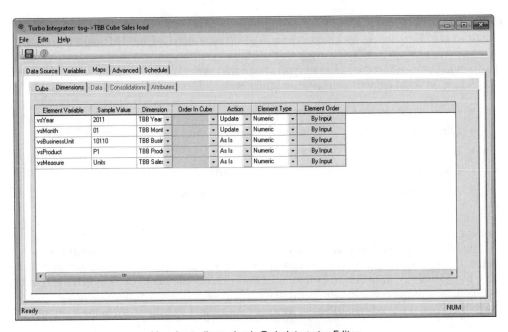

Mapping a dimension in TurboIntegrator Editor

In Table 7-2 we have summarized all definitions you can make in the TurboIntegrator Editor. In the last column of the table you can find the code that is generated by these definitions.

TM1 Object	Field	Value	Generated Code
Cube	Cube Name		Is used as <Cube> in the code.

	Cube Action	Create Cube	**Prolog:**
			`if ( CubeExists('<Cube>') <> 0 );`
			`  CubeDestroy('Test');`
			`  endif;`
			`CUBECREATE('<Cube>','<Dimension1>',`
			`'<Dimension2>',...,`
			`  '<DimensionN>');`

		Recreate Cube	
		Update Cube	No code
	Zero Out Portion/ ViewName		**Prolog:** `VIEWZEROOUT('<Cube>','<ViewName>');`

	Data Action	Store Value	**Data:**
			`CELLPUTN(<DataVariable>,'<Cube>',`
			`<ElementVariable1>,`
			`<ElementVariable2>,...,`
			`<ElementVariableN>);`
			(CELLPUTN is used for N-cells. Similar code (CELLPUTS) is generated for S-cells.)

		Accumulate Value	**Data:**
			`CELLPUTN(CellGetN('<Cube>',`
			`<ElementVariable1>,`
			`<ElementVariable2>,...,`
			`<ElementVariableN>)`
			`+ <DataVariable>,'<Cube>',`
			`<ElementVariable1>,`
			`<ElementVariable2>,...,`
			`<ElementVariableN>);`

	Enable Cube Logging		**Prolog:**
			`OldCubeLogChanges = CUBEGETLOGCHANGES`
			`('<CubeName>');`
			`CUBESETLOGCHANGES('<Cube>', 0);`
			Epilog:
			`CUBESETLOGCHANGES('<Cube>',`
			`OldCubeLogChanges);`

TABLE 7-2 Definitions for Code *(continued)*

TM1 Object	Field	Value	Generated Code
Dimensions	Element Variable	Name of the variable or "(Data Variables)"	Is used as `<ElementVariable>` in function calls.
	Sample Value		No code.
	Dimension		Is used as `<Dimension>` in the code.
	Order In Cube		Defines the position of the `<Dimension>` in: `CUBECREATE(..)` and the position of the `<ElementVariable>` in: `CELLPUTN()`, `CELLPUTS()`, `CELLGETN()`, `CELLGETN()`

	Action	Create	**Prolog:**
			`DIMENSIONDESTROY('<Dimension>');`
			`DIMENSIONCREATE('<Dimension>');`

		Recreate	**Prolog:**
			`DIMENSIONDELETEALLELEMENTS`
			`('<Dimension>');`

		Update	**Data:**
			`DIMENSIONELEMENTINSERT`
			`('<Dimension>','',`
			`<ElementVariable>,'n');`

		As Is	No code generated.

	Element Type	Numeric	**Metadata:**
			`DIMENSIONELEMENTINSERT('<Dimension>',`
			`'',<ElementVariable>,'n');`

	Element Type	String	**Metadata:**
			`DIMENSIONELEMENTINSERT('<Dimension>',`
			`'',<ElementVariable>,'s');`

	Element Order	By Input	**Prolog:**
			`DIMENSIONSORTORDER('<Dimension>','','`
			`','ByInput','ASCENDING');`

		By Name	**Prolog:**
			`DIMENSIONSORTORDER('<Dimension>','','`
			`','ByName','ASCENDING');`

		By Level	**Prolog:**
			`DIMENSIONSORTORDER('<Dimension>','','`
			`','ByLevel','ASCENDING');`

		By Hierarchy	**Prolog:**
			`DIMENSIONSORTORDER('<Dimension>','','`
			`','ByHierarchy','ASCENDING');`

TABLE 7-2   Definitions for Code *(continued)*

TM1 Object	Field	Value	Generated Code
Data	Data Variable		Is used as `<DataVariable>` in `CELLPUTN` and `CELLPUTS` functions.
	Element		Is used in `CELLPUTN` and `CELLPUTS` functions. It is inserted in the code as parameter for the dimension element of the dimension, which is defined as `"Data Variables."`
	Element Type		Controls whether `CELLPUTN` or `CELLPUTS` is generated.
	Sample Value		No code generated.

Consolidations	Cons.Variable		**Metadata:**
			`DIMENSIONELEMENTINSERT('<Dimension>',`
			`'',<ConsVariable>,'c');`
			`DIMENSIONELEMENTCOMPONENTADD`
			`('<Dimension>',`
			`<ConsVariable>,<ChildVariable>,`
			`<Weight>);`

	Dimension		Is used as `<Dimension>` in the code.
	Child Variable		Is used as `<ChildVariable>` in the code.
	Weight		Is used as `<Weight>` in the code.
	Sample Value		No code generated.

	Component Order	By Input	If the dimension is not set to "As Is", this option will enhance the `DIMENSIONSORTORDER` function, which is generated by the Dimensions tab.
			Prolog:
			`DIMENSIONSORTORDER('<Dimension>',`
			`'ByInput','ASCENDING',`
			`'<Element Order>','ASCENDING');`

		By Name	**Prolog:**
			`DIMENSIONSORTORDER('<Dimension>,`
			`'ByName','ASCENDING',`
			`'<Element Order>','ASCENDING');`

		By Level	**Prolog:**
			`DIMENSIONSORTORDER('<Dimension>,`
			`'ByLevel','ASCENDING',`
			`'<Element Order>','ASCENDING');`

		By Hierarchy	**Prolog:**
			`DIMENSIONSORTORDER('<Dimension>,`
			`'ByHierarchy','ASCENDING',`
			`'<Element Order>','ASCENDING');`

TABLE 7-2 Definitions for Code *(continued)*

PART II

TM1 Object	Field	Value	Generated Code
Attributes	Attribute Variable		Is used as `<AttributeVariable>` in the code.
	Sample Value		No code generated.
	Dimension		Is used as `<Dimension>` in the code.
	Element Variable		Is used as `<ElementVariable>`.
	Attribute		Is used as `<Attribute>` in the code.

	Action	Create	**Prolog:**
			`ATTRDELETE('<Dimension>',`
			`'<Attribute>');`
			`ATTRINSERT('<Dimension>','',`
			`'<Attribute>',`
			`'<AttributeType>');`
			Data:
			`ATTRPUTS(<AttributeVariable>,`
			`'<Dimension>',`
			`<ElementVariable>,'<Attribute>');`

		Update	**Data:**
			`ATTRPUTS(<AttributeVariable>,`
			`'<Dimension>',`
			`<ElementVariable>,'<Attribute>');`

	Attribute Type	Text	`'<AttributeType>'` is set to `'S'`.
		Numeric	`'<AttributeType>'` is set to `'N'`.
		Alias	`'<AttributeType>'` is set to `'A'`.

TABLE 7-2 Definitions for Code *(continued)*

Advanced (the Script)

The fourth step is the generation of the code. The following illustration shows some of the generated code, which you can see in the Advanced tab. All generated code is encapsulated in the lines

```
#****Begin: Generated Statements***
```

and

```
#****End: Generated Statements****
```

Before and after this code section, the developer can add custom code.

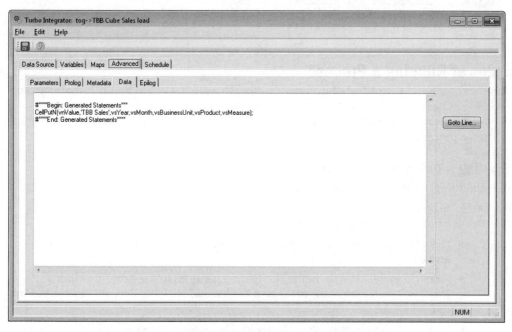

Advanced scripting in TurboIntegrator

In the following listing you can see the complete generated code of our example. Using Table 7-2, you can compare the mapping and the generated code and find out which line of code is generated by which definition in the Maps tab.

Prolog:
```
#****Begin: Generated Statements***
DIMENSIONSORTORDER('TBB Year','','','ByInput','ASCENDING');
DIMENSIONSORTORDER('TBB Month','','','ByInput','ASCENDING');
OldCubeLogChanges = CUBEGETLOGCHANGES('TBB Sales');
CUBESETLOGCHANGES('TBB Sales', 0);
#****End: Generated Statements****
```

Metadata:
```
#****Begin: Generated Statements***
DIMENSIONELEMENTINSERT('TBB Year','',vsYear,'n');
DIMENSIONELEMENTINSERT('TBB Month','',vsMonth,'n');
#****End: Generated Statements****
```

Data:
```
#****Begin: Generated Statements***
CellPutN(vnValue,'TBB Sales',vsYear,vsMonth,vsBusinessUnit,vsProduct,
vsMeasure);
#****End: Generated Statements****
```

Epilog:
```
#****Begin: Generated Statements***
CUBESETLOGCHANGES('TBB Sales', OldCubeLogChanges);
#****End: Generated Statements****
```

Principles of Running a Process

After we create and save a TurboIntegrator process we want to explain how a TurboIntegrator process can be started and what happens during the execution. The next two sections explains several way of starting a TurboIntegrator process and the steps which are involved when the process is executed.

Starting a TurboIntegrator Process

A TurboIntegrator process can be executed in several ways:

- A TurboIntegrator process can be started by a user. If a user has READ permission on a process, he can start this process in several ways:

  - From Server Explorer (Cognos TM1 Perspectives/Architect): Select the process and click Run (Process | Run).

  - From Cognos TM1Web: In the Navigation pane, go to the Administration/ Processes node. Select the process in the list and click the Execute Process button in the toolbar.

  - From an Action button (see Chapter 8). The Action button is available for Excel sheets and Cognos TM1 Websheets.

  A developer (member of the security group ADMIN) can also start a TurboIntegrator process from the TurboIntegrator Editor.

- A TurboIntegrator process can be started by a Cognos TM1 chore. A Cognos TM1 chore can consist of multiple processes that are executed in a sequence; a Cognos TM1 chore can also be started manually or by the Cognos TM1 scheduler (please refer to the TM1 documentation: *TM1 TurboIntegrator Guide*, Chapter 8: "Scheduling a Process for Automatic Execution with Chores"). If you use the Schedule tab, the last tab of the TurboIntegrator Editor, a Cognos TM1 chore with the name of the process is created automatically. If a user is not a member of the security group ADMIN, he has to have READ permissions for a chore to start it manually. If you are using Cognos TM1 10.1 and higher, you can also set up the TM1 server to start one or multiple chores on startup. In this case, you have to set the parameter StartupChores in the tm1s.cfg file:

  ```
  StartupChores=ChoreName1:ChoreName2:ChoreName3:ChoreNameN
  ```

- A TurboIntegrator process can be executed by a TurboIntegrator process using the ExecuteProcess function:

  ```
  ExecuteProcess(ProcessName, [ParamName1, ParamValue1,ParamName2,
  ParamValue2]);
  ```

- A programmer can use the Cognos TM1 API to start a TurboIntegrator process from outside the Cognos TM1 server. This can be used to write a little program that can be called by schedulers other than the Cognos TM1 scheduler. With this mechanism you can schedule a TurboIntegrator process with the Windows scheduler (for instance). IBM provides such a program since Cognos TM1 9.5.2 Hot Fix 1: tm1runti .exe. You can find a description of this program in the Cognos TM1 documentation: *TM1 Operations Guide*, Chapter 6, "Using TM1runTI."

Executing a TurboIntegrator Process

In the earlier section "Automating Cognos TM1 Models with TurboIntegrator," we showed how to create a sample process. Now we will take a look what happens when the process is executed. If you have defined a data source for the TurboIntegrator process, the script is executed in six steps (see Figure 7-1).

- **Step 1.**   All lines of code in the Prolog section are executed.

- **Step 2.**   After the Prolog and before the code in the Metadata section is executed, the Cognos TM1 server opens the data source and retrieves the data. Because the data source is opened in step 2, you can modify any information regarding the data source in the Prolog. For example, you can change the name of the file or the SQL statement. For each field in the Data Source tab, TM1 provides a local built-in variable that can be used to retrieve or modify the value. The next four illustrations show which of the most important fields can be accessed by which variable:

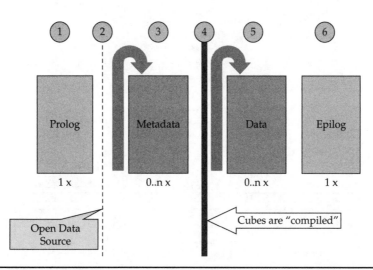

FIGURE 7-1   Execution of a TurboIntegrator process in six steps

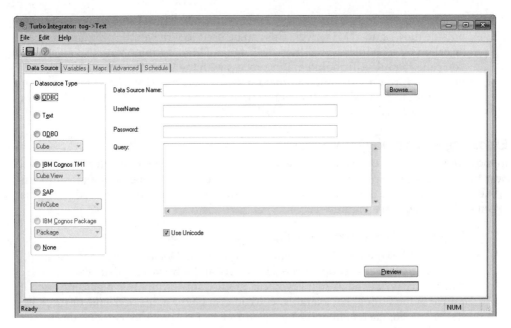

Fields for ODBC

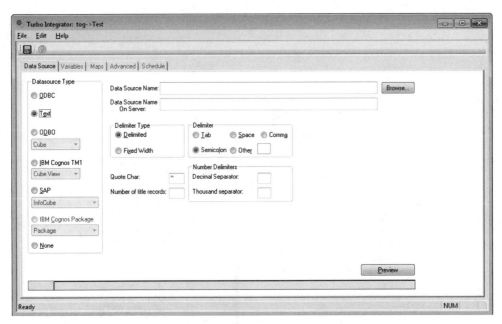

Fields for text

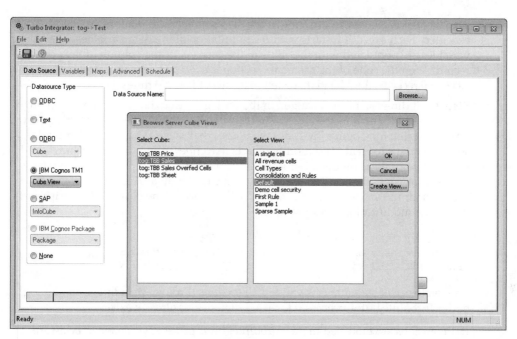

Fields for view

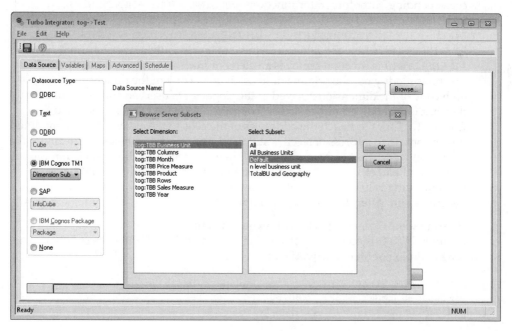

Fields for subset

- **Step 3.**   For each data record/line of the data source, the Metadata section is executed. Each execution starts with the population of the data variables. The variables are populated with the value in the corresponding column of the actual record. Then the code of the Metadata section is executed. If your data source has 1,000,000 records, the Metadata code is executed 1,000,000 times.

- **Step 4.**   If dimensions are changed in the Prolog or Metadata section, these changes become valid for all affected cubes. This is called "compiling the cubes." It's a very important step for Cognos TM1. But what does that mean? Cognos TM1 provides some functions to create and modify objects like cubes, dimensions, attributes, and so on. Some of these model modifications are available to the process immediately, but some are not. If you create a dimension, a cube, or an attribute by the corresponding TurboIntegrator function, you can access the object in the script and do further modifications. For example:

```
CUBECREATE('TBB Sales','TBB Year','TBB Month',
   'TBB Business Unit','TBB Product','TBB Sales Measure');
CELLPUTN(1,'TBB Sales','2011','01','UK','P1','Units');
```

This sequence of statements is valid in all sections (Prolog, Metadata, Data, Epilog) of the TurboIntegrator process if the used dimensions already exist.

If dimensions are modified in the TurboIntegrator process, you have to be aware that any element that was added to a dimension is available in a cube only after step 4. A modification of a dimension has to be made in Prolog or Metadata. The corresponding TurboIntegrator functions are: DIMENSIONELEMENTINSERT, DIMENSIONELEMENTDELETE, DIMENSIONDELETEALLELEMENT, DIMENSIONELEMENTCOMPONENTADD, DIMENSIONELEMENTCOMPONENTDELETE, ATTRINSERT (this function adds an element to an attribute dimension), and ATTRDELETE (this function removes an element from an attribute dimension). These functions modify not the original dimension but a copy of the dimension. In step 4, each copy of the dimension is saved in the Cognos TM1 server, and each cube that depends on a modified dimension is "compiled." When a cube is "compiled," Cognos TM1 tries to match the addresses of the cells to the elements of the modified dimensions. If an address of a cell is still valid, the cell keeps the old value; if not the cell is removed. This mechanism is used when you rebuild a dimension. You can remove and add elements from a dimension in the Prolog and Metadata sections without losing values in the cubes. Values will be lost if removed elements are not inserted again. After the cubes are "compiled," you can put a value into new cells.

Here are some examples to clarify the mechanism:
Example 1: 'UK' is an existing element in the dimension "TBB Business Units." The code in Prolog or Metadata would be:

```
DIMENSIONDELETEALLELEMENTS('TBB Business Units');
DIMENSIONELEMENTINSERT('TBB Business Units', '', 'UK', 'n');
```

All values that were referenced by 'UK' before the execution of the TurboIntegrator process will still exist after step 4.

Example 2: "Italy" does not exist in dimension "TBB Business Units." The code in Prolog or Metadata would be:

```
DIMENSIONELEMENTINSERT('TBB Business Units', '', 'Italy', 'n');
CELLPUTN(1, 'TBB' Sales', '2011','01','Italy','P1','Units');
```

This will throw an error, because "Italy" does not exist in cube "TBB Sales." "TBB Sales" is still using the original version of dimension "TBB Business Units." The code in the Prolog or Metadata section modifies a copy of the dimension.

Example 3: "Italy" is an existing element in dimension "TBB Business Units." The code in Prolog or Metadata would be:

```
DIMENSIONELEMENTDELETE('TBB Business Units', 'Italy');
CELLPUTN(1, 'TBB' Sales', '2011','01','Italy','P1','Units');
```

This will not throw an error because all the cells that are referenced by the element "Italy" will still exist until step 4.

After this step, you can also create or delete Cognos TM1 objects like cubes or dimensions, but you cannot modify dimensions. If you place a function like `DIMENSIONELEMENTINSERT` in the Data or Epilog section, you won't see any changes to the dimension. Changes to dimensions are also made to temporary dimensions only. These "temporary dimensions" will never be committed to the model.

- **Step 5.** For each data record/line of the data source, the Data section is executed. Each execution starts with the population of the data variables. The variables are populated with the value in the corresponding column of the actual record. Then the code of the Data section is executed. If your data source has 1,000,000 records, the Data code is executed 1,000,000 times. Usually you will populate cubes here. Also attribute values are assigned to the elements here. Attribute values are stored in attribute cubes. So attributes values are treated as data from a technical perspective.

- **Step 6.** All lines of code in the Epilog section are executed. Usually this section is used for cleanup code.

These six steps are also valid for the execution of a TurboIntegrator process that has no data source. In this case, steps 2, 3, and 5 are skipped, as you can see in Figure 7-2.

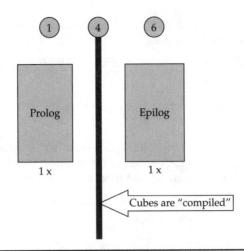

FIGURE 7-2 Execution steps of a process with no data source

Using Cognos TM1 TurboIntegrator Processes as Building Blocks

With the information presented so far in this chapter, you should now be able to understand Cognos TM1 TurboIntegrator processes as building blocks. In a Cognos TM1 solution you can use TurboIntegrator processes for different purposes. Here are some examples:

- Loading dimensions from a data source
- Loading cubes from a data source
- Loading permission rights from a data source
- Changing permissions based on data or attributes
- Implementing workflow by using TurboIntegrator processes as the transition between workflow states
- Transforming cube data: freezing rule-based values to stored values
- Precalculating values

We would like to mention some TurboIntegrator process hints that should help you in developing a Cognos TM1 solution. Some hints will be explained by the following

TurboIntegrator process: "TBB Element Security set recursively." Here are the parameters and the code of this TurboIntegrator process:

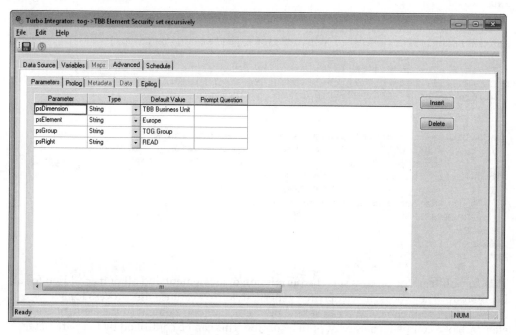

Sample process (parameters)

```
sThisProcess = GetProcessName();

# Check if the first parameter is a valid dimension name:
IF ( psDimension @= '' % DIMENSIONEXISTS(psDimension) = 0);
  # is not valid: stop with an error here
  PROCESSERROR;
ENDIF;

# Check if the second parameter is a valid dimension element:
IF ( psElement @= '' % DIMIX(psDimension,psElement) = 0);
  # is not valid: stop with an error here
  PROCESSERROR;
ENDIF;

# Check if the third parameter is a valid group name:
sGroupDimension = '}Groups';
IF ( psGroup @= '' % DIMIX(sGroupDimension,psGroup) = 0);
  # is not valid: stop with an error here
  PROCESSERROR;
ENDIF;

# Check if the fourth parameter is a valid access right:
IF ( psGroup @= '' % ~ ( psRight@= 'WRITE' % psRight@= 'READ' % psRight@=
'NONE' ));
```

```
    # is not valid: stop with an error here
    PROCESSERROR;
ENDIF;

# Set security for the element:
ELEMENTSECURITYPUT(psRight, psDimension, psElement, psGroup);

# If this element has children, set the same right to all children
# ELOMPN will return 0 if the element is an N-Element
iChildrenCount = ELCOMPN(psDimension, psElement);
index = 1;
WHILE ( index <= iChildrenCount );
    sChildElement = ELCOMP(psDimension, psElement, index);
    iReturn = EXECUTEPROCESS(sThisProcess,'psDimension', psDimension,
        'psElement', sChildElement, 'psGroup', psGroup, 'psRight', psRight);
    # Check if the execution was successful
    IF ( iReturn <> PROCESSEXITNORMAL() );
        # it was not successful: stop here
        PROCESSERROR;
    ENDIF;
    index = index +1;
END;
```

This TurboIntegrator process sets the permission of an element and all of its children for a
User Group. The process is written in a generic style: You can use this process for a
dimension of your choice. You can set the permission of one element (if the element is a leaf
element), of a complete hierarchy, or of a subtree. This can be controlled by the parameter
values.

Now we would like to explain some specific points:

- **Parameters**   You can use parameters to make your TurboIntegrator process more
  generic. Use prefixes for parameter variables. We recommend using the prefix "p"
  followed by a type indicator (again, "s" for string, "i" for integer (parameter type
  number), and "n" for numbers (parameter type number). (See the preceding
  illustration.)

- **Using parameter variables in the Variables tab**   You can use parameter variables
  in formula variables that are added in the Variables tab. Unfortunately, TurboIntegrator
  Editor checks the syntax of a formula with variables of the Variables tab only. So
  you will get an error message if you use parameter variables here. But you can
  ignore the message. The TurboIntegrator process can be saved to the Cognos TM1
  server and executed.

- **EXECUTEPROCESS function**   With the EXECUTEPROCESS function, you can run a
  TurboIntegrator process within a TurboIntegrator process. It is also possible to run
  a TM1 process recursively. Each process will have its own memory for variables.
  This is called the "stack." The "stack" can have a size of 100. That means: A process
  can run itself, which calls itself, which can call ..., and this can repeat 100 times.
  Regarding our example, this means that you can use the process to set the permissions
  of a whole hierarchy, if the hierarchy has 100 levels or less.

- **EXECUTEPROCESS** **function with parameters and using default values**   In our example we call a process with parameters. Cognos TM1 allows you to skip from one to all parameters when you execute a process. If you skip a parameter, Cognos TM1 will replace the parameter value with its default value. Using the default values of our example (see in the earlier illustration of the Advanced tab), the code

```
EXECUTEPROCESS('TBB Element Security set recursively')
```

is equal to

```
EXECUTEPROCESS('TBB Element Security set recursively',
    'psDimension', 'TBB Business Unit', 'psElement', 'Europe',
    'psGroup', 'TBB Group', 'psRight', 'READ');
```

- **Formulas in the Variables tab**:
  - When you want to use variables in formulas, you have to be careful about the sequence. A variable that is used in a formula has to be defined beforehand.
  - With the options "Metadata," "Data," and "Both," you can define in which section the formula will be inserted. We recommend not inserting the formula into a section where it is not needed. Unnecessary lines of code do not throw an error, but they could lead to longer execution time. Table 7-3 presents some rules of thumb regarding when to put a formula in which section.

- **Formatting with ASCIIOUTPUT/TEXTOUTPUT**   You can use ASCIIOUTPUT or TEXTOUTPUT to create a semicolon-separated file:

```
TEXTOUTPUT ('.\sample.csv',Line 1 Field 1',
    'Line 1 Field 2', 'Line 1 Field 3');
TEXTOUTPUT ('.\sample.csv',Line 2 Field 1',
    'Line 2 Field 2', 'Line 2 Field 3');
```

These lines of code will create a file when the section of this code is finished. The content of the file looks like this:

```
"Line 1 Field 1","Line 1 Field 2","Line 1 Field 3"
"Line 2 Field 1","Line 2 Field 2","Line 2 Field 3"
```

Content of Variable	Option
Element (and Dimension is set to "As Is")	Data
Element (and Dimension is *not* set to "As Is")	Both
Element (only updating Dimension/no Cube population/no Attributes)	Metadata
Consolidation	Metadata
Attribute (Update)	Data
Attribute (Create)	Data
Data	Data

TABLE 7-3   Destinations of Variable Formulas

But what if you need another separator, or you want to get rid of the quotes? You can format the output by using the local TurboIntegrator variables `DatasourceASCIIDelimiter` and `DatasourceASCIIQuoteCharacter`. For instance, you could insert

```
DatasourceASCIIDelimiter=':';
DatasourceASCIIQuoteCharacter = '';
```

before the `TEXTOUTPUT` sample code. The content of the created file will be:

```
Line 1 Field 1:Line 1 Field 2:Line 1 Field 3
Line 2 Field 1:Line 2 Field 2:Line 2 Field 3
```

You also can create files other than field-separated files. Here is an example of creating a rule object by a TurboIntegrator process:

Prolog:
```
DatasourceASCIIDelimiter='';
DatasourceASCIIQuoteCharacter = '';
sCube = 'TBB Sales';
sRuleFile = '.\' | sCube | 'Rule.txt';
sLine = '[''Price''] = N: DB(''TBB Price'', !TBB Year,
!TBB Month, !TBB Product, ''Price'');';
TEXTOUTPUT (sRuleFile, sLine);
sLine ='          C: [''Revenue''] \ [''Units''];';
TEXTOUTPUT (sRuleFile, sLine);
```

Epilog:
```
RULELOADFROMFILE(sCube, sRuleFile);
```

As you can see in the sample code, the single quote can be masked by an additional single quote.

- **Neutralizing generated code**   Sometimes you need to get rid of the generated code. You can neutralize the generated code by encapsulating the code in an `IF` clause:

```
IF(1=0);
#****Begin: Generated Statements***
DIMENSIONELEMENTINSERT('TBB Year','',vsYear,'n');
DIMENSIONELEMENTINSERT('TBB Month','',vsMonth,'n');
#****End: Generated Statements****
ENDIF;
```

ODBO, SAP, and IBM Cognos Package

There are three additional data sources in TurboIntegrator. We will discuss them in this separate section because there are some differences between these and the other data sources:

1. OLE DB for OLAP (ODBO), SAP, and IBM Cognos Package are multidimensional data sources, so you can connect to objects like cubes or dimensions.

2. These data source types are also using the principle of populating variables, which can be used with TurboIntegrator functions, but you cannot modify the name of the variable or add new variables in the Variables tab.

3. Depending on the data source type, multiple TurboIntegrator processes are generated. If you choose the data source type Cube for ODBO, Package for an IBM Cognos Package, or InfoCube for SAP, the TurboIntegrator Editor creates a main process to populate a target cube and a subprocess for each dimension of the target cube. In the following illustration, you can see an example of generated processes: TBB ODBO load is the name of the main process and TBB ODBO load_<Dimensionname> is the pattern for the name of its subprocesses.

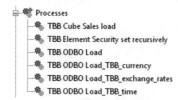

Process and subprocesses

4. In the generated script code you will find some TurboIntegrator functions that are not documented.

Now we will take a look at some special aspects of the multidimensional data sources.

ODBO

ODBO is a data provider to connect to OLAP databases. When you choose the ODBO data source, you can select to load a cube, to load a dimension, or to perform an MDX Query. For each option you get a different set of tabs. Let's take a look at how to load cubes. In the Connection tab you can choose a provider. This provider has to be installed on the Cognos TM1 server machine. In the following illustration, you can see that you can access another Cognos TM1 server via ODBO. The ODBO connection to Microsoft Analysis Services is another ODBO provider that is often used.

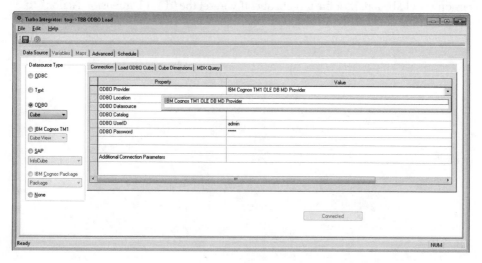

ODBO Connection tab

In the Load ODBO Cube tab (see the following illustration), you can select a cube from the data source and define the Cognos TM1 cube to populate the data. At this point we want to mention that the ODBO Provider is the only data source that can be used to create a virtual cube. If you select the virtual cube option, only an empty cube and its dimension will be created by the TurboIntegrator process. All the connection information will be stored in the properties of the target cube. If a user accesses the cube, Cognos TM1 performs a query on the data source to retrieve the requested data. So this is the one and only case when Cognos TM1 performs an "implicit drill-through" to external data.

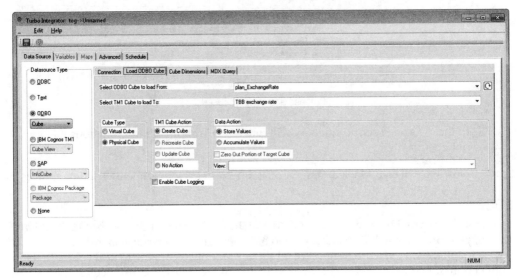

Load ODBO Cube tab

In the Cube Dimensions tab (see the following illustration), you can define which dimension should be a part of the target cube. If you set the "TM1 Dimension Action" to "Don't Load," the data will be retrieved on the highest aggregation of the affected dimension.

Furthermore, you can select which levels and which elements (members) should be loaded to TM1.

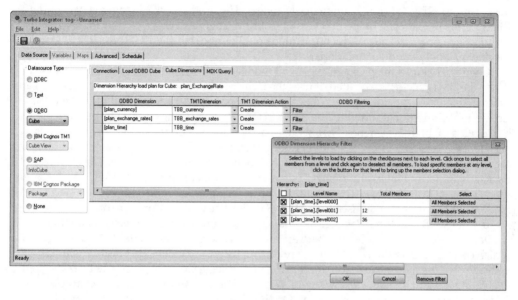

Cube Dimensions tab

For all your settings in the tabs, the TurboIntegrator Editor will create an MDX query to retrieve the data and the TurboIntegrator process script (see the following illustration).

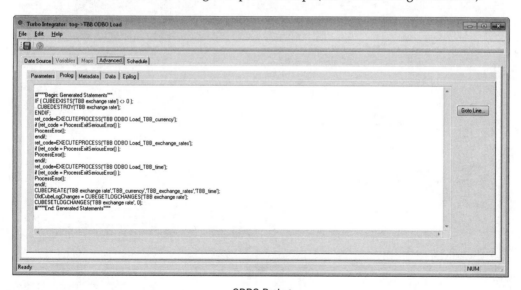

ODBO Prolog

As you can see in the prolog of the sample process, each of the subprocesses is called by the EXECUTEPROCESS function.

IBM Cognos Package

The IBM Cognos Package data source enables TurboIntegrator to utilize a package that was designed with IBM Cognos Framework Manager. The Framework Manager is part of the IBM Cognos BI Platform. In the first versions of IBM Cognos Package Connector, Cognos TM1 could utilize only Packages, which is dimensionally modeled (DMR-Model; DMR stands for dimensionally modeled relational).

Cognos TM1 uses the package to gain all model information of a Cognos BI data source. When the TM1 process is executed, it uses the Cognos BI Connectors to retrieve data from an external database. The link between Cognos TM1, the Cognos Package, and the Cognos BI Connectors is additional software: the Cognos TM1 Package Connector. This software has to be installed on both the Cognos TM1 server machine and the Cognos TM1 client, which is used by the developer of the TurboIntegrator process. If the Package Connector is missing on the developer's machine, the data source "IBM Cognos Package" is disabled. The Cognos TM1 Package Connector makes all Cognos BI data sources available to Cognos TM1, which can be modeled as a DMR-Package. The main purpose of the Package Connector is to connect to SAP NetWeaver Business Warehouse and SAP R/3 Enterprise Central Component.

If you use IBM Cognos Package as a data source, you will find a mechanism that is similar to the ODBO connection. There are two data source types available. "Package," which corresponds to the ODBO cube, and "Dimension." "Dimension" is also using a package. But the focus is to load a dimension via Package Connector only. Let's take a look at creating a script by using a "Package." With the Package Connector, you get access to a Cognos BI system in your environment. On the Connection tab you have to enter all the credential information. In the Package tab (see the following illustration), you can select a cube from the data source and define the TM1 cube to populate the data.

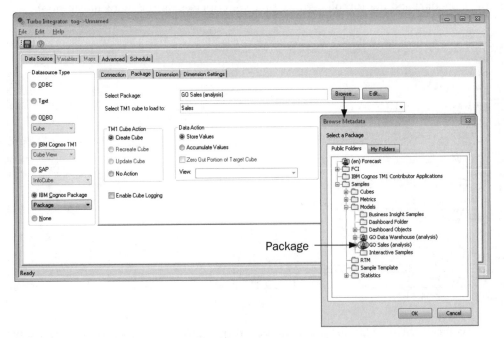

Choosing a package

The Dimension tab (as shown in the following illustration) is slightly different from the ODBO data source. Instead of "Filters," you can choose multiple "Hierarchies" and "Attributes" to be imported. Also there is an additional button on the tab, which is very important for importing mass data from a data source like SAP BW. In the Framework Manager you can define prompts to have a parameter for the query, which is sent to the external database. So you can define a query that retrieves only one month, and the parameter determines which month. This enables you to partition the retrieval of a whole year. So the prompts are called "Segmenter" prompts.

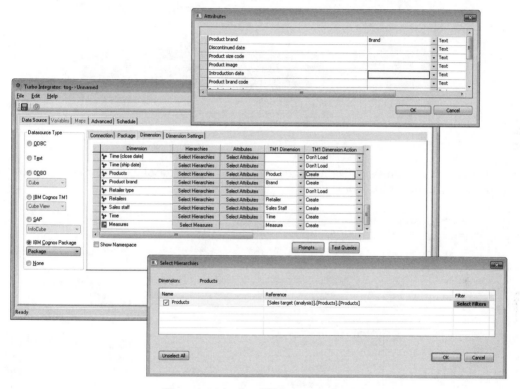

Dimension tab of an IBM Cognos package

The Prompts button invokes a dialog to set the query parameters (see the following illustration). The Attributes dialog shows all available parameters. You can set a value for each parameter. If you leave the value blank, you can utilize the Cognos TM1 Package Connector to run parallel multiple queries with different segments. To activate this capability, you have to modify the configuration of the Cognos TM1 Package Connector. In the installation folder of the Cognos TM1 Package Connector, you will find the file cogtr. xml. Add the following entry to the "Transformer" section:

```
<Preference Name="SegmenterParallelQueryCount" Value="<Number>"/>
```

For instance, if you set <Number> to 5, the TM1 Package Connector will run up to five queries in parallel. You can monitor the parallel process if you watch the running processes on the TM1 server machine. In this case you will find five instances of a process called TM1Interface.exe.

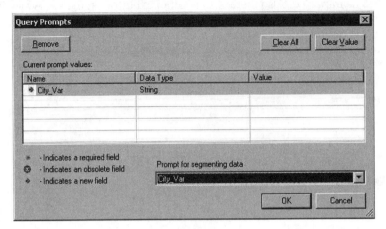

Prompts dialog

In the last tab, Dimension Settings. you can define a Top Consolidation for each Cognos TM1 dimension that is loaded.

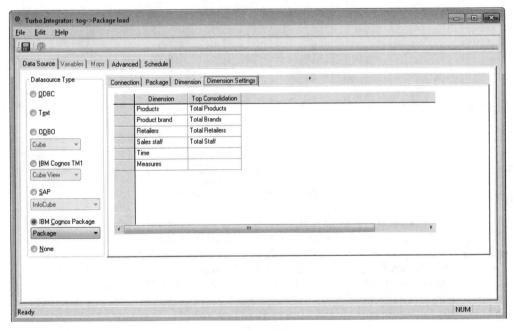

Dimension settings

After you have stepped through all these tabs, TurboIntegrator will create code for you. Again a main process with subprocesses for all dimensions is created.

NOTE *In Cognos TM1 Version 10.1 and higher, the Cognos TM1 Package Connector can also be used with a non-dimensionally modeled package. When defining the source, select "Custom query." The TurboIntegrator Editor will now provide settings to select Cognos BI "Query Items" and "filters." A preview option shows a listing of the requested data. With the "Custom query" data source, the tabs Variables and Maps are enabled. So you can map the data and define variables in the same way as you would for a text or ODBC data source.*

SAP

The SAP data source is based on a third-party program that has to be installed on the SAP BW system. Because the tabs of this data source are very similar to the tabs of the IBM Cognos Package, we will not explain each dialog, and instead, will take a look at the special aspects:

1. There are more data source types available:

   - **InfoCube**   Corresponds to Cube or Package.

   - **Characteristic**   Corresponds to Dimension.

   - **Security**   Creates a TurboIntegrator script to retrieve users and roles from SAP BW 3.5 Security and to create Cognos TM1 users and Cognos TM1 groups.

   - **SAP table**   Enables you to create a SELECT statement on a base SAP table. You need the knowledge of the underlying table model of SAP BW in order to utilize this feature.

   - **ODS table**   This option enables a TurboIntegrator process to write back into an ODS/DSO object. So the ODS table is actually not a data source but the data target. The real source is a Cognos TM1 view in this case. You also need the permissions in SAP BW to write back. (This is often denied by the SAP BW administrators.)

   - **Currency**   This option allows a TurboIntegrator process to retrieve data from the SAP BW Currency Cube.

2. The segmentation of the data retrieval is per number of records. You can set the number of records in the field Package Size in the Connection tab.

3. The SAP data source allows you to retrieve security information together with the data.

4. You can add restricted characteristics to retrieve only data that is identified by the restricted characteristics. The restrictions can be added by using a dialog or by using a TurboIntegrator function that can be added to the prolog script manually.

Finally, we will discuss which restrictions we have to face when we use an OLAP-based data source. The restrictions are due to the fact that the code generation is different from the record-based data sources (Text, ODBC, and TM1). If you use an OLAP-based data source, the usage of the data is fixed by the TurboIntegrator Editor. A cube in the source system can become a Cognos TM1 cube, a dimension (characteristic) can become a Cognos TM1 dimension, and an attribute can become a Cognos TM1 attribute. Unfortunately, this often does not match the requirements when you design a Cognos TM1 model. For instance, a navigational attribute of a SAP BW InfoCube is a Cognos TM1 dimension rather than a Cognos TM1 attribute. Another example is that you can reduce the number of dimensions of the Cognos TM1 cube comparing the number of dimensions of the source cube, but you cannot enhance the Cognos TM1 cube to a higher dimensionality. For instance, you want to have a Version or a Scenario dimension in the Cognos TM1 cube, and the source cube provides the "Actual" data only.

The main reason for the restrictions is the lack of the Variables tab. But there is a way to work around these restrictions:

1. Find out which variables are available and what the content of these variables is: After you have defined your load process, go to the Advanced tab of the TurboIntegrator Editor and analyze the generated code. In the code you will find the names of the variables. Based on the TurboIntegrator functions, you can determine the content of each variable. If not, use the TurboIntegrator function textoutput to dump the values of the variables into a text file. Here is an example of code that was generated by using an IBM Cognos Package data source.

```
IF(TRIM(V1) @= '');V1_Mod='#';ELSE;V1_Mod=V1;ENDIF;
IF(TRIM(V2) @= '');V2_Mod='#';ELSE;V2_Mod=V2;ENDIF;
IF(TRIM(V3) @= '');V3_Mod='#';ELSE;V3_Mod=V3;ENDIF;
IF(TRIM(V4) @= '');V4_Mod='#';ELSE;V4_Mod=V4;ENDIF;
IF(TRIM(V5) @= '');V5_Mod='#';ELSE;V5_Mod=V5;ENDIF;
IF(V1 @= '' % V2 @= '' % V3 @= '' % V4 @= '' % V5 @= '');
NCellOldValue=CELLGETN('Sales',V1_Mod,V2_Mod,V3_Mod,V4_Mod,
V5_Mod,'Quantity');
CELLPUTN(V6+NCellOldValue, 'Sales',
V1_Mod,V2_Mod,V3_Mod,V4_Mod,V5_Mod,'Quantity');
NCellOldValue=CELLGETN('Sales',V1_Mod,V2_Mod,V3_Mod,V4_Mod,V5_Mod,
'Unit cost');
CELLPUTN(V7+NCellOldValue, 'Sales',
V1_Mod,V2_Mod,V3_Mod,V4_Mod,V5_Mod,'Unit cost');
NCellOldValue=CELLGETN('Sales',V1_Mod,V2_Mod,V3_Mod,V4_Mod,V5_Mod,
'Unit price');
CELLPUTN(V8+NCellOldValue, 'Sales',
V1_Mod,V2_Mod,V3_Mod,V4_Mod,V5_Mod,'Unit price');
NCellOldValue=CELLGETN('Sales',
V1_Mod,V2_Mod,V3_Mod,V4_Mod,V5_Mod,'Unit sale price');
CELLPUTN(V9+NCellOldValue, 'Sales',
V1_Mod,V2_Mod,V3_Mod,V4_Mod,V5_Mod,'Unit sale price');
NCellOldValue=CELLGETN('Sales',V1_Mod,V2_Mod,V3_Mod,V4_Mod,
V5_Mod,'Revenue');
CELLPUTN(V10+NCellOldValue, 'Sales',
V1_Mod,V2_Mod,V3_Mod,V4_Mod,V5_Mod,'Revenue');
NCellOldValue=CELLGETN('Sales',V1_Mod,V2_Mod,V3_Mod,V4_Mod,
V5_Mod,'Product cost');
CELLPUTN(V11+NCellOldValue, 'Sales',
V1_Mod,V2_Mod,V3_Mod,V4_Mod,V5_Mod,'Product cost');
ELSE;
CELLPUTN(V6, 'Sales', V1_Mod,V2_Mod,V3_Mod,V4_Mod,V5_Mod,'Quantity');
CELLPUTN(V7, 'Sales', V1_Mod,V2_Mod,V3_Mod,V4_Mod,V5_Mod,'Unit cost');
CELLPUTN(V8, 'Sales', V1_Mod,V2_Mod,V3_Mod,V4_Mod,V5_Mod,'Unit price');
CELLPUTN(V9, 'Sales', V1_Mod,V2_Mod,V3_Mod,V4_Mod,V5_Mod,'Unit sale
price');
CELLPUTN(V10, 'Sales', V1_Mod,V2_Mod,V3_Mod,V4_Mod,V5_Mod,'Revenue');
```

Variable	Type	Content
V1	String	Element: Dimension "Product" (could be blank)
V2	String	Element: Dimension "Brand" (could be blank)
V3	String	Element: Dimension "Retailer" (could be blank)
V4	String	Element: Dimension "Sales Staff" (could be blank)
V5	String	Element: Dimension "Time" (could be blank)
V6	Numeric	Data: value for "Measure" "Quantity"
V7	Numeric	Data: value for "Measure" "Unit cost"
V8	Numeric	Data: value for "Measure" "Unit price"
V9	Numeric	Data: value for "Measure" "Unit sale price"
V10	Numeric	Data: value for "Measure" "Revenue"
V11	Numeric	Data: value for "Measure" "Product cost"

TABLE 7-4 Content of Variables

```
CELLPUTN(V11, 'Sales', V1_Mod,V2_Mod,V3_Mod,V4_Mod,V5_Mod,
'Product cost');
ENDIF;
```

If you want to find out the content of the variables, you need to know the structure of the target cube. In the prolog of the sample process, you find the following statement:

```
CUBECREATE('Sales','Product','Brand','Retailer','Sales Staff',
'Time','Measure');
```

So you can get the information shown in Table 7-4.

2. Now you can neutralize the generated code by encapsulating it in an IF clause.

3. Write your own code using the known variables.

Implement Business Logic and Workflow with TurboIntegrator Processes

Now we will discuss three of the purposes mentioned in the beginning of the chapter ("implement business logic with TurboIntegrator processes," "implement workflow with TurboIntegrator processes," and "export data"). We have joined two of them ("implement business logic with TurboIntegrator processes" and "implement workflow with TurboIntegrator processes") into this section because "workflow" is just a special case of "business logic." For both cases you almost always use the data source type "None" or "IBM Cognos TM1." These data sources are used to manipulate data that already exist in the model. Here are some examples:

- Copy data from one scenario to another
- Precalculate values in a cube

- Implement iterative calculations
- Provide administrative functions to non-admin users (for example, add an element to a dimension)
- Write into a solution-specific protocol cube
- Set permissions (workflow)
- Change a status in a status cube (workflow)

A good example of how to implement workflow with TurboIntegrator is the Cognos TM1 Workflow Manager. The whole configuration of the workflow is managed by the Cognos TM1 Workflow Manager control objects (cubes, dimensions, and processes, which are indicated by the "}sm"-prefix; "sm" stands for the first name of the Workflow Manager, Submission Manager). The "}sm-cubes" and dimensions are fully maintained by }sm-processes. The }sm-processes are also responsible for the change of the status of a task and the change of the permissions. Because a TurboIntegrator script is saved in clear text, you can analyze the processes. Maybe you will get some good ideas to implement your own workflow mechanism. Sometimes this could be necessary, if you have special requirements that do not match with the Cognos TM1 Workflow Manager or Cognos TM1 Contributor Workflow.

Export Data

"Export data" is the last main purpose of TurboIntegrator mentioned in the beginning of this chapter. If you export information from Cognos TM1 with a TurboIntegrator process, you will use "IBM Cognos TM1" data source in most cases. You can export information to files with the functions ASCIIOUTPUT and TEXTOUTPUT (please be aware of the output format, which can be controlled by the built-in variables; we mentioned this earlier in the section "Executing a TurboIntegrator Process"). But you can also write to an ODBC data source. For that you need to use the functions ODBCOPEN (or ODBCOPENEX), ODBCOUTPUT, and ODBCCLOSE. Each of the functions has the parameter "Datasourcename," which should be a valid name of an ODBC data source. This ODBC data source has to exist on the machine of the Cognos TM1 server. With ODBCOUTPUT you can send a SQL statement to the data source. For instance, you can send UPDATE, DELETE, and/or INSERT statements to the SQL database. The SQL statement is provided as a string to the ODBCOUTPUT function and has to be created in the script of the process. If your process has a "IBM Cognos TM1" data source, it makes sense to place the ODBCOPEN into the Prolog section, the ODBCOUTPUT into the Data section, and the ODBCCLOSE into the Epilog section.

Summary

In this chapter we discussed one of the main building blocks of a Cognos TM1 solution: TurboIntegrator. We discussed the main purposes of TurboIntegrator: creating and populating the model, implementing business logic, implementing workflow, and exporting data. We also looked at how you set up a TurboIntegrator process and how to customize the script code. In the next chapter you will learn how to access the building blocks using Excel and Cognos TM1Web and how to create a user interface.

Deploying Cognos TM1 Solutions via Microsoft Excel

The goal of this chapter is to review how to create rich planning and analysis applications with Cognos TM1 through the use of Microsoft Excel and/or Cognos TM1 Web. These Cognos TM1 components provide an excellent development environment for users who are familiar with Microsoft Excel. Excel and Cognos TM1 Web are taking the role of the user front end. In this role they are very important for user acceptance of the solution. But this chapter is not only about the user front end. A Cognos TM1 solution consists of all Cognos TM1 building blocks. We have already discussed the Cognos TM1 model, the business rules and the roles of TurboIntegrator. In this chapter we focus first on user front ends, and later in this chapter, we discuss the whole "building."

Cognos TM1 Web provides two ways of presenting the Cognos TM1 content to the user: the Cognos TM1 Web Cube Viewer, which is based on the Cube Viewer of the Cognos TM1 Perspectives/Architect, and the Cognos TM1 Websheet, which is based on a Microsoft Excel workbook. The Cube Viewer is discussed in Chapter 5. In the following sections we will take a closer look at the interaction between Cognos TM1 and Microsoft Excel. We will show how to use Excel capabilities to build a user front end and how to provide this front end via the web to the user. All user clients that are discussed in this chapter have their roots in the Cognos TM1 Perspectives Add-In for Microsoft Excel. So let's start here.

Cognos TM1 Perspectives

Cognos TM1 Perspectives is an Excel add-in that comes with an installation on the user's desktop. Cognos TM1 Perspectives combines administrative, developer and user functions. A user takes advantage of Cognos TM1 Perspectives by using its tight integration into Mircosoft Excel. In this section we will look at the interaction with Microsoft Excel only. Since Cognos TM1 supports various versions of Microsoft Excel, we will indicate if there is a different integration of TM1. For instance, the Perspectives Add-In adds the "TM1" menu and some toolbars to Excel 2003 and lower versions; Perspectives adds the "TM1" ribbon to

Excel 2007 and 2010. In any case, you can access the Server Explorer to open cube viewers (see the following illustration).

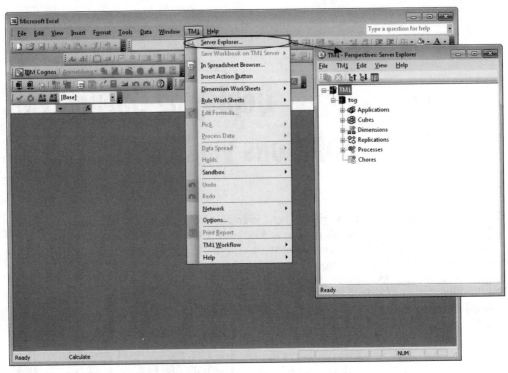

Opening the Server Explorer in Excel 2003

Usually the Cube Viewer is the starting point to build an Excel workbook that interacts with a Cognos TM1 server. You have various options for "slicing" the cube view into an Excel sheet, as shown in the following illustration:

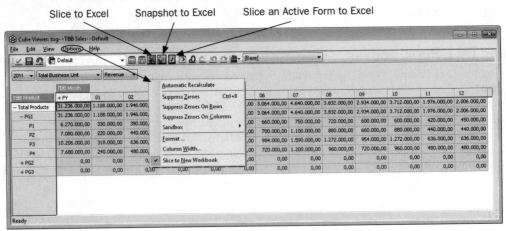

Slice a cube view to Excel

- You can slice the view to Excel by generating formulas to keep the sheet connected to TM1 (the Slice to Excel button).

- You can slice the view to Excel to keep values only in the sheet (the Snapshot to Excel button).

- You can create an Active Form based on the cube view (the Slice an Active Form to Excel button). An Active Form generates a preformatted view with formulas to keep the sheet connected to Cognos TM1, and also exhibits dynamic behavior such as expansion, collapse, and self-maintenance for newly added row items. Active Forms are discussed in the section "Active Forms."

The menu option Slice to New Workbook has an impact on all three kinds of a slice. If this option is turned on (see the Options menu in the preceding illustration), each time you use one of the "Slice" functions, a new workbook is created. If the option is turned off, a new sheet is appended to the active workbook (if there is no active workbook, a new workbook is created).

Classic Slice to Microsoft Excel

In the following illustration you can see an example of a slice to Excel of the "connected" kind. The connection to a Cognos TM1 server is established by formulas. Each time you recalculate the Excel sheet, the Cognos TM1 Excel formulas retrieve the requested data from the TM1 server. In the example you can see a SUBNM formula. This formula is not only for getting data from a Cognos TM1 server but also to maintain interaction with the Cognos TM1 Perspective Add-In. If you double-click on an Excel cell that contains the SUBNM formula, you will invoke the Subset Editor (see Chapter 5). In the Subset Editor you can choose a different dimension element. The chosen element will appear in the cell with the SUBNM formula. If you recalculate the sheet, the data for the modified slice will be retrieved.

A slice in Excel

Now let's take a closer look at the Excel formulas and how the calculation is performed. From an Excel perspective, all Cognos TM1–specific Excel formulas work like any other Excel formula. The most frequently used Cognos TM1 formula is the DBRW. This formula is placed in all Excel cells by the slice mechanism, which should show the values of a Cognos TM1 cube. With this formula you "link" an Excel cell with a Cognos TM1 cube cell one to one. Because the formula is a "link," the Excel cell gets functionality similar to that of the Cognos TM1 cube cell in a Cube Viewer. So you can read and write to a Cognos TM1 cell via the linked Excel cell. If you enter a value into the linked cell, the Cognos TM1 Add-In will send the value to the Cognos TM1 server, while the Excel cell keeps the formula.

In the preceding illustration, you can see an example of a DBRW formula in cell B8:

```
=DBRW($B$1;$B$2;B$7;$B$3;$A8;$B$4)
```

The DBRW formula retrieves a value from a cube cell. The parameters of the formula define which cell should be linked: The first parameter has to be the name of the cube. All other parameters should be valid element names of the dimensions of the linked cube. For the element parameters, the sequence of the names is relevant. The sequence of the element name has to match the sequence of the dimensions in the cube (see the following illustration). Instead of an element name, you can also provide an alias of that element to the DBRW formula. The sequence of the cube dimensions is defined when the cube is created. This original dimension order is always used for Cognos TM1 cell references. Cognos TM1 allows an administrator to change this dimension order to optimize performance. This optimization changes only the internal order. DBRW dimension references always match the original dimension order for the cube.

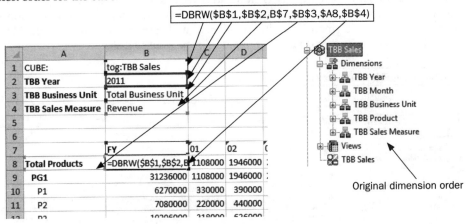

Parameters of a DBRW formula

If the sequence or the element name is not valid, the formula will return the error "KEY_ERR." Depending on the size (dimensionality) of a cube, the DBRW formula has fewer or more parameters (at least three parameters). As you can see in the example, the name of the cube begins with the name of the Cognos TM1 server. This is common to all Cognos TM1 Excel formulas. If the parameter of a Cognos TM1 formula has to be the name of Cognos TM1 object (a cube or a dimension), the name of the Cognos TM1 server has to be added in this way: *<name of the Cognos TM1 server>:<name of the Cognos TM1 object>*.

If you want to create a Microsoft Excel view on Cognos TM1 data on your own, you should use the Cognos TM1 formulas in the same way that a slice from a cube viewer is created. What does that mean? DBRW is the abbreviation for "Data Base Reference Wide" area network. The DBRW formula is optimized regarding network traffic and Cognos TM1 server-side calculation. Cognos TM1 also provides formulas that are not optimized. The formula that corresponds to "DBRW" is the "DBR" formula. Consider what happens if we use the "DBR" formula instead of DBRW. When MS Excel calculates a sheet, it will calculate cell by cell. If a formula refers to another cell, the referenced cell has to be calculated first. So each DBR formula is calculated separately, which means that all values are retrieved from the TM1 server cell by cell and not in a whole bunch. This might result in heavy network traffic and in slow response times.

The DBRW formula works in a different way. If you calculate an Excel sheet containing this formula, the Cognos TM1 Add-In will collect the DBRW requests and retrieve the requested values in one or more chunks. To make this work, the Cognos TM1 Add-In will take over the calculation mechanism of Excel. TM1 changes the Excel calculation into a three-step process:

1. In the first step, all necessary Excel cells have to be calculated. The DBRW formula can refer to other Excel cells with formulas. The DBRW formula needs the values of these cells as coordinates for a Cognos TM1 cube cell.

2. Now the Cognos TM1 Add-In can evaluate which DBRW formula can be grouped. All DBRW formulas are bundled if they have the same Excel cell reference in the first parameter and the referenced cell contains a VIEW formula. The VIEW formula just returns the name of a Cognos TM1 server. But this formula also provides some additional information for the first calculation phase. The parameters of the VIEW formula are used to communicate with a "Stargate view" in the Cognos TM1 server memory. Stargate views are used to collect, calculate, and cache cell values. For instance, if you request cell values by a Cube Viewer view on the Cognos TM1 client, the Cognos TM1 server uses a Stargate view on the server side to answer the request. The Cognos TM1 server always tries to reuse existing Stargate views. A new Stargate view is created if no appropriate Stargate view can be found. Whether a Stargate view can be reused or not is identified by matching title elements. If a request has the same title elements as an existing Stargate view, this Stargate view can be reused.
   In a Cube Viewer view, you can see which element are title elements. The VIEW formula supports this mechanism by providing the information about the title elements. In the sequence of the cube dimension, title element names are passed as parameters to the VIEW formula. An "!" is passed to all other parameters. The Excel cell reference in the DBRW formula to the VIEW formula identifies all DBRW requests that can be used by the same Stargate view. The result is retrieved from the Stargate view as a bundle and can be populated to the Excel cells (Stargate views are also discussed in Chapter 10).

3. In the third step, the Excel sheet has to be recalculated again. The result value of the DBRW formulas does not exist during the first calculation. But some other formulas or Excel charts can refer to cells with DBRW formulas. They need a value during the calculation phase. This is the reason why the Cognos TM1 Add-In forces the second calculation.

This mechanism is also used by the DBSW formula, which can be used to send a numeric value to a Cognos TM1 cube cell. All other Cognos TM1 formulas are calculated in one step or better: They already provide a value in step 1 during the first calculation. This is the reason why a DBRW formula can refer to any other Cognos TM1 formula except another DBRW or DBSW formula.

An example of such a "single-step" formula is the DBRA formula. This formula accesses the value of an element attribute. To work around the "single-step" mechanism, you can use a DBRW formula on an attribute cube instead. Another very common example of using a "single step" formula is the usage of a parameter cube to control the output of multiple reports. The parameter values that are used by DBRW formulas are retrieved from a parameter by the DBR formula. You can find this kind of example in the next few illustrations.

The DBRW formula is the central building block of a Cognos TM1 Excel report. If you use this formula, you just need to make sure that all element parameters are populated with a valid element name. A valid element name is also the alias name of an element. The DBRW formula does not care how the element name is provided. You can use all the Excel functions to create those names.

	A	B	C	D
1				
2		CUBE:	tog:TBB Sales	
3		TBB Year	2011	
4		TBB Month	06	
5		PG1		
6				
7		P1		
8		P2		
9		P3		
10		P4		
11		TBB Product	P2	
12				
13			Revenue	Units
14		Total Business Unit	700,000.00	3,500
15		Europe	660,000.00	3,300
16		North America	40,000.00	200
17		PacRim	0.00	0
18		ROW	0.00	0
19				

The preceding illustration shows two samples of how to provide element names to DBRW formulas:

1. Providing an element name by a Cognos TM1 cell value (TBB Year element and TBB Month element)

2. Providing an element name by pure Excel calculation (TBB Product element)

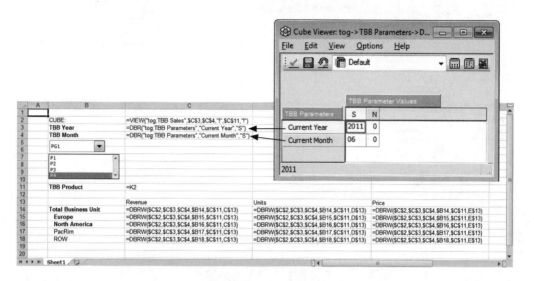

In the preceding illustration, you can see that the element names for the TBB Year and TBB Month coordinates are retrieved from the cube "TBB Parameters." In this case we have to use the DBR formula to make sure that the "TBB Parameters" values are retrieved by the first Excel calculation of Step 1 and are passed to the DBRW formula before the Cognos TM1 cell references are bundled (Step 2):

	A	B	C	D	E	F	G	H	I	J	K	L
1												
2		CUBE:	tog:TBB Sales				1	PG1		4	P2	
3		TBB Year	2011									
4		TBB Month	06					PG1		1	P1	
5		PG1 ▼						PG2		2	P2	
6								PG3		3	P3	
7		P1								4	P4	
8		P2										
9		P3										
10		P4										
11		TBB Product	P2									
12												

The content of the listbox depends on the selection of the checkbox.

The preceding two illustrations show how a "TBB Product" element could be selected by the user and provided to the DBRW formulas using Excel toolbox objects and formulas. In this example, a combo box is used to select a product group, and a list box is used to show and select products. The list box shows only products of the selected product group and will change if you select another product group. Both objects are linked to a range of values that represents the selectable content and to a cell that represent the selected entry as an index number. To convert the index to the selected value, we use the Excel formula INDEX. The list of product groups is static. The list of products is dynamic because it has to depend on the selected product group (cell H2). You can retrieve the children of a consolidated element by using the Cognos TM1 formula ELCOMP ("ELement COMPonent").

	A	B	C	D	E	F	G	H	I
1		CUBE:	tog:TBB Sales		tog:TBB Price				
2		TBB Year	2011						
3		TBB Product	P1						
4		TBB Month	01						
5									
6									
7			Units		Price		Units		
8									
9		UK	1,000.00		30.00		1,000		
10		Germany	2,000.00		30.00		2,000		
12		Europe	3,000.00				3,000		
13									
14		Canada	1,000.00		30.00		1,000		
15		US	6,000.00		30.00		6,000		
17		North America	7,000.00				7,000		
18									
19		PacRim	0.00		30.00		0		
20		ROW	1,000.00		30.00		1,000		
22		Total Business Unit	11,000.00				11,000		
23									
24									
25									

Sheet1

	A	B	C	D	E	F	G	H
1		CUBE:	=VIEW("tog:TBB Sales",$C$2,$C$4,"T",$C$3,"T")		=VIEW("tog:TBB Price",$C$2,$C$4,$C$3,"T")			
2		TBB Year	=SUBNM("tog:TBB Year","Current Year","2011")					
3		TBB Product	=SUBNM("tog:TBB Product","","P1")					
4		TBB Month	=SUBNM("tog:TBB Month","","01")					
5								
6								
7			Units		Price		Units	
8								
9		UK	=DBRW($C$1,$C$2,$C$4,$B9,$C$3,C$7)		=DBRW($E$1,$C$2,$C$4,$C$3,E$7)		=DBRW($C$1,$C$2,$C$4,$B9,$C$3,C	
10		Germany	=DBRW($C$1,$C$2,$C$4,$B10,$C$3,C$7)		=DBRW($E$1,$C$2,$C$4,$C$3,E$7)		=DBRW($C$1,$C$2,$C$4,$B10,$C$3,	
12		Europe	=DBRW($C$1,$C$2,$C$4,$B12,$C$3,C$7)				=DBRW($C$1,$C$2,$C$4,$B12,$C$3,	
13								
14		Canada	=DBRW($C$1,$C$2,$C$4,$B14,$C$3,C$7)		=DBRW($E$1,$C$2,$C$4,$C$3,E$7)		=DBRW($C$1,$C$2,$C$4,$B14,$C$3,	
15		US	=DBRW($C$1,$C$2,$C$4,$B15,$C$3,C$7)		=DBRW($E$1,$C$2,$C$4,$C$3,E$7)		=DBRW($C$1,$C$2,$C$4,$B15,$C$3,	
17		North America	=DBRW($C$1,$C$2,$C$4,$B17,$C$3,C$7)				=DBRW($C$1,$C$2,$C$4,$B17,$C$3,	
18								
19		PacRim	=DBRW($C$1,$C$2,$C$4,$B19,$C$3,C$7)		=DBRW($E$1,$C$2,$C$4,$C$3,E$7)		=DBRW($C$1,$C$2,$C$4,$B19,$C$3,	
20		ROW	=DBRW($C$1,$C$2,$C$4,$B20,$C$3,C$7)		=DBRW($E$1,$C$2,$C$4,$C$3,E$7)		=DBRW($C$1,$C$2,$C$4,$B20,$C$3,	
22		Total Business Unit	=DBRW($C$1,$C$2,$C$4,$B22,$C$3,C$7)				=DBRW($C$1,$C$2,$C$4,$B22,$C$3,	
23								

Sheet1

The preceding two illustrations show another example with a DBRW formula. Here you can see that you are not bound to the table structure that is generated by the "slice" function of the Cube Viewer. In this case we add some empty rows and columns and retrieve the price value directly from the cube "TBB Price."

This is a good place to mention that you are not forced to start with the Cube Viewer to create such an Excel report. You also can start from an empty Excel sheet:

1. Get the name of the cube with the Cognos TM1 Pick function:

   a. Click the Pick Cube button located in the Cognos TM1 ribbon (Excel 2003: choose TM1 | Pick | Cube); select a cube (a small dialog opens with instructions); double-click an Excel cell where the cube name should be inserted.

   b. Or: Open Server Explorer; select a cube; choose Cube | Pick. The Pick function will copy the name of the cube including the server name as prefix to the clipboard. You can now paste the picked cube to an Excel cell.

2. Add Title elements with the TM1 Pick function:

   a. Click the Pick Element button located in the Cognos TM1 ribbon (Excel 2003: choose TM1 | Pick | Element); select a dimension; the Subset Editor opens; select a single element; click OK (a small dialog opens with instructions); double-click an Excel cell where the element name should be inserted.

   b. Or: Open Server Explorer; open the Subset Editor, select an element, and copy to clipboard. You can now paste the picked element to an Excel cell.

   c. Or: Open the Subset Editor. Arrange the Subset Editor and the Excel window to see both windows, and drag a single element to an Excel cell.

3. Set up row headers:

   a. Click the Pick Element button located in the Cognos TM1 ribbon (Excel 2003: choose TM1 | Pick | Element); select a dimension; the Subset Editor opens; select a range of elements; click OK (a small dialog opens with instructions); double-click an Excel cell where the first element name should be inserted (the Select Way To Store Names dialog opens); click the Vertical button.

   b. Or: Open Server Explorer; open the Subset Editor, select a range of elements, and copy to clipboard. You can now paste the picked elements to an Excel cell.

   c. Or: Open Server Explorer; open the Subset Editor, select a range of elements, and pick the elements vertically (Excel 2003: choose Edit | Pick Elements | Vertical). You can now paste the picked elements to an Excel cell.

   d. Or: Open the Subset Editor. Arrange the Subset Editor and the Excel window to see both windows; select a range of elements and drag the elements to an Excel range.

4. Set up column headers:

   a. Click the Pick Element button located in the Cognos TM1 ribbon (Excel 2003: choose TM1 | Pick | Element); select a dimension; the Subset Editor opens; select a range of elements; click OK (a small dialog opens with instructions); double-click an Excel cell where the first element name should be inserted (the Select Way To Store Names dialog opens); click the Horiz. button.

   b. Or: Open Server Explorer; open the Subset Editor, select a range of elements, and pick the elements horizontally (Excel 2003: choose Edit | Pick Elements | Horizontal). You can now paste the picked elements to an Excel cell.

As you can see, there are many ways to get the name of a Cognos TM1 object and populate it to an Excel sheet. The following illustration is an example of the ways we've discussed so far:

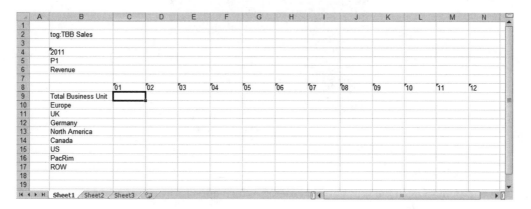

We can go on with the DBRW formula now.

1. Select the top left cell of the range where you want to insert the DBRW formulas (C9 in the preceding illustration).

2. Add a DBRW formula with the Formula Wizard of the Cognos TM1 Add-In:

   a. Click the Edit Formula button located in the Cognos TM1 ribbon (Excel 2003: choose TM1 | Edit Formula); click the DBRW button in the Edit Formula dialog; when the Select Cube dialog appears, double-click on the cell that holds the name of the cube; in the next dialog (Select Type Of Cell Reference), click "Absolute."

   b. The Cognos TM1 Add-In now scans the sheet for element names that match the dimensions of the selected cube. The result is displayed in the next dialog. If a value is found, a cell reference and the cell value is displayed for each dimension. If no element name could be found for a dimension, the field behind the dimension name will be blank. The dialog shows the parameters of the DBRW formula that will be generated. You can correct references or fill blank fields now, or you can edit the DBRW formula in Excel later. To change a cell reference, select the field you wish to change and double-click the new cell in the Excel sheet. The Select Type Of Cell Reference dialog is shown again to ask you for the type of the reference. If no appropriate element name for a dimension exists in the Excel sheet, you can pick an element from a Subset Editor by clicking the button with the dimension name. The picked element will be placed as text in the DBRW formula later on. If all elements can be found, the result looks like the following illustration. If all element names appear only once in the sheet, all referenced cells including the type of the reference will fit in almost all cases.

Click OK.

c. Click OK in the Edit Formula dialog, which appears again, as in the following illustration.

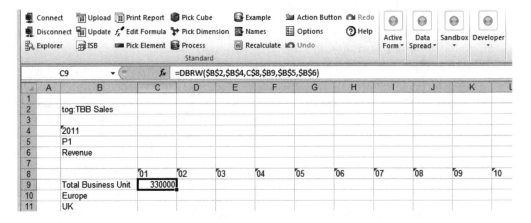

3. The TM1 wizard generates the references in the DBRW formula so that you can copy and paste this formula to all other cells of the appropriate range.

4. In the last step we have to make sure to use the VIEW formula with the DBRW formula. In our example we have to replace the text "tog:TBB Sales" in cell B2 with the VIEW formula. Unfortunately, the formula wizard of the TM1 Add-In doesn't support the VIEW formula. But the VIEW formula is structured very similarly to the DBRW formula. We recommend creating the VIEW formula from a DBRW formula with the following steps:

   a. Select a cell with a DBRW formula and change to the edit mode of the Excel formula editor by clicking into the Editor field or pressing F2.

   b. Select the first parameter as shown in the following illustration.

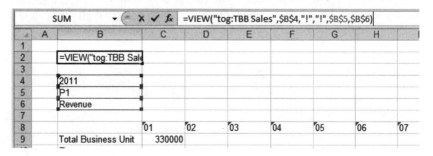

	SUM	▾ ⊙ ✕ ✓ *fx*	=DBRW(	$B$2	,$B$4,C$8,$B9,$B$5,$B$6)		
◢	A	B	C	D	E	F	G
1							
2		tog:TBB Sales					
3							
4		2011					
5		P1					
6		Revenue					
7							
8			'01	'02	'03	'04	'05
9		Total Business Unit	=DBRW($				
10		Europe					

c. Press F9. Excel will calculate only the selection. In this case, the reference will be resolved and be replaced by the value:

	SUM	▾ ⊙ ✕ ✓ *fx*	=DBRW("tog:TBB Sales",$B$4,C$8,$B9,$B$5,$B$6)						
◢	A	B	C	D	E	F	G	H	I
1									

d. Select the whole formula including the "=" and copy the selection to the clipboard. Leave the editor without saving the changes by pressing ESC or clicking on the red "X" (we do not want to change the DBRW formula).

e. Select the cell with the name of the cube and enter the Excel formula editor again.

f. Replace the value of the cell by pasting the clipboard contents into the Editor field.

g. Change the name of the formula from DBRW to VIEW.

h. All references that are pointing to title elements should be absolute references. All other references should be references to column dimension elements or row dimension elements. Replace these references with an "!".

	SUM	▾ ⊙ ✕ ✓ *fx*	=VIEW("tog:TBB Sales",$B$4,"!","!",$B$5,$B$6)						
◢	A	B	C	D	E	F	G	H	I
1									
2		=VIEW("tog:TBB Sale							
3									
4		2011							
5		P1							
6		Revenue							
7									
8			'01	'02	'03	'04	'05	'06	'07
9		Total Business Unit	330000						

Active Forms

Using Active Forms is the second way to slice a Cube Viewer view into an Excel sheet. If you click the Active Form button (in the second illustration in this chapter this button is labeled with "Slice an Active Form to Excel"), an Excel sheet will be populated with Cognos TM1 formulas. Some of the formulas are the same as those used in the classic slice. The following illustration shows an example:

Active Form

You can see some differences. The rows are formatted. Parent elements of the row dimension are indicated if they are expanded or collapsed. Child elements are indented relative to their parents. Some columns and rows of the Excel sheet are hidden. So let's look at the whole slice and unhide the hidden ranges (see the following illustration). (The Cognos TM1 function "Show format area" will unhide almost all ranges. You can access this function via the Cognos TM1 ribbon/toolbar or in the Active Form menu, which is added to the Excel right-click menu. Of course, you can unhide the ranges using the standard Excel Unhide function.)

	A	B	C	D	E	F	G	H	I	J	K	L
1	[Begin Format Range]											
2	0											
3	1											
4	2											
5	3											
6	D											
7	N											
8	[End Format Range]											
10												
11		TBB Year	2011									
12		TBB Product	P1									
13		TBB Month	01									
14												
15												
16			Revenue	Units	Price							
17	0	- Total Business Unit	330,000.00	11,000	30.00							
18	1	- Europe	90,000.00	3,000	30.00							
19	N	UK	30,000.00	1,000	30.00							
20	N	Germany	60,000.00	2,000	30.00							
21	1	- North America	210,000.00	7,000	30.00							
22	N	Canada	30,000.00	1,000	30.00							
23	N	US	180,000.00	6,000	30.00							
24	N	PacRim	0.00	0	30.00							
25	N	ROW	30,000.00	1,000	30.00							
26												

Sheet1

Active Form with format areas

Active Forms are similar to classic Excel slices regarding the use of DBRW and the SUBNM formulas. The difference is that Active Forms are much more dynamic. An Active Form takes control over a range of rows of the Excel sheet to perform the following functions:

- Filter elements of the row dimension by zero suppression
- Filter elements of the row dimension by cube values (for example, the top five business units)
- Use elements of the row dimension by using a predefined list
- Use elements of the row dimension by using a subset (including dynamic subsets [see Chapter 5])
- Filter elements of the row dimension by using an expression (MDX expression; see also dynamic subsets in Chapter 5)
- Provide user interaction by expanding and collapsing parent elements. This interaction can be performed when the user double-clicks the cell with the name of the parent element.

To make this work, the Cognos TM1 Add-In has to tie together several parts of Active Forms that are spread over the Excel sheet. This is done by using named ranges and Excel cell references. The following illustration shows the different components that are involved.

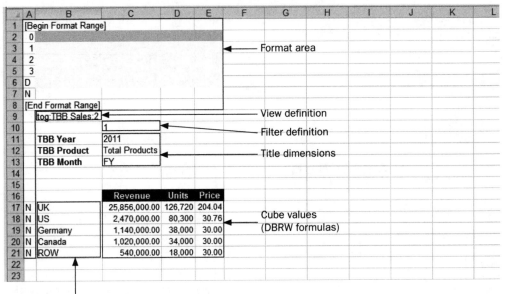

Components of an Active Form

In the following illustration, you can see the named ranges.

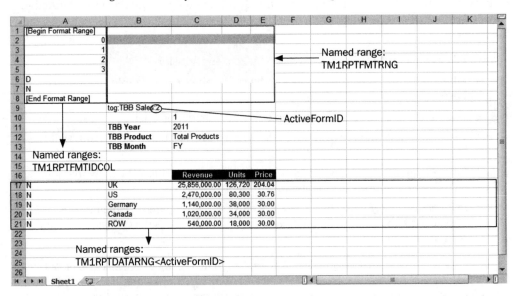

Named ranges in an Active Form

In Figure 8-1 you can see how these Active Form components are connected.

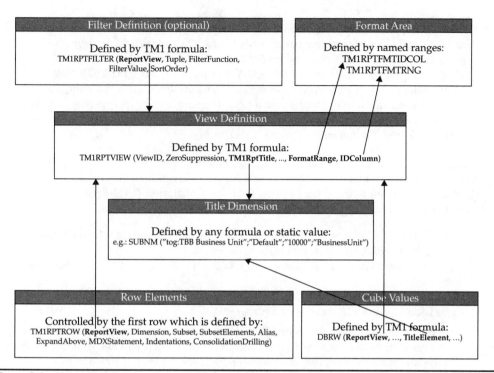

FIGURE 8-1   How Active Form components are connected

How Active Forms Work

Now let's look at how the Active Form works. There are two different recalculation modes:

- **Recalculate**   Press F9; all Excel formulas are recalculated twice (as described in the preceding section: Cognos TM1 hooks into the Excel calculation).
- **Rebuild**   Press ALT-F9; all Active Forms are rebuilt.

When you rebuild Active Forms, the Cognos TM1 Add-In evaluates the list of row elements. The top element of all row elements is calculated by the TM1RPTROW formula. This formula defines how the row elements are evaluated. The list of elements can be defined by:

- **A stored subset**   The name of the subset should be passed to the third parameter: "Subset."
- **A list of elements**   A reference of a cell range should be passed to the fourth parameter: "SubsetElements."
- An MDX statement that returns a set of "members" (MDX name for elements). The MDX could be passed to the seventh parameter ("MDX statement") as text. We recommend placing the MDX statement in a separate cell and passing the cell reference to the seventh parameter. This way is better for the maintenance of the sheet.

NOTE *In the third parameter of the TM1RPTROW formula, you can pass the name of a subset. This subset could be a dynamic one that consists of an MDX statement. But, there is an advantage to using the MDX statement in the TM1RPTROW instead.*

When using the MDX in the TM1RPTROW, you are able to make the MDX statement dynamic. You can modify the statement with Excel formulas. If you do so, not only is the list of elements dynamic (the result of the statement), but the query statement is dynamic too, and it can be built by using values from the current workbook. The expression in a dynamic subset is static (only the result is dynamic).

After the list of elements is evaluated, an optional filter and/or the zero suppression is applied. This can result in a new sort order and/or a further reduced set of elements.

At this point we refer you to the Cognos TM1 documentation (*TM1 Reference Guide*) for a detailed description of all parameters, but here are some hints and notes:

- The TM1RPTROW doesn't need all parameters. Depending on which parameter is used, the length of the parameter list is different:
  Using a subset: `TM1RPTROW($B$9;"tog:TBB Business Unit";"All Business Units")`
  Using MDX: `TM1RPTROW($B$9;"tog:TBB Business Unit";;;;;"{[TBB Business Unit].[Europe].children}")`

- We recommend using subsets or MDX statements as element list definitions. You can create an Active Form with a subsets definition when you assign named subsets to the row dimension in the Cube Viewer and click the Active Form button. If no named subset is assigned to the row dimension, the Cognos TM1 Add-In will create a hidden sheet containing a range of cells filled with the elements currently shown in the Cube Viewer. The TM1RPTROW formula will look like this:
  `TM1RPTROW($B$9;"tog:TBB Business Unit";`
  `"";'{AR}01'!$B$17:$B$25;"BusinessUnit";0)`
  {AR}01 is the name of the hidden sheet that holds the elements of the "unnamed subset." Slicing an Active Form with a large "unnamed subset" is detrimental to performance. A named subset is recommended at all times because the reference to the elements is maintained on the server.

- Use the Subset Editor to create and test MDX statements (see Chapter 8). With the Subset Editor you can record an MDX expression. You can copy and paste the result from the Expression Window to an Excel cell. Make sure that the MDX statements do not include the `TM1SubsetBasis()` function. The TM1RPTROW formula has no access to the "Subset Basis" (use `TM1SUBSETALL(...)` instead).

Now we have a list of row elements that has to be added to the Excel sheet. For that purpose, the rows of an Active Form are bundled into a named range: TM1RPTDATARNG<ID>. The ID can be found in the first parameter of the TM1RPTVIEW formula. The first row of this range is the master row. This row contains a TM1RPTROW formula for each row dimension (you can have multiples if you use stacked dimensions). It doesn't matter in which column the TM1RPTROW formula is placed. If the Active Form is rebuilt, all rows except the first row are deleted from the Excel sheet, and for each element of the evaluated list, a new Excel row is inserted under the first row. Now the formulas or values of each column of the first row are copied to the new rows. So if you want to modify or add a formula to your Active Form, you just have to do this in the first row. Changes in the other cells of the TM1RPTDATARNG<ID> range will be overwritten. Because the rows of an Active Form are deleted and re-inserted, the rows have to be reformatted by the TM1 Add-In. For that purpose TM1 uses the "Format Area."

In the same column as the TM1RPTFMTIDCOL is defined, the TM1 Add-In is looking inside the TM1RPTDATARNG<ID> range for a format ID. This ID could be a number, text, or a TRUE/FALSE value. The TM1 Add-In compares the ID with the IDs in the TM1RPTFMTIDCOL-range and copies the formats of the matching row in the TM1RPTFMTRNG range to the row in the TM1RPTDATARNG<ID> range. All kind of formats are copied including validations, conditional formats, and cell protection.

Regarding conditional formats: Make sure that you define cell references relative to formatted cells if you want the condition to compare cells of the TM1RPTDATARNG<ID> range. Excel uses absolute cell references as defaults when you define a conditional format. A copy of a conditional format will still point to these cells.

The default formula that evaluates the format ID is quite complex:

```
=IF(TM1RPTELISCONSOLIDATED($B$17;$B17);IF(TM1RPTELLEV($B$17;$B17)<=3;
     TM1RPTELLEV($B$17;$B17);"D");"N")
```

This formula means: The format ID is the report level number of a consolidated element if the level is less than or equal to 3. If the level is greater than 3, the ID is "D." If the row dimension element is a leaf, the ID is "N." The level is evaluated by the TM1RPTELLEV formula, which is different than the classic ELLEV formula. ELLEV returns the absolute level of an element. This level is the count from a leaf element (Level 0) to the topmost consolidated element. The report level is a relative level with reverse counting. Level 0 is now the topmost element of the element list of the Active Form.

You can create your own formula to evaluate a format ID. The next two illustrations show two examples:

	A13	▼	fx	=IF(A12="LIGHT","DARK","LIGHT")						
	A	B	C	D	E	F	G	H	I	J	K
1	[Begin Format Range]										
2	LIGHT										
3	DARK										
4	[End Format Range]										
6											
7		TBB Year	2011								
8		TBB Business Unit	Total Business Unit								
9		TBB Month	01								
10											
11											
12	LIGHT		Revenue	Units	Price						
13	DARK	P1	330,000.00	11,000	30.00						
14	LIGHT	P2	220,000.00	1,100	200.00						
15	DARK	P3	318,000.00	1,060	300.00						
16	LIGHT	P4	240,000.00	800	300.00						
17	DARK	P5	0.00	0	0.00						
18	LIGHT	P6	0.00	0	0.00						
19	DARK	P7	0.00	0	0.00						
20	LIGHT	P8	0.00	0	0.00						
21	DARK	P9	0.00	0	0.00						
22	LIGHT	P10	0.00	0	0.00						
23	DARK	P11	0.00	0	0.00						
24	LIGHT	P12	0.00	0	0.00						
25											
26											
27											

H ◀ ▶ H   Sheet1

Active Form Format Sample 1

In the preceding illustration, you can see an example of alternating formats. You just need to modify the format formula of the master row. Often financial data requires a number of different data formats based on hierarchy or type, like the accounts in a Profit and Loss statement (you can find an example in Chapter 19). The rebuild process will also copy this formula to the other rows of the Active Form. In this example you can see that we use a relative reference (A12). So you can read this formula like this: If the value above the current cell is "LIGHT," the value of the current cell should be "DARK"; if not, it should be "LIGHT."

	A	B	C	D	E	F	G	H	I	J	K
				A14			▼	fx	=DBRA("tog:TBB Product",B14,"Type")		
1	[Begin Format Range]										
2	Total										
3	Group										
4	Product										
5	[End Format Range]										
6		tog:TBB Sales:2									
7											
8		TBB Year	2011								
9		TBB Business Unit	Total Business Unit								
10		TBB Month	01	02							
11											
12											
13			Revenue		Units	Price					
14	Total	- Total Products	0.00		0	102.85					
15	Group	- PG1	0.00		0	102.85					
16	Product	P4	0.00		0	300.00					
17	Product	P3	0.00		0	300.00					
18	Product	P2	0.00		0	200.00					
19	Product	P1	0.00		0	30.00					
20	Group	+ PG2	0.00		0	0.00					
21	Group	+ PG3	0.00		0	0.00					
22											
23											
24											
25											
26											
	Sheet1										

Active Form Format Sample 2

The preceding illustration shows how to get the format ID from an element attribute. Be aware that this sample could lead to bad performance, because the DBRA formula is not network-optimized. You cannot replace the DBRA formula by a DBRW formula retrieving data from the attribute cube because the DBRW formula will deliver the values in the second phase of calculation (see the earlier section "Classic Slice to Microsoft Excel"), which is too late for formatting.

As already mentioned, Active Forms interact with the user. The user can expand and collapse consolidated elements that are indicated by a "+" or "−" sign. When the user expands a consolidated element, the children of this element will be shown with an indentation. (By the way, you can disable this interaction with the ninth parameter of the TM1RPTROW formula. You can also disable this indentation with the eighth parameter. The "+", "−" sign and the indentation are special formatting that is added to the copied format.) If you expand a node for each child element, a row is inserted into the Excel sheet that is formatted in the same way as described earlier in this section. If you collapse a node, the "child" rows are deleted from the Excel sheet. You will always go back to the starting list of elements when you rebuild the Active Form.

As shown in Figure 8-1, the TM1RPTVIEW formula is the central formula of the Active Form. This formula also defines how the TM1 server should evaluate the usage of a Stargate view as the classic VIEW formula does. The TM1RPTVIEW formula also defines whether zero suppression is applied or not. For zero suppression, the Cognos TM1 server needs to know which range of cells is affected by zero suppression. In the case of an Active Form, this range is all cells in the TM1RPTDATARNG<ID> range that are calculated by a DBRW formula referencing with the first parameter to the TM1RPTVIEW formula.

The connections shown in Figure 8-1 are a critical factor to make sure that an Active Form is working. If the Active Form does not work, please check the connections first. The example in the following illustration shows you how to set up an Active Form if you need columns with values that must vary from the default sliced view.

	SUM		▾ ✖ ✔ *fx*	=DBRW($F$9,$F$11,$F$13,$B17,$C$12,F$16)				
	B	C	D	E	F	G	H	I
8								
9	tog:TBB Sales:2			tog: TBB Price	tog:TBB Sales			
10								
11	TBB Year	2011			2010			
12	TBB Product	Total Products						
13	TBB Month	FY			12			
14								
15								
16		Revenue	Units	Price	Units			
17	- Total Business Unit	31,236,000.00	304,020	39,960.00	=DBRW($F$9,$F			
18	- Europe	26,996,000.00	164,720	39,960.00	16,254.19			
19	UK	25,856,000.00	126,720	39,960.00	12,504.44			
20	Germany	1,140,000.00	38,000	39,960.00	3,749.75			
21	- North America	3,490,000.00	114,300	39,960.00	11,278.86			
22	Canada	1,020,000.00	34,000	39,960.00	3,355.04			
23	US	2,470,000.00	80,300	39,960.00	7,923.82			
24	PacRim	210,000.00	7,000	39,960.00	690.74			
25	ROW	540,000.00	18,000	39,960.00	1,776.20			
26								
27								
28								

Active Form Format Sample 3

The example in the preceding illustration shows an additional column that should display the units of 12/2010. The month and the year are title dimensions that are referenced in the TM1RPTVIEW formula. But the formulas in column F refer to different titles. So we disconnect the DBRW formulas in column F and let them point to their own VIEW formula. Use the same mechanism if you want to query cells from different cubes in the same Active Form. We used this for the Price column (column E). The values of this column are retrieved from the "TBB Price" cube.

Using Charts with Active Forms

Now we have Excel reports with dynamic rows. But because the rows are dynamic, this leads to a challenge when you want to visualize the data with Excel charts. If you create a chart on an Active Form in the standard Excel way, the references of the chart to the cells of the Active Form will break each time you rebuild the Active Form. The references in the chart become invalid (#ref-error) because the rows are deleted and re-inserted. Here is the workaround.

You have to create named ranges on the Active Form and use these ranges as references in the chart. Here is a step-by-step example:

1. Slice the Active Form from a Cube Viewer.

2. Create a named range for each section of the chart that should refer to a dynamic range. In our example we need two ranges, one for the data (we want to visualize the revenue only and one for the title of one axis [row dimension elements]). So let's look at the title first (see the following illustration). If you define the named range from the first row element to the last row element, the named range will also be broken if you rebuild the Active Form. But if you include the first line beneath the Active Form (in this example it's row 22), the range is maintained by Excel automatically.

	B	C	D	E	F	G	H	I	J
	B17			f_x	=TM1RPTROW($B$9,"tog:TBB Business Unit","Default")				
10									
11	TBB Year	2011							
12	TBB Product	P1							
13	TBB Month	01							
14									
15									
16		Revenue	Units	Price					
17	- Total Business Unit	330,000.00	11,000	30.00					
18	+ Europe	90,000.00	3,000	30.00					
19	+ North America	210,000.00	7,000	30.00					
20	PacRim	0.00	0	30.00					
21	ROW	30,000.00	1,000	30.00					
22									
23									

Now we define a range for the data too.

3. Insert a chart and set up the series and titles:

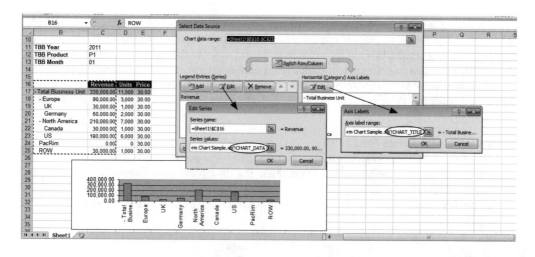

As you can see in the preceding illustration, the chart will work after the rebuild of the Active Form and after expanding and collapsing the rows. But the chart will always visualize the blank line beneath the Active Form, too. To get rid of this blank line, we have to enhance the named ranges.

4. Use the OFFSET formula to evaluate the named range. To change the named range, you have to open the dialog to maintain the named ranges and change the cell references to the formula:

```
CHART_DATA: =Sheet1!$C$17:$C$22 change to =OFFSET(Sheet1!$C$1
7;;;ROWS(Sheet1!TM1RPTDATARNG1);1)
CHART_TITLE: =Sheet1!$B$17:$B$22 change to
=OFFSET(Sheet1!$B$17;;;ROWS(Sheet1!TM1RPTDATARNG1);1)
```

In the following illustration you see this example with some modification. We just enhance the TM1RPTROW formula and add some selection capabilities. Even though we made these changes, the named ranges CHART_DATA and CHART_TITLE are still valid. So the chart still works. We have to change the formula in B18:

```
=TM1RPTROW($B$9,"tog:TBB Business Unit","","","Business Unit",0,$B$15)
```

The last parameter of this formula refers to an MDX statement (B15) that is created by another formula:

```
="{TM1FILTERBYLEVEL( {TM1DRILLDOWNMEMBER( {[TBB Business Unit].["&C14&"]},
    ALL, RECURSIVE )}, 0)}"
```

The result of the MDX statement is a list of elements that are leaf elements of the selected Business Unit (selected in a combo box).

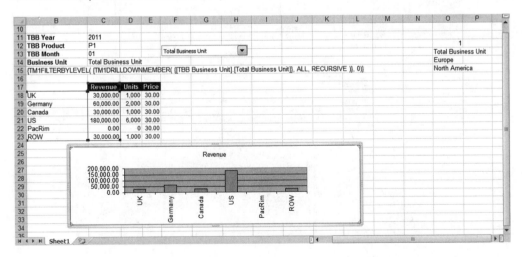

Cognos TM1 Web

As mentioned in Chapter 4, Cognos TM1 Web is one of the TM1 clients. This client is a full HTML browser client with zero footprint on the user's desktop. All web pages are created on demand by a web server component. The main web page is divided into three parts (see Figure 8-2): the title, the navigation pane, and the main display area. The navigation pane can be hidden by the user. An administrator/developer can exclude the navigation pane for each user; in this case the user is not able to open the pane. In the navigation pane you can see the applications tree as defined in the Cognos TM1 Architect/Perspectives. Items of the applications tree that are not valid for the Web are hidden. The following items are valid:

- Views
- Excel sheets
- Cubes
- Other files

If the user clicks on an application item, the various items are treated depending on their type: Views and cubes are opened as a web cube view in the display area. Excel sheets are opened as Cognos TM1 Websheets in the display area. Other files are downloaded or opened in a separate browser window (this depends on the setting of the user's web browser).

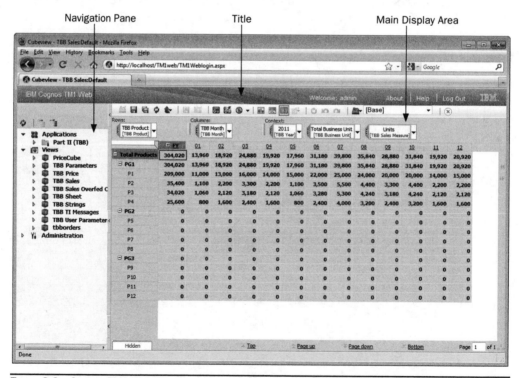

FIGURE 8-2   Cognos TM1 Web Client

Cognos TM1 Architect/Perspectives	Cognos TM1 Web
Create Active Form (Perspectives only)	–
Replace view by another view (drop-down list)	Open a new Cube Viewer from navigation pane
Slice/Snapshot to Excel (Perspectives only)	Export to Excel
Print Report to multiple Snapshots (Excel)	Export to Excel
Print Report to PDF	Export to PDF
–	Charts
Format	–
Column width	–
Layout right to left	–

TABLE 8-1 Comparing Cube Viewers

The view node in the navigation tree is a collection of all cubes that are available to the user with all their views. The Administration node gives the user the ability to start TurboIntegrator processes and to change the password. The Views node and the Administration node can be excluded from the navigation pane by configuration setting.

The Cube Viewer of Cognos TM1 Web has almost the same functionality as the Cube Viewer of Cognos TM1 Architect/Perspectives. The differences are outlined in Table 8-1.

With Cognos TM1 Web, the user also gets access to the Web version of a subset editor. The editor can be called from a Cube Viewer or Websheets. Table 8-2 lists the differences between the subset editors in Cognos TM1 Web and Cognos TM1 Architect/Perspectives.

Cognos TM1 Architect/Perspectives	Cognos TM1 Web
Properties window	–
Expression window/record expression	–
Filter by View Extract	–
Open multiple subset editors for exchange elements	Split view in advance mode to incrementally add elements to an existing subset
–	Find in Subset (search)
Filter... (Top Count etc.)	–
Security settings (reserve, lock)	–

TABLE 8-2 Comparing subset editors

Delivering Components to a User's Desktop

Since you are familiar with the components of Cognos TM1 Web now, we should look at how these components are delivered to a user's desktop. The web server (MS Internet Information Server) has to be extended by the installation of the Cognos TM1 Web server components. These components are Cognos TM1 libraries, which enable the web server to create dynamic HTML files directly from Cognos TM1 cubes, views, and subsets. To create a Cognos TM1 Websheet, the web server needs the help of an additional service: the Cognos TM1 Excel service. Because the generation of a Websheet is more complex, we will take a closer look at this mechanism now.

Figure 8-3 shows the architecture of Cognos TM1 web. The web server component always "renders" (= creates HTML code on demand and sends it to the client's browser) a Cognos TM1 Websheet from a corresponding XML file. The XML version of the Websheet is

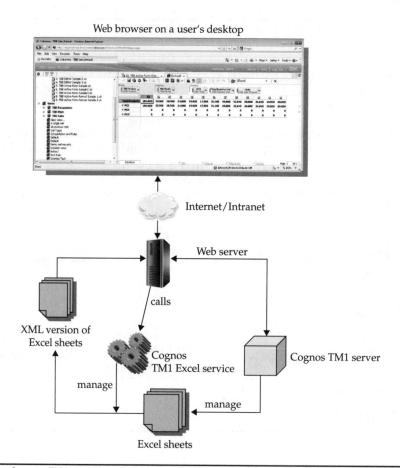

FIGURE 8-3   Cognos TM1 Web Architecture

closer to the final HTML page than the original Excel sheet. The XML version can be created in two different ways:

- **XML creation on demand**   If a user requests to open a Websheet, the web server forwards the request to the Cognos TM1 Excel service. The Cognos TM1 Excel service checks whether a corresponding XML file already exists and whether an existing XML file is up to date. The check is based on the files in the directory <*web server root directory*>\TM1WebEx\ExcelSheet. Here you can find the file ExcelReport.bin. This file contains the information about which Excel file is already converted to which XML file, including a conversion timestamp. The timestamp is for checking whether the original Excel sheet has changed and the XML file has to be re-created. If the corresponding XML file doesn't exist, the Cognos TM1 Excel service gets the origin Excel file from the TM1 server and saves a temporary copy into the <*web server root directory*>\TM1WebEx\ExcelSheet directory. The temporary copy is opened in Excel and saved as XML plus supporting files like images. For this step, the Cognos TM1 Excel service needs access to Excel on the same machine. Excel is invoked "in the background." That means that Excel is not visible to a user. You can find all temporary files and generated files in the <*web server root directory*>\TM1WebEx\ExcelSheet directory. Now these files can be used by the web server to create the HTML page. Creating the XML files in this way requires an MS Excel version installed on a server machine where the Cognos TM1 Excel service is running.

- **XML creation on the user's desktop**   If your company has a policy of not installing Excel on a server machine, you need to use Excel on the user's machine to do the XML conversion. In this case, you have to add `ExcelWebPublishEnabled =T` to the Cognos TM1 server configuration file tm1s.cfg. If the server is switched to that mode, you will find some additional menu entries for Excel sheets in the applications tree: "Publish to TM1Web" and "Remove from TM1Web." If an Excel sheet is not published to Cognos TM1 Web, the node is grayed in the application tree of Cognos TM1 Architect/Perspectives and is not visible in the navigation pane of Cognos TM1 Web. If a user publishes a sheet, the local Excel version is used to generate the XML file (including the supporting files). The files are stored in the directory "publish," which is a subdirectory of the Cognos TM1 server directory. Now the Excel sheet is visible in Cognos TM1 Web. If a user requests the Websheet, the Cognos TM1 Excel service just needs to make the already generated files available in the <*web server root directory*>\TM1WebEx\ExcelSheet directory. If a user "removes" the Excel sheet from Cognos TM1Web, the generated files are deleted and the Excel sheet becomes invisible again in Cognos TM1 Web.

We recommend using the first method (Excel is installed on the server) because there are fewer steps to deploy a Websheet. Furthermore, the server-side Excel is used for printing. If you use the XML creation on the users' desktop, the printing is done by PDF Creator software, which is installed with the Cognos TM1 Excel service. The result of this type of printing is very different from a "what you see is what you get" style.

PART II

Creating a Guided Web Application

In this section we will demonstrate how to use the Cognos TM1 building blocks to create a guided web application. First, we have to define what a guided application is. According to Wikipedia, "application software, also known as an application or an app, is computer software designed to help the user to perform singular or multiple related specific tasks." We call an application "guided" if the user's interface provides only data and functions that are related to the tasks that have to be performed. Such an application has to be careful to provide only data and functions that make sense in the context of a task. If the application does so, the user is guided, which means that he doesn't need to have much knowledge about the application (only about his tasks), and therefore less training is needed. Be aware that the "task" is not a workflow task but a business task of the user, which is supported by the application. Of course, you can implement a workflow task in Cognos TM1, which corresponds to the business task. In this case the application can take control of the status of the business task, which is also a kind of "guidance." Especially if the user has to perform multiple tasks with the application, implementing a workflow is very useful.

In our case the interface is Cognos TM1 Web, so we talk about a web application. You can also build a guided application with Excel sheets as interface. But with Cognos TM1 Web, it is easier to hide functions from the user that are not useful for the context of the task. And Cognos TM1 Web is easier to deploy to the user's desktop (just provide the URL of Cognos TM1 Web).

The following Cognos TM1 components are the building blocks of guided applications (Figure 8-4):

Figure 8-5 shows an extract of the Cognos TM1 architecture, which we have discussed in Chapter 4.

We already discussed the components Data, Business Logic, and Workflow in the previous chapters. We already introduced Cognos TM1 Web in the earlier sections of this chapter. Now we will look at how we can bring these components together to create a guided application.

Cognos TM1 Web is the building block that represents the user interface. With Websheets you can create the presentation of an application that can guide the user. In this context the

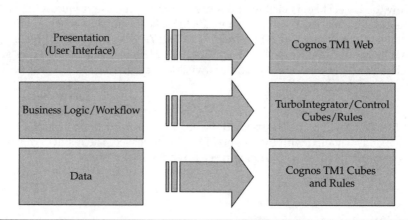

Figure 8-4   Cognos TM1 components as application building blocks

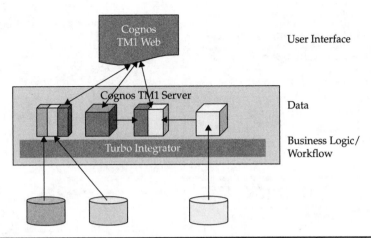

User Interface

Data

Business Logic/
Workflow

FIGURE 8-5   Cognos TM1 building blocks

Action buttons play a major role. The Cognos TM1 Excel Add-In provides a function to insert a Cognos TM1 Action button into an Excel sheet. This Action button is also available in a corresponding Websheet. The following illustration shows which actions you can perform:

1. **Run a TurboIntegrator process**   You can run a process by providing parameter values from Excel cells.

2. **Go to another worksheet**   You can go to another sheet including passing values to cells or SUBNM formulas in the called sheet. By passing values, you can keep the context of the data (for example, the user has selected "Business Unit" "US" as the title element and the same "Business Unit" is selected in the called sheet) and the task. The name of the called sheet can be retrieved from an Excel cell. So the called sheet can depend on the context of a task.

3. **Run a process, then go to a worksheet**   This is a combination of actions 1 and 2. But the other worksheet is opened only if the process does not terminate with an error (to control this, you can use the TurboIntegrator function ProcessError in the process script).

4. **Calculate/Rebuild Only**   You can use this action to attach the function Calculate (F9) or Rebuild an Active Form (ALT-F9) to a button. This action can always be used in combination with actions 1 to 3.

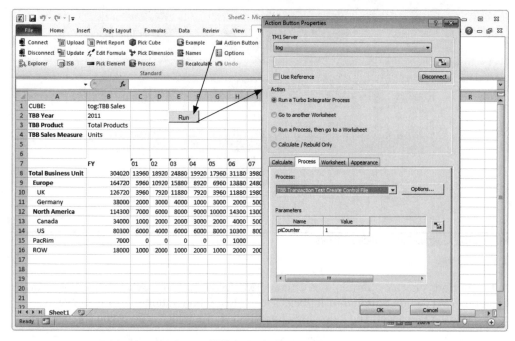

Cognos TM1 Action button properties

Figure 8-6 shows an example of how to use Action buttons to provide interactions to guide the user from one Websheet to another and functions (TurboIntegrator processes) that make sense in the context of a task.

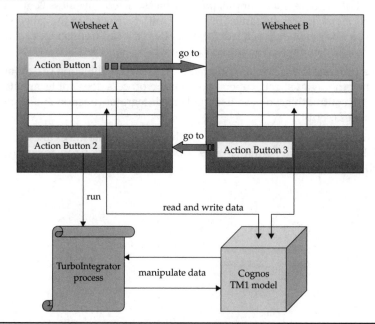

FIGURE 8-6   Using Cognos TM1 Action buttons in an application

If you want to make your application "fully guided," you can hide some standard Cognos TM1Web functions from the user. The configuration can be accomplished by using a Cognos TM1 control cube per user. The control cube is called "}ClientSettings" (see the following illustration). In this cube you find some settings that can be edited using a standard dialog in Cognos TM1 Architect/Perspectives: Select the server node in the Server Explorer, choose Server | Security | Client/Groups, and in the Clients/Groups dialog:, click the Settings button.

Client Settings cube

In a "fully guided" application, the user should not be able to choose a Websheet by himself. So you should hide the navigation tree for the user by setting "Web Hide NavTree" to "true." The context of the task should be the only criteria to decide which sheet is available. It is possible that a user may have opened multiple Websheets at one time. The open Websheets can be accessed by the TabBar (see the following illustration). If the user can change the Websheet by the TabBar, it is almost impossible to guarantee that the data context is the same for all open Websheets. To prevent this situation, you should disable the TabBar by setting "Web Hide TabBar" to "true." Now you can control which Websheet is used by the user. But you need a starting point: the first Websheet. With the setting "Home Page Object Type" (set to "Websheet") and "Home Page Object" (set to an Excel sheet in the Cognos TM1 URI notation for sheets that are uploaded to the application tree or set to an absolute path for other sheets; we recommend using the Client Setting dialog to set the Home Page Object), you can define the starting point of your guided web application for each user. (The TM1

URI notation has to conform to the pattern: TM1://<TM1 server name>/blob/PUBLIC/.\}
Externals\<Name of the uploaded file>.) If a Home Page object is set, a Home button is
added to the Cognos TM1 Web Banner (see the following illustration). The Home Object (the
Websheet where the application starts) cannot be closed by the user. Optionally, you can
prevent a user from closing other Websheets: Set "Web Hide Websheet Toolbar" to "true."
In this case the user cannot access the functions of the toolbar, including the Close button.
You can hide the toolbar if only the Calculate or Rebuild function is needed, because these
functions can be provided by Action buttons as an alternative to the toolbar.

NOTE *The parameters in the Client Settings cube can also be set globally for all users in the
web.config file in the Cognos TM1 Web directory.*

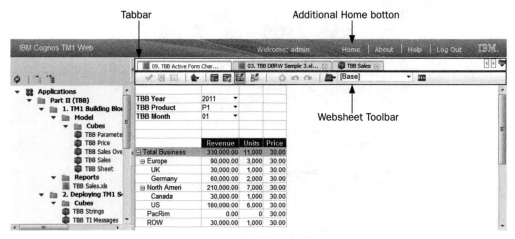

Tabs and toolbar in Cognos TM1 Web

Building a Common Framework

All samples in the previous sections of this chapter were built from scratch. Every Excel report
could look different. When you are developing a Cognos TM1 solution, we recommend
having a common look and feel for all your Excel sheets/Websheets. This is one reason to
define and build a framework for your Cognos TM1 solution. If you are going to develop
more than one solution, you should consider defining a common framework for all your
solutions. A Cognos TM1 solution framework should consist of the following items:

1. Definition of a naming convention for

    a. Dimension names

    b. Cube names

    c. Process names

    d. Parameter names

  e. Variable names (TurboIntegrator)

  f. Element names

2. Definition of standard attributes

3. Definition of sequences of dimensions that are similar for all cubes

4. Definition of how to handle messages

5. Definition of templates for Excel sheets/Websheets

To give you an idea of a framework, we will introduce a framework we used for our solution. Please take the following framework as an example.

Naming Conventions

We decided to name all dimensions and cubes with a plural name. For instance, we call the dimensions "Months," "Years," "Regions," and so on. If you can divide your solutions into smaller modules, you should use prefixes for the Cognos TM1 objects (cubes, dimensions, processes, and so on), which can be assigned to a single module. For instance, we used TBB for the sample objects in this book regarding the "TM1 Building Block." Probably you can reuse single modules for various solutions. In this case the prefix helps you to identify objects of a module and to copy a module from one solution to another. When we define a TurboIntegrator process, we use prefixes for variables to identify the type and the origin of the variable. We use the following prefixes:

- ps = Parameter String

- pn = Parameter Number (float or decimal)

- pi = Parameter Integer

- pb = Parameter Boolean (1 or 0 only)

- vs to vb = Variable from a data source with the same pattern we are using for parameters (use v instead of p)

- gs to gb = Global variables with the same pattern we are using for parameters (use g instead of p)

- s to b = All other variables with the same pattern we are using for parameters (use no prefix instead of p)

Prefixes help you to read TurboIntegrator script code. For instance, if you find the variable "psDimension," this variable holds a name (String) of a dimension that was passed by a parameter to the TI process.

We use IDs as element names. In most cases, elements of a dimension are loaded from a data source. The advantage of using IDs is that they actually do not change. We use aliases for the element names that should be presented to the user. If a dimension has one root element name, we name this element "Total <Dimension name>". This is more comfortable in Cube Viewer when you can identify the dimension by its top element in the Cube Viewer, especially if you have a view with some title elements set to the top element.

Standard Attributes

Because we use element names, we add an alias attribute with the same name to all dimensions. If you work with only one language in your solution, you can add an alias like "Name" or "Description." If you work with multiple languages, add an alias attribute for each language. Please make sure that for each language, you use the same alias name for each dimension. If you have the same alias attribute per dimension per language, it is easier to create Excel sheet templates with multilanguage capability. In our solutions we use the "locale" name of a language for alias names (for example,"EN" for English, "DE" for German, "FR" for French, and so on).

For time dimensions like Months, Years, Periods, and so on, we recommend adding the attributes "prev" and "next." These attributes help you to calculate with previous/next periods in Rules or in Excel sheets. If you use the "prev" attribute in Rules to calculate with the previous Period, you often need the "next" attribute in a corresponding feeder as a counterpart (and the reverse).

Sequences of Dimensions

Here we would like to remind you of the suggested sequence of dimensions mentioned in Chapter 5:

- Versions/scenarios
- Years
- Periods
- Others
- Organizations
- Organizations IC
- Positions
- Measures

Handling Messages

When we talk about messages, we mean messages that are generated by TurboIntegrator processes. There are two kinds of messages: server-side and client-side.

Server-Side Messages

We add a protocol cube to our models to hold messages that are inserted by TurboIntegrator processes. One dimension of the cube is the system dimension "}Processes" (other dimensions are timestamp and a "measure" dimension with elements like message, message code, and/ or message type (INFO, WARNING, ERROR). The name of the process that generates the message can be evaluated by using the TurboIntegrator function GetProcessName(). We do not write directly into the message cube, but we provide a Turbo Integrator process that does this work and is run by ExecuteProcess from other TurboIntegrator processes.

Client-Side Messages

If a user starts a process by clicking an Action button, you want to inform the user about the status of this process, but not just with "OK" and "Not OK." In the Action Button Properties dialog you can set messages for "Success," "Failure," and "Confirmation." In the following illustration, you can see that the messages are entered as text in the Process Options dialog (a child dialog of Action Button Properties).

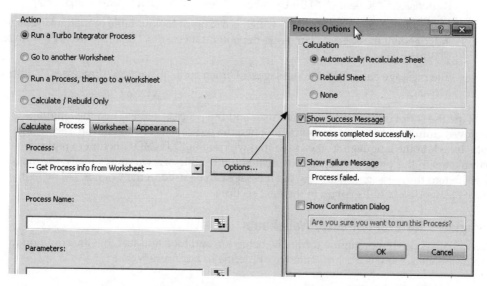

You can make this user message more flexible if you enter an Excel cell reference instead. The cell reference should be a cell that refers to a message cube. (We will introduce an example in the next section). At this point the handling of client messages is similar to server messages. We create a message cube that consists of the system dimension "}Clients," the system dimension "}Processes," and a "Message Measure" dimension. With these dimensions, you can create user-specific messages. The message cube can hold only the last message. If you want to have a message history, you can also add the message to a server message cube. Here is a code segment to show how we populate a message cube:

```
sMessageCube = 'TBB TI Messages';
sStringCube = 'TBB Strings';
sParameterCube = 'TBB User Parameters';
sUser = TM1USER();
sThisProcess = GETPROCESSNAME();
sLanguage = CELLGETS(sParameterCube,sUser,'TBB Language','S');
IF ( sLanguage @= '' );
  sLanguage = 'EN';
ENDIF;
 . .
sMessageParameter1 = …;
sMessage = EXPAND(CELLGETS(sStringCube, 'TBB Message 1001', sLanguage));
CELLPUTS(sMessage, sMessageCube, sUser, sThisProcess, 'Message');
 . .
```

This code handles the language of the user. There are three cubes involved:

- The control cube "TBB User Parameters," which holds the language of the user. Dimensions: "}Clients," "TBB User Parameters," "TBB Parameter Values"

- The control cube "TBB Strings," which is a kind of lookup table to match language-independent messages to language-dependent messages. Dimensions: "TBB Strings," "TBB Languages"

- The message cube "TBB TI Messages." Dimension: "}Clients," "}Processes," "TBB TI Messages"

First the script evaluates the current user and the process name. Then the language is retrieved from the user's parameter cube. Then the message is retrieved from the String cube based on the language. You can see that we use the EXPAND function to replace parameters in the language-dependent string by the value of a variable. Finally, the message is written to the message cube. Now the message can be used in the Cognos TM1 client. How this works we will explain in the next section.

Templates for Excel Sheets/Websheets

A template is used to predefine formulas, behavior, and look and feel that are common to multiple sheets. Here is a list of what we predefine in our framework:

- Name of the server
- Name of the user
- Names of control cubes that are often used (for example, message cubes, parameter cubes)
- Action buttons with standard functions (for example, go back to the calling sheet)
- Ranges to handle messages
- Colors/palette
- Titles and headers

All predefinitions can be positioned on the template sheet into a range that can be hidden later on the final Excel/Websheet. An alternative is to put all predefinitions on an extra sheet and hide the whole sheet in the final version.

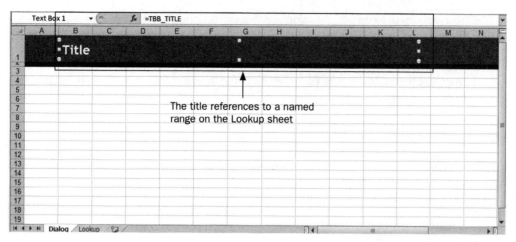

Dialog sheet of a template workbook

The preceding and following illustrations show a sample template. As in this template, we recommend using named cells/ranges as often you can. Especially if you use references in Action button properties, you should use names. The reason is that the references saved with the Action button properties are not updated when a referenced cell is moved. After you insert or remove cells from the Excel sheet, the Action button may refer to cells other than what you intended. The references of a name are always up to date and maintained by Excel.

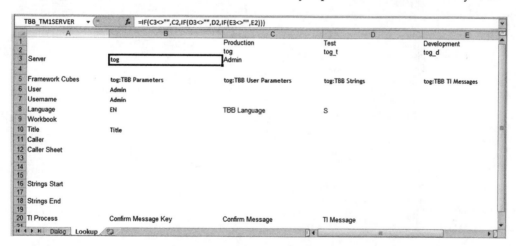

Lookup sheet of a template workbook

Now we want to use a template for our solution. There are two ways to use a template:

- You can create your sheet by slicing a Cube Viewer view to an Excel sheet. After you have your TM1 cell references arranged in the sheet, you can copy your predefinitions from the template to the new sheet. Now you can use Action buttons, names, strings, and messages to finalize the sheet.

- You can create a copy of the template as a starting point. Now you can add slices to the sheet by using the TM1 Add-In function "Insert Active Form" (right-click in the Excel cell where you want to position the slice; choose Active Form | Insert Active Form; select a view from the dialog). (Hint: Populate at least one cell of the Title rows to prevent the Active Form from overwriting the title.) Go on with Action buttons, names, strings, and messages.

As you can see, both versions need many manual steps. You can simplify that by building a library of Excel macros that automate these steps.

We would like to demonstrate the creation of a new sheet based on the template. For that we will use the second method. In addition, we will show you how to define standard Action buttons that could be part of a template and how you can use the messages.

Let's take a look at the following steps:

1. Create a copy of the template file.

2. Insert the Active Form.

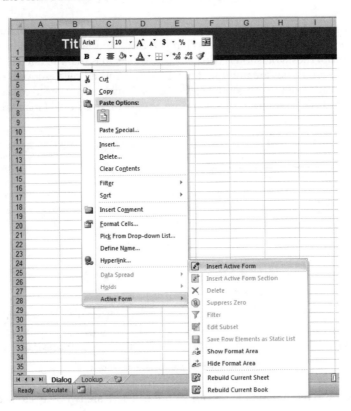

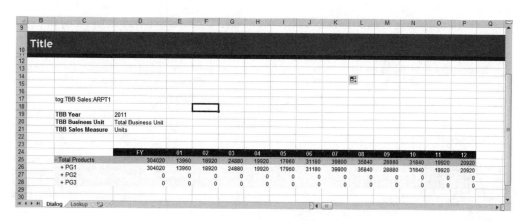

(Hint: If you want to have different standard colors for the Active Form, you can change the colors that are used in the format area of the active form in the palette of the template file.)

3. Insert a standard Action button to go to another sheet.

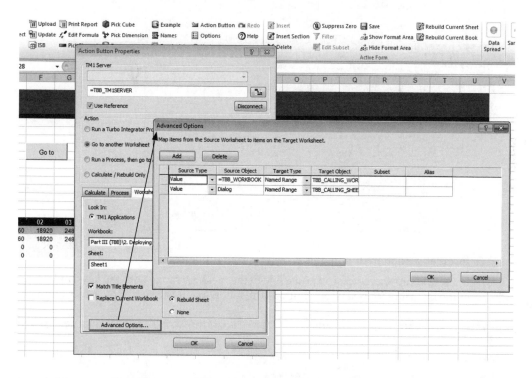

The preceding illustration shows how to provide values to the called sheet. These values are used for automatic navigation, which is explained later.

4. Insert an Action button to go back to the calling sheet.

The following illustration shows how you can use cell references for the name of the called workbook and worksheet. Again, we use names instead of native cell addresses.

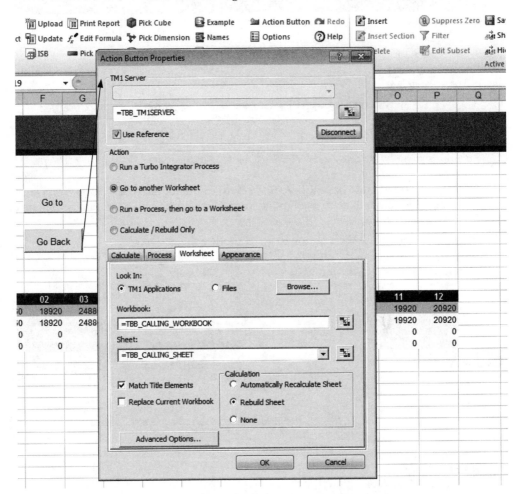

5. Insert an Action button that uses the message framework:

In the Lookup sheet, you can add a line in the message range with the keys and values of the messages for one Action button. The following illustration shows an example:

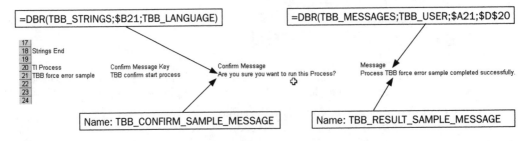

In the first column of the new line, you find the name of the Turbo Integrator process that should be run by the Action button. The name of the process is also used in the fourth column to retrieve the message from the message cube. In the second column, we enter the name of an element name of the dimension "TBB Strings." In the third column the confirmation message is retrieved in the language version. The DBR formula uses the element name of the second column to identify the message. As we already recommended, we add names for the cells in columns three and four. Now we add the Action button and set the option "Action" to "Run a TurboIntegrator Process." In our example the TI process has one parameter. If you want to provide the parameter by the value of an Excel cell, you should always use Names. This is shown in the example in the following illustration.

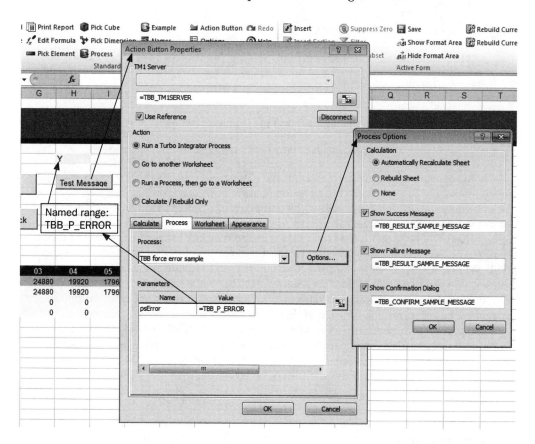

In the example we have used the same cell reference for the "Success Message" and the "Failure Message." This will work properly only if the called TI Process writes error messages to the messages cube just before the function ProcessError is executed and writes a success message just before the process terminates. Here is the code of the TI process of our example:

```
sMessageCube = 'TBB TI Messages';
sStringCube = 'TBB Strings';
sParameterCube = 'TBB User Parameters';
sUser = TM1User();
sThisProcess = GETPROCESSNAME();
sLanguage = CELLGETS(sParameterCube,sUser,'TBB Language','S');
IF ( sLanguage @= '' );
  sLanguage = 'EN';
ENDIF;
# Error message
IF ( psError @<> 'N' );
    sMessage = EXPAND(CELLGETS(sStringCube,
            'TBB TI standard error message', sLanguage));
    CELLPUTS(sMessage, sMessageCube, sUser, sThisProcess, 'Message');

    PROCESSERROR;
ENDIF;
# Success message
sMessage = EXPAND(CELLGETS (sStringCube, 'TBB TI standard success message',
sLanguage));
CELLPUTS (sMessage, sMessageCube, sUser, sThisProcess, 'Message');
```

There are some additional points about the navigation buttons in Step 3 and 4: There is a dependency between the Go To button (Step 3) and the Go Back button (Step 4). The Go Back button will work properly only if the named range "TBB_CALLING_WORKBOOK" is set to a valid workbook name. (The "TBB_CALLING_SHEET" can be empty. In this case the default sheet will be shown.) If a workbook is called by a Go To button, the named range "TBB_CALLING_WORKBOOK" is set by the Action button (assuming the named range "TBB_WORKBOOK" is set to the correct value). If your template already has these two buttons, you just need to maintain the lookup cell TBB_WORKBOOK. If you want to go from one worksheet to various worksheets, you just have to copy the Go To button and change the target workbook for each of them.

Finally, we recommend using the name "TBB_TM1SERVER" instead of the literal server name in all Cognos TM1 formulas if you want to make sure that your Excel sheets can work with various Cognos TM1 servers (for example, production, test, and development). The following formulas are candidates to replace the server name by the named reference:

- VIEW
- SUBNM
- TM1RPTVIEW
- TM1RPTTITLE
- TM1RPTROW
- TM1USER

Here is an example of how a TM1RPTVIEW formula should look:

```
=TM1RPTVIEW(TBB_TM1SERVER & ":TBB Sales:ARPT1"; 0;
TM1RPTTITLE(TBB_TM1SERVER & ":TBB Year";$D$19);
TM1RPTTITLE(TBB_TM1SERVER & ":TBB Business Unit";$D$20);
TM1RPTTITLE(TBB_TM1SERVER & ":TBB Sales Measure";$D$21);
TM1RPTFMTRNG;TM1RPTFMTIDCOL)
```

As you can see, this is a great deal of work if you do this manually. We recommend using the Find and Replace function or creating a macro.

Summary

In this chapter we looked at how to assemble the building blocks to have a whole Cognos TM1 solution. As the front end of a solution is very important for the user's acceptance, we discussed the usage of Microsoft Excel as a front-end editor. For the assembly of the building blocks, we recommend creating the framework first. The conventions of a common framework help to make maintenance and enhancements easier.

PART II

## 9

CHAPTER

Enhancing the User Experience

The goal of this chapter is to continue our conversation about developing Cognos TM1-based solutions. With the release of Cognos TM1 10.1, there are exciting new application development tools that will ease the development of Cognos TM1-based applications but will also enrich the application environment for users. These new tools include Cognos TM1 Performance Modeler and Cognos Insight as well as integration with Cognos Business Insight, which gives application developers a rich toolbox to develop industry-leading planning and analysis applications. So let's begin our discussion with Performance Modeler.

Cognos TM1 Performance Modeler

Cognos TM1 Performance Modeler is an application development environment that extends the current Cognos TM1 toolset by creating a guided development environment that makes it easier to create planning and analysis applications. The goal for this modern development environment is to support and promote prototyping and experimentation and make application design more accessible. Cognos TM1 Performance Modeler uses a simple notion (see Figure 9-1) of a guided modeling and application development environment that can deploy a variety of integrated applications. Cognos TM1 applications share a single multicube architecture; therefore, as your models evolve, your application will inherit these changes in business logic, metadata, and data, reducing your application maintenance and creating more agile applications to meet your organization's requirements.

To support this integrated application view for development, Cognos TM1 Performance Modeler provides a guided development process through two main steps, or modes: *model design* and *application design*. For readers who are familiar with Cognos TM1 Contributor Administrator, Cognos TM1 Performance Modeler is the next generation of this development environment, which not only allows the deployment of Contributor-style applications, but also a broader range of planning and analysis solutions coupled with a new modeling environment. Let's start with the basics of model design.

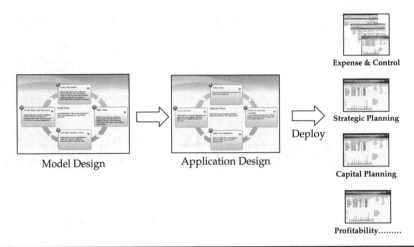

Expense & Control

Strategic Planning

Deploy

Capital Planning

Profitability.........

Model Design

Application Design

FIGURE 9-1 Model-to-application relationship

Performance Modeler is launched from the Cognos Application Portal, as shown in Figure 9-2.

Please note that you need administrator rights to the Cognos TM1 server to launch Cognos TM1 Performance Modeler (see Figure 9-3). Cognos TM1 Performance Modeler is an Eclipse-based Java client that will be provisioned the first time using the client.

After Cognos TM1 Performance Modeler is launched, you will be asked to select the TM1 server to log in to validate your credentials, as shown in Figure 9-4. You will be required to have administrator rights to the server in order to create and maintain Cognos TM1-based solutions.

Now that we have launched Cognos TM1 Performance Modeler and have logged in to the Cognos TM1 server, we want to develop an application. Let's start our journey in developing a TM1-based solution. The first step is developing our model.

FIGURE 9-2 Cognos Application Portal

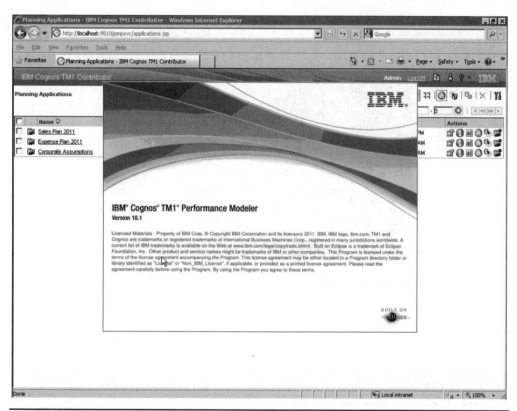

FIGURE 9-3   Launching Performance Modeler

Model Design

At the heart of every Cognos TM1 solution is a model. For our conversation in this chapter, a model is a collection of TM1 cubes that are linked together to solve a specific business problem. One of the advantages that Cognos TM1 Performance Modeler brings to Cognos TM1 is that it provides a guided process for the development of Cognos TM1 models. This process includes four steps (see Figure 9-5):

1. Define dimensions

2. Build cubes

3. Link data between cubes

4. Create rules and processes

The development environment has three main panels, which include a *navigation panel* on the left that displays all Cognos TM1 objects; a *center panel*, which provides a guided process for model creation; and a *properties panel* below the center panel, which displays key information on the objects developed. We will discuss the properties panel in more detail shortly.

Let's take a look at each of these steps in a little more detail and highlight some of the key advantages Cognos TM1 Performance Modeler provides in model development.

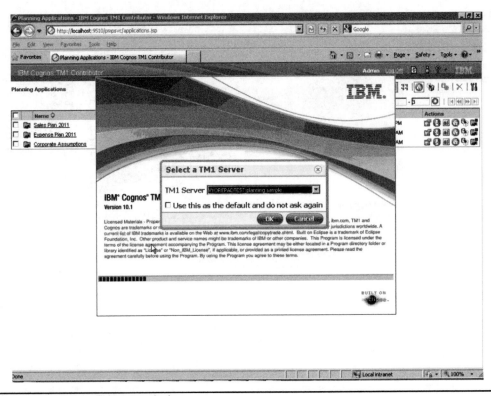

FIGURE 9-4   Cognos TM1 server login

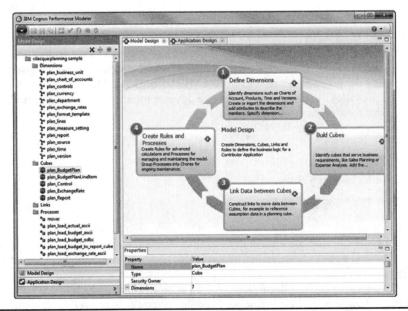

FIGURE 9-5   Performance Modeler model design environment

Defining Model Dimensions

The first step in any Cognos TM1-based model is to define dimensions. With the release of Cognos TM1 Performance Modeler, we now support a number of dimension types, which include the following:

- **Basic** The *basic dimension* is the default type of a Cognos TM1 dimension that was previously defined outside of Performance Modeler.

- **Generic** A *generic dimension* contains general members, such as lists of department products, or customers. A generic dimension can be used when you do not know the precise dimension type.

- **Hierarchy** A *hierarchy dimension* represents a child-parent relationship between element structures that can be used for workflow or reporting structure for summary levels.

- **Calculation** A new *calculation dimension* contains formulas that perform mathematical and other operations on your data. For example, you can use calculation dimensions to set up profit and loss statements for your company or when you use pick lists to provide structured data entry to end users.

- **Time** A *time dimension* contains time members that are meaningful to your users, such as financial accounting periods or the dates of sales transactions.

- **Version** A *versions dimension* contains data from various iterations of a member in an application. Some common examples are actual, budget, forecast, and calculated members for variance analysis such as Actual versus Forecast, and so on.

Each of these dimension types will contain specific attributes that will drive specific behavior within your model. These dimension types can also be changed after their creation, allowing a developer to prototype and to experiment with different logic. Let's look at each of these types in a little more detail as we review the creation of a dimension in Cognos TM1 Performance Modeler.

Creating Hierarchy Dimensions Dimensions can be created in Performance Modeler in three main ways: manually, by importation, and by automation through a process or chore. Since processes and chores were covered in previous chapters, we will focus on manual creation and guided imports. This chapter will focus on the four new dimension types (hierarchy, time, calculation, and version) introduced in the current release of Cognos TM1 Performance Modeler, given the simplicity of both generic and basic dimensions. So let's begin with a hierarchy dimension, which is commonly used for dimensions that have parent-child relationships between members. Some common examples are Approval hierarchies to be used in workflow applications like product families, organizational structures, or perhaps a chart of accounts. Figure 9-6 shows that a dimension can be created by right-clicking in the TM1 object panel. From here you can see a number of options. For this example, we select New and then Dimension. This process is the same for creating all Cognos TM1 objects.

The first step in creating your new dimension is to select a name and then the dimension type. For our example, we will create a Channel dimension, which is a Hierarchy type dimension, as shown in Figure 9-7.

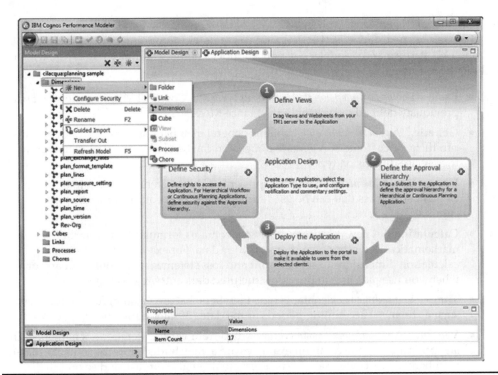

Figure 9-6   Dimension creation

A hierarchy dimension allows the creation of parent-child relationships. As you can see in Figure 9-8, the default is a weight of 1.0, but it can be changed to –1 to represent a scenario like Cost of Goods Sold Netting with Sales when both are rolling into parent Gross Margin, or it can be increased or decreased based on your business requirements.

Also there is a new properties panel below the center panel that displays the key attributes of the elements. For example, this dimension has a

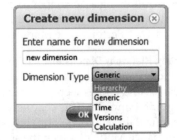

Figure 9-7   Creating a hierarchy dimension

number of attributes like aliases for BusinessUnit in various languages, as well as text attributes for currency, as shown in Figure 9-9. These attributes can be organized as well as selected for viewing.

Let's review and add some new member properties. As shown in Figure 9-10, you can easily customize the property columns you want to see. For example, let's display BusinessUnit, Index, Weight, and Invariant Name, as well as set BusinessUnit alias as the default to make it easier to build views later.

If we select all five properties, the following columns will be displayed, as shown in Figure 9-11. Note that the Index and Invariant Name are system-assigned; this is represented through shading and cannot be changed.

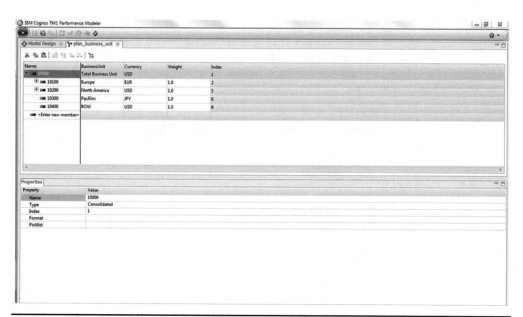

FIGURE 9-8 Default weight of a hierarchy dimension

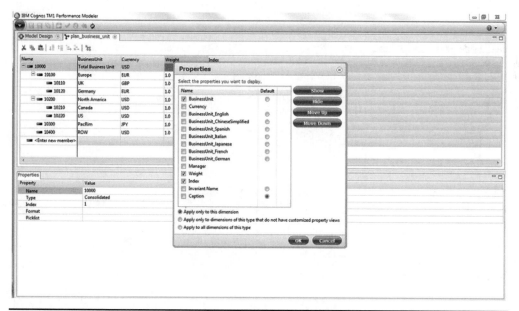

FIGURE 9-9 Dimension attributes

FIGURE 9-10 Customizing the display of property columns

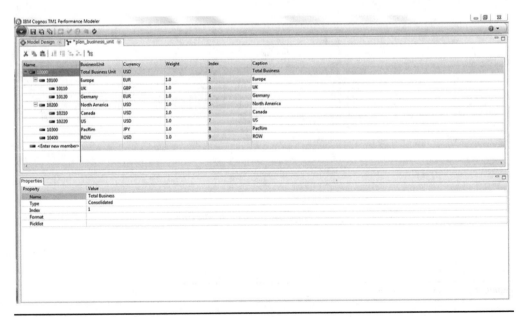

FIGURE 9-11 Property columns

Now let's create a new element called 10500, which represents South America, as shown in Figure 9-12. This is a simple process of selecting the cell and typing in the new element.

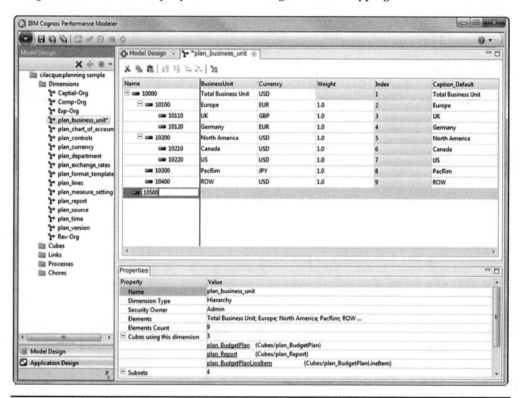

FIGURE 9-12   Creating a new element

Now that we have a new element, we can change the alias and caption to a more specific term like South America, remembering that this is what will be displayed when the user hovers over this element. Again, the editing of an alias and caption is done by selecting the cell and typing in the text as shown in Figure 9-13.

We have one last step, which is to add 10500/South America to the 10000/Total Business Unit. This can be done in a number of ways, but we will select Demote Selected Members from the context menu (see Figure 9-14). Also note that there are a large number of other options not only to navigate through large dimension sets but also to change their relationship and add additional attributes.

And finally, let's save this dimension and move on to our discussion on the other three new dimension types. When you exit the dimension, you will be prompted to save changes, as seen in Figure 9-15 with the default of Yes highlighted.

Now let's take a look at creating a time dimension.

Creating Time Dimensions   Earlier we mentioned that time dimensions are assigned to help manage the aggregation of data by a specific period. These periods can be calendar-based, fiscally based, or based on the solution periodicity. One of the values of Cognos TM1

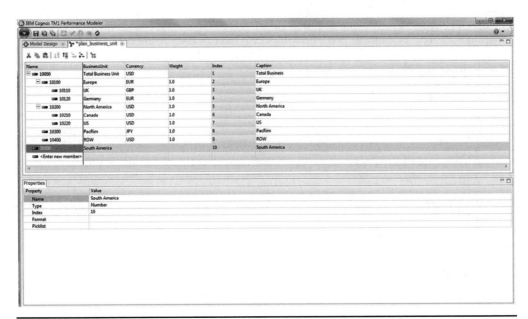

FIGURE 9-13   Editing an alias and caption

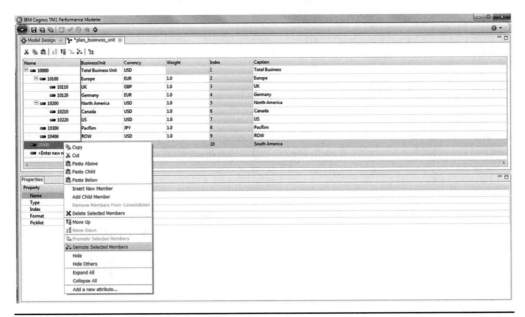

FIGURE 9-14   Adding the alias

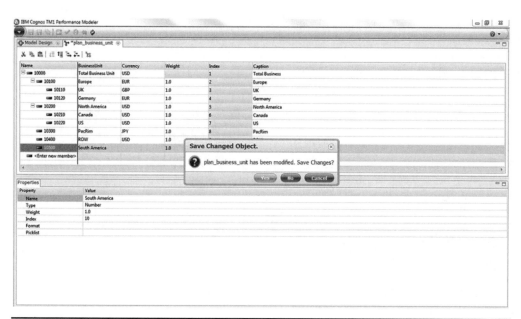

Figure 9-15   Saving changes

Performance Modeler is the new dimension types, which have predefined attributes to help speed up the development of dimension logic. In our example we have created a time dimension named plan_fiscal_year (see Figure 9-16).

In Figure 9-17, you can see the specific attributes for a time dimension. They include Start Date, End Date, Last Period, First Period, Previous Period, and Next Period. Each of these attributes provides parameters to generate time elements. For additional information on these attributes, please refer to the user manual for Cognos TM1 Performance Modeler.

Figure 9-16   Creating a time dimension

So let's begin generating our new time dimension using the new Time Dimension tool, which will generate time elements based on period level, duration, and member names. Let's generate a time dimension that supports a monthly rollup to year by quarters for 2011 and 2012. The first step is to define the Period level; in this case, we will be selecting years, quarters and months, which is our lowest level of periodicity, as shown in Figure 9-18.

Now let's move on to duration, and since we would like this time dimension to span 2011 and 2012, we have selected Jan 1, 2011 to Dec 31, 2012 as shown in Figure 9-19.

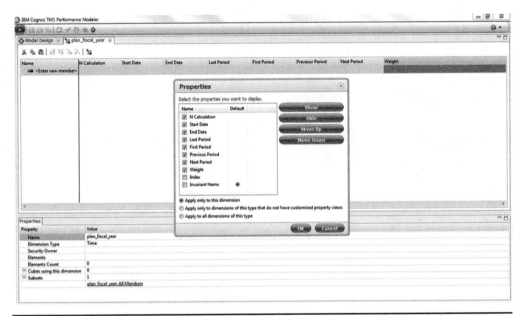

FIGURE 9-17   Time dimension attributes

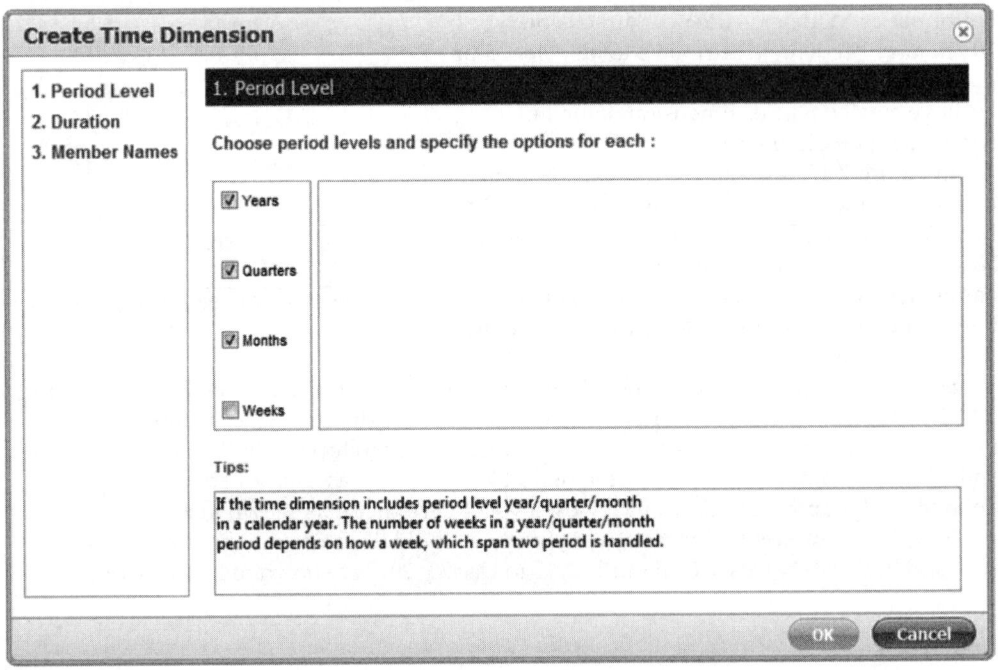

Create Time Dimension

1. Period Level
2. Duration
3. Member Names

1. Period Level

Choose period levels and specify the options for each :

☑ Years

☑ Quarters

☑ Months

☐ Weeks

Tips:

If the time dimension includes period level year/quarter/month
in a calendar year. The number of weeks in a year/quarter/month
period depends on how a week, which span two period is handled.

OK   Cancel

FIGURE 9-18   Period level

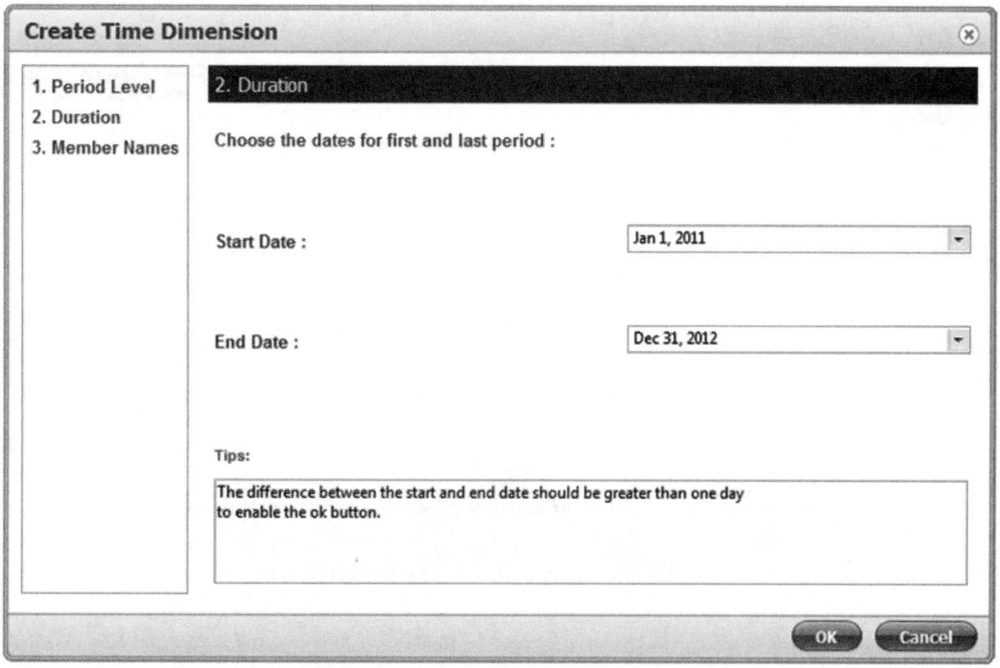

FIGURE 9-19 Time dimension duration

Our final step is to define the member naming convention. Cognos TM1 Performance Modeler provides a number of ways to format, prefix, and suffix your member names. As shown in Figure 9-20, we have selected the default format for member names.

When you click the OK button, the 34 elements are generated with proper parent-child relations defined, as shown in Figure 9-21. Also, additional attributes can still be added or modified after generation. Attributes like Previous Period and Next Period can be leveraged when designing TM1 business logic (rules, TI processes) to navigate data along the time dimension.

Creating Version Dimensions   Now let's turn our attention to how Cognos TM1 Performance Modeler helps define version dimensions. As mentioned earlier, version dimensions are commonly used to create alternatives or categories of plans and analysis, or to compare different versions of similar data.

Most often, version dimensions are used for gap or variance analysis between actual data and a budget or forecast. Given their popular use in planning and analysis solutions, a new dimension type has been created to make it easier to create them. A version dimension has the following default attributes:

- Name (member name)
- Format (user-defined: number, date/time and text formats)
- Version calculation
- Weight

Create Time Dimension

| 1. Period Level |
| 2. Duration |
| 3. Member Names |

3. Member Names

Choose the naming pattern for the selected period :

Member name
Years : 2011-12
Quarters : Q4 2011-12
Months : 12 2011-12

Format : yyyy-yy ▼

Prefix :

Suffix :

Tips:

Use the above tree to select the different period to specify the naming pattern for the members in a period.
Date Format is available for only Week period.
Format is available for all periods except Quarter.

OK   Cancel

FIGURE 9-20 Member names

IBM Cognos TM1 Performance Modeler

Model Design | plan_fiscal_year

Name	N Calculation	Start Date	End Date	Last Period	First Period	Previous Period	Next Period	Weight
2011		Jan 1, 2011	Dec 31, 2011	Q4 2011	Q1 2011		2012	
Q1 2011		Jan 1, 2011	Mar 31, 2011	Mar 2011	Jan 2011		Q2 2011	1.0
Jan 2011		Jan 1, 2011	Jan 31, 2011				Feb 2011	1.0
Feb 2011		Feb 1, 2011	Feb 28, 2011			Jan 2011	Mar 2011	1.0
Mar 2011		Mar 1, 2011	Mar 31, 2011			Feb 2011	Apr 2011	1.0
Q2 2011		Apr 1, 2011	Jun 30, 2011	Jun 2011	Apr 2011	Q1 2011	Q3 2011	1.0
Apr 2011		Apr 1, 2011	Apr 30, 2011			Mar 2011	May 2011	1.0
May 2011		May 1, 2011	May 31, 2011			Apr 2011	Jun 2011	1.0
Jun 2011		Jun 1, 2011	Jun 30, 2011			May 2011	Jul 2011	1.0
Q3 2011		Jul 1, 2011	Sep 30, 2011	Sep 2011	Jul 2011	Q2 2011	Q4 2011	1.0
Jul 2011		Jul 1, 2011	Jul 31, 2011			Jun 2011	Aug 2011	1.0
Aug 2011		Aug 1, 2011	Aug 31, 2011			Jul 2011	Sep 2011	1.0
Sep 2011		Sep 1, 2011	Sep 30, 2011			Aug 2011	Oct 2011	1.0
Q4 2011		Oct 1, 2011	Dec 31, 2011	Dec 2011	Oct 2011	Q3 2011	Q1 2012	1.0
2012		Jan 1, 2012	Dec 31, 2012	Q4 2012	Q1 2012	2011		
Q1 2012		Jan 1, 2012	Mar 31, 2012	Mar 2012	Jan 2012	Q4 2011	Q2 2012	1.0

Properties

Property	Value
Name	2012
Type	Consolidated
Index	18
Format	
Picklist	
N Calculation	
Start Date	Jan 1, 2012
End Date	Dec 31, 2012
Last Period	Q4 2012
First Period	Q1 2012

FIGURE 9-21 Generated time dimension

Let's create a version dimension named plan_type that will include actual, budget, forecast, and two calculated members to track variances of budget and forecast from actual results. These will be named ActvsBud and ActvsForc, as shown in Figure 9-22.

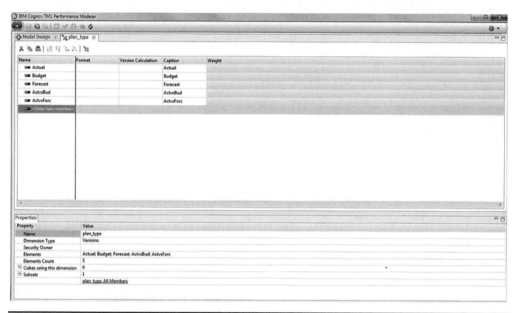

FIGURE 9-22   Version dimension

As with any Cognos TM1-based dimension, you can add additional attributes that are text, numeric, and/or an alias. In this example we will not need to extend the default attributes. Now let's focus on a new attribute, the version calculation. The version calculation has an editor that can be invoked by selecting the Version Calculation field for a particular element, for example, the ActvsBud member. The editor appears as an additional tab in the properties panel, as shown in Figure 9-23.

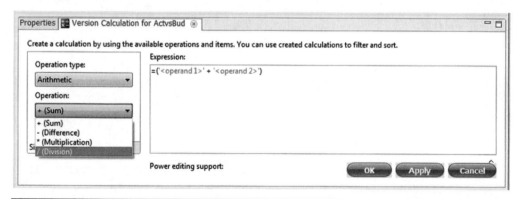

FIGURE 9-23   Version Calculation editor

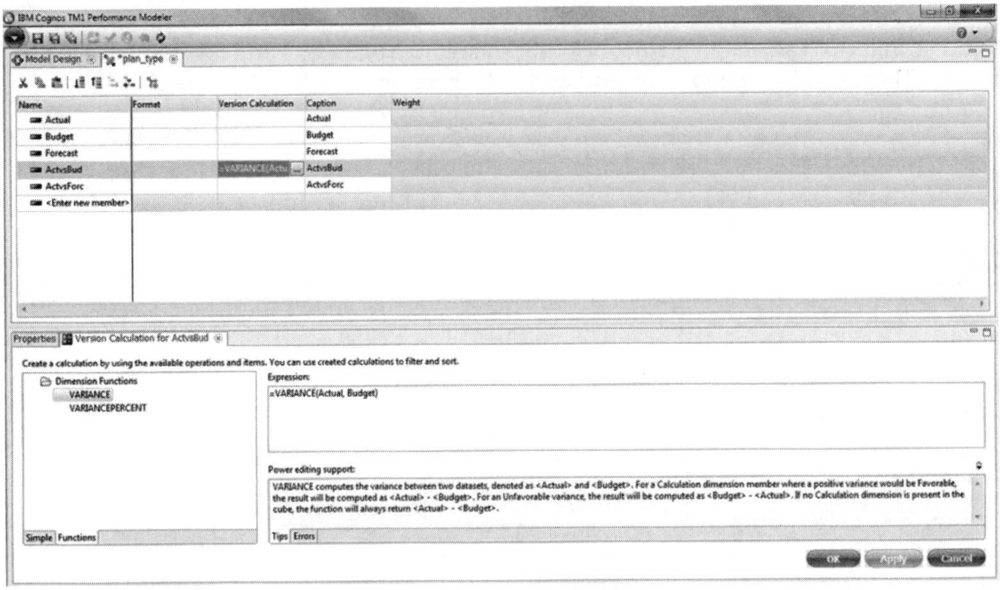

FIGURE 9-24 Variance calculation

The editor supports simple calculations, but it also supports dimension functions, as shown in Figure 9-24. For our example we will use the VARIANCE function to define ActvsBud.

We have repeated the process using the VARIANCE function for the dimension ActvsForc, as shown in Figure 9-25.

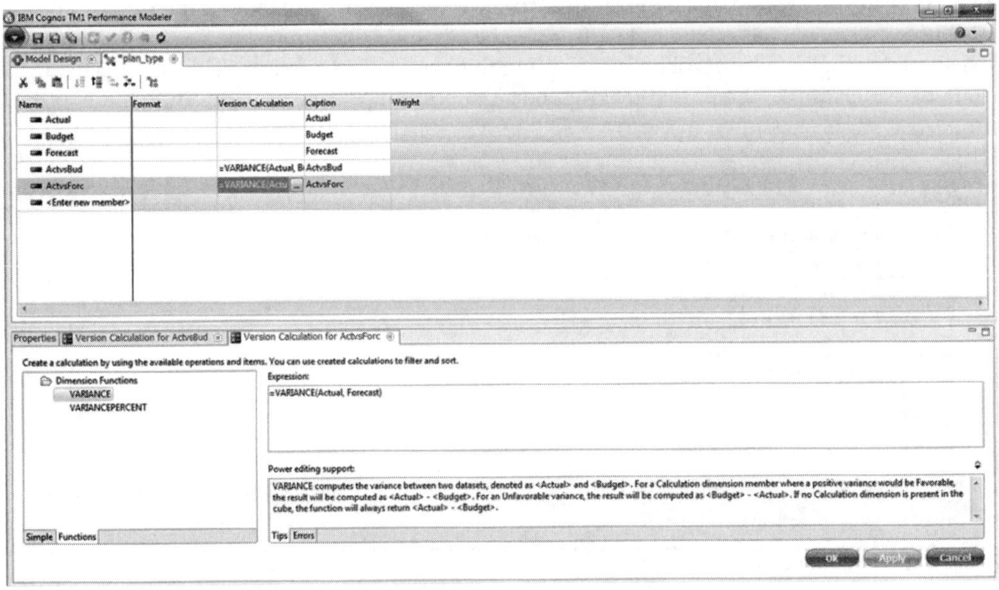

FIGURE 9-25 Defining ActvsForc

Now let's save our version dimension and move on to our last new dimension type introduced in Cognos TM1 Performance Modeler, the calculation dimension.

Creating Calculation Dimensions   Calculation dimensions, also known more generally as measure dimensions, are typically defined for calculations and measurements on numeric data. For example, you might use a calculation dimension for a profit and loss dimension where calculations beyond the typical hierarchy aggregations are needed. Calculated dimensions have the following predefined attributes:

- **Name**   The member name
- **Format**   User-defined: number, date/time and text formats
- **Pick list**   A link to a predefined dimension or subset
- **Nature of positive variance**   The result of a positive value, either favorable or unfavorable. This attribute is only used in conjunction with a version dimension. For example, a positive value for sales and price would be favorable, but a positive value for cost of sales would be unfavorable.
- **N calculation**   A simple calculation performed at the leaf level.
- **C calculation**   A calculation performed on aggregated results.
- **Weight**   A factor usually of minus 1 applied to change a positive value to a negative value. For example, if the unit price for a product is EUR 50 and the discount is EUR 5, a weight of –1 applied to the discount keeps an addition result logical.
- **Index**   A numerical value to allow quick access to the members.

As with all dimensions, these attributes can be changed to meet your specific application requirements. Now let's take a look at a calculated dimension in Figure 9-26. The plan_p&l dimension contains a hierarchy of key elements in a profit and loss statement. This starts with key consolidated elements such as Net Operating Income, Revenue, Cost of Sales (COS), Operating Expense, and so on. These all roll up from specific cost centers, except Adv & Marketing, which is calculated as a percentage of revenue.

A new feature in Performance Modeler is the ability to have calculations at the element level beyond a weighted aggregation. The calculation editor supports a broad range of arithmetic and average functions (see Figure 9-27). These are complemented by supported Cognos TM1 functions that are available on the tab in the properties panel.

In our example we will be allocating advertising and marketing expenses as a percentage of revenue. Although the Performance Modeler provides an easy drag-and-drop expression editor, you are free to edit and type your expressions as well. In this example we will do a little of both, as shown in Figure 9-28.

In this example we have created an allocation calculation for Adv & Marketing as percentage revenue. This new approach will allow all cubes built on the basis of this dimension to inherit the calculation. Now that we have reviewed the new dimension types, let's move on to the second step in model design, which is building cubes.

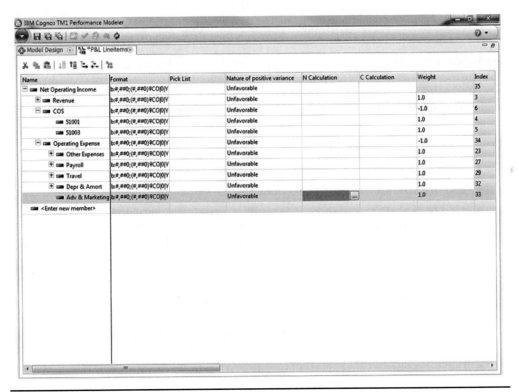

FIGURE 9-26 Calculated dimension

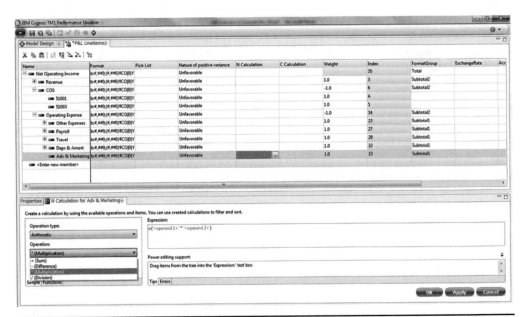

FIGURE 9-27 Calculation editor

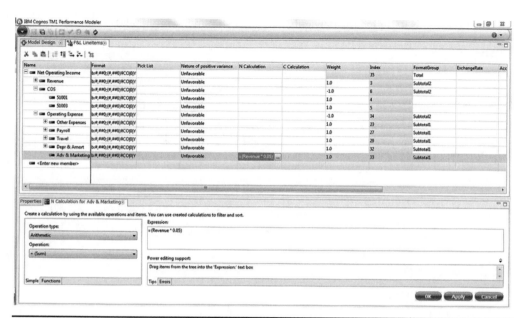

FIGURE 9-28   Adv & Marketing calculation definition

Building Cubes

Performance Modeler has a number of innovations to help facilitate cube building in Cognos TM1. Let's start off by building our plan_p&l cube, which will hold a consolidated p&l for our application, as shown in Figure 9-29.

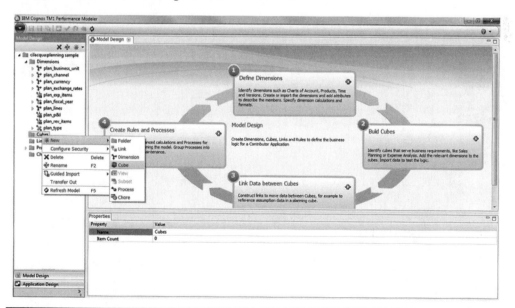

FIGURE 9-29   Building a new cube

The first step is to define the new cube name, as shown in Figure 9-30.

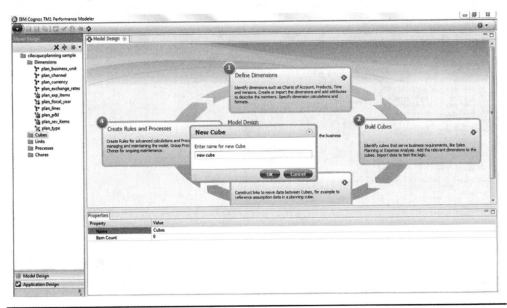

FIGURE 9-30 Defining a new cube

One of the new innovations with Performance Modeler is the WYSWIG cube designer. The cube designer, shown in Figure 9-31, provides all the capabilities to build a Cognos TM1 cube with easy-to-use drag-and-drop features. As you can see, there are drag-and-drop

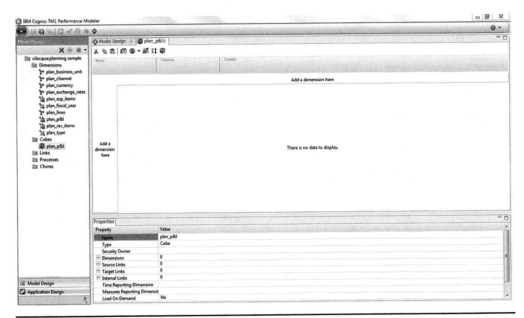

FIGURE 9-31 Cube designer

areas for the row, column, and context areas where dimensions can be placed to build Cognos TM1 cube structures.

So with that, let's start to build our plan_p&l cube. As shown in Figure 9-32, the analyst has placed the plan_p&l dimension on the rows and has dragged the plan_fiscal_year onto the columns.

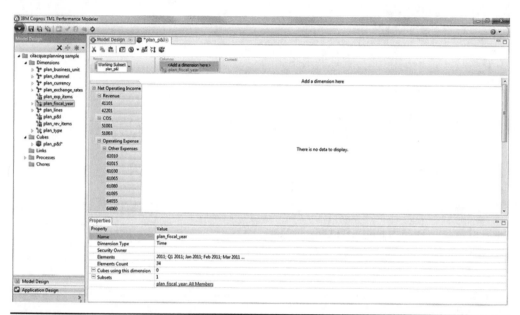

FIGURE 9-32   Building the plan_p&l cube

Our final dimension for this cube will be plan_type, which we will use for storage and P&L variance analysis from our planning process. One of the advantages of this approach is the interactive nature of cube building in Performance Modeler. A developer is able to interact with both the structure and data at the same time as well as optimize the cube structure for better performance through reordering cube dimensions and the cube optimizer, as shown in Figure 9-33.

For example, in the creation of the plan_p&l dimension, the item Adv & Marketing is a calculated element, which is 5 percent of revenue allocated to this expense. With Performance Modeler, an analyst can test calculations as part of the cube design approach. In Figure 9-34, an analyst has entered 100,000 in Revenue for Jan 2011. Adv & Marketing is automatically calculated as well as all defined aggregations. Although this is a very simple example, this capability will facilitate the development of complex cubes and calculations in advanced models.

After we have tested our cube calculations, we notice that we have forgotten an important dimension, plan_business_unit, which will not only allow us to plan and analyze on a business unit level but will be used as our approval hierarchy for planning submissions. Fortunately, one of the unique features of Performance Modeler is the ability to add or remove dimensions of cubes dynamically even if there is existing data in the cube. In this case, we have entered 100,000 dollars in revenue for account 41101 for Jan 2011 to test the Adv &

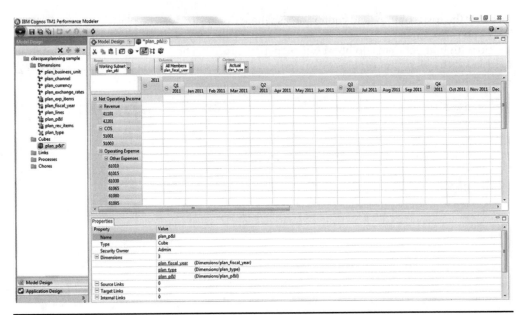

FIGURE 9-33   Structure of the plan_p&l dimension

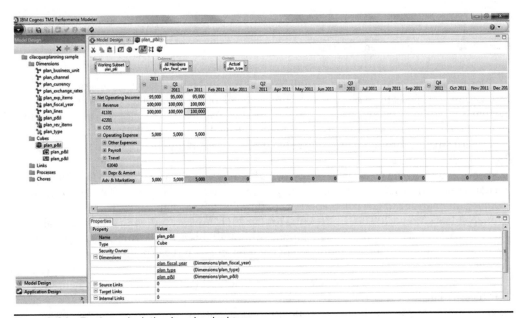

FIGURE 9-34   Testing calculation in cube designer

Marketing operating expense allocation. When you drag the plan_business_unit dimension to the content panel, Performance Modeler will ask the analyst where to allocate the current data, as shown in Figure 9-35.

In our simple case, the data is primarily test data, but if this were a redesign of an existing production cube, these options would become increasingly important if the cube is expanding to add additional dimensions like channels and so on. In this example, shown in Figure 9-36, the analyst will allocate all current data to the plan_business_unit element, which is Canada.

Let's take a closer look at what was generated by Performance Modeler for this cube. When this cube is saved, two new TM1 objects are generated—a default cube view with full access to the Subset Editor, as well as cube rules. Figure 9-37 shows the generated cube view, which has full access to

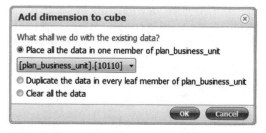

FIGURE 9-35   Add a dimension to a cube

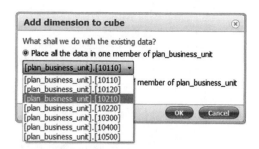

FIGURE 9-36   Adding a dimension data allocation

both the Subset Editor as well as the dimension editor. This allows an analyst to move seamlessly between cube views for application development and cube data structures in support of these cube views.

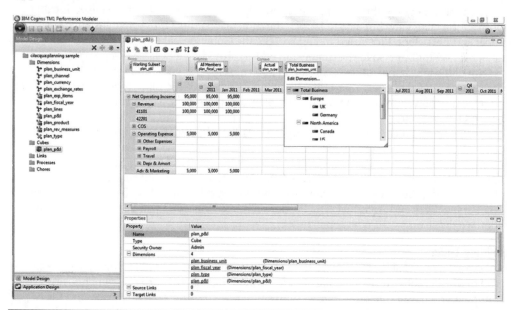

FIGURE 9-37   plan_p&l default cube view

As TM1 cube views are the building blocks of applications, the ability to create highly flexible cube rules is critical to delivering value in an application. Creating a cube view can be done quickly and easily by right-clicking on the cube object (see Figure 9-38).

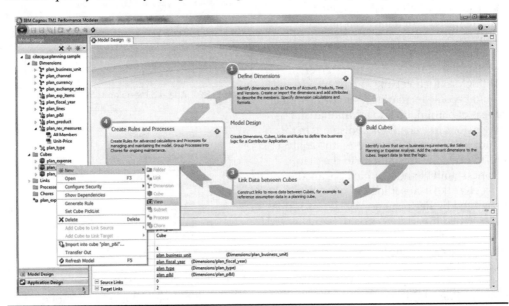

Figure 9-38   Creating a cube view

An advancement within Performance Modeler is the ability not only to create flexible subsets for a cube view but also to launch the dimension editor if the changes are more global and persistent. Illustrated in Figure 9-39, the Cube Viewer editor has access not only to the Subset Editor but also to the dimension editor, providing a holistic design environment.

Now let's take a look at the generated cube rules for this cube. In Figure 9-40, we see that rule sections were generated for calculated members of the plan_type, which used the variance function as well as the calculation element, the Adv & Marketing member of the plan_p&l dimension.

As we dive a bit deeper, we see in Figure 9-41 that the generated cube rules follow the same syntax that an analyst would generate in developing these calculated values.

Also, a rule and feeders are generated for the calculation of Adv & Marketing in the plan_p&l dimension, as shown in Figure 9-42. As with all generated rules, they cannot be edited, but the cube rules can be extended with the traditional TM1 cube editor found in TM1 Perspectives and Architect. The Feeder section of this cube will be further extended when we move on to our next topic, links.

Building Links

Links are a new capability designed to facilitate the movement of data from one cube to another or internally from one cube area to another. Based on your requirements, links can be implemented as a rule or as a process. We will be exploring each approach and the advantages and disadvantages to consider in a solution design. Performance Modeler

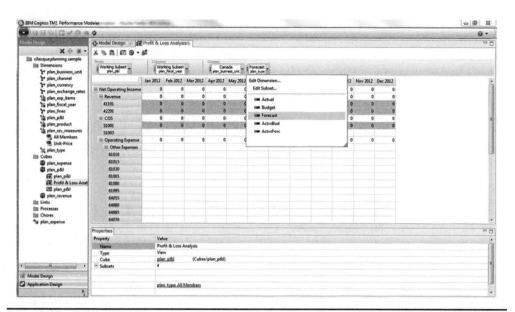

FIGURE 9-39   Editing dimension and subsets

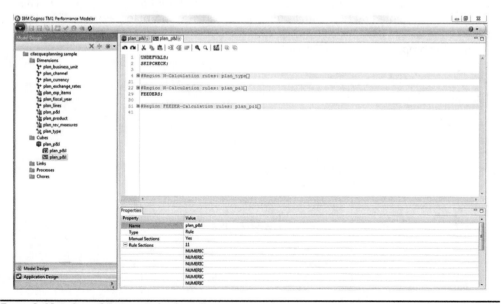

FIGURE 9-40   plan_p&l generated cube rules

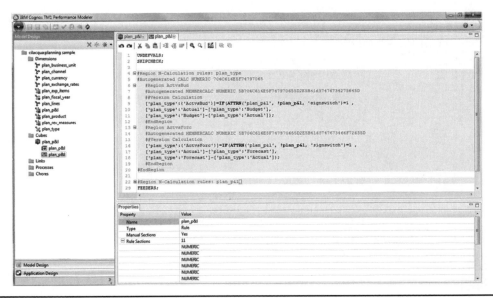

Figure 9-41   plan_type generated rules

supports both approaches in an easy WYSIWYG environment that is highly interactive. So with that, let's return to our application. Previously we had built the plan_p&l cube. This cube will be augmented by two source cubes, plan_expense and plan_revenue. The plan_ expense cube will be used for collecting expenses and is a three-dimensional cube, as shown in the properties panel in Figure 9-43.

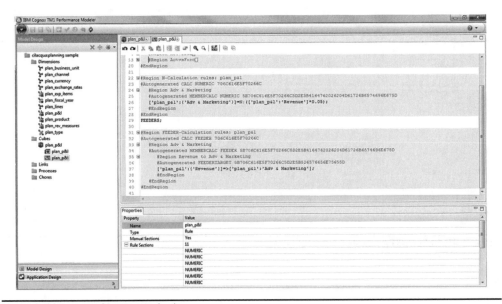

Figure 9-42   plan_p&l generated rules

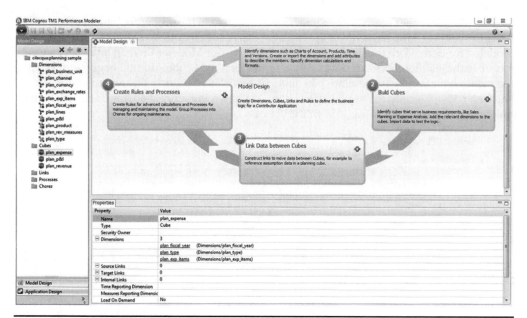

Figure 9-43   plan_expense cube

Similarly, the plan_revenue cube will be used to capture the revenue forecasts for the current period, as shown in Figure 9-44.

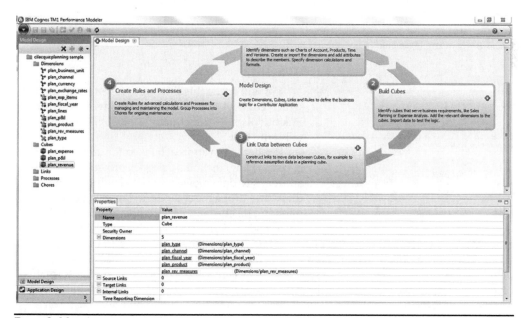

Figure 9-44   plan_revenue cube

The plan_revenue cube has five dimensions, as shown in the properties panel in Figure 9-44. Expenses and revenue have very different analysis requirements, so a different cube was modeled for each. With the flexibility of the Performance Modeler link, an analyst can easily reconcile these differences as a data source for the plan_p&l cube. We will begin with linking the plan_revenue cube to the plan_p&l cube. Our goal is to capture our revenue forecast and link it dynamically to the plan_p&l cube. As shown in Figure 9-45, the creation of a new link is as easy as right-clicking to start the process.

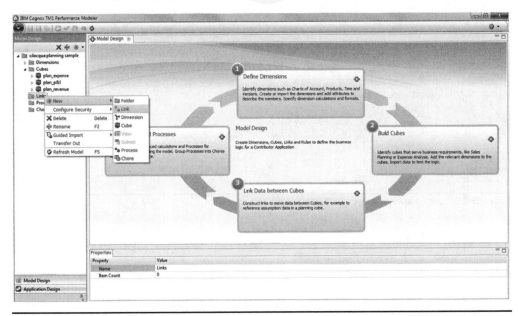

FIGURE 9-45 Creating a link

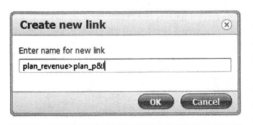

FIGURE 9-46 Naming a link

We will name this link plan_revenue>plan_p&l, which conveys not only the cubes involved with the link but also the direction of the data flow, as shown in Figure 9-46.

Similar to the approach taken for dimension and cube building, the links designer provides a visual approach to data movement. The analyst simply drags and drops the source and target cubes onto the mapping palette, and Performance Modeler will do a quick review of dimensions with common names in order to map elements. In this case, plan_business_unit, plan_fiscal_year, and plan_type are all automatically mapped, leaving plan_channel, plan_product, plan_rev_measures, and plan_p&l to be resolved by the analyst, as shown in Figure 9-47. Other important information on the link is available in the properties panel, also shown in Figure 9-47. This includes the security owner, the link implementation type (rules), and four validation errors based on differences of dimensionality between the cubes.

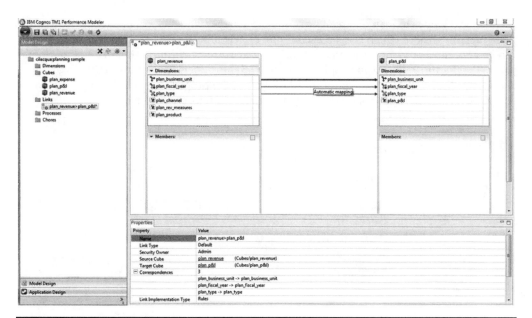

Figure 9-47   Defining mapping

So let's start with the plan_channel dimension. Given that our plan_p&l does not require plan_channel, we will select Total so that only an aggregate of all channel information is sent to the plan_p&l cube, as shown in Figure 9-48.

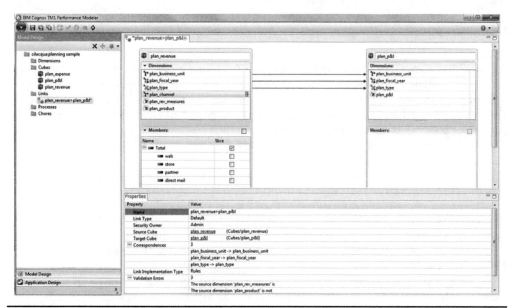

Figure 9-48   Total channel

The next step is to map our plan_revenue dimension, which is at a product level to our plan_p&l dimension, which is at an account level. Fortunately, Performance Modeler links can be very flexible to meet the types of mapping requirements through a manual mapping process. In Figure 9-49, the analyst has mapped Total Products to account 41101, Total Services to 42201, and COS to account 51001. And as the properties panel shows, we have one more dimension in the plan_revenue cube to account for in this link.

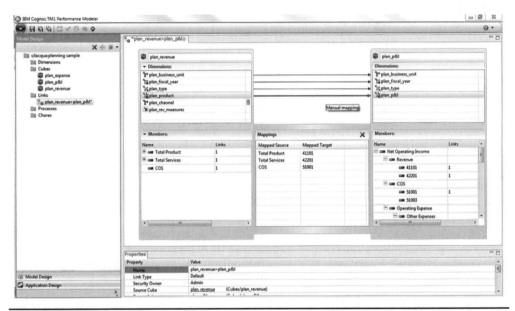

Figure 9-49 Manual mapping

Since the plan_revenue cube is the source for revenue forecasts, the plan_rev_measures dimension will be limited to provide just revenue. This is accomplished in the same way in which we limited the plan_channel dimension, with the selection of a single element. Figure 9-50 shows the selection of revenue, the resolution of all validation errors in the properties panel, and the saving of this link.

Our final step is to generate the rule to activate this link in our plan_p&l model, as shown in Figure 9-51.

Once the link rule is generated, it is available in the target cube, in this case plan_p&l as shown in Figure 9-52.

The Link Generate rule is no different than a cross-rule calculation that can be developed in the Cognos TM1 rules editor. The key difference is the ease with which it was generated for the developer. Now let's do a quick test to see if the plan_revenue>plan_p&l link is working. First let's enter the number of units forecasted for L Series 1.6 L Convertibles in plan_revenue for Jan 2012, as shown in Figure 9-53.

Note that when we entered 35 units for L Series 1.6 L Convertibles, the program immediately calculated revenue for the period and all aggregations. Also services are

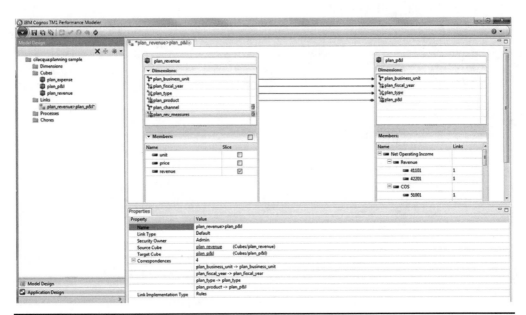

Figure 9-50   plan_rev_measures resolution

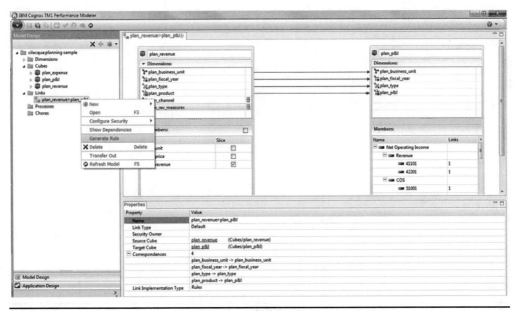

Figure 9-51   Generating the plan_revenue>plan_p&l link rule

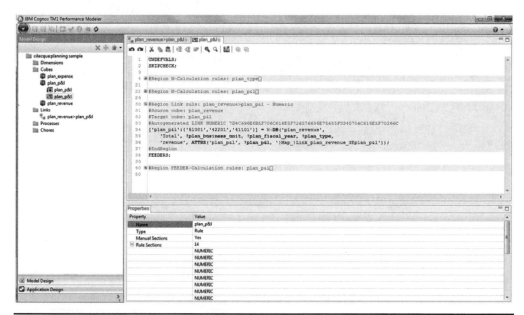

FIGURE 9-52   plan_revenue>plan_p&l Link Generate rule

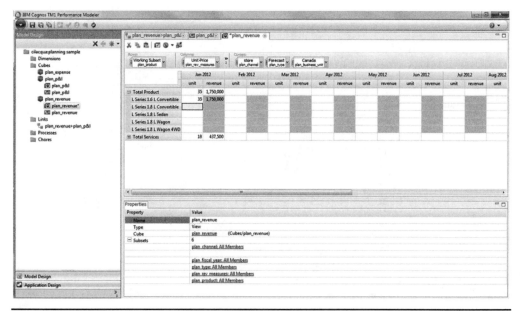

FIGURE 9-53   Entering units forecasted for L Series 1.6 L Convertibles

calculated as a percent of revenue by model. This is because revenue is a calculated member based on units and price. Figure 9-54 shows that account 41101 has a balance of 1,750,000, which is the Total Product revenue, as well as account 42201, which has a balance of 435,500, which is the Total Service revenue that was calculated by plan_revenue.

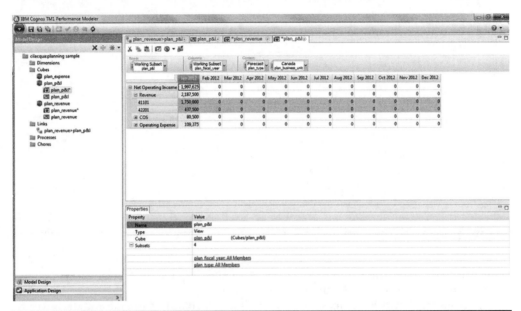

Figure 9-54   plan_p&l revenue validation

Rule-based links have a number of advantages and disadvantages that need to be considered when building an application. Rule-based links keep data in the source cube and reduce redundant data and data management across an application. If data changes in the source cube, then these changes are automatically reflected in the target cube. This creates a highly dynamic application. But there are some design considerations that we need to evaluate. Since this is a rule-based link, all data changes in this example must be done in the source cube, plan_revenue.

Now let's take a look at a process-based link for capturing expense-based data in our plan_p&l cube. One of the advantages of a process-based link is that data from the source cube is copied to the target cube. After you copy data from the source cube to the target cube by running the process, there is no longer a connection between the two cubes. You can freely edit data in either the source cube or target cube.

Based on this, let's create the plan_expense>plan_p&l link. The process for creation is the same as with plan_expense>plan_p&l link. As shown in Figure 9-55, Performance Modeler has automatically set associations between common dimensions.

Note that in the properties panel, the Link Implementation Type has been set to a process. As a result, this link definition will generate a process instead of a cube rule. Now let's turn our attention to the two link violations that need to be resolved before we can execute and test this link. Since the names of the final dimension between plan_expense and

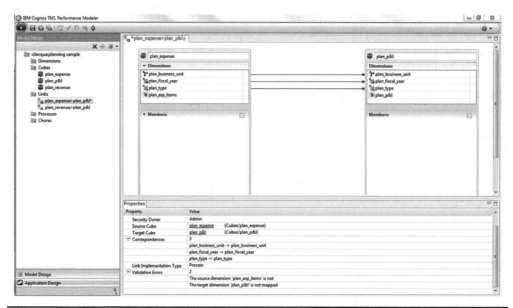

FIGURE 9-55 Creation of plan_expense>plan_p&l link

plan_p&l are different, the analyst will have to drag and drop the source dimension on the target dimension, as shown in Figure 9-56.

Although the dimension names are different, the contents are the same and the analyst can automatically map the expense accounts between the common dimension elements, as shown in Figure 9-57.

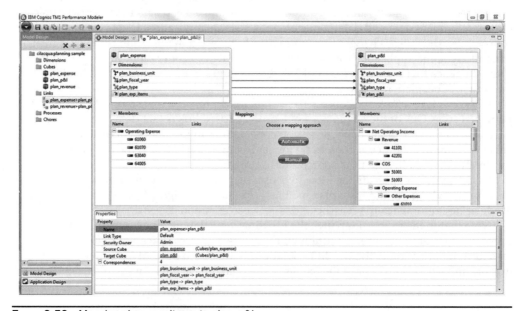

FIGURE 9-56 Mapping plan_exp_items to plan_p&l

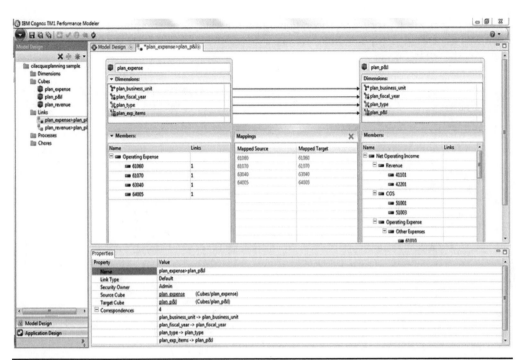

Figure 9-57 Automatic mapping of plan_exp_items>plan_p&l

Once the mapping is completed, all link validations are done, and we are now ready to save the link and generate the process, as shown in Figure 9-58.

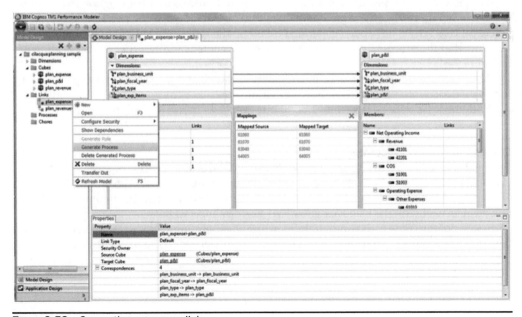

Figure 9-58 Generating a process link

Now that the link process has been generated for plan_expense>plan_p&l, let's inspect what was generated. To open a link process, a developer simply selects the link and right-clicks, as shown in Figure 9-59.

FIGURE 9-59 Opening a link process

The generated link process is similar to a generated process in other Cognos TM1 clients. As shown in Figure 9-60, there are Parameters, Prolog, Metadata, Data, and Epilog tabs where process scripts have been generated based on the scope of the defined link process.

Now that the process has been generated, let's execute it and test the results, as shown in Figure 9-61.

The process executed successfully and payroll, travel, and Depr & Amort expense data has been loaded into plan_p&l as shown in Figure 9-62.

With the links defined, let's move on to our final area in model design, creating rules and processes.

Creating Rules and Processes

The final step in the model design process is to create rules and processes. Cognos TM1 rules have traditionally been developed manually and with the rules editor. With the release of Cognos TM1 10.1, rules can be generated (see Figure 9-63) both at the dimensional and link level as well with the use of Cognos TM1 Performance Modeler.

A key point to note is that although the ways of generating rules have become easier in Performance Modeler, the results of these rules are still stored in the rules files for review

Figure 9-60 Generated plan_expense>plan_p&l script

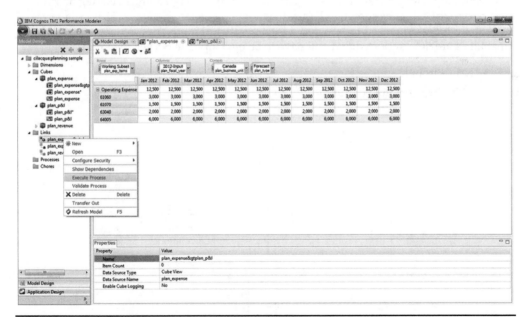

Figure 9-61 Executing process plan_expense>plan_p&l

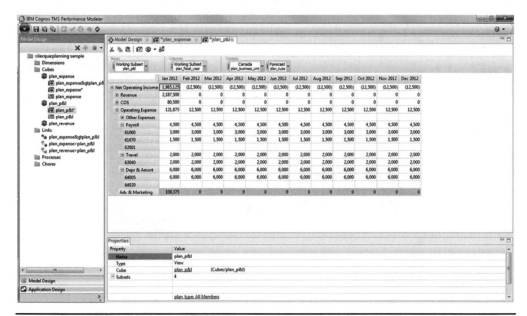

FIGURE 9-62 Expense data loaded to plan_p&l

and debugging. The generated rules are easy to identify through a preceding tag of
#Autogenerated... as shown in Figure 9-64.

Although Performance Modeler provides a number of innovative features, the following
capabilities are not supported and will have to be developed in Server Explorer:

- Drill-through
- MDX Expression Recorder

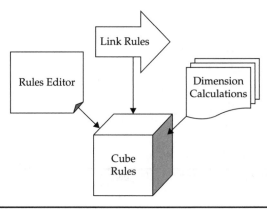

FIGURE 9-63 Cognos TM1 Rules Generation

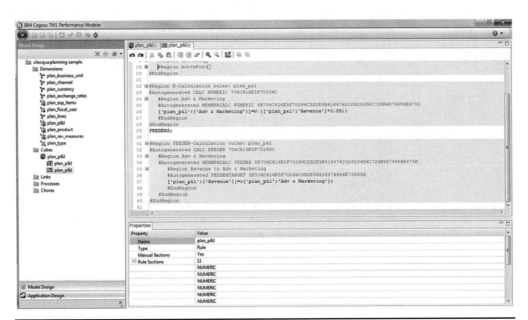

FIGURE 9-64   Generated rules

- Capability assignment
- Replication and synchronization
- Application folders

Fortunately, you can open and edit rules and TI process files created in either Performance Modeler or Server Explorer. For additional information on these features, please refer to the *Cognos TM1 User Guide*.

Now let's turn our attention to processes. Two types of processes can be created. The first type is the link process for internal movement of data between cubes, which was discussed in the previous section. The second is processes that are focused on external data outside of Cognos TM1. With the release of Cognos TM1 10.1, the source type has expanded to include IBM Cognos report data, as shown in Figure 9-65.

Once a source is identified, in this case a text file, it will be used to update the plan_ expense cube with 2011 actuals to support our forecasting for 2012.

Once the data source is identified, the mapping of the data and advanced tab performance uses the same functions as with Cognos TM1 other clients, as shown in Figure 9-66.

Defining Cognos TM1 Model Security

Cognos TM1 Performance Modeler defines application security on two levels. The first is the model level, which we will discuss in this section. Later in the chapter we will review

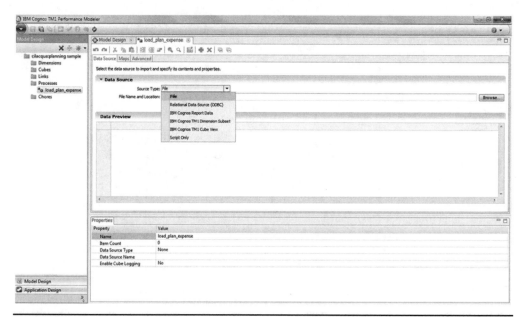

FIGURE 9-65   Process data sources

application rights in the context of application design. As shown in Figure 9-67, Performance Modeler provides the ability to define both users and groups.

This model has been defined based on users and their area of responsibility. Figure 9-68 highlights the user groups, which are a regional responsibility, and roles.

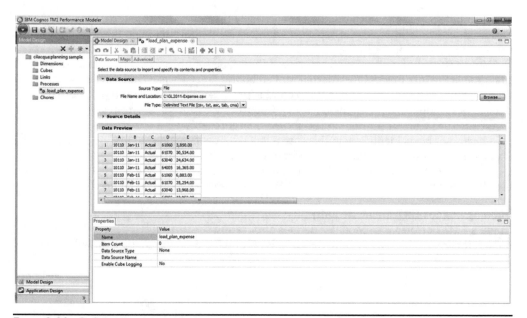

FIGURE 9-66   Defining the data source

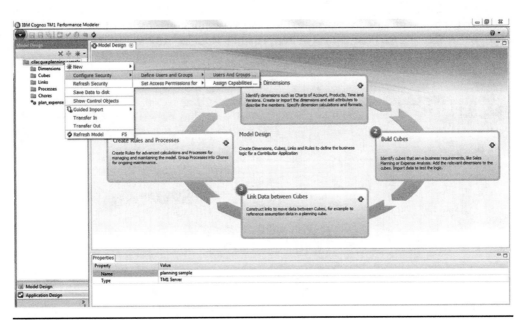

FIGURE 9-67 Model-based security

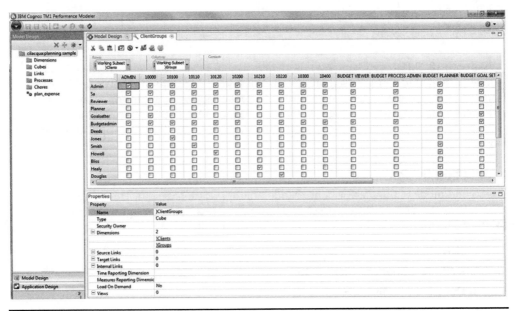

FIGURE 9-68 User and work group security

Once users and groups are assigned, then access permissions can be set for each group, as shown in Figure 9-69. Permissions in Performance Modeler are consistent with TM1's historical security models. Access is based on TM1 objects, which include dimensions, cubes, processes, and elements.

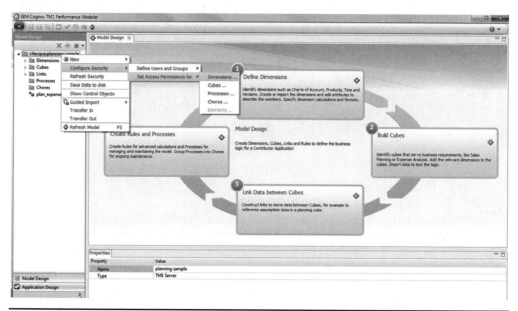

FIGURE 9-69   Setting access permissions

As with all TM1-based security, it is always best to set security at the highest level to ease security maintenance. Based on dimensions and user groups, as shown in Figure 9-70, read, write, lock, none, or reserve permissions can be set. For more information on these settings, please refer to the user guide for IBM Cognos TM1 Performance Modeler.

Now let's turn our attention to constructing an application through application design mode.

Application Design

The second mode within Performance Modeler is application design. This mode guides an analyst through the four main phases of defining and deploying a Cognos TM1-based solution. The four phases include the following (see Figure 9-71):

1. Define views.

2. Define the approval hierarchy.

3. Deploy the application.

4. Define security.

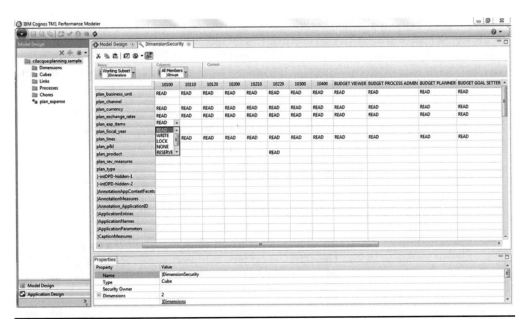

FIGURE 9-70   Dimension-based security

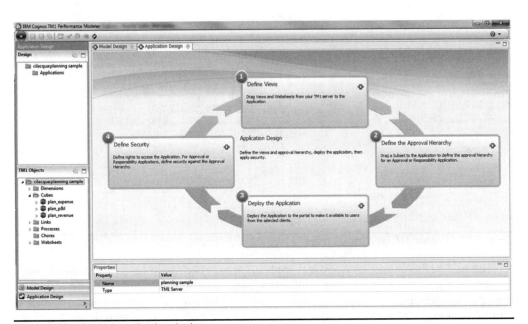

FIGURE 9-71   Guided application design

The first step in the application design process is to define an application that will hold the specific views, approval hierarchy, and security that will govern the roles and access to the application. With the release of Performance Modeler, there are a broader range of application styles that can be supported by Cognos TM1. As shown in Figure 9-72, Performance Modeler supports the following application types:

- **Approval**   The traditional "Contributor style" applications that create a hierarchical approval workflow structure to manage the submission of organizational plans.

- **Central**   A Cognos TM1-based solution with no approval hierarchy, which is typically used in solutions with a small group of users who equally share the task of performing central planning or analysis. Key attributes of this application type are: taking ownership is an option (but not enforced), and this type of application cannot be deployed through Cognos Insight in Distributed mode. This is primarily due to lack of enforcement of taking ownership.

- **Responsibility**   An Approval hierarchy–based solution in which a user cannot submit a node to lock it. This application type is typically used for rolling or continuous forecast processes with no defined end date.

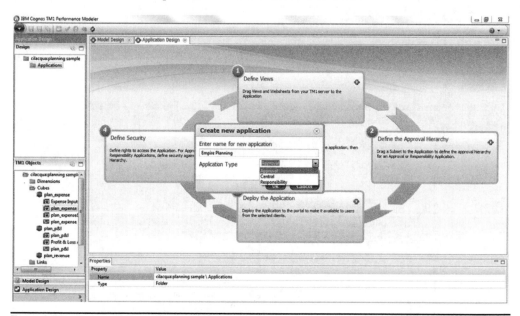

Figure 9-72   Cognos TM1 application types

The analyst has chosen an Approval application type because it holds a superset of all capabilities for illustration. Once an application name is chosen and saved, an application framework is set up in the design window, as shown in Figure 9-73. The application name is Empire Planning, and folders for Approval Hierarchy and Views have been defined for the user. The user drags and drops objects from the left-hand navigation panel key TM1 objects.

Performance Modeler uses the same building blocks for applications as other TM1 clients, namely, dimension subsets for Approval Hierarchy and cube views and/or

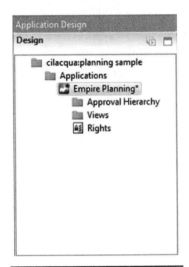

FIGURE 9-73 Application framework

Websheets for application tabs. The choice of cube views versus highly formatted Websheets will be a design choice based on your application requirements and client deployment strategy. Table 9-1 highlights some key differences to consider in your application design. Note that with the release of Cognos TM1 10.1, there are a broad range of application options; for example, TM1 Websheets can now be deployed with workflow.

Once the level of application interaction based on client features is decided, then the application properties need to be set. There is an Application Design properties panel to manage the global setting that governs key feature enablement as well as clients.

As shown in Figure 9-74, the analyst has selected key features that will allow the users to chart, create multiple sandboxes, and export and create new views through the Subset Editor. Sandboxes are a unique capability of TM1 that allow users to create an unlimited number of private workspaces to test different business scenarios. These scenarios can be based

Feature/Client	Cube View	Websheet	Cognos Insight (Central and Distributed)
Menu bar	X	X	X
User-defined subsets	X	X	
User-defined charting	X		X
Sorting and filtering	X		X
User-defined calculations	X		X
Sandbox support	X	X	
User-defined dimension nesting	X		X
Workflow	X	X	X
Distributed processing			X
Hide row/column elements for asymmetrical definitions			X
Combining data from multiple cubes into one UI display	X (via stacking views)	X	X (via stacking views)
Custom forms-based layout		X	
Custom formatting and branding		X	
Action buttons		X	X
In cell pick lists	X	X	X

TABLE 9-1 Client Feature Differences

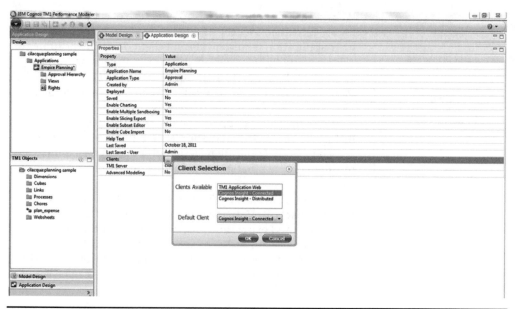

Figure 9-74 Key features

on baseline data defined by the application author or based on a previously defined scenario. Once a scenario is committed, it becomes the base data for the application.

Application Properties

Based on these application requirements, the analyst has chosen Cognos Insight as the client in connected mode. With these decisions made, it is time to build our application. Since this is an Approval application, the All Business Unit dimension subset of plan_business_unit will define our submission process, as well as three cube views, Revenue Input, Expense Input, and Profit & Loss Analysis. Each of these views was specifically created to facilitate input and analysis in support of the business users' forecast submission. Once the approval hierarchy and views are assigned, the final step is to validate the application prior to deployment. Application validation checks the following (see Figure 9-75):

- The correct structure is used for approval hierarchy.
- All objects in the application definition are available on the IBM Cognos TM1 server.
- The correct client is used for the application.
- For the application types, Approval, Central and Responsible, the Approval Hierarchy folder includes the dimension that contains the approval hierarchy.
- The Approval hierarchy dimension is defined in at least one of the cube views.

Once the application is validated, we are ready to deploy, as shown in Figure 9-76. Deployment generates the application and creates an entry within the IBM Cognos TM1 Applications Portal.

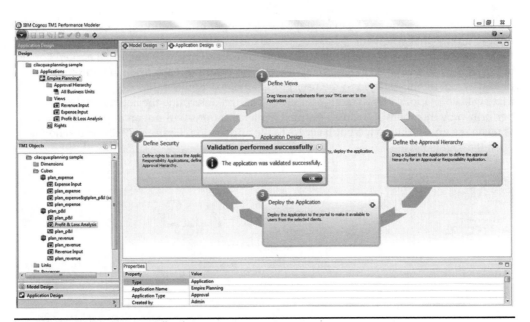

FIGURE 9-75   Validating an application

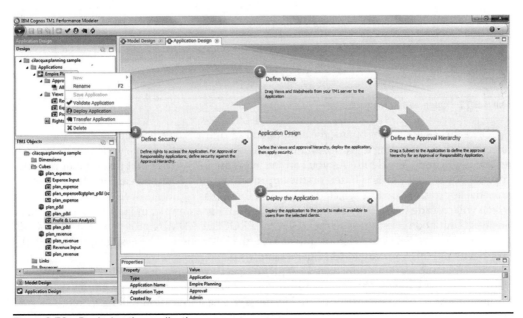

FIGURE 9-76   Deploying the application

After an application has been deployed, a developer must define application rights for all user groups that you want to have access to the application. These rights are based on the users and groups defined in the model-based security that was discussed earlier. For an application with an approval hierarchy, as with this example, each node in your approval hierarchy has rights assigned to the user groups that exist on the IBM Cognos TM1 server that hosts your application. The rights that you assign determine the actions that can be performed by members of the user groups. For applications without an approval hierarchy, you can assign a group to have full access to the application. Figure 9-77 illustrates how to open the Rights Editor.

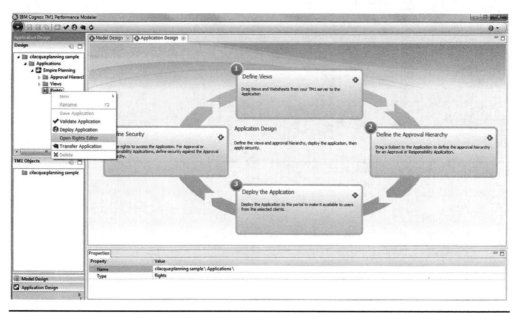

FIGURE 9-77   Opening the Rights Editor

Once the Rights Editor opens, the assignment of rights is a three-step process of selecting a node, selecting a group, and finally, defining security rights, which includes review depth and view depth. As you can see in Figure 9-78, given that this is an approval application, adding rights is based on the approval hierarchy defined earlier. This process links the approval node to a selected group and the access rights allowed by the group, which will cascade to all users assigned to the group. For example, in Figure 9-78, the Total Business Unit node is assigned to the BUDGET PROCESS ADMIN group, which allows full access across to review submissions. In contrast, the UK node will be assigned to the 10110 group with submission only to this business unit's plans.

Now that application rights have been defined, let's review what has been deployed through the IBM Cognos TM1 Applications Portal. When you enter the portal, an entry with the application will appear, as shown in Figure 9-79. The application will have to be activated to be made visible to nonadministrative users.

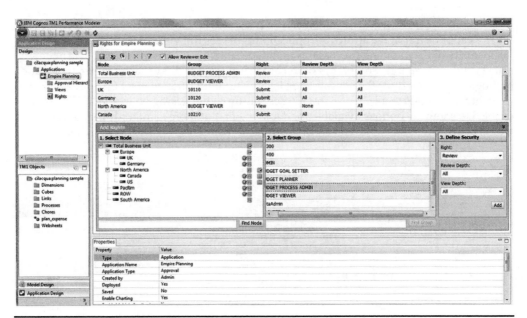

FIGURE 9-78   Assigning rights

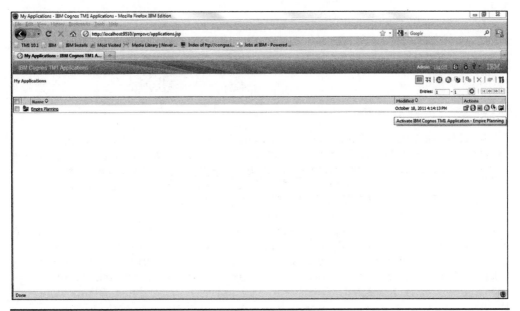

FIGURE 9-79   Activating the application

Once the application is activated, it can be launched, as shown in Figure 9-80. When you log in as administrator, the approval application provides full view of all workflow nodes, the maturity of the planning process through node status, and all permissions. The node state includes: Available, Reserved, Locked at the leaf level and, Available, Incomplete, Work in Progress, and Ready at the consolidated level. This application was set up with a default client but also access to all clients. You can see this by right-clicking on the node. This was enabled to show the options available for deployment, but more commonly a single client would be chosen based on design considerations as mentioned earlier in this chapter.

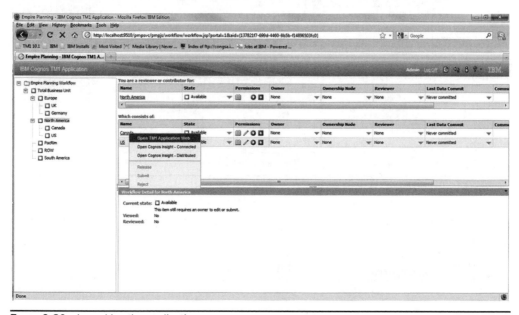

FIGURE 9-80   Launching the application

So with that, let's start our planning and analysis process in Canada with Cognos Insight – Connected. This is the newest client for Cognos TM1. The first step in the planning and analysis process is to take ownership, which grants the user exclusive write access to data represented by the ownership node and signals the initiation of the planning process by updating the workflow page node status (see Figure 9-81).

The views that were defined in the Application Design phase appear as tabs for navigation between Revenue Input, Expense Input, and Profit Loss Analysis. Let's start our planning process by entering 100,000 units as our product goal for 2011 for Canada across all our channels. Earlier in our cube design, we defined units as a driver of revenue in the calculation of Revenue = Units * Price. Cognos Insight supports the full range of spreading capabilities within Cognos TM1. Entering 100,000 units as a consolidated 2011 for Total Product, Total plan_channel, and forecast will prompt the analyst to decide on how to spread the 100,000 units, as shown in Figure 9-82. Given that this is our first entry, the analyst selected Equal Spread. Proportional Spreading is extremely helpful, with more complex spreading requirements; for example, an analyst may want to proportionally spread against prior history of revenue or any other values within the model to take advantage of seasonal changes in product demand.

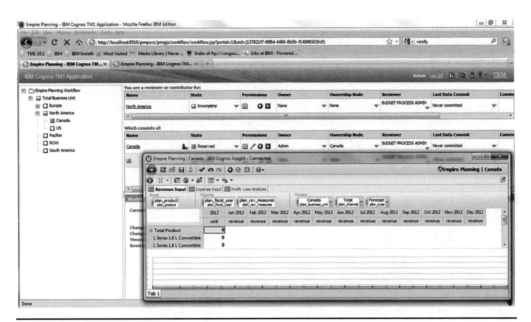

FIGURE 9-81   Taking ownership

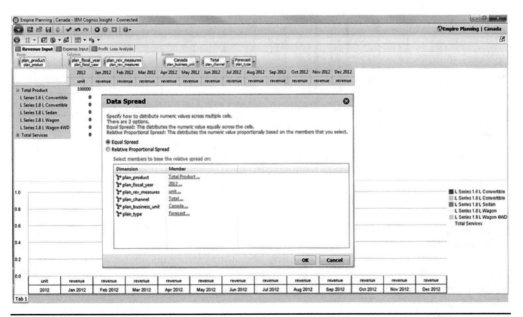

FIGURE 9-82   Data spreading

NOTE *The data entry example described in the preceding paragraph can be streamlined by leveraging a data entry shortcut and automatic spreading techniques. Entering 100,000 into a Consolidation cell having ALL null/zero child leaf cell values will perform an automatic Equal Leaves Spread of 100,000—evenly allocating the value to each eligible child leaf cell. If one or more child leaf cells have a non-zero value, the system will perform a Proportional Spread, allocating the 100,000 proportionally to child leaves based on their value as a percentage of the Consolidation cell value. Pressing the shortcut key of M implies million (2M = 2,000,000).*

As Figure 9-83 shows, the analyst can now see the equal distribution units and corresponding revenue across product models, time, and channel. Also, based on our previous definition of Services as a percentage of revenue, all service revenue is calculated as well.

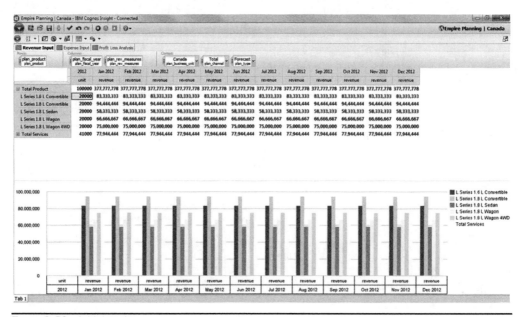

FIGURE 9-83   Initial goals

Now that the base revenue is calculated, the analyst needs to make adjustments in the unit, and consequently revenue changes due to seasonal customer demand. For example, in Canada, due to the harsh winters, there is less demand for convertible models in January, February, March, October, November, and December. As shown in Figure 9-84, Cognos Insight supports TM1 Hold capability to highlight other months, protecting their values from subsequent spreading.

Now that convertible products for spring and summer months are held, the analyst can adjust these by decreasing them by 50 percent in the winter months. As shown in Figure 9-85, an analyst can simply use the dec50 command in the 2012 column for the convertible product lines.

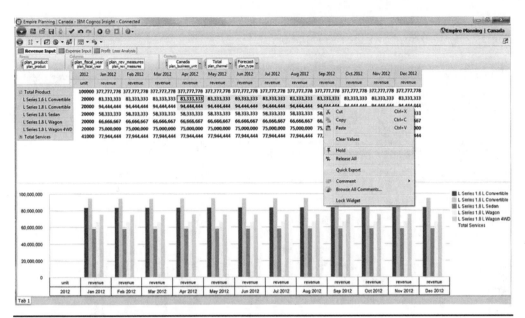

FIGURE 9-84   Holding values in Cognos Insight

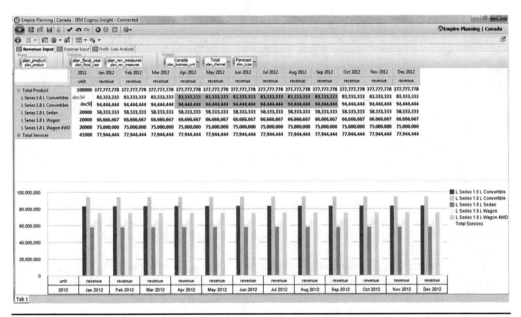

FIGURE 9-85   Adjusting a forecast for seasonality

Cognos TM1 instantly recalculates only the hold values to decrease winter month sales forecast. Figure 9-86 shows the recalculation.

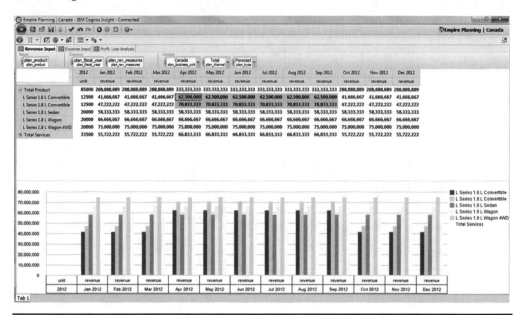

FIGURE 9-86 Convertible adjustment results

Now that the analyst has addressed the seasonal product demand portion of the plan, let's turn our attention to channel strategy changes that will affect units and consequentially revenue expectations. To address this portion of the forecast, the analyst simply drags the plan_channel tab down to the row access, and immediately the forecast view changes to channel across time. Shown in Figure 9-87, knowing that there is a greater emphasis being placed on web revenue to low cost and a decrease of store hours in Canada, the analyst chooses to increase unit sales for the web by using the command inc20, which increased the 2012 unit sales by 20 percent. Then a reduction of 5 percent of unit sales in stores is entered, using the TM1 command dec5.

As with all changes within TM1, the values for units and their impact on revenue are instantly calculated, as shown in Figure 9-88.

Now with the forecast for revenue entered, let's review the impact of this forecast on the P&L. As shown in Figure 9-89, the Profit & Loss Analysis is automatically updated with the latest revenue forecast numbers. Note that this update is automatic due to the rules-based link that was developed earlier. As we dive a bit deeper, notice that the Operating Expense has also been updated.

In a prior section of this chapter, the link between the plan_expense cube and plan_p&l cube was defined as a process link, which requires it to be run manually or through a chore. The question that arises is: why has Operating Expense been impacted by the revenue forecast? As shown in Figure 9-90, Adv & Marketing has been updated due to the revenue forecast. Adv & Marketing is an allocated expense based on revenue.

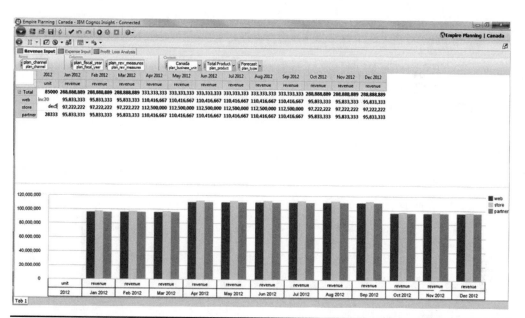

FIGURE 9-87   Adjusting channel forecast

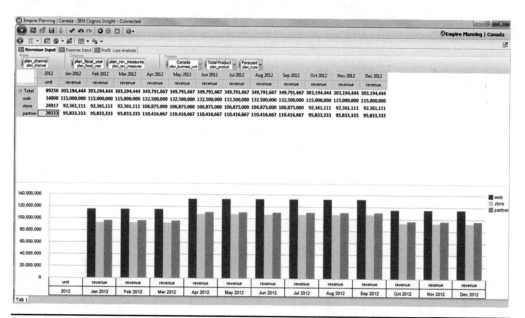

FIGURE 9-88   Channel forecast adjustment results

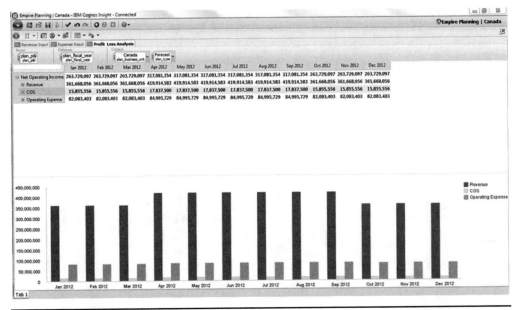

FIGURE 9-89 Profit & Loss Analysis

The next step is to add some comments to the forecast to document the assumption in the decision process. Right-clicking brings up a menu where you can add a comment to this tab (see Figure 9-91).

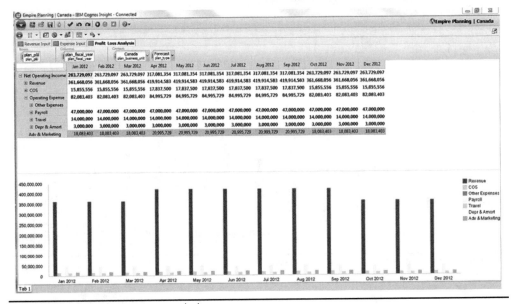

FIGURE 9-90 Operating expense analysis

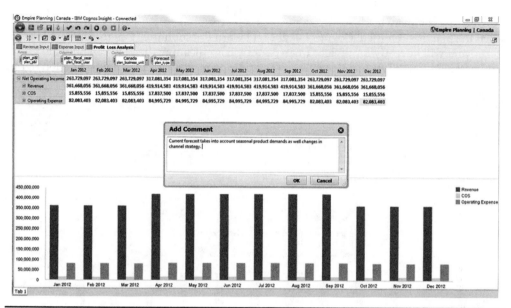

FIGURE 9-91   Adding a comment

Once a comment has been added, Cognos Insight provides the ability to browse all comments that have been created as well as the ability to delete any comments that are no longer relevant to the submission. Figure 9-92 shows the capability.

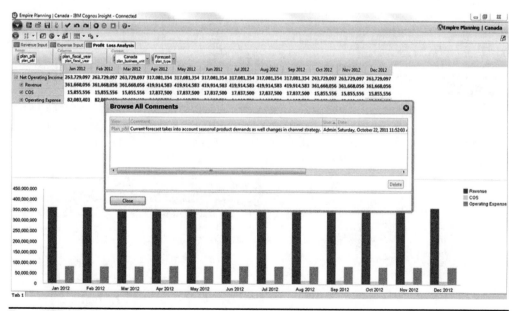

FIGURE 9-92   Browsing comments

Once the comment has been saved, the plan can be submitted. As shown in Figure 9-93, when the plan is submitted, Cognos Insight will warn the submitter that the data will be locked and will be ready for review. In an Approval application, the plan can only be resubmitted by a user who has the ability to reject the plan, which is set in the application rights.

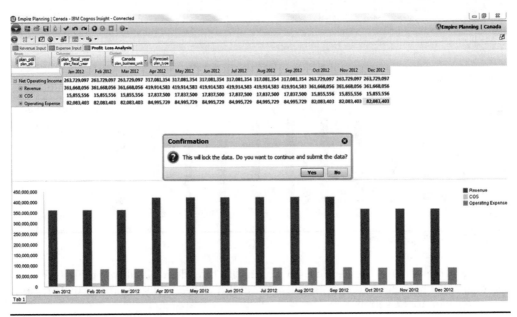

FIGURE 9-93   Submitting the plan

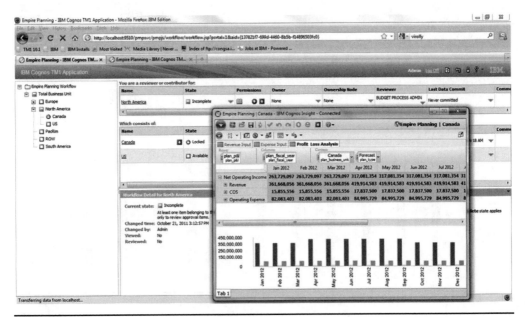

FIGURE 9-94   Workflow update after plan submittal

After the plan has been submitted, the data becomes locked and is shaded gray to notify the user that it is read-only, and the workflow is updated to the state of the submittal, as shown in Figure 9-94.

The deployment of Cognos Insight provides a number of new capabilities to extend a planning and analysis process. Although this example was of Cognos Insight running in Central mode, it can also be deployed in Distributed mode, which downloads the slices of the Cognos TM1 models locally, taking advantage of local PC processing power. This configuration may be desirable if bandwidth of a network is limited. Now let's turn our attention to Cognos Insight as a personal analytic client that is wired to the enterprise.

Cognos Insight

In the preceding section we have discussed Cognos Insight as an extension of Cognos TM1 10.1 deployment options to extend enterprise planning and analysis solutions. Cognos Insight can also be deployed as an agile personal analytic client to support exploration, discovery, and scenario analysis with both personal and corporate data. These capabilities are also wired for the enterprise to support publishing to workgroups and the enterprise to reduce silos of information and promote collaboration across an organization (see Figure 9-95).

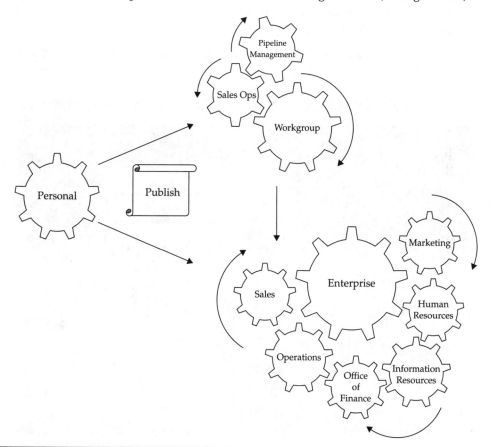

FIGURE 9-95   Cognos Insight wired for enterprise

Cognos Insight provides a broad range of analytic capabilities that include the following personal, interactive, and collaborative areas:

- **Personal** Users work with their data of choice, on their desktop, without IT.
  - Zero configuration
  - Multiple data sources; managed or personal
  - Easily import, merge, and enrich data
- **Interactive** Discover trends and explore scenarios using speed-of-thought interactions.
  - Intuitive gestures for exploration
  - Rich visualizations and instant recalculation
  - Detect and understand trends and outliers
  - Evaluate scenarios and make decisions
- **Collaborative** Share findings and results within a workgroup or throughout the enterprise.
  - Extend as a scalable enterprise client
  - Promote to server for broad distribution
  - Create and contribute to plans

Let's take a look at these features in a bit more detail. As shown in Figure 9-96, Cognos Insight has an intuitive startup screen that allows analysts to create a number of workspaces

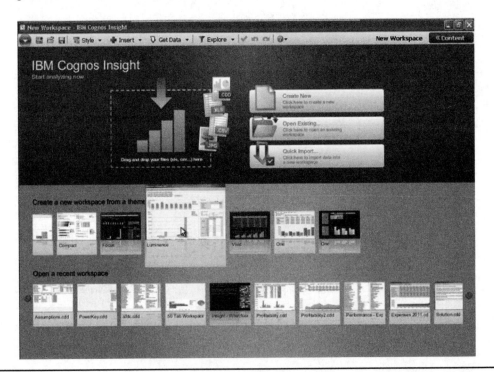

Figure 9-96 IBM Cognos Insight

where they can import and organize or visualize data, create new information through write-back, and finally share this information across an organization. Cognos Insight can import Microsoft Excel files, delimited text files, non-prompt-based reports from Cognos BI, Cognos TM1 cube views, Cognos TM1 dimension subsets, and ODBC data sources. These import options are complemented by a number of prebuilt workspace themes to make formatting easier and create a consistent look and feel across your analysis.

After creating a new workspace to start the analysis process, let's start our profitability analysis by importing a Microsoft Excel CSV file. As Figure 9-97 shows, a workspace allows the dragging and dropping of import files directly into the workspace.

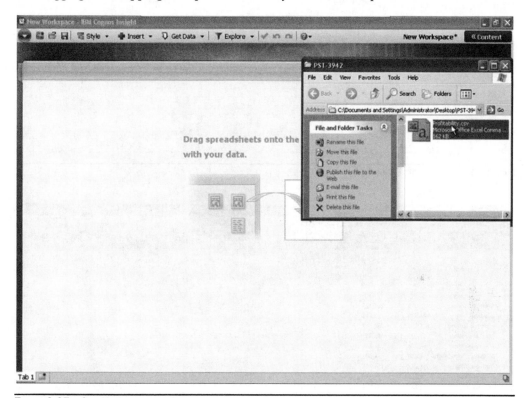

FIGURE 9-97   Creating a new workspace

Before we begin this process, let's take a closer look at what is contained in the Microsoft Excel file. This file contains common information that has been exported by a number of management reporting systems within an organization. As shown in Figure 9-98, the file contains channel, sales division, product, month, actual, plan, and target information.

When you drag and drop this file into the workspace, Cognos Insight immediately transforms this data into a multidimensions view and creates consolidated totals. Figure 9-99 shows the result of this transformation; columns have been transformed into dimensions as well as totals. Additionally, a comparative bar chart for each channel is displayed.

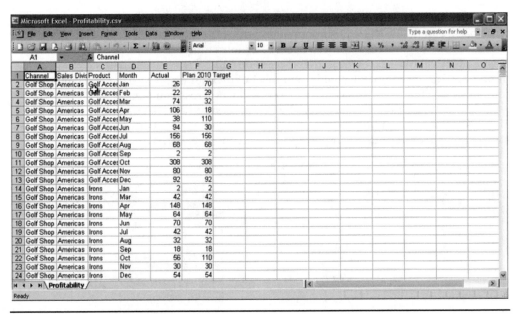

FIGURE 9-98 Microsoft Excel file

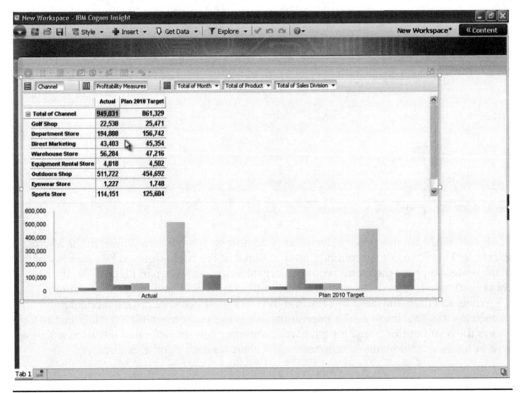

FIGURE 9-99 Microsoft Excel import

This new Cognos Insight object supports full pivot and drill-up and drill-down navigation to facilitate the exploration of this new information. Additionally, Cognos Insight allows users to extend this information through user-defined calculations. The analyst can create a full range of predefined calculations as well as additional custom calculations (see Figure 9-100).

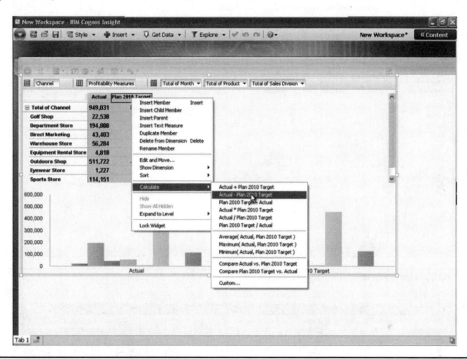

FIGURE 9-100   User-defined capabilities

The ability to extend information easily is a key attribute of Cognos Insight. As shown in Figure 9-101, the initial information is extended through the creation of status indicators that create a visual cue about the variance between actual versus plan; the actual variance is shown as well as a comment area to collect qualitative information on the status of sales problems in the Golf Store. All these enhancements are done using simple right-clicks and pull-down menus.

Now that this information is in a form that supports the analyst's requirements, he or she is free to explore the current performance and comment on key issues. As shown in Figure 9-102, this new workspace supports full pivoting of information to create an interesting view of profitability by Sales Division. Again, this is as easy as dragging and dropping the Sales Division dimension on the rows.

Now that the view is consistent with our analysis requirements, let's expand this analysis to create a new forecast. Figure 9-103 shows how easy it is to create a new column through the use of duplicate members. A duplicate member creates a new member with accompanying data within the cube that can be renamed.

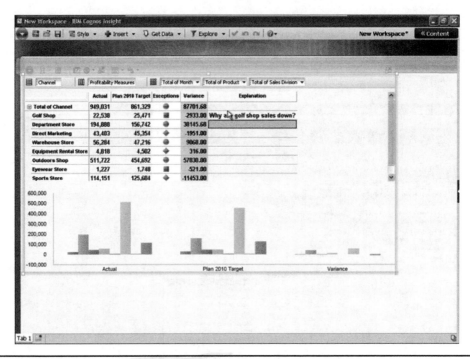

Figure 9-101   Variance and Comment columns

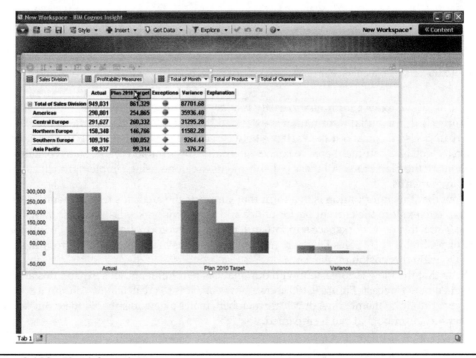

Figure 9-102   Pivot information

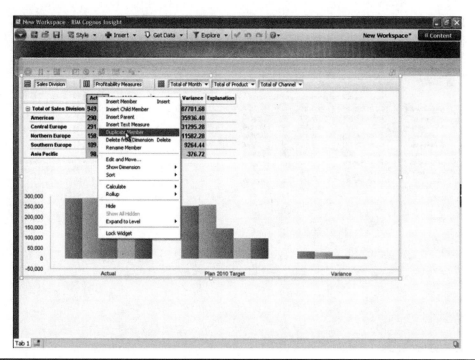

FIGURE 9-103   Adding a new member

In this example we will be using the duplicated Actuals as the basis for the new plan. Once the column is duplicated, it is renamed New Plan, and we can start to modify the new plan. In Figure 9-104, we can see that in the New Plan column we have held the channels Total Channel, Direct Marketing, Warehouse Store, Equipment Rental Store, Eyewear Store, and Sports Store. This is designated by the gray shaded cells in the New Plan column. Now to improve our new plan, let's start by decreasing Department Store by 10 percent. Notice that Customer Insight uses the same shorthand notation that Cognos TM1 uses.

Now that we have decreased our Department Store revenue to $175,399, let's add a proper title for this analysis as well as add additional context for our plan from the corporate profitability application. Cognos Insight provides a data panel to access corporate information and merge TM1-based application information into a personal analysis for greater context (see Figure 9-105). Based on a user's access rights to the TM1 application, an analyst can simply drag and drop a cube, in this case profitability, directly into the personal workspace with the same navigation that was used with external data. The chart created shows the actual trend of revenue by channel.

The next step is to unite these two views of data under common filters. Again, this process is a simple drag-and-drop operation. In Figure 9-106, we can see the dimensions within the corporate profitability cube in which Sales Division is dropped into the workspace.

This analyst also required the ability to filter on product. Again, this is accomplished by dragging and dropping the product dimension to the workspace, as shown in Figure 9-107.

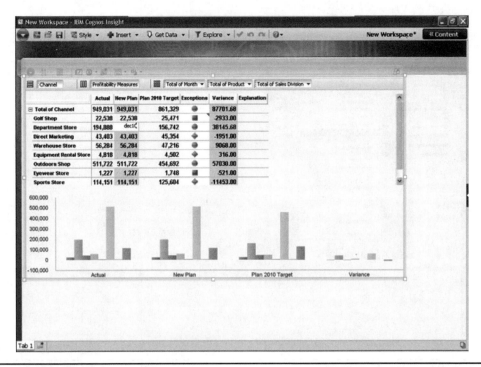

FIGURE 9-104   Creating a new plan

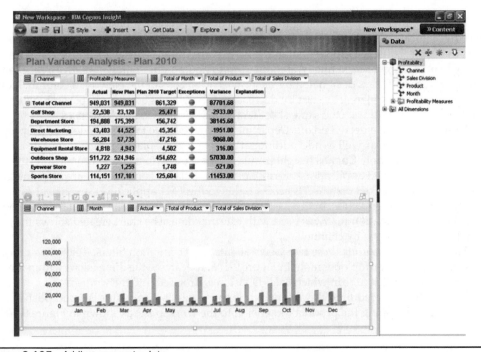

FIGURE 9-105   Adding corporate data

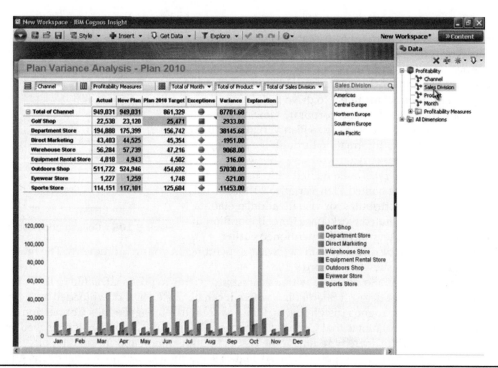

FIGURE 9-106   Adding filters

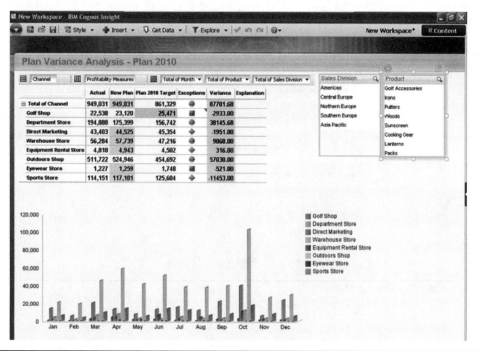

FIGURE 9-107   Final dashboard

Cognos Insight automatically listens across common dimensions, so in this case Product and Sales Division widgets are automatically linked to the personal data imported and the corporate data widget. This provides the ability to select any number of combinations of Sales Division and Product members to drive the viewing across both personal data and corporate views seamlessly.

Once the data has been saved as Plan Variance 2010, we are ready to share this information through the sharing and publishing process. When you save this workspace, Cognos Insight generates a file named <file_name>.cdd. In this case the file is named Plan Variance 2010.cdd. This file contains all the attributes for visualization, metadata and data of the generated workspace for collaboration in a number of interesting ways. As mentioned earlier, Cognos Insight can be distributed in two ways depending on your requirements. The first is through sharing, as shown in Figure 9-108.

Figure 9-108 Collaboration options

The Share option allows a user with administrator rights to post a CDD file to IBM Connects as well as Microsoft SharePoint, where it can be posted and downloaded and consumed by other Cognos Insight users. One advantage of using Cognos Connection over Microsoft SharePoint is that Cognos Connection downloads Cognos Insight as well as the CDD file for users, thereby reducing the cost of administration and installation of Cognos Insight across your organization. As Figure 9-109 shows, to share a Cognos Insight workspace, a user needs to identify the location of the IBM Cognos System, log in, and identify the Cognos Insight CDD file. In this example, the name would be the saved file name Plan Variance 2010.cdd.

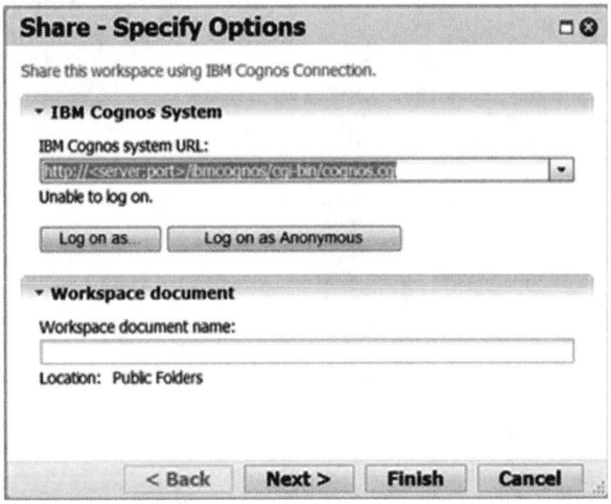

Share - Specify Options ▢ ⊗

Share this workspace using IBM Cognos Connection.

▾ IBM Cognos System

IBM Cognos system URL:

http://<server:port>/ibmcognos/cgi-bin/cognos.on ▾

Unable to log on.

[Log on as...]　　[Log on as Anonymous]

▾ Workspace document

Workspace document name:

Location: Public Folders

[< Back]　[Next >]　[Finish]　[Cancel]

Figure 9-109 The Share process

This uploads the CDD file into the Cognos 10 content store and creates a link to it in Cognos Connection, as shown in Figure 9-110.

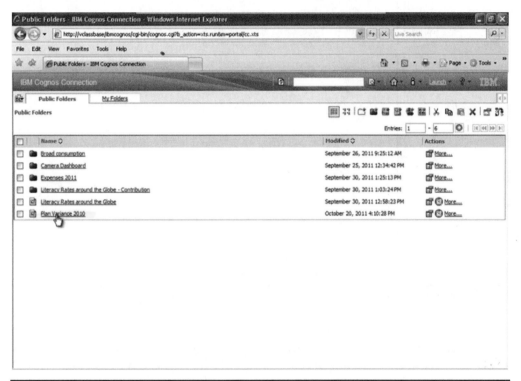

FIGURE 9-110   Cognos Insight shared

This approach distributes the content of the Plan Variance 2010.cdd to all users with access to Cognos Connection and permission to the folder. For additional control and the ability to enhance Cognos Insight, there is a publish capability, as shown in Figure 9-111. The Publish option allows the CDD to create a new Cognos TM1 Server instance and deploys a new application, which is made available through the TM1 Application Portal, mentioned earlier in the section "Cognos TM1 Performance Modeler." Publish also makes the output of the Cognos Insight analysis available for enterprise enrichment through TM1 Performance Modeler. This enrichment can include the following requirements as this analysis matures to a corporate application that needs to span broader user requirements:

- Create additional dimensionality
- Automate the update of data through TM1 processes
- Implement role-based security
- Additional deployment options (TM1 Web, Cognos Insight [Central or Distributed], Business Insight)

FIGURE 9-111 Publish process

The second option is Publish & Distribute, which additionally creates a Cognos 10 data source deployment package and publishes a Cognos 10 report for each widget in the CDD file. Given that Publish & Distribute is a superset of Publish, our example will cover Publish & Distribute together in a single example.

After you've selected Publish & Distribute, the next step is to identify the location of the TM1 gateway, as shown in Figure 9-112. Identifying the TM1 gateway specifies the TM1 system you want to publish your workspace(s) to. Once the location is identified, a user name and a password that has administrative access rights need to be entered as well as the application name. In this example, the application name will be Plan Variance 2010. Also note that, given the varied application types now available, the publisher can identify a dimension to control access. If you select a dimension, you are publishing an Approval application type. If you do not select a dimension, you are publishing a Central application type. These application types were covered in the earlier section "Cognos TM1 Performance Modeler."

The second half of this process is making this available to Cognos 10 BI. As shown in Figure 9-113, there are a number of options to generate Cognos packages. To be consistent in

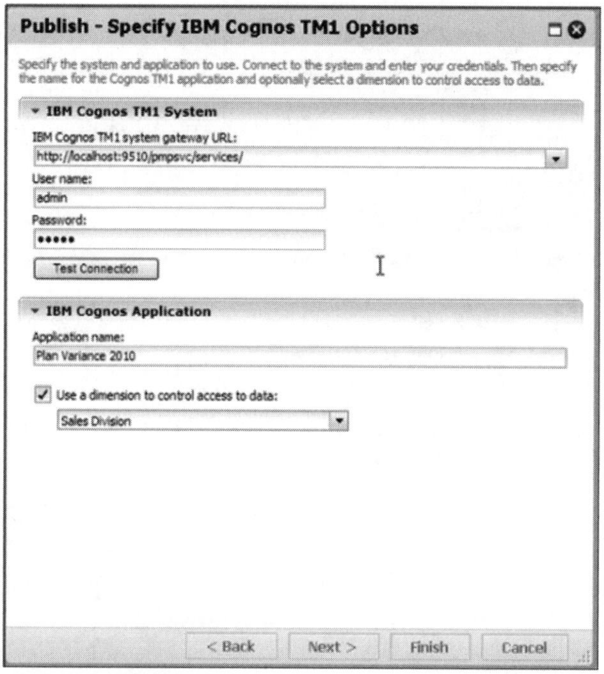

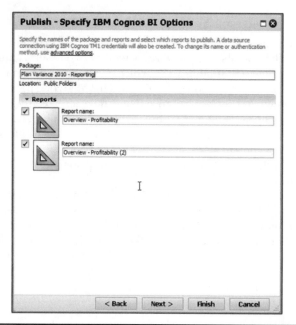

FIGURE 9-112   Publish & Distribute options

FIGURE 9-113   Defining the Cognos BI package and reports

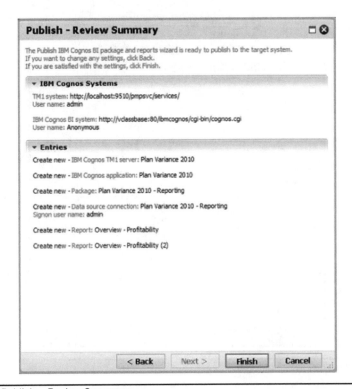

Publish – Review Summary

The Publish IBM Cognos BI package and reports wizard is ready to publish to the target system.
If you want to change any settings, click Back.
If you are satisfied with the settings, click Finish.

▼ IBM Cognos Systems

TM1 system: **http://localhost:9510/pmpsvc/services/**
User name: **admin**

IBM Cognos BI system: **http://vclassbase:80/ibmcognos/cgi-bin/cognos.cgi**
User name: **Anonymous**

▼ Entries

Create new - IBM Cognos TM1 server: Plan Variance 2010

Create new - IBM Cognos application: Plan Variance 2010

Create new - Package: Plan Variance 2010 - Reporting

Create new - Data source connection: Plan Variance 2010 - Reporting
Signon user name: **admin**

Create new - Report: Overview - Profitability

Create new - Report: Overview - Profitability (2)

< Back   Next >   **Finish**   Cancel

FIGURE 9-114   Publish – Review Summary

this example, we will name the package Plan Variance 2010 – Reporting. This package will be made available in the Cognos 10 data store, as well as two reports named Overview – Profitability and Overview – Profitability (2), which can be modified in Report Studio.

At this point the Publishing portion of the Cognos Insight workspace has been completed to Cognos TM1 as a new TM1 service instance that can be accessed by the purpose-built TM1 clients. The final step, as shown in Figure 9-114, is the Publish and Review Summary. This dialog box provides a summary of all key entries to both the Cognos TM1 system as well as the Cognos 10 BI content store. If additional changes are made to these settings, an analyst can click the Back button to make modifications prior to completing the final stages of the publishing process.

With the Cognos Insight workspaces published, let's turn our attention to what applications were generated in Cognos TM1 as well as in Cognos 10. In Figure 9-115, we can see the TM1 application-generated Plan Variance 2010. When you select the application link, an approval application is generated based on the Sales Division selected previously. After you've selected the Americas, Cognos Insight is invoked and launched with the developed workspaces.

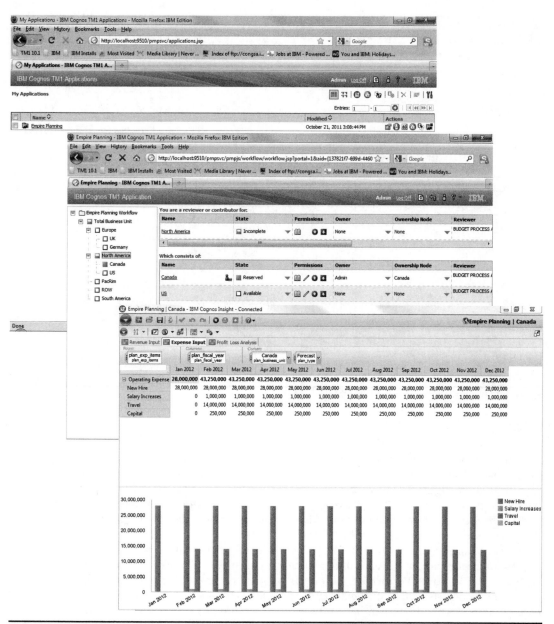

FIGURE 9-115   Publish to TM1 Applications Portal

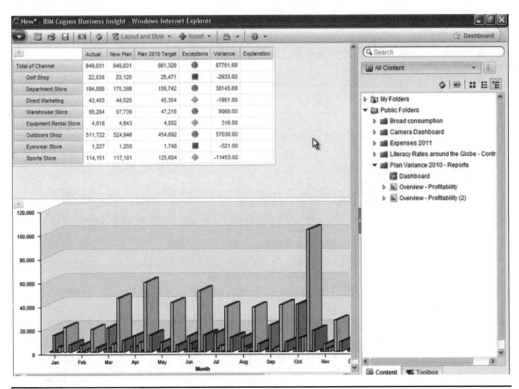

Figure 9-116 Available in Business Insight

Now that we have closed the loop from Cognos Insight through the deployment through Cognos TM1, let's examine how Cognos Insight workspaces have been made available to Cognos 10 BI. In Figure 9-116, we can see that the Plan Variance Reports 2010 – Reports package is now available in the Business Insight content panel, and it can now be dragged and combined with disparate data sources into a Business Insight dashboard. We will discuss Business Insight in more depth in the next section.

Often, prior to making the published Cognos Insight personal workspaces available to a broader audience, additional dimensionality, measures, and security are required. As Figure 9-117 shows, Performance Modeler can play an important role in enriching the generated models as well as automating the data feeds to meet a broader range of user requirements. As mentioned earlier in the section "Cognos TM1 Performance Modeler," the published Cognos TM1 server Plan Variance 2010 is available for further model enrichment and application development.

Our next topic for extending the Cognos TM1 user experience is through Cognos Business Insight.

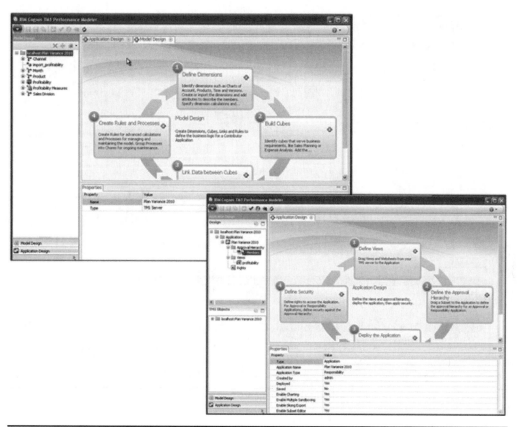

FIGURE 9-117   Plan Variance 2010 available in Performance Modeler

Application Development with Business Insight

IBM Cognos Business Insight can be used to extend the value of Cognos TM1 models to provide a new user experience. Cognos Business Insight is a unified workspace for the creation of highly interactive dashboards that can span data sources. With the release of Cognos TM1 9.5.2, Business Insight supports a Cognos TM1 widget that allows a developer to embed a Cognos TM1 cube view, contributor application, or Websheet into a Business Insight dashboard. In most cases a Websheet is chosen to provide a highly formatted view of Cognos TM1 data, and because it is based on a TM1 view, it supports the full range of write-back, spreading, sandboxes, and so on. So let's begin with a quick review of the components of a Business Insight dashboard. A Business Insight dashboard is made of the following key components, as shown in Figure 9-118 (see *IBM Cognos Business Insight User Guide*, Version 10.1.0).

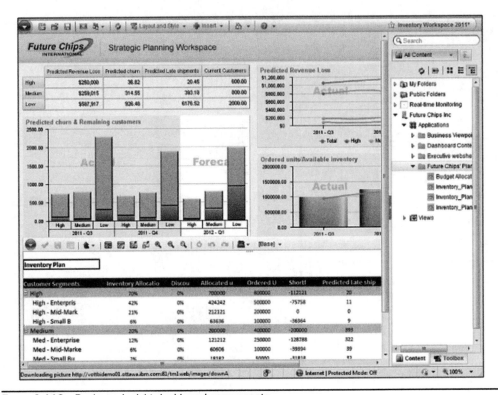

Figure 9-118 Business Insight dashboard components

As already noted, Business Insight dashboards are an amalgamation of content widgets that are managed from the content panel (see Figure 9-119). Business Insight has a specific widget to support the full range of TM1 capabilities. Let's now dive a bit deeper into the content panel, where TM1 can be a source for information.

The content panel provides access to a broad range of Cognos content. For the purposes of this chapter, we will focus primarily on TM1-generated content and how it is integrated into a Business Insight dashboard. Business Insight provides full access to TM1 Websheets and cube views with varying levels of interaction that can be defined by the author. For example, each TM1 widget can turn on or off the Widget Action button. The menu that appears when we click the Widget Action button is shown in Figure 9-120.

The Widget Action button gives users full control over the widget operation within the dashboard. These actions include the following:

- Remove the widget from the dashboard
- Refresh content
- Reset
- Restart
- Turn on/off listening for widget events (used for common based navigation between multiple widgets)

- Content placement
- Properties of the widget

Along with this Widget Action button is a TM1 toolbar, as shown in Figure 9-121.

This toolbar provides all the key features you expect from a TM1-based object, whether it is used in a cube view, Websheet, or contribution application. Also note that sandboxes are also available to facilitate scenario analysis without the overhead of premodeling each scenario by an administrator.

The TM1 Widget toolbar can also be turned off depending on your application requirements. For more formal input planning processes, often an application requires a less flexible interface that provides a standard view with areas for input. Fortunately, the TM1 Widget has the ability to turn off the Widget Action button and toolbar, as shown in Figure 9-122.

Figure 9-123 shows an example of a TM1 Websheet with a deactivated Widget Action button and toolbar.

As mentioned earlier, TM1 Contributor can also be used within a widget, as shown in Figure 9-124. In this case, the author chose to deactivate the toolbar for a cleaner look to the dashboard. This dashboard provides a manufacturing workspace that monitors key production metrics globally that span both production performance and demand forecast. The TM1 Contributor widget is in the lower right-hand corner.

The TM1 Contributor widget provides a view of the current maturity of the forecast in progress through TM1 workflow. This also can be used to launch the Contributor application and start a new forecasting process, as shown in Figure 9-125.

In this example, we chose to enable the Widget toolbar, and we can navigate the Contributor application and, upon submission of a forecast, return to the previous dashboard to continue to monitor the manufacturing performance of the organization.

Figure 9-119 Cognos Business Insight content panel

Figure 9-120 Widget Action button menu

FIGURE 9-121   TM1 Widget toolbar

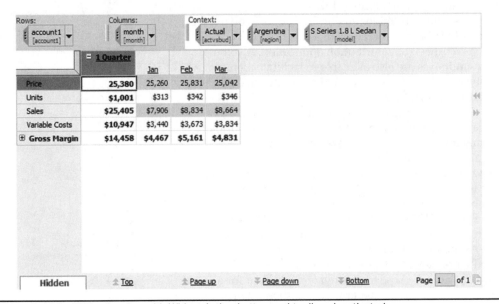

FIGURE 9-122   TM1 cube view with Widget Action button and toolbar deactivated

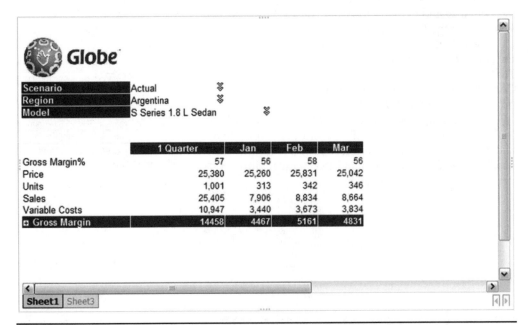

FIGURE 9-123   TM1 Websheet with Widget Action button and toolbar deactivated

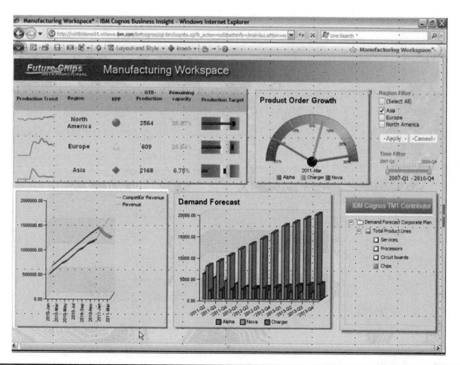

FIGURE 9-124   Business Insight with TM1 Contributor widget

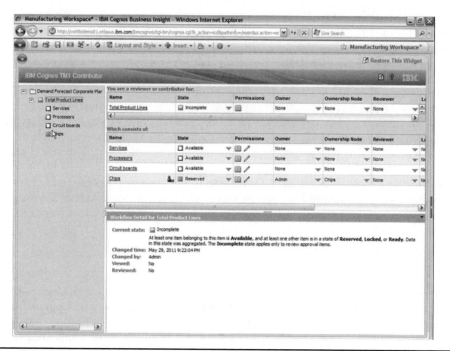

FIGURE 9-125   TM1 Contributor widget

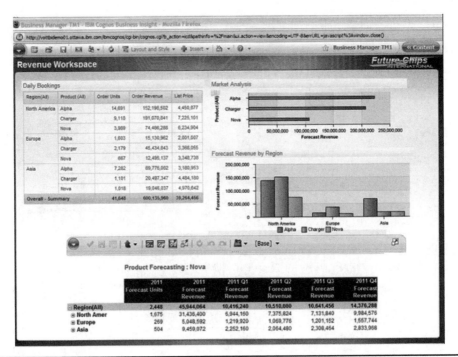

Figure 9-126 Business Insight Revenue workspace

So as we look at this myriad of options, ideally we should think through the use of each widget and the interrelationship of one widget to another in providing key information to the end user. For example, is there a common business unit or time period that each widget references to provide a consistent reference point? Fortunately, Business Insight allows widgets to listen for widget events, and listening is automatically enabled. A key point is that as of the release of Cognos TM1 10.1 Contributor, widgets cannot listen to events. For example, in Figure 9-126 a dashboard contains four widgets as part of a revenue workspace.

The Daily Bookings, Market Analysis, and Forecast Revenue by Region widgets have limited navigation requirements and are read-only; thus, the Widget menu is deactivated. The Product Forecasting widget provides a read-write experience for the user and requires broader interaction with the data to generate a new forecast. As such, the Widget toolbar is activated to allow for the full range of TM1-based interactions and submissions of forecasts. Also, each widget is aligned to the same products and time period so that as the forecast is updated, all widgets will refresh, providing an instant view of the impact the new forecast will have on the organization.

Summary

This chapter highlighted key new capabilities of Cognos TM1 10.1 as well Cognos BI version 10. This review included Cognos TM1 Performance Modeler and Cognos Insight as well as integration with Cognos Business Insight, which provides application developers with a rich toolbox to develop industry-leading planning and analysis applications. Now let's turn our attention to the engine that is driving these applications in Chapter 10.

Under the Hood

There are two sides of a coin. On the one side, we like to solve business requirements with a software solution. On the other side, we have to operate this solution, and there may be many users who want to use the solution. So it is important to know how a solution works under the hood, especially if the solution should work in a multiuser environment. This chapter is about how Cognos TM1 caches data and how Cognos TM1 ensures that multiple users can write to the same cube. As the developer of a Cognos TM1 solution, you have almost no control over these Cognos TM1 mechanisms. This makes your knowledge about the mechanisms even more important. With this knowledge, a developer can take account of these mechanisms in his Cognos TM1 solutions.

Cognos TM1 uses locks to prevent inconsistency when multiple users change objects. Caches are used to enhance the query performance of Cognos TM1. But there are also dependencies between both aspects. For instance, building a cache (and the reverse operation: invalidating a cache) creates locks. In the next section we will take a look at how Cognos TM1 does caching and how the object locking is managed.

Cognos TM1 Caching

Why do we need caching in Cognos TM1? We remind you that Cognos TM1 is an OLAP engine, which calculates "on demand." "Calculation on demand" is one of the four performance factors of Cognos TM1 (see Chapter 6). Caching of calculated values improves the performance of "calculation on demand." This feature has to coexist with the user's ability to write to a cube. Why is this important? When values are written to a cube (for example, by simple user data entry, or TurboIntegrator executes a CELLPUTx function), the related cache becomes invalidated. *Invalidation* means that the cache is destroyed and has to be rebuilt again. This happens even if one value is written to a single cell only. A cache is associated with a cube. Cubes can be dependent on other cubes if the cube has rules with reference to other cubes (DB or ATTRS/N functions in rules; see Chapter 6). These dependencies also affect the caches. So caches are destroyed (or become invalidated) if values are written to dependent cubes, too. In addition, cube dependency information is stored in a separate cache. This is discussed later in the section "Cube Dependency."

Figure 10-1 shows how the cubes in the sample model depend on each other. The arrows in the figure show the direction of the impact if the data has changed. For instance, the data in cube "TBB Price" has changed. In this case the cache of "TBB Price" is invalidated. This invalidates the cache of "TBB Sales" and (the chain is going on) invalidates the cache of "TBB Revenue." If a value has changed in cube "TBB Sales," the cache of "TBB Price" is not affected, but the cache of "TBB Revenue" becomes invalidated. If we talk about "dependencies," we have to read the arrows in the reverse direction: We say "TBB Revenue" depends on "TBB Sales" ("TBB Revenue" is the base cube and "TBB Sales" is the dependent cube) and "TBB Sales" depends on "TBB Price."

Each cube can have various caches. This is shown in Figure 10-2. Cognos TM1 manages two different kinds of caches that are bound to a cube:

- **Cell cache or calculation cache**   The calculation cache holds all values that are calculated by rules. This cache improves the performance of rule calculation. If a rule-calculated cell is requested, the value of this cell is calculated on demand (see Chapter 6) and stored in this cache. There is one calculation cache associated with a cube.

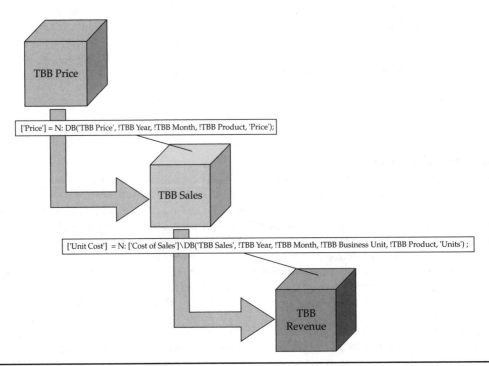

FIGURE 10-1   Cube dependencies of the sample model

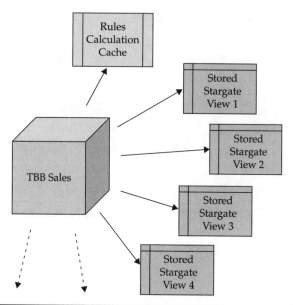

FIGURE 10-2   Associated caches of a cube

- **"Stargate" views or view cache**   This cache improves the performance of views and is also used by rule calculations. There could be multiple "Stargates" associated with a cube. We will give you a detailed description of view caching in the next section.

"Stargate" or View Caching

We already mentioned "Stargate views" when we talked about the Cognos TM1 Excel formula VIEW and Cube Viewer views in Chapter 8. A Stargate view optimizes consolidation of leaf cells and caches these values to improve the performance of views. But how does Cognos TM1 create and store a Stargate view (cache a view)? Cognos TM1 uses a Stargate view if data is requested by a Cube Viewer, the Excel formula VIEW, views accessed by TurboIntegrator, or the Cognos Excel formula TM1RPTVIEW. However, a Stargate view is also used by every client request to a cube and by the rules calculation mechanism. If a cell is calculated by a rule, Cognos TM1 knows if the calculation is performed in the context of a Stargate view. If the rule-calculated cell is calculated by a consolidated cell and the context is a Stargate view, the rule calculation will create a new Stargate view. The new Stargate is created with the same row and column dimension as in the origin Stargate. So the new Stargate is caching not only a single value but many values that are likely requested by the rule, too.

We want to show you how the Stargate views are stored to give you an insight into this important mechanism of Cognos TM1:

- **Step 1.**   The following illustration shows a sample view of the Cube Viewer that is requested by a user.

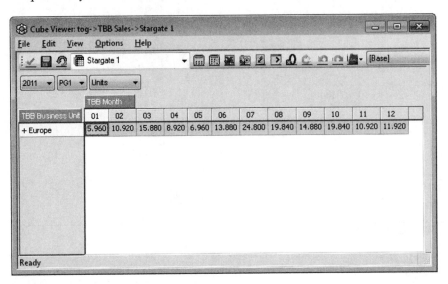

Stargate views are identified by their title elements. In our example we request a view with the elements "2011," "PG1," and "Units." So we can call the Stargate view "Stargate 2011-PG1-Units." Cognos TM1 is now looking for a "Stargate 2011-PG1-Units" view, which is already stored in the memory of the Cognos TM1 server. We assume that there is no such Stargate stored. So Cognos TM1 will cache "Stargate 2011-PG1-Units" as a new stored view. But the view that is stored looks different from the view you can see in the Cube Viewer. Cognos TM1 stores values and element names of all leaf children of the consolidated elements of the row and the column dimensions (dimensions that are shown on the row and column axes of the Cube Viewer view). In our example we already have only leaf elements on the column axis, but we have "Europe" on the row, which is a consolidated element. In this case Cognos TM1 will store the elements "UK" and "Germany" (the leaf children of "Europe") with the new Stargate view. The cells that are referenced in the Stargate are calculated and cached with this stored view. All requested values are now satisfied from this Stargate. At this point we note that no Stargate calculation is needed if the user would drill down on "Europe" (as shown in the preceding illustration), because all leaf children are already cached.

- **Step 2.** Now another user is using an active form on the same cube. You can see the sample in the following illustration:

	B17	▼		*fx*	=TM1RPTROW($B$9;"tog:TBB Business Unit";"";{AR}011'$B$17;"BusinessUnit";0)								
	B	C	D	E	F	G	H	I	J	K	L	M	N	O
9	tog:TBB Sales:1													
10														
11	TBB Year	2011												
12	TBB Product	PG1												
13	TBB Sales Measure	Units												
14														
15														
16		01	02	03	04	05	06	07	08	09	10	11	12	
17	+ North America	7000	6000	8000	9000	10000	14300	13000	13000	12000	9000	6000	7000	
18														
19														
20														
21														

In this example the requested view has also the title elements "2011," "PG1," and "Units." So Cognos TM1 is looking for a stored view "Stargate 2011-PG1-Units" again. Now Cognos TM1 finds such a stored view and checks the sets of elements of the row and column dimensions. The sets of the column dimension are equal in both views (the stored view and the requested view), but the sets of the row dimensions do not match. Cognos TM1 evaluates the children of the consolidated element "North America" ("US" and "Canada") first when the row dimensions are compared. These "new" elements (which do not already exist in the Stargate) are now added to the existing Stargate. The values of the view are calculated, returned, and cached.

- **Step 3.** We go back to our first user. This user has changed the subset of the row dimension in the meantime. This example is shown in the following illustration.

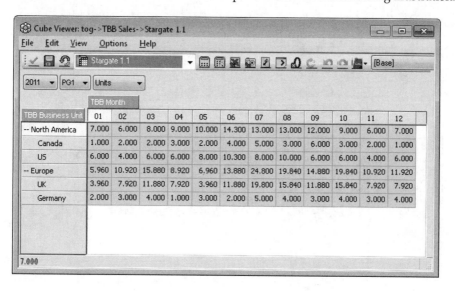

In this example Cognos TM1 is also looking for a stored Stargate "Stargate 2011-PG1-Units." Cognos TM1 can find a stored view. Again, the stored view and the requested view are compared regarding the leaf children of the row and column dimension. In this case all requested leafs can also be found in the stored view. The requested view can be fulfilled by the stored view (cache) without any further action.

- **Step 4.** In this step the user does some OLAP gestures (Slice & Dice). The user changes one title dimension (from "Units" to "Revenue"; see the following illustration) and recalculates the view. After that, the user replaces the row dimension "TBB Business Unit" with the title dimension "TBB Product" (see the second following illustration) and recalculates the view again. This gesture leads to the creation of two new Stargate views: "Stargate 2011-PG1-Revenue" and "Stargate 2011-North America-Units."

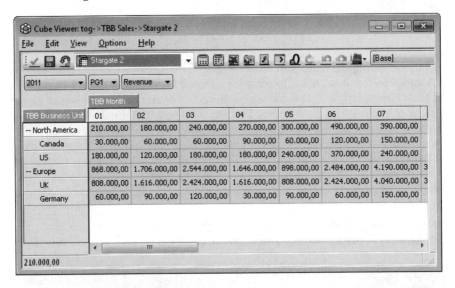

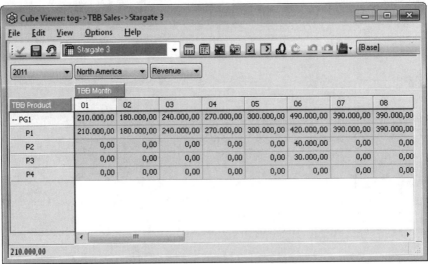

As we mentioned in the introduction of this chapter, the developer has little control over the Cognos TM1 caching. Regarding Stargate, the developer can control the behavior of caching by setting the cube properties VMM (View Maximum Memory) and VMT (View Minimum Time). You can find these properties in the system cube "}CubeProperties", as shown in the following illustration:

At this point we refer you to the Cognos TM1 documentation, *Cognos TM1 Operations Guide*. Here is an excerpt from this documentation:

VMM	For each cube, this property determines the amount of RAM reserved on the server for the storage of Stargate views. The more memory made available for Stargate views, the better performance will be. You must, however, make sure sufficient memory is available for the Cognos TM1 server to load all cubes.
	If no VMM value is specified, the default value is 65,536 bytes. The valid range is from 16,384 to 42,934,943,296 bytes.
VMT	For each cube, this property defines the time threshold, in seconds, beyond which the algorithm that stores Cognos TM1 Stargate views is triggered.
	If the time required to calculate a cube view surpasses the specified threshold, Cognos TM1 attempts to store a Stargate view. If there is not enough memory available to store the Stargate view, Cognos TM1 purges the oldest Stargate view that is not currently in use, and continues to purge views in this manner until sufficient memory is made available.
	If no VMM value is specified, the default value is five seconds. The valid range is from 1 to 259,200 seconds.

The VMM (View Maximum Memory) property is set for the RAM per cube. That means the value is a threshold that should not be passed by the amount of the RAM used per view of the cube.

If you set these properties, the next view will use them to create and store a Stargate view.

Cube Dependency

Once a cube dependency is established, it remains valid for the duration of the server session unless it becomes invalidated by changing a rule object or a dimension. Establishing the cube dependency on demand is a quick operation, but when it is performed as part of a long-running view or TI process, a write lock on the dependencies cache will block concurrent readers and writers from accessing the dependent cube (see also the next section). In the newest versions of Cognos TM1, there are some changes in the locking methodology. For that reason we alternate between older and newer versions in the following sections.

Cognos TM1 Versions 10.1 and Higher

Virtually all cube dependencies are established automatically at server startup, following dimension updates, or during rule file compilation. Rules that derive cube names conditionally in rule syntax will establish cube dependencies "on the fly" when data represented by the rules is invoked. If that cube dependency is established by a long-running TurboIntegrator process, it may cause contention issues for users attempting to update the cubes involved concurrently with the TurboIntegrator process execution. If you have such a rule, we recommend you establish the cube dependency "up front" with a quick-running TurboIntegrator process containing the function AddCubeDependency(base cube, dependent cube) following server startup or after related dimension changes (dimensions in either of these cubes).

Cognos TM1 Versions 9.5.2 FP1 and Earlier

Some cube dependencies are established during server startup, namely those that Cognos TM1 can determine based on feeders. Therefore, any cube relationship that can be determined by cross-cube feeders will result in cube dependencies being created at server startup. However, cube dependencies not represented by feeders—for instance, relationships to }Element_ Attribute cubes required as a result of using ATTRN or ATTRS functions in TM1 rule files— will be created "on the fly" when data represented by the rules is invoked. Further, related cube dependencies will be invalidated following any dimension updates. See the chapter "Understanding Cube Dependencies" in the *Cognos TM1 Operations Guide* for more details.

Garbage Collection

In case of invalidation of a cache, the memory that is allocated by the cache is released and goes to garbage collection. Cognos TM1 controls its own garbage collection, so no memory is released to the underlying operating system (such as Windows). If the Cognos TM1 server needs additional memory, it will first check the garbage collection to reuse the released memory. If the garbage collection is empty, Cognos TM1 will allocate new memory from the operating system. That means Cognos TM1 never gives back allocated memory to the operating system.

Understanding Object Locking

In this section we will dive deeply into the core of Cognos TM1. Before we start, we want to mention that IBM introduced the new concept of "Parallel Interaction" with Cognos TM1 version 9.5.2. This concept changes the mechanism of locking. "Parallel Interaction" is the default behavior of Cognos TM1 9.5.2 FP 2 and higher. So let's have a look at this feature.

Parallel Interaction

Parallel Interaction is one of the outstanding features of the current Cognos TM1 version. It was subsequently established as a default capability with Version 10.1. Parallel Interaction enables concurrent reading and writing to a cube. With Parallel Interaction the Cognos TM1 server can handle concurrent writers without blocking multiple threads/transactions. This feature solves the contention problem with the cost of slightly more memory consumption. The exact memory usage varies depending on the specific cubes in your TM1 server and the amount of read/write activity on those cubes. Customers upgrading from versions prior to TM1 9.5.2 should allow for between 10 and 30% more RAM consumption in their TM1 server to accommodate Parallel Interaction structures.

The mechanisms of object locking that are discussed in this section are valid for manipulating metadata. They are also valid for manipulating data if you are using Cognos TM1 versions between 9.1 and 9.5.1 (including these versions), or if you have deactivated "Parallel Interaction" (it can be deactivated by setting the parameter ParallelInteraction=F in the configuration file tm1s.cfg). We do not discuss the locking model of older versions in this book.

Cognos TM1 Transactions and Locking

To understand object locking, you have to first understand the aspects of a "Cognos TM1 transaction" because objects are locked in the context of a transaction. (We call it "Cognos TM1 transaction" to underline that a transaction in Cognos TM1 is not equal to a transaction in a relational database. Additionally, the Cognos TM1 transaction mentioned here is not a transaction in the Cognos TM1 transaction log.)

Figure 10-3 shows the flow of a Cognos TM1 transaction. Some terms in this figure need to be explained. A Cognos TM1 transaction is a collection of one or many operations. In Cognos TM1 a *transaction* is a predefined function inside the Cognos TM1 server. These functions are visible outside the Cognos TM1 server as Application Programming Interface (API) calls. As a programmer you can use the API functions in a programming environment. As a Cognos TM1 solution developer or Cognos TM1 user, you can explicitly call some of the API functions by the user interface. Here are some examples of these Cognos TM1 transactions (all samples are treated as single transactions in Cognos TM1):

- Executing a chore (job)
- Executing a TurboIntegrator process, especially executing nested TurboIntegrator processes (execute a process inside a process via the ExecuteProcess function)
- Calling SaveDataAll from the menu
- Calling RefreshSecurity from the menu
- Creating or opening a view (for example, Cube Viewer)
- All Data Spread functions
- All Hold functions
- Changing the value of a cell (for example, entering a value in a websheet)
- Accessing a dynamic subset

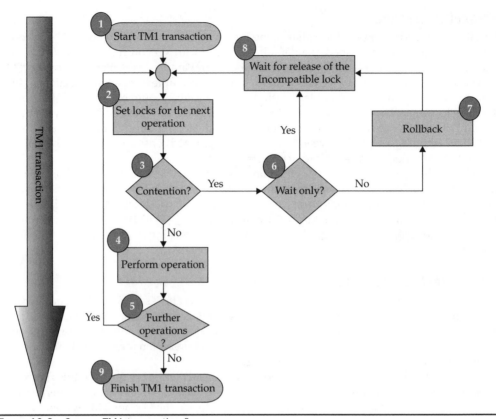

FIGURE 10-3   Cognos TM1 transaction flow

It is possible for a Cognos TM1 function to call another Cognos TM1 function. For instance, in a TurboIntegrator process, another TurboIntegrator process is executed or the SaveDataAll function is called. This is treated as one single Cognos TM1 transaction. The start of the first function (topmost function in a function call stack or the enclosed function) starts the transaction. The transaction is finished when this topmost function is terminated. All nested functions do not run in transactions.

Let us explain the other terms now by going step by step through the transaction flow (see Figure 10-3):

- **Step 1.**   The Cognos TM1 transaction starts (a Cognos TM1 API function is called).

- **Step 2.**   In this step Cognos TM1 starts to lock objects for the upcoming operation. It depends on the operation that is going to be executed if only one object or more objects are locked. Which lock mode is used for the different objects also depends on the operation. If the operation is going to modify an object, Cognos TM1 will create a temporary copy (the "Before Image") of the object. This copy is needed to do the "Rollback" later on (Step 5). Table 10-1 lists the lock modes.

Cognos TM1 Lock Mode	Description
R (READ)	The READ lock is used when an object is read. For instance, a cube is locked by a READ lock, if a user queries that cube.
IX (intent to write lock)	The IX lock is used when you intend to modify an object. However, if a transaction holds an IX lock on an object, it is allowed to modify the object. Only one transaction at a time is allowed to have an IX lock on an object. For instance, an IX lock is acquired on a dimension (the object) if an element is inserted or removed.
W (WRITE)	The WRITE lock is used when the modification of an object is committed. In order to request a WRITE lock, the transaction has to hold an IX lock first. No other transaction can read or modify an object that is locked by a W lock.

TABLE 10-1   Lock Modes

- **Step 3.**   For each object lock, Cognos TM1 checks whether a contention occurs. What does "contention" mean? If two or more concurrent Cognos TM1 transactions try to access the same Cognos TM1 object, they both try to lock this object. As we mentioned in Step 2, which lock mode is used for the intended lock depends on the object and the operation. So if the current transaction tries to lock an object, it has to first check if the object is already locked. If the object is not locked, the lock can be set (which means that no contention occurs). If the object is already locked, the transaction can set its own lock if the existing lock and the intended lock are compatible. Table 10-2 shows which locks are compatible and which are not.

  The compatibility of the locks controls the flow of the transaction. If the locks are compatible (Yes), the flow continues with Step 4. If the locks are not compatible, the flow continues with Step 6. (The empty cells indicate combinations that never occur. The reason is that a transaction can set an IX lock only if it had set an R lock in a previous operation, and the transaction can set a W lock only if it already holds an IX lock on the objects.)

- **Step 4.**   The operation is performed on the locked object(s).

- **Step 5.**   If all operations of the Cognos TM1 transaction are done, the flow will go to Step 9. Otherwise, the flow will go on with Step 2.

	Intended Lock		
Existing Lock	**R**	**IX**	**W**
R	Yes	Yes	No
IX	No	No	
W	No		

TABLE 10-2   Lock Compatibility

- **Step 6.**   In this step the flow branches to Step 7 or Step 8. The flow continues with Step 7 if the transaction intends an IX lock on an object that is already locked by another transaction with an R or an IX lock. The flow continues with Step 8 for all other cases.

- **Step 7.**   Now the Cognos TM1 transaction has to roll back. On rollback, the transaction restores all "Before Images." The objects that are already modified by the transaction return to the same state that they were in at the start of the transaction. The Cognos TM1 transaction is reset to the first operation, and all locks are released.

- **Step 8.**   In this step the Cognos TM1 transaction has to wait until all incompatible locks of other transactions are released. While the transaction is waiting, you can monitor this wait state with the Cognos TM1 Top Utility or the Cognos TM1 Operations Console. At this point, the state of the flow is indicated by the word "Wait" in these utilities followed by additional information. This additional information could be one from the following list (excerpted from the *Cognos TM1 Operations Guide*):

  - **WR** (WaitForWriterEvent)   The thread is waiting for R locks to be released so it can obtain a W lock on the object.

  - **IXR** (WaitForIXReaderEvent)   The thread is waiting for a W lock to finish so it can get either an R lock or an IX lock on an object.

  - **IXC** (WaitForIXConflictEvent)   The thread is requesting an IX lock, but is waiting for another thread with an IX lock on the same object to finish and release the lock.

  - **IXCur** (WaitForIXCurrentEvent)   The thread is requesting an IX lock for an object, but is waiting for a thread with an R lock on the same object to release its lock.

  - **WC** (WaitForCompletionEvent)   The thread is waiting for another thread to complete and release its locks.

  - **DRR** (Data Reservation Release)   The thread is waiting for data.

- **Step 9.**   Reservation to be released.

- **Step 10.**   The Cognos TM1 transaction finishes and releases all locks.

In Figure 10-3 we used the phrase "operation." An operation is meant to be a granular step in a transaction. Let's explain this with an example: Writing a value to a cell is performed by the transaction (API call) DimensionElementInsert. This transaction consists of single operations:

1. Set a READ lock on the dimension.

2. Set an IX lock on the dimension and write to a temporary copy of the dimension.

3. Set a WRITE lock to the dimension and commit the modification to the original dimension.

With the following example, you can force the occurrence of a contention in order to observe the behavior of Cognos TM1 when concurrent transactions try to manipulate the same object. You need to create two TurboIntegrator processes. The first TurboIntegrator process inserts an element into a dimension and waits for an event before it continues. The second

TurboIntegrator process fires the event for the first process. How do we extend the time of a lock and therefore the time of the contention? To understand the mechanism of the example, you have to understand that a TurboIntegrator process works as a single transaction (see Figure 10-4). Regarding the transaction flow (Figure 10-3), the execution of a TurboIntegrator process starts with Step 1 and ends with Step 9. A TurboIntegrator process can consist of many statements that manipulate Cognos TM1 objects. Therefore it can acquire many different locks before it reaches the last step. Only in this last step, all locks are released that are owned by the transaction of the TurboIntegrator process. If, during the execution of the process, a contention is detected that leads to a "rollback" (Step 7), the whole process will roll back and restart from the beginning of the script.

NOTE *A TurboIntegrator process that is called by another process via the* `ExecuteProcess` *function is not treated as a separate transaction. All operations of this process are embedded in the transaction of the parent process.*

Now we will prove this mechanism with our example. For this example we use the fact that the release of the locks happens only in Step 9. We add a loop to our TurboIntegrator process so that this process does not continue to the last step until an event occurs. The loop is implemented by a WHILE statement. The condition to leave the loop is the existence of a file in the log directory of the Cognos TM1 server. Our sample process will wait until a specified file is created. After the execution has left the loop, this file is deleted to make sure that the next time the TurboIntegrator is executed, it will wait again. A parameter is passed to this TurboIntegrator process. This parameter is used to specify the name of the file. So you can start the TurboIntegrator process with different parameter values to simulate multiple concurrent transactions. Each concurrent TurboIntegrator process can wait on its own event (file).

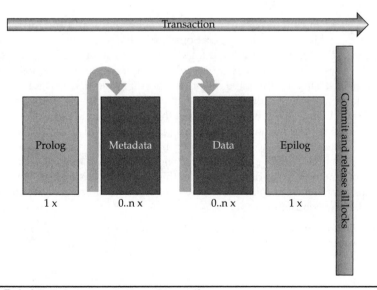

FIGURE 10-4 TurboIntegrator process as one transaction

Here you find the definition of the first TurboIntegrator process:

TBB Test Transaction (Numeric Parameter: piCount)
Prolog:

```
sDimension = 'TBB Test';
sElement = 'Element ' | NumberToString(piCounter);
sFileName = '.\logs\TestTransaction' | NumberToString(piCounter) | '.log';

DimensionElementInsert(sDimension, '', sElement, 'N');
```

Epilog:

```
#  wait for event/file
WHILE( FILEEXISTS(sFileName) = 0);
    iCount = 1;
    WHILE( iCount <= 100000);
        iCount = iCount +1;
    END;
END;

ASCIIDELETE(sFileName);
```

The second TurboIntegrator process just creates the file (creates the event). You can pass the same parameter to the process, as in the first process. This parameter also specifies the file that has to be created. The second TurboIntegrator process is defined as follows:

TBB Transaction Test Create Control File (Numeric Parameter: piCount)
Prolog:

```
sFileName = '.\logs\TestTransaction' | NumberToString(piCounter) | '.log';

TEXTOUTPUT(sFileName ,'Test');
```

To run the check, you should log in three times concurrently and run the monitor tool Cognos TM1 Top or the Cognos TM1 Operations Console if you have installed Cognos TM1 10.1. The Cognos TM1 Top tool shows and logs the state of each thread that is running in the Cognos TM1 server. Each concurrent user who is logged in to the Cognos TM1 server has his own thread. Each user can have only one thread per login. If a user is logged in with multiple clients, he will open multiple threads. In our example we have created three users: User 1, User 2, and User 3. We start the Architect three times and log in with these three users. In the following illustration, you can see a screenshot of this situation. Only one transaction can be executed at the same time per thread. So we have a one-to-one relation of a thread to a transaction. Now we also start the Cognos TM1 Top tool (please refer to the Cognos TM1 documentation for details). To run this tool, open a command console and change the directory to the bin folder of your Cognos TM1 installation. Execute the tool by issuing the following command:

```
TM1top.exe -adminhost <Name of the AdminHost> -servername <Name of the
Cognos TM1 server> -refresh 1
```

and follow these steps:

- **Step 1.** User 2 starts the process "TBB Test Transaction" with parameter value = 1.

- **Step 2.** User 1 starts the process "TBB Test Transaction" with parameter value = 2. Now you can observe in the Cognos TM1 Top window that User 2 is waiting with "IXC" state (see the wait state list earlier). At this point the thread of User 1 is running the TurboIntegrator, which is executing the loop, and the thread of User 2 is waiting for the release of the incompatible lock (Step 8 in Figure 10-3).

- **Step 3.** If you are finished with observing the transactions, you can stop the first transaction by running the TurboIntegrator process "TBB Transaction Test Create Control File" with the parameter value = 1. Run the process as User 3. After the process has finished, the process of User 1 will also terminate and the process of User 2 will enter the loop.

- **Step 4.** To finish the process of User 2, you can run the TurboIntegrator process "TBB Transaction Test Create Control File" again. This time you should set the parameter of the process to value = 2.

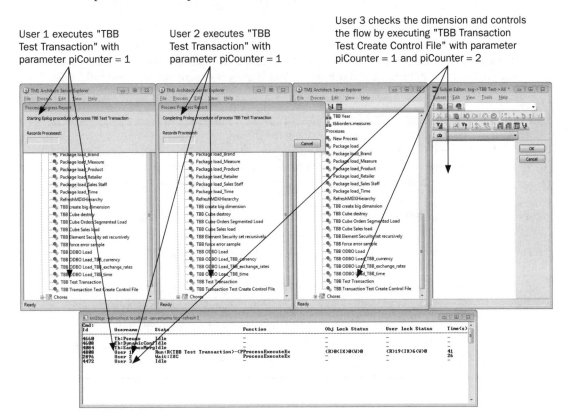

User 1 executes "TBB Test Transaction" with parameter piCounter = 1

User 2 executes "TBB Test Transaction" with parameter piCounter = 1

User 3 checks the dimension and controls the flow by executing "TBB Transaction Test Create Control File" with parameter piCounter = 1 and piCounter = 2

The following illustration shows an example of monitor information in Cognos TM1 Operations Console.

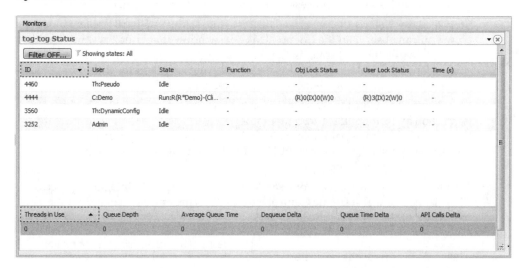

Both monitoring tools (Cognos TM1 Top and Cognos TM1 Operations Console) display the thread/transaction information in columns. Here is a short description of these columns:

ID	The ID of the Thread
Username	The name of the user who is running the thread. System threads: Th:Pseudo (used to clean up "user-defined consolidations"), Th:DynamicConf (used to update dynamic configurations set in the tm1s.cfg file) Chores: Chores that are running by schedule are displayed as C:<Name of the chore>
State	The state of the thread, like "Idle," "Run," "Login," "Commit," "Rollback," or "Wait:<Contention Type>"
Function	The name of the API call, like "CubeCellValueGet," "CubeCellValueSet," "CubeCellSpread"
Obj Lock Status	The number of READ (R), IX, and WRITE (W) locks on the object that is currently accessed by the thread (these are the counterpart locks of the user locks)
User Lock Status	The number of READ (R), IX, and WRITE (W) locks that are already set by the thread
Time(s)	The time in seconds the thread is already running

TABLE 10-3   Columns in the Monitor Tools

As you now understand how Cognos TM1 locks objects in the Cognos TM1 server, we will take a look at some common transactions in Cognos TM1. Table 10-4 shows these transactions and what potential conflicts could occur.

Transaction/Operation	Locks/Objects	Potential Conflicts
Execute TurboIntegrator	Commonly READ and IX locks	The locks are held for a long time because the locks are released when the process terminates
SecurityRefresh	READ lock on the most objects in the Cognos TM1 server	High potential for contention
SaveDataAll	READ lock on every cube and IX lock on every modified object	High potential for contention **Note:** The function SaveData(<cubeName>) was introduced with Version 10.1. This function allows you to save data for single cubes with fewer contention issues
ViewArrayConstruct	READ lock on cube	READ lock prevents other transactions from modifying the cube and dependent objects. This could be an issue if the view takes a long time to be generated
CubeSetLogChanges	IX lock on cube on system cube "}CubeProperties"	Parallel running TurboIntegrator processes are blocked even if they intend to write to a different cube than the process that executed CubeSetLogChanges
Element maintenance and updating an alias	IX lock on dimension and all cubes containing the modified dimension (updating an alias is also a modification of a dimension)	There may be contention issues when a dimension is maintained as part of a longer-running TurboIntegrator process. We recommend that you separate modification of metadata (including updating aliases) and loading of data into different processes

TABLE 10-4 Potential Transaction Conflicts

To complete this section we would like to add some information regarding "Parallel Interaction" and chores.

Chore Transaction
You can execute multiple TurboIntegrator processes in a chore (see also Chapter 7). The processes are executed in the defined sequence. A chore can also execute the same process multiple times (optional with different parameters). An example is shown in

the following illustration. A chore can be scheduled to run frequently. If the chore runs on a scheduled event, it will run in its own thread.

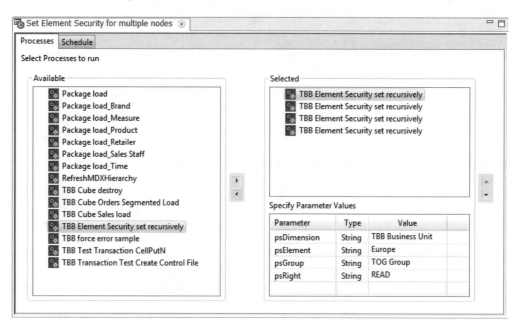

Chore definition with Performance Modeler

All operations of all TurboIntegrator processes executed by the same chore are embedded in only one transaction. The modifications that are made are committed when the last process terminates. In Cognos TM1 version 10.1 or higher, there is an option to commit each TurboIntegrator process in a chore. In this case, locks from each TurboIntegrator process are not held for the duration of the chore, but you get the benefit of sequentially executed processes. In the following illustration, you can see the two options "Single Commit Mode" and "Multiple Commit Mode." "Single Commit Mode" is the "old version" of the Transaction mode. If you choose "Multiple Commit Mode," each TurboIntegrator process of the chore commits all modifications and releases all locks.

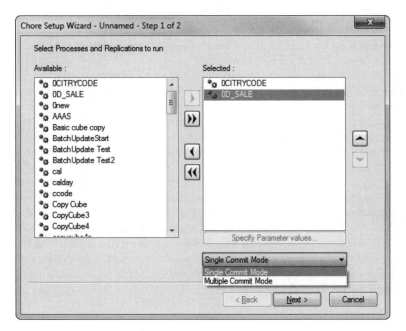

Regarding Cache and Locks

In the next two sections we will discuss some issues involving caches and locks.

Locks and Cube Dependency

We already talked about cube dependency when we discussed caching earlier in this chapter. Cube dependencies are also relevant for locking. There are two issues regarding cube dependencies:

1. If a cube is locked by a Cognos TM1 transaction, then all dependent cubes are also locked. Let us explain this by an example: Cube 1 depends on Cube 2 because a rule is applied to Cube 1, which accesses Cube 2 by a DB function (see also Chapter 6). If a transaction reads from Cube 1, a READ lock is set on both cubes. If a transaction writes to Cube 2, an IX lock is set on both cubes. But: If a transaction reads from Cube 2, no lock is set on Cube 1. If a transaction writes to Cube 1, no lock is set on Cube 2.

2. We already discussed the following in the section "Cognos TM1 Caching." But for the sake of completeness, we repeat: The information about the cube dependencies is cached in the Cognos TM1 server. If a dependency is not already cached, the information has to be evaluated when it is needed. The detected dependency has to be added to the cache. This is a modification of a system object, which leads to a lock of this system object.

Please refer to the chapter "Understanding Cube Dependency" in the *Cognos TM1 Operations Guide* for additional information.

Dynamic Subsets in Older Versions

The following section is only valid for older Cognos TM1 versions. Dynamic subsets will not cause contention with Cognos TM1 9.5.2 FP2 and higher.

If you open a dynamic subset in the Subset Editor, or a dynamic subset is used in a view, the element list needs to be calculated. If the content of the dynamic subset is calculated, the result will be cached in the Cognos TM1 server and can be reused by the next request of the subset. If any object in the Cognos TM1 server is modified, the cached subset is invalidated and has to be recalculated because the expression of a dynamic subset can depend on any data and metadata of the Cognos TM1 server (for example, cell values, attributes, elements of different dimensions). When the content of a dynamic subset needs to be calculated, the parent transaction locks the subset with an IX lock (plus a READONLY lock on the parent dimension). This may causes contentions. If you observe unacceptable performance of your application, you should investigate whether this is an issue caused by dynamic subsets. A workaround to avoid dynamic subsets is to create adequate static subsets by TurboIntegrator processes. Dynamic subset contentions occur when you use a dynamic subset as the data source of a TurboIntegrator process and this process modifies an object (for example, CellPutN). For each modification, the dynamic subset has to be recalculated. This leads to a decrease of the speed of the process.

Summary

In this chapter we took a look under the hood of Cognos TM1 and discussed important mechanisms of Cognos TM1. Please be aware that you must consider which Cognos TM1 version you are running. Only the new versions of TM1 have the feature of Parallel Interaction. If you run an older version, every input of data (by user entry, by TurboIntegrator process) could lead to lock contentions on the underlying cube. So we recommend using the versions with Parallel Interaction. This gives you more freedom when you develop a Cognos TM1 solution for many concurrent users, because Parallel Interaction manages the concurrent write access of multiple users in the background.

Data Loading and Scaling

A s the developer of a Cognos TM1 application, you should focus on the requirements of your application first. What are the business requirements? How can I meet these business requirements and build a Cognos TM1 model with the Cognos TM1 building blocks? These are the questions you probably asked yourself while you were reading the previous chapters in this part of the book. Now we will move on to another perspective.

As we discussed in Chapter 4, the Cognos TM1 model is "disconnected" from data sources. You can use data sources to build up and load your model, and/or you can populate an existing model with data from an external data source. But some Cognos TM1 applications require loading a large amount of data to the Cognos TM1 server. For this kind of application, you have to have a second focus on your application: performance and how to manage large data volumes. This second focus should be your second step after the design of the model concerning business requirements. This chapter is about how to load large volumes of data and how to manage this amount of data in a Cognos TM1 model. (The next chapter also concerns performance but from a different angle: a large number of concurrent users.) So this chapter is divided into two sections: the loading of data and the scaling of data in a Cognos TM1 model.

Before we start, we want to note that we often mention the locking model of Cognos TM1, which was explained in Chapter 10. Please be aware that with Cognos TM1 9.5.2, the locking model changed with Parallel Interaction. Parallel Interaction is an option that can be deactivated or activated by the administrator. The default setting for the Cognos TM1 server in Version 9.5.2 is the deactivated Parallel Interaction. In Version 10.1 and higher, Parallel Interaction is the default mode. In addition, many customers are still using older versions of Cognos TM1, so we want to give hints for users of the old versions in the next sections.

Loading Metadata and Data

You can create a TurboIntegrator process that connects to a data source and loads data and metadata. In the case of loading a large amount of data, you have to consider the following issues:

- **Locking (see Chapter 10)** The TurboIntegrator process sets a lock to the cube, which is loaded if a dimension maintenance function is executed. This lock forces the users who are interacting with the application to wait (the users will see the hourglass icon). The lock is released when the TurboIntegrator process terminates. Loading a large amount of data leads to a long-running process, which leads to long-lasting locks. The users who are waiting a long time perceive this as poor performance. Best practice is to separate Metadata maintenance from data maintenance in separate TurboIntegrator processes, and run them together in a chore which commits changes to each process as it completes.

- **Completeness of data** Reporting and analysis on data make sense only if you are using data that is complete. So a Cognos TM1 model is ready to be used when all data is already loaded but loading a large amount of data could take much time. At this point your application runs into an issue when the loading is still in progress and the users want to start their daily work.

Because of these two issues, you have to decide *when* to load the data. The best time to load data and prevent these issues is the period when the application is not being used. In most cases, the data is loaded during the night. Unfortunately, there is a possibility that a load can run out of time. Especially if the Cognos TM1 application is used in more than one time zone around the world, the window for loading data can be very small, if it exists at all. The only way to solve the problem is to shorten the loading time. How can you do that? The answer to that question is parallel loading. (Of course, you can also optimize the loading by tuning the data source. If you are using a relational database, you can optimize the indexes of the requested tables and/or optimize the SQL query.)

NOTE *Using Parallel Interaction eliminates lock contentions when loading data. There are still lock contentions when metadata is modified. If you are using the older version without a Parallel Interaction, this issue occurs even when you load the data only.*

Parallel Loading

Parallel loading means running multiple TurboIntegrator processes at the same time. This includes executing the same TurboIntegrator process multiple times concurrently. Parallel loading is also called "multithreaded loading." When you define parallel loading, you have to make sure that all concurrent processes are loading a different portion of the data. That leads into data segmentation. It is obvious that you can do parallel loading if the model of your Cognos TM1 application is already segmented by the business requirements. That means you have to load data into different cubes. In this case, you should already have different TurboIntegrator processes, which can be executed concurrently. We will explain later how you can run parallel multiple processes.

Now we will take a closer look at parallel loading from the same data source to the same cube. In this case, you have to define different portions of the data source to load the data into different portions of the cube. The next few sections provide some examples of this data segmentation.

Loading from a Relational Database

When you load data from a relational database, you can divide the SQL query into segments by using the WHERE clause. Of course, you can create a single TurboIntegrator process for each segment, but it is best practice to have one process per cube that can load different segments controlled by parameters. We now want to create a TurboIntegrator process that supports segmentation on a relational database (we are assuming that we define segmentation per month; see also the section "How to Do the Segmentation"). We already discussed in Chapter 7 how to create a TurboIntegrator process with the Architect client. In the following example we took the screenshots when we were using Performance Modeler for each step. Of course, you can do this with Architect, too. There are only a few differences. For instance, the Performance Modeler does some additional code generation when you map the data source items to Cognos TM1 objects, and it creates two additional parameters that are used in the generated script. Here are the steps:

- **Step 1.** Create a new TurboIntegrator process with relational data source type "ODBC" (see also Chapter 7). See the following two illustrations.

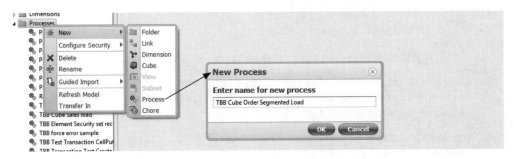

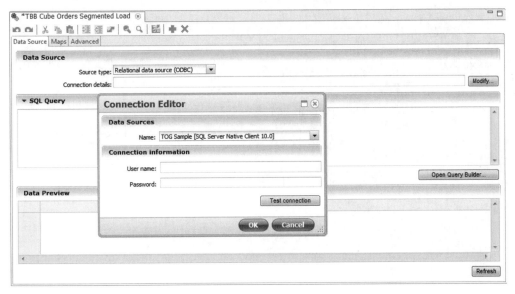

- **Step 2.**   Choose the "Data Source Name" and enter the appropriate SELECT statement. If you are using Performance Modeler, you can create your query with the Query Builder. The query should be defined to request only one segment from the data source. In other words, you should create a SQL query with an appropriate WHERE clause to get a sample segment. This helps you find out which part of the SQL statement should be parameterized to access different segments. Here is our sample query:

```
select
     T1."orderid" as "orderid",
     T1."customerid" as "customerid",
     T1."date" as "date",
     T1."productid" as "productid",
     T1."units" as "units"
from
     "TOG Sample"."dbo"."orders" T1
where
     (Month(date) = 01) and (Year(date) = 2006)
```

The WHERE clause depends on the month and the year of the table column date. So we have to change the year and/or the month to get another segment. (In Performance Modeler you can use the Query Builder, as shown in the following two illustrations.)

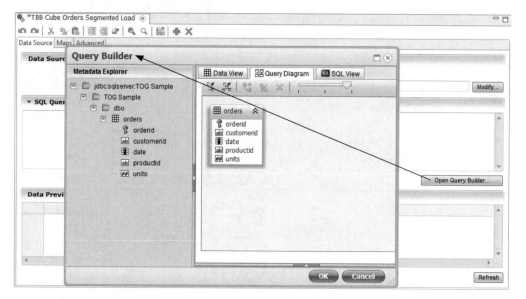

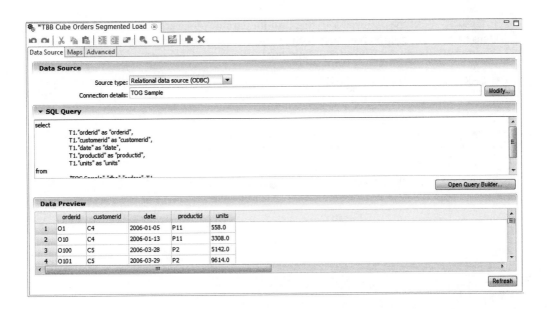

- **Step 3.** Use variables and mapping in the same way as you would create a single load process for your target cube, as shown in the following illustration.

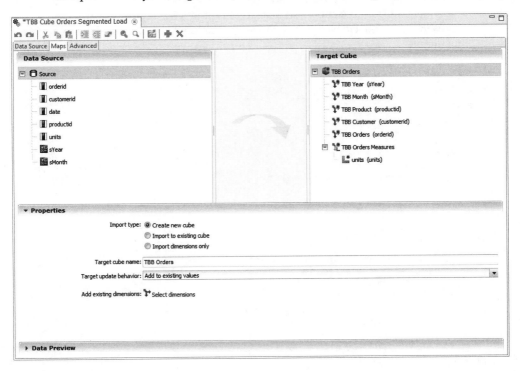

- **Step 4.**   Add the parameter to the TurboIntegrator process (in our example, we want to have segmentation by one month of one year, so we add the parameters psYear and psMonth, as shown in the following illustration).

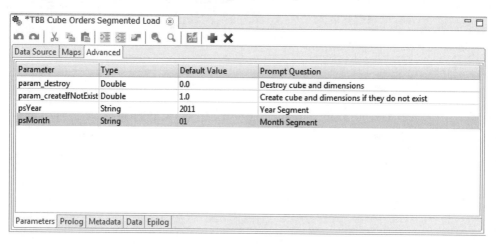

- **Step 5.**   Copy the query statement from the Data Source tab.

- **Step 6.**   Go to the Prolog tab and add the following code to the script (use the copied SQL statement from the clipboard instead of typing it in, and replace the static values in the WHERE clause by the process parameters as needed). See the following illustration.

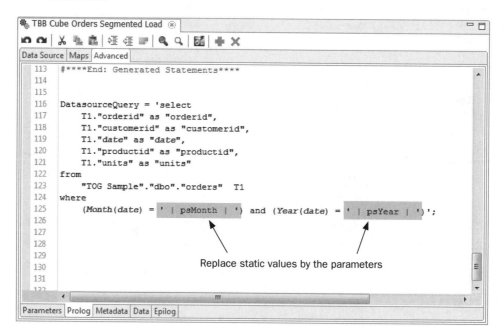

Loading from Files

When you load data from files, you have to create separate files for each segment because a file cannot be opened by multiple TurboIntegrator processes at the same time. As we explained for relational data sources, you should create only one TurboIntegrator process per cube and use a parameter to control which file should be loaded. We recommend naming the segment files using a pattern and storing the files in the same folder (the folder has to be accessible by the Cognos TM1 server). This allows you to access different files by modifying the value of the "Data Source Name for Server." The steps to create this kind of process are very similar to the steps described in the previous section, "Loading from a Relational Database":

- **Step 1.** Create a new TurboIntegrator process with data source type "Text" (this is called "File" in Performance Modeler).

- **Step 2.** Choose one of the segment files as a sample (a pattern for the columns in each segment file).

- **Step 3.** Use variables and mapping in the same way as you would create a single load process for your target cube.

- **Step 4.** Add the parameter to the TurboIntegrator process as needed. Which parameters are needed depends on how you have defined the pattern of the segment files. For instance, if your segment files are named "orders_2010-01.csv," "orders_2010-02," "orders_2010-03," and so on, you can have one parameter to pass a value like "2010-01," or you can have two parameters to pass "2010" and "01" to the process. If you do not use a pattern, you have to pass the whole filename to the process. Let's use the "orders_YYYY-MM.csv" pattern and the two-parameters version as an example. We add psYear and psMonth to the process parameters.

- **Step 5.** Go to the Prolog tab and add the following code to the script:

```
#Add here the path of the folder where the segment files are stored
sSegmentFolder = '.......';
DataSourceNameForServer = sSegmentFolder | 'orders_' |
                  psYear | '-' | psMonth | '.csv';
```

How to Do the Segmentation

First, you should be aware that segmentation depends on the number of cores on the machine where the Cognos TM1 server is running. Each segment is represented by a TurboIntegrator process. If you load the segments concurrently, the operating system must be able to support each parallel TurboIntegrator process with the appropriate resources. If you run more TurboIntegrator processes concurrently than the number of cores that are available, the processes have to share these cores. In this case, the processes will not run concurrently in real time. But let's go back to the segmentation.

You can do the segmentation by various criteria:

- Segmentation by time (for example, one segment per month)
- Segmentation by products
- Segmentation by regions
- Segmentation by business units and so on

To choose the best segmentation, you should observe the following consideration:

- The segments should not overlap. That guarantees that different segments do not contain the same data. Loading the same data with different processes would be a waste of time. The objective should be loading separate portions of the cube.

How to Run Concurrent TurboIntegrator Processes

Each concurrent segment process has to run in a separate thread. A thread is created if a user has logged in to the Cognos TM1 server (user thread) or if a chore is started by the Cognos TM1 scheduler. So there are the following options to start multiple TurboIntegrator processes concurrently (this includes the fact that you can start the same process multiple times):

1. Open multiple clients (for example, Architect) and log in. Run a process manually.
2. Use a command-line tool to run a TurboIntegrator process. Such a command-line tool is based on the Cognos TM1 API. A command-line tool creates a user thread because all Cognos TM1 API-based tools must log in with a user account to the Cognos TM1 server first. IBM provides such a tool since Cognos TM1 9.5.2 HF1, which is called tm1runti.exe (see also Chapter 7).
3. Schedule a chore for each segment process at the same time. In the chore you can specify the segment parameters (see also Chapter 7), as shown in the following illustration.

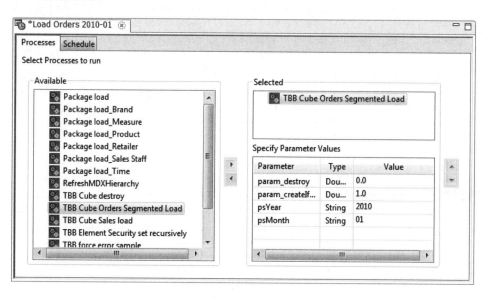

At this point we have to discuss how to work around lock contentions (see Chapter 7). When we run multiple segment processes concurrently, these processes access the same cube. The following discussion is not related to segmented loads only.

Generally, if you run multiple TurboIntegrator processes, you have to find out which Cognos TM1 objects are accessed and which the potential contentions are. You'll need to know this if you have to work around contentions. For instance, suppose that you want to load two different cubes with two different TurboIntegrator processes, which are running concurrently. You should know that you won't get contentions on the cubes you are loading, but you will get contention on the system cube "}CubeProperties" if both processes are executing the CUBESETLOGCHANGES function. TurboIntegrator processes that are running concurrently are very common if you provide Action buttons (see Chapter 8) to the users, which allow a user to start a process (for example, to proceed with workflow), or if you are using Cognos TM1 Contributor, which executes TurboIntegrator processes for different events in the Cognos TM1 Contributor client (for example, "Take Ownership," "Submit," "Save," and so on).

There are two ways to work around the contentions and to make sure that multiple processes are running concurrently. We will discuss these mechanisms in the next section.

Using BatchUpdate with Cognos TM1 9.5.1 and Lower

The batch update method is only relevant for older TM1 versions. With Parallel Interaction (Cognos TM1 9.5.2 and higher) there is no need for using BatchUpdate because multiple data sources could be simply loaded at the same time. For that reason we just like to mention how to set up BatchUpdate in a TurboIntegrator process:

When you develop the TurboIntegrator process you should place the BatchUpdateStart function as the first statement in the Prolog script and the BatchUpdateFinishWait function as the last statement in the Epilog script. Now all data modifications which are performed by the TurboIntegrator process are written to the temporary space and no locks are acquired. This mode continues until the process executes the BatchUpdateFinishWait function. Now all necessary locks (R, IX) are set to the cubes which are going to be modified. When the TurboIntegrator process terminates, the modification will be committed.

With this mechanism you shorten the time of holding locks when a long-running TurboIntegrator process is executed (it's like moving all locks to the end of the process).

NOTE *For compatibility reasons there is still an older function called* BatchUpdateFinish. *The difference between* BatchUpdateFinish *and* BatchUpdateFinishWait *is that if on commit a contention occurs,* BatchUpdateFinish *rolls back the current transaction and* BatchUpdateFinishWait *waits until the commit can be done.*

Using Parallel Interaction with Cognos TM1 9.5.2 and Higher

Parallel Interaction is a feature that has been available since Cognos TM1 version 9.5.2. We have already discussed Parallel Interaction in Chapter 10. Parallel Interaction can be switched on or off for the Cognos TM1 server. With Cognos TM1 10.1, Parallel Interaction becomes the default mode.

With Parallel Interaction, you do not need to use Batch mode for parallel loading because Parallel Interaction is already utilizing a multithreaded environment. We recommend using Parallel Interaction instead of Batch mode if available. Using Parallel Interaction, you will eliminate the disadvantages of Batch mode. To use your existing load process with Parallel Interaction, you should remove BatchUpdateStart and BatchUpdateFinishWait statements from the code.

Serial Loading

Although this chapter is about scaling data, to complete this section, we want to mention the method of loading that's the opposite of parallel loading. In some cases it is necessary to serialize data loading. For instance, it could be necessary to prevent any interaction while you are loading data. Another reason could be that the data has to be loaded in a certain sequence in order to be valid. For instance, a value has to be calculated during the loading based on another value that has to be loaded first.

In the next two sections we show two methods to serialize data load.

Bulk Load Mode

In some cases it is necessary to make sure that loading information to the Cognos TM1 server is not disturbed by any access by other threads (users who interact with the Cognos TM1 server or chores that are running processes). You can control a serialized load with the Bulk Load mode.

Use the following TurboIntegrator function to enable Bulk Load mode:

```
EnableBulkLoadMode();
```

Use the following TurboIntegrator function to disable Bulk Load mode:

```
DisableBulkLoadMode();
```

NOTE *The* `DisableBulkLoadMode` *function can only be used on the last line in the Epilog section.*

If you enable the Bulk Load mode, the current transaction will wait for the termination of all other transactions in the Cognos TM1 server. Then the Bulk Load mode is activated and prevents any start of new transactions in the Cognos TM1 server. That means that users cannot log in to the server and create a new thread. Threads that already exist will go into a sleep mode. The current transaction becomes the only active transaction in the Cognos TM1 server. The Cognos TM1 server runs in a single-thread mode. If the current transaction terminates or the `DisableBulkLoadMode` function is executed, all sleeping threats are woken up and users are allowed to log in to the Cognos TM1 server again. During the Bulk Load mode, the TurboIntegrator process (= the transaction) can modify Cognos TM1 objects without any conflict. But there is another advantage: During the Bulk Load mode, the transaction doesn't create any "Before Image" (see Chapter 10). For instance, if you want to manipulate large dimensions or huge cubes, the creation of a "Before Image" would take a long time. In this case, loading in Bulk Load mode would be faster than loading in "normal" mode.

Using Semaphores

A *semaphore* is an abstract object. In general, it's used as a flag that indicates a special mode to control access to parallel running threads. Which mode is indicated, what the flag means, and how a semaphore is implemented—all of this is up to the developer. To explain semaphores, we like to use the following analogy: Imagine that ten wise men are sitting in a circle. Each one wants to explain an important fact to the other ones. But if all men talk at the same time, nobody can hear. So the wise men put a stone in the middle of the circle. One man is allowed to grab the stone. Only the holder of the stone is allowed to speak. When the man with the stone has finished, he puts back the stone and another man can pick up the stone. The stone is the semaphore and the wise men are the processes. We will use a semaphore to indicate that a TurboIntegrator is manipulating objects and other TurboIntegrator processes should wait.

We want to mention that there are different approaches to implementing semaphores depending on which version you are using. The recommended approach is available with Cognos TM1 10.1. Cognos TM1 10.1 provides an explicit object for semaphores. Using an older version, you have to use an appropriate object as a semaphore. First, we want to mention the approach when you use older Cognos TM1 versions (without Parallel Interaction).

For this approach we need a Cognos TM1 object that can indicate to other processes that it is already in use. Now you might say: "We already have an indicator of this kind: the Cognos TM1 object lock." Indeed, we will use this lock; however, with the implementation of a semaphore, we want to have more control over when the lock should be set. Our semaphore object is a cube. This should be a small cube. You may create a new cube "Semaphore" with only two dimensions, or you can use an existing cube (for instance, an application control cube like "TBB Parameters"). In a TurboIntegrator process, you should set a semaphore by putting a value into this cube. The appropriate $CellPutX$ function should be one of the first statements in the script. For instance:

```
CellPutN(1, 'TBB Parameters', 'Counter', 'N');
```

If you intend to serialize different TurboIntegrator processes, you should make sure that all processes use the same cube as the semaphore.

In Figure 11-1, you can see the difference between the behavior of a standard TurboIntegrator process and the behavior of a process that is using a semaphore. With the semaphore, we force a lock contention very early in the flow of the process instead of having a contention late in

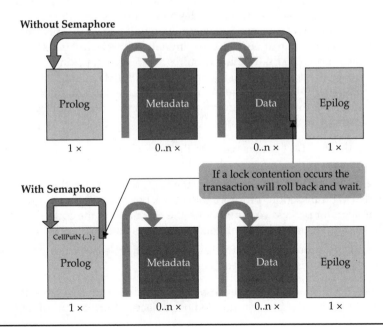

FIGURE 11-1 Process flow with and without a semaphore

the process flow. Of course, if the TurboIntegrator runs in a short time, it may not matter when the contention occurs. But imagine what happens during the data load of a large number of records (worst case: the last statement in the data section performing on the last data record of a huge data source leads to a contention). In this case, all data that is already loaded is rolled back and has to be loaded again. If you run multiple processes concurrently using a semaphore, the first of these processes will pass the semaphore (CellPutX). All other processes will roll back (in the best case, only the first statement, which should be the semaphore), wait, and race again to be the first process that passes. This will continue until all processes have passed the semaphore. The semaphore is like a small door, which can only be entered by one process after another. The result is a serialization of the processes.

This kind of semaphore does not work with Parallel Interaction because in Parallel Interaction mode, the access to the semaphore object does not lead to a contention and so the TurboIntegrator processes can always pass the semaphore.

Now we want to discuss the second approach to implementing semaphores. If you want to serialize TurboIntegrator processes with Parallel Interaction activated, you have to use a different semaphore object. In Parallel Interaction mode, Cognos TM1 transactions still block other transactions if you are modifying metadata. So you can use a dimension as a semaphore object. The semaphore should be a dedicated dimension that is not used by a cube. Otherwise, a modification of the dimension would also lock all cubes that contain this dimension.

Here is an example, which can be inserted in the Prolog section:

```
sThisProcess = GetProcessName();
sSemaphoreDim = 'TBB Semaphore';
DimensionElementInsert(sSemaphoreDim , '', sThisProcess,'N');
```

Our last approach is the recommended one, which is only available for Cognos TM1 10.1 and higher. Cognos TM1 10.1 provides a new TurboIntegrator function: synchronize(<LockObjectName>). This function will force only one execution of the TurboIntegrator process to run at one time to eliminate rollback situations where locks are encountered. The synchronize function acquires a lock on a new kind of Cognos TM1 object (the Lock object), which is not visible in any Cognos TM1 client. The purpose of a Lock object is to be a built-in semaphore. A Lock object is created automatically when it is used for the first time. If the TurboIntegrator process executes the synchronize statement, Cognos TM1 performs the following steps:

- **Step 1.**   Cognos TM1 checks whether the Lock object with the name that is passed in the function parameter exists. If the Lock object doesn't exist, it is created.

- **Step 2.**   Cognos TM1 checks whether the Lock object is already locked by another Cognos TM1 transaction (process). If the Lock object is not locked, the TurboIntegrator process continues with the execution of the code. Otherwise, if the Lock object is locked, the TurboIntegrator process goes to Step 3.

- **Step 3.**   The TurboIntegrator process waits for the release of the lock. If the lock is released, the process goes back to Step 2.

A developer of a TurboIntegrator process can place the synchronize statement everywhere in the code and can use multiple Lock objects. Multiple TurboIntegrator processes that have to be serialized have to use the same Lock object. By using different Lock objects (different names in the synchronize parameter), you can "group" TurboIntegrator processes.

NOTE *For newer Cognos TM1 versions synchronization is only useful if the TurboIntegrator processes are performing Metadata Updates.*

Scaling the Application

In the last section we divided the loading of the data into portions. In this section we take a look at how to divide the Cognos TM1 application into portions. This is often called "partitioning." But be careful with the word "partitioning." This word has a special meaning in the world of server applications. In many cases partitioning is understood as a feature of the software. That means server application software supports partitioning when you can configure parameters which tell the software how to scale data and/or process time. But from this point of view the Cognos TM1 server is a monolith which is using the RAM which it can allocate from the underlying operation system. For instance a Cognos TM1 server doesn't support partitioning if you expect that this Cognos TM1 server is spread over some physical machines to utilize RAM and CPU resources of multiple machines. Of course you can spread an application across multiple servers as we have shown in the section "Partitions by Cognos TM1 Servers" later in this chapter. But what are the criteria to divide an application and therefore to divide the Cognos TM1 Model?

Here are some drivers:

- Long query time because of huge amount of data and/or complex calculations
- Better maintenance of the model (logical partitions)
- Security and company compliance (logical partitions)
- Separation of planning data and report data (logical partitions)
- Lock contentions, if you are using an older Cognos TM1 versions (no Parallel Interaction)

Before we take a look at the various methods of scaling we want to say something about "lock contentions."

Scaling the application driven by lock contentions is only necessary for planning solutions (user modifies objects) if you use older Cognos TM1 versions without Parallel Interaction or if the metadata is frequently changed by the planning users (for instance, a dimension can be changed by end users via Cognos TM1 Action buttons and TurboIntegrator processes). Only in these cases locking contention will occur.

Let's take a look at the various methods of scaling a Cognos TM1 application.

Large Cubes and Complex Calculations

Simply having a huge amount of data is not a sufficient criterion for partitioning your application. For instance, you can have a cube with a huge amount of data, but the users are only used to request small parts of a cube. If these small parts are close to the leaf level of the cube, the Cognos TM1 server does not have to calculate many cells for each request. If the users are used to request views on the top level of each dimension, the query performance of a request could be an issue. So the reason for poor performance is the calculation time. The method to improve performance is "precalculation." To store precalculated values, often the partitioning of a model is needed. Here are two examples to give you an idea of when and how to partition your model.

Precalculation of Consolidated Values

Cognos TM1 can precalculate values with the TurboIntegrator. Instead of calculating the Revenue by a rule like ['Revenue'] = ['Units'] * ['Price'], you can define a TurboIntegrator process that reads Units and Price from a cube, multiplies them, and writes the result back into the cube. This works fine if you do not have to calculate on the C level. Of course, Cognos TM1 can calculate the consolidated values, but you need a separate cube to store these consolidated values. In addition, you also need a third cube to present the precalculated data in its hierarchies. The cube that stores the calculated data has to be completely flat. That means that the cube should consist only of leaf cells. For that you need, for each dimension in the original cube, a flat dimension in the precalculated cube. The third cube consists of the same dimensions as the original cube. But this cube will be a full virtual cube. That means all cells of the cube are rule-calculated. Now you can say that we have rules again. That's correct, but the needed rules just get corresponding values. There is no calculation, just DB references. Figure 11-2 shows these three cubes.

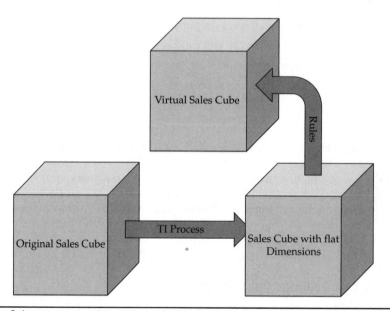

Figure 11-2 Cubes to store and report precalculated values

NOTE *If the original Sales cube is loaded by TurboIntegrator from an external data source, you can modify this process to load and calculate all values and populate the precalculated cube instead. In this case the original cube becomes obsolete.*

The following illustration shows an example with our TBB Sales cube. In the illustration you can also see the flat Product dimension. The TBB Sales Measure is already flat, so you do not need to make it flat.

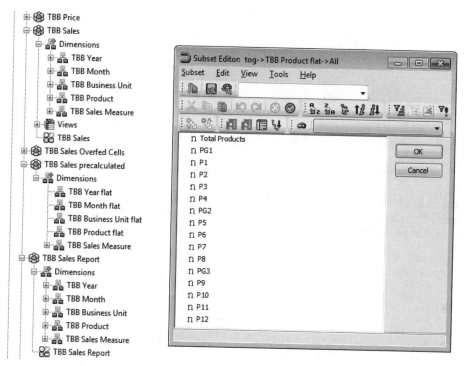

There is only one rule in the TBB Sales Report cube:

```
[]=DB('TBB Sales precalculated',!TBB Year,!TBB Month,
!TBB Business Unit,!TBB Product,!TBB Sales Measure);
```

NOTE *Of course, in a real-life solution, you need SKIPCHECK and feeders in this model (see Chapter 6).*

Report Partitions

You can use Report Partitions if you just want to reduce the calculations. This approach is a mix of online calculation and precalculation. It partitions a cube along a dimension. In Figure 11-3, you can see that a Sales cube is split into three regional cubes.

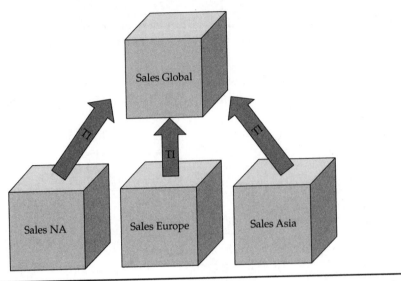

FIGURE 11-3   Precalculation on defined levels

For this example, we define one dimension of the original cube as a partition dimension. For instance, the original Sales cube would have a Region dimension, which can be split into separate dimensions, as we did in the following illustration.

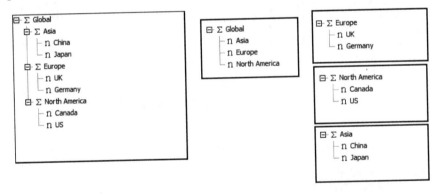

We will have a similar example in the section "Logical Partitions." In this Planning example we will get all global sales values by rules from the partitions. In this example, we use TurboIntegrator processes to copy consolidated values from the partitions to the leaf cells of the global cube. In each of the new cubes, the calculation time should be improved now.

Logical Partitions

Probably you already have divided your application into logical parts incidentally. If you already use the multi-cube architecture of Cognos TM1 you may have various cubes in our model. This is called a *natural partition*. There are various criteria for partitioning the Cognos TM1 Applications into logical units.

Separation of Planning Data and Report Data

You can separate your model to have cubes that are intended for reporting and to have cubes that are intended for planning. In most cases the reason for that is that the planned values are only valid for reporting if the users who are responsible for the planning process commit the data. Figure 11-4 shows an example of such partitioning:

The two cubes are synchronized by a TurboIntegrator process. The TurboIntegrator process is scheduled or executed by an event. The event could be the submission of a planning version which is part of a workflow process. For instance, it could be a business requirement that planning data is available to report users only if the version is approved by a business line manager.

Logical Separation by Organizational Structures

This concept of separating cubes is used if you want to have a model which is more maintainable. "More maintainable" means that the model is easier to understand because it reflects the organizational structure, which leads also to simpler security administration. In some cases this method meets the company requirements of data separation (for instance, by business unit or regions). In the following example we split a "Plan Sales" cube into separate cubes. As a developer you have to decide how to split this cube. One option is to choose one of the "Plan Sales" dimensions as the "partition dimension" (it is also possible to have more than one "partition dimension"). Typical partition dimensions are "Departments," "Business Units," "Divisions," "Regions," or "Organization." In our example the best partition dimension may be "Regions." Figure 11-5 shows an example of a model which combines "natural partition" (Financial Statement consists of Cash Flow, Costs and Sales) and a regional partition (Sales data comes from various regions).

Combination of Separation by Organizational Structures and Separation by Planning and Reporting

Let's enhance our example. Figure 11-6 shows you an example where a natural partition (Financial Statement, Costs, Cash Flow, and Sales) is multiplied by regions (so the regional models do not need a "Region" dimension). All regional Financial Statements are collected

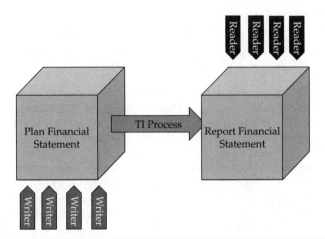

Figure 11-4 Separate Reporting and Planning cubes

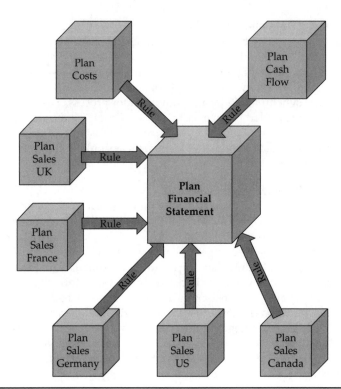

FIGURE 11-5 Multi Planning cubes

together into a global one by TurboIntegrator processes. An advantage of this model is that each region could have different "micro" models which are consolidated into the global cube.

Partitions by Cognos TM1 Servers

With partitioning by Cognos TM1 servers, you can additionally utilize the resources (RAM and CPU) of different server machines and bring the data physically closer to the users in different geographical regions. The separation is very similar to that described in the last section. In the section "Combination of Separation by Organizational Structures and Separation by Planning and Reporting ," we separated the model into groups of cubes that are "dedicated" to different user groups. Now you can put these different cube groups on different servers. In that same section, the connection between the cube groups was a TurboIntegrator process. This is now replaced by a Replication/Synchronization connection between the servers that are hosting the different groups. In Figure 11-7 you can see an example of Replication/Synchronization (Rep/Sync) that corresponds to the example shown in Figure 11-8.

The Rep/Sync connection has two participants: two Cognos TM1 servers, which can be run on the same or different machines. One of the servers takes the part of the "Star" and one takes the part of the "Planet." You can use this connection for Replication or Synchronization. With Replication you can "copy" metadata (dimensions, subsets, views, rules) and data (cell values) from a source (this is always the "Star" server) to the target (the "Planet" server).

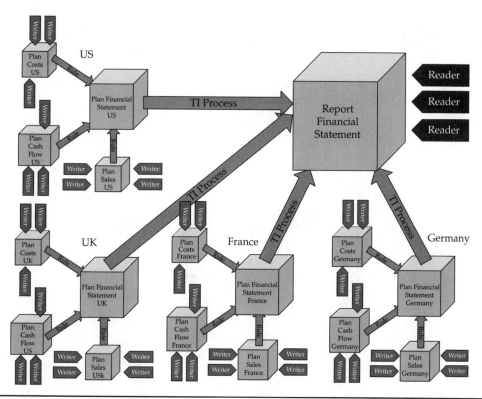

FIGURE 11-6   Module partitioning

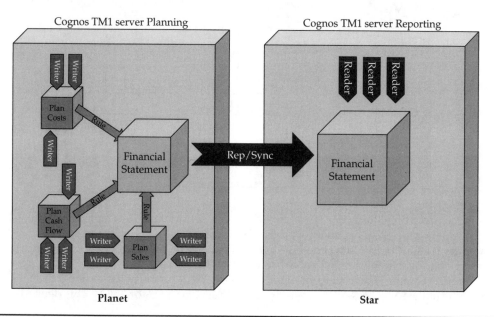

FIGURE 11-7   Replication/Synchronization

With Synchronization you can "synchronize" unidirectional metadata from "Star" to "Planet," and you can "synchronize" bidirectional data between "Star" and "Planet." The connection is always defined in the "Planet" server (see the following illustration).

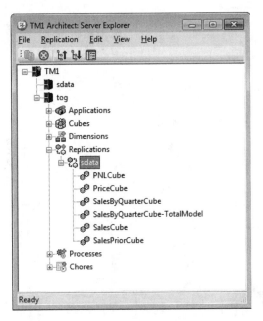

Replications

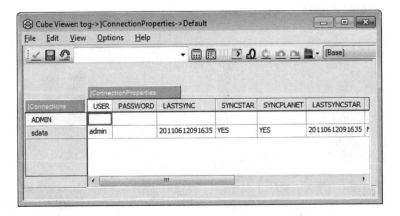

In the preceding illustration, you can see that the definition of the connection is stored in the system cube "}ConnectionProperties." Here you can also define whether the "synchronization" of the data should be bidirectional (default) or if you want to restrict the connection to synchronize only in one direction (see Table 11-1).

For our example shown in Figure 11-8, the SYNCSTAR property has to be set to "YES." The value of the SYNCPLANET properties could be set to "YES" or "NO." This depends on

Connection Property	Description
SYNCSTAR = YES	Data of the Planet server is synchronized to the Star server
SYNCPLANET = YES	Data of the Star server is synchronized to the Planet server

TABLE 11-1 Synchronization Properties

our business requirements. For instance, if you host central Planning cubes in a Star server and regional Planning cubes in several Planet servers (see Figure 11-9), you may want to provide the central figures to the regions. So you have to set SYNCPLANET properties to "YES" for each Planet server.

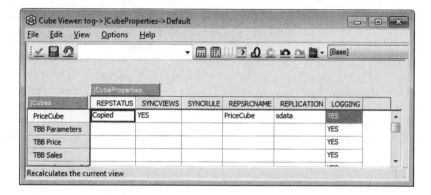

In the system cube "}CubeProperties" (shown in the preceding illustration), you can find the Rep/Sync configuration for each cube.

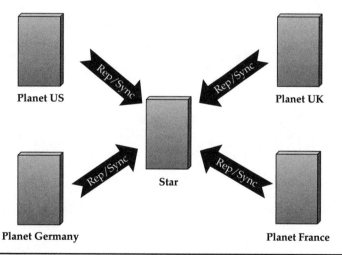

FIGURE 11-8 Multiple planets

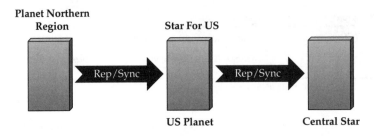

FIGURE 11-9 Cascading Rep/Sync

For further information regarding Rep/Sync, please refer to the Cognos TM1 documentation (*Cognos TM1 Operations Guide*). We just want to note that the synchronization of the data is based on the transaction logs of the servers that are involved. The log is used to identify which cell has changed since the last synchronization (see the earlier illustration labeled "Replications": LASTSYNC property). The synchronization only works properly if you have turned on the log for all involved cubes (see the earlier illustration labeled "Cube properties": LOGGING property = YES). With Rep/Sync you can set up various scenarios. You can have a configuration that looks like a "Star system" (see Figure 11-8; that's where the names "Star" and "Planet" come from). You can also cascade Stars and Planets. That means a Planet could become a Star for another server (see Figure 11-9). You also can configure a combination of both.

Summary

In this chapter we provided a technical perspective on treating data in Cognos TM1. We have discussed how to load large amounts of data. We also discussed how and when you should scale your model. We want to remind you that your first priority when you design a Cognos TM1 model is to solve business requirements. These design aspects should be merged with further scaling aspects if needed.

User Scaling

In the last chapter we talked about how to scale the data of a Cognos TM1 model. In this chapter we want to cover the methods of user-related scaling. The purpose of scaling users is to prevent performance issues when many users access a Cognos TM1 server at the same time. This concurrency can lead to performance issues if queries take a long time and/or contentions arise when modifying Cognos TM1 objects. You will see that there is a small overlap between Chapter 11 and this chapter. While Chapter 11 deals with the amount of data, this chapter deals with the number of users. The focus in the next section is on concurrency.

Spreading Users over Multiple Server Machines

Concurrency could be a performance issue even if your Cognos TM1 application is a read-only application (for example, Reporting or Analysis only).

Each user who is connected to the Cognos TM1 server runs a thread inside Cognos TM1. As described in Chapter 10, you can observe these threads with Cognos TM1 Top or Cognos TM1 Operations Console. The underlying operating system is aware of these threads and can schedule each thread to be executed on a CPU core. If the server machine has four CPU cores (for instance, on a quad-core CPU or two dual-core CPUs), only four threads can be executed simultaneously in real time. In this case, a thread is not necessarily a Cognos TM1 thread. Other programs and services on the same machine also have threads, which use the resources of the CPU.

If two users open the same view, both will share the data and the cache of a cube. But they do not share the request. In this case we have two requests running in two threads. Each request takes time. If the operating system can provide enough resources (CPU time), both requests may run simultaneously. The same behavior occurs if more than two users request data from the Cognos TM1 server. Each request runs in a thread that requests to be executed by the hardware. If more active threads (see also Chapter 10; threads can be idle if there is nothing to compute) exist than cores are installed on the machine, the operating system has to serialize the active threads (the time for executing is scheduled). But a thread is not executed as a whole (see Figure 12-1). The operating system tries to give each thread only a small slot for execution in order to run the threads virtually parallel. If more and more threads become active, the scheduling of these threads becomes more and more challenging. Be aware that the number of active threads is not equal to the number of connected users. But what is an active Cognos TM1 thread? In Cognos TM1 Top or Cognos

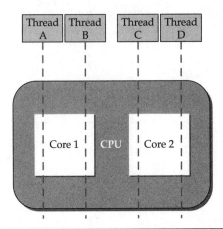

Figure 12-1   Parallel threads

TM1 Operations Console, active threads are indicated with a status that is different from "idle" or "wait." For instance, a Cognos TM1 thread could be a data query from a user, the spreading of data, the execution of a TurboIntegrator process, and so on.

If too many threads are active, the performance could be downgraded. How can you solve this issue?

In Chapter 11 we talked about how to split a Cognos TM1 model into partitions on different Cognos TM1 servers. You can use this method to run different Cognos TM1 servers on different machines and assign different groups of users to each Cognos TM1 server. With this method, you can manage the number of concurrent users per Cognos TM1 server (see also the section "Sizing" in Chapter 13), and therefore the number of active threads on each machine. Of course, if the data of the Cognos TM1 server has to be shared or consolidated on a central server, you have to use the Replication/Synchronization mechanisms.

For instance, you split a Cognos TM1 server into two instances to reduce the concurrency of users' requests. Both servers should have the same data and no data partitioning is necessary. We make this assumption to make clear that we are talking about "user scaling," not "data scaling," to stay within the scope of this chapter. Now you can have two scenarios to share the model, as shown in Figures 12-2 and 12-3.

- **Scenario 1 (Figure 12-2)**   You can create the model in one Cognos TM1 server and load the data from the appropriate data source. Then you replicate/synchronize this model to the other server. You just have to decide which Cognos TM1 server is the master of the Cognos TM1 model (the star). Of course, you can use this scenario if you have one star server and multiple planet servers.

- **Scenario 2 (Figure 12-3)**   You can use this scenario only if your Cognos TM1 model is completely derived from an external data source. That means all cubes, dimension, attributes, security, and so on are built and loaded by TurboIntegrator processes. In this case, you just provide these TurboIntegrator processes to all Cognos TM1 servers. This enables each server to load all needed information on its own. (For distribution of Cognos TM1 models, see Chapter 13.)

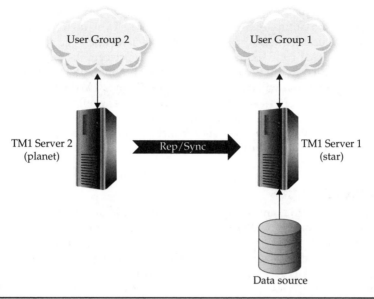

FIGURE 12-2   Scenario 1

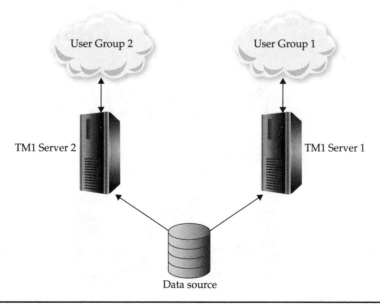

FIGURE 12-3   Scenario 2

Now you have different Cognos TM1 servers on different hardware machines. The next task is to assign users to Groups/Cognos TM1 servers. When you do this, you should consider the behavior of each user's interactions. You should keep an open eye on how often a user is requesting a Cognos TM1 cube and how long it takes to perform the requests. So you will have users who use Cognos TM1 with a low frequency but request a huge amount of data, which takes a long time. You will have users who use Cognos TM1 with a high frequency, but their requests are very short. And you will have all other combinations. You have to assign these different kinds of users to leverage the resources of your hardware. Often you can decide which users should be assigned to which server after observing the behavior of these users and the behavior of the Cognos TM1 server machine over a time span.

Avoiding Contention Issues

Before we start, we want to mention again that contention issues are more relevant if you are not using Parallel Interaction. If you are using Parallel Interaction, contention issues occur if the TM1 model is modified frequently. The following section assumes that you are using the old locking methodology of Cognos TM1. (Remember, the new locking methodology is available since Cognos TM1 9.5.2 and can be deactivated.)

A read-only application leverages the CPU resources by default, as explained in the last section. What if you have a mixed read/write application? Write operations are not compatible with read operations (see Chapter 10). In the worst case, a thread that wants to write to a Cognos TM1 object has to wait. This is indicated in Cognos TM1 Top or Cognos TM1 Operations Console by the state "wait:…" Threads in a wait state are not scheduled to be executed by the CPU. The example in Figure 12-4 shows such a situation when multiple threads are waiting for the termination of a single thread (all threads intend to modify the same object, but only one thread gets the right to modify the object at one time). In an application with

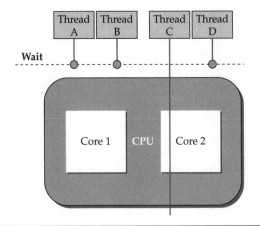

FIGURE 12-4 Single thread

heavy writing activities, it could happen that over a long time, only one thread is executing at a time. If you take a look using a monitoring tool of the operating system (such as Task Manager in Windows), only one core is active during this state. Some Cognos TM1 customers have complained that Cognos TM1 is not a multithreading-application. This is not true. The truth is that the customers' application does not avoid blocking contentions.

Let's look at the different methods of avoiding blocking contentions.

Using Parallel Interaction

Parallel Interaction is a feature that has been available since Cognos TM1 version 9.5.2. We have already discussed Parallel Interaction in Chapter 10. Parallel Interaction is an option that can be switched on or off for the Cognos TM1 server.

If Parallel Interaction is activated, no blocking contention will occur when multiple users want to modify the same data. But be aware if multiple users want to modify the same metadata (for example, maintaining a dimension); it's still the same behavior of waiting threads.

Scaling the Model

We already discussed the method of scaling the model in Chapter 11. Scaling the model also helps to scale the user and to avoid blocking contentions. The principle of this method is to make sure that multiple users are modifying different Cognos TM1 objects. There is no blocking contention if two users write to different cubes at the same time or one user reads and another user writes at the same time. When you partition the model, you reduce the ratio of writers to Cognos TM1 objects, and therefore you reduce the probability of blocking contention. So it's not really avoiding them at all.

Using Sandboxes

Sandboxes provide ad hoc "Personal What If" scenarios to a Planning user. This is the user perspective of sandboxes. So a sandbox is not only a scaling feature of Cognos TM1. But in this section we take a more technical look at this Cognos TM1 feature.

When more and more customers began using Cognos TM1 as their planning application, the demand arose to have a built-in feature to reduce contention. This was the reason for the introduction of sandboxes with version 9.1.

From a user's perspective, a sandbox is a private space to enter values and simulate with this value. At any time, the user can commit the data in this private space to the real Cognos TM1 cubes. The modification of the data is only visible to the owner of the sandbox until the sandbox is committed to the base cube.

From a technical perspective, a sandbox is a private version of all cube data (including system cubes). You can compare it to the partitioning of the model, but on a private basis.

As with Parallel Interaction, you can activate and deactivate the sandbox feature. Sandboxes can be activated per user group. An administrator can set up the sandbox feature in the Capability Assignments dialog (Server | Capability Assignments), as shown in the following illustration.

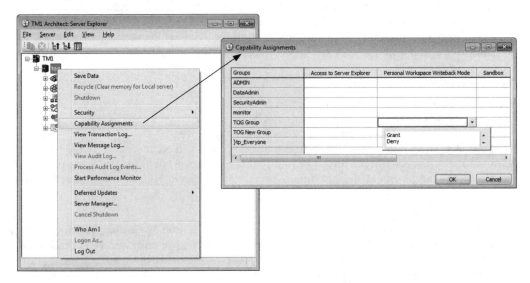

In the dialog you will find two settings that are responsible for the behavior of the sandbox feature:

- Personal Workspace Writeback Mode
- Sandbox

The combination of these settings determines how your data changes are stored and processed. In Tables 12-1 through 12-4, you will find explanations of the valid settings and a screenshot of the relevant toolbar. The screenshot is taken from a Cognos TM1 Web Cube

Mode	Description
Enabled Sandboxes	Sandbox is enabled. Each user of the group can create his own sandboxes. He can choose if he wants to write back to the base cube or to a sandbox. If he chooses a sandbox, the Commit button is enabled.

Option	Setting
Personal Workspace Writeback Mode	Empty or Deny
Sandbox	Empty or Grand

TABLE 12-1 Settings for Enabled Sandboxes (Default Mode)

Mode	Description
Disabled Sandboxes	Sandbox and Personal Workspace are disabled. The user will always write back to the base cube. A similar mode can be set by a tm1s.cfg parameter: If you set the parameter `DisableSandboxing=T`, you will get the same result. However, this is global for all users and takes precedence over Capability Assignments.
Option	**Setting**
Personal Workspace Writeback Mode	Empty or Deny
Sandbox	Deny

TABLE 12-2   Settings for Disabled Sandboxes

Viewer. The appearance of the toolbar reflects the current settings for the sandbox capabilities. These indicators are also valid for the corresponding toolbars of an Excel sheet (since Excel 2007, the sandbox feature, and the Commit button are found in the Cognos TM1 ribbon) or for Cognos TM1 Web.

In Tables 12-1 through 12-4, we mentioned three terms that may be new to you: Personal Workspace, sandbox, and base cube. A *base cube* is a regular Cognos TM1 cube. It is just named "base cube" to distinguish it more clearly from a sandbox or a Personal Workspace. A Personal Workspace is just a special sandbox. This special sandbox is automatically maintained by the system if the "Personal Workspace Writeback Mode" is turned on. The Personal Workspace cannot be deleted by the user. So the term "sandbox" remains. Let's look at this in more detail.

Mode	Description
Personal Workspace	Only the Personal Workspace is enabled. The user will always write to a "default" sandbox, which is called the "Personal Workspace." He never writes back to the base cubes directly. The Commit button is always enabled.
Option	**Setting**
Personal Workspace Writeback Mode	Empty or Deny
Sandbox	Deny

TABLE 12-3   Settings for Personal Workspace

Mode	Description
Combination of Personal Workspace and Sandboxes	Sandbox and Personal Workspace are enabled. The user will always write back to a sandbox. He can never access the base cubes. A "Default" sandbox, which is called the "Personal Workspace," is always available. In addition to that sandbox, the user can create new sandboxes, which can be deleted. The user cannot delete the "Default" sandbox. The Commit button is always enabled.

Option	Setting
Personal Workspace Writeback Mode	Grand
Sandbox	Empty or Grand

TABLE 12-4 Settings for Combination of Personal Workspace and Sandboxes

First, we want to mention that a sandbox is not a copy of a cube. A sandbox is a private area in a Cognos TM1 server for each user. Sandboxes are not local on the client machine. Each sandbox (which is created by a user) or the Personal Workspace (which is created for each user by the Cognos TM1 system) is a separate area to store personal data. This separate area is "spanned over" all cubes of a Cognos TM1 server. If a user is working in a sandbox (or Personal Workspace) and he writes values to a cube, all modifications will go to the sandbox. The sandbox will store only the modifications. If the user requests data from the cube, he will get this data from the base cube overlaid by the modifications of the sandbox. A sandbox or the Personal Workspace can be committed at any time by the owner. If a sandbox is committed, all modifications are written to the base cube in a single transaction.

The mode shown in Table 12-1 enables a user to choose whether he writes to the base cube or to one of his sandbox areas. If the user has chosen a sandbox or he is assigned to the modes that are described in Table 12-3 or Table 12-4, all data entry is redirected to such a separate sandbox area.

For a better understanding, let us compare the following two illustrations. Both illustrations display some sample values of the "TBB Price" and the "TBB Sales" cube. In the first following illustration, the data scope is the base cube. The base cube data is the data of the real Cognos TM1 cubes. So this is the data that could be accessed by any other user. In the second illustration, the data scope is set to the sandbox "My Sandbox." Furthermore, the user has changed the price of product "P1" from 30 to 100. This data entry was redirected to the active sandbox. When a sandbox is active, all values of the sandbox that are different from the base cubes are marked. In the Cube Viewer, the Cognos TM1 Web Cube Viewer, Cognos TM1 Contributor, and Cognos Insight, the values are colored blue. In Excel these values are marked by a small blue triangle. In the second illustration, you can also see that not only the changed value is marked. Also, four values in the "TBB Sales" cube changed color from black to blue. These values are derived from the "TBB Price" cube by Cognos TM1 rules and consolidations. So these values are also different from the base cube now. This is a useful side effect. If you change a value, you can track which are the dependent values. Figure 12-5 illustrates this behavior.

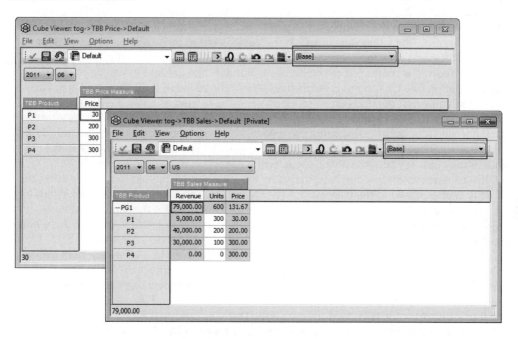

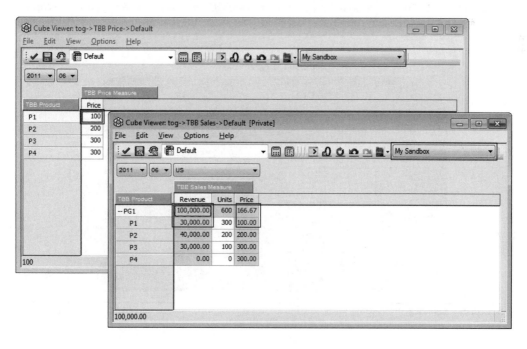

Figure 12-5 shows the two cubes of our example. As a part of the whole model, these cubes are covered by the active sandbox "My Sandbox." All requests and value entries are now redirected to this sandbox. When the user enters the value 100, this value is not stored in the cube but in the sandbox. Now the user requests the values of the view. The Cognos TM1 server looks into the sandbox because the request is redirected. If the requested value is in the sandbox, the value is returned. If the value is not in the sandbox, the request is passed to the base cube. In the next step, the user requests the view on the TBB Sales cube. Again the request is redirected to the sandbox. But now the values have to be calculated. The calculation (see Chapter 6) is performed within the scope of the active sandbox. Each calculated value that depends on a "sandbox value" is treated as a value stored in this sandbox. As shown in Figure 12-5, a sandbox is like a window pane that overlays all cube data. If a cell value exists in the sandbox, it covers the corresponding cell in the underlying cube. If a cell value doesn't exist in the sandbox, you can see (request) the value in the underlying cube. If you write a value, you will write it "on the window pane."

Just as requests that cannot be satisfied by the sandbox are passed to the base cube, the security is also passed to the base cube. Even though the sandbox is private, a user can only write values to cells to which he has write access. But be careful if the sandbox already holds values when the write access is withdrawn. The user is not able to commit the whole sandbox if only one value cannot be written because of the loss of write access.

We want to mention here that the "sandbox values" are not treated like normal cell values. For each sandbox, a subdirectory is created in the user directory of the owner (the user directory can be found in the data directory of the server and has the same name as the user; this is the place where all private objects like subsets and views are stored). In the sandbox directory a file is created for each cube that was modified by the user. The sandbox values are stored in these files and in a limited user space in RAM. This space is limited to the default size of 100MB on a 32-bit system, and 500MB on a 64-bit system. This size can be customized by the tm1s.cfg parameter `MaximumUserSandboxSize=n`.

Sandbox "My Sandbox"

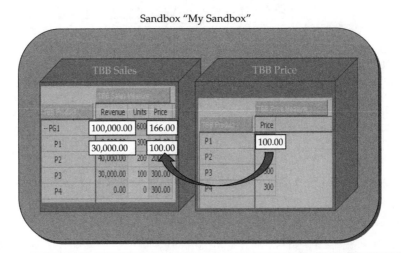

FIGURE 12-5 Sandbox

Data requests that are redirected to a sandbox could be slower than requests to the base cube because the sandbox itself doesn't maintain a cache. That means that a calculated value that is derived by a sandbox value is not cached and has to be recalculated for each request. Of course, all base cube values that are requested by the same query are retrieved with the well-known mechanisms of Cognos TM1. So the performance depends on the number of sandbox values in a query. The performance of a large query on a sandbox could be dramatically slower. But sandboxes are for writing back, and writeback will clear the cache. So you are not giving up much with sandbox usage. If your application is a read-only application, it makes no sense to turn on the Sandbox/Personal Workspace mode.

We do not want to forget the focus of this chapter: scaling users to avoid or reduce contention issues. To conclude, we can say that writing to a sandbox minimizes contentions to zero. As users write to a private space, no locks on the Cognos TM1 cubes are needed. But with the old locking methodology, a contention can occur if a sandbox is committed. During the commit of a sandbox, the user acquires the IX lock (see Chapter 10) on each cube that has corresponding data in that sandbox. In sum, the contention issues are reduced because the chance that multiple users would commit at the same time is less than the chance that multiple users would write to a base cube at the same time.

But let us assume that multiple users would commit their sandboxes at the same time. Cognos TM1 has an answer for that type of contention issue since version 9.5.1: Job Queuing.

Job Queuing is a Cognos TM1 server mode that is available for users who are using sandboxes or Personal Workspace. In this mode Cognos TM1 queues the sandbox commits of multiple users. The Job Queuing mode is enabled when you set the parameter JobQueuing=T in the Cognos TM1 server configuration file tm1s.cfg. If Job Queuing is activated, all sandbox users will get a new Job Queue button in their toolbars (ribbons) (see the following illustration).

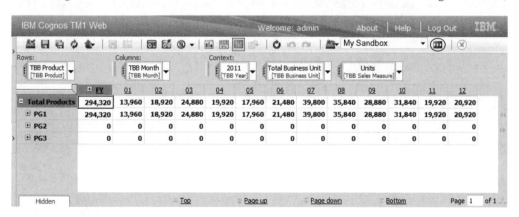

What does Job Queuing mean?

The Cognos TM1 server does not commit a sandbox/Personal Workspace immediately when the user clicks the Commit button. When Job Queuing is enabled, the commit request is queued. The commit proceeds as soon as the update of all cubes that are affected by the sandbox is possible. In other words, the thread that requests to commit the data has to successfully acquire the IX lock on all necessary cubes, and no blocking contention occurs. In many cases, sandbox submission will be instantaneous.

NOTE *The usage of Job Queuing is only required when there is overwhelming demand on the server, which the server cores cannot manage.*

The user can observe the status by clicking the Job Queue button. The Job Queue dialog will open (see the following illustration). In this dialog the user can watch the status of all queued jobs of all users, and he can cancel (stop the commit of) his own jobs (an admin user can cancel jobs of all users).

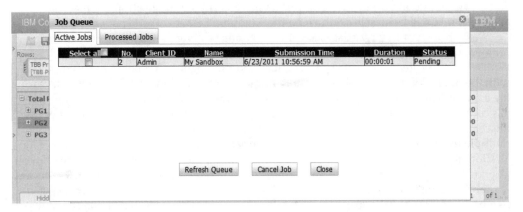

The status of the Job Queue can also be observed in the Cognos TM1 Operations Console (see the following illustration) or Cognos TM1 Top. (You have to change the Cognos TM1 Top mode by parameters to see the Job Queue. Please refer to the Cognos TM1 documentation for details.)

While the commit is queued, the user can go on with his work. But Cognos TM1 pays attention to whether this user read the data from the committed sandbox only. When the user changes data in this sandbox, the message shown in the following illustration will display:

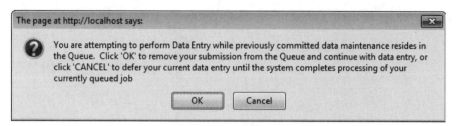

Now the user can decide if he wants to withdraw his changes or to cancel his job.

Regarding sandboxes, we want to mention the slightly different behaviors with Cognos TM1 Contributor.

If you are using Cognos TM1 Contributor, you need to know that the setting for Personal Workspace Writeback Mode in the Capability Assignment dialog is ignored. Instead of that, the Cognos TM1 Contributor works with special Contributor workspaces. If the setting "Sandbox" in the Capability Assignment dialog is not set to "Deny," a user who is using the Cognos TM1 Contributor client will get the Sandbox drop-down box in the toolbar. This user will see "Personal Workspace "[Default]." But this is a special sandbox that is created for each Contributor node (the "[Default]" sandbox is created when the user takes ownership of the node). These Contributor sandboxes are created with a special name pattern: "[Default]_<Node ID>_<ID of the Contributor application>." But the user of the Cognos TM1 Contributor client will only see the first part of the name: "[Default]." If the Sandbox capability is not disabled, a user of the Cognos TM1 Contributor client can create a new sandbox. Again this will be a special Contributor sandbox, created by using the following name pattern: "<Name of Sandbox>_[Default]_<Node ID>_<ID of the Contributor Application>." Again, the user sees the first part of the name only.

For instance, a user creates the sandbox "My Sandbox." He is now able to decide if he wants to write to the "[Default]" sandbox or "My Sandbox" (see the following illustration labeled "Cognos TM1 Contributor toolbar"). When the same user will now use another client (for example, Cognos TM1 Perspectives), he will see the original name in the Sandbox list (see the following illustration labeled "Cognos TM1 Web Cube Viewer toolbar"). On the other hand, a sandbox that is created in another client than Cognos TM1 Contributor client is not visible to a Cognos TM1 Contributor user.

We just want to say a word about the difference between "Commit" and "Submit." "Submit" also commits the sandbox or the Personal Workspace. In addition "Submit" controls the workflow of the Cognos TM1 Contributor application. In a Cognos TM1 Contributor Application the user works in the context of node which belongs to a submission hierarchy.

If the user submits, the access rights of the data which is associated with this node will change to read-only.

Cognos TM1 Contributor toolbar

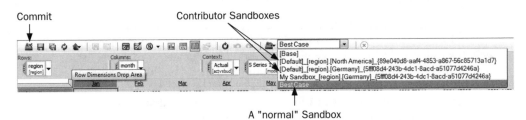

Cognos TM1 Web Cube Viewer toolbar

Distributed Clients

Using Distributed Clients is the last method to avoid contention issues that we will describe in this chapter. This method is available if you are using Cognos TM1 10.1 or higher.

The Distributed Clients feature is similar to sandboxes. The difference is that this method uses data that is really local. If a user is using the Distributed Client, he will load the data to his machine and modify the data only on his machine. So the user can work "disconnected" from the Cognos TM1 server. But be aware that the user has to be connected anyway. Only the data is "disconnected" from the server. After modifying the data, the user can submit or commit the data. In this case, the data will be uploaded to the Cognos TM1 server. Obviously, there are no contention issues when the "disconnected" data is modified.

How can you set up your application to work with Distributed Client? Distributed Client is a feature that is provided by the Cognos TM1 Contributor, which is included in Cognos TM1 version 10.1 or higher. Cognos TM1 Contributor can be configured to be used with various clients: TM1 Contributor Client (based on Cognos TM1 Web Cube Viewer; this client is also known from former TM1 Contributor versions), Cognos Insight – Connected, or Cognos Insight – Distributed. As you can see, the Distributed Client is using the client Cognos Insight. Depending on how your Cognos TM1 Contributor application is configured, the user can choose a client or is forced to use one type of client.

This chapter is not about how to design a Cognos TM1 Contributor application. So we will just take a look at what to do if you want to use the Distributed Client.

After you have designed your Cognos TM1 Contributor application in Performance
Modeler, you can set the properties of this application.

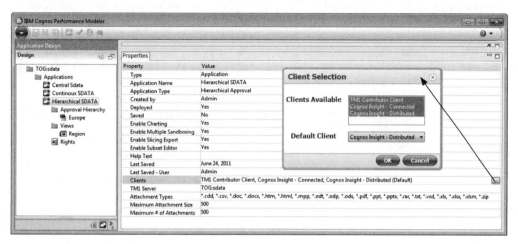

Properties of a Cognos application

As you can see in the preceding illustration, if you select the application in the Application
Design tree, all properties of the application are displayed. You can now select the property
"Clients." An Ellipse button appears to open the Client Selection dialog. In this dialog you
can select all available clients and set a default client. (The available clients are defined in
the server setup of the Cognos TM1 Contributor.)

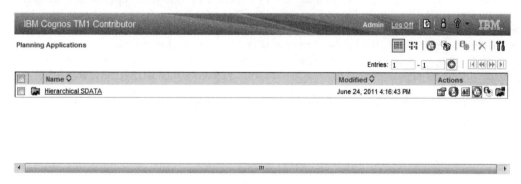

Cognos application portal

If a user has selected an application to work with the "Planning Applications" page
(see the preceding illustration), he will see all his assigned application nodes in the Cognos
TM1 Contributor portal (see the following illustration). Now the user can work with a node
in two ways: With a left click on an underlined node name, he will open the node with the
"Default Client." With a right click on a node name, he will get a popup menu to choose
a client.

We are interested in the Cognos Insight – Distributed client now. So we assume that the user chooses this option. If the Cognos Insight client is not installed on the user's machine, it will be downloaded and installed by the Cognos TM1 Contributor application. Now Cognos Insight is started.

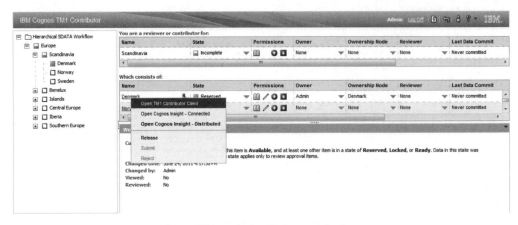

Approval hierarchy in a Cognos application

When starting Cognos Insight, the Cognos TM1 Contributor application creates a partition of the model. We already discussed in Chapter 11 that you can partition a model by using a "partition dimension." This is the exactly how the partition is created in this case: The partition dimension is the approval hierarchy of the Cognos application, as shown in the preceding illustration. All cubes that are used by the application (the dependency between a cube and an application is defined by the views that are used in that application) have to consist of the Approval Hierarchy dimension. This is a mandatory condition to use a cube view in an application. These cubes are now sliced into "subcubes," which are loaded by the central Cognos TM1 server into a local Cognos TM1 server on the user's machine. Furthermore, all dependent objects are loaded into the local Cognos TM1 server:

- All dependent cubes (see the section "Cube Dependencies" in Chapter 10)
- All views that are used by the application
- All dimensions that are used by the cubes
- All subsets of these dimensions that are used in the views
- Rules
- Attributes

The local Cognos TM1 server is fully embedded into the Cognos Insight client software (you won't see any Cognos TM1 process like tm1s.exe or tm1sd.exe). After the partition is loaded, you will see the local data in the Cognos Insight Cube Viewer (see the following illustration). Now the user can modify the data in the local Cognos server. If the user clicks the Commit or Submit button, the data is synchronized with the central Cognos TM1 server.

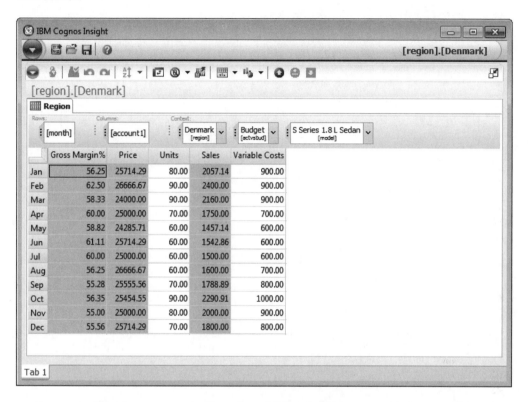

From a scaling perspective, the Distributed Client behaves very similar to sandboxes. Distributed Clients are avoiding contention issues, as sandboxes do. But Distributed Clients also utilize hardware resources, as we have discussed in the first section of this chapter. Distributed Clients utilize the hardware resources of the user's machine and discharge the central server resources.

Summary

In this chapter we have discussed how to make sure that many users can use a Cognos TM1 solution at the same time. The main aspect is the leveraging of computer processor time. This can be achieved if your solution ensures that concurrent users do not block each other. We described various methods to avoid such blocking.

Cognos TM1 Server in Production

I n this chapter we will discuss how you can operate a Cognos TM1 server environment. From the perspective of an IT administrator, the best case would be that he or she does not need to know the content (the model) of the Cognos TM1 server. Unfortunately, an IT administrator needs to understand the model and the user requirements for most aspects of the operation of a Cognos TM1 server. There are only a few tasks that are independent from the content of the Cognos TM1 server:

- Backup
- Reliability
- External scheduling of chores/TurboIntegrator processes
- Managing Cognos TM1 server uptime/restart

In addition to these points, we want to talk about some tasks that depend on the Cognos TM1 model and the user requirements:

- **Security** Security depends on the Cognos TM1 model and the requirements of the departmental users.
- **Sizing** Sizing depends on the requirements concerning which level of detail has to be loaded into the cubes. Sizing depends on the number of concurrent users and how the users access the Cognos TM1 application.
- **Monitoring** Monitoring doesn't depend on the Cognos TM1 model, but it spans the entire application. To understand and analyze the monitoring key figures, you need to know what the user requirements are. Otherwise, the figures are only numbers.

From these facts, we can conclude that operating a Cognos TM1 server in production is not just a task for the IT department. An IT administrator has to work closely with the Cognos TM1 users and developers of the Cognos TM1 application.

Now we will take a look at each of these points.

Security

When we talk about security, we have to differentiate between authorization and authentication. *Authentication* describes how a user ensures that he is the user he claims to be. Authentication is about usernames and passwords. *Authorization* describes what a user can do and/or access. Authorization is about permissions. Cognos TM1 can delegate the authentication to other systems, but authorization can only be managed by Cognos TM1. Let's start with authorization.

Authorization

Cognos TM1 manages security by control objects like security dimensions and security cubes.

The security dimensions are as follows:

- **}Clients**   Each element of this dimension represents a user of the Cognos TM1 system.
- **}Groups**   Each element of this dimension represents a security group.

The security cubes are

- **}Capabilities**   This cube manages the capabilities of each security group.
- **}ClientGroups**   This cube manages the assignments of a user to a security group.
- **}CubeSecurity**   This cube manages the permissions of each cube per security group.
- **}DimensionSecurity**   This cube manages the permissions of each dimension per security group.
- **}ProcessSecurity**   This cube manages the permissions of each process per security group.
- **}ChoreSecurity**   This cube manages the permissions of each chore per security group.
- **}ApplicationSecurity**   This cube manages the permissions of each application and application entries per security group.
- **}ElementSecurity_<Dimensionname>**   These cubes manage the permission of each element of a dimension (for example, }ElementSecurity_TBB Business Unit).
- **}CellSecurity_<Cubename>**   These cubes manage the permission of each cell of a cube (for example, }CellSecurity_TBB Sales).

Each of these security cubes contains the security dimension "}Groups" to assign an access right to the Cognos TM1 object per security group. The access rights are

- ADMIN (highest permission)
- LOCK
- RESERVE
- WRITE
- READ
- NONE (lowest permission)

The permission for each user is evaluated when he accesses a Cognos TM1 object. The evaluation of the permission is performed in the following sequence:

A user is assigned to one or multiple security groups. For each assigned group, the access right is retrieved for the requested object. If different access rights are retrieved for different groups, the highest permission will be used. In other words, a higher permission of one group will overrule a lower permission of another group. For instance, suppose that a user is assigned to Group A and Group B. Group A has WRITE access to cube "TBB Sales" and Group B has READ access to cube "TBB Sales." The user can write to this cube because WRITE overrules READ. In the case of using element security, you can have competing permissions for one cube cell, because the permission of a cell is evaluated by the intersection of the security of the corresponding dimension elements. For instance, when a security group has WRITE access to element A and READ access to element B, the data at the intersection of A and B is assigned the lower security—in this case, READ.

There are a few important points about the permissions LOCK and RESERVE, which are special TM1 features. A group that has these rights on an object can lock and/or reserve this object. If a user locks an object, this object will be read-only for every user (including the user who locks and ADMIN users). Only ADMIN users can unlock the object. If a user reserves an object, he is the only user who can modify the object (ADMIN users are also able to modify the object). The object can be released by the user who has reserved the object or by an ADMIN user. The object is also released automatically if the user terminates the connection to the Cognos TM1 server.

In the Cognos TM1 documentation, *Developer Guide*, in Chapter 6, you will find a table that lists all valid access rights for each object.

Some of the security cubes consist of system dimensions which represent Cognos TM1 objects.:

- }CubeSecurity -> }Cubes
- }DimensionSecurity -> }Dimensions
- }ProcessSecurity -> }Processes
- }ChoreSecurity -> }Chores
- }ApplicationSecurity -> }ApplicationEntries

These system dimensions are self-maintaining. That means the elements of these dimensions are updated if you add or delete a Cognos TM1 object with Performance Modeler, Architect, or Perspectives, or by an API call, or by a TurboIntegrator function. These dimensions are also updated on server startup. For example, if you copy a TI process file (let's name it "abc.pro") into the database directory, Cognos TM1 will add the process to the dimension "}Processes" automatically when the Cognos TM1 server is started.

All control objects exist in the memory of the Cognos TM1 server. Therefore Cognos TM1 creates the control objects on demand to reduce memory consumption. This mechanism has an impact on the behavior of Cognos TM1 security. Cognos TM1 creates the security cubes on demand when permissions are assigned to a TM1 object the first time (except cell security cubes, which are created by the developer or by TurboIntegrator processes). The security works differently whether a security cube exists or not. Cognos TM1 assumes that if a security cube does not exist, every group has WRITE permissions on the corresponding object. To make it more clear, we want to give you an example of when the element security object exists or does not exist:

- If element security exists for a dimension, and a new element is added, all groups will default to NONE security on that element.
- If no element security exists for a dimension, and a new element is added, all groups will default to WRITE security on that element.
- If element security exists for a dimension, and a new group is added, that group will default to having NONE access to all elements.
- If no element security exists for a dimension, and a new group is added, that group will default to having WRITE security on that element.

What happens in the Cognos TM1 server if a security object is created? We like to use the creation of the cube security object as an example to explain this behavior:

You can write to all cubes if the "}CubeSecurity" cube does not exist (assuming there is no security on elements or cells). If you assign a single access right to one cube for one group only, the "}CubeSecurity" cube will be created. The security cube will be filled with the default permission WRITE for all cubes and groups except the one for which you have set the security (in our example we set the permission to READ; see the following illustration).

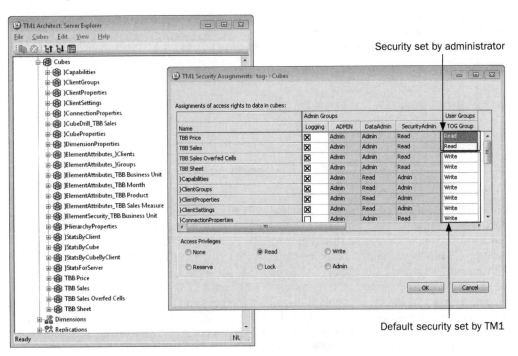

Creation of the cube security object

After the creation, the default behavior is different. If you add a new cube or a new group, the corresponding control dimensions are maintained by Cognos TM1 automatically. This leads to new cells in the "}CubeSecurity" cube, which are empty cells (again, this is housekeeping of memory performed by the Cognos TM1 server). Empty security information corresponds to the permission NONE (see the following illustration). The same mechanism is used when you assign security to other Cognos TM1 objects except cell security.

The cell security object (cell security cube) has to be created by the administrator (or you can create this object by using a TurboIntegrator script). After the creation of this object, the cell security cube is empty (like any other new cube). See the following illustration. But in this case, an empty cell does not correspond to the permission NONE.

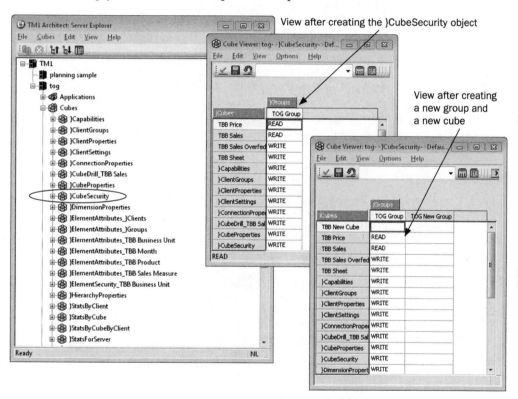

Security after the cube security object is created

The cell security cube is more like a window pane to its data cube. If you have an empty cell in the security cube, you can "see" through this cell to the data cube where the element security restricts the cube access. In the next illustration, you see three views on similar ranges. The cell security overlays the element security (except the permission NONE), but it cannot overrule the cube security. Also, the cell security cannot overrule a NONE permission of the element security, because this permission makes an element invisible.

You can set an access right for every cell. It is almost impossible to maintain cell security for larger cubes manually. It is recommended to set the cell security by using TurboIntegrator processes instead of managing the cell permissions manually. You can use the `CellPutS` function to write the valid permissions directly into a cell security cube. An alternative is to set the permissions by rules. Because a security cube is a regular cube, you can attach a Rule object to these cubes. All security cubes are text cubes (the last dimension of each security cube is the "}Groups" dimension, and the group elements are S elements). So each rule in a security cube has to be an "S rule."

For instance, the following rule

```
['TOG Group'] = S: 'READ';
```

will set the cell permission of a cube to READ for the security group "TOG Group."

NOTE *However, if the permissions are calculated by a rule on demand, you have to be aware that the permission for Cognos TM1 objects is armed only after the function RefreshSecurity is executed (from the menu: Server | Security | Refresh Security; or use the TurboIntegrator function RefreshSecurity). This is valid for all objects except cells. If cell security is calculated by rules, the permissions will be calculated on demand without the need for RefreshSecurity.*

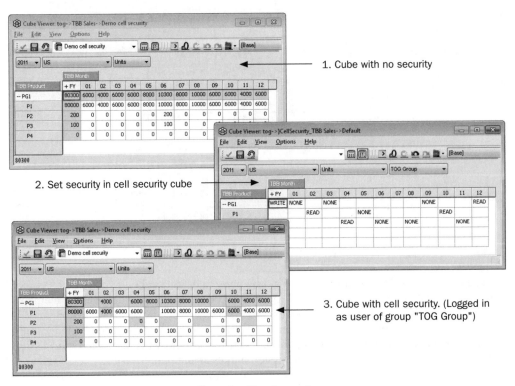

Example with cell security

Let's take a glance at how Cognos TM1 security treats dimension elements. Using permissions on dimension elements is the most frequently used method of managing security in a Cognos TM1 solution.

NOTE *Even though you want to manage security by a dimension, you should be aware that the appropriate method is to secure dimension elements, not the dimension itself.*

You can assign security rights to dimensions and/or to dimension elements. Security rights on dimensions are not relevant to secure data. Instead, it is more common to secure elements. You can assign a security right to every single element. The right of an element doesn't depend on other elements like parent elements or children. With the right NONE, you can hide elements from users. For instance, imagine you are a user who is allowed to see values of the business unit "PacRim" and of the whole company ("Total Business Units"), as shown in the following illustration. So the security for your security group on the elements "PacRim" and "Total Business Units" is set to READ. The security of all other elements is set to NONE.

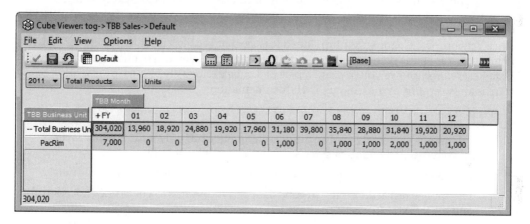

Sometimes you will have the requirement that if a user group gets permission on a parent element, this group should have the same permission on all children recursively. This requirement can be solved by a TurboIntegrator process, which can set necessary permissions for a group if the access right changes for a parent element.

Now you have the building blocks of security to design our concept of securing the data in a cube. If you design your security concept, you should consider the following topics:

- Do you need security on a cube?
- Do you need security on elements? Which dimension would be the best? The first candidate to be a "secured" dimension is an "organizational" dimension, like

business units, regions, cost centers, and so on. Be aware that the element security has an effect on all cubes where the dimension is used. Do you need additional "secured" dimensions? The more dimensions are secured, the more maintenance effort is generated.

- If there is no way to implement your security requirements with cube or element security, then consider using cell security. This is often the case when two or more dimensions drive the security requirements. For instance, if a user should only see certain products in region A and different products in region B, cell security is necessary. Because a cell security cube can hold a potentially huge number of security values, you should also consider how to populate the cell security cube. You can populate the cell security cube by using a TurboIntegrator script or by rules.

- Security could consume a notable amount of memory, depending on your requirements.

- Rules on security cubes can lead to reduction of performance. If this is the case, consider using TurboIntegrator to populate the security cubes. In general, you should prefer to use TurboIntegrator. You should use rules only if your application requires on-demand permissions, which can be implemented by cell security.

Data Reservation

Since Version 9.5.2 Cognos TM1 provides a feature that is called Data Reservation. We want to mention this at this point because with Data Reservation, you can overlay the TM1 security. Data Reservation allows you to grant a part of a cube exclusively to a user for write access. Here is an excerpt from the Cognos TM1 documentation:

Data Reservation (DR) is different from TM1 security in the following ways:

- DR does not override TM1 security assignments, but only adds another layer of write restriction on top of standard security for cube objects.

- DR applies to individual users, while TM1 security applies to groups of users.

- DR applies restrictions only to cube data and individual users. It does not control any other TM1 objects.

Data Reservation can only be managed by TurboIntegrator functions and/or Cognos TM1 API functions. For further information regarding Data Reservation, refer to the Cognos TM1 documentation: *Cognos TM1 Developers Guide*, Chapter 9.

Authentication

This section is about authentication. As already mentioned, Cognos TM1 can delegate authentication to other systems. This is configured by a security mode in the Cognos TM1 server configuration file tm1s.cfg. The parameter is called `IntegratedSecurityMode` and could have a value between 1 and 5, as shown in Table 13-1:

IntegratedSecurityMode Value	Description
1	The Cognos TM1 default security mode. The user and the assignment of the user to security groups are managed by Cognos TM1. Upon logon, the user will get the Cognos TM1 logon dialog to provide username and password. The Cognos TM1 server validates the username and password. Depending on the tm1s.cfg parameter `PasswordSource`, Cognos TM1 validates the password internally (`PasswordSource=TM1`) or delegates it to an LDAP source (`PasswordSource=LDAP`) (see the Cognos TM1 documentation: *Cognos TM1 Operations Guide*, Chapter 11).
2	This is a mixed mode of security modes 1 and 3. This mode enables the user to choose between Integrated Login and the native Cognos TM1 authentication.
3	In this mode Cognos TM1 uses Integrated Login. Integrated Login uses Microsoft Windows network authentication. Cognos TM1 delegates the validation of the username and password to Microsoft Windows. The assignment of the user has to be set in the Cognos TM1 security or can be imported by the ETLDAP Utility (see the Cognos TM1 documentation: *Cognos TM1 Operations Guide*, Chapter 9).
4	In this mode Cognos TM1 uses the IBM Cognos BI security (CAM). Cognos TM1 delegates the validation of the username and password and the security group assignment to the IBM Cognos BI Utility (see the Cognos TM1 documentation: *Cognos TM1 Operations Guide*, Chapter 12). So that Cognos TM1 can delegate the security group assignment, security groups have to be imported from IBM Cognos BI. Upon logon, the username and password are validated first. If a validated username does not exist in Cognos TM1, it is added to the Cognos TM1 users automatically. Then Cognos TM1 deletes all existing group assignments for this user and renews these assignments for all imported groups by retrieving the actual information from IBM Cognos BI. Assignments to the built-in Cognos TM1 admin groups are not deleted and are managed independently from this mechanism.
5	This mode is very similar to security mode 4. The difference is that Cognos TM1 renews only the group assignments of the imported groups. Assignments to groups that exist only in Cognos TM1 are not touched. So Cognos TM1 can manage users who are assigned to groups that are originated from IBM Cognos BI security and to groups that are pure Cognos TM1 groups. (This is the same mechanism that is used in mode 4 for the Cognos TM1 admin groups.) You have to use this mode if you want to operate Cognos TM1 Contributor with IBM Cognos BI security.

TABLE 13-1   Values for the Parameter `IntegratedSecurityMode`

Backup and Reliability

Backup and reliability are based on the principle of how Cognos TM1 manages its resources when it is up and running. At startup time, the Cognos TM1 server loads all Cognos TM1 objects from the "DataDirectory" into memory. Each Cognos TM1 object has a corresponding file on hard disk, as shown in Table 13-2. (In the table, folder names are printed in *italics*; also, the backslash "\" is only valid for Windows operating systems; on UNIX it is replaced by a forward slash "/").

After startup, all Cognos TM1 objects that are loaded into the memory are in sync with their corresponding files in the "DataDirectory." Now the users, developers, and administrators are modifying these objects. If you change metadata, the modification is written to the "DataBaseDirectory" when you save the object (for example, if you click Save/Save As in the Subset Editor) or if the object is modified by a TurboIntegrator process when the modification is committed at the end of the process.

If you change a cell value, the modification is written immediately to memory. But it is not written only to memory when the Logging property of the cube is set to "On"; it's also written to the Transaction log. You can set this in the Cognos TM1 Security Assignments dialog for cube security (select Cubes-Node in the Server Explorer; Cubes | Security Assignments) or in the }CubesProperties cube (see the following illustration). The Logging is "On" if the "LOGGING" value is empty or set to "YES." The Logging is "Off" if the "LOGGING" value is set to "NO."

If the Logging of a cube is "Off," the changes are only written to memory. If the Logging is "On," the changes are also written to the Transaction log. The Transaction log is a file that

Cognos TM1 Object	*Folder*\File on Hard Disk
Cube	<CubeName>.cub
Dimension	<DimensionName>.dim
Public view	*<CubeName>}vues*\<ViewName>.vue
Public subset	*<DimensionName>}subs*\<SubsetName>.sub
Private view	*<UserName>**<CubeName>}vues*\<ViewName>.vue (if you are using Cognos Security (CAM), you have to replace *<UserName>* with *<Domain>**<UserName>*)
Private subset	*<UserName>**<DimensionName>}subs*\<SubsetName>.sub
Process	<ProcessName>.pro
Chore	<ChoreName>.cho
Rule	<CubeName>.rux
Feeders	<CubeName>.feeders

TABLE 13-2 Cognos TM1 Objects in Memory and on Hard Disk

is created on every startup of the Cognos TM1 server. Cognos TM1 writes the following information into this log file:

- When was a value changed (timestamp)?
- Who has changed the value (username)?
- What was the old value?
- What is the new value?
- Where is the value stored (cube and all element names in the sequence of the dimensions)?

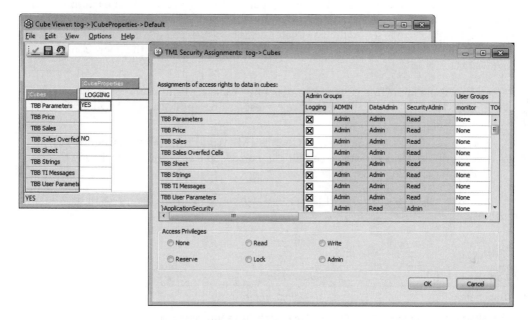

This mechanism is valid for all cubes including the system cubes. So if you change an attribute of an element, the modification is written to memory and to the Transaction log.

After the first modification of data in a cube, the memory and the files on disk are out of sync. But then in the Transaction log you will find the delta stored on disk (assuming that logging is "On" for all modified cubes). The Transaction log is stored in the "LoggingDirectory." You can set this parameter in the tm1s.cfg file. If this parameter is not set, the Transaction log is stored in the "DataBaseDirectory." The filename of the log is "tm1s.log." When the Cognos TM1 server is shut down, all modifications of all cubes (there are no exceptions) are written to the cube files. The Transaction log is closed and renamed to "tm1s<shut down timestamp>.log." Now all data of the Cognos TM1 server is written to the Cognos TM1 object files.

What if the Cognos TM1 server has crashed and the data in the memory could not be saved on disk? In this case, on startup the Cognos TM1 server recognizes a tm1s.log file that is not properly closed (not renamed). Now all the Cognos TM1 objects are loaded without the modifications. Then the Cognos TM1 server uses the old tm1s.log to "replay" all modifications that are "recorded" in that file. After startup, your data will be in the same state as before the crash. The Transaction log is also used by the Undo/Redo function and the Replication/Synchronization mechanism.

The Transaction log is not the only log file of a Cognos TM1 server. Table 13-3 gives a list of the log files.

Some additional points about the Audit log: The Audit log has to be switched on by the tm1s.cfg parameter AuditLogOn=T. If the Audit log is "on," the Cognos TM1 server doesn't write directly to the audit file. A temporary file is created in the "DataBaseDirectory": tm1rawstore.<Timestamp>. The entries in this log are moved frequently to the final Audit log. The frequency in minutes is set by the tm1.cfg parameter AuditLogUpdateInterval. If the final Audit log has reached a defined size, the Cognos TM1 server will create a new Audit log file. The size is set by the parameter AuditLogMaxFileSize.

There are some other files/objects that could be modified during the operation of the Cognos TM1 server:

- The Application Tree is stored on disk only. Table 13-4 shows the corresponding files. The files are created when the corresponding application or application entry is created.

- Cognos TM1 Web Cube Viewer, Cognos TM1 Workflow Manager, Cognos TM1 Contributor, and Performance Modeler create some additional files during the operation, as shown in Table 13-5.

As we have now discussed the foundations, we can go on with the topics of backup and reliability.

Log	*Folder*\File
Transaction log	*<LoggingDirectory>*\tm1.log
Message log: All messages of the Cognos TM1 server	*<LoggingDirectory>*\tm1server.log
Sandbox transaction log: Modification in a sandbox	*<LoggingDirectory>**sandboxlogs**<User Name>**<Number of Sandbox>*\tm1s.log
Audit log: Logs changes to the system and metadata	*<LoggingDirectory>*\auditstore<Timestamp>.log
TurboIntegrator process log: Error messages during process execution	*<LoggingDirectory>*\ ProcessError_<Timestamp>_<ProcessName>.log
Replication log: Message during Replication/Synchronization	*<LoggingDirectory>*\ TM1ReplicationLog_<Timestamp>_<StarServerName>.log

TABLE 13-3 Cognos TM1 Logs

Cognos TM1 Object	*<Folder>*\File on Hard Disk
Public application	*}Applications\<Public Application Tree>*
Public application entry: Cube-Link Dimension-Link View-Link Subset-Link Process-Link Chore-Link Uploaded file (uploaded files are stored in the folder *}Externals*) File reference	 *}Applications\<Public Application Tree>\<EntryName>*.cube *}Applications\<Public Application Tree>\<EntryName>*.dimension *}Applications\<Public Application Tree>\<EntryName>*.view *}Applications\<Public Application Tree>\<EntryName>*.subset *}Applications\<Public Application Tree>\<EntryName>*.process *}Applications\<Public Application Tree>\<EntryName>*.chore *}Applications\<Public Application Tree>\<EntryName>*.blob *}Applications\<Public Application Tree>\<EntryName>*.extr
Private application	*}Applications\<Public Application Tree>\}<UserName>\<Private Application Tree>* (If the whole Application Tree is private, the *}<UserName>* folder is below the *}Application* folder, and the private Application Tree may consist of one folder only)

TABLE 13-4   Cognos TM1 Objects Stored on Hard Disk Only

Backup

Backing up a Cognos TM1 server is an easy task. You just need to copy and/or archive the "DataBaseDirectory" of the Cognos TM1 server. As explained in the previous section, the "DataBaseDirectory" contains the whole content of a Cognos TM1 server: data, metadata, applications, uploaded files (application entries), processes, replications, chores, the whole security, and so on. Backing up a Cognos TM1 server that is down is easier than backing up a running Cognos TM1 server: Just copy the whole folder. To recover the Cognos TM1 server, just delete the content of the "DataBaseDirectory" and copy your backup into this folder.

Cognos TM1 Tool	*Folders*\Files
Cognos TM1 Web Cube Viewer	<cubename>.<viewname>.blb stores additional information like chart settings of a view in Cognos TM1 Web
Cognos TM1 Workflow Manager	• client_groups_<timestamp>.blb • sm_version_task_bindings_<timestamp>.blb • version_tasks_<timestamp>.blb are created by the Cognos TM1 Workflow Manager Console
Cognos TM1 Contributor/ Performance Modeler	• *distributed_temp* • *tunit*

TABLE 13-5   Files of Cognos TM1 Tools

If the Cognos TM1 server is up and running, you have to pay attention to the Transaction log (and the Audit log if it is activated by the tm1s.cfg parameter). The Transaction log and the temporary Audit log (see the previous section) are always opened by the Cognos TM1 server process. "Open" means that the Cognos TM1 server has the exclusive access right to these files. The files are locked. No other program can access these files including an archiving tool or a simple "copy" command-line statement. If you back up the "DataBaseDirectory" of a running Cognos TM1 server, you have to exclude these files from the copy operation. In this case, your backup doesn't include the delta between data in the .cub files and the data in the memory. But you can synchronize the .cub files and the memory by using the `SaveDataAll` function or `CubeSaveData` function (new in TM1 10.1). Use `CubeSaveData` when serializing a designated cube to minimize the locking impact of `SaveDataAll`, which takes longer as it serializes all cubes that have had data updates since they were last serialized. Only the `SaveDataAll` function is available as a menu option (TM1 | Save Data All [for all Cognos TM1 servers in the environment] or Server | Save Data). Both functions are available as TurboIntegrator functions. In addition to synchronizing the data, the `SaveDataAll` function saves the tm1s.log to the "timestamp version" and creates a new empty Transaction log.

The Audit log doesn't contain information to recover modifications of the Cognos TM1 server. The Audit log is just a protocol. If you want to synchronize the temporary Audit log with the final one, you can use the menu option Process Audit Log Events in the Server menu.

NOTE *Cognos TM1 10.1 provides a utility which is called "tm1xfer". This utility can be used for backup. Please refer to the* Cognos TM1 Operations Guide *for further information.*

Reliability

In this section we will discuss various methods to operate a Cognos TM1 server with a "high" degree of reliability. We use quotes because "high" degree is relative and is defined differently in some circumstances. Members of the IT department like to define "failover" as a high degree of reliability. But what is failover? Here is a definition from Wikipedia:

> In computing, failover is the capability to switch over automatically to a redundant or standby computer server, system, or network upon the failure or abnormal termination of the previously active application, server, system, or network. Failover happens without human intervention and generally without warning, unlike switchover.

Switchover is necessary for critical applications, which have to be available every time. A real switchover is not possible with Cognos TM1 because the memory and the "DataBaseDirectory" cannot be shared by two or more Cognos TM1 server processes. But a user can switch from one Cognos TM1 server to another Cognos TM1 server that has the same content. In this case "switching" means logging out from one server and logging in to another.

You have to ask yourself if your Cognos TM1 application is actually a critical application regarding failover. We think that moderate reliability is sufficient for an analytical or planning application.

How can that kind of reliability of a Cognos TM1 server be achieved? Reliability of a Cognos TM1 application is based on the principle of having two or more identical

Cognos TM1 servers on different machines (in our examples we will talk about two Cognos TM1 servers). We will discuss three methods. Each method has a different down time for the Cognos TM1 application. "Down time" means the time span between the termination of one Cognos TM1 server (the primary Cognos TM1 server) and the login to the second one (the secondary Cognos TM1 server). Depending on the methods, the content of the two servers is identical or only almost identical.

- **Reliability with two Cognos TM1 servers running concurrently** A primary and a secondary Cognos TM1 server with almost the same content are running concurrently (see Figure 13-1). Frequently the secondary server is replicated and synchronized with the content of the primary one. The frequency of Replication/Synchronization defines the degree of identity and how much data will be lost if the primary Cognos TM1 server terminates. The lost data is the delta of modifications since the last Replication/Synchronization. The down time is the time to log in to the secondary Cognos TM1 server.

  You can use this method if you can accept some loss of modifications and/or if only a few modifications are made by users.

NOTE *Replication/Synchronization is not designed for failover. There could be a loss of data depending on when the last synchronization was. The availability of Replication/Synchronization is not guaranteed if network issues occur.*

- **Reliability based on a backup** The second method is based on a backup of your primary Cognos TM1 server (see Figure 13-2). The frequency of backup defines the degree of identity and how much data will be lost if the primary Cognos TM1 server terminates. The lost data is the delta of modifications since the last backup. The down time is the time to copy the backup folder to the secondary Cognos TM1 server, start up this Cognos TM1 server, and log in.

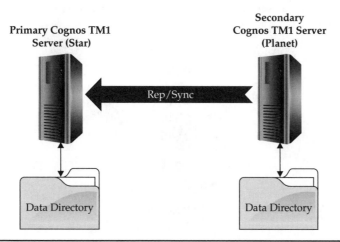

FIGURE 13-1   Reliability with two Cognos TM1 servers running concurrently

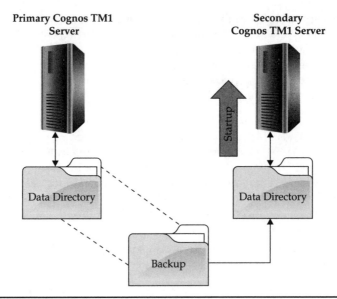

FIGURE 13-2   Reliability based on a backup

We recommend not using this method with planning applications or applications with many modifications made by the users. This is a good method for reporting or analysis applications.

- **Reliability based on a "DataBaseDirectory" in a SAN**   This method has the highest degree of identity.

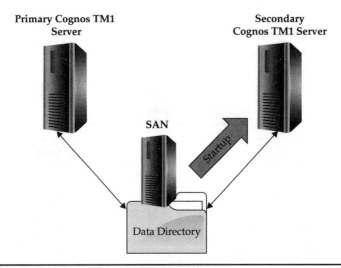

FIGURE 13-3   Reliability based on a data directory in a SAN

The primary Cognos TM1 server uses a "DataBaseDirectory," which is stored in a SAN (Storage Area Network) (see Figure 13-3). To explain SANs, we quote from Wikipedia again:

> ...SANs primarily are used to make storage devices (such as disk arrays, tape libraries, and optical jukeboxes) accessible to servers so that the devices appear as locally attached to the operating system. A SAN typically has its own network of storage devices that are generally not accessible through the regular network by regular devices....

SANs could be implemented with a high degree of reliability. The reliability of a Cognos TM1 server based on this method delegates a major part of the reliability to the infrastructure of a SAN.

In the case of an abnormal termination of the primary Cognos TM1 server, the secondary Cognos TM1 server can start up by using the same "DataBaseDirectory." Note that a "DataBaseDirectory" can be used by only one Cognos TM1 server at the same time. After startup, the secondary Cognos TM1 server will be identical because it will find a tm1s.log file that is not closed properly and it will "replay" all modifications that are done in the memory of the primary Cognos TM1 server.

The down time is the time to start up the secondary Cognos TM1 server and to log in. We recommend using this method for planning applications.

Sizing

In this section we will show how you can evaluate the hardware environment of a Cognos TM1 server. But please note that the sizing of a Cognos TM1 server is a fuzzy science. Sizing is a forecast, not a calculation. Nevertheless, we will talk about how to "calculate" the amount of memory for your Cognos TM1 application.

Calculation Criteria

NOTE *The system environment that you set up actually may deviate from your forecast.*

The calculation of the sizing is based on the principle on which Cognos TM1 operates. There are three main components of a hardware environment that can be forecasted. Each of these components depends on a different aspect of the Cognos TM1 operation. The components are

- The amount of memory (RAM)
- The number of CPU cores
- The amount of hard disk space

If you are using Cognos TM1 Web, we recommend having a separate server machine for the Cognos TM1 Web server. It is possible to user a single server machine for both: Cognos TM1 server and Cognos TM1 Web server. But you have to be aware that both compete for system resources (memory and execution time). A user who is using Cognos TM1 Web will allocate resources on the Cognos TM1 Web server and the Cognos TM1 server.

There are relations between an aspect of Cognos TM1 server operation and the type of resources which is needed. These relations are

- **Number of cores**   Number of concurrent users
- **Processor speed**   Calculation time and therefore query time before calculation is stored
- **Amount of memory (RAM)**   Size of the Cognos TM1 model
- **Hard disk space**   Amount of used memory (RAM), log files, import files, uploaded files

You have to consider the following factors in order to forecast your Cognos TM1 environment:

- Number of concurrent users
- The role of each concurrent user
- Number of concurrent users using Cognos TM1 Web
- Number of data in the cubes
- Server topology

In the next few sections we estimate the various factors step by step. With these factors in total, we can forecast the sizing of the hardware.

Forecasting the Number of Concurrent Users

The number of concurrent users is derived (forecasted) from the number of users who are going to use the Cognos TM1 application (named users). This "calculation" is based on the role of each user. You have to separate the users into the following three groups of roles:

- **Power users**   Power users are used to being connected to the Cognos TM1 application all the time during their working hours. They load data, modify the model, and create complex views and reports. Power users are allocated with 100 percent to the number of concurrent users.
- **Read/Write users/Planning users**   Read/Write users are writing data to the Cognos TM1 cubes on a regular basis. They are using and creating complex views and reports. Read/Write users are allocated with 33 percent to the number of concurrent users.
- **Read-Only users/Reporting users**   Read-Only users do not enter values into a Cognos TM1 cube. They are used to working with existing Excel reports and Cognos TM1 Web or Cognos BI. Read-Only users are allocated with 10 percent to the number of concurrent users.

In the next few sections, we will refer to the sample in Table 13-6. In this example we assume a number of named users (510) with the different roles. Based on those roles, we calculate 83 concurrent users.

Role	Number of Users (Sample)	Percentage of Concurrent Users	Forecast Concurrent Users (Sample)
Power Users	10	100%	10
Read/Write users	100	33%	33
Read-Only users	400	10%	40
Total	**510**		**83**

Table 13-6   Sample Forecast of Concurrent Users

Forecasting the Number of CPU Cores

The number of cores used by a Cognos TM1 server depends on the number of concurrent users and their roles. As a "calculation" rule, we use a rule of thumb:

- Read/Write and Power users per core: 25
- Read-Only users per core: 100
- In a mixed environment (Read-Only and Read/Write users), you should calculate 25 users per core.

This rule of thumb accounts for the fact that contentions may occur in an application with Read/Write users. With Parallel Interaction (introduced in Cognos TM1 9.5.2), contention is reduced to a minimum. You may work with 100 users per core in a Read/Write application if "Parallel Interaction" is turned on (see Chapter 12).

If we look at the example in Table 13-6, the rule of thumb would forecast four cores for the 83 users. As you get hardware servers with the second power of numbers of CPU, there are systems available with 1, 2, 4, 8, and so on CPUs available. A CPU can consist of multiple cores (for instance, single-core, dual-core, quad core, six cores [AMD]). Based on our forecast, you can use a single CPU machine with four cores or a dual-CPU machine with dual-core processors. Actually almost all available CPUs are quad core or six core processors.

Note *Intel provides the feature "hyperthreading" with their CPU chips. This feature makes a CPU function as if it has double the number of cores. In fact, there are not more cores physically. The Cognos TM1 threads do not take advantage of the feature. We recommend turning off hyperthreading.*

Forecasting the Amount of Memory for Concurrent Users

In this section we "calculate" the used memory for user sessions only. This excludes the memory used by the Cognos TM1 model. Per concurrent user we estimate 20MB of RAM for the user session (user thread in Cognos TM1 Top/Cognos TM1 Operations Console). Regarding our example, we estimate 1.62 GB RAM for the concurrent user sessions:

20MB * 83 Users = 1660MB

Forecasting the Amount of Memory for the Cognos TM1 Model

In this section we estimate the amount of RAM for the Cognos TM1 model. These estimations are based on some assumptions and average values, which can be deferred in the actual application. A more accurate estimation is possible if you forecast on the basis of a reference model. A *reference model* is the prototype of your application, which is running in a development environment with only a partition of the data. For instance, you load data only for one month into your prototype. In the actual Cognos TM1 model, you intend to load the data from two years. For the forecast you need to evaluate the memory consumption of this prototype. There are various tools to find out what amount of memory is consumed by Cognos TM1:

- In a Windows environment, you can use the Task Manager to get the memory consumption of the Cognos TM1 server.

- You can use the property window of the Server Explorer to see the "Used Memory" property of a cube, dimension, view, or subset.

- You can use the Cognos TM1 Performance Monitor, which is discussed later in this chapter.

After you know the memory consumption of the data portion, you have the choice to do the forecast by two different methods.

The first method is to calculate the amount of memory by multiplying one month by 24 (two years). With this method you will also multiply the memory consumption of the metadata (for instance, dimension elements). Usually the metadata does not grow on a monthly basis. So your calculation result may be too high.

With the second method, you also evaluate the amount of memory for one month. But then you load an additional month into your prototype. After the second month, you will be able to observe the growth of memory. Using this factor, you can calculate the memory consumption of two years: memory of first month + (23 * growth of memory).

You can use these methods only if you can assume that each month has a similar volume of data. In many cases, you do not have the opportunity to forecast the memory consumption by these empirical methods. Then you have to "calculate" the amount of memory. But before we explain the calculation, you should know which Cognos TM1 objects consume memory.

Memory Consumption by Objects

The following objects consume memory in a Cognos TM1 application:

- Cubes
- Stored calculated values
- Metadata: Dimensions, views, and subsets

Normally metadata do not take up a significant portion of memory. There is an exception if you are using large dimensions. In this case the dimension and subsets with a big portion of the dimensions are consuming a significant amount of memory (do not forget subsets that are owned by a view: the private "All" subset of a view). For instance, we create a dimension with 1,000,000 elements. This dimension consumes approximately 230MB (the size depends also on the length of the element names). A subset of all elements consumes approximately 27MB. Even the memory consumption of metadata could be significant. We will now concentrate on cubes and stored calculations.

Memory Consumption in Cubes

Memory consumption in a cube depends on two factors:

- Values that are stored in the leaf cells of a cube
- Leaf cells in a cube that are calculated by rules and fed (see Chapter 6)

If you want to estimate the memory consumption of leaf cells in a cube, you can "calculate" 10 to 20 bytes per stored leaf cells and 1 to 8 bytes per fed leaf cell. These factors are averages because the memory consumption of leaf cells depends on the size, sequence, and density of the cube dimensions (see also Chapter 5). Consolidated cells are not stored in the cube. These cells consume memory when they are cached. This is discussed in the next section.

If your cubes are loaded by external data sources, you can forecast the memory consumption by counting the number of loaded records. Let's take a look at an example:

We want to load sold units of various products into our "TBB Sales" cube. The data source contains the sold units of one month. The "TBB Sales" cube stores "Units" and calculates "Revenue" on the leaf level:

```
Rule: ['Revenue'] = N: ['Units'] * ['Price'];

Feeder: ['Units'] => ['Revenue'];
```

The data source contains 100,000 records. Each record contains one unit value. In this example, each unit value will be stored in a leaf cell and feed a corresponding revenue cell. So we can calculate the forecast of the memory consumption in the following way:

```
Number of records * (memory per leaf cell + memory per fed cell)

100,000 * (20 bytes + 8 bytes) = 2,800,000 bytes = 2.67MB
```

NOTE *If you are using conditional feeders in your model, it is very hard to estimate the number of fed cells. In this case you have to use the empirical way, which was discussed earlier.*

Memory Consumption for Stored Calculations

Memory consumption for stored calculations is a Cognos TM1 calculated requested value only. The calculation is performed on demand. Cognos TM1 stores the calculated value in memory to utilize the calculation for other requests (see also Chapter 10). The following calculated values are stored:

- Values calculated by rules
- Stargate views

Unfortunately, you cannot forecast these kinds of memory consumption by a calculation. You have to "go" the empirical way. You cannot calculate the memory consumption up front because the memory is allocated on demand and depends on which data is requested by the users.

NOTE *The memory consumption for Stargates could be significant. This depends on the number of requested rows and columns and the number of non-empty cells. You can limit the size of all Stargate views per cube by the cube property VMM, which is explained in Chapter 10.*

Considerations for 64-Bit Systems

If you want to run the Cognos TM1 server on a Windows operating system, you can choose between 32-bit Windows and 64-bit Windows. Both server systems are supported server platforms. What impact does this have on the Cognos TM1 server? On a 32-bit operating system, you can run only the 32-bit version of the Cognos TM1 software. On the 64-bit system, you have the option to run either the 32-bit or 64-bit version of the Cognos TM1 server software. But what is the difference from the perspective of Cognos TM1?

The 64-bit server removes the memory address space limit of 32-bit servers, which can be between 2 and 3GB on 32-bit Windows systems. The 32-bit limit depends on an option of the Windows operating system. (Theoretically, a 32-bit system can address 4 GBs of memory, but 32-bit Windows limits the memory to applications running on that operating system.) If you run the 32-bit Cognos TM1 server software on 64-bit Windows, the limit is 4GB of memory. So the 64-bit Windows offers the full 32-bit address space to 32-bit applications. If you run the 64-bit Cognos TM1 server, only the hardware limits the memory. The Cognos TM1 model, which is loaded to the memory, is not affected by the Cognos TM1 server software version. For instance, a model that was created on a 64-bit Cognos TM1 server can be moved to a 32-bit environment and vice versa (of course, the model must fit into the address space of the 32-bit environment). Please be aware that the same model could consume more memory when loaded in a 64-bit Cognos TM1 server. The reason is that address pointers in 64-bit systems take 8 bytes instead of 4 bytes. A Cognos TM1 model may take between 30 percent and 100 percent more memory in 64-bit architecture than in 32-bit.

We predominantly recommend 64-bit architecture, as most TM1 models these days will exceed the 3GB RAM ceiling of a 32-bit architecture.

Forecasting the Amount of Hard Disk Space

Cognos TM1 mainly utilizes RAM. For that reason Cognos TM1 doesn't make high demands on hard disk space. All Cognos TM1 objects that are stored in RAM memory during the operation of the Cognos TM1 server have corresponding images on disk. In addition to these objects, Cognos TM1 stores all log files on hard disk. These logs are: Transaction log, Audit log, TurboIntegrator error logs, Replication logs, and Cognos TM1 Message log. So the log size is always growing during the operation of a Cognos TM1 server. Often a Cognos TM1 application consists of many Excel reports. These reports are stored in the Cognos TM1 "DataBaseDirectory" if you have uploaded them to the Cognos TM1 Application Tree. Cognos TM1 allows you also to upload other files (documentation, presentations, and so on). All uploaded files require hard disk space. Last but not least, if you have input files (for example, txt, comma-separated (csv), or tab-separated files) as data sources for your Cognos TM1 model, these files are often stored on the server machine, too.

With this information we can forecast the amount of hard disk space:

- Cognos TM1 software installation:
  - 1.5GB Cognos TM1 10.1 or higher (older versions: 600MB)
- Cognos TM1 database:
  - Size of RAM
  - Size of log files
  - Size of uploaded files
  - Size of import files

Because of this calculation we recommend having 80GB of free disk space at least. But be aware of the log files. The Cognos TM1 server does not delete any logs. To watch the size of the log files is an administrative task. If you do not want to delete log files, we recommend having more appropriate free disk space.

Cognos TM1 Web Server

The Cognos TM1 Web server requires additional resources. If your Cognos TM1 application is used by a few users at the same time, you can operate the Cognos TM1 Web server on the same machine as the Cognos TM1 server. But both servers will compete for resources. These resources are primarily RAM memory and CPU time. We recommend separating the Cognos TM1 Web server and the Cognos TM1 server on different machines.

Let's take a look at how Cognos TM1 Web uses the system resources. If a user opens Cognos TM1 Web, he has to log on first. The user is able now to open a Cognos TM1 Web object (Cognos TM1 Web Cube Viewer or Cognos TM1 Websheet) in the main display frame. A Cognos TM1 Web object can be opened by selecting an entry in the Navigation tree or by clicking an Action button (Cognos TM1 Websheets only). In the following illustration, you can see an example when a user has open one Cognos TM1 Web Cube Viewer and a Cognos TM1 Websheet.

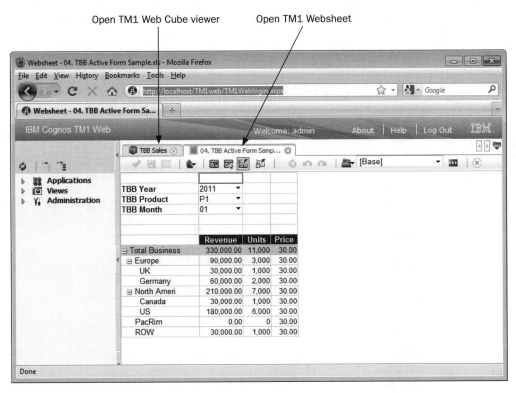

We will explain what happens on the Cognos TM1 Web server using this example. When the user opens Cognos TM1 Web, the request to the web server opens a user session on the web server. When the user logs on to the Cognos TM1 server, the created connection is held in the user's web session. The user now opens a Cognos TM1 Web Cube Viewer. This action creates a corresponding object in the session of the user. The same happens when the user opens a Cognos TM1 Websheet. For each open object in the user's browser, there is a corresponding object on the Cognos TM1 Web server. These objects exist as long as the user closes the object in the web browser (closes the tab or clicks the Close button in the toolbar). This scenario is displayed in Figure 13-4.

NOTE *You can configure Cognos TM1 Web to hide the tab bar. In this case, only the topmost Cognos TM1 Web object is displayed because all objects are stacked behind each other. But it could be that some objects are still open and have corresponding objects on the web server. These hidden objects can be accessed only by closing the topmost object.*

If we want to size a Cognos TM1 Web server machine, we have to consider these issues:

- Each user who is using Cognos TM1 Web has opened a web session.
- Each session requires memory (RAM).
- Multiple concurrent users utilize CPU time of the web server machine.
- Each open Cognos TM1 Web object on the Cognos TM1 Web server uses memory (RAM).

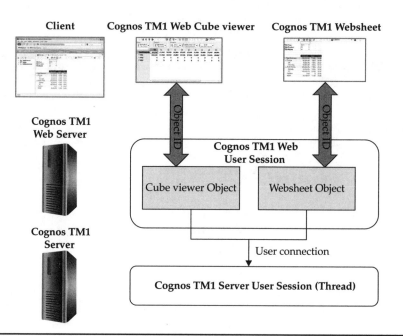

FIGURE 13-4 Objects in the Cognos TM1 Web environment

Cognos TM1 Client	LAN	WAN
Cognos TM1 Perspectives (Excel Add-in)/Cognos TM1 Architect/ Performance Modeler/Cognos Insight	X	
Cognos TM1 Clients via "Remote Screen"	X	X
Cognos TM1 Web	X	X

TABLE 13-7   Deployment Methods

Although concurrent user sessions exist, there are no contentions on the Cognos TM1 Web server. The Cognos TM1 Web objects are "private" to each session. A rule of thumb for the number of TM1 Web servers is ~50 to 100 active (logged in at once) web users per Cognos TM1 Web server. If you have more concurrent web users, you should have multiple Cognos TM1 Web servers, which can be virtualized on a single physical server.

The utilization of memory depends on how many objects are opened per session at the same time and what is the size of a single object (size of rows and columns of a view or number of populated cells in the Cognos TM1 Websheet). A rule of thumb is to have a similar amount of RAM on the Cognos TM1 Web server as on the Cognos TM1 server machine.

Network Considerations

A Cognos TM1 application is a client/server application and therefore a "networked application." For that reason, a Cognos TM1 application is affected by network capacity and latency. There are some rules to follow regarding networks:

- Consider if your connections are using LAN or WAN.
- For performance reasons, we do not recommend using the Cognos TM1 Excel Add-in over a WAN. If you have to, please consider whether you can use the Cognos TM1 Excel Add-in via "Remote Screen" software like Citrix.
- In almost all scenarios, Cognos TM1 Web will perform better.
- WAN latency is <100ms for your connections.

These rules lead to some recommended deployment methods and bandwidths, as shown in Table 13-7 and Table 13-8.

Method	Minimum Bandwidth
LAN	100BASE-T Ethernet (100Mbps) to clients and server
WAN (server side)	2Mbit synchronous Internet connection
WAN (client-side Cognos TM1 Web or Screen Remoting)	256Kbit synchronous Internet connection (that is, 2Mbit ADSL) <100ms latency

TABLE 13-8   Recommended Bandwidth

General Sizing Recommendations

Let us mention again that all calculations we showed in the previous sections are forecasts only. In the real world, the operation of a Cognos TM1 application could be different from these forecasts. So there is only one true rule:

- **More is better.**

    Here are some detailed examples of what we mean by "more":

    - Use more RAM to have a buffer. This buffer can be used for temporary objects like "Before Images" when you load your model by TurboIntegrator (see Chapter 10) or for optimizing the order of cube dimensions.

    - Use more cores to have real parallel execution. (Imagine, you can have one core per concurrent user. This would guarantee that all user transactions could get CPU time at the same time. But this makes no sense because the cores would be idle most of the time.)

    - Use more hard disk space to have enough space for log files. With enough hard disk space, you do not have to worry about the log files for a long time.

    - Use faster processors. The faster the processor is, the faster Cognos TM1 can calculate and retrieve values.

Monitoring and Logging

Using monitoring and logging information, you can understand what happens during the operation of a Cognos TM1 server. There are different areas, which we discuss in the next few sections.

Cognos TM1 Logging

We already introduced the various logs created by the Cognos TM1 server operation. This section provides a description of the log files.

Audit Log

The Audit log contains the following information, as shown in the following illustration:

- Date (when)
- User (who)
- Event/Description (what)
- Object Type
- Object Name
- Details

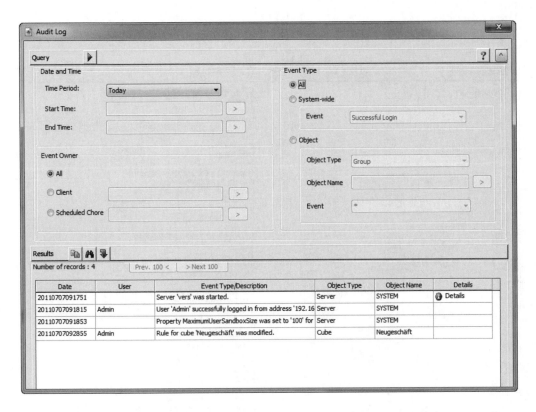

The following list and Table 13-9 describe the different object types and the events that are logged.

System logs (object type: Server) log the following parameters:

- Connection Synchronized Successful (Replication)
- Connection Synchronized With Errors
- Dimensions Attribute Delete
- Dimensions Attribute Insert
- Property Set: <PropertyName> (logs the change of a dynamic tm1s.cfg parameter)
- Shutdown
- Shutdown Request Cancelled
- Shutdown Requested
- Startup
- Successful Login
- Unsuccessful Login

Table 13-9 describes Cognos TM1 object-related logs.

Object Type	Event
Application	Created Deleted Entry Added Entry Deleted Entry Privatized Entry Published Entry Renamed Privatized Property Set: EntryAdditionalProperties Property Set: EntryPublishUrl Property Set: EntryReference Published Renamed Security Changed
Cube	Attribute Delete Attribute Insert Attribute Value Set Cell Security Changed Created Data Reservation: Acquired Data Reservation: Released Data Reservation: Rollback Acquire Data Reservation: Rollback Release Default View Set Deleted Dimensions Reordered Property Set: ChangedSinceLoaded Property Set: CubeDataReservationM Property Set: IsVirtual Property Set: LoadOnDemand Property Set: LogChanges Property Set: MeasuresDimension Property Set: PerspectivesMaxMemor Property Set: PerspectivesMinTime Property Set: ReplicationConnection Property Set: ReplicationSourceObjec Property Set: ReplicationStatus Property Set: ReplicationSyncRule Property Set: ReplicationSyncViews Property Set: TimeDimension Rule Added Rule Deleted Rule Modified Security Changed Unloaded
View	Created Deleted Modified Published

TABLE 13-9 Cognos TM1 Object-Related Logs

Object Type	Event
Dimension	* Attribute Delete Attribute Insert Attribute Value Set Created Default Subset Set Deleted Element Deleted Element Inserted Property Set: ChangedSinceLoaded Property Set: DefaultHierarchy Property Set: LastRepSyncChangedTime Property Set: LoadOnDemand Property Set: ReplicationConnection Property Set: ReplicationSourceObjectNa Property Set: ReplicationStatus Property Set: ReplicationSyncAttributes Property Set: ReplicationSyncSubsets Property Set: SortComponentsSense Property Set: SortComponentsType Property Set: SortElementsSense Property Set: SortElementsType Renamed Security Changed Subset Published Updated
Subset	* Created Deleted Modified Property Set: Alias Property Set: ExpandAbove Property Set: Expression Property Set: FormatStyle Property Set: IsAll Renamed
Element	* Added to Consolidation Attribute Value Set Removed from Consolidation Security Changed Type Change Weight Changed
Process	* Created Deleted Executed GrantSecurityAccess disabled GrantSecurityAccess enabled Modified Security Changed
Chore	* Created Deleted Executed Property Set: Active Property Set: Frequency Property Set: StartTime Property Set: Steps Security Changed

TABLE 13-9   Cognos TM1 Object-Related Logs *(continued)*

Object Type	Event
User (Client)	Created Deleted Password Assigned Property Set: MaximumPorts Property Set: PasswordExpirationDays Property Set: ReadOnly Property Set: UniqueID Property Set: WebCollapseNavTreeOnSt. Property Set: WebHideCubeviewerToolB; Property Set: WebHideCubeviewerToolB; Property Set: WebHideNavTree Property Set: WebHideNavTreeAllowOve Property Set: WebHideTabBar Property Set: WebHideTabBarAllowOver Property Set: WebHideWebsheetToolBar Property Set: WebHideWebsheetToolBar Property Set: WebHomePageObject Property Set: WebHomePageObjectAllow Property Set: WebHomePageObjectDesc Property Set: WebHomePageObjectType Property Set: WebToggleNavTreeAllowO Property Set: WebUserStyle Property Set: WebUserStyleAllowOverwr
Security group	Client Assigned Client Removed Created Deleted

TABLE 13-9   Cognos TM1 Object-Related Logs *(continued)*

Transaction Log

The Transaction log records all modification of data in cube cells, as shown in the following illustration. This includes all system cubes such as attribute cubes or security cubes.

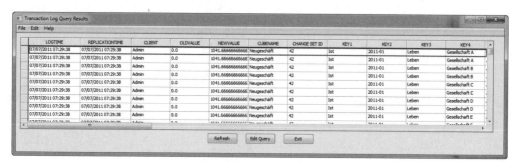

The Transaction log contains the following information:

- **Logtime**   When does the modification occur?
- **Replicationtime**   Used for Replication/Synchronization.
- **Client**   Who modifies?
- **Old Value**

- **New Value**

- **Change Set ID**   This brings together multiple modifications that are made by a single action (for instance, the modifications made by data spreading).

- **Cubename**   Which cube was affected.

- **Key1...KeyN**   Dimension elements in the order of the dimensions of the affected cube. This element identifies the modified cell.

Cognos TM1 Server Message Log

In this section we take a closer look at the message log. The message log is stored in the "LoggingDirectory" and has the name "tm1server.log."

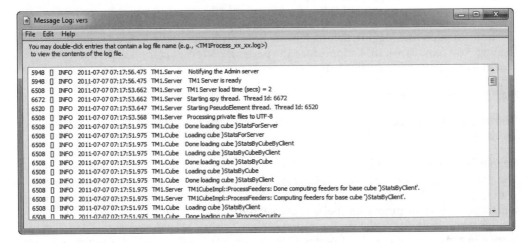

The message log contains the following information, as shown in the preceding illustration:

- ThreadID

- Logging severity: DEBUG, INFO, WARNING, ERROR, FATAL

- Logging timestamp

- Scope (for example: Server, Cube, Lock, API, Process)

- The message

As already mentioned, you can configure the Cognos TM1 server to log more details in the message log. This configuration is made in the "tm1s-log.properties," which can be found in the "DataBaseDirectory." Here is a basic example of the log configuration, which can be enhanced:

```
#
# Enable INFO level logging through the shared memory appender,
# by default. The server will write informational messages,
# as well as errors and warnings to the log file.
#
```

```
log4j.rootLogger=INFO, S1
log4j.logger.TM1=INFO
log4j.logger.TM1.TI=DEBUG

# S1 is set to be a SharedMemoryAppender
log4j.appender.S1=org.apache.log4j.SharedMemoryAppender
# Specify the size of the shared memory segment
log4j.appender.S1.MemorySize=5 MB
# Specify the max filesize
log4j.appender.S1.MaxFileSize=100 MB
# Specify the max backup index
log4j.appender.S1.MaxBackupIndex=20
# Specify GMT or Local timezone
log4j.appender.S1.TimeZone=GMT
```

Unfortunately, the logging parameters are not documented. If you need some more logging, you have to ask IBM support for the parameters for your special scenario. We would like to give you just one example:

```
Log4j.logger.TM1.Process=DEBUG
```

With this parameter, you can get more information on the execution of TurboIntegrator processes.

Cognos TM1 Admin Server Log

You can also log the operation of the Cognos TM1 Admin Server. In the "bin" directory of your Cognos TM1 installation, you can create or modify the configuration file tm1admsrv-log.properties. In the properties file, you can set the name and the path of the log file. The configuration is similar to the configuration of the Cognos TM1 server message log. For further information, refer to the Cognos TM1 documentation (*Cognos TM1 Operations Guide*, Chapter 6).

Cognos TM1 Web Logs

You can find an error log in the log directory, which is a subdirectory of the Cognos TM1 Web directory. Furthermore, if you use Cognos TM1 Websheets, the Cognos TM1 Excel service is involved in creating the HTML versions of your Excel sheets. This Cognos TM1 Excel service is configured by the TM1ExcelService.exe.config file. You can find this file in the same directory where the TM1ExcelService.exe is installed (default: the bin directory of your installation). In the configuration you can set the path and filename of the log file. The default setting lets the Cognos TM1 Excel service create a log file in the same directory. The file is called tm1excelservice.log.

Cognos TM1 Client Logs

Since Cognos TM1 9.5.1, you can also log in to the Cognos TM1 clients Cognos TM1 Perspectives and Cognos TM1 Architect. In the same location you can find the tm1p.ini file. You can create or modify the configuration file tm1p-log.properties. In the properties file, you can set the name and the path of the log file. The configuration is similar to the configuration of the TM1 Server Message log. For further information, refer to the Cognos TM1 documentation (*Cognos TM1 Operations Guide*, Chapter 6).

Performance Monitor

The Performance Monitor is a built-in logging capability that logs various information to system cubes (control cubes). The Performance Monitor is deactivated by default. You can activate the monitor on demand using the Server Explorer menu: Server | Start Performance Monitor. If the Monitor is started, the menu item changes to Stop Performance Monitor. With this option you can turn off the Monitor again, but it is also an indicator for a running monitor.

It is also possible to activate the Performance Monitor on Cognos TM1 server startup. This is controlled by the tm1a.cfg parameter `PerformanceMonitorOn=T`.

The Performance Monitor creates and populates the following control cubes:

- }StatsByClient
- }StatsByCube
- }StatsByCubeByClient
- }StatsForServer

Cognos TM1 populates these cubes with some system measures every minute.

You can find a detailed description of the cubes and the measures in the Cognos TM1 documentation: *Cognos TM1 Operations Guide*: Appendix A, Performance Monitoring Control Cubes, and Appendix B, Control Dimensions.

Cognos TM1 Performance Counters

Performance counters are Cognos TM1 server measures that are exposed by a Cognos TM1 server. These counters can be tracked by two different tools: the Cognos TM1 PerfMon utility and the Microsoft Windows Performance Monitor. Currently Cognos TM1 provides 59 counters.

The Cognos TM1 PerfMon Utility is a command-line tool that can be used on Microsoft Windows or UNIX operating systems. The name of the executable file is "tm1perfmon.exe" on both systems. The next illustration shows an example of the Cognos TM1 PerfMon Utility executed in a Windows console (see the Cognos TM1 documentation: *Cognos TM1*

Operations Guide; Chapter 6, Using Cognos TM1 Performance Counters). This also shows all available counters.

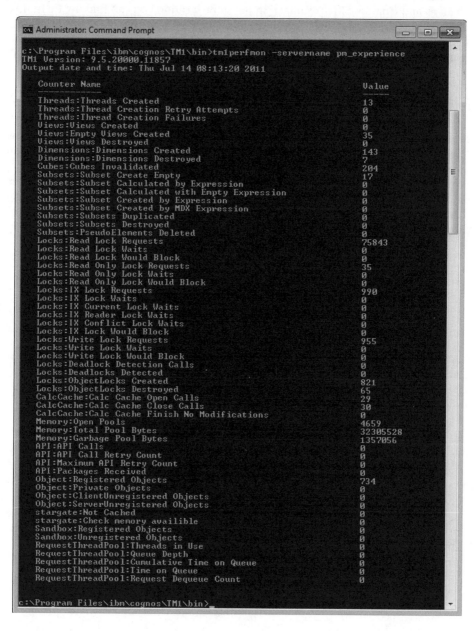

On a Microsoft Windows system, you can also use the Windows Performance Monitor, as shown in the following illustration:

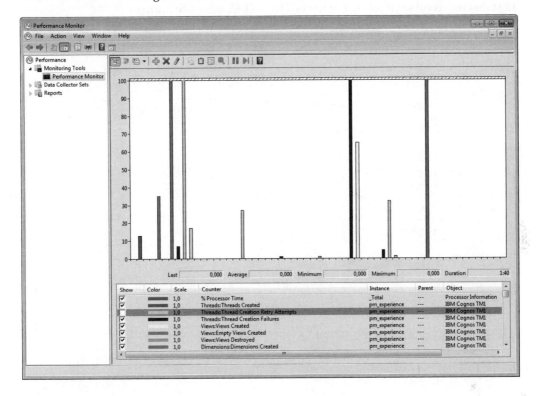

PART II

Using this utility, you can choose one or more Cognos TM1 counters to be displayed in the monitor. You can add a counter using the Add Counters dialog. Here you get also a short description of each counter, as shown in the following illustration.

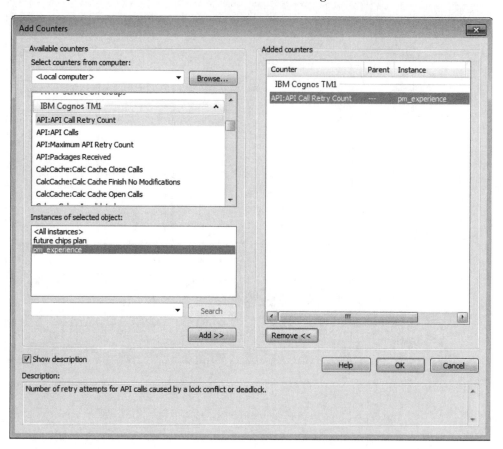

Sharing Cognos TM1 Models Between Environments

Larger applications and applications that have to be enhanced over time require an environment that is split into production and development environments. In addition, you can have a third environment for testing. For this reason you have to move single Cognos TM1 objects from one environment to another. We want to mention that some Cognos TM1 model information is stored in system cubes and dimensions. Please use the transport method for cubes and dimensions to transfer these kinds of objects. Relevant objects are: Security, Attributes, all kinds of properties, and Replications (Connections).

There are various methods to accomplish this transport. These methods are discussed in the next sections.

Transport by File Copy

The first and most frequently used method is to copy the corresponding files of the files from a source "DataBaseDirectory" to a target "DataBaseDirectory." The copies of the Cognos TM1 objects can be used only after the restart of the target Cognos TM1 server. Cognos TM1 will maintain the system dimensions "}dimensions, }cubes, }processes, }chores, and }ApplicationEntries" automatically on startup time.

Of course, there are some challenges.

Some Cognos TM1 objects consist of multiple files. Some of them are mandatory, and some are optional. So you have to be careful to copy all necessary files into the target Cognos TM1 server (see the section "Backup" for information regarding folders and private objects). Table 13-10 provides information on the files for these objects.

Cognos TM1 Object	Files	Remarks
Dimension	\<DimensionName>.dim Additional (optional) files for Element Attributes: }ElementAttribute_\<DimensionName>.cub, }ElementAttribute_\<DimensionName>.dim	
Subset	\<SubsetName>.sub	
Cube	\<CubeName>.cub Additional (optional) file for Rules object: \<CubeName>.rux	Ensure that all dimension files of the cube dimension exist on the target server. Also make sure that all dependent cubes exist on the target server if you transport the Rules object.
View	\<ViewName>.vue	
Process	\<ProcessName>.pro	Ensure that the data source is also available on the target server: ODBC Data Source Name, import file, Source cube + view or dimension + subset.
Chore	\<ChoreName>.cho	Ensure that all processes and replications of the chore exist on the target server.
Application Entry	Just copy files and subfolders of the }Application folder	Ensure that the links are valid in the target server. If your copy of a application contains uploaded files, you have to copy the corresponding files from the }Externals folder.

TABLE 13-10   Cognos TM1 Objects Consisting of Multiple Files

NOTE *Cognos TM1 10.1 provides a utility which is called "tm1xfer". This utility can be used to transport a TM1 Database. Please refer to the* Cognos TM1 Operations Guide *for further information.*

Transport by Replication

The second transport method is using Replication/Synchronization. With this method you can transport cubes, public views, rules, dimensions, and public subsets only. If you replicate a cube, you should be aware that you also transport the data from the source environment to the target environment. Views and rules can be transported only in the context of their cube, and subsets only in the context of their dimension. In general, Replication/Synchronization is about transporting a cube. If you want to transport a dimension only, just replicate the Element Attribute cube of this dimension.

For detailed information, refer to the Cognos TM1 documentation: *Cognos TM1 Operations Guide*, Chapter 5.

Transport with Performance Modeler

The Performance Modeler provides the capability to "transfer" an "application." From the perspective of the Performance Modeler, an application is not the whole Cognos TM1 model but an application that is used by the Cognos TM1 Contributor. Such an application consists of an approval hierarchy and views on various cubes. Based on these views and subset, all dependent Cognos TM1 objects are determined and transferred to an output folder as files (see the following illustration). These dependent objects are all cubes that are affected by the views, all dependent cubes, all dependent dimensions with Element Attributes, and all subsets that are used in the views (plus the Approval Hierarchy subset).

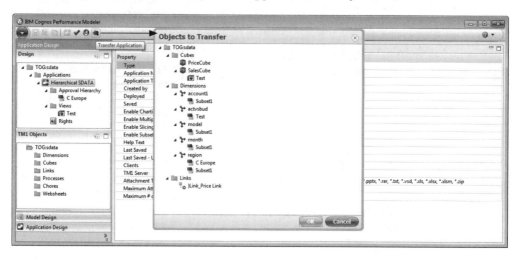

Instead of transferring an application, you can transfer single objects. This capability is available in the Model Design Tree. From here you can call the "Transfer Out" (export to an output folder) and the "Transfer In" (import from a folder), as shown in the following illustration.

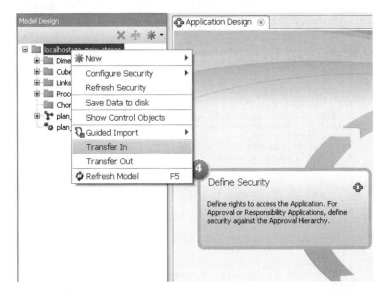

The "Transfer Out" function invokes a dialog where you can select single objects. Again, all dependent objects will also be transferred automatically (see the next illustration).

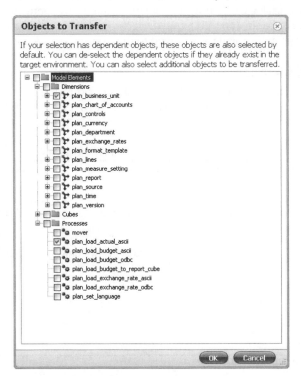

Regardless of whether you transfer an application or single objects, the output folder can now be moved to the target server (for instance, as a zip file). On the target Cognos TM1 server, you can "Transfer In" this folder with all exported Cognos TM1 objects. The next illustration shows the dialog that is invoked when you use the "Transfer In" function.

This method of the Performance Modeler does not transfer cube data. Therefore, the Performance Modeler has logic to handle the data of the target environment if the dimensionality of a cube has changed. For instance, if a transferred cube has an additional dimension compared to the target cube, the data is moved to the first leaf element in the new dimension.

Mixing Transport Methods

Because not all methods can transport all kind of objects, you have to mix the methods we discussed in the last few sections. Table 13-11 provides an overview of transport methods.

Cognos TM1 Object	Transport Method		
	Copy Files	Replication	Performance Modeler
Dimensions	X	X	X
Subsets	X	Public subsets only	Public subsets only
Cubes	With data	With data	Without data
Views	X	Public views only	Public views only
Rules	X	X	X
Processes	X		X
Chores	X		
ApplicationEntries	X		

TABLE 13-11 Matrix of Transport Methods

Transport Method	Advantages	Disadvantages
Copy files	Easy mechanism; the Cognos TM1 object files can be stored in a version control tool; all objects are supported	Restart of the target Cognos TM1 server is needed; you have to be careful about all dependencies of the various objects
Replication	Transport is supported by a tool; one-step transport.	Not all objects are supported; there is no external version of the objects that can be stored in a version control tool; you have to be careful about cube dependencies
Performance Modeler	Transport is supported by a tool; takes care about dependencies; easy to use; the content of the output directory can be stored in a version control tool	Not all objects are supported

TABLE 13-12 Advantages and Disadvantages of Transport Methods

To give you more information for the decision about which method to use, we summarize the advantages and disadvantages in Table 13-12.

Summary

In this chapter we have discussed how to operate a Cognos TM1 server. We have discussed the following points:

- Security
- Backup and reliability
- Sizing
- Monitoring and logging
- Model transport

All of these points are relevant for IT administrators. Security is also important for the design of a Cognos TM1 application. Cognos TM1 developers should be interested in model transport.

PART II

PART III

Business Solutions with IBM Cognos TM1

14 CHAPTER

Business Modeling with Cognos TM1

N ow that you have become familiar with Cognos TM1 as a tool by working through the previous chapters, we want to help you get the necessary business background, too. And more important, you will get a lot of hints about how to map this business knowledge to Cognos TM1.

The reason for the 25-year-long success story of Cognos TM1 is its capability to map business requirements very effectively into an IT solution. "Effectively" means that the method of implementation is very business-oriented. Some can argue that doing the same thing with pure spreadsheet design is business-oriented, too. So what's the difference? The key requirement might be that the solution is built to last. Although ad hoc modeling, as is often done with spreadsheets, might be helpful in some areas, your attention will mostly be directed toward building longer-lasting solutions. For this, you need more powerful modeling tools like the Cognos TM1 rules, or automatic aggregation across hierarchies.

The usage of a tool depends on the stability of the business environment. If you reinvent your business quite often, you need a way to combine ad hoc tools with a business model. It should be possible to adapt your solution to environmental changes easily. Hence the tool used to solve business problems should support change. If you try to change something, like adding a cost center, in a complex and intensively linked spreadsheet, you will find that it's not easy. Perhaps you would have to start from scratch. That is the biggest advantage of Cognos TM1 over pure spreadsheet modeling.

In this final part of the book we will show important business scenarios and how to implement them with Cognos TM1. It could be seen as a cookbook or a toolbox. We avoid creating huge complex models but provide small examples that we hope are easy to understand (and easy to adapt to your individual requirements as well). Naturally, you will not need all of these concepts for your own projects. But maybe the suggested solutions will give you some good hints and inspire you to be innovative and develop your own creative approaches. And "creative" is the keyword. The most fascinating thing with Cognos TM1 is that each time you try to solve a problem, you can find new insights into business solutions and how to map these insights into multidimensional structures.

But first we want to present a short discussion about the principles of modeling and why it is necessary to spend some time contemplating them.

Complexity and Dynamics

If you have already been working in the area of software development for a while, one of your biggest concerns might be complexity. A typical situation could be that you have to change a certain aspect of the system or enhance the system with an additional function. Hopefully, you have a clear understanding how to implement it. But often you don't feel comfortable because you can't assess all the ramifications. What is the effect on other parts of the system? Are existing calculations still working correctly? And even if you feel more or less safe, you may discover during testing that you have overlooked some consequences. And testing is hardly comprehensive. Are there still risks of malfunction? You can never be sure.

What is complexity? It is not simply the number of cubes, dimensions, and elements. Huge cubes with many dimensions and elements can be astonishingly simple. It is the dependency of elements that drives complexity. It doesn't have to be only rules that cause complexity. TI scripts and all kind of reports can also significantly drive complexity.

But it isn't complexity alone that makes modeling such a challenging task. The second important driver is change. Complexity alone is not critical per se because you can rely on classic software engineering principles like modularization and information hiding. But change alone (without complexity) is also easy to handle because you understand all the consequences of change. What usually bothers us is the combination of both: a dynamic and complex environment. This is critical for development because traditional engineering principles handle complexity very well but also make a development process inflexible.

Complexity and change affect the system design even before implementation. Complexity and change should influence the buying decision. When you start to think about possible automation of a performance management process, these drivers should be considered. Take, for instance, typical planning and budgeting requirements. You can choose between spreadsheet, ERP, dedicated planning solutions, or Cognos TM1. Although our preference is, of course, Cognos TM1, a recommendation to always use Cognos TM1 would be rather marketing-oriented. If you are in a stable environment with only a few users, little change, and limited requirements, why not use your existing ERP? Most of the available ERP systems in the market have some budgeting functions included. They are limited and inflexible, but in a steady and simple environment, this could be sufficient. If complexity increases, but business processes remain stable, it might be interesting to use a pure spreadsheet approach simply because ERP systems usually support only simple business modeling. You can define some complex rules with spreadsheets. Usually you will have to copy formulas a lot, so later changes are risky. But with the assumption of a stable environment, this shouldn't be critical.

On the other hand, when you are in a very unstable environment but with low complexity, perhaps a situation where only one person works with the system, a spreadsheet solution might be appropriate. A lot of changes must be adopted but within simple models, this shouldn't be critical.

But the most common situation nowadays is, of course, complexity and change. And this is exactly the real-life situation where Cognos TM1 can provide its greatest strengths. Rules scripting is a perfect means to handle complexity: Instead of copying formulas, the scope of the rules is automatically enhanced to include new elements. Hence no redundancy of definitions exists. And rules are also the perfect weapon for change. Rules are automatically applied to dimension elements. In combination with a good design, change results in few adaptations.

A problem, of course, is how to measure complexity and change. There are ideas to make these terms more operational. We are skeptical that a formal approach could help in making fundamental system decisions. Our impression is that most companies are facing medium to high complexity and change.

Another aspect shouldn't be neglected. Maturity is a further key driver. People with little experience or with experience in only one system often tend to stick with one single tool. There is nothing wrong with that. However, there is a potential risk of doing inappropriate things with a tool. We have seen ERP systems (and not the worst one) implemented with office tools. But maintenance becomes really painful. Of course, a good understanding of alternative concepts—for example, multidimensional and relational modeling—is helpful.

And last but not least a warning: the first steps with Cognos TM1 are very often motivating. But always try to assess the final complexity. As the number of business requirements increases, complexity increases exponentially. And more than that: working intensively with Cognos TM1 often leads to complex systems, particularly if basic software engineering principles are not considered. The ease of use of Cognos TM1 supports rapid prototyping. And the new Performance Modeler makes it even easier to start with a limited understanding of the business challenge. When new insights are discovered, almost all aspects of a system can be adjusted. But this is only the technical part of the problem. All business ramifications must be considered. In overly complex systems, this is nearly impossible.

Build or Buy

An important aspect is the old question: make or buy? Can you buy a packaged solution or do you have to write the program yourself? The huge success of ERP solutions speaks for a buy solution. But can this simply be the rule: "If a packaged application is available, take it"? That is definitely too simple. Cognos TM1 is very often used in areas where packaged solutions are available. Although there are not many predefined applications for performance management available yet, the number is growing. Some examples include

- Statutory consolidation
- Activity-based costing
- Balanced scorecard
- Integrated financial planning
- Risk management

Packaged solutions are strong in well-defined areas like bookkeeping or operational purchasing. When it comes to more operational questions like manufacturing, individual requirements are becoming more and more important. It's the same with planning: the term "planning" spans such a broad area of functions that a packaged application for planning does not seem possible. Specific planning applications for budgeting or sales forecasting may be more realistic.

Another aspect is important: is the domain mission-critical or not? Bookkeeping isn't mission-critical for most companies (although we have seen accounting departments that really believed in their central roles for the company's success). The more mission-critical a process is, the more important a competitive advantage could be. However, it is not very likely to achieve such an advantage with packaged software that every company could use. If it is about industry-specific solutions, it is likely that your competitors use or will use the same functionality. So a strategic advance is quite unlikely with packaged applications. And very often companies are not willing to adjust their mission-critical processes to a predefined process that a vendor has developed.

Performance Management software is slightly different from typical ERP systems:

- Process standards are not that established. For instance, take processes like rolling forecasts or balanced scorecards. Although there are initiatives to standardize, it is a long way from an accepted standard.

- Companies change their approach more often. We know companies that start each year with a new planning process design.

- The users are either less computer trained or used to working with office tools. They often don't accept rigid entry forms.

- Experimental problem solving is a common requirement. Hence flexible ad hoc simulation capabilities are important.

We are aware that you can challenge these statements. Of course, there are parts within the ERP scope that need to be flexible and include simulation. Take shop floor planning, for example. On the other hand, rigid performance management processes like budgeting are very close to transactional processing. These statements are tendencies, not strict rules. But one conclusion should be clear: you need more flexibility than common packaged software can provide.

How could we position Cognos TM1? The strength of Cognos TM1 is exactly in coping with less standardized solution areas. Although Cognos TM1 has some strong planning features like workflow, distribution rules, and more, it is not a packaged solution. It is a toolbox to define individual solutions. On the other hand, it is not a programming tool. The confusing thing might be that you can use Cognos TM1 as a programming tool with an integrated database. Or you can use the API to embed it into a programming environment.

We have seen situations where this definitely made sense. A lot of IBM's business partners encapsulate Cognos TM1 into their specific performance management applications. Each company that uses Cognos TM1 can do the same. However, we recommend using the built-in capabilities of Cognos TM1 as often as possible.

So when should you use packaged applications and when should you use Cognos TM1? There is no hard rule for this. But a simple principle might be: the more general acceptable principles are available, the bigger is the tendency to use packaged applications. This is obvious with statutory consolidation. Not many individual requirements exist. So it doesn't make sense to invest in a custom-built Cognos TM1 application.

It is different with costing. There is no standard, and a broad set of calculation methods are available. Specific costing applications, for instance, for activity-based costing, only map a part of common costing requirements. In particular, product or service calculations can be very specific.

If packaged applications map with your requirements, that is fine and the recommendation is to use packaged applications. If you need additional functions or you need enhanced functionality in the future, it may make sense to think about Cognos TM1 because building workarounds with packaged applications can be cumbersome. Often, built-in intelligence restricts individual workarounds.

To choose between build or buy is a trade-off. How big is the fit, and how expensive will possible workarounds and enhancements be? The best thing is to do a TCO-based assessment.

Potential Limitations of Business Modeling with Cognos TM1

Another important question goes beyond the question of what you could do with Cognos TM1. It is the opposite question: what should you *not* do with Cognos TM1? Where are its limitations? This is not easy to answer. The developers have included a lot of new concepts in recent years to broaden the scope.

A good example may be line items. This is a relational rather than a multidimensional concept: Below a cell identified by a set of dimensional elements, you need a potentially unlimited number of detailed entries. The same concept must be applied when it is about accounting: below the account balance is the document level. In the early days of OLAP, this was not possible to solve. At that time, we built a lot of workarounds, most of which included a relational database to store the line items. But synchronization between multidimensional and relational databases is not simple stuff and always took a lot of time. We will describe how we solve this nowadays in Chapter 17.

Another aspect is transactions handling, such as bookkeeping. We don't want to go into detail, but early OLAP wasn't very strong even in handling multiuser requests, particularly when it was about write-back. However, when it is about classic transaction handling with a lot of concurrency, we think there are better tools available on the market. Cognos TM1 wasn't built for operational transactional handling. That shouldn't surprise anyone. So the ease of data definition and the comfort of spreadsheet-based forms development should not hide the challenges of dealing with massive transaction handling with locking and so on. However, with version 10, a lot of work has been invested in improving this area.

There are also limitations in the graphical representation. That is where Cognos BI comes into play. However, in the following chapters we won't talk about the possibilities of using Cognos BI. To provide conceptual solutions is the key task of these chapters.

The last limitations we see are optimization and statistics. CPLEX and SPSS are the leading tools available. We show some minor approaches to solve statistical and operations research problems. A complex allocation, for instance, is solved with linear equations. But this is far from professional optimization or statistical algorithms. So our recommendation is: when you start with optimization or limited statistical analysis, try Cognos TM1. When your analysis is established and you want more, think about a specific solution. We have had the experience that integration between these tools is not a big challenge.

Modeling Principles

What you do with Cognos TM1 is usually very quickly implemented (at least a prototype). That is a dream for business analysts. They can discuss the requirements in business language. With this short distance between business requirements and technical implementation, prototyping is possible.

But even though ad hoc modeling is simple, we all know that a lot of things can go wrong with a Cognos TM1 model. There are design decisions that are hardly reversible. An absolutely necessary prerequisite is to have a clear understanding about the business background and the problems you would like to solve with Cognos TM1. Simply stated, the better your business background and its typical challenges are understood, the more efficient the discussion between analyst and business department can be. This definitely means that you should have experience in business. Of course, you can't be an expert in all business areas. But there is a core knowledge set that includes planning, budgeting, forecasting, and management accounting, which really helps. We added some additional business areas—for instance, risk management—that could be of interest to you.

What you implement can be very stable if you stick to some principles. This is simply software engineering. Although our book should not be an academic treatise on business modeling, it is necessary to understand at least the basic principles of business modeling. But relax: we won't spend too much time on theoretical aspects. Other books are available for business modeling. Our objective is to show how smooth an implementation can be.

What does business modeling mean? It is simply something you always do when you try to solve business problems with Cognos TM1. You can do this intuitively or—which is definitely more appropriate with complex requirements—with a more formal approach. The chosen approach is often related to the level of experience. Sometimes an experienced Cognos TM1 consultant is able to design an excellent model completely in his mind. From a conceptual point of view, there is nothing wrong with that. But to get a clear understanding is only a fraction of the method. Another thing might be more important: communication. A good model representation helps to transfer the ideas from a business perspective to the technical implementation.

Good business modeling doesn't have to be complex. On the contrary, a good business design is most often surprisingly simple. A good orientation uses the old principle "dividere et impere" (divide and conquer), which means divide your problem into smaller parts and thus be able to understand and model them. The key in software engineering is modularization. Try to build small models and link them together by the smallest possible interface. And respect the inner secrets of the module and use only what is specified as external. All good programming languages work in this way.

But this is not always easy with Cognos TM1. One of the strengths of Cognos TM1 is openness. You can access every object in every part of Cognos TM1. On the one hand, this is really helpful because you can easily bring everything together, even across totally different topics. On the other hand, this is somewhat risky. The more links you have between objects like cubes, the harder it is to maintain integrity.

- So try to limit the connections between cubes. For instance, limit the links between cubes. When you use links, try to document them and keep them clearly marked within the rules. Or better: use the new link mechanism within the Performance Modeler.

- Another important thing is dependencies between TI processes and dimension elements. There are elements that can be generic, like scenarios or periods. To link TIs to specific accounts can be more risky.

What about using a modeling language like ADAPT or Entity Relationship Modeling? We think that the value is limited. Sometimes it can be helpful, but don't spend too much time on it. The cube model and the right dimension are important, without any question. But model languages neglect an important type: the rules. As you will see later in this book, we spend more time on rule generation than on what are the right dimensions.

Don't expect strict rules from us. They don't exist. There is another problem with rules or the softer form principles: they can kill creativity. We think it is better to run in the wrong direction in the beginning than to take an excessively strong formal approach. The important thing is that you discover early enough if you started in a wrong direction. So steps in prototyping should always include critical reviews about data modeling.

There are only minor recommendations, which can't be seen as strong rules. However, there are some experiences we would like to share:

- Start with small prototype models. Most of our models are good examples of how to work with small prototypes. First of all, you should have a clear understanding about the business requirements and how to map them into a multidimensional model with a rule language.

- Although there is no "component deployment" (sometimes also referred to as "transportation system" before version 10), you should always test on a separate model. The good thing is that you can generate a test model within minutes. It lets you do prototyping. Don't test with a complete set of calculated measures. Instead, split them up into separate models. It is not a big job to combine them later into a productive system. Focus on a small fraction of your company, product, or customer structure. To include at least two or three levels is often important to test the rule behavior. The fewer objects you define, the easier it is to go a step back or even start with a fresh model again

- What is the right design approach? Or more concretely: should you strive to limit the number of cubes? It is about balancing multicubing versus single cubing. The good thing is that Cognos TM1 is not restrictive. The bad thing is that you must make a decision. It is also somewhat related to your experience. For instance, if you haven't started with Cognos TM1 but with Oracle/Hyperion Essbase, for instance, it is very likely that you will work with only a few cubes because Essbase was originally designed as a single-cube approach. Cognos Planning, by contrast, requires the designer to build many cubes. The reason is mainly capacity restrictions due to a missing sparsity concept. There is no right or wrong modeling unless you go to the extreme. We think that objects with the same dimensions or at least with a similar dimensions structure should be included in one cube. A typical example is the model of profit and loss, balanced sheet, and cash flow. Although they have different behaviors—take the flow and stock behavior, for example—we think they belong in a single cube. The strongest argument is that cash flow is simply an aggregation of balance (as fund flow) and profit and loss (see Chapter 19). Another practical advantage is that rules design could be simpler. You could use short references instead of the DB function. Short references are more stable from a modeling point of view, and you can check whether the referenced elements exist.

Another aspect to consider with cube design is the restriction that cube views may only contain data from one cube. While data can be virtually (rules) or physically (TI) moved between cubes to satisfy the need for per-cube views, you must consider their interface options as a factor in building the model. Excel and Websheets can effectively pull data from multiple cubes into the same UI, often reflecting data from different cubes in a single grid driven by common row dimensions.

A sign of a model with too few cubes is the intense use of elements of "no element," "dummy," "not assigned," or similar. It shows that a lot of object types don't really fit into the cube scheme. Although you can profit from simpler rules, the complexity increases. Multicubing can be used for modularization. We recommend rather short rule scripts to avoid side effects. Since the rule script is not fired in a procedural order (which is definitely a strength, not a disadvantage), the backtracking mechanism of Cognos TM1 sometimes leads to surprising side effects. To control such side effects within hundreds of lines of code is hard work. And don't forget the effect of later changes. Due to the missing module concept within Cognos TM1, module structured testing becomes very complicated.

- Start to build your own idea repository. Each Cognos TM1 expert should have a set of small applications with sometimes hundreds of cubes and dimensions.

- Be creative. Could such advice really help? Yes and no. A lot of business problems are already solved with Cognos TM1 methods. Fortunately you don't have to think about the solution. You only have to map the business problems to Cognos TM1. But this is not always straightforward. Don't stick too closely to procedures others have developed.

- Use rules intensively, or better yet, try to limit calculations to rules. The performance of rules calculation with Cognos TM1 has increased steadily. The advantage of rules instead of TI is the higher stability and, even more important, the stronger business orientation. You can calculate in TI scripts and reports, but we clearly recommend rules. Avoiding calculations in reports should be clear: since we want to map business knowledge into Cognos TM1, it should be independent of single reports but be reusable. If you have to change the calculation, for instance, for a measure, you are responsible to update all reports that contain this calculation.

Sometimes performance is offered as the argument for why a TI script is preferred for calculation. This is indeed an aspect to consider. Long calculation chains definitely affect calculation time. And sometimes you need iterative calculations like interest iteration (Chapter 19) or iterative allocations (Chapter 18). On the other hand, the rules definitions are very compact: you don't have to think about loops and sequences. Our recommendation is: always use rules for business calculations. For iterations and batch calculation, use TI only to copy rule-calculated results into base elements and to define loops. Use dynamic subsets as input for the copying process to reflect possible changes. You can find examples of this concept in Chapter 18 and Chapter 19. With this concept it is possible to let business experts maintain the rules. TI scripting is rather something for programmers.

Although our recommendations regarding modeling are limited, this can't be an excuse for missing documentation. Cognos TM1 is business-oriented. But even experts have problems understanding their own complex rules after a certain time. The setup time to understand even our own older models is quite high. With good documentation, this time can be drastically reduced. What is good documentation? It must be easy to understand. And even more important—the effort for creation must be minimal. Consider that you do a lot of prototyping.

To document the results is time-consuming. Very often the parts of a concept are spread across different tools:

- Calculation in rules files
- Active Forms
- TI process
- Attributes and dimensions
- How can you document your models?
- Always take screenshots.
- Document directly within the screenshots (for instance, by saving them into Microsoft PowerPoint and using boxes and callouts for documentation as close as possible to the solution). You can also use the speaker notes.
- Use small examples to show how the model works. Particularly for rules, it is comfortable to have small examples.

In our examples we avoid intensive discussion of performance. We are aware that performance issues are one of the main causes of unhappy users. Does this diminish the value of our efforts? We don't think so. First of all, you need correct results. So there is no way to neglect good business understanding. And secondly, the strength of Cognos TM1 is prototyping, which means that solutions must be easy to adapt. However, you have to avoid the following situation: You used classical waterfall engineering, developed, tested everything, and went live—and then you and the users realized that performance is unacceptable. Too much work has already been spent to change the business method. Your toolbox might be limited to smaller improvements. So what can you do?

We suggest the following steps:

1. Find an appropriate business solution, also known as a good algorithm (perhaps in our book).
2. Test it with a minimal set of elements.
3. Enlarge the dimensions with a more realistic set and test it.
4. If performance is not satisfying, use common optimization methods. (For example, use SKIPCHECK, avoid overfeeding, precalculate with Turbo Integrator processes, optimize the dimension order, and so on.)
5. If performance is still not optimal, start with a new approach. Since you are still in a prototype mode, not much time should be wasted.

This approach is, of course, no silver bullet, and the more you know about how Cognos TM1 behaves and calculates, the closer to the final solutions your first models will be. However, don't stick too long to an algorithm that may be the right one from a theoretical point of view but can't be implemented efficiently.

What to Expect in the Following Chapters

Now you should be well prepared for the following chapters. We prepared a set of business examples that should cover a major part of common business requirements. The selection is still subjective, of course.

The examples we will introduce should help you to understand typical business challenges. However, they are not intended to use immediately as professional solutions. Those solutions are often called "blueprints." What is the difference between our examples and blueprints? Blueprints often have been discussed to provide a quick start. Simply said, a best practice model has been implemented in advance for another customer or out of experience. Such a blueprint is delivered to customers for a concrete project. The customer or a consultant takes the model and includes the individual structures. This sounds easy and compelling: less time for solution finding, less time for design and implementation. But this hardly works. Blueprints are mainly used as a solution finder. And for this they are good. But blueprints are built with the target of mapping realistic situations with real complexity. We think, from a learning point of view, simpler models are more appropriate.

Most of the solutions were not developed exclusively for this book, but have been collected from implementation projects during the last 15 years. We have tried to reduce these models to their essence. Not all concepts are the result of real business projects. For instance, we haven't implemented linear equation models yet. But our intention is not only to provide proven working examples, but also to inspire you to think beyond the typical project scope.

The following chapters will be presented with a specific structure:

- What is the business challenge?
- How can Cognos TM1 help?
- More or less simple Cognos TM1 models for a better understanding of the concepts.

There is always more than one way to solve problems with Cognos TM1. Particularly with version 10, new tools like the Performance Modeler or Cognos Insight are introduced. In many respects, the way you work with the system will change basically. However, we don't think that the way you fundamentally model design will change significantly . We admit that almost all of our models were developed for version 9 and earlier. But this shouldn't be a problem because from a conceptual point of view, there is no change regarding Cognos TM1 Model architecture.

But don't misunderstand us: Cognos TM1 version 10 is a big move forward, but mostly in the way that model creation will be simplified so that Cognos TM1 users with less experience can benefit from the strengths of Cognos TM1. And experienced users can profit from more user-friendly tools like the link mechanism. However, in the end, the core concepts like rules or Turbo Integrator scripts are automatically generated from the more user-friendly development tools. Hence the proven principles are still valid even with the new tools.

Given this short introduction, enjoy our modeling suggestions in the following chapters. They should give you some ideas about creating your own solutions in your individual environment.

Sales and Profitability Analysis

S ales and distribution are "classic" areas for OLAP models. In this domain multidimensionality is obvious. You can intuitively identify dimensions like customers, products, regions, channels, and more and assign them to your sales and cost transactions. Hence it is very natural to model sales structures with OLAP. Also, the typical sales and profitability questions directly lead to multidimensional models and OLAP:

- Which products, customers, and regions provide the highest and lowest sales and contribution margins?

- In which area do the biggest variances occur?

- Are there changes during the specified time period?

- …and many more.

These questions are often related. For instance, when you have identified the highest negative sales variance, you would like to investigate how long this potential problem has existed and how strong the contribution margin (still) is. It is not surprising that the first OLAP approaches were developed to cope with typical sales problems.

Cognos TM1 for Sales and Profitability Analysis

Cognos TM1 is the perfect tool for sales and profitability analysis: Cognos TM1 can handle a huge amount of data, which usually is a prerequisite for sales and profitability planning. And it can let you analyze multidimensional situations in real time at the speed of thought. But more important for complex sales analysis are Cognos TM1's calculation capabilities. It must be possible to split variances, disaggregate numbers, and more. The combination of scalability and KPI/driver calculation makes Cognos TM1 unique. With the understanding you have already accumulated in the previous chapters, sales analysis should not be complicated. We want to focus on more specific and somewhat more complex challenges:

- **Best practices in how to model a sales and contribution cube**   How to calculate cross-dimensional measures (for instance, percent of sales).

- **How to design a meaningful variance analysis**   Sales and profitability analysis means to analyze variances. This is not only classical drilldown or slice and dice: sophisticated variance splitting helps find causes of potential problems.

- **How to assign volume and prices to base level and group elements**   Pure direct costing means to avoid allocations. From a theoretical point of view, it is not always appropriate to allocate costs to the lowest level, that is, the product or the customer. It is sometimes more appropriate to assign costs to a group level or even to the top level. For instance, marketing activities sometimes support not a single product but a product group. Most administration costs cannot be assigned to any specific product or customer/group.

- **How to use complex filters in sales reports**   Complex filtering in a sales cube is an important requirement because there are a lot of dimensions, and OLAP behaves differently than relational databases. However, the expectations of users are often driven by experience with SQL.

- **How to create specific analysis, like ABC analysis**   Another important thing is flexible grouping. A typical example is the ABC analysis where you build categories on current values like sales or contribution margin. Dynamic grouping has consequences for the aggregation mechanism.

We will not show all related aspects of sales with Cognos TM1 in this chapter, but we promise to cover everything in detail in later chapters. For instance, sales and profitability planning are crucial steps in the planning process. Sales is typically the starting point for company-wide planning. In global company structures, intercompany relations, profit adjustments, and currency conversions are also crucial. In Chapter 23 we will cover typical best-practice concepts for holdings and groups.

A Simple Multidimensional Model

A good starting point is to create a simple profitability calculation. This is something that is always helpful when you begin to work with an OLAP tool. It looks rather intuitive; however, meeting all specific requirements can result in a very complex model.

Let's start with the definition of a cube. What dimensions are needed? This is, of course, industry-specific and depends on what questions you want to answer now and in the future. For our examples we will assume a retail company and therefore we suggest the following dimensions:

- Products and product groups

- Customers and/or Customer Groups

- Channels like direct sales, Internet

- Regions

- Time (years, months, and so on)

- The scenario dimensions contain elements like "Actuals," "Budget," and various variances like price, volume, and mixed variances.

- The central logic is part of the measure dimension. Typical elements of a contribution margin are gross sales, discounts, direct costs, fixed costs, and various contribution margins.

You should also consider whether you need a currency calculation. We chose to skip this dimension in this chapter. The art of currency calculations is handled in Chapter 23, where the requirements are much more sophisticated. After you have worked through the paragraph about currency conversion in Chapter 23, a simple currency calculation needed for sales analysis should not be any challenge for you.

With the following dimensions, we can easily set up our example cube.

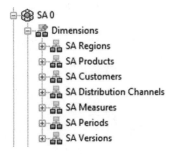

The most important topic to discuss is the calculations of measures and variances. With Cognos TM1 we have at least three approaches to calculating measures:

- Use aggregations together with weighting (+/−). The margin calculation, for instance, can be seen as an aggregation of revenue (weighting 1) and costs (weighting − 1).

- Rules

- TurboIntegrator processes for static calculations

We prefer hierarchies for simple profit calculation instead of rules. There are some advantages:

- You don't have to optimize rules (that is, skipcheck and feeders).

- If you don't work with the new Performance Modeler and you share this dimension between cubes, you don't have to set up the same behavior for each cube.

- You can use built-in drilldown capabilities in many report generators to start, for instance, with profit and drilldown to sales or costs details.

However, this method is only possible for simple +/− calculation. In a typical sales model you usually need more complex calculations. For instance, in many cases the profitability calculation contains prices and costs per units, not to mention variance calculation in percent or cost in percent of sales.

Although most measures and variance calculations are more or less simple, you should be aware of possible miscalculations when it comes to aggregation. That is why it is always necessary to review the results. Some results might be nonsense. For example, it doesn't make sense to aggregate prices or costs per unit along the various dimensional hierarchies. To define the rule for prices and costs per unit on the aggregate level is important, because otherwise these items will be aggregated.

A typical calculation looks like the following:

```
['Sales']=N:['Volume']*['Price'];
['Costs']=N:['Volume']*['Costs per Item'];
```

The result is perfect. But it is not completed. Since we work with multipliers, we have to consider the aggregation effects. You can argue about the need for the aggregated volume, but the price calculation in the following illustration is definitely useless.

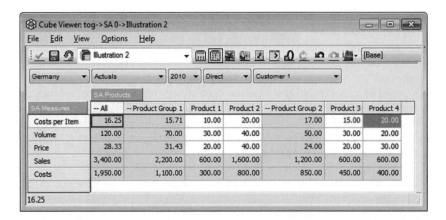

There are two possibilities:

- Either you set all aggregated elements for the "price" element to "no value";
- Or you calculate average values for aggregated elements. The average price can be helpful for various comparisons. We usually prefer this option.

Most often you need the "C:" rule. Here are the aggregate price/costs formulas:

```
['Price']=C:['Sales']\['Volume'];
['Costs per Item']=C:['Costs']\['Volume'];
```

The result looks much better:

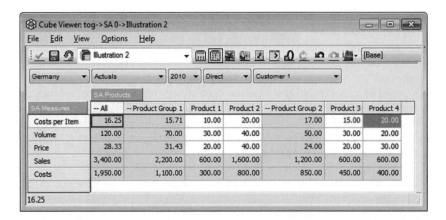

So price is a typical measure type, which you shouldn't aggregate. But there are more. Other examples are

- Percentage

- Time aggregation of stock

- KPIs, which can show behavior similar to that of percentage, but it is sometimes more complex or even impossible to define rules for calculation on an aggregate level. An good example might be ROCE (return on capital employed).

Up to now we have only used measures with the same dimensionality. But is this realistic for prices or costs? Do we really have a separate price for each customer? It can be, but in many business areas this assumption is not very realistic. Hence you either model price in a separate cube or work with specific dimension elements in a single cube: For each dimension for which you don't want to specify price, you should enter a dummy element, "No Element." This enables you to assign pricing data to a cube with a customer dimension where you don't want to assign a price to specific customers.

We prefer to create a new cube with prices and costs. Do we have specific costs per region? It is worth having a discussion. Be aware that modeling decisions can limit your flexibility. If you plan to change your pricing policy, you should consider more dimensions as actually needed. Let us take the following cube structure:

And we need a rule in the main cube "SA 0":

```
['Price']=N:DB('SA Prices', !SA Regions, !SA Products, !SA Measures, !SA
Periods, !SA Versions);
```

For contributions analysis, you perhaps need some further measures:

- "% of Sales" (for all positions). This gives you a better impression about the cost structure for each product. You can easily compare products.

- "Return on Sales" also lets you compare dimension elements like customer regions. You can create rankings to find out where your engagement is most effective.

- "Average Sales" can be defined for all aggregations.

First, one correction: "% of Sales" is actually not a measure in the classical sense. Typically the measures are defined in the measure dimension. But "% of Sales" will be calculated for all cost and revenue positions (for sales too). We define this element within the dimension "SA Versions." To let the calculation work efficiently, neither "C:" nor "N:" is necessary since the rule should be always fired regardless of the level.

The calculation of "% of Sales" in our example is set on the first position in the rule script. And we need a further restriction. This definition of "% of Sales" is only valid for value positions, not for volume and others. This is a good opportunity to introduce a commonly used type attribute for the measure dimension. This is very often used to control the behavior of the measures. With this definition we are able to avoid miscalculations. See the type attribute in the following illustration.

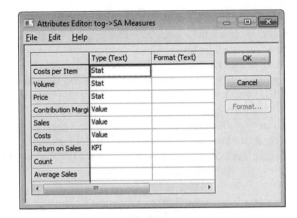

The following rule limits the calculation to attributes with the type "Value":

```
['% of Sales'] = IF(ATTRS('SA Measures',!SA Measures,'Type')@=
'Value',['Actuals']/ ['Actuals','Sales']*100,CONTINUE);
```

An easy measure calculation is Return on Sales (ROI). Consider that this calculation is also without specifying C: or N:. This measure should be calculated after all aggregation.

```
['Return on Sales'] = ['Contribution Margin'] \ ['Sales']*100;
```

The rule calculation is correct on every level, as the following illustration shows.

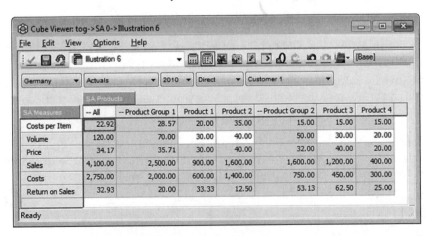

The final type of calculation is a simple statistical one: Show me the average sales per product group, per customer group or quarter. To calculate average elements, an intermediate step is necessary. With Cognos TM1 it is easy. In older versions a count function is not available. We define average sales as follows:

```
['Count']=N:1;
['Average Sales'] = ['Sales'] \['Count'];
```

The result:

We have new statistical functions in Cognos TM1 9.5.2: Min, Max, Average, Count, and Distinct Count. We should make reference to them here; this is a new best practice for statistical calculations.

This is a quick shot, but you have some aspects to consider: First, which level is the base for the average calculation? With our definition we assume that we only refer to basic elements. But is the average sales really the average of each customer and each product sales? Or should average sales be defined across all products?

You also have to think about zero values. Does this mean you have sold nothing this period, or are you looking at a combination that is not valid for sales? In the first case, you want to include this number in the second case. This is a quite complex discussion. However, if you want to suppress zero, simply change the Count calculation to

```
['Count']=N:IF (['Sales']=0,0,1);
```

Calculating Variances

After you have successfully implemented a base model, you want to do some analysis. An important step is to do a variance analysis. There's nothing fancy about it: A variance analysis compares actual data either with previous periods, with plan, forecast, or budget data, or with similar structured data of other similar objects (for instance, similar regions or projects or products).

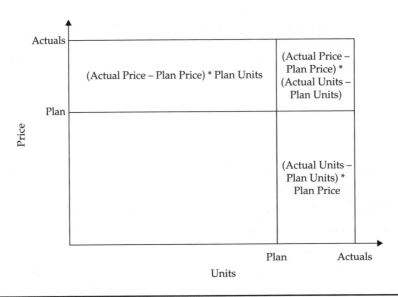

FIGURE 15-1 Concept of variance calculations

But you can get more out of a structured analysis. Usually several effects are responsible for variances. An important thing is to separate relevant from irrelevant variances. One example: Is the sales department responsible for higher production costs? Not very often. So if you want to identify reasons for contribution margin variances in the sales department, you should not focus on production cost variances.

Another question: Are they responsible for high discounts? You may say yes. This should be mostly the case. That is exactly the art of variance analysis: to split variances so you can define appropriate adjustments. A diagram (see Figure 15-1) shows how the calculation of these variances works. Combined variances (Price variances * Unit variances) are usually assigned to the price variance. However, in our example we show this variance as "mixed effect."

But there can also be a third variance, which is called structure or product mix effect. This variance is only valid on an upper level and explains movement from one element (that is, product or customer) to another. We built a small cube to explain the concept, as follows:

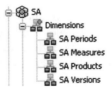

We will show a way to split the variances into price, unit, and mixed variances. Take the following scenario dimension:

```
n Plan
n Actuals
n % of Sales
⊟ Σ Variance
    ├ n Price Effect
    ├ n Volume Effect
    ├ n Structure Effect
    └ n Mixed Effect
```

For Units, Price, and costs per unit, the variance calculation is rather simple: We can't split up variances into parts.

```
['Variance',{'Costs per item','Volume','Price'}]=['Actuals'] - ['Plan'];
```

For costs and sales, we want to break down variances into a price effect, a unit effect, a combined effect, and finally a so-called structure effect. The price effect is usually defined as:

```
['Price Effect','Sales']=N: (['Price','Actuals']-
['Price','Plan'])*['Volume','Plan'];
```

The volume effect can be defined as:

```
['Volume Effect','Sales']=['Price','Plan']*(['Volume','Actuals']-
['Volume','Plan']);
```

There is a residual amount, which is often described as price/unit variances:

```
['Mixed Effect',{'Sales','Costs'}]=
['Price Effect']*(['Volume','Actuals']/['Volume','Plan']-1);
```

On the aggregate level, the calculation of a fourth variance is necessary. It is the second residual variance. The last effect is called structure effect and can be defined as follows:

```
['Structure Effect',{'Sales','Costs'}]=['Actuals']-['Plan']-
['Price Effect']-['Volume Effect']-['Mixed Effect'];
```

The structure effect can be calculated because the volume effect is individually calculated on each level and not a simple aggregation. What is the meaning of the structure variance?

It simply says how many of the unit variances are explained by a shift of sales from one product to another product. Let's take a look at how this calculation works:

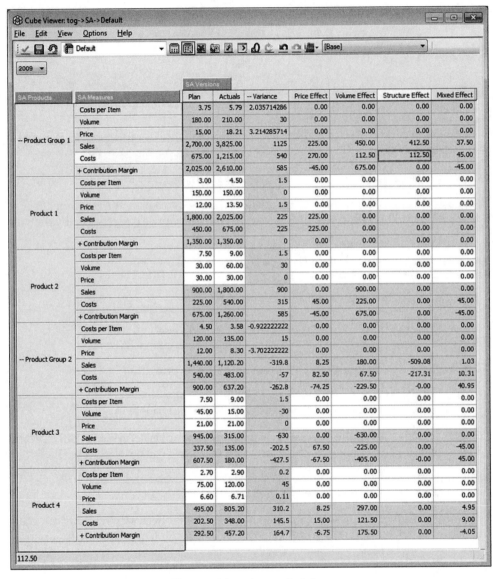

SA Products	SA Measures	Plan	Actuals	-- Variance	Price Effect	Volume Effect	Structure Effect	Mixed Effect
-- Product Group 1	Costs per Item	3.75	5.79	2.035714286	0.00	0.00	0.00	0.00
	Volume	180.00	210.00	30	0.00	0.00	0.00	0.00
	Price	15.00	18.21	3.214285714	0.00	0.00	0.00	0.00
	Sales	2,700.00	3,825.00	1125	225.00	450.00	412.50	37.50
	Costs	675.00	1,215.00	540	270.00	112.50	112.50	45.00
	+ Contribution Margin	2,025.00	2,610.00	585	-45.00	675.00	0.00	-45.00
Product 1	Costs per Item	3.00	4.50	1.5	0.00	0.00	0.00	0.00
	Volume	150.00	150.00	0	0.00	0.00	0.00	0.00
	Price	12.00	13.50	1.5	0.00	0.00	0.00	0.00
	Sales	1,800.00	2,025.00	225	225.00	0.00	0.00	0.00
	Costs	450.00	675.00	225	225.00	0.00	0.00	0.00
	+ Contribution Margin	1,350.00	1,350.00	0	0.00	0.00	0.00	0.00
Product 2	Costs per Item	7.50	9.00	1.5	0.00	0.00	0.00	0.00
	Volume	30.00	60.00	30	0.00	0.00	0.00	0.00
	Price	30.00	30.00	0	0.00	0.00	0.00	0.00
	Sales	900.00	1,800.00	900	0.00	900.00	0.00	0.00
	Costs	225.00	540.00	315	45.00	225.00	0.00	45.00
	+ Contribution Margin	675.00	1,260.00	585	-45.00	675.00	0.00	-45.00
-- Product Group 2	Costs per Item	4.50	3.58	-0.922222222	0.00	0.00	0.00	0.00
	Volume	120.00	135.00	15	0.00	0.00	0.00	0.00
	Price	12.00	8.30	-3.702222222	0.00	0.00	0.00	0.00
	Sales	1,440.00	1,120.20	-319.8	8.25	180.00	-509.08	1.03
	Costs	540.00	483.00	-57	82.50	67.50	-217.31	10.31
	+ Contribution Margin	900.00	637.20	-262.8	-74.25	-229.50	-0.00	40.95
Product 3	Costs per Item	7.50	9.00	1.5	0.00	0.00	0.00	0.00
	Volume	45.00	15.00	-30	0.00	0.00	0.00	0.00
	Price	21.00	21.00	0	0.00	0.00	0.00	0.00
	Sales	945.00	315.00	-630	0.00	-630.00	0.00	0.00
	Costs	337.50	135.00	-202.5	67.50	-225.00	0.00	-45.00
	+ Contribution Margin	607.50	180.00	-427.5	-67.50	-405.00	-0.00	45.00
Product 4	Costs per Item	2.70	2.90	0.2	0.00	0.00	0.00	0.00
	Volume	75.00	120.00	45	0.00	0.00	0.00	0.00
	Price	6.60	6.71	0.11	0.00	0.00	0.00	0.00
	Sales	495.00	805.20	310.2	8.25	297.00	0.00	4.95
	Costs	202.50	348.00	145.5	15.00	121.50	0.00	9.00
	+ Contribution Margin	292.50	457.20	164.7	-6.75	175.50	0.00	-4.05

112.50

The complete variance calculation

Product 4 shows the following sales variances:

- A price variance of 8.25 = (6.71 − 6.60) * 75

- A unit variance of 297 = (120 − 75) * 6.60

- A mixed variance of 4.95. For Product Group 2, a structure effect of −509.08 is calculated. You can see a massive shift from product 3 to product 4. That is why this variance shows the highest effect.

Practice a little bit with the model. And use the trace calculation as shown in the following illustration to understand how the calculation works.

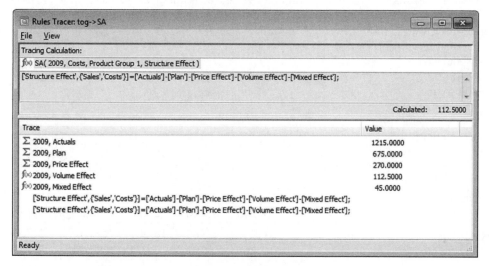

Trace calculations

To better understand the model, build up your own scenarios with this model.

Stepwise Fixed Costs Assignment

In the preceding examples we simply assumed that there is a rate for direct costs and (preallocated) indirect costs. But this is not always the appropriate way to work with indirect costs. A long academic discussion about relevant costs revealed that allocation of indirect cost could lead to wrong decisions. A typical example might be a decision whether to accept a sales offer with a price below the total costs. The traditional recommendation would be to refuse this offer because the contribution margin (including allocated indirect costs) is negative. However, in many cases the contribution margin (without indirect costs) would be positive. In consequence, the overall profit would increase with the additional sales order. So to refuse the sales offer results reduces the possible profit. This argumentation might be too simple, and of course, you have to consider more aspects. But with this discussion we are in the heart of the academic discussion of direct and indirect costs.

A proposed (and often accepted) approach is to assign costs to a higher level in the products or customer hierarchy. We will call it relative direct costs. For example, a manufacturing machine that can produce more than one product can be only assigned to the product group, not to a single product. The same can be done with various overhead cost types. This is not always easy and requires good business understanding. Look at Figure 15-2. This can be a typical stepwise assignment of indirect costs.

To map this calculation to Cognos TM1, it is necessary to assign data to an aggregate element. We all know that Cognos TM1 cannot store data on aggregate levels. Not a problem at all, you may think; perhaps we can use data distribution. But this doesn't solve the problem, because costs are distributed to the lowest level. And this is what we want to avoid because this results in invalid allocation (at least in the point of view of academic purists).

The usual proposal to overcome this kind of problem is to define a so-called dummy element: A group "Product Group A" could consist of

Product Group A E
Product A1
Product A2
and so on…

Business Units	1			2	
Products	I	II	III	IV	V
Product Groups	A		B	C	
Gross Sales	18,700	7,200	17,250	16,050	12,250
- Discount	3,740	1,440	3,450	3,210	2,450
Net Sales	14,960	5,760	13,800	12,840	9,800
- Direct Costs	10,259	2,257	9,278	8,021	4,791
Contribution Margin	4,701	3,503	4,522	4,819	5,009
Direct Costs Product			100		
Contribution Margin II	4,701	3,503	4,422	4,819	5,009
Contribution Margin II	8,204		4,422	9,828	
Product Groups					
- Direct Costs Product Groups	150			250	
Contribution Margin III Business Units	8,054		4,422	9,578	
Contribution Margin III Business Units	12,476			9,578	
- Direct Costs Business Unit	4,295			4,795	
Contribution Margin IV	8,181			4,783	
Contribution Margin IV	12,964				
Company					
- Indirect Costs Company	690				
EBIT	12,274				

FIGURE 15-2   Example of a multilevel contribution margin calculation

where "Product Group A E" is the dummy element, and the postfix "E" stands for entry. This works fine, because the fixed costs are assigned to Product "Group A E." When you assign costs to "Product Group A E," costs are not allocated down to the granular level. On the higher level, "Product Group A," you can show product-related direct costs and indirect costs. This is much better, or is it?

However, there is a disadvantage: If you report or you want to implement a drilldown, you always see the dummy element. In standard reports you must always suppress this element. Hence this workaround is always visible and, to be honest, it looks nasty (at least in our eyes).

Let's try another approach. We created the following cube:

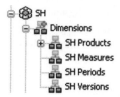

To solve this problem, we work with a "shadow hierarchy" in the dimension "SH Products." We have two hierarchies: the original "natural" hierarchy, and the so-called "shadow hierarchy." The shadow hierarchy contains all dummy elements:

- An element per aggregation node with the postfix "E," as shown in the following illustration.

- An element per aggregation node with the postfix "T." "T" stands for "Transfer." These nodes are referred by the nodes of the natural hierarchy.

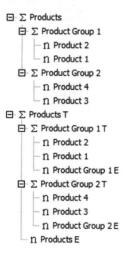

But this is not enough. Furthermore, we need a calculation since we want the aggregate levels to be assigned with directly assigned values. To calculate the "natural" tree, you need only one rule:

```
skipcheck;
[]=IF(  DIMIX('SH Products',!SH Products | ' T') = 0,
 continue,
 DB('SH', insrt(!SH Products,' T',1),
 !SH Measures,!SH Periods, !SH Versions));
```

You can see that we used a string transformation rule. It depends on whether we use a postfix or a suffix. We used a postfix, but feel free to change it. The only obvious restrictions are that the postfix or suffix shouldn't be confused with an element with the same "natural" ending (perhaps you have products named "product a," "product b,".... "product e").

The IF statement tests whether a "T" element exists for the current member. This is only the case for "natural" aggregations. For all other elements (Level 0, "E" Elements, "T" Elements) the DIMIX function returns 0.

The result of this formula is shown in the following illustration. It is a surprising behavior of Cognos TM1. For instance, the fixed costs on Product Group 1 are obviously not calculated by summing up its children.

		-- Products	-- Product Group 1	Product 2	Product 1	+ Product Group 2
Actuals	Sales	460	210	110	100	250
	Cost of Sales	182	102	50	52	80
	-- Contribution Margin	278	108	60	48	170
	Fixed Costs	42	12	0	0	30
	-- Contribution Margin 2	236	96	60	48	140
	Cost of Administation	35	0	0	0	0
	-- Profit	201	96	60	48	140
Plan	Sales	110	110	0	110	0
	Cost of Sales	61	61	0	61	0
	-- Contribution Margin	49	49	0	49	0
	Fixed Costs	4	4	0	0	0
	-- Contribution Margin 2	45	45	0	49	0
	Cost of Administation	39	0	0	0	0
	-- Profit	6	45	0	49	0

Fixed costs on a higher dimension level

There is one caveat: Don't try zero suppression. Since we work on the N/C level, a sufficient feeder concept would slow down enormously.

This looks almost perfect. But what about maintaining this shadow hierarchy? Manually, it could be a huge effort to maintain this second hierarchy with all dummy elements. But it is easy to use a program to reduce the maintenance effort. We developed a small TurboIntegrator process to minimize the effort. We defined a process that runs through a dynamic subset that contains all elements (alternatively, you can program the loop within the TI process). This is the code of the metadata section in the TurboIntegrator editor.

```
vsDimname = 'SH Products';
IF(SUBST(V1,LONG(V1)-1,2) @<> ' E' &
   SUBST(V1,LONG(V1)-1,2) @<> ' T' );
IF( ELLEV(vsDimname,V1)= 0);
   DimensionElementInsert( vsDimname, '',
   INSRT(ELPAR(vsDimname,V1,1),' T',1),'C');
   DimensionElementComponentAdd ( vsDimname,
   INSRT(ELPAR(vsDimname,V1,1),' T',1)   ,V1, 1);
  ELSE;
   DimensionElementInsert( vsDimname, '',
   INSRT(V1,' T',1),'C');
   IF (ELPARN(vsDimname, V1)<>0);
     DimensionElementInsert(vsDimname, '',
     INSRT(ELPAR(vsDimname,V1,1),' T',1),'C');
     DimensionElementComponentAdd ( vsDimname,
     INSRT(ELPAR(vsDimname,V1,1),' T',1),
     INSRT(V1,' T',1) , 1);
   ENDIF;
   DimensionElementComponentAdd( vsDimname,
   INSRT(V1, ' T',1)   ,INSRT(  V1, ' E',1) , 1);
  ENDIF;
ENDIF;
```

This program should always run after you have changed the dimension structure. You can integrate this into a TI load routine.

The last thing is to provide a convenient way to collect data in Excel forms. We created a small Active Forms template. You could start with the lowest level in the product hierarchy and see the result as shown in the following illustration. Only on the direct elements of the hierarchy is data entry possible.

The cells with the light gray characters are only shown for purposes of explanation. In practice they should be invisible and locked to avoid unintentional changes.

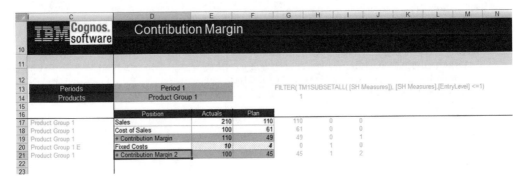

Let's now change the product element to an element of level 1. You can see in the following illustration that sales and cost of sales cannot be manipulated any more. Figures for fixed costs can be entered now.

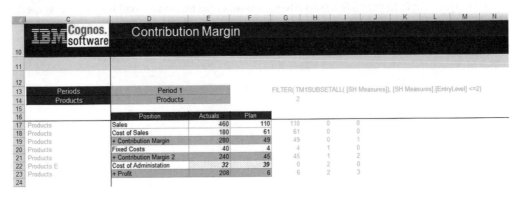

Finally, take a look at the top level. Only numbers for cost of administration can be entered.

	C	D	E	F	G	H	I	J	K	L	M	N
10	IBM Cognos software	Contribution Margin										
11												
12												
13	Periods	Period 1				FILTER(TM1SUBSETALL([SH Measures]), [SH Measures].[EntryLevel] <=2)						
14	Products	Products				2						
15												
16		Position	Actuals	Plan								
17	Products	Sales	460	110	110	0	0					
18	Products	Cost of Sales	180	61	61	0	0					
19	Products	+ Contribution Margin	280	49	49	0	1					
20	Products	Fixed Costs	40	4	4	1	0					
21	Products	+ Contribution Margin 2	240	45	45	1	2					
22	Products E	Cost of Administation	32	39	0	2	0					
23	Products	+ Profit	208	6	6	2	3					
24												

The impression of this entry form is that the user directly enters data on a higher level. In the reporting, he doesn't see the shadow hierarchy at all.

How is this developed? Only the "SH Measures" elements relevant for this level should be visible. This is the row definition:

```
=TM1RPTROW($C$9,"TOG:SH Measures",,,,,$G$13)
```

This filter query can be defined with an MDX statement:

```
G13:="FILTER( TM1SUBSETALL( [SH Measures]), [SH Measures].[EntryLevel]
<="&$G$14& ")"
G14:=ELLEV("tog:sh products";$D$14)
```

In plain English: show only elements with the attribute EntryLevel smaller or equal to the level of the selected product (or group). This attribute must be entered for each measure because the Cognos TM1 level functions don't provide the right information.

Please consider that the SH Measure dimension must have the following order:

- ⊓ Cost of Sales
- ⊓ Sales
- ⊞ Σ Contribution Margin
- ⊓ Fixed Costs
- ⊞ Σ Contribution Margin 2
- ⊓ Cost of Administation
- ⊞ Σ Profit

As mentioned, the product entry level drives the behavior of the active form. The level for SH Products is calculated as follows:

```
G14:=ELLEV("TOG:sh products",$D$14)
```

We also need a level assignment for the measure dimension. The entry level is defined as an attribute, as shown in the following illustration.

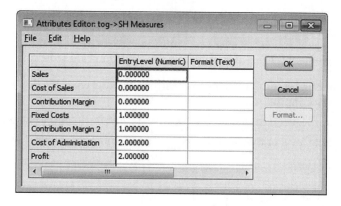

What happens if the entry level changes from <=0 to <= 1 is easy to understand. The MDX filter changes and more elements are returned.

The second task is to mark the entry cells. Entry elements are shown in yellow, in the box labeled "Preview of format to use when condition is true." This is represented by a conditional formatting standard, as shown in the following illustration:

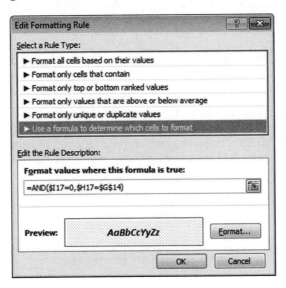

We want to enter data to level 1. But this is not possible because "Product Group 1" is not a leave element. For this purpose the dummy element with a prefix or postfix like "E" is used. The first idea might be to select "Product Group 1 E" for the whole form. But this doesn't work, because we wouldn't get the aggregated values from product 1 and product 2. The report must contain a flexible combination of the original and the dummy element.

We decided to use Column C for a dynamic calculation of the hierarchy elements. Have a look at cell c20:

```
c20:=IF(AND($G$14<>0,AND(H20=$G$14,$I20=0)),
$D$14&" E",$D$14)
```

The dummy element ("E") is used when three conditions are true:

- The product level (G14) must be greater than 0; otherwise, we don't need an E-element for input.

- The measure level (I20) must be 0, because it must be an entry element.

- The attribute level of the current measure (H20) must be identical with the org level.

For a better understanding, we show the referenced cell formulas:

```
G14:=ELLEV("TOG:SH Products",$D$14)
H20:=ELLEV("TOG:sh measures",$D20)
I20:=ELLEV("TOG:sh measures",$D20)
```

There is a additional column, G, which contains a DBRW formula too and is set to invisible. Why is this? For the active form to work properly, it is necessary to have at least one correct column with the DBRW formula. The visible DBRW formulas in columns E and F are not correctly defined because the reference to the product dimension can change dynamically. Thus the calculations might be wrong. You can use the DBR formula instead, but an active form needs at least one DBRW column. We choose to let E and F refer to the cube, not to the report definition cell. For example:

```
E17:=DBRW("TOG:sh",$C17,$D17,$D$13,F$16)
```

The DBRW formula in column G refers to the Active Forms definition.

```
G17:=DBRW($C$9,$C17,$D$13,$D17,G$16)
```

This example might look very specific to you. However, entering data to a non-zero level element without data distribution can be a common requirement. We will refer to this from time to time in later chapters.

Multidimensional Cost Assignment

Multidimensional modeling with product-related direct costs is very intuitive. We also showed how we can handle cost assignment to upper levels of the product structure. But this isn't truly a multidimensional assignment. For instance, in addition to product group–related costs, customer groups or regions can cause costs that can be assigned directly. Generally speaking, all elements on a higher level can cause costs. But this doesn't have to be always a single-dimensional element. This can also be a combination. From an academic point of view, these costs are not indirect costs but relative direct costs because the point of view drives the assignment.

For instance, take indirect service costs in a specific region. This can include all office costs for the service department (and doesn't include sales costs). This amount can't be assigned to a single service product. But it can be assigned to a specific region.

With this information a structure analysis is possible (see Figure 15-3). You can see that the situation in Services isn't positive because the contribution margin is negative. You can also estimate what the effect on the loss would be if you eliminate the service unit.

Let us use the following cube to explain how to transform the idea into Cognos TM1. In addition to the Products dimension, the cube has two further dimensions: Regions and Customers, as shown in the following illustration.

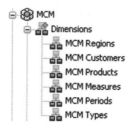

	Computer				Services			
	New York		Berlin		New York		Berlin	
	Standard	Key	Standard	Key	Standard	Key	Standard	Key
Sales	90,000	83,000	60,000	30,000	60,000	40,000	70,000	40,000
Direct Costs	40,000	22,000	24,000	8,000	15,000	14,000	26,000	14,000
Var. Indirect Costs	30,000	16,000	18,000	3,000	25,000	9,000	40,000	20,000
CM I	20,000	45,000	18,000	19,000	20,000	17,000	4,000	6,000
	65,000		37,000		37,000		10,000	
	35,000		10,000		45,000		25,000	
CM II	30,000		27,000		–8,000		–15,000	
	57,000				–23,000			
	34,000							
	44,000							
Profit/Loss	–10,000							

FIGURE 15-3   Multidimensional cost assignment

Again we are working with shadow elements. But this time we have to adapt this concept to all three dimensions: Regions, Customers, and Products. For instance the customer dimension looks like this:

We have defined a view where we entered a list of upper-level costs and comments for explanations, as shown in the following illustration.

			Value					Comment
MCM Products	MCM Customers	MCM Regions	Sales	Direct Costs	+ CM I	Indirect Costs	+ CM II	Indirect Costs
Computers	Standard	Berlin	1000	600	400	0	400	
		New York	350	250	100	0	100	
	Key	Berlin	500	300	200	0	200	
		New York	350	250	100	0	100	
	All E	All E	0	0	0	300	-300	Computer Production
Services	Standard	Berlin	1500	800	700	0	700	
		New York	300	200	100	0	100	
	Key	Berlin	500	300	200	0	200	
		New York	400	300	100	0	100	
	All E	Berlin	0	0	0	300	-300	Service Office
		New York	0	0	0	200	-200	Service Office New York
All E	Standard	Berlin	0	0	0	200	-200	Sales Cost for Key Customers in Berlin
		New York	0	0	0	100	-100	Sales Cost for Key Customers in New York
	All E	Berlin	0	0	0	100	-100	Headquarters Berlin
		New York	0	0	0	200	-200	Office Twente
		All E	0	0	0	300	-300	Not assignable

Data collection for multidimensional cost assignments

We can assign costs to every possible combination including aggregated elements. This is only the entry form we need and it should be easy to understand. Now we need a formula that enables us to analyze the consequences. The rule is a little bit more complex because three dimensions must be taken into account.

```
skipcheck;
[]=IF(DIMIX('MCM Regions',!MCM Regions | ' T')=0,
    IF(DIMIX('MCM Products', !MCM Products | ' T')=0,
        IF(DIMIX('MCM Customers',!MCM Customers | ' T')=0,
        CONTINUE,
        DB('MCM', !MCM Regions, INSRT( !MCM Customers,' T',1),
        !MCM Products,  !MCM Measures,!MCM Periods, !MCM Types)),
        DB('MCM', !MCM Regions, !MCM Customers, INSRT (!MCM Products,
'          T',1), !MCM Measures, !MCM Periods, !MCM Types)),
        DB('MCM', INSRT (!MCM Regions,' T',1), !MCM Customers,
        !MCM Products, !MCM Measures, !MCM Periods, !MCM Types));
```

Again the same situation: feeders don't help much. What is this rule doing? Only for standard C-level elements of the three dimensions, it fetches the value from the respective T elements.

Let us see how this rule works, in the following illustration. On level 0 CM I equals CM II. On a higher level this isn't the case any more.

MCM Products	MCM Customers	MCM Regions	Sales	Direct Costs	+ CM I	Indirect Costs	+ CM II
		Berlin	1000	600	400	0	400
	Standard	New York	350	250	100	0	100
		-- All	1350	850	500	0	500
		Berlin	500	300	200	0	200
Computers	Key	New York	350	250	100	0	100
		-- All	850	550	300	0	300
		Berlin	1500	900	600	0	600
	-- All	New York	700	500	200	0	200
		-- All	2200	1400	800	300	500
		Berlin	1500	800	700	0	700
	Standard	New York	300	200	100	0	100
		-- All	1800	1000	800	0	800
		Berlin	500	300	200	0	200
Services	Key	New York	400	300	100	0	100
		-- All	900	600	300	0	300
		Berlin	2000	1100	900	300	600
	-- All	New York	700	500	200	200	0
		-- All	2700	1600	1100	500	600
		Berlin	2500	1400	1100	200	900
	Standard	New York	650	450	200	100	100
		-- All	3150	1850	1300	300	1000
		Berlin	1000	600	400	0	400
-- All	Key	New York	750	550	200	0	200
		-- All	1750	1150	600	0	600
		Berlin	3500	2000	1500	600	900
	-- All	New York	1400	1000	400	500	-100
		-- All	4900	3000	1900	1700	200

Multidimension cost assignment

You can see that some specific combinations lead to a negative contribution margin. New York has a negative CM II. What does this mean? You should ask whether to continue with this combination because you lose money.

Filter Dimensions vs. Dynamic Aggregation

Hierarchies in Cognos TM1 are static. Sometimes we need more flexibility. Here's a simple example: You have created a multiproject hierarchy and want to sum up the revenue across various product groups. But you have active and inactive projects and also projects that are assigned to a specific project manager. Perhaps you only want to get results for the active and/or assigned projects. The flags for active/inactive and assigned/not assigned can be simple attributes.

We see basically two approaches:

- **Model it in the nearest way**   Use the Cognos TM1 attributes and filter with dynamic subsets. Sounds easy but there are some disadvantages. For instance, what is with the hierarchy elements? If you use the filter, the project groups are suppressed. An idea might be to use a rule to calculate the hierarchy attribute. However, how should you aggregate text attributes? But what we could also do is to use Active Forms. The biggest challenge is the aggregation of values. The aggregation always includes the nonrelevant values.

- **Another approach might be to use filter dimensions**   Their only purpose is to act as a filter. You can use zero suppression to apply the filter.

Let's take a deeper look into the second proposal. We created a cube with two filter dimensions, DS Filter Active and DS Filter Assigned, as shown in the following illustration.

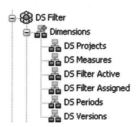

The project dimension looks like this:

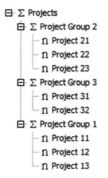

PART III

The following illustration shows a filter dimension (e.g. DS Active).

```
⊟ Σ All
   ├ n Yes
   └ n No
```

With this structure we can create a view according to our requirements. You can see two selections. In the first view the filter "assigned" is set to "No." All projects that do not fit show zero. When we change the "assigned" filter to "All," all project values are shown. You can work with zero suppression to filter out the nonrelevant projects. The next two illustrations show the results of applying the filters.

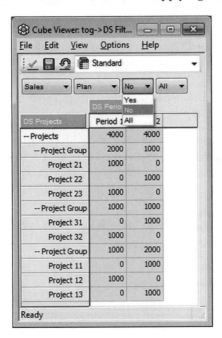

It works, but you can see that this inflates the cube. And you must consider this structure when you import data. Simple example: If you change the status of a project from inactive to active and reload data, the data is loaded into different cells. However, with TurboIntegrator, this should not be a big challenge.

However, let us discuss an alternative approach. The cube will be leaner because we don't need filter dimensions. The following illustration shows the alternative cube:

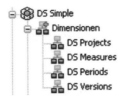

In this approach we are using the attributes for filtering. We defined the following attributes:

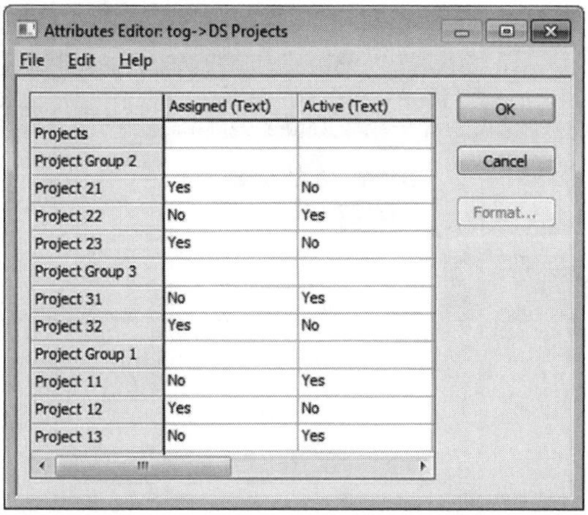

The most complicated aspect is the design of the active form, of course. Also it is not critical to filter the attributes, but we have to consider that aggregated elements don't have attributes.

There are MDX functions that allow filtering and remaining hierarchies. One statement is Cognos TM1-specific. First, we need the filter. It can become more complex if we want to increase the filter term, so we like to structure it a little bit (M15, N16, and N17 are cell references of the spreadsheet example shown in the next illustration):

```
M15:="FILTER( TM1SUBSETALL([DS Projects]),1=1 "&N16&N17&"  )"
N16:=IF(G13="Yes"," AND [DS Projects].[Active]='Yes' ","")
N17:=IF(H13="Yes"," AND [DS Projects].[Assigned]='Yes' ","")
```

The filter returns a subset of relevant projects. But we also want the hierarchy:

```
M13:="hierarchize(distinct(TM1rollup(TM1rollup(TM1rollup(
"&M15&",TM1subsetall([DS Projects])),TM1subsetall(
[DS Projects])),TM1SUBSETALL([DS Projects]))))"
```

The MDX function `TM1rollup` is TM1-specific. It adds the parent element to the result set. `Hierarchize` rebuilds the structure according to the stored hierarchy but without the suppressed elements.

Let's review what this view could look like. You can see the reduced hierarchy of projects. From the structural aspect we are fine.

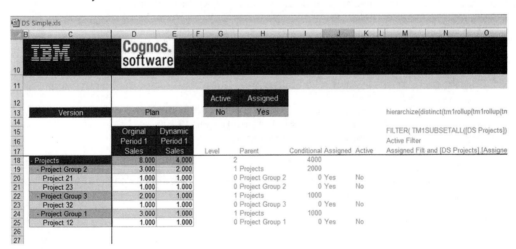

Dynamic filtering without selection

Now change the filter for the assignment flag. You can see the effect. The hierarchy calculation is dynamic.

Dynamic filtering with selection

The only problem is the values. Look at the first value column (D). It looks odd but it is formally right: Because some elements are suppressed, the aggregated value needs not to be identical with the shown children. But we want something different: a dynamic summation.

So the last step is to use the conditional sum. It is a little bit tricky:

- First we need the level:

  ```
  G18:=ELLEV("TOG:DS Projects",C18)
  ```

- We need the parent of the current element:

  ```
  H18:=ELPAR("TOG:DS Projects",C18,1)
  ```

- And we use the conditional sum function of Excel, SUMIF:

  ```
  I18:=SUMIF(H18:H$27,C18,E18:E$27)
  ```

  What does SUMIF do? It scans through a range (H18:H$27) for the search key C18 (the current element name). This is matched with the Parent column. Range E18:E$27 contains the values to sum up. The range must be defined across the Active Forms area so that a rebuild of the Active Forms sets the range correctly.

- Finally you only need to mix level 0 with the conditional calculation. It is recursive, but Excel doesn't care about that.

  ```
  E18:=IF(G18=0,DBRW(("TOG:DS Simple",$C18,E$17,E$16,$D$13),I18)
  ```

The only drawback is that you shouldn't do a drillup and a following drilldown. You see the result in the following illustration:

	Orginal Period 1 Sales	Dynamic Period 1 Sales
- Projects	8,000	5,000
- Project Group 2	3,000	3,000
Project 21	1,000	1,000
Project 22	1,000	1,000
Project 23	1,000	1,000
- Project Group 3	2,000	1,000
Project 32	1,000	1,000
- Project Group 1	3,000	1,000
Project 12	1,000	1,000

Which approach is more appropriate? It depends. It is obvious that you generate several additional dimensions when you appreciate approach 1. The performance can be also critical since you use massive zero suppression.

ABC Analyses

A common requirement if you work with large sets of elements is the ABC analysis. Simply put, it is a dynamic grouping mechanism. Based on periodic numbers like sales, contribution margin, or cost, you split up products, customers, or other elements into groups according to the rank of the current value.

What is the need for this? The idea is to focus on the important elements if you have to handle a large group of elements and the numbers are not distributed equally. The Pareto rule is well known: Doing 80 percent of your business with 20 percent of your customers might be a good example. Obviously there are few customers with high sales figures and a lot of customers with minor sales. So why should we treat all customers in the same way? This is the principle of ABC analysis, but instead of having two classes, three classes are used. Here's an example of how to work with the results of an ABC analysis:

- Class A customers are customers with high revenue, which are visited very often and get special offers.
- Class B customers are treated in a very standardized way.
- Class C customers are handed over to business partners.

Grouping that is close to classes is a base concept of Cognos TM1. But it isn't that easy. What is the difference from Cognos TM1 groups? Cognos TM1 groups are static and thus must be predefined. The ABC classification is based on values and thus can change from period to period and even if you change another dimension (for example, switching from Actual to Forecast). Time-dependent groups are not the right solution: You need a lot of overhead to keep dimensions time-dependent (see the paragraph about organization by period in Chapter 23).

Of course, it is possible to create static classes within Cognos TM1 on a specific request. It could make sense if you want to use the classes for planning purposes. An example: detailed planning on class A, high-level planning on class B, and only forecasting for class C. You could create a TI process for the generation. This would be possible as well but it has some limitations:

- We want to provide solutions that can be maintained by subject experts, not programmers.
- It should be easily adapted from one application to another.
- It should work in a multiuser environment and within simulations.

We want to show a concept based on dynamic calculation. Cognos TM1 doesn't support dynamic classes as mentioned. However, it is very easy to create this with Cognos TM1 in combination with Excel and Active Forms. The easiest method is to use the Active Forms because it supports a dynamic sort based on the recent selections. Hence the classes only exist in the report. This, of course, has the disadvantage that you can't continue working with these groups in other parts of your system.

The result should look like the following illustration:

ABC Analysis

ABC Periods	Period 1	A	30%
		B	80%

	Value	Share		Class
Prod 5	188.00	15.78%	15.78%	1
Prod 11	168.00	14.10%	29.88%	1
Prod 22	67.38	5.66%	35.54%	2
Prod 23	64.58	5.42%	40.96%	2
Prod 33	63.86	5.36%	46.32%	2
Prod 10	61.12	5.13%	51.45%	2
Prod 9	60.72	5.10%	56.55%	2
Prod 32	55.50	4.66%	61.21%	2
Prod 12	55.45	4.65%	65.86%	2
Prod 15	54.46	4.57%	70.44%	2
Prod 26	49.54	4.16%	74.60%	2
Prod 8	43.00	3.61%	78.21%	2
Prod 35	43.00	3.61%	81.81%	3
Prod 21	43.00	3.61%	85.42%	3
Prod 28	39.43	3.31%	88.73%	3
Prod 24	15.00	1.26%	89.99%	3
Prod 25	12.00	1.01%	91.00%	3
Prod 34	10.00	0.84%	91.84%	3
Prod 16	9.58	0.80%	92.65%	3
Prod 3	8.44	0.71%	93.35%	3
Prod 18	8.09	0.68%	94.03%	3
Prod 17	5.97	0.50%	94.53%	3
Prod 7	5.43	0.46%	94.99%	3
Prod 36	5.43	0.46%	95.45%	3
Prod 13	5.43	0.46%	95.90%	3
Prod 31	5.43	0.46%	96.36%	3
Prod 1	5.43	0.46%	96.81%	3
Prod 2	5.34	0.45%	97.26%	3
Prod 6	4.59	0.39%	97.65%	3
Prod 4	4.55	0.38%	98.03%	3
Prod 27	4.34	0.36%	98.39%	3
Prod 20	4.32	0.36%	98.76%	3
Prod 29	3.45	0.29%	99.05%	3
Prod 19	3.32	0.28%	99.32%	3
Prod 30	3.32	0.28%	99.60%	3
Prod 14	3.23	0.27%	99.87%	3
Prod 37	1.50	0.13%	100.00%	3

ABC analysis with Excel diagrams

The class boundaries are not static but are saved with the sheet. Every user can change them locally to regroup the classes. How do we come to this diagram? We created this simple cube with three dimensions:

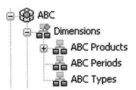

Further, we need a simple rule to calculate the share per product. This rule should be independent of the period or the scenario dimension:

```
['ABC Types':'Share']=N:['ABC Types':'Value']\
['ABC Types':'Value','ABC Products':'All'];
```

With this Cognos TM1 calculation we have done enough to start working on the active form. The needed active form is not a standard one because it is necessary to create dynamic MDX. Let's look at the row formula:

```
=TM1RPTROW($C$9,"TOG:ABC Prod",,,,,O13)
```

The last parameter refers to the cell O13. With longer MDX statements we recommend this kind of referencing; otherwise, the formula would be too long to digest. The referenced cell can itself refer to other cells so that the dynamic MDX can be quite sophisticated and, even more important, dynamically constructed based on various user input.

The cell O13 contains the following statement.

```
="ORDER( TM1FILTERBYLEVEL( TM1SUBSETALL( [ABC Products] ), 0),
[ABC].([ABC Periods].["&Period&"],[ABC Types].[Value]), BDESC) "
```

You can see that we use an Excel name (Period) to reference to a cell. You don't have to be an Excel expert to conclude that this name refers to the cell containing the SUBNM formula for the period. In consequence, the active form is dynamically sorted dependent on the selected period. We limit the subset to level zero. You can change it, but it should contain only one level otherwise the result might be confusion when you rank a town with a country for example.

In row E we use the calculated element share. The next step is to cumulate the percentage for the class assignment. That is why the column name in cell F16 is empty: We need a starting period.

The following formula does the class assignment:

```
G17:=IF(F17<AClass,1,IF(F17<BClass,2,3))
```

AClass and BClass are Excel names for the data entry.

The diagram is a little bit tricky because we need the color coding. We need three columns for the respective classes.

```
I17:=IF(G17=1,D17,"")
J17:=IF(G17=2,D17,"")
K17:=IF(G17=2,D17,"")
```

You reference this cell area as the data source for the diagram. Choose bar graph as the diagram type. However, when you do this, you will see some disturbing zero numbers. To overcome this challenge, we need a small formatting trick: Use the formatting attributes for the data names. Select User Defined. You can enter three formats separated by a comma with the following meaning:

```
Positive, Negative, Zero
```

Simply leave the last element out so that zero numbers are suppressed. See the formatting dialog in Excel:

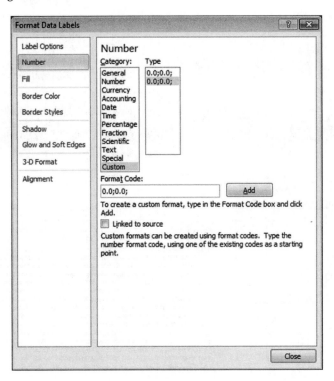

Although it would be helpful to have this active form also in the web, the result is not very satisfying; it's far from being perfect.

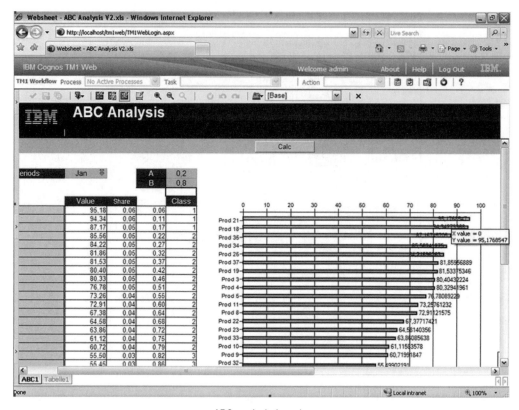

ABC analysis in web

However, what you can do is to define your own cell-based diagram with character symbols. There is a formula for this. In column H we create the formula

```
H17:=REPEAT("I",F17*100)
```

And you also need conditional formatting for column H. See the conditional formatting parameters in the following illustration:

It is important to choose the right relative address. The result might not be that fancy, but now it also works in the web:

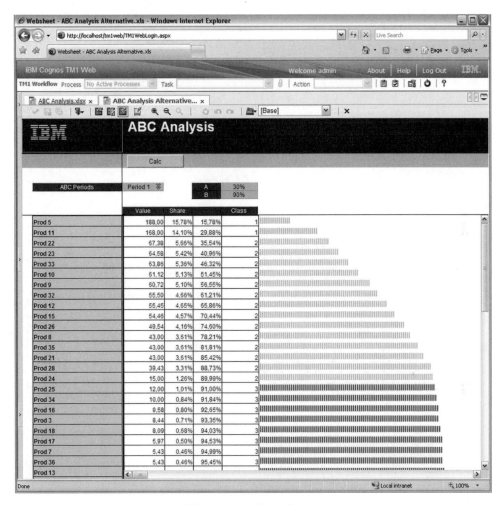

ABC analyses without diagrams

Summary

As you have seen, Cognos TM1 is a great tool for sales and profitability analysis. Standard sales analysis isn't a challenge. Almost everybody even with limited Cognos TM1 experience can do that. However, when you dig into details, some specific problems have to be solved. Variances have to be analyzed by splitting up into details. Data such as costs and revenue must be assigned to non-zero-level elements, and dynamic sorting and filtering are some of these aspects. It is also important to look at sales and profitability analysis in a wider context. In the following chapters we will work further on this context. Some examples are cost calculations, planning, budgeting, and forecasting, and don't forget doing profitability analysis across borders of companies.

16
CHAPTER

Budgeting

Budgeting is a key task within the yearly planning process. Typically after the multiyear and the program planning are completed, the budgeting process starts to work out the financial consequences. Financial targets for a specific timeframe and organizational units are set. Budgeting is a tool to delegate decisions. Plan measures are defined and are supported by various activities that are the responsibility of the business unit owner.

The process of budgeting even in midsize companies is cumbersome and almost not practical without IT support. This process is enterprise-wide and requires coordination across all functions. Hence the right software support is crucial. Although Cognos TM1 is not a dedicated budgeting tool, it includes all functions necessary to build a powerful budgeting application for all sizes of companies. Here are some typical challenges a company has to face:

- Heterogeneous data sources (GL, HR, Sales, Payroll, and so on)
- Coordination between finance business acumen and IT technology knowledge
- Connecting personal analysis (spreadsheet models) to structured plan templates
- Establishing business models to facilitate driver-based budgets
- Different levels of data detail—unlikely to budget at same level as actuals
- Requirement for multiple versions
- Budgeting to the wall/need for rolling forecasts
- Engaging occasional users (managers) in a controlled workflow process
- Facilitating collaboration
- Frequent data refreshes
- Frequent metadata changes

The challenges go beyond the scope of this chapter. Other aspects will be handled in later chapters. For instance, Chapter 20 is about rolling forecasts and Chapter 18 is about driver-based planning. In this chapter we will outline tools to support the budgeting process. The goals of these tools are to

- Organize a top-down process
- Increase data quality by using validations
- Enable individual bottom-up planning with line item detail
- Enhance flexibility by adding new elements on a local base
- Reduce the planning effort with seasonal factors
- Enable multiyear investment planning with depreciation and interest calculation
- Introduce simple concepts for a workflow-controlled process
- Increase automation with a planning calendar, including e-mail and automatic period opening and closing

The Business Challenge

Budgeting can be described as follows:

- Budgeting is a means to allocate the resources. The aligned budget is the foundation of profit and cash planning.
- Instead of defining specific tasks, value targets are set. The budget owner is more or less free to choose the appropriate means to meet the targets. This freedom to act should motivate.
- Budgeting is the starting point for operational performance measurement. Greater variances from the budget must be explained and lead to further analysis.

It is not easy to separate the various planning terms like planning, forecasting, activity planning, or budgeting. An important term to separate from budgeting is activity planning. Budgeting is focused on a commitment on a certain amount to spend for an area (that is, cost center or project), whereas activity planning focuses on a concrete action item. With Figure 16-1, at least our understanding should be clearer: activity planning and budgeting are the two essential parts of an operational planning system. Both tasks are supported by forecasting. Budgeting and activity planning actively design the future by making decisions, whereas forecasting is simply the process of estimating future development. Forecasting is the basis of budgeting and activity planning.

Budgeting means setting targets for a certain period. Most often the horizon is limited to one single year. A crucial question that is often discussed is how fixed the budget should be. There are different opinions. Most often the budgets are not changed during the year. Any adjustments are done in a so-called year-end forecast. The "fixed" budget is also related to a later variance analysis. If you had planned a certain output level, but it turned out later that you realized a different output level, it could make sense to adjust the budget numbers to the changed output. Within a fixed budget, there is no adaptation. With a flexible budget, the allowed costs are adapted to the new output level. Or, simply said, if you produce more, you are allowed to spend more. We will discuss this in more detail in Chapter 17.

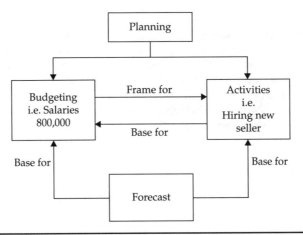

FIGURE 16-1   Functions of planning

Budgets are defined for different areas. For example, typical areas are sales, production, material, administration, or investment (see Figure 16-2).

Let's spend some time on the planning direction: Budgeting can be more than just collecting data. It is very often a negotiation process with the objective of aligned and reconciled values. There are at least three types of budget flow: bottom-up, top-down, and iterative. The top-down allocation is mostly derived from financial key performance

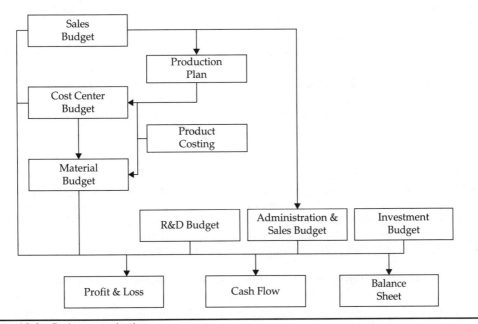

FIGURE 16-2   Budget organization

indicators like EVA (economic value added) and/or strategic initiatives. Bottom-up usually stems from last year's adjustments and the collection of planned operational activities. Both methods are often combined: You start with a targeting process. Then it is operationally founded by concrete plans and aggregated from the bottom up. This process can be iterative: In further cycles, adjustments are made top-down and/or bottom-up.

The budget is often based on constraints. Usually the possible sales numbers are the limiting factor, so it makes sense to start with the sales budget. From these numbers you can derive the inventory and production plan. The resulting production demand is the basis for the cost center output plan. With this information, a qualified cost-center budgeting is possible.

There are two ways to start:

- Starting from scratch. The idea is to plan all costs in an analytical way. This is often called *zero-based budgeting* (ZBB). This term is not quite right, because ZBB is a more complex management system developed at Texas Instruments in the sixties. However, it is widely used for the process that I am describing.

- Copying the actual or the plan from the previous period as a starting point and working with specific adjustment elements. This can be called *continuous budgeting*.

Although a zero-based process better reflects the real demand, the continuous budget is more familiar. With this kind of process, there are only very limited connections to the target-setting process, where targets are distributed down from top management to the departments. Based on last year's values and more or less rough adjustments, the new budget numbers are derived. There might be implicit planned activities; however, these activities are not part of the budgeting process. There is also a tendency to focus only on existing elements and procedures. Only significant changes between previous periods and the upcoming period are planned from scratch.

Various cost planning methods can be integrated with budgeting models. Activity-based budgeting might be a quite popular method but also a very time-consuming one. For activity-based budgeting you need a comprehensive business model. The budgeted costs should be in relation to the output of the budgeted unit. For this it is necessary to have a transparent model of the dependencies. Also, a direct link to the strategic target is helpful. A company or business unit model where cause-and-effect relations are clearly worked out is necessary.

Budgeting is often seen as an unloved duty that blocks resources for a longer time. Some leading international managers have spoken very negatively about budgeting. Jack Welch, legendary CEO of General Electric, has said: "… making a budget is an exercise in minimalization. You're always trying to get the lowest number out of people, because everyone is negotiating to get the lowest number…." Bob Lutz, former COO of Chrysler, has stated: "…budgets are tools of repression, rather than innovation. What if I got a market opportunity mid-year?…" And the founders of the so-called "Beyond Budgeting" movement wrote an article, "Figures of Hate. What Are the Key Points?"

- Budgeting requires time. Hackett Groups revealed an average planning cycle of 4.5 months.

- Budgeting is expensive. Investigations of PriceWaterhouseCoopers (PWC) revealed 25,000 man-days per billion sales on average.

- A survey of the magazine *Financial Director* showed that most who are responsible see the budgeting process as inefficient with a big potential for improvement.

- In a survey of the magazine *CFO*, only seven percent of the investigated companies link strategy with operational planning. Most of the people in middle management don't understand the strategy.

The question is whether there are practical ways to achieve improvement without destroying the whole budgeting process (as is suggested by the Beyond Budgeting roundtable). A complete ban does not seem to be the right approach for most companies. What could be done better? Various items are under discussion:

- Budgeting is very much focused on financials. Concrete business activities and the dependencies remain nontransparent. An enhancement might be to also include drivers to improve business understanding. Although a budget is mostly based on values, it is possible to include volumes and other drivers. We will discuss this in chapter 20.

- There is often a missing link between strategic and operational planning. To take over just the financial consequences of strategic KPIs into operational planning is not enough. There should be a way to transfer the strategic initiatives into a budgeting system.

- The replacement of the budget by a rolling forecast system is often discussed. The crucial question is why do we have a year-long (static) process when the environment significantly changes within months? We will show a way to implement a rolling forecast system in chapter 20. But this also requires streamlining the whole process. Otherwise, a quarterly revision and update on the rolling forecast is hardly possible. It is also a good means to a closer integration with cash forecasting. This calculation has a rolling structure too.

- Several budgeting processes impress through exact numbers. A typical example might be an automatic cost allocation; from a technical point of view it is easy to implement. The meaning on the other hand could be very limited. It is more important to focus on the important objects and thus reduce the number of plan items, organizational levels, and allocations. This is sometimes referred to as "lean budgeting."

A lot of inappropriate software is in use. Budgeting is very often based solely on spreadsheets. We don't want to claim that spreadsheets are per se not the right tool for budgeting. They are helpful for specific tasks, but they are not the right tool to control the overall budgeting process when a lot of people are involved. Our biggest concerns are typical macros to support distribution and collection of distributed spreadsheets. They are often developed by programming amateurs to overcome limitations. The consequences are often embarrassing: errors that weren't discovered for years. On the other hand, there are a lot of specified applications comparable to classic ERP solutions. But budgeting is not ERP. Budgeting solutions need much more flexibility to cope with the variations and changes and to bring budgeting closer to target and driver orientation.

- Planning and budgeting must become more professional. This is a development started with the corporate governance discussion. The forecast figures must be trustworthy and auditable. Errors in the forecasting communication can be quite expensive, as some big companies have experienced. Also the planning quality must be improved by a better understanding of the environment conditions. This requires a more professional approach to budgeting. Due to increased volatility and the complexity of global organizations, organizations need to automate and transform their planning processes to meet business demands. So the right software is crucial. But there is still a lot of discussion. Typical aspects to consider are

- How to create a budget in a simple way
- How to automate and streamline the process
- What can you do to increase data quality? It is not about data from transactional systems or about miscalculation. It is more about how valid the entered information is.
- How can you integrate drivers and non-financials into the process?

Top-Down versus Bottom-Up Budgeting

Look at the following structure with the three budgeting directions in Figure 16-3. The budgeting process is

- Hierarchical
- Iterative
- Distributed and disconnected
- Periodical
- Dynamic

But what does "top-down" really mean? Is it an automatic distribution of target numbers? We think it is more a negotiation process where different opinions and objectives come together.

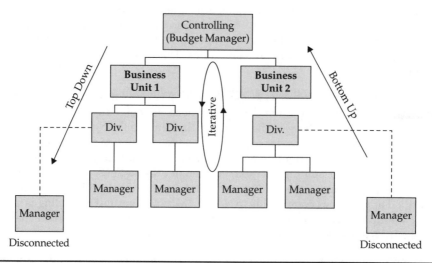

FIGURE 16-3   Top-down/bottom-up process

Hence each level might model its structure and dependencies separately. On the basic level you might have a very good understanding of input-output relations, for example, production processes. On higher levels, softer relations, for instance between customer behavior and sales, are more important.

In a top-down process we also need to plan on a higher level. We show a concept requiring a planning cube for each level. An alternative could be adding so-called dummy elements for each aggregate element. The decision depends on how flexible the process is and how balanced the budget organizational tree is.

To explain the idea we created a very simple model with only two levels. The cube "BUD Bottom Up" contains the granular data.

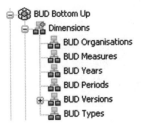

"BUD Level 1" is an aggregated view of the planning model. It contains target data coming from multiyear planning or strategic management.

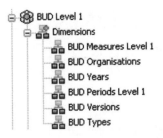

The difference between these cubes is simple:

- "BUD Level 1" requires planning on a quarterly level, "BUD Bottom Up" on a monthly level.
- "BUD Level 1" contains only aggregated measure elements.

First we enter the targets on a quarterly level and in cost type groups. To show the top-down process, we focus on one cost type group (Material) and allocate costs down to the zero-level elements. For this activity you can use the built-in distribution functions including holds.

Independent of the target planning, the bottom-up process can start. However, it can be helpful to have the targets available when you plan the details. The combined view with targets and bottom-up budget can look like this:

BUD Measures	Target + Year	Var Budget Target + Year	Var Budget Target % + Year	Budget + Year	Jan	Feb	Mar	Apr	May	Jun
-- All Costs	30,460.00	2,712.00	8.90%	33,172.00	2,742.31	2,854.09	2,800.50	2,841.90	2,741.50	2,741.50
-- Material	9,000.00	1,800.00	20.00%	10,800.00	900.00	900.00	900.00	900.00	900.00	900.00
Material 1	0.00	0.00	.00%	3,600.00	300.00	300.00	300.00	300.00	300.00	300.00
Material 2	0.00	0.00	.00%	3,600.00	300.00	300.00	300.00	300.00	300.00	300.00
Material 3	0.00	0.00	.00%	3,600.00	300.00	300.00	300.00	300.00	300.00	300.00
-- Salaries	8,460.00	2,340.00	27.66%	10,800.00	900.00	900.00	900.00	900.00	900.00	900.00
Salaries Group 1	2,960.00	640.00	21.62%	3,600.00	300.00	300.00	300.00	300.00	300.00	300.00
Salaries Group 2	3,000.00	600.00	20.00%	3,600.00	300.00	300.00	300.00	300.00	300.00	300.00
Salaries Group 3	2,500.00	1,100.00	44.00%	3,600.00	300.00	300.00	300.00	300.00	300.00	300.00
+ Other Costs	13,000.00	(2,200.00)	-16.92%	10,800.00	900.00	900.00	900.00	900.00	900.00	900.00
Travel	0.00	0.00	.00%	172.00	0.00	113.00	59.00	0.00	0.00	0.00
Marketing	0.00	0.00	.00%	100.00	0.00	0.00	0.00	100.00	0.00	0.00
Heating	0.00	0.00	.00%	100.00	8.98	7.76	8.16	8.57	8.16	8.16
Energy	0.00	0.00	.00%	400.00	33.33	33.33	33.33	33.33	33.33	33.33

You can see the entry items for Material 1 and so on on a monthly level. But you also can see the target numbers on the upper level for the year in the cost type groups. Why do we see an asymmetric view? We simply are using zero suppression.

The rules are easy to create: The target version can be referenced from the cube "BUD Level 1" with a DB function.

```
['Target']=
DB('BUD Level 1', !BUD Measures , !BUD Organisations,
!BUD Years, !BUD Periods, !BUD Versions, !BUD Types);
```

Although we prefer variance calculation by hierarchies, we decide to let the variance be calculated by a formula. The reason is that we can suppress the variance calculation if a budget value exists but not a target.

```
['Var Budget Target','Year'] = C:
IF(['Target']=0,0, ['Budget']-['Target']);

['Var Budget Target %','Year'] = C:
['Var Budget Target']\['Target']*100;
```

Improve Data Quality with Validation

Data quality is always an important aspect even in budgeting, particularly when data is entered manually. When you load data from transactional systems, you can use specific extract, transfer, and load (ETL) tools to improve data quality. But what can you do when data is entered manually within the budgeting process? How can you avoid entering wrong data? The key word is "validation." You can create routines that prevent users from entering the wrong data. This can be enforced by very simple checks like the following:

- A value for a specific cell must be entered. For instance, the salary costs must not be zero.
- Avoid or enforce negative values.
- Only allow a specific selection. You can usually support this by using a drop-down or the new feature Cognos TM1 picklist.

Sometimes the requirements could be more complex, so that a calculation is the basis for another validation. More complex validations are:

- Budget cells must equal other cells. The classic example is the balance sheet equation "Asset = Equity and Liabilities."
- Budget cells must be higher and/or lower than a certain target.
- Avoid exaggerated data. The problem is to find a reasonable limit.

There is a simple mechanism within Excel. You can use the Excel built-in validation feature. This also works in the Cognos TM1 Web in a limited way. This could only be used for simple validation. Please be aware that not all Excel validations are transferred to the Web. The most flexible one, a user-defined validation, is not transformed into the Web. Another problem might be that you need more than one validation per number. You can do complex calculations within Excel, which we don't think is a good idea because it increases the maintenance effort.

The following example shows the setup within Excel to avoid negative values. We can define our own individual error message on the last tab.

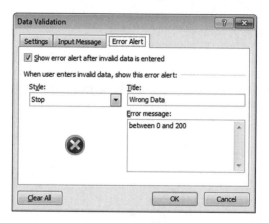

This is the result in Cognos TM1 Web when you try to enter a number that breaks a rule.

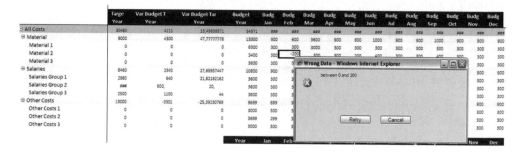

If you have to check more complex calculations, we recommend using Cognos TM1 rules. The advantages are:

- It is more flexible because you can use generic rules and you have direct access to all cells.

- It is more dynamic because you can change the validation in one area ("single place of truth") if you allow entering a certain number in different forms.

- The Excel entry forms remain simple. You can use alternatives like Contributor or third-party tools for data entry.

- An important aspect is that you can connect validation directly with processes (workflow).

We now briefly describe the validations with Cognos TM1 rules. You define a rule for every validation and show the result in a section within the entry form. The implementation is simple. Usually you define the validation elements within the measure dimension:

- Each rule provides a 1 if the validation fails.

- The overall validation is an aggregation of single validations.

The following Cognos TM1 rules show a validation system:

```
['V']=ConsolidateChildren('BUD Measures');
['V1']= N:IF(['Other costs']=0,1,0);
['V2']= N:IF(['Other costs']> ['Material'],1,0);
['V3','Year']= IF(['All costs','Budget']>
['All Costs','Target'],1,0);
```

Why do we use ConsolidateChildren? It gives us more flexibility within the rules system because we have to aggregate the result of "C" rules. Look at the rule V3. This is a rule to be applied on the N and C levels. So we cannot simply use the standard aggregation. The standard aggregation would leave out V3 because part of the calculations are applied on the C-level and this calculation takes place after the aggregation.

We use an alias to create the messages.

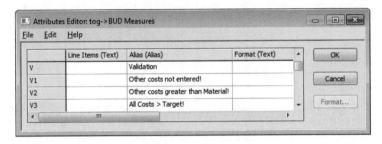

The following view shows the result.

BUD Measures	Budget + Year	Jan	Feb	Mar	Apr	May	Jun	Jul	Aug	Sep	Oct	Nov	Dec
-- All Costs	32,872.00	2,742.31	2,854.09	2,800.50	2,841.90	1,541.50	2,741.50	3,641.90	2,742.31	2,741.90	2,741.90	2,741.50	2,740.68
-- Material	10,500.00	900.00	900.00	900.00	900.00	600.00	900.00	900.00	900.00	900.00	900.00	900.00	900.00
Material 1	3,300.00	300.00	300.00	300.00	300.00	0.00	300.00	300.00	300.00	300.00	300.00	300.00	300.00
Material 2	3,600.00	300.00	300.00	300.00	300.00	300.00	300.00	300.00	300.00	300.00	300.00	300.00	300.00
Material 3	3,600.00	300.00	300.00	300.00	300.00	300.00	300.00	300.00	300.00	300.00	300.00	300.00	300.00
-- Salaries	10,800.00	900.00	900.00	900.00	900.00	900.00	900.00	900.00	900.00	900.00	900.00	900.00	900.00
Salaries Group 1	3,600.00	300.00	300.00	300.00	300.00	300.00	300.00	300.00	300.00	300.00	300.00	300.00	300.00
Salaries Group 2	3,600.00	300.00	300.00	300.00	300.00	300.00	300.00	300.00	300.00	300.00	300.00	300.00	300.00
Salaries Group 3	3,600.00	300.00	300.00	300.00	300.00	300.00	300.00	300.00	300.00	300.00	300.00	300.00	300.00
-- Other Costs	10,800.00	900.00	900.00	900.00	900.00	0.00	900.00	1,800.00	900.00	900.00	900.00	900.00	900.00
Other Costs 1	3,300.00	300.00	300.00	300.00	300.00	0.00	300.00	300.00	300.00	300.00	300.00	300.00	300.00
Other Costs 2	4,200.00	300.00	300.00	300.00	300.00	0.00	300.00	1,200.00	300.00	300.00	300.00	300.00	300.00
Other Costs 3	3,300.00	300.00	300.00	300.00	300.00	0.00	300.00	300.00	300.00	300.00	300.00	300.00	300.00
Travel	172.00	0.00	113.00	59.00	0.00	0.00	0.00	0.00	0.00	0.00	0.00	0.00	0.00
Marketing	100.00	0.00	0.00	0.00	100.00	0.00	0.00	0.00	0.00	0.00	0.00	0.00	0.00
Heating	100.00	8.98	7.76	8.16	8.57	8.16	8.16	8.57	8.98	8.57	8.57	8.16	7.35
Energy	400.00	33.33	33.33	33.33	33.33	33.33	33.33	33.33	33.33	33.33	33.33	33.33	33.33
-- V	3.00	0.00	0.00	0.00	0.00	1.00	0.00	1.00	0.00	0.00	0.00	0.00	0.00
V1	1.00	0.00	0.00	0.00	0.00	1.00	0.00	0.00	0.00	0.00	0.00	0.00	0.00
V2	1.00	0.00	0.00	0.00	0.00	0.00	0.00	1.00	0.00	0.00	0.00	0.00	0.00
V3	1.00	0.00	0.00	0.00	0.00	0.00	0.00	0.00	0.00	0.00	0.00	0.00	0.00

32,872.00

But the result isn't meaningful to the end user, or is it? Of course, this is not a very user-friendly format. We use character symbols in Excel to make this a little more impressive. We create a simple Excel sheet with two active form sections. To enable a separate formatting for the second section, it is necessary to overwrite the standard formula in column A for the second section: We simply entered "D" for section two.

						Budget	Budget	Budget	Budget	Budget	Budget	Budget	Budget	Budget	Budget	Budget	Budget

	BUD Organisations	Org 11		Limit		Submitted				⊗							
	BUD Years	2010		400		Submit				⊗							
	BUD Types	Value															

			Target Year	Var Budget Target Year	Var Budget Target % Year	Budget Year	Budget Jan	Budget Feb	Budget Mar	Budget Apr	Budget May	Budget Jun	Budget Jul	Budget Aug	Budget Sep	Budget Oct	Budget Nov	Budget Dec
0	All Costs		30480	4111	13,50	34571	2741,31	2554,09	5500,5	2841,9	1741,5	2841,5	2741,9	3442,31	2841,9	1841,9	2741,5	2740,68
1	- Material		9000	4300	47,78	13300	900	600	3600	900	800	1000	900	900	1000	900	900	900
N	Material 1		0	0	-	6300	300	300	3000	300	300	300	300	300	300	300	300	300
N	Material 2		0	0	-	3400	300	0	300	300	200	400	300	300	400	300	300	300
N	Material 3		0	0	-	3600	300	300	300	300	300	300	300	300	300	300	300	300
1	- Salaries		8460	2340	27,66	10800	900	900	900	900	900	900	900	900	900	900	900	900
N	Salaries Group 1		2960	640	21,62	3600	300	300	300	300	300	300	300	300	300	300	300	300
N	Salaries Group 2		3000	600	20,00	3600	300	300	300	300	300	300	300	300	300	300	300	300
N	Salaries Group 3		2500	1100	44,00	3600	300	300	300	300	300	300	300	300	300	300	300	300
1	- Other Costs		13000	-3301	- 25,39	9699	899	900	900	900		900	900	1600	900		900	900
N	Other Costs 1		0	0	-	3000	300	300	300	300	0	300	300	300	300	0	300	300
N	Other Costs 2		0	0	-	3699	299	300	300	300	0	300	300	1000	300	0	300	300
N	Other Costs 3		0	0	-	3000	300	300	300	300	0	300	300	300	300	0	300	300
						Year	Jan	Feb	Mar	Apr	May	Jun	Jul	Aug	Sep	Oct	Nov	Dec
D	- Validation					⊗	⊗	⊗	⊗	⊗	⊗	⊗	⊗	⊗	⊗	⊗	⊗	⊗
D	Other costs not entered!					⊗	☺	☺	☺	☺	⊗	☺	☺	☺	☺	⊗	☺	☺
D	Other costs greater than Material!					⊗	☺	⊗	☺	☺	☺	☺	☺	⊗	☺	☺	☺	☺
D	All Costs > Target!					☺	☺	☺	☺	☺	☺	☺	☺	☺	☺	☺	☺	☺

We want to define a fourth validation rule for tolerances. Sometime it makes sense to define a separate cube to hold tolerances. We created the cube "BUD Tolerances." The following illustration shows a simple example. It shows the allowed variances in percent.

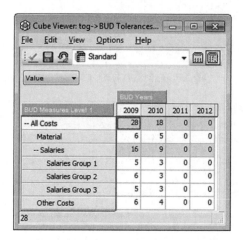

But there is one remarkable aspect: The new validation rule is not part of the measure dimension unless we want to define a separate validation for each relevant position. This would be time-consuming, and even more important, it would be error-prone because every time you create a new account, you have to add a new validation rule. So we add an element V4 in the dimension "BUD Version." The related rule is :

```
['V4','Year']= IF(['Target']<>0 & ['Budget']/['Target'] -1 >
DB('BUD Tolerances', !BUD Measures, !BUD Years, !BUD Types)/100,1,0);
```

The result is as desired. See element V4 in the last column.

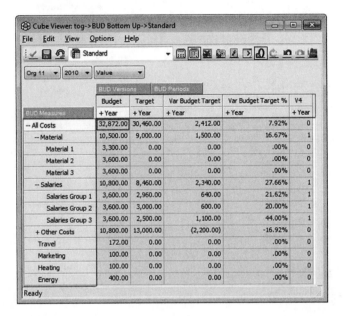

The open aspect we don't cover is that you should suppress further actions like submitting your numbers to your boss if validation rules are breached. This workflow step should not be possible to perform. To let this happen, you must modify the workflow coding.

Working with Line Item Detail

A very important concept particularly for budgeting purposes is the so-called line item detail. Look at Figure 16-4. The smallest item of an OLAP cube is the cell. A cell is directly addressed by a unique set of dimension elements. The problem is that not more than one value for a cell can exist. Sometimes this is not adequate because you need more granular data to describe your budget. You can create a dedicated dimension to hold this type of data. But in your administrator role, it is very likely that you don't know either the name of the elements or the possible number of items your budgeting client will create. And each individual planner usually would like to name elements differently. Typical examples are:

- Marketing activities
- Travels
- Contracts and so on

Therefore we need an enhancement, which is called line item detail. This is a feature many planning applications have been offering for a long time. Many experts say that OLAP can't handle line item details. This might be true for other OLAP tools; it is definitely not true for Cognos TM1.

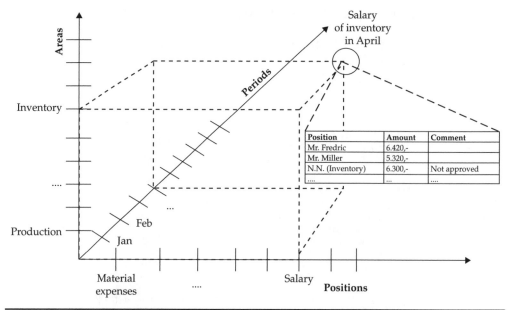

FIGURE 16-4   OLAP and line item detail

It is not an "out of the box" feature, but it is easy to implement. You don't have to do very much to create your line item solution. We will go through the cooking list step by step. Figure 16-4 shows a typical planning scenario: Several positions should be planned. Some of the positions should be planned on a more granular level.

We use our simple "BUD Bottom Up" cube. We define two cost types where we want to show line item detail: Travel and Marketing. You see the two cost types shaded in the following illustration.

			Line Item Detail													
13	BUD Organisations	Org 11														
14	BUD Years	2010														
15	BUD Types	Value														
16	BUD Versions	Budget														

		Year	Jan	Feb	Mar	Apr	May	Jun	Jul	Aug	Sep	Oct	Nov	Dec
20	- All Costs	34.322	2.700	2.722	5.400	2.800	1.800	2.800	2.700	3.400	2.800	1.800	2.700	2.700
21	+ Material	13.700	900	900	3.600	900	900	1.000	900	900	1.000	900	900	900
22	+ Salaries	10.800	900	900	900	900	900	900	900	900	900	900	900	900
23	+ Other Costs	9.700	900	900	900	900	0	900	900	1.600	900	0	900	900
24	LI Travel	22	0	22	0	0	0	0	0	0	0	0	0	0
25	LI Marketing	100	0	0	0	100	0	0	0	0	0	0	0	0

We use a flag "T" in column B to mark the line-item-enabled items in the cost planning form (as an active form) where we allow line item detail. It is simply an attribute.

In the Excel sheet put the cursor on the line item you want to specify and click the Line Item Detail button. The button opens the Excel sheet "BUD Line Item Details." All title elements should be passed to the new sheet. To pass the row information, the enhanced options of the button must be filled out in the following way:

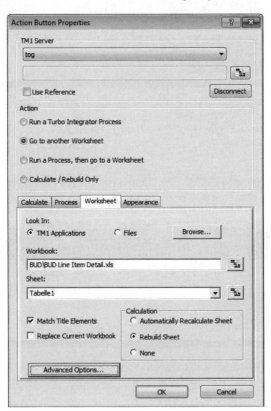

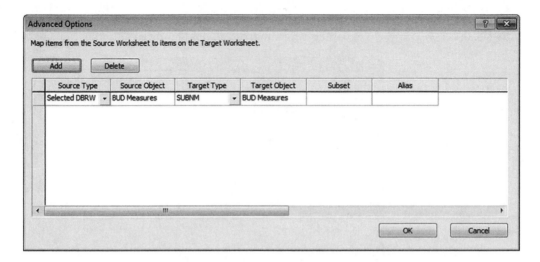

You see the line item forms in the following illustration. All title elements are accurately set.

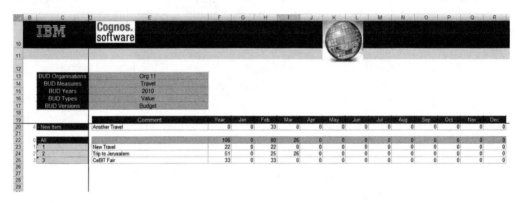

Enter a new description in Cell E20 and some new values and rebuild the sheet (press ALT-F9). You see that the row number of the active form is increased by a line.

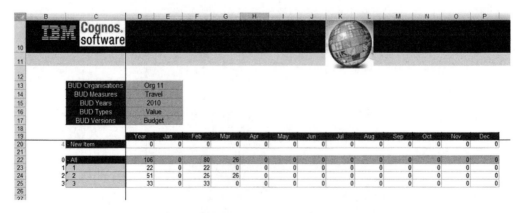

When you return to the periodic planning, you will also see that the position is updated accurately.

	Year	Jan	Feb	Mar	Apr	May	Jun	Jul	Aug	Sep	Oct	Nov	Dec
- All Costs	34.406	2.700	2.780	5.426	2.800	1.800	2.800	2.700	3.400	2.800	1.800	2.700	2.700
+ Material	13.700	900	900	3.600	900	900	1.000	900	900	1.000	900	900	900
+ Salaries	10.800	900	900	900	900	900	900	900	900	900	900	900	900
+ Other Costs	9.700	900	900	900	900	0	900	900	1.600	900	0	900	900
LI Travel	106	0	80	26	0	0	0	0	0	0	0	0	0
LI Marketing	100	0	0	0	100	0	0	0	0	0	0	0	0

BUD Organisations — Org 11
BUD Years — 2010
BUD Types — Value
BUD Versions — Budget

Line Item Detail

How is this implemented? It is not complex but very powerful. For this example we created two cubes. "BUD Bottom up" is the conventional cube with six dimensions.

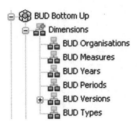

We create a second cube with the additional dimension. The "BUD Line Items" cube contains the line items. It has the same structure as the "BUD Bottom Up" cube with one exception: It has an additional dimension, "BUD Line Items," which is simply a dimension with count elements and an aggregation, "All," which is linked to the main cube. For the form design, it is necessary to name the elements from 1 to n. N is the maximum number of elements below a single Cognos TM1 cell in the cube "BUD Bottom Up."

The main cube "BUD Bottom Up" refers to the Line Items cube. We defined an exception: not every position should contain line items. An attribute to the cost types drives the availability of line items.

```
['Budget']=N:
IF(ATTRS('BUD Measures',!Bud Measures, 'Line Items') @= 'T',
DB('BUD Line Items', !BUD Organisations, !BUD Measures, !BUD Years,
!BUD Periods,  !BUD Versions, 'All', !BUD Types), Continue);
```

The "BUD Line Items" cube only has one simple rule: the cross cube feeder:

```
FEEDERS;
['Bud Line Items':'All']=>DB('BUD Bottom Up', !BUD Organisations, !BUD
Measures,!BUD Years,
!BUD Periods, !BUD Versions, !BUD Types);
```

But also the entry form is important. The key concept is "zero suppression." The report definition must contain all line items. But only the line items that contain data should be shown in the report. The second parameter in the TM1RPTVIEW report definition ("1") controls the zero suppression:

```
C9:=TM1RPTVIEW("tog:BUD Line Items:5",1,
TM1RPTTITLE("tog:BUD Organisations",$D$13), TM1RPTTITLE("tog:BUD
Measures",$D$14),
TM1RPTTITLE("tog:BUD Years",$D$15), TM1RPTTITLE("tog:BUD Versions",$D$17),
TM1RPTTITLE("tog:BUD Types",$D$16), TM1RPTFMTRNG,TM1RPTFMTIDCOL)
```

In addition we need a row for new elements. This row must refer to the next free element. How can we get this element? It is a simple Excel formula:

```
MAX(<Line Item Count>) + 1
```

What will happen if the entry number is higher than the maximum element? To avoid this case, it makes sense to limit the generation of lines. And you should generate a warning. However, you should be generous with the number of elements within the count dimension. Cognos TM1 has an excellent sparsity mechanism. We enhance the formula definition:

```
MIN(<MaxElement>, MAX(<Line Item Count) + 1)
```

To calculate the maximum allowed element, we can use the Cognos TM1 formula DIMSIZ. We need the following Excel formulas. B20 creates the element reference for the new key:

```
B20:=MIN(DIMSIZ("tog:bud line items")-1,MAX(B22:B26)+1)
```

B22 is copied down the active form's lines and transforms the keys into a number. You need the IF statement to transform all. And it is also possible that no element at all is available. In that case C22 contains a blank cell.

```
B22:=VALUE(IF(OR(C22="All",LEN(C22)=0),0,C22))
```

C19 generates a warning if no additional line item is available.

```
C19:=IF(B20>= DIMSIZ("tog:bud line items")-1;"No more elements
available!";"")
```

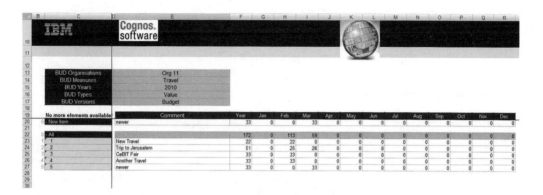

Let's have a final discussion. Why do we need two cubes? Of course, you can also do this with a single cube. It is a question of modularization. Usually you don't have line items on each line. With this concept you can modularize and focus in one cube on the concept and in the other cube on line items.

Reducing Budgeting Effort with Seasonal Factors

Very often you don't want to budget on a monthly level because this granular way of planning is time-consuming and perhaps you want to save some of your time. However, for a later variance analysis and other purposes, it could be helpful to have plan data on a monthly level. You can do this with a minor loss of information particularly when you have similar distribution figures across the year. Typical examples are:

- Work days
- Christmas and/or summer business
- Steady growth

This can be done by various means.

- Using the built-in spreading functions. For instance, you can distribute your numbers according to the distribution of the previous year. This method is quite flexible. A possible disadvantage is that it could be a little bit too complex for inexperienced users to use the built-in function for distribution.
- Distribution could be predefined by a TI process. It can be triggered by a button with parameters.
- In many projects we prefer distribution by a rule because it is simple and easy to understand for developers and end users.

First we define a simple cube to hold the distributions. We limit the cube to two dimensions. But it also could make sense to define seasonal figures per organization or scenario. Enhance the cube with additional dimensions if you need. The dimension "BUD Seasonal Factors" contains the figures.

The data collection is simple:

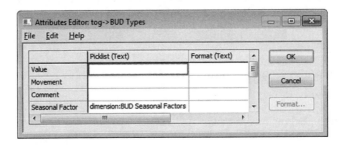

We enhanced the cube "BUD Bottom Up" a little bit. We need to enter the yearly values. Therefore we add a dummy element in the BUD Periods dimension ("Year Entry"). We also need another element to hold the seasonal factor. We want to set the factor per measure. We add a string element to the BUD Types dimension and assign a picklist to it with the link to the BUD Seasonal factors.

Finally we have to write a rule. The calculation is easy: Simply take the "Year Entry" amount, multiply this by the monthly seasonal factor, and divide it by the year sum of the seasonal factors. The following rule looks a little bit more complex because we have to get the relevant seasonal factor from the "BUD Bottom Up" cube and we have to do this twice:

```
['Budget']=N:
IF(ATTRS('BUD Measures',!Bud Measures, 'Line Items') @= 'S'
& !BUD Periods @<> 'Year Entry',
DB('BUD Seasonal Factors',DB('BUD Bottom Up',
```

```
!BUD Organisations, !BUD Measures, !BUD Years, 'Year Entry',
!BUD Versions, 'Seasonal Factor'),!BUD Periods)
\ DB('BUD Seasonal Factors',DB('BUD Bottom Up',
!BUD Organisations, !BUD Measures, !BUD Years, 'Year Entry',
!BUD Versions, 'Seasonal Factor'), 'Year')
*['Year Entry'],continue);
```

With these additions we can adapt the standard form. In row R you can enter the yearly value. The seasonal factor is chosen in column S.

Please keep in mind not to use the reference to the TM1RPTVIEW within the DBRW cell for the seasonal factor because the cube address doesn't fit into the view and doesn't work properly. Instead use the direct link to the cube:

```
S20:=DBRW("TOG:BUD Bottom Up";$D$13;$C20;$D$14;S$18;$D$16;"Seasonal Factor")
```

You see that the distribution is immediately calculated.

New Elements During the Budget Process

Budgeting is usually a well-defined process and all elements are known beforehand, hopefully. So why do we need new elements during the planning process? In a perfect world we have "one single source of truth," which means that only one place should exist where dimension elements are maintained. And for business structures like cost centers, cost types, products, and so on, the best place for creating, changing, and deleting the definitions is usually the ERP system. Every change should be created in the ERP system first and then transferred to other systems.

But this is very idealistic: The creation process in ERP is very slow. Particularly when you handle complex objects like products, it can take days to run through the creation workflow. This is problematic when you are in a planning process where the pressure to complete the planning activities is very high. Sometimes you want to plan on elements that don't exist in the ERP system. And you are not sure whether they will exist at all. Sometimes it is also a problem of different responsibilities. This is very often the case with products, orders, or cost centers.

What should we do? In Cognos TM1 you can delegate administrative tasks so that everybody can change dimensions. The problem is that you can't control this sufficiently. To let several, sometimes inexperienced users change dimension structures might result in chaotic data. So it must be very controlled. For instance, users can only enter elements in a certain area. The administrator should identify the newly added elements later to synchronize the new elements with the ERP system.

So the best way to allow users to change the structure is to use TI. The good thing is that you can run these modifications also via the Web. We like this to do as generically as possible since such a function can be used in various areas. So we need some parameters to hand over to the TI process:

- Elementname
- Alias
- Parent
- Dimension

Within the TI process we only need one row to create the new element (if we don't need the alias):

```
DimensionElementComponentAdd(psDimension,psParent, psElement, 1);
```

This looks pretty easy. However, reality is more complex. For instance, what should happen if the element already exists? And how can you guarantee that the requested element is unique? Sometimes it makes sense to generate an automatic key because then we can be sure that the key scheme is consistent. It is also important to store information about the date of creation and the status, whether it is a new or an imported element. So we have to invest a little bit more time.

We created a parameter dimension "BUD Parameters," where we hold the needed values like the next new key for automatic key generation and error texts.

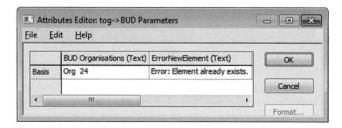

Let's start with the process. The function should be used in two ways: First, an element key should be automatically generated. But it should also be possible to hand over the new key with a parameter.

Parameter	Type		Default Value	Prompt Question
psElement	String	▾		
psParent	String	▾	Org 2	
psAlias	String	▾	New Org	
psDimension	String	▾	BUD Organisations	

Let's have a look at the prolog code. Most of the code is about consistency checks. Because we cannot give an error code, we write messages about possible errors into the parameter attribute.

```
IF (TRIM(psAlias) @= '');
AttPuts('Error: No Alias provided.', 'BUD Parameters',
'Basis', 'ErrorNewElement');
ProcessError;
ENDIF;
IF(TRIM (psParent) @= '');
AttrPuts ('Error: No Parent provided.', 'BUD Parameters',
'Basis', 'ErrorNewElement');
ProcessError;
ENDIF;
i = 1;
WHILE(i<DIMSIZ(psDimension));
IF(psAlias @=ATTRS(psDimension, DIMN(psDimension, i), 'Alias'));
AttrPuts ('Error: Alias already exists.', 'BUD Parameters',
'Basis', 'ErrorNewElement');
ProcessError;
ENDIF;
i = i + 1;
END;
IF(psElement @= '');
psElement =  ATTRS('BUD Parameters','Basis',psDimension);
ELSE
i = 1;
```

```
WHILE ( i < DIMSIZ(psDimension));
  IF (psElement @= DIMNM(psDimension, i);
ProcessError ('Error: Element already exists.', 'BUD Parameters',
  'Basis', 'ErrorNewElement');
  ProcessError;
 ENDIF;
 i = i + 1;
END;
ENDIF;
DimensionElementComponentAdd(psDimension, psParent,psElement, 1);
ExecuteProcess('BUD Generate Key', 'psAttribute',psDimension);
```

In the epilog section we fill in the attributes. It is necessary to put the attribute modification into the epilog section because the new dimension elements are not generated immediately in the prolog section.

```
AttrPuts(psAlias, psDimension, psElement, 'Alias');
AttrPuts ('New', psDimension,psElement, 'Status');
AttrPuts (Today, psDimension, psElement, 'Created On');
```

We need a function that generates the unique new key. Within the prolog session, the process "BUD Generate Key" is executed. The process "BUD Generate Key" separates the prefix from a number and increases the number by 1 each time it is executed:

```
sCurrentKey = ATTRS('BUD Parameters','Basis', PAttribute);
sNewKey= psPrefix|STR(NUMBR(SUBST
(CurrentKey,LONG(psPrefix)+1,5))+1,5,0);
AttrPuts (NewKey, 'BUD Parameters','Basis', psAttribute);
```

After running the process you can see the following results:

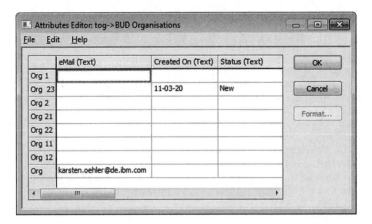

Investment Planning

Investment planning is closely related to budgeting activities. However, the time aspect becomes more important since a non-current asset is usually in use longer than just for the next year. Furthermore, if you want to calculate an ROI (return on investment) or the present value, you need more complex calculations with interest rates. Within an integrated plan, you often need to generate a so-called statement of changes of non-current assets. Another challenge is to create planned depreciations for the new investment. A further aspect is to consider is that we usually need depreciation forecasting for existing investments. We won't cover this, but keep it in mind when you discuss asset planning.

Hence there are a lot of tasks to do. What structure do we need? Let's focus on the necessary cubes. We defined two cubes, one to store all attributes ("IM Assets") and one for the calculations ("IM Planning"):

IM Assets should contain a "dynamic" dimension. We don't know the number of possible objects when we start. In our little example we prefer a single time dimension instead of using a year and a period dimension. It is simpler to define the carryover calculations between years.

An aspect to consider is dealing with classes or categories (although we haven't implemented this in our little example). Why? We need to assign the assets to the balance sheets. And furthermore, it could be comfortable to assign the lifetime automatically according to the relevant class. For the data collection we use the picklist feature.

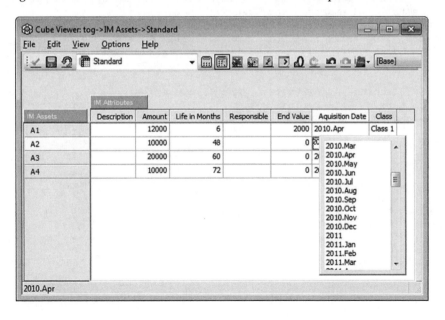

We need four rules to develop the basis module.

- We define the carry-forward logic (#4). This rule should stop after life end.
- We have to trigger the activation. The condition becomes true when the current period is identical with the respective attribute (#1).
- We want to check out all values on the life-end period. This is the case when the net value is identical with the respective attribute (#2). Be aware that we need the depreciation for this.
- And finally we have to create the depreciation. The calculation is easy: Amount minus residual value divided by the month. The depreciation should stop when the cumulated depreciation amount is bigger than the starting value minus the residual value.

And don't forget the feeders. The carry-forward rules must be feeders from the opposite side. And the depreciation must be fed.

```
SKIPCHECK;
#1
['In','Asset']=N:
IF(DB('IM Assets', !IM Assets, 'Aquisition Date')@=!IM Periods,
DB('IM Assets', !IM Assets, 'Amount'),STET);
#2
['Out','Asset'] =N:IF(['Asset Net','Opening']= DB('IM Assets', !IM Assets,
'End Value'),DB('IM Assets', !IM Assets, 'End Value'),0);

#3
['Out','Depreciation']=N:IF((['Opening','Asset'] >0 % ['In','Asset']> 0) &
['Depreciation','Opening'] > (- DB('IM Assets', !IM Assets, 'Amount')+
DB('IM ssets', !IM Assets, 'End Value')),
(DB('IM Assets', !IM Assets, 'Amount') -DB('IM Assets',
!IM Assets, 'End Value')) \ DB('IM Assets', !IM Assets,
 'Live in Month'),0);
#4
['Opening']=N:
IF(DB('IM Planning', !IM Assets, 'Asset', 'Out',
ATTRS('IM Periods',!IM Periods,'Prev'), !IM Versions, !IM Types)=0,
DB('IM Planning', !IM Assets, !IM Measures, 'Closing',
ATTRS('IM Periods',!IM Periods,'Prev'), !IM Versions, !IM Types),
CONTINUE);
FEEDERS;
['Closing']=>DB('IM Planning', !IM Assets, !IM Measures, 'Opening',
ATTRS('IM Periods',!IM Periods,'Next'), !IM Versions, !IM Types);

[{'Opening','In'},'Asset']=> ['Out','Depreciation'];
['Opening','Asset']=>['Out'];
```

Let's have a deeper look at the carry-forward. This is something we also need very often in inventory calculation. Also if you have to cumulate a carry-forward, this method can be helpful. Why do we use the "Prev" attribute? Although you can also use the function pair DIMNM/DIMIX for relative addresses, the attribute method is more flexible. For instance, if you handle aggregations like quarters and years, you have to consider the order. For the carry-forward function, you always need this rule and feeder pair:

```
['Opening']=n:DB(<this cube>, <!elements>,... 'Closing',
ATTRS('Periods',!Periods, 'Prev'),<!elements>...);
Feeder: DB(<this cube>, <!elements>... 'Opening',
ATTRS('Periods',!Periods, 'Next'),<!elements>...);
```

Something is still missing. The 'In' element feeds all other elements. But what drives the 'In' element? This can be only triggered by the "IM Asset" cube:

```
FEEDERS;
['Aquisition Date']=>
DB('IM Planning', !IM Assets, 'Asset', 'In', DB('IM Assets', !IM Assets,
!IM Attributes), 'Plan', 'Value');
```

The following screen shows the result. We chose a very short lifetime for A1 to show the correct values for all periods. In the last period, instead of depreciation, the object is checked out with the residual value.

And the consolidated statement looks like this:

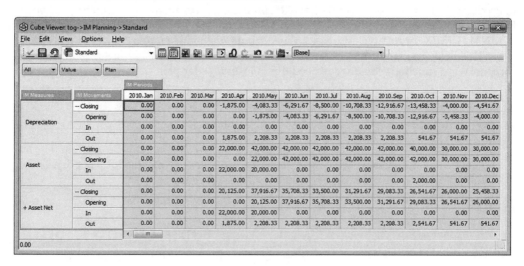

Of course, this example is simpler than the real world:

- Sometimes you need nonlinear depreciation (for instance, degressive depreciation).
- From time to time, partial activation of an asset is necessary, for instance, if you create your own production machines.

Create Your Own Workflow

There are tools in Cognos TM1 available to model your workflow (explained in Chapter 9): Using Cognos TM1 Contributor Application deployments, a completely predefined workflow is available. In addition to that, the more flexible Cognos TM1 Workflow can be used to structure the budgeting process. Why should you use your own concept? (Why should you use Cognos TM1 Workflow or why should you build your own?) Here are some possible answers:

- **You need more flexibility**   The Contributor workflow is out of the box with limited possibilities for adjustments. An example might be to have two approvers.
- **You need something rather simple**   The Cognos TM1 Workflow is open for extensions. However, this makes the tool complex. The workflow manager supports features you may never need.

In other cases you should really try to use the existing tools.

An interesting aspect is to do workflow without TI. Usually you need programming to establish typical workflow transitions. We like to show an approach without any TI. With the picklist feature and some security rules it is possible. What do we need?

First we define a workflow cube. Three dimensions we already discussed in our budgeting examples. The additional dimension "BUD WF Type" contains the necessary text elements like Status, Action, Comment, Owner, Approver, and so forth.

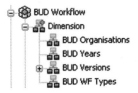

With this cube we can generate the first view showing all status information.

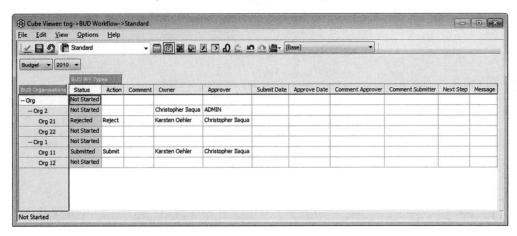

For the owner and the approver we only want to allow existing elements. For simplification we assume that each client is also a group with the same name. So we simply assign the dimension to the picklist.

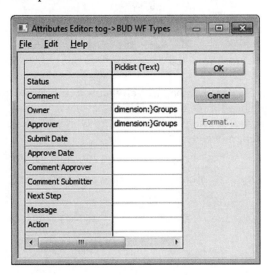

You can also restrict the picklist to a subset.

The next step is about transition. We have to map actions and states. To keep the approach simple, we write the relation directly into the picklist cube of the workflow. Before you can do this, you have to create the picklist cube "}PickList_BUD Workflow" by clicking on the right mouse button and selecting Create Pick List Cube.

Look at the structure of the picklist cube. It has the same structure with the additional dimension "}PickList".

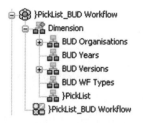

For each attribute in "BUD WF Type" we can define a rule. We want to define this for the element "Action." We need three transitions. Because we have a simple definition, we simply use a rule. It is of course also possible (and surely more flexible) to store the transition relations in a separate cube.

```
['Action']=S:
IF(SCAN(DB('WF', !A OEs, !A Time, !A Scenarios, 'Status'),
'Not Started In Progress Rejected')>0,
'Static:Submit',
IF(DB('WF', !A OEs, !A Time, !A Scenarios, 'Status')@='Submitted',
```

```
'Static:Approve:Reject',
#Approved
'Static:Rejected'));
```

To avoid multiple text comparisons, we often use the function SCAN.

Depending on the action, we can set the resulting status in the rule file for the cube "BUD Workflow":

```
['Status']=s:
IF(DB('WF', !A OEs, !A Time, !A Scenarios, 'Action') @= 'Reject','Rejected',
IF(DB('WF', !A OEs, !A Time, !A Scenarios, 'Action') @= 'Approve','Approved',
IF(DB('WF', !A OEs, !A Time, !A Scenarios, 'Action') @= '', 'Not Started',
'Submitted')));
```

Now you can test the behavior. Change the status from "Approve" to "Reject." First you can see that the status changed. Also the Action picklist changed.

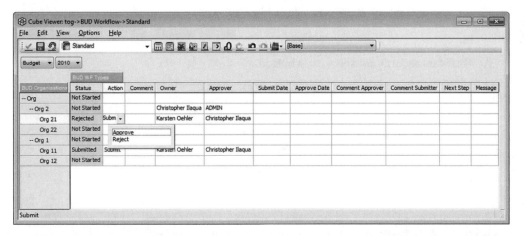

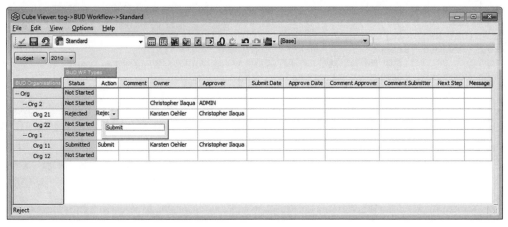

Next we need a cell security cube for the Cube "BUD Bottom Up".

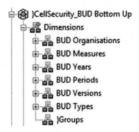

We create a rule for the element "Value":

```
['BUD Types': 'Value'] =S:
IF(SCAN(DB('BUD Workflow', !BUD Organisations, !BUD Years, !BUD Versions,
'Status'),'Rejected In Progress, Not Started')>0,
'WRITE',
'READ');
```

We also want security for the Action button.

```
['Action']=S:IF(
(SCAN(DB('BUD Workflow', !BUD Organisations, !BUD Years,
!BUD Versions,'Status'),'Rejected In Progess Not Started')>0 &
!}Groups @= DB('BUD Workflow', !BUD Organisations, !BUD Years,
!BUD Versions, 'Owner')) %
(SCAN(DB('BUD Workflow', !BUD Organisations, !BUD Years,
!BUD Versions,'Status'), 'Submitted Approved')>0 &
!}Groups @= DB('BUD Workflow', !BUD Organisations, !BUD Years,
!BUD Versions, 'Approver')), 'WRITE','READ');
```

With this preparation, we can now design our little process. Open the file "BUD Workflow.xls" and test the behavior.

			Status	Submitted
BUD Organisatio	Org 11	⩘		
BUD Years	2010	⩘	Action	Submit
BUD Types	Value	⩘		

	Budg Year	Budg Jan	Budg Feb	Budg Mar	Budg Apr	Budg May	Budg Jun	Budg Jul	Budg Aug	Budg Sep	Budg Oct	Budg Nov	Budg Dec
⊞ All Costs	34200	2700	2700	5400	2700	1800	2800	2700	3400	2800	1800	2700	2700
⊟ V	4	0	0	0	0	1	0	0	1	0	1	0	0
V1	2	0	0	0	0	1	0	0	0	0	1	0	0
V2	1	0	0	0	0	0	0	0	1	0	0	0	0
V3	1	###	###	###	###	###	###	###	###	###	###	###	###
⊟ Material	13700	900	900	3600	900	900	1000	900	900	1000	900	900	900
Material 1	6300	300	300	3000	300	300	300	300	300	300	300	300	300
Material 2	3800	300	300	300	300	300	400	300	300	400	300	300	300
Material 3	3600	300	300	300	300	300	300	300	300	300	300	300	300
⊟ Salaries	10800	900	900	900	900	900	900	900	900	900	900	900	900
Salaries Gro	3600	300	300	300	300	300	300	300	300	300	300	300	300
Salaries Gro	3600	300	300	300	300	300	300	300	300	300	300	300	300
Salaries Gro	3600	300	300	300	300	300	300	300	300	300	300	300	300
⊟ Other Costs	9700	900	900	900	900	0	900	900	1600	900	0	900	900
Other Costs	3000	300	300	300	300	###	300	300	300	300	###	300	300
Other Costs	3700	300	300	300	300	###	300	300	1000	300	###	300	300
Other Costs	3000	300	300	300	300	###	300	300	300	300	###	300	300

A Planning Calendar with E-mail Notification

The keyword for budgeting is automation. You usually have activities that should be processed automatically. This is something that can be done by a chore. Typical tasks are:

- Open a period on a certain date
- Close a period on a certain date
- Send a reminder by e-mail; for instance, that a period will be closed on a certain date.

In a complex environment it can be helpful to define this only for an area for the events, not for the whole organization.

We need a cube to store the events:

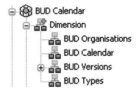

With this cube we can create a simple form. In row 15 new actions for a certain day are created. The sheet contains an active form with zero suppression. You simply delete an item by clearing the cells.

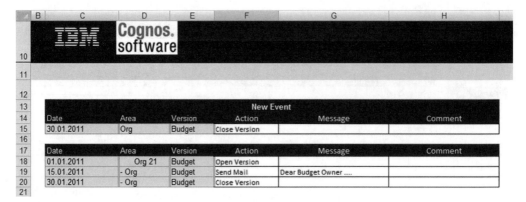

	Date	Area	Version	Action	Message	Comment
				New Event		
14	Date	Area	Version	Action	Message	Comment
15	30.01.2011	Org	Budget	Close Version		
17	Date	Area	Version	Action	Message	Comment
18	01.01.2011	Org 21	Budget	Open Version		
19	15.01.2011	- Org	Budget	Send Mail	Dear Budget Owner	
20	30.01.2011	- Org	Budget	Close Version		

The next step is to store the status of the versions. We could use the security cube directly. However, we want more flexibility. For instance, it is sometimes necessary to change the state manually. Hence we define the cube "BUD State." It holds status information for the three relevant dimensions.

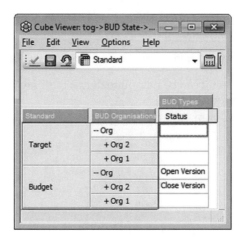

With this preparation we are now empowered to define the process. The TI process "BUD Calendar Action" frequently checks whether actions are due to start. For this we have to create a chore directly from the process.

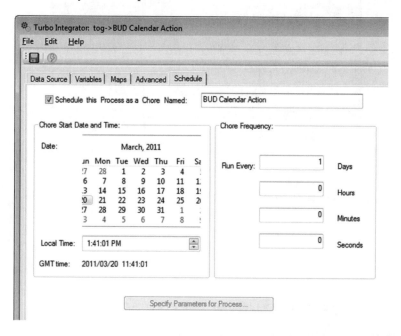

The process is based on the view "Actions" of the cube "BUD Calendar." This view simply lists all dates and events. The performance can be improved, of course. What you can do is to overwrite the assigned subset definition with the current day. However, this view is very small, so this process is not critical.

```
dt=SUBST(TODAY(1),9,2)|'.'|SUBST(Today(1),6,2)|'.'|
SUBST(TODAY(1),1,4);
IF (V1 @= dt);
IF (SVALUE @= 'Send Mail');
ExecuteProcess('Bud Send Mail', 'psOrg', V2,
'psMessage', '....');
ELSE
#****Begin: Generated Statements***
V6='Status';
if (VALUE_IS_STRING=1, CellPutS(SVALUE,'BUD State',V2,V3,V6),
 CellPutN(NVALUE, 'BUD State', V2,V3,V6));
#****End: Generated Statements****
ENDIF;
ENDIF;
```

This process simply executes the defined activity. If a period is to open or to close, it simply writes the action into the budget state. If a mail is to be sent, it invokes another process, "BUD Send Mail."

The process "BUD Send Mail" changes the subset to focus only on the chosen element and all descendants. We need the following parameter.

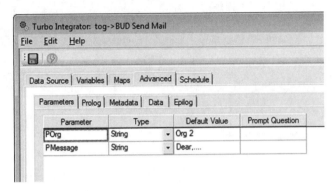

In the prolog section we create the new subset.

```
IF (SubsetExists('BUD Organisations', 'SendTo') = 1);
SubsetDestroy('BUD Organisations', 'SendTo');
ENDIF;
SubsetCreateByMDX('SendTo', 'DESCENDANTS( [BUD Organisations].['
| psOrg | '])');
```

In the metadata section we generate the e-mail per organizational unit.

```
S_Run='cmd /c C:\Sendmail /smtpserver 127.0.0.1  /to ' |
 attrs('BUD Organisation',V1,'eMail')   |' /from TM1@demo-vm
/subject Reminder /Body  ' | psMessage;
ExecuteCommand(S_Run,0);
```

Summary

As we discussed, budgeting with Cognos TM1 is a huge topic. In this chapter we focus mostly on organizational and process aspects. We will cover important topics like driver-based planning or version handling in other chapters.

We present various tools instead of an integrated budgeting application. A budgeting toolbox fits the variety of requirements better. Although budgeting is established for a long time, its very concrete implementations vary immensely. A concrete budgeting implementation usually will need concepts out of other chapters such as allocations (Chapter 17) or versioning and forecasting (Chapter 20).

17

CHAPTER

Costing

The world of costing is dominated by enterprise resource planning (ERP) systems. Costing has a long tradition, particularly in manufacturing companies. ERP systems have been working well for standard tasks like inventory valuation, but are inflexible when it comes to real decision support. There are still gaps and uncertainties about how to create a decision-supporting costing system in many industries, for instance, in service-oriented companies. Existing manufacturing-oriented cost accounting systems and especially transaction systems are often cited as inflexible and too complex, particularly for service organizations. New development or significant structural changes are often hard to integrate into the existing accounting flow.

On the other hand, when OLAP is used for costing purposes, it is only used for reporting and analysis with very limited use of more sophisticated costing methods like allocations. But some companies are doing interesting costing calculations with Cognos TM1 to get better costing information. A European manufacturer, for instance, reduced his effort in ERP costing drastically and modeled with TM1 to do profit simulation on a complex costing system.

We think that the power of Cognos TM1 is underestimated. We think that more companies can profit from the enormous costing capabilities of Cognos TM1. There is not much regarding costing that you can't solve effectively with Cognos TM1. As you will see in this chapter, Cognos TM1 can provide a lot of options. We will show various costing methods to give you an impression of what is possible with Cognos TM1. Although the literature about costing is huge, we hope to cover the most important models.

A caveat: A complex cost system still will be complex within Cognos TM1. Hence you need a good understanding of cost methods and a structured method to avoid being overwhelmed by complexity. However, the result of using Cognos TM1 in costing is convincing: It is more flexible, and what is more important, business users are able to change the system by themselves.

The Business Challenge

When defining a standardized cost structure, there are three main requirements to address: multipurpose, granularity, and flexibility:

- **Different costs for different purposes.** This is an old requirement. For instance, you need different values for inventory valuation as the base for your (external) closing statement (full costs), and on the other hand, perhaps you need decision support for short-term decisions like price limits (only direct and variable indirect costs). There are a lot of additional needs for using other alternative costing approaches, which result in the rather theoretical need for several costing systems. To solve this problem, there are two developments: Some experts are working on standardization. The objective is to come to a commonly agreed-upon costing process similar to International Financial Reporting Standards (IFRS) in external accounting. A bias between the various needs and a standard for external and internal cost calculation will be accepted. Other experts are searching for the possibility of parallel valuation to fulfill more than one purpose. The result of having more than one margin for the same product must be understood, of course.

- The second challenge is **granularity**. By allocation and cost assignments, important information is lost. A typical requirement is the effect of currency volatility on specific projects. Granularity can be also a means to support multiple purposes because it is possible to leave out certain valuation parts within an analysis without changing the cost calculation flow.

- **Flexibility** means the capability to adapt an existing cost model, for instance standard costing, to new requirements or to changed context (for instance, implement activity-based costing). It can be seen as structure-related and reporting-related. The first one is harder to archive because it is not enough to change the reporting system when new requirements occur. This is very closely related to the overall architecture. There has been a long discussion about architectures, and there is a movement away from an open-based calculation to a more case-based calculation. Tools like Cognos TM1 are able to support this requirement (Figure 17-1).

This is a move from the intensively discussed base calculation, which was discussed even earlier in the last 30 years of the twentieth century by American and German professors Clark and Schmalenbach. This approach should provide basic precalculations, but they should be "purpose neutral." All-purpose specific calculation should be part of case-based calculation. Because the base calculation is completely free of purpose-related valuations, the idea is very similar to a data warehouse. But with the same argument for OLAP as a need on top of a data warehouse, we can argue that there is a need for a purpose-related costing flow. The problem is that valuation is something that is done already in the early phases of cost accounting. Hence a base calculation can't provide much, and too much complexity is built into the case base calculation. Hence a base calculation must be accompanied by some flexible standard calculations.

An important question is: how specific should a tool for costing be? Packaged applications for cost accounting are very specifically implemented: They provide concrete calculation objects like cost centers, orders, projects, products, and processes, to name only a few calculation objects. Perhaps this might be the reason that they are usually seen as quite

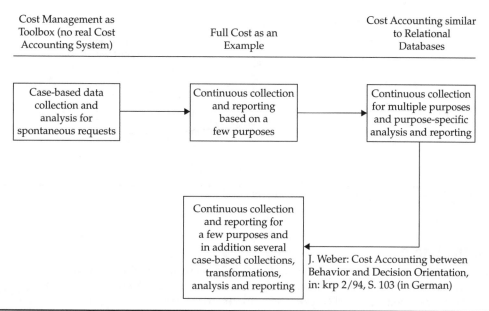

Cost Management as Toolbox (no real Cost Accounting System)	Full Cost as an Example	Cost Accounting similar to Relational Databases

FIGURE 17-1 Development of costing systems

inflexible: All methods are based on specific objects, and thus new concepts like life cycle costing, target costing, and so on are complex to integrate.

The opposite approach might be to program every function during an implementation. Giving the complexity of cost accounting, this is perhaps not the best idea. A good tool must support the implementation in an efficient way so that it is possible to implement individual structures. Let us investigate how Cognos TM1 meets these requirements.

When you design a costing system, you can start on a rather abstract level. For instance, you don't model cost centers or products, but instead you define a rather abstract object type, "Cost object." In consequence, the possibility of adapting new concepts increases because you can use all the core methods already defined for the generic cost object. This is positive, but on the other hand, the costs for adaptation also increase because more parts of a system must be configured. Basic functions like allocation, for instance, are not available.

Decisions about the "right costing system" are about cost optimization on the meta level. We have trade-offs with two cost drivers. We have costs of adaptations and we have the cost of configuration. When we talk about costing with Cognos TM1, the cost of configuration might be higher. However, the costs of adaptation over time are lower. This is different in comparison to classical programming. Here Cognos TM1 provides a lower cost of ownership (Figure 17-2).

With Cognos TM1 you usually start with a generic database. Nevertheless we think (and you will see) that Cognos TM1 is a good fit because it starts with minimal restrictions and very strong features to model cost management functions.

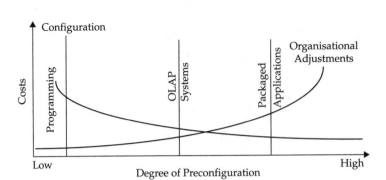

FIGURE 17-2   Degree of abstraction of software systems for accounting

Costing Is Simple

What is costing from a formal point of view? Is it double-entry bookkeeping or multidimensional analysis? We think that it is a mixture of both. Double-entry bookkeeping describes the value flow. For analysis purposes, the costing output is modified to enable multidimensional analysis.

Costing is often seen as complex. A helpful means to reduce this complexity is to be generic. It is crucial to start with a high-level cost mapping.

We would like to look into different aspects of cost accounting. A simple cost calculation is usually based on very few dimensions. The basic dimensions should be "Scenarios" ("Actuals," "Plan," "Forecast"), "Cost Types," "Cost Objects," and "Periods." To collect amounts, currency calculations, and texts such as comments, we added the dimension "Types."

The following example shows a simple calculation with supporting and production cost centers and two products. In the first simple version, we will not split costs into variable and fixed costs.

We split up cost objects into cost centers and products. Furthermore, we have production cost centers (PCCs) and supporting cost centers (SCCs), for instance, for heating, energy, or administration (Figure 17-3).

With this model it is possible to create a simple cost calculation. And since this structure is simple, we only need one cube for all tasks.

Costing items can be entered in a planning scenario, and actual data can automatically be loaded from ERP systems. The usual cost allocation can be done by using Cognos TM1 rules. The advantage is that all allocations are calculated instantly. Hence you can use Cognos TM1 for simulation.

Start with Allocations

Let's first focus on the heart of cost accounting: allocations. Allocation is a widely used term in cost management. A lot of different methods are available. The available cost accounting methods in ERP systems set a high standard. For instance, in sophisticated ERP systems like SAP ERP, transfer price calculation and vector-oriented allocations with mutual dependencies are supported.

CM Objects	CM Measures	CM Periods	CM Scenarios	CM Types
All	Calculation	Year	Actual	Value
Cost Centers	Sales	Jan	Plan	Comments
PCC	Costs	Feb	Variance	Currency Values
PCC1	Primary Costs	Mar		
PCC2	Material	Apr		
SCC	Salaries	May		
SCC1	Secondary Costs	Jun		
SCC2	PCC1	Jul		
Products	PCC2	Aug		
Product 1	All Costs	Sep		
Product 2	Primary Costs	Oct		
	Material	Nov		
	Salary	Dec		
	Secondary Costs			
	SCC1			
	SCC2			
	Statistics			
	SqMtrs			

FIGURE 17-3   Dimensions for cost management (basic model)

Existing OLAP systems usually don't directly support allocation methods. Sometimes specific allocation formulas are offered. Cognos TM1 doesn't offer this. The good thing is that Cognos TM1 provides generic tools to get the same result with little effort. With rules it is possible to implement all types of allocations. We start with this simple cube:

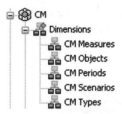

The magic allocation formula is simple:

```
A*B/C
```

A is the allocation amount, and B and C refer to the allocation base. B is the single driver number and C is the summation of all driver numbers. For example, the heating costs of 1000 (A) can be allocated by square meters and the production cost center has 100 SQM (B) and the whole plant has 500 SQM (C). Hence 200 are allocated to the production cost center (1000 × 100/500).

Let's start with the first version. We want to allocate costs from the cost center SCC1 to other cost centers by using the square meters as allocation base. Our first rule would be:

```
['CM Measures':'SCC1']=N:['CM Objects': 'SCC1',
'Primary Costs']*['SqMtrs']\['SqMtrs','Cost Centers'];
```

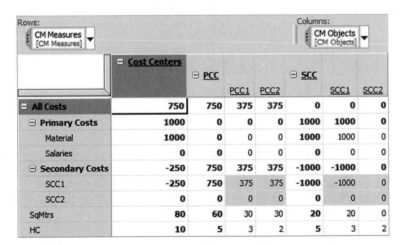

But there should be also a respective cost reduction of the sending cost center to zero because all costs are allocated. But you can see that the costs of the service cost centers are doubled. You can simply ignore this fact in your analysis; however, we want to provide a solution that is always consistent. You simply solve this problem with an IF statement.

```
['CM Measures': 'SCC1']=N:
['CM Objects': 'SCC1','Primary Costs']*
IF (!CM Objects @= 'SCC1',-1,
['SqMtrs']\['SqMtrs','Cost Centers']);
```

By using the IF statement, the primary costs are eliminated when the current cost center is identical with 'PCC1'. The result is better now:

	Cost Centers	PCC	PCC1	PCC2	SCC	SCC1	SCC2
All Costs	750	750	375	375	0	0	0
Primary Costs	1000	0	0	0	1000	1000	0
Material	1000	0	0	0	1000	1000	0
Salaries	0	0	0	0	0	0	0
Secondary Costs	-250	750	375	375	-1000	-1000	0
SCC1	-250	750	375	375	-1000	-1000	0
SCC2	0	0	0	0	0	0	0
SqMtrs	80	60	30	30	20	20	0
HC	10	5	3	2	5	3	2

But there is still something wrong. Although the whole amount is eliminated from the cost center, the total costs are not allocated. Perhaps you should consider that no square meters are collected on this cost center. But most of the time, it is a fact that the chosen cost center has allocation drivers, too. If you import this data, it can be automatically assigned to all cost centers. So you must ensure that all costs are allocated by a modification of the driver base. A simple addition can solve this:

```
['CM Measures': 'SCC1']=N:
['CM Objects': 'SCC1','Primary Costs']*
IF (!CM Objects @= 'SCC1',-1,
['SqMtrs']\(['SqMtrs','Cost Centers']-['SqMtrs','CM Objects': 'SCC1']));
```

Now it is perfect:

Rows: CM Measures [CM Measures]		Columns: CM Objects [CM Objects]					
	Cost Centers	**PCC**			**SCC**		
			PCC1	PCC2		SCC1	SCC2
All Costs	1000	1000	500	500	0	0	0
Primary Costs	1000	0	0	0	1000	1000	0
Material	1000	0	0	0	1000	1000	0
Salaries	0	0	0	0	0	0	0
Secondary Costs	0	1000	500	500	-1000	-1000	0
SCC1	0	1000	500	500	-1000	-1000	0
SCC2	0	0	0	0	0	0	0
SqMtrs	80	60	30	30	20	20	0
HC	10	5	3	2	5	3	2

A Generic Allocations Approach

As you see, allocation is not that simple. However, with this basic understanding you can write additional allocations by yourself. However, if you have hundreds of allocations, this can become quite painful. Hence we want to provide you with a more generic proposal. We will write a rule that automatically runs across all service cost centers.

First we define an attribute "base" to define the allocation base for each cost center. This is necessary because more than one service cost center can use the same driver as a base for its allocation.

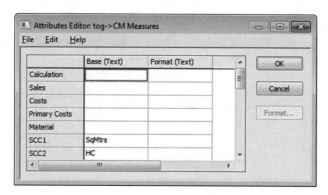

The new allocation formula looks quite different. And it looks complex. As always, you have to balance between ease of understanding and maintenance effort.

The rule is only executed for children of the element "Secondary costs." The structure (A*B/C) remains the same.

```
SKIPCHECK;
[]=N:IF(ELPAR('CM Measures',!CM Measures,1) @= 'Secondary Costs',
DB('CM', 'Primary Costs', !CM Measures, !CM Periods, !CM Scenarios, !CM Types)*
IF (!CM Objects @= !CM Measures,-1,
DB('CM', attrs('CM Measures',!CM Measures,'Base'), !CM Objects, !CM Periods,
!CM Scenarios, !CM Types)\(
DB('CM', attrs('CM Measures',!CM Measures,'Base'), 'Cost Centers', !CM Periods,
!CM Scenarios, !CM Types)-
DB('CM', attrs('CM Measures',!CM Measures,'Base'), !CM Measures, !CM Periods,
!CM Scenarios, !CM Types))),CONTINUE);
FEEDERS;
['Statistics']=>['Secondary Costs'];
```

Here is the result:

	Cost Centers	PCC	PCC1	PCC2	SCC	SCC1	SCC2
All Costs	**2000**	**1625**	**875**	**750**	**375**	**375**	**0**
Primary Costs	**2000**	**0**	**0**	**0**	**2000**	**1000**	**1000**
Material	**2000**	**0**	**0**	**0**	**2000**	1000	1000
Salaries	**0**	**0**	**0**	**0**	**0**	0	0
Secondary Costs	**0**	**1625**	**875**	**750**	**-1625**	**-625**	**-1000**
SCC1	**0**	**1000**	500	500	**-1000**	-1000	0
SCC2	**0**	**625**	375	250	**-625**	375	-1000
SqMtrs	**80**	**60**	30	30	**20**	20	0
HC	**10**	**5**	3	2	**5**	3	2

Rows: CM Measures [CM Measures] Columns: CM Objects [CM Objects]

The positive consequence is that you don't have to change the rules when you enter a new cost center that should be allocated to other cost centers or products. Users only have to work with the dimension editor and the attribute editor.

Of course, some practice is necessary to create such a rule. But the result is pretty flexible. Imagine what will happen when you add a cost center, a cost type, or a scenario. You don't have to adapt the rule. Compare this with the classical spreadsheet allocation. Even with simple models, the effort is much higher.

A word about rounding issues. In our examples we don't have to face rounding issues. Why? Because we don't round so that a cost center is always completely set to zero. However, if you want to only allocate amounts rounded on cents, it is not guaranteed that all costs are allocated.

You can simply calculate the difference between allocated costs and the cost base. We recommend that you collect these rounding differences on a specific element in the "CM Measures" dimension. By summing this up across the "CM Organization" dimension, you get the amount of rounding difference to reconcile your profit calculations with the input costs.

Another aspect might be important to discuss: Depending on the size of the model, number of calculated cells, and the dependency of allocations, rule-based allocations may be sluggish. Reports based on allocated costs can be slow. In these situations it might be helpful to use the TurboIntegrator. Although you lose the instant simulation capability, the system might be significantly faster. So should we throw away the examples we've seen so far?

The good thing is that you don't have to create new allocations when you realize that your rule-based allocations are slow. Simply copy the target values of your allocations produced by rules into a rule-free area. For this you can use the "CM Types" dimension. Simply add an element "Result" and copy from "Value" to "Result." We will show how this works in the section about cyclic allocations.

Differentiate Cost Allocation with Cost Vectors

There is a caveat using simple allocations introduced in earlier chapters. Through allocation procedures, important cost information for the allocation target gets lost. Cost accounting has several purposes, and with an aggregation the possibility to provide insufficient information is increasing. An important proposal to overcome this limitation is a vector- or matrix-oriented allocation. Instead of transferring a single cost value, it is possible to allocate a certain number of cost values, a cost vector. With this modification you can see what primary cost parts are allocated. So specific questions like the percentage of $ or Euro parts or salaries can be answered from analysis of the allocation target object.

Usually the measure dimension is used for this concept. To avoid data explosion, you usually use aggregated cost types.

For multidimensional modeling, this has to be considered. It is possible to allocate values directly to the primary cost type of the receiving cost center. However, the source of the cost positions is no longer available for analysis, and thus accountability is harder to achieve. A short example: Costs of the Facility department are "Salaries" (100) and "Miscellaneous" (50). These costs are allocated to the cost centers Production 1 and 2 by square meters.

	Facilities	Production 1	Production 2	Total
Salaries	1000	800	1200	3000
Miscellaneous	1000	500	400	1900
Sum	2000	1300	1600	4900
SqrM		30	70	

After Allocation				
Salaries	0	1100	1900	3000
Miscellaneous	0	800	1100	1900
Sum	0	1900	3000	4900

This is why we suggest a second parallel cost type. A cube would contain both cost types and dimensions. The elements of these dimensions should be identical. You can mirror this dimension with a TI script so that the maintenance effort is limited.

A simple example should clarify the discussion. Suppose that a cost center CC10 has three cost types. These costs are allocated to CC20 and CC21. Therefore we use an additional cost type, the secondary maintenance costs.

To keep the primary cost type, the cubes need two cost type dimensions, "Primary cost types" and "Cost Type." The "Primary cost types" can be a copy or contain aggregation elements of "Cost Type."

The calculation of secondary costs is simple: "price * numbers." The Price is specified by the dimensions "Period," "Primary costs," "Output," and "Sending cost center."

To keep the primary costs part, the primary costs of cost center "CC10" must be divided by the output measure number (Figure 17-4). The number is specified by "Period," "Output," "Sending cost center," and "Receiving cost center."

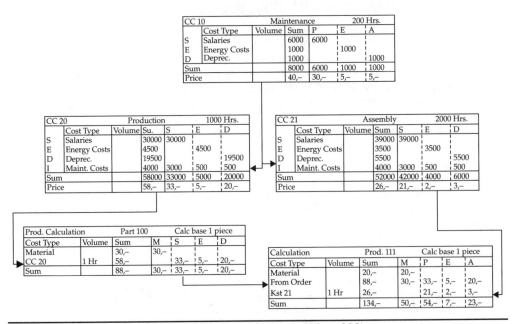

FIGURE 17-4 Example of a primary cost calculation (Müller, 1996, p. 206)

It is simple to map this concept to Cognos TM1. We use the following cube:

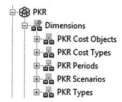

- Cost Types also contains the sales
- Cost Objects (cost centers and products)

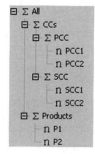

- Scenarios (Plan, Actuals)
- Periods
- Types. We use this dimension also to store the primary parts. You can, of course, use an additional dimension. But as an explanation of the concept, it is sufficient.

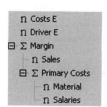

The example shows the cost center planning. The secondary cost centers SSC1 and SSC2 plan originally shows the costs for material and employees respectively. The production cost centers request the services of the secondary cost centers. The secondary cost centers don't deliver to each other.

We use a very simple cost center planning structure. PCC1 and PCC2 use services from SCC1 and SCC2. And Products P1 and P2 are requiring work from cost centers PCC1 and PCC2.

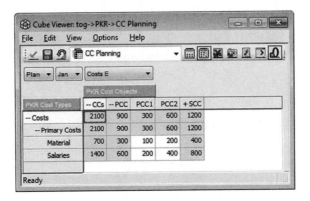

We created a small set of dependencies.

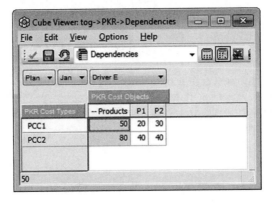

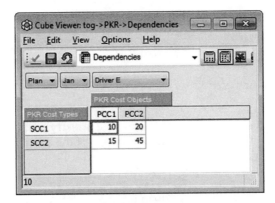

Let's first look to the cost center costing.

			Costs E	Driver E	Material	Salaries	⊞ Primary Costs
⊟ **PCC**		⊟ **Total Costs**	900	90	700	1400	2100
		⊟ **Primary Costs**	900	0	300	600	900
		Material	300	0	300	0	300
		Salaries	600	0	0	600	600
		⊟ **Secondary Costs**	0	90	400	800	1200
		SCC1	0	30	300	600	900
		SCC2	0	60	100	200	300
	PCC1	⊟ **Total Costs**	300	25	225	450	675
		⊟ **Primary Costs**	300	0	100	200	300
		Material	100	0	100	0	100
		Salaries	200	0	0	200	200
		⊟ **Secondary Costs**	0	25	125	250	375
		SCC1	0	10	100	200	300
		SCC2	0	15	25	50	75
	PCC2	⊟ **Total Costs**	600	65	475	950	1425
		⊟ **Primary Costs**	600	0	200	400	600
		Material	200	0	200	0	200
		Salaries	400	0	0	400	400
		⊟ **Secondary Costs**	0	65	275	550	825
		SCC1	0	20	200	400	600
		SCC2	0	45	75	150	225
⊟ **SCC**		⊟ **Total Costs**	1200	0	400	800	1200
		⊟ **Primary Costs**	1200	0	400	800	1200
		Material	400	0	400	0	400
		Salaries	800	0	0	800	800
	SCC1	⊟ **Total Costs**	900	0	300	600	900
		⊟ **Primary Costs**	900	0	300	600	900
		Material	300	0	300	0	300
		Salaries	600	0	0	600	600
	SCC2	⊟ **Total Costs**	300	0	100	200	300
		⊟ **Primary Costs**	300	0	100	200	300
		Material	100	0	100	0	100
		Salaries	200	0	0	200	200

Rows: PKR Cost Objects [PKR Cost Objects]   PKR Cost Types [PKR Cost Types]

You see that the material costs of SCC1 are allocated to 100 to PCC1 and PCC2.

The process is simple. We define a rule to map the costs, which are collected on "Cost E" to the primary dimension.

```
[]=N:IF(!PKR Types @= !PKR Cost Types, ['Costs E'],CONTINUE);
```

The second rule is slightly more complicated. We avoid referring to specific elements (we see primary costs and secondary costs as generic). Thus this rule works dynamically.

```
[]=N:IF(!PKR Types @= !PKR Cost Types, ['Costs E'],CONTINUE);
[]=N:IF((Elispar('PKR Cost Types','Secondary Costs',!PKR Cost Types)=1 %
ELISPAR('PKR Cost Types','Overhead',!PKR Cost Types)=1)
& ELISPAR('PKR Types','Primary Costs',!PKR Types)=1,
DB('PKR', !PKR Cost Types, 'Primary Costs', !PKR Periods, !PKR Scenarios,
!PKR Types)* ['Driver E']/['Driver E','All'],        CONTINUE);
```

Some explanations:

- The formula should only be calculated for secondary costs (cost center allocation) and indirect costs (product calculation).
- The primary cost part of the sending cost center is taken and weighted with the demand.

The good thing is that we use the same rule for product calculation. The following illustration shows a report for product calculation:

Cognos. software

CUBE:	tog:PKR
PKR Scenarios	Plan
PKR Periods	Jan

P1

		costs E	driver e	margin	revenue	primary costs	material	salaries
Revenue		1,500		1,500.00	1,500			
Costs		300		720.00		720.00	240.00	480
Primary Costs		300		300.00		300.00	100.00	200
material		100		100.00		100.00	100.00	
salaries		200		200.00		200.00		200
Overhead				420.00		420.00	140.00	280
PCC1	Hrs		20.00	120.00		120.00	40.00	80
PCC2	Hrs		40.00	300.00		300.00	100.00	200
Margin		1,200		780.00	1,500	−720.00	−240.00	−480

Primary costs %							33%	67%

Effect of increase on material costs			Margin	756.00		Increase	10%	

P2

		costs E	driver e	margin	revenue	primary costs	material	salaries
Revenue		2,000		2,000.00	2,000			
Costs		500		980.00		980.00	360.00	620
Primary Costs		500		500.00		500.00	200.00	300
material		200		200.00		200.00	200.00	
salaries		300		300.00		300.00		300
Overhead				480.00		480.00	160.00	320
PCC1	Hrs		30.00	180.00		180.00	60.00	120
PCC2	Hrs		40.00	300.00		300.00	100.00	200
Margin		1,500		1,020.00	2,000	−980.00	−360.00	−620

Primary costs %							37%	63%

Effect of increase on material costs			Margin	984.00		Increase	10%	

Products

		costs E	driver e	margin	revenue	primary costs	material	salaries
Revenue		3,500		3,500.00	3,500			
Costs		800		1,700.00		1,700.00	600.00	1,100
Primary Costs		800		800.00		800.00	300.00	500
material		300		300.00		300.00	300.00	
salaries		500		500.00		500.00		500
Overhead				900.00		900.00	300.00	600
PCC1	Hrs		50.00	300.00		300.00	100.00	200
PCC2	Hrs		80.00	600.00		600.00	200.00	400
Margin		2,700		1,800.00	3,500	−1,700.00	−600.00	−1,100

Primary costs %							35%	65%

Effect of increase on material costs			1,740.00			10%	
Primary costs %						35%	65%

Allocation with Cycles

Now we want to discuss another typical costing problem: recursive relationships. Here's a simple example: The energy cost center delivers energy to all other cost centers. One of these cost centers is the maintenance unit. They also maintain the devices of the energy cost center. Do you already see the problem? Energy costs are allocated to the maintenance cost center and other cost centers, and so this number is set to zero. After-maintenance costs are allocated to requesting cost centers where energy is one of them. Now a small amount is again booked on the energy cost center, although it is already set to zero. Our rather simple allocations don't cover this problem. See the principle design in Figure 17-5.

To enter the input-output relations we need mirror positions. In the base model we have already defined them: The cost centers are included in the dimensions "Cost Objects" and "Cost Types."

In Cognos TM1 there are several ways to solve recursive independencies:

- The easiest one is to avoid recursive relations. Try to allocate step by step.

- The traditional way is called iteration. Let the allocation run as often as value remains on a certain group of cost centers (usually secondary cost centers).

- The last and most elegant way is to use linear algebra.

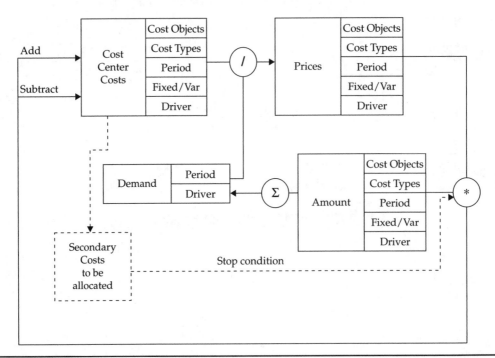

FIGURE 17-5   Recursive relationships

For the first method, we assume that you don't need help. Let us focus on the second method. We use the following cube:

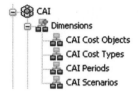

We use a simple allocation script:

```
['CAI Cost Types':'Facilities']=N:
IF (!CAI Cost Objects @= !CAI Cost Types, -1,['SM']\['SM','All'])*
['CAI Cost Objects':'Facilities','Allocation Basis'];
['CAI Cost Types':'HR']=N:
IF (!CAI Cost Objects @= !CAI Cost Types, -1,['HC']\['HC','All'])*
['CAI Cost Objects':'HR','Allocation Basis'];
```

To build up an iterative allocation, you need a little programming within TI scripts. Then you need stop conditions. Usually the following two conditions are used:

- A residual value
- Number of iterations

We created two TI scripts:

The starting point, "CAI Iteration," contains a simple WHILE loop:

```
Index = 0;
Value = 99;
WHILE( (Index < PnCounter) & (Value > PnLimit));
EXECUTEPROCESS('CAI Allocation');
Index= Index + 1;
Value=CELLGETN('CAI', 'Allocation', 'Total Costs',PsPeriod,PsScenario);
END;
```

To increase the flexibility we want to hand over some parameters. The limit parameters are interesting. We want to stop the allocation definitely after certain runs. This is necessary because there are situations where the iteration doesn't terminate. And it doesn't make sense to have an allocation down to the smallest fraction. Consider that sometimes these iteration nets can contain thousands of objects.

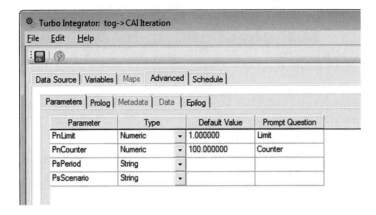

The second process ("CAI Allocation") simply copies the results of an allocation into a starting area, so that the subsequent allocation run only uses the residual value.

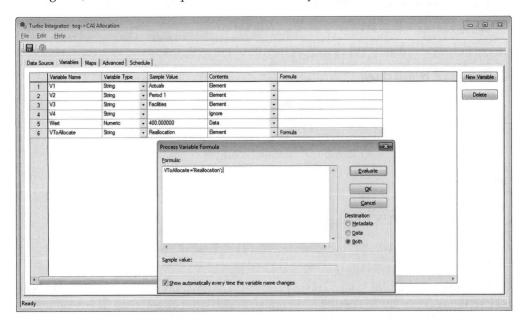

The following illustrations show how to work with iterations. The Action button is used to start the iteration.

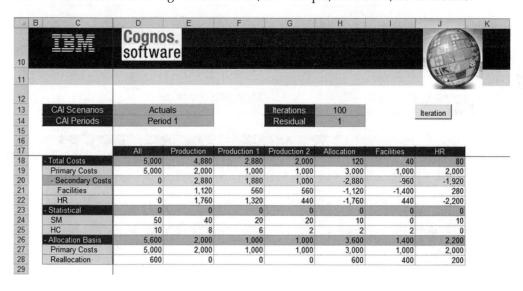

	All	Production	Production 1	Production 2	Allocation	Facilities	HR
- Total Costs	5,000	4,400	2,600	1,800	600	400	200
Primary Costs	5,000	2,000	1,000	1,000	3,000	1,000	2,000
- Secondary Costs	0	2,400	1,600	800	-2,400	-600	-1,800
Facilities	0	800	400	400	-800	-1,000	200
HR	0	1,600	1,200	400	-1,600	400	-2,000
- Statistical	0	0	0	0	0	0	0
SM	50	40	20	20	10	0	10
HC	10	8	6	2	2	2	0
- Allocation Basis	5,000	2,000	1,000	1,000	3,000	1,000	2,000
Primary Costs	5,000	2,000	1,000	1,000	3,000	1,000	2,000
Reallocation	0	0	0	0	0	0	0

Although the iteration process runs several times, let's look at the result after the first run. The allocation base has grown. Facilities, for example, has now 1,400 to allocate.

	All	Production	Production 1	Production 2	Allocation	Facilities	HR
- Total Costs	5,000	4,880	2,880	2,000	120	40	80
Primary Costs	5,000	2,000	1,000	1,000	3,000	1,000	2,000
- Secondary Costs	0	2,880	1,880	1,000	-2,880	-960	-1,920
Facilities	0	1,120	560	560	-1,120	-1,400	280
HR	0	1,760	1,320	440	-1,760	440	-2,200
- Statistical	0	0	0	0	0	0	0
SM	50	40	20	20	10	0	10
HC	10	8	6	2	2	2	0
- Allocation Basis	5,600	2,000	1,000	1,000	3,600	1,400	2,200
Primary Costs	5,000	2,000	1,000	1,000	3,000	1,000	2,000
Reallocation	600	0	0	0	600	400	200

After the second run, Facilities has to allocate 1,440.

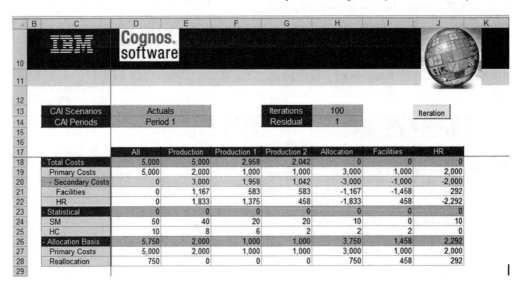

	All	Production	Production 1	Production 2	Allocation	Facilities	HR
- Total Costs	5,000	4,976	2,944	2,032	24	16	8
Primary Costs	5,000	2,000	1,000	1,000	3,000	1,000	2,000
- Secondary Costs	0	2,976	1,944	1,032	-2,976	-984	-1,992
Facilities	0	1,152	576	576	-1,152	-1,440	288
HR	0	1,824	1,368	456	-1,824	456	-2,280
- Statistical	0	0	0	0	0	0	0
SM	50	40	20	20	10	0	10
HC	10	8	6	2	2	2	0
- Allocation Basis	5,720	2,000	1,000	1,000	3,720	1,440	2,280
Primary Costs	5,000	2,000	1,000	1,000	3,000	1,000	2,000
Reallocation	720	0	0	0	720	440	280

And finally (after one of the conditions has terminated the iteration), the allocation basis of Facilities is 1,458. This is the amount that is necessary to relieve primary and secondary costs.

	All	Production	Production 1	Production 2	Allocation	Facilities	HR
- Total Costs	5,000	5,000	2,958	2,042	0	0	0
Primary Costs	5,000	2,000	1,000	1,000	3,000	1,000	2,000
- Secondary Costs	0	3,000	1,958	1,042	-3,000	-1,000	-2,000
Facilities	0	1,167	583	583	-1,167	-1,458	292
HR	0	1,833	1,375	458	-1,833	458	-2,292
- Statistical	0	0	0	0	0	0	0
SM	50	40	20	20	10	0	10
HC	10	8	6	2	2	2	0
- Allocation Basis	5,750	2,000	1,000	1,000	3,750	1,458	2,292
Primary Costs	5,000	2,000	1,000	1,000	3,000	1,000	2,000
Reallocation	750	0	0	0	750	458	292

Using Linear Algebra

Let's look at the cost calculation from a more mathematical point of view. Cost accounting is nothing more than working with matrix operations. This is nothing new and has been well discussed in the sixties. The mutual input-output relations can be elegantly mapped and thus can be calculated exactly.

For communication, this model might be not very helpful because the customers often do not have a strong mathematical background.

Figure 17-6 shows a typical analytical cost planning by using vectors and matrices. The costs (r1 to r13) are a result from the matrix multiplied by the drivers (e1 to e6). The first column in the matrix contains the driver-neutral costs.

With this "lite" introduction to linear algebra, it should be possible to solve this with Cognos TM1. The approach for the method we are using is called the "Gauss Elimination Method." This is a procedural method. But it is a finite process, which means we know how many iterations are necessary.

Let's take a simple example, as shown in Figure 17-7. We have five cost centers. The first step is to define the volume. We start with the external demand. The dependencies and the equations are as follows:

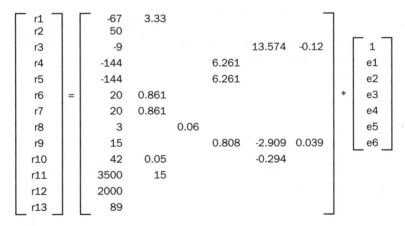

r1 = Wages		r2 = Training		r3 = Overtime wages		
r4 = Gas		r5 = Gas side costs		r6 = Gasoline		
r7 = Gasoline for heating		r8 = Dolomite		r9 = Sintered dolomite		
r10 = Wages for Maintenance		r11 = Depreciation		r12 = Interests		
r13 = Taxes						
e1 = Melting time		e2 = Time to melt		e3 = Cooking time		
e4 = # of melting machines		e5 = liquidity generation		e6 = Monthly factor		

FIGURE 17-6   Matrix calculation

$$m_{KON} = \qquad\qquad\qquad\qquad\qquad\qquad\qquad\qquad 22.500[KH]$$

$$m_{MON} = \qquad\qquad\qquad\qquad\qquad\qquad\qquad\qquad 7.500[MH]$$

$$m_{SER} = 0{,}06*m_{KON} + 0{,}06*m_{MON} \qquad +0{,}001*m_{Strom} + 150[SH] + 48.000[SH]$$

$$m_{Strom} = 0{,}75*m_{KON} + 0{,}75*m_{MON} +0{,}3*m_{SER} \qquad +12.500[KWH]$$

m(Construction)	=				22.500 [KH]
m(Assembly)	=				7.500 [KH]
m(Service)	= 0,06*m(Construction)	+ 0,06*m(Assembly)	+ 0,001*m(Energy)	+	150 [SH]+48.000 [SH]
m(Energy)	= 0,75*m(Construction)	+ 0,75*m(Assembly)	+ 0,3*m(Service)	+	12.500 [KWH]
vk(Kon)	= 0,06*vk(Ser)	+ 0,75*vk(Strom)		+	42
vk(Mon)	= 0,06*vk(Ser)	+ 0,75*vk(Strom)		+	44
vk(Ser)	=		0,03*vk(strom)	+	44
vk(Strom)	=	0,001*vk(ser)		+	0.2

Figure 17-7   A simple demand model

You see the mutual dependencies: Service demand is driven by Construction, Assembly, and Energy demand. Energy is driven by Construction, Assembly, and Service.

But we also want to know the price for the various services. Hence the second model is about pricing and costing. It has a similar structure. However, the resulting matrix is transposed, as shown in Figure 17-8.

$$m_{KON} = \qquad\qquad\qquad\qquad\qquad\qquad\qquad\qquad 22.500[KH]$$

$$m_{MON} = \qquad\qquad\qquad\qquad\qquad\qquad\qquad\qquad 7.500[MH]$$

$$m_{SER} = 0{,}06*m_{KON} + 0{,}06*m_{MON} \qquad +0{,}001*m_{Strom} + 150[SH] + 48.000[SH]$$

$$m_{Strom} = 0{,}75*m_{KON} + 0{,}75*m_{MON} +0{,}3*m_{SER} \qquad +12.500[KWH]$$

m(Kon)	=				22.500 [KH]
m(Mon)	=				7.500 [KH]
m(Ser)	= 0,06*m(Kon)	+ 0,06*m(Mon)	+ 0,001*m(strom)	+	150 [SH]+48.000 [SH]
m(Strom)	= 0,75*m(Kon)	+ 0,75*m(Mon)	+ 0,3*m(Ser)	+	12.500 [KWH]
pc(Construction)	= 0,06*pc(Service)	+ 0,75*pc(Energy)		+	42
pc(Assembly)	= 0,06*pc(Service)	+ 0,75*pc(Energy)		+	44
pc(Service)	=		0,03*pc(Energy)	+	44
pc(Energy)	=	0,001*pc(Service)		+	0.2

Figure 17-8   A costing model

We take this minimalistic model as reference. Take the following cube:

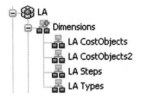

"LA CostObjects" and "LA CostObjects 2" are almost identical. The latter also contains input and output for the independent numbers.

n CO1
n CO2
n CO3
n CO4
n CO5
n In
n Out

And LG Types contains the calculation steps. For each equation we need one step.

n Basis
n CO1
n CO2
n CO3
n CO4
n CO5

First question is: How high is the demand on energy, service hours, and so on? This is the answer:

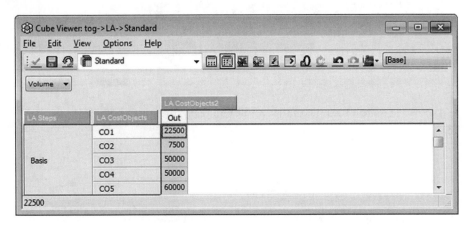

As you can see, the elimination is done step by step.

LA Steps	LA CostObjects	CO1	CO2	CO3	CO4	CO5	In	Out
Basis	CO1	1	0	0	0	0	22500	22500
	CO2	0	1	0	0	0	7500	7500
	CO3	-0.06	-0.06	1	-0.001	0	48150	50000
	CO4	-0.75	-0.75	-0.3	1	0	12500	50000
	CO5	0	0	0	0	1	60000	60000
CO1	CO1	1	0	0	0	0	22500	22500
	CO2	0	1	0	0	0	7500	7500
	CO3	0	-0.06	1	-0.001	0	49500	50000
	CO4	0	-0.75	-0.3	1	0	29375	50000
	CO5	0	0	0	0	1	60000	60000
CO2	CO1	1	0	0	0	0	22500	22500
	CO2	0	1	0	0	0	7500	7500
	CO3	0	0	1	-0.001	0	49950	50000
	CO4	0	0	-0.3	1	0	35000	50000
	CO5	0	0	0	0	1	60000	60000
CO3	CO1	1	0	0	0	0	22500	22500
	CO2	0	1	0	0	0	7500	7500
	CO3	0	0	1	-0.001	0	49950	50000
	CO4	0	0	0	0.9997	0	49985	50000
	CO5	0	0	0	0	1	60000	60000
CO4	CO1	1	0	0	0	0	22500	22500
	CO2	0	1	0	0	0	7500	7500
	CO3	0	0	1	-0.001	0	49950	50000
	CO4	0	0	0	1	0	50000	50000
	CO5	0	0	0	0	1	60000	60000
CO5	CO1	1	0	0	0	0	22500	22500
	CO2	0	1	0	0	0	7500	7500
	CO3	0	0	1	-0.001	0	49950	49950
	CO4	0	0	0	1	0	50000	50000
	CO5	0	0	0	0	1	60000	60000

The trick is to create a triangle matrix and then, using the input, start from the last element.

```
# Step 2: replacement of variables

['Out','LA Steps':'CO5']=N:['In'];
['Out']=N:IF(!LA CostObjects @= !LA Steps,0,
-DB('LA', !LA Steps, 'Out', ATTRS ('LA Steps',!LA Steps,'Next')),!LA Types)*
DB('LA', !LA CostObjects, !LA Steps, 'CO5'        ,!LA Types))+
DB('LA', !LA CostObjects, !LA CostObjects2,
ATTRS('LA Steps',!LA Steps,'Next'),!LA Types);
```

```
# Step 1: Eliminiation towards triangle matrix
[]=N:IF(!LA Steps @<> 'Basis',
IF(!LA CostObjects @= !LA Steps ,DB('LA', !LA CostObjects, !LA CostObjects2,
ATTRS ('LA Steps',!LA Steps,'Prev'),!LA Types)
\DB('LA', !LA CostObjects, !LA CostObjects, ATTRS('LA Steps',!LA Steps,'Prev'),
!LA Types),
IF(DIMIX('LA CostObjects',!LA CostObjects)>= DIMIX('LA CostObjects',!LA Steps) ,
-DB('LA', !LA CostObjects, !LA Steps, ATTRS ('LA Steps',!LA Steps,'Prev'),
!LA Types)\
DB('LA', !LA Steps, !LA Steps, !LA Steps,!LA Types)
* DB('LA', !LA Steps, !LA CostObjects2, !LA Steps,!LA Types)
+ DB('LA', !LA CostObjects, !LA CostObjects2,
ATTRS ('LA Steps',!LA Steps,'Prev'),!LA Types),
DB('LA', !LA CostObjects, !LA CostObjects2,
ATTRS ('LA Steps',!LA Steps,'Prev'),!LA Types))), CONTINUE);
```

We could use the same model to calculate the costs. For this we transform the matrix because now we want to calculate in the opposite direction. We have to push the prices.

```
['Prices','Basis']=N:IF(!LA Costobjects2 @<> 'In',
DB('LA', !LA CostObjects2, !LA CostObjects, !LA Steps, 'Volume'),CONTINUE);
```

And here is the result:

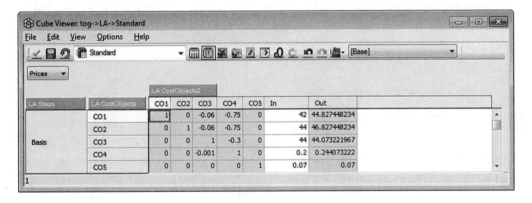

Dynamic Budgeting: Splitting Costs into Fixed and Variable Parts

Cost accounting is often used for budgeting and consequently also for variance analysis. Static budgets are not always appropriate when it comes to variance analysis. What if you have variable costs and output is much lower (or higher) than budgeted? If the costs remain the same, this is bad (or good), but the static budget doesn't show it. Hence you need a modified base for the variance. You can call it "allowed costs." An example for further clarification:

> You planned to produce 100 bicycles and budgeted 10,000 Euros. Now you produce 110 bicycles and spend 11,000 Euros. So you overspend by 10 percent. Is this fair? Why not take the production increase into account? However, not all costs vary with the output. Let's assume that only 50 percent of the costs can be adjusted to the output level. Hence your allowed costs are $5000 + 5000 \times 1.1 = 10,500$. So you only overspend 500 Euros.

For this situation, it is common to split costs into a fixed and a variable part during the planning process. The variable costs are assigned to an output measure. This measure should describe the output of a cost unit/center. For instance, the machine hours or working hours can be used to measure the output of a construction unit.

We like to show a typical flexible plan cost formula for the "allowed costs." The usual definition is:

Fixed plan costs +
variable plan costs *
actual output/planned output

Or we can show this in a more formal manner:

$$C^A_{CC,CT} = C^P_{CC,CT,f} + C^P_{CC,CT,pr} \bullet \frac{D^A_{CC}}{D^P_{CC}}, \text{ with}$$

C	Costs	CC	Cost Center
A	Adjusted Plan	D	Driver
P	Plan	f	Fix
CT	Cost Type	pr	Proportional

With the diagram in Figure 17-9 it is easier to understand the variance calculation.

With this modification we can calculate different variances due to responsibilities. The allocated plan cost shows which full cost parts are allocated:

$$Allocated\ Costs = Total\ Costs \bullet \frac{Actual\ Output}{Planned\ Output}$$

The efficiency variance is defined as

Actual Costs – Allowed Costs

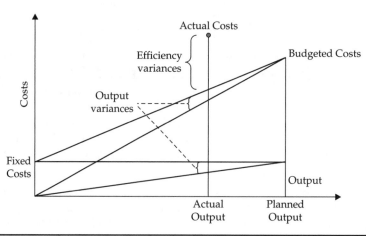

FIGURE 17-9   Variance calculation

The output variances can be calculated as follows:

Output variances = Allowed Costs – Allocated Costs

An enhancement is to increase the scenario dimension to fixed plan and variable plan. In the second step we enhanced the cost object dimension by the type of output. The variable costs are planned dependent on the output. Or simply said, when the output varies, the variable costs vary in a linear mode.

A second enhancement is to add the calculation objects with a type "output type." So we don't need a new dimension. The costs can be planned per output type. A cost center is simply an aggregation of different outputs. Why do we need more than one output per cost center?

The next picture shows the necessary enhancements. You don't need additional dimensions because we use scenarios.

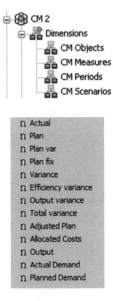

But we have to consider that we have costs that must be assigned without a direct connection to the output. The problem is that we need a dummy element. Another aspect is that we need to allocate these costs to the output figures. In the first step we need the performance:

```
['CM Measures':'Output','Plan var'] =N:
DB('CM 2',  'Products', !CM Objects,!CM Periods, 'Planned Demand');
['CM Measures':'Output','Actual'] =N:
DB('CM 2',  'Products', !CM Objects,!CM Periods, 'Actual Demand');
```

The modified budget is calculated by a rule.

```
['Adjusted Plan']=['Plan fix']+['Plan var']*
['CM Measures':'Output','Actual']\['CM Measures':'Output','Plan'];
['Allocated Costs'] = ['Plan'] *
['CM Measures':'Output','Actual']\['CM Measures':'Output','Plan'];
```

With this information it is possible to split between efficiency variance and output variance. Variances can be split up.

```
['Efficiency variance'] = ['Actual']-['Adjusted Plan'];
['Output variance'] = ['Adjusted Plan'] -['Allocated Costs'];
['Total variance'] = ['Actual'] - ['Plan'];
```

Price can be calculated like this:

```
['Price',{'Plan var','Plan fix'}] = N:['All Costs']\['Plan var',
'CM Measures':'Output'];
```

Here is the product calculation:

```
['Actual']=N: IF (ELISANC('CM Measures','Indirect Costs',!CM Measures)=1,
['Actual Demand']* DB('CM 2', !CM Measures, 'Price', !CM Periods, 'Plan')
,CONTINUE);
['Plan']=N: IF (ELISANC('CM Measures','Indirect Costs',!CM Measures)=1,
['Planned Demand']* DB('CM 2', !CM Measures, 'Price', !CM Periods, 'Plan')
,CONTINUE);
```

And here's the calculation for the Earned figure:

```
['Earned']=N:DB('CM 2', 'Products', !CM Objects, !CM Periods,
!CM Scenarios);
```

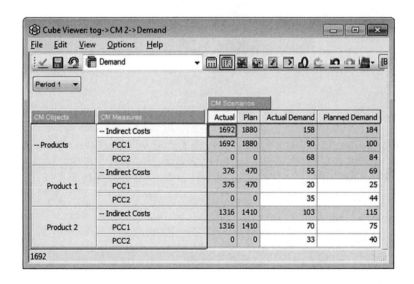

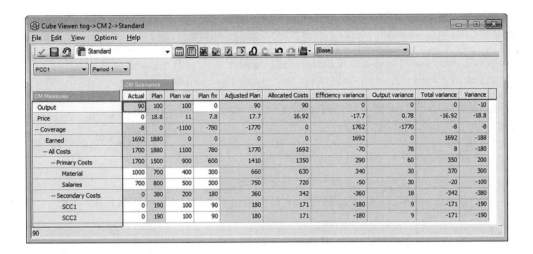

Activity-Based Costing

Are you interested in activity-based management and looking for a dedicated system? If you have Cognos TM1, you might not need such a tool. Cognos TM1 provides all means to create an ABC system. But first we will provide some statements to clarify our understanding.

The re-engineering wave in the 1990s brought some new ideas into cost accounting. The favorite process orientation was also the foundation for activity-based costing. Instead of the traditional "cost plus" method, a more accurate tracing was requested to better show the cost dependencies.

This became more and more necessary because the relationship between direct and indirect costs changed in the last few years due to higher automation. Direct costs are often only a small fraction in relation to indirect cost.

In the past, highly customized products bore the same indirect costs as standard products. This was sufficient because the assumption that all products consume the same amount of resources was more or less realistic in a mass environment. The production of variances increases the complexity more and more.

This is not realistic any more. It often becomes unfair because the exotic products need much more time and resources. Standard products can profit from economy of scale. Look at the following simple example.

		A	B
Material Costs		500	500
Production Volume		10,000	10
Purchase Order Size		200	1
Number of Orders		50	10
Order Costs	500000		
Calculation Base	5005000	5,000,000	5,000
	9.99%		
Allocated Order Costs		499,500	500
Total Costs		5,499,500	5,500
Total Costs per Piece		549.95	549.95

Also it is problematic to control the so-called indirect areas. The efficiency of indirect areas is hard to assess. You need more input-output relations.

The idea was to use activities for a better cost allocation. The process is simple. From cost pools, costs are allocated to activities. In a second step, activities are aggregated to processes. In a third step, cost drivers are used to allocate to products or services. Cost drivers could be number of purchase order, product weight, and so on. The focus of ABC is the indirect areas. As you can see in Figure 17-10 costs are collected in cost pools and aggregated or allocated to processes.

A simple example shows the method of activity-based costs. The purchasing department has the following activity output for one month:

Process	Effort in Man-days
Create Orders	89
Negotiate Standard Contracts	42
Manage Departments	14
SUM	**145**

Regardless of salary differences between the cost center employees, we allocate the costs of the department (500,000) to the various processes according to the man-days spent.

Process	Effort in Man-days	Costs
Create Orders	89	306,896.55
Negotiate Standard Contracts	42	144,827.59
Manage Departments	14	48,275.86
SUM	**145**	**500,000.00**

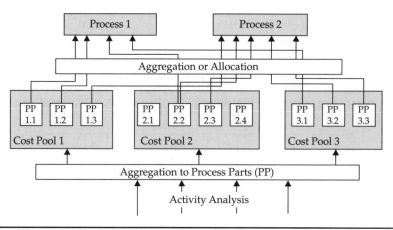

FIGURE 17-10   Modified ABC allocation process

The calculation can be modified as follows:

	A	B
Material Costs	500	500
Production Volume	10,000	10
Purchase Order Size	200	1
Number of Orders	50	10
Activity Costs	416,667	83,333
Total Costs (ABC)	5,416,667	83,333
Total Costs per Piece (ABC)	542	8,833
Total Costs (conventional)	5,499,500	5,500
Total Costs per Piece (conv.)	549.95	549.95

What is the result? Product B is far more expensive because the purchasing costs are much higher.

Activity costing can be integrated into traditional cost accounting systems. There is no need to change the whole system. Only the cost plus areas are to be adapted. It is also possible to use ABC as an add-on method.

But pure accounting doesn't change much. To actively control the activity-based costs is important. That is why the term is more and more replaced by activity-based management. The scope is the design and management of processes. The cost manipulation is crucial.

The only thing that might be missing is the graphic representation. However, in the end the results are important.

Let us define the following cube. It is a standard costing cube we have already seen.

There is one specific addition: We model processes and activities. Activities are aggregated to processes and alternatively to cost centers.

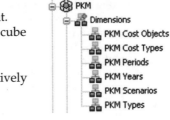

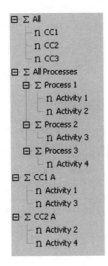

The idea is simple:

- First, we collect the costs on the cost centers.

- We allocate the cost center costs to activities based on working hours.

- Not all cost center costs can be assigned to activities. For example, managing the department is not usually an activity. For this we allocate the indirect costs in a second step to the activities.

- We aggregate the activities to processes.

- Finally, we use cost drivers to allocate process costs to products (is not part of the example).

```
SKIPCHECK;
# Cost Center Costs which can be directly
# collected with the activities
['Direct']=N:STET;
# Calculate the Price per Cost Center
['Price per HR']=N:['Salaries']\(['HC']*['Hrs']);
# Direct Salaries for an activity= Price of the cost center * HRS
['Direct Salaries'] = N:
DB('ABM', SUBST(ELPAR('ABM Cost Objects',!ABM Cost Objects,2),1,
LONG(ELPAR('ABM Cost Objects',!ABM Cost Objects,2))-2),
'Price per HR', !ABM Periods, !ABM Years, !ABM Scenarios, !ABM Types)
* ['Hrs'];
# Indirect Salaries for an activity =
# Not allocated costs * % of CC Work
['Indirect Salaries'] =N:
( DB('ABM',SUBST(ELPAR('ABM Cost Objects',!ABM Cost Objects,2),1,
LONG(ELPAR('ABM Cost Objects',!ABM Cost Objects,2))-2), 'Salaries',
!ABM Periods, !ABM Years, !ABM Scenarios, !ABM Types)
- DB('ABM',ELPAR('ABM Cost Objects', !ABM Cost Objects,2),
 'Direct Salaries', !ABM Periods, !ABM Years, !ABM Scenarios,
!ABM Types)) *['Hrs'] \ DB('ABM',
ELPAR('ABM Cost Objects', !ABM Cost Objects,2),
 'Hrs' , !ABM Periods, !ABM Years, !ABM Scenarios, !ABM Types);


['Direct Costs','Value'] =N: ['Indirect Costs','Direct'];
[{'Material','Rental Costs'}] = N:IF (ELISANC('ABM Cost Objects',
'All', !ABM Cost Objects)=1, CONTINUE,
( DB('ABM', subst( elpar('ABM Cost Objects',!ABM Cost Objects,2),1,
long(elpar('ABM Cost Objects',!ABM Cost Objects,2))-2),
!ABM Cost Types, !ABM Periods, !ABM Years, !ABM Scenarios,
!ABM Types)
- DB('ABM', elpar('ABM Cost Objects', !ABM Cost Objects,2),
!ABM cost types, !ABM Periods, !ABM Years, !ABM Scenarios, 'Direct'))
*DB('ABM', !ABM Cost Objects, ATTRS('ABM Cost Types',!ABM Cost Types,
'Base'), !ABM Periods, !ABM Years, !ABM Scenarios, !ABM Types)
 \ DB('ABM',ELPAR('ABM Cost Objects', !ABM Cost Objects,2),
ATTRS ('ABM Cost Types',!ABM Cost Types,'Base'), !ABM Periods,
!ABM Years, !ABM Scenarios, !ABM Types));
```

```
FEEDERS;
['HC']=>['Price per HR'];
['Hrs']=> ['Direct Salaries'];
['Value','Direct Costs']=> ['Indirect Costs'];
['Hrs']=> ['Indirect Salaries'];
['Indirect costs','direct']=>['Direct Costs','Value'];
```

We also are able to collect other costs directly on the activities.

This is the process calculation:

The total costs of CC1 (2750) are allocated to Activity 1 (1810.67) and Activity 2 (939.33).

Coordination Process

We saw that cost allocation is usually based on cost center output, and on the other side, demand from products and cost centers. The calculation is easy, and if the output and/or the consumption are easy to measure, there shouldn't be a problem. However, in the cost planning, the output level is very often the result of an intensive discussion. How high the demand is can be usually seen as a function of the transfer price.

We want to discuss the way demand is planned. There are several ways to coordinate this process. We don't want to organize the negotiation process. But from the administration point of view, it is necessary to have agreed-upon and consistent numbers. What can you do to align the two parties?

- The so-called "follower-leader principle" simply says that either the vendor or the seller plans, and this number is automatically transferred into the partner's position. The negotiation process should take place in advance.

- Autonomous planning with adjustment. This makes sense when the plan numbers are created from different points of view. For instance, the vendor starts with capacity-oriented planning, whereas the seller uses demand-oriented planning. Hence it is very unlikely that both numbers are the same.

It is important to link this activity with a workflow. The activities of the planning process should only be finished when both partners agree.

For this we define a dimension with collection attributes:

- Approved vendor
- Approved seller
- Comment vendor
- Comment seller
- The final approval

We "reuse" the CM cube for this. We create a rule that "calculates" an overall status based on both seller's and vendor's approval status. Since Cognos TM1 rules do not support case statements, the conditional statement looks a little bit ugly, but it is simple to understand.

```
['Final Approval'] =s:
 IF(DB('CM',!CM Measures,!CM Objects,!CM Periods,!CM Scenarios,
'Approved Vendor')@='OK' &
DB('CM',  !CM Measures, !CM Objects,!CM Periods, !CM Scenarios,
'Approved Seller') @='OK','OK',
IF (DB('CM',!CM Measures, !CM Objects,!CM Periods, !CM Scenarios,
'Approved Vendor') @= 'Rejected' %
DB('CM', !CM Measures, !CM Periods,!CM Objects,  !CM Scenarios,
'Approved Seller') @='Rejected','Conflict',
IF (DB('CM', !CM Measures, !CM Objects, !CM Periods, !CM Scenarios,
'Approved Vendor')@<>
DB('CM', !CM Measures, !CM Objects, !CM Periods, !CM Scenarios,
'Approved Seller'),'In Progress','')));
```

In the example we allow only one partner to enter data. The user interfaces could look like this:

You have to set up security rights so that status and amount can only be changed by one partner.

From Costing to Multidimensional Profitability Analysis

Traditional costing methods usually use a limited number of dimensions, as we have shown in our previous examples. When you are integrating costing with profitability analysis, additional dimensions are required.

Take project costing as an example. Often you collect costs on cost centers, orders, and so on. But the target for the cost calculation is the project. So you use the allocation methods we showed in the previous paragraphs. But very often you want to do analysis not only for the project but also for regions, customers, project groups, and many more.

These objects can sometimes be simple aggregation. But what if you want to do a cross analysis? Give the revenue of customer group 1 in the region North. This is nothing you can get by a simple aggregation. You need different dimensions.

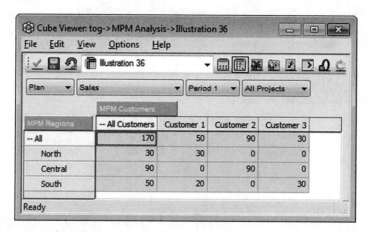

Let us do some further work on this example. We have defined a simple project structure.

First, we define project attributes in a cube.

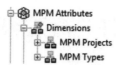

With a picklist we can define an entry form like this.

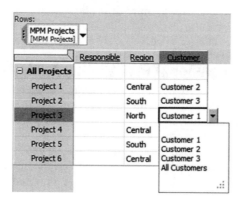

The dimension "MPM Types" needs the following picklist entries:

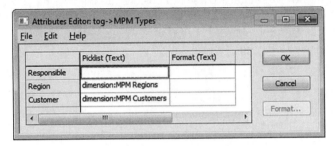

You can, of course, use subsets to suppress the "All" selection. The syntax is

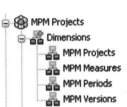

```
subset:<dim name>:<subset name>
```

We want to collect the values on a periodical base for different versions. So we define a separate cube.

It is pretty easy to collect some data for the projects.

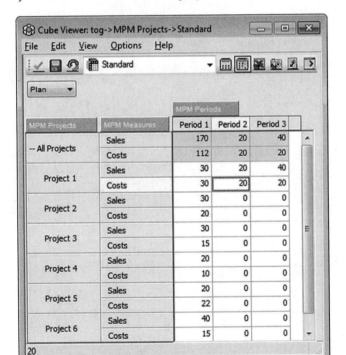

The last cube is the analysis cube. Here we add some dimensions: MPM Customers and MPM Regions. These dimensions are the target of the picklist attributes.

You can get the results with a simple rule. For each additional dimension we need a part in a condition statement:

```
SKIPCHECK;
['Plan']=N:IF
(!MPM Regions @= DB('MPM Attributes',!MPM Projects,'Region') &
!MPM Customers @= DB('MPM Attributes',!MPM Projects,'Customer'),
DB('MPM Projects', !MPM Projects, !MPM Measures, !MPM Periods,
!MPM Versions),STET);
FEEDERS;
```

How should we now set up the feeder for this? The MPM Projects cube is usually quite dense in comparison to the analysis cube. So we can use a generic feeder.

```
SKIPCHECK;
FEEDERS;
[ ]=>DB('MPM Analysis', !MPM Projects,
DB('MPM Attributes',!MPM Projects,'Customer'),
DB('MPM Attributes',!MPM Projects,'Region'),
!MPM Measures, !MPM Periods, !MPM Versions);
```

This is a precise feeder. You see the result in the following screenshot:

An alternative with bigger cubes might be to use a TI script. This can be done without programming. Define a transfer view with all values you want to transfer. You can skip the aggregate level if you want to transfer all details into the analysis cube. This could be a (simple) transfer view:

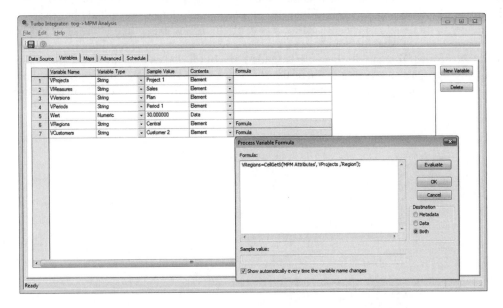

You have to define a new variable per addition dimension. To get the relevant dimension, you need the following function:

```
VRegions=CellGetS('MPM Attributes', VProjects ,'Region');
```

With this, the assignment to the analysis cube is easy:

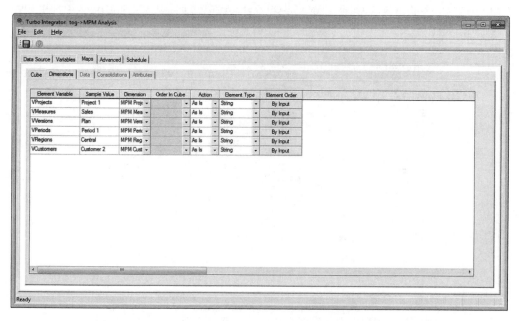

Again, this proposal is very individual: Depending on what dimensions are necessary in your profitability analysis, the matching model changes.

Summary

There is no standard for costing systems. Due to the long tradition of cost calculation, several methods appeared, and seldom disappeared completely. Cognos TM1 has the flexibility to model all aspects of costing. There might be one exception: Some old concepts were based on bookkeeping principles; even allocations were booked, resulting in documents with two entries. You can do this with Cognos TM1, but it makes the value flow inflexible.

Some approaches go quite to the limits of Cognos TM1. We showed a way to solve linear equations, but most companies that we have seen avoid circular references. However, there are business problems that can only be solved simultaneously.

Production Planning and Costing Analysis

Welcome to the world of production. It is typically a rather complex environment. Hence there is a valid need to use computers to support decision making. To create a working production plan and coordinate material delivery and routing is still a big challenge for all companies.

A lot of excellent ERP systems support various tasks of production planning. Even innovative methods like the so-called "theory of constraints" are supported. But as always when it comes to decision support, ERP solutions are well-defined, sophisticated, well-implemented—and inflexible.

That is the reason why a new class of planning tools appeared in the '90s. So-called advanced planning and scheduling tools (APS) were quite successful because they address the slowness and inflexibility of traditional solutions. Systems like I2, Manugistics, or later APO of SAP focus on decision support methods. They provide specific algorithms based on data that is stored in memory. So this development is not very different from the development in the business intelligence world.

These systems are highly sophisticated but expensive. Companies who need only a fraction of the offered function must invest a lot, perhaps only to solve one or two specific problems. In addition, the more specific those problems are, the more complex the customization of these systems might be. So the question is: why not use a rather generic system? Why not use Cognos TM1? The side effect is that Cognos TM1 can be used for far more, as we are about to explain in this part of the book.

But can Cognos TM1 support complex production challenges in the same way that the tools we've mentioned do? In various projects we have had some good experiences. We were really surprised how flexible production decision support is possible with Cognos TM1. In this chapter we want to share our experiences.

The Business Challenge

What are the typical challenges? There are usually the traditional production planning problems to solve. Algorithms like bill of materials (BOM) explosion and adjusting capacity constraints are very typical. Starting with a sales forecast, you break down the demand to the material level. So you know which parts you have to produce or order externally, and most important, you know when. But real life is not that easy: you have to consider batch sizes, lead times, and constraints, like machine time.

And what is even more important: you can plan, but you must be able to react quickly to changes. What if a machine is out of order? Or a worker is ill? You need some buffer, usually higher inventory stock. But inventory, for instance, as a means to make your company more flexible to react to variations in demand, is expensive due to the finance costs of working capital.

There is no perfect solution. Approaches vary from industry to industry. It is obvious that a ship manufacturer has different problems than a producer of mass consumer goods. So flexibility is a key element to meet industry-specific requirements.

How Cognos TM1 Can Help

The rationale is obvious: If Cognos TM1 has a storage architecture similar to that of APS, why shouldn't it be possible to use Cognos TM1 as a planning system? But let's look at it from another side: Why should we use Cognos TM1 to do something that is already available? Think about the following reasons:

- APS tools are expensive. There are many companies that only need a fraction of the offered functions.
- Very specific functions are needed, which are not always supported.
- Integration with non-production systems. APS systems are usually well integrated in the manufacturing world. But what about integration with other plans like strategic, long-term, and finance?

We want to address the use of rules not only for simple analysis but also for decision support.

- Bill of materials explosion with time differences
- Routing and capacity planning
- Product calculation
- Production costing
- Target costing

But we can't stress this often enough: Complexity is growing fast and the speed of change is increasing as well. The more algorithms you have to support, the more inflexible Cognos TM1 becomes. And highly sophisticated algorithms are not likely to work properly on Cognos TM1—at least not without a reasonable effort.

So our recommendation is: start with rather simple solutions. And some advice to the business experts: if you have a working solution and the pain is not too great, stay with your system. However, perhaps you can use Cognos TM1 as an add-on to support some very specific challenges.

Bill of Materials (BOM) Explosion

Let's start with a simple example (see Figure 18-1). We have two products that consist of subassemblies. These assembly parts can be used by multiple final parts. Raw material is needed in order to build the subassemblies. We have three levels in this example. However, such graphs can contain more than ten levels with millions of parts. Hence performance is very important.

A typical requirement is to calculate the so-called BOM explosion: How many pieces of a certain raw material do I need to a produce a finished good? In the example it is obvious that I need 8 times A7 to produce one A1. With more than three levels, it gets more complex.

A consequent question is to map this to an external demand. You have a demand for 100 A1 and 200 A2. How many raw material pieces do you need to produce that? For A6 it is still easy: $100 * 1 * 2 = 200$. But to calculate A7, for instance, is more complex: $100 * 2 * 4 + 200 * 2 *4 + 100 * 1 * 3 = 2700$. Imagine a complex net with millions of items. The complete (small) example is shown in Figure 18-1.

Cognos TM1 can help to calculate this. A good TI programmer can do this within a short time frame. However, programming might not be the best solution. Cognos TM1 rules are leaner and easier to understand for somebody who has no or only limited programming experience.

The first challenge is to find the right representation of the bill of materials. We can propose at least two approaches:

- Use of the weighting factor. This seems to be very easy and natural. Simply write the amount of lower material that the upper material needs. The good thing is that Cognos TM1 supports multiple parent-child assignments within hierarchies. And you get nice hierarchical reports with drill-down and so on.

  However, there is an important limitation: You can only collect one weighting factor per parent-child combination. But what if the relation changes from time to time? A second disadvantage is that this number cannot be changed with an Excel formula. And finally, you cannot assign work plans like assembling to the materials, since work plans are mainly assigned to non–level-zero elements.

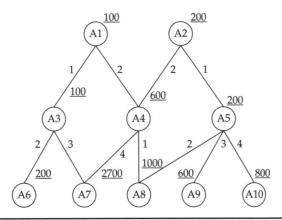

FIGURE 18-1   BOM structure

- Use of a demand matrix where we have the products and subassemblies in one dimension and raw material and subassemblies in the other dimension. In cells we enter the needed parts.

  The good thing is that the assignment is not limited to one single (factor) number. With a third dimension, you can define as many assignments as you want. It is also possible to design a time-variant bill of materials.

Thus we prefer the matrix. It is definitely more flexible. With this decision we are able to collect period-specific and simulation-specific bills of material. Further, we decide to do the calculation in a single cube. Feel free to adapt this to a multiple-cube scenario. We define the following planning cube:

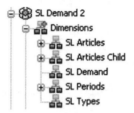

The dimension "SL Articles Child" is a copy of "SL Articles." We call this dimension "child" because we store parent-child relations in a matrix spanned by the dimensions "SL Articles" (parent) and "SL Articles Child." But as mentioned earlier, "SL Articles" and "SL Articles Child" don't have to be identical. You can reduce "SL Articles" by the raw material items (no child) and the SL Articles Child by final products. The next two illustrations show "SL Article" and "SL Article Child."

The elements necessary for the calculation steps are part of the "SL Types" dimension:

```
n BOM
n BOM Explosion
n Costs
n total costs
⊟ Σ Constraints
  ⊟ Σ Demand
    ├ n Primary Demand
    └ n Secondary Demand
  └ n Capacity
```

Let's go through the calculation step by step. First we can enter the bill of material. You can see the BOM we already introduced in our small example in the following illustration:

Value ∨	Jan ∨												
		SL Articles Child											
SL Demand	SL Articles	A1	A2	A3	A4	A5	A6	A7	A8	A9	A10	NoArticle	+ Total
	A1	0	0	1	2	0	0	0	0	0	0	0	3
	A2	0	0	0	2	1	0	0	0	0	0	0	3
	A3	0	0	0	0	0	2	3	0	0	0	0	5
	A4	0	0	0	0	0	0	4	1	0	0	0	5
	A5	0	0	0	0	0	0	0	2	3	4	0	9
BOM	A6	0	0	0	0	0	0	0	0	0	0	0	0
	A7	0	0	0	0	0	0	0	0	0	0	0	0
	A8	0	0	0	0	0	0	0	0	0	0	0	0
	A9	0	0	0	0	0	0	0	0	0	0	0	0
	A10	0	0	0	0	0	0	0	0	0	0	0	0
	+ Total	0	0	1	4	1	2	7	3	3	4	0	25

Given the dependencies between the articles, we can now enter the sales plan. We enter the primary demand. We assume that we need 100 parts of A1 and 200 of A2. For this we enter the primary demand in the "SL Articles Child" element "No Article":

		SL Articles Child											
SL Demand	SL Articles	A1	A2	A3	A4	A5	A6	A7	A8	A9	A10	NoArticle	+ Total
	A1	0	0	0	0	0	0	0	0	0	0	100	0
	A2	0	0	0	0	0	0	0	0	0	0	200	0
	A3	0	0	0	0	0	0	0	0	0	0	0	0
	A4	0	0	0	0	0	0	0	0	0	0	0	0
	A5	0	0	0	0	0	0	0	0	0	0	0	0
Primary Demand	A6	0	0	0	0	0	0	0	0	0	0	0	0
	A7	0	0	0	0	0	0	0	0	0	0	0	0
	A8	0	0	0	0	0	0	0	0	0	0	0	0
	A9	0	0	0	0	0	0	0	0	0	0	0	0
	A10	0	0	0	0	0	0	0	0	0	0	0	0
	+ Total	0	0	0	0	0	0	0	0	0	0	300	0

The "Secondary Demand" element holds recursive calculated demand:

SL Demand	SL Articles	A1	A2	A3	A4	A5	A6	A7	A8	A9	A10	NoArticle	+ Total
	A1	0	0	100	200	0	0	0	0	0	0	0	300
	A2	0	0	0	400	200	0	0	0	0	0	0	600
	A3	0	0	0	0	0	200	300	0	0	0	100	500
	A4	0	0	0	0	0	0	2400	600	0	0	600	3000
	A5	0	0	0	0	0	0	0	400	600	800	200	1800
Secondary Demand	A6	0	0	0	0	0	0	0	0	0	0	200	0
	A7	0	0	0	0	0	0	0	0	0	0	2700	0
	A8	0	0	0	0	0	0	0	0	0	0	1000	0
	A9	0	0	0	0	0	0	0	0	0	0	600	0
	A10	0	0	0	0	0	0	0	0	0	0	800	0
	+ Total	0	0	100	600	200	200	2700	1000	600	800	6200	6200

In the "NoArticle" column, you see the recursively calculated (secondary) demand. When you enter 1 as primary demand, you can directly see the BOM explosion, which simply means how many parts of material you need to produce a finished good.

SL Demand	SL Articles	A1	A2	A3	A4	A5	A6	A7	A8	A9	A10	NoArticle	+ Total
	A1	0	0	1	2	0	0	0	0	0	0	0	3
	A2	0	0	0	2	1	0	0	0	0	0	0	3
	A3	0	0	0	0	0	2	3	0	0	0	1	5
	A4	0	0	0	0	0	0	16	4	0	0	4	20
	A5	0	0	0	0	0	0	0	2	3	4	1	9
Secondary Demand	A6	0	0	0	0	0	0	0	0	0	0	2	0
	A7	0	0	0	0	0	0	0	0	0	0	19	0
	A8	0	0	0	0	0	0	0	0	0	0	6	0
	A9	0	0	0	0	0	0	0	0	0	0	3	0
	A10	0	0	0	0	0	0	0	0	0	0	4	0
	+ Total	0	0	1	4	1	2	19	6	3	4	40	40

So how is this calculated? The rule must be independent of the number of levels. Thus the calculation should work recursively. This is not a big challenge for the Cognos TM1 rules engine. The only thing you have to consider is to avoid any cycles. This is something the Cognos TM1 rules engine cannot handle. In the first step (#1) we have to multiply the demand by the BOM.

BOM(A1,A4) * Demand A2 = 2 * 100 = 200

BOM(A2,A4) * Demand A2 = 2 * 200 = 400

We sum it up to 600. This is the total demand for article 4 (no primary demand).

In the second step (#2), we have to bring this demand into the secondary demand matrix. The demand for A4 is 600.

The second level must be calculated. For instance:

BOM(A4,A8) * Demand A4 = 1 * 600 = 600

and

BOM(A5,A8) * Demand A5 = 2 * 200 = 400

We can sum up to 1000.

The following rule script makes Cognos TM1 work recursively.

```
#2 Copy
['Secondary Demand','No Article']= N:
DB('SL Demand 2', 'Total', !SL Articles, !SL Demand, !SL Periods,
!SL Types);

#1 Multiply Demand with BOM
['Secondary Demand']= N:
DB('SL Demand 2', !SL Articles, !SL Articles Child, 'BOM',
attrs('SL Periods',!SL Periods,'Ref'),!SL Types)
*DB('SL Demand 2', !SL Articles, 'NoArticle', 'Demand', !SL Periods,
!SL Types);
```

As contemplated, setting the feeders is necessary:

```
['BOM','Value']=>['Secondary Demand'];
['SL Articles':'Total']=>DB('SL Demand 2', !SL Articles Child,
'No Article', !SL Demand, !SL Periods, !SL Types);
```

Cost Calculation

The good thing is that we can do another recursive calculation for cost calculation exactly with the same structure. Calculation simply uses the other direction in the graph (meaning bottom up). This is a very typical phenomenon in accounting: The flow of value goes in the opposite direction of the material flow.

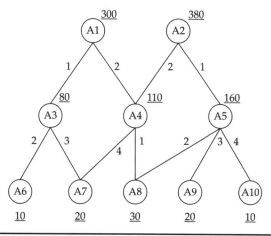

FIGURE 18-2   Cost calculation in the BOM structure

Cost calculation on the basis of the bill of materials is sufficiently implemented in many ERP systems. If a company has already implemented such a calculation and is happy with it, we don't see a valid reason to implement this with OLAP. So why do we show how to do calculation? Sometimes it is necessary to have a more flexible valuation structure.

We define a simple calculation in the "SL Types" dimension:

```
n Value
⊟ Σ Costs
    ├ n Material Costs
    └ n Material Overhead
```

The elements below the cost elements represent the "granularity" of the cost calculation. In our small example we limit it to two elements. However, the strength of Cognos TM1 is that you can simply enhance this structure, for instance, by adding elements for assembly costs, setup costs, and so on.

The cost calculation per part simply needs two rules:

```
['SL Demand':'Costs']= N:IF( !SL Articles @= !SL Articles Child, STET,
DB('SL Demand 2', !SL Articles, !SL Articles Child, 'BOM',
ATTRS('SL Periods',!SL Periods,'Ref'),'Value')*
DB('SL Demand 2', !SL Articles Child, 'Total', 'Costs',
!SL Periods, !SL Types));

['Total Costs','SL Articles Child':'No Article']=N:
['SL Demand':'Costs','SL Articles Child':'Total']*['Demand','Value'];
```

And don't forget the feeders.

```
['BOM','Value']=>['SL Demand':'costs','SL Types':'costs','Year'];
['SL Demand':'Costs','SL Articles Child':'Total','SL Types':'Costs']=>
DB('SL Demand 2', !SL Articles, 'No Article', 'Total Costs', !SL Periods,
!SL Types);
```

We differentiate between cost per item and total costs (costs for the periodical demand). The costs of raw material are entered in the cells where the elements of "SL Articles" and "SL Articles Child" are identical, as shown in the following illustration:

Parts List	SL Types	SL Articles	A3	A4	A5	A6	A7	A8	A9	A10	NoArticle	+ Total
BOM	Value	A1	1	2	0	0	0	0	0	0	0	3
		A2	0	2	1	0	0	0	0	0	0	3
		A3	0	0	0	2	3	0	0	0	0	5
		A4	0	0	0	0	4	1	0	0	0	5
		A5	0	0	0	0	0	2	3	4	0	9
		+ Total	1	4	1	2	7	3	3	4	0	25
Costs	-- Costs	A1	120	330	0	0	0	0	0	0	0	450
		A2	0	330	240	0	0	0	0	0	0	570
		A3	0	0	0	30	90	0	0	0	0	120
		A4	0	0	0	0	120	45	0	0	0	165
		A5	0	0	0	0	0	90	90	60	0	240
		A6	0	0	0	15	0	0	0	0	0	15
		A7	0	0	0	0	30	0	0	0	0	30
		A8	0	0	0	0	0	45	0	0	0	45
		A9	0	0	0	0	0	0	30	0	0	30
		A10	0	0	0	0	0	0	0	15	0	15
		+ Total	120	660	240	45	240	180	120	75	0	1680
	Material Costs	A1	80	220	0	0	0	0	0	0	0	300
		A2	0	220	160	0	0	0	0	0	0	380
		A3	0	0	0	20	60	0	0	0	0	80
		A4	0	0	0	0	80	30	0	0	0	110
		A5	0	0	0	0	0	60	60	40	0	160
		A6	0	0	0	10	0	0	0	0	0	10
		A7	0	0	0	0	20	0	0	0	0	20
		A8	0	0	0	0	0	30	0	0	0	30
		A9	0	0	0	0	0	0	20	0	0	20
		A10	0	0	0	0	0	0	0	10	0	10
		+ Total	80	440	160	30	160	120	80	50	0	1120
	Material Overhead	A1	40	110	0	0	0	0	0	0	0	150
		A2	0	110	80	0	0	0	0	0	0	190
		A3	0	0	0	10	30	0	0	0	0	40
		A4	0	0	0	0	40	15	0	0	0	55
		A5	0	0	0	0	0	30	30	20	0	80
		A6	0	0	0	5	0	0	0	0	0	5
		A7	0	0	0	0	10	0	0	0	0	10
		A8	0	0	0	0	0	15	0	0	0	15
		A9	0	0	0	0	0	0	10	0	0	10
		A10	0	0	0	0	0	0	0	5	0	5

PART III

The element "total costs" shows the costs for the calculated demand:

SL Articles	total costs -- Costs	Material Costs	Material Overhead
A1	45000	30000	15000
A2	114000	76000	38000
A3	12000	8000	4000
A4	99000	66000	33000
A5	48000	32000	16000
A6	3000	2000	1000
A7	81000	54000	27000
A8	45000	30000	15000
A9	18000	12000	6000
A10	12000	8000	4000
+ Total	477000	318000	159000

Building a Bill of Material Structure

Until now we have been working with two flat article structures. However, a hierarchical representation of the bill of material is more intuitive. To use "drill-down" could also be a nice feature. The idea is to reference a hierarchical model to our data to combine the flexibility of the matrix model with a good analysis representation. We have all the information we need to generate this structure automatically. We create a cube per a different structure.

We define two dynamic data sets:

```
{ EXCEPT( {TM1FILTERBYLEVEL( {TM1SUBSETALL( [SL Articles] )}, 0)},
{ [SL Articles].[No Article] }) }
```

We do the same for the dimension "SL Articles Child." With these subsets we define the BOM view, as shown in the following illustration:

BOM	BOM	Value									
		Jan									
		A1	A2	A3	A4	A5	A6	A7	A8	A9	A10
BOM	A1	0.00	0.00	1.00	2.00	0.00	0.00	0.00	0.00	0.00	0.00
	A2	0.00	0.00	0.00	2.00	1.00	0.00	0.00	0.00	0.00	0.00
	A3	0.00	0.00	0.00	0.00	0.00	2.00	3.00	0.00	0.00	0.00
	A4	0.00	0.00	0.00	0.00	0.00	0.00	4.00	1.00	0.00	0.00
	A5	0.00	0.00	0.00	0.00	0.00	0.00	0.00	2.00	3.00	4.00
	A6	0.00	0.00	0.00	0.00	0.00	0.00	0.00	0.00	0.00	0.00
	A7	0.00	0.00	0.00	0.00	0.00	0.00	0.00	0.00	0.00	0.00
	A8	0.00	0.00	0.00	0.00	0.00	0.00	0.00	0.00	0.00	0.00
	A9	0.00	0.00	0.00	0.00	0.00	0.00	0.00	0.00	0.00	0.00
	A10	0.00	0.00	0.00	0.00	0.00	0.00	0.00	0.00	0.00	0.00

The process "SL CreateHierarchy" needs the period where the BOM is stored. In the Prolog section, we adjust the predefined BOM view:

```
NewView = 'BOM';
SubsetElementDelete('SL Periods', NewView, 1);
SubsetElementInsert('SL Periods', NewView, PScenario, 1);
IF(CubeExists('SL Hierarchy' | PScenario )=1);
CubeDestroy('SL Hierarchy' | PScenario);
ENDIF;
IF(DimensionExists('SL Hierarchy' | PScenario )=1);
DimensionDestroy('SL Hierarchy' | PScenario );
ENDIF;
DimensionCreate('SL Hierarchy' | PScenario);
CubeCreate('SL Hierarchy' | PScenario, 'SL Hierarchy' | PScenario,
'SL Types');
```

In the Metadata section we create the new dimension.

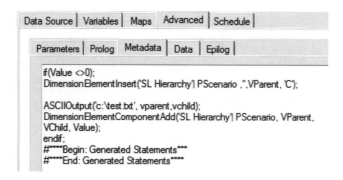

A subset can be easily created (in the Epilog section) with an MDX statement:

```
SubsetCreatebyMDX('BOM','HIERARCHIZE(TM1SUBSETALL([SL
Hierarchy'|PScenario|']))');
```

The result of the TI process looks like the following illustration:

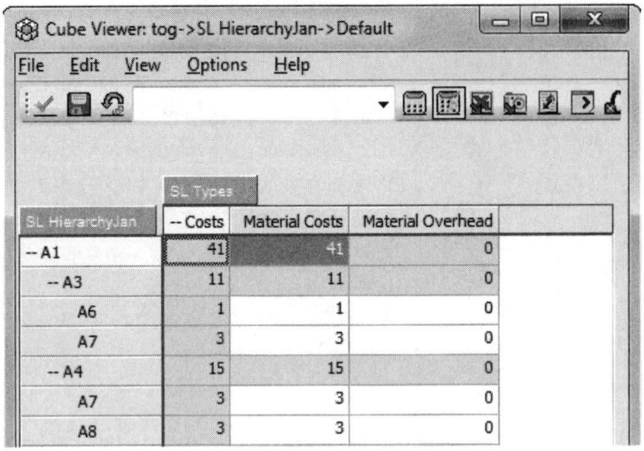

Working with Lead Times

But the world isn't that simple. We cannot assume that production starts in an instant when a primary demand occurs. To produce goods and subassemblies, you need setup time. Various demands have to be combined into production orders. Material must be ordered, to name some restrictions.

We want to introduce a simple enhancement. We define an attribute "Delay" in the BOM structure. Per BOM relation, we entered a number. In our example we only work with integers. Our planning scheme with months might be too rough. But feel free to extend the granularity. The following illustration shows the production delay. For instance, if you want to produce A2, you have to start one month earlier to produce A4 and two months earlier to produce A5.

| | | Parts List | | | | | | | | | |
	SL Demand	A1	A2	A3	A4	A5	A6	A7	A8	A9	A10
A1	BOM	0.00	0.00	1.00	2.00	0.00	0.00	0.00	0.00	0.00	0.00
	Delay	0.00	0.00	1.00	1.00	0.00	0.00	0.00	0.00	0.00	0.00
A2	BOM	0.00	0.00	0.00	2.00	1.00	0.00	0.00	0.00	0.00	0.00
	Delay	0.00	0.00	0.00	1.00	2.00	0.00	0.00	0.00	0.00	0.00
A3	BOM	0.00	0.00	0.00	0.00	0.00	2.00	3.00	0.00	0.00	0.00
	Delay	0.00	0.00	0.00	0.00	0.00	1.00	2.00	0.00	0.00	0.00
A4	BOM	0.00	0.00	0.00	0.00	0.00	0.00	4.00	1.00	0.00	0.00
	Delay	0.00	0.00	0.00	0.00	0.00	0.00	1.00	1.00	0.00	0.00
A5	BOM	0.00	0.00	0.00	0.00	0.00	0.00	0.00	2.00	3.00	4.00
	Delay	0.00	0.00	0.00	0.00	0.00	0.00	0.00	1.00	2.00	1.00
A6	BOM	0.00	0.00	0.00	0.00	0.00	0.00	0.00	0.00	0.00	0.00
	Delay	0.00	0.00	0.00	0.00	0.00	0.00	0.00	0.00	0.00	0.00
A7	BOM	0.00	0.00	0.00	0.00	0.00	0.00	0.00	0.00	0.00	0.00
	Delay	0.00	0.00	0.00	0.00	0.00	0.00	0.00	0.00	0.00	0.00
A8	BOM	0.00	0.00	0.00	0.00	0.00	0.00	0.00	0.00	0.00	0.00
	Delay	0.00	0.00	0.00	0.00	0.00	0.00	0.00	0.00	0.00	0.00
A9	BOM	0.00	0.00	0.00	0.00	0.00	0.00	0.00	0.00	0.00	0.00
	Delay	0.00	0.00	0.00	0.00	0.00	0.00	0.00	0.00	0.00	0.00
A10	BOM	0.00	0.00	0.00	0.00	0.00	0.00	0.00	0.00	0.00	0.00
	Delay	0.00	0.00	0.00	0.00	0.00	0.00	0.00	0.00	0.00	0.00

We need a delay function for the BOM explosion. We take the algorithm that we already discussed and enhance it by the delay part. Therefore we need a distance function in the time dimension, which is not available. In some other examples we worked with attributes like "previous" or "next." But this wouldn't work since we don't know the distance beforehand. So we have to use the function pair DIMIX and DIMN. The limitation is that we are responsible for the index order. A change in the period structure, that is, a new aggregation level, can destroy the calculation. However, there is no working alternative—at least for us—that we can use to avoid TI programming.

We only need to adapt the first rule. The key is to refer to a distance period. We get this result with this enhancement:

```
DIMNM('SL Periods',DIMIX('SL Periods',!SL Periods)+
DB('SL Demand 2', !SL Articles, !SL Articles Child, 'Delay',
ATTRS('SL Periods',!SL Periods,'Ref'),!
```

The whole algorithm looks like this:

```
# Time Differences

#2 Copy
['Secondary Demand Delay','SL Articles Child':'No Article']= N:
DB('SL Demand 2', 'Total', !SL Articles, !SL Demand, !SL Periods,
!SL Types);


#1 Multiply Demand with BOM
['Secondary Demand Delay']= N:
DB('SL Demand 2', !SL Articles, !SL Articles Child, 'BOM',
ATTRS('SL Periods',!SL Periods,'Ref'),!SL Types)
*DB('SL Demand 2', !SL Articles, 'NoArticle', 'Demand Delay',
DIMNM('SL Periods',dimix('SL Periods',!SL Periods)+
DB('SL Demand 2', !SL Articles, !SL Articles Child, 'Delay',
ATTRS('SL Periods',!SL Periods,'Ref'),!SL Types)), !SL Types);
```

The feeder must be adapted accordingly.

```
['SL Articles':'Total'] => DB('SL Demand 2', !SL Articles Child,
'No Article', !SL Demand, !SL Periods, !SL Types);
['BOM','Value']=>DB('SL Demand 2', !SL Articles, !SL Articles Child,
'Secondary Demand Delay', 'Year', !SL Types);
```

However, the feeder is not optimal. We have to feeder each period. But the result is motivating. With limited changes, we get our result.

Value

SL Demand	SL Articles	NoArticle					+ Total				
		Aug	Sep	Oct	Nov	Dec	Aug	Sep	Oct	Nov	Dec
-- Demand Delay	A1	0	0	0	0	100	0	0	0	300	0
	A2	0	0	0	0	200	0	0	200	400	0
	A3	0	0	0	100	0	0	300	200	0	0
	A4	0	0	0	600	0	0	0	3000	0	0
	A5	0	0	200	0	0	600	1200	0	0	0
	A6	0	0	200	0	0	0	0	0	0	0
	A7	0	300	2400	0	0	0	0	0	0	0
	A8	0	400	600	0	0	0	0	0	0	0
	A9	600	0	0	0	0	0	0	0	0	0
	A10	0	800	0	0	0	0	0	0	0	0
	+ Total	600	1500	3400	700	300	600	1500	3400	700	0
Primary Demand	A1	0	0	0	0	100	0	0	0	0	0
	A2	0	0	0	0	200	0	0	0	0	0
	A3	0	0	0	0	0	0	0	0	0	0
	A4	0	0	0	0	0	0	0	0	0	0
	A5	0	0	0	0	0	0	0	0	0	0
	A6	0	0	0	0	0	0	0	0	0	0
	A7	0	0	0	0	0	0	0	0	0	0
	A8	0	0	0	0	0	0	0	0	0	0
	A9	0	0	0	0	0	0	0	0	0	0
	A10	0	0	0	0	0	0	0	0	0	0
	+ Total	0	0	0	0	300	0	0	0	0	0
Secondary Demand Delay	A1	0	0	0	0	0	0	0	0	300	0
	A2	0	0	0	0	0	0	0	200	400	0
	A3	0	0	0	100	0	0	300	200	0	0
	A4	0	0	0	600	0	0	0	3000	0	0
	A5	0	0	200	0	0	600	1200	0	0	0
	A6	0	0	200	0	0	0	0	0	0	0
	A7	0	300	2400	0	0	0	0	0	0	0
	A8	0	400	600	0	0	0	0	0	0	0
	A9	600	0	0	0	0	0	0	0	0	0
	A10	0	800	0	0	0	0	0	0	0	0
	+ Total	600	1500	3400	700	0	600	1500	3400	700	0

SL Articles Child   SL Periods

PART III

Let's check whether Cognos TM1 calculates correctly: Take A9 as an example. It is required from A5 with a delay of 3. A5 is required of A2 with a delay of 1. Hence A9 must be produced in August to fulfill an A2 request in December, which is correctly represented.

Here's a more complicated example: A7 is required (3) of A3 with a delay of 2 and is required of A4 with a delay of 1:

A3 is required of A1 with a delay of 1.
And of A2 with a delay of 1.

Check it yourself. But don't be too optimistic. There are still a lot of limitations. Some necessary enhancements are

- Month seems to be too rough. The day level would be appropriate.
- We neglect the batch size building.
- We don't consider purchasing or inventory constraints.
- We neglect the available inventory.
- We don't consider BOM alternatives or construction versions.
- We don't discuss planning levels. We have short-term and mid-term planning (and sometimes even more levels).

As a result, for very complex elements, we still recommend dedicated tools.

Routing and Capacity Planning

Material planning is only half of the planning process. We also need to understand how much capacity is needed to produce the parts. Given this delay, we now are able to calculate capacity restraints. What are typical constraints?

- Machines
- Materials
- Workers
- Also financing and purchasing can be constraints.

We define a cube for the routings:

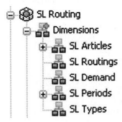

A new dimension, "SL routing," contains the routings (that is, melding, quality check, and so on):

We need a matrix to store the resource demand:

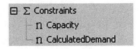

SL Articles	R1	R2	R3	R4
A1	30	20	0	0
A2	0	30	0	20
A3	0	20	0	0
A4	0	0	20	20
A5	20	0	20	0
A6	0	20	0	0
A7	0	0	0	0
A8	0	0	0	0
A9	0	0	0	0
A10	0	0	0	0

For the constraint calculation, we enhanced the dimension "SL Demand" slightly:

"Capacity" is weighted by –1. The capacity is entered manually per period. We only need a simple rule for the capacity calculation:

```
['CalculatedDemand']=N:DB('SL Demand 2', !SL Articles,'NoArticle' ,
'Demand Delay', !SL Periods, !SL Types)* ['ResourceNeeded','Jan'];
```

	Value ⌄ All ⌄												
	SL Demand		SL Routings										
	-- Constraints				Capacity				CalculatedDemand				
SL Periods	R1	R2	R3	R4	R1	R2	R3	R4	R1		R2	R3	R4
Jan	2000	6500	-1000	2600	1000	1500	1000	1400		3000	8000	0	4000
Feb	-1000	-1500	-1000	-1400	1000	1500	1000	1400		0	0	0	0
Mar	-1000	-1500	-1000	-1400	1000	1500	1000	1400		0	0	0	0
Apr	-1000	-1500	-1000	-1400	1000	1500	1000	1400		0	0	0	0
May	-1000	-1500	-1000	-1400	1000	1500	1000	1400		0	0	0	0
Jun	-1000	-1500	-1000	-1400	1000	1500	1000	1400		0	0	0	0
Jul	-1000	-1500	-1000	-1400	1000	1500	1000	1400		0	0	0	0
Aug	-1000	-1500	-1000	-1400	1000	1500	1000	1400		0	0	0	0
Sep	-1000	-1500	-1000	-1400	1000	1500	1000	1400		0	0	0	0
Oct	-1000	-1500	-1000	-1400	1000	1500	1000	1400		0	0	0	0
Nov	-1000	500	11000	10600	1000	1500	1000	1400		0	2000	12000	12000
Dec	2000	6500	-1000	2600	1000	1500	1000	1400		3000	8000	0	4000

As you can see, in December and November we have massive capacity problems. There are several aspects missing in our small model:

- What to do if capacity constraints occur?
- Are there alternative production processes?
- and so on

Product Calculation with BOM and Routing

We now want to turn to a larger calculation problem where we can use Cognos TM1 effectively. We created a scenario where we include order costing, target costing, and inventory management. With target costing, our calculation will change from a bottom-up calculation to a top-down calculation. Figure 18-3 shows the data model.

As we already discussed, the hierarchical structures of Cognos TM1 are not always appropriate for production calculation. In some industries even cycles within the BOM are possible (in the chemical industry, for example). A matrix calculation is more flexible.

Let's start with our example. We have a bicycle and we want to calculate the overall costs. Typically we need more than the overall costs. A typical requirement is to transfer the

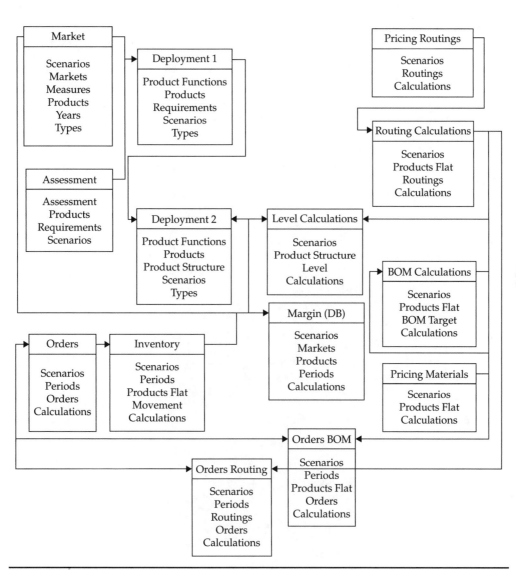

FIGURE 18-3   The big picture

primary cost structure to the final assembly goods when we use the BOM to calculate the
total costs. We want to have cost information for the following cost types:

- Material
- Material overhead costs
- Production
- Production overhead

We defined the following cube:

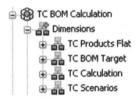

The most interesting part of this cube is the calculation dimension, as shown in the following illustration:

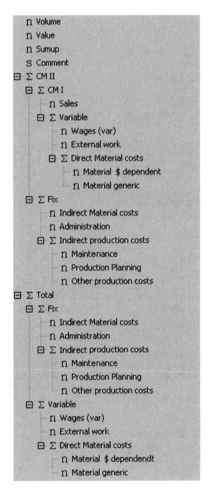

Part of this definition is the valuation vector below "Total." We use a valuation vector instead of a single price value. The vector contains granular price components. Each element that this vector contains is part of the total price. The more granularly we define this vector, the more detailed later analysis can be. As you can see, we also create a margin calculation (Sales minus costs), using elements of the valuation vector.

First we enter the BOM structure into the cube "TC BOM Calculation," as shown in the following illustration. To keep the example simple, we don't use time-dependent product structures.

		TC Calculation		
TC BOM Target	TC Products Flat	Volume	-- Total	+ Variable
City Bike	Main group	1	0.00	0.00
	Drive unit	1	50.00	50.00
	Brake system	1	170.00	170.00
	spare units	1	0.00	0.00
Main Group	handlebar	1	80.00	80.00
	Plates	3	165.00	165.00
	Accessories	1	40.00	40.00
	Rack	1	120.00	120.00
	Fitting	1	55.00	55.00
	Gear shift	1	140.00	140.00
	Frame	1	0.00	0.00
Frame	Aluminium frame	3	540.00	540.00
	Bottom bracket	1	90.00	90.00

Plan

The two last columns already contain the calculation. We assume that all material costs are variable. Material overhead costs can be calculated with a simple allocation rule.

The calculation is done by multiplying the needed amount by a price vector. Changes in the calculation vectors are immediately visible:

```
[]=N:IF(!TC Calculation @= 'Volume',CONTINUE, ['Amount']*
DB('TC Pricing Materials V3', !TC Calculation,!TC Products Flat,
!TC Scenarios));
```

We have the production structure defined within the cube shown in the following illustration:

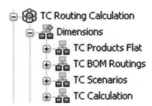

We simply enter the resource demand per part:

TC Products Flat	TC BOM Routings	Volume	-- Total	+ Fix	+ Variable
Main group	Final Assembly	45	108.00	49.50	58.50
Main group	Assemble AddOn Parts	30	33.00	0.00	33.00
City Bike	Final Check	1	40.00	40.00	0.00
City Bike	Prepare Shipping	25	85.00	0.00	85.00
Frame	Weld Frame	20	70.00	26.00	44.00
HB drive	Final Assembly	15	36.00	16.50	19.50

Here we have variable and fixed valuation parts. The calculation looks like this:

```
[]=N:IF(!TC Calculation @='VOLUME',CONTINUE,['Amount']*
DB('TC Pricing Routings V2', !TC BOM Routings, !TC Calculation,
!TC Scenarios));
```

The valuation of Routing and BOM calculation is done through the use of two price cubes. The material price cube should be filled by the purchasing department. The routing prices are delivered by cost center planning (see Chapter 17).

TC Pricing Materials V3
  Dimensions
    TC Calculation
    TC Products Flat
    TC Scenarios

TC Pricing Routings V2
  Dimensions
    TC BOM Routings
    TC Calculation
    TC Scenarios

Let's take a look at the valuation vector (as part of the dimension "TC Calculation"). It is important to understand that this structure is used throughout the whole system. We split up between fixed and variable costs. You can see right away that material costs are split up into a common part and a dollar-related part. This is a common requirement to analyze what cost effect a currency rate change will have on specific products. Products with a higher percentage of dollar-related parts will react more intensively to currency rate variations and thus may be inefficient to produce due to high currency rates.

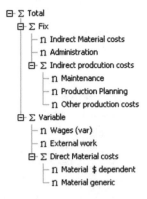

Σ Total
  Σ Fix
    n Indirect Material costs
    n Administration
    Σ Indirect prodcution costs
      n Maintenance
      n Production Planning
      n Other production costs
  Σ Variable
    n Wages (var)
    n External work
    Σ Direct Material costs
      n Material $ dependent
      n Material generic

This vector can be quickly adapted by the business experts. Using a flexible OLAP approach enables you to enhance it even to a valuation matrix or a valuation cube. Why would this be interesting to do? Some examples:

- Intercompany elements (we will discuss later in Chapter 23)
- More granular split between fixed and variable. For instance, if you want to split the variables into "variable within 3 months," variable within 6 months," and so forth.

With this information we can create the product calculation. We define a cube to bring part costing and routing costing together, as shown in the following illustration:

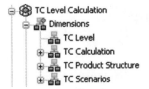

We define an additional dimension, "TC Level," to capture the costs per BOM level:

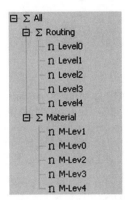

Furthermore, we use a Cognos TM1 hierarchy to represent the BOM, as shown in the following illustration. We discussed how to generate this out of the matrix in this chapter.

This gives us the chance to calculate level by level. With this preparation work completed, we are now able to create the plan calculation, as shown in the following illustration.

TC Product Structure	-- All			+ Routing			+ Material		
	-- Total	+ Fix	+ Variable	-- Total	+ Fix	+ Variable	-- Total	+ Fix	+ Variable
-- City Bike	1,736.00	115.50	1,620.50	336.00	115.50	220.50	1,400.00	0.00	1,400.00
-- Main Group	1,441.00	75.50	1,365.50	211.00	75.50	135.50	1,230.00	0.00	1,230.00
-- Frame	700.00	26.00	674.00	70.00	26.00	44.00	630.00	0.00	630.00
Bottom Bracket	90.00	0.00	90.00	0.00	0.00	0.00	90.00	0.00	90.00
Aluminium Frame	540.00	0.00	540.00	0.00	0.00	0.00	540.00	0.00	540.00
Handlebar	80.00	0.00	80.00	0.00	0.00	0.00	80.00	0.00	80.00
Plates	165.00	0.00	165.00	0.00	0.00	0.00	165.00	0.00	165.00
Accessories	40.00	0.00	40.00	0.00	0.00	0.00	40.00	0.00	40.00
Rack	120.00	0.00	120.00	0.00	0.00	0.00	120.00	0.00	120.00
Fitting	55.00	0.00	55.00	0.00	0.00	0.00	55.00	0.00	55.00
Gear Shift	140.00	0.00	140.00	0.00	0.00	0.00	140.00	0.00	140.00
Drive Unit	50.00	0.00	50.00	0.00	0.00	0.00	50.00	0.00	50.00
Brake System	120.00	0.00	120.00	0.00	0.00	0.00	120.00	0.00	120.00
Spare Units	0.00	0.00	0.00	0.00	0.00	0.00	0.00	0.00	0.00

As you can see, we have a typical OLAP aggregation with an interesting effect: the rules "overrule" the aggregation. Look at the product "City Bike" and the level element "Routing." The routings are assigned directly to the City bike. The costs follow: The total costs are higher than the simple aggregation. This is exactly what we want to have.

One nice feature is the drill-down capability. We can use drill-down to get details for the cost types and also for the levels.

TC Product Structure	-- All	-- Routing	Level0	Level1	Level2	Level3	Level4	-- Material	M-Lev1	M-Lev0	M-Lev2	M-Lev3	M-Lev4
	+ Total	+ Total	+ Total	+ Total	+ Total	+ Total	+ Total	+ Total	+ Total	+ Total	+ Total	+ Total	+ Total
-- City Bike	1,736.00	336.00	0.00	70.00	141.00	125.00	0.00	1,400.00	630.00	0.00	600.00	170.00	0.00
-- Main Group	1,441.00	211.00	0.00	70.00	141.00	0.00	0.00	1,230.00	630.00	0.00	600.00	0.00	0.00
-- Frame	700.00	70.00	0.00	70.00	0.00	0.00	0.00	630.00	630.00	0.00	0.00	0.00	0.00
Bottom Bracket	90.00	0.00	0.00	0.00	0.00	0.00	0.00	90.00	0.00	90.00	0.00	0.00	0.00
Aluminium Frame	540.00	0.00	0.00	0.00	0.00	0.00	0.00	540.00	0.00	540.00	0.00	0.00	0.00
Handlebar	80.00	0.00	0.00	0.00	0.00	0.00	0.00	80.00	0.00	80.00	0.00	0.00	0.00
Plates	165.00	0.00	0.00	0.00	0.00	0.00	0.00	165.00	0.00	165.00	0.00	0.00	0.00
Accessories	40.00	0.00	0.00	0.00	0.00	0.00	0.00	40.00	0.00	40.00	0.00	0.00	0.00
Rack	120.00	0.00	0.00	0.00	0.00	0.00	0.00	120.00	0.00	120.00	0.00	0.00	0.00
Fitting	55.00	0.00	0.00	0.00	0.00	0.00	0.00	55.00	0.00	55.00	0.00	0.00	0.00
Gear Shift	140.00	0.00	0.00	0.00	0.00	0.00	0.00	140.00	0.00	140.00	0.00	0.00	0.00
Drive Unit	50.00	0.00	0.00	0.00	0.00	0.00	0.00	50.00	0.00	50.00	0.00	0.00	0.00
Brake System	120.00	0.00	0.00	0.00	0.00	0.00	0.00	120.00	0.00	120.00	0.00	0.00	0.00
Spare Units	0.00	0.00	0.00	0.00	0.00	0.00	0.00	0.00	0.00	0.00	0.00	0.00	0.00

Let's look at how the calculation works. To make the calculation more flexible, we use "CONSOLIDATECHILDREN." On the one hand, this gives us more flexibility. On the other hand, be aware that this calculation might not be very efficient.

```
SKIPCHECK;
['TC Level':'All']= CONSOLIDATECHILDREN ('TC Level');
['Routing']= CONSOLIDATECHILDREN ('TC Level');
['Material']= CONSOLIDATECHILDREN ('TC Level');
['Level0']=IF( ELLEV('TC Product Structure', !TC Product Structure)=0 ,
DB('TC Routing Calculation', !TC Product Structure, 'All', !TC Scenarios,
!TC Calculation), CONSOLIDATECHILDREN ('TC Product Structure'));
['Level1']=IF( ELLEV('TC Product Structure', !TC Product Structure)=1,
DB('TC Routing Calculation', !TC Product Structure, 'All', !TC Scenarios,
!TC Calculation), CONSOLIDATECHILDREN ('TC Product Structure'));
['Level2']=IF( ELLEV('TC Product Structure', !TC Product Structure)=2,
DB('TC Routing Calculation', !TC Product Structure, 'All', !TC Scenarios,
!TC Calculation), CONSOLIDATECHILDREN ('TC Product Structure'));
['Level3']=IF( ELLEV('TC Product Structure', !TC Product Structure)=3,
DB('TC Routing Calculation', !TC Product Structure, 'All', !TC Scenarios,
!TC Calculation), CONSOLIDATECHILDREN ('TC Product Structure'));

['M-Lev0']=IF( ELLEV('TC Product Structure', !TC Product Structure)=0 ,
DB('TC BOM Calculation', !TC Product Structure, 'All',  !TC Calculation,
!TC Scenarios),0);
['M-Lev1']=IF( ELLEV('TC Product Structure', !TC Product Structure)=1,
DB('TC BOM Calculation', 'all', !TC Product Structure,!TC Calculation,
!TC Scenarios), CONSOLIDATECHILDREN ('TC Product Structure'));
['M-Lev2']=IF( ELLEV('TC Product Structure', !TC Product Structure)=2,
DB('TC BOM Calculation', 'all',!TC Product Structure,  !TC Calculation,
!TC Scenarios), CONSOLIDATECHILDREN ('TC Product Structure'));
['M-Lev3']=IF( ELLEV('TC Product Structure', !TC Product Structure)=3,
DB('TC BOM Calculation','All', !TC Product Structure,  !TC Calculation,
!TC Scenarios), CONSOLIDATECHILDREN ('TC Product Structure'));

FEEDERS;
['Total','TC Level':'All']=>DB('TC Deployment 2', 'Basis',
!TC Product Structure,
'City Bike', !TC Scenarios, 'Standard Costs');
```

Production Costing

We already described several production structures. However, we have always been in a planning mode. But we must calculate the actual costs, too. This is not the same because accounting is somewhat different from planning. This is different because the BOM is not relevant, but the actual production order structure, which can vary from the planned structure for various reasons like unavailability of parts, cheaper prices of alternatives, and so on, is relevant.

This can be called *order calculation*, and it is also possible with Cognos TM1. However. it can be quite complex because such a calculation should reveal several variances. And in addition, it should be the link between production costing and profitability analyses.

We will refer to our simple example. We produce goods in series and use production order. This is not a must, but it is kind of an industry standard. Our first cube represents the result of our efforts: the profitability calculation.

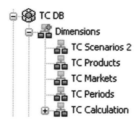

We use the already introduced dimension "TC Calculation" to create the profitability calculation. The following illustration shows a typical analysis.

City Bike ▾   Germany ▾

TC Calculation	-- Year		Jan		Feb		Mar	
	Plan	Actuals	Plan	Actuals	Plan	Actuals	Plan	Actuals
Volume	360	357	30	28	30	31	30	31
Sales	635,040.00	606,900.00	52,920.00	47,600.00	52,920.00	52,700.00	52,920.00	52,700.00
Material $ dependent	10,800.00	0.00	900.00	0.00	900.00	0.00	900.00	0.00
Material generic	493,200.00	612,481.48	41,100.00	48,037.76	41,100.00	53,184.67	41,100.00	53,184.67
+ Direct material costs	504,000.00	612,481.48	42,000.00	48,037.76	42,000.00	53,184.67	42,000.00	53,184.67
Wages (var)	59,580.00	61,885.36	4,965.00	4,853.75	4,965.00	5,373.80	4,965.00	5,373.80
External work	19,800.00	24,266.35	1,650.00	1,903.24	1,650.00	2,107.16	1,650.00	2,107.16
+ Variable	583,380.00	698,633.19	48,615.00	54,794.76	48,615.00	60,665.63	48,615.00	60,665.63
-- CM I	51,660.00	(91,733.19)	4,305.00	(7,194.76)	4,305.00	(7,965.63)	4,305.00	(7,965.63)
Sales	635,040.00	606,900.00	52,920.00	47,600.00	52,920.00	52,700.00	52,920.00	52,700.00
+ Variable	583,380.00	698,633.19	48,615.00	54,794.76	48,615.00	60,665.63	48,615.00	60,665.63
+ Indirect production costs	41,580.00	42,127.07	3,465.00	3,304.08	3,465.00	3,658.09	3,465.00	3,658.09
Indirect material costs	0.00	0.00	0.00	0.00	0.00	0.00	0.00	0.00
Administration	0.00	0.00	0.00	0.00	0.00	0.00	0.00	0.00
+ Fix	41,580.00	42,127.07	3,465.00	3,304.08	3,465.00	3,658.09	3,465.00	3,658.09
+ CM II	10,080.00	(133,860.26)	840.00	(10,498.84)	840.00	(11,623.72)	840.00	(11,623.72)

The profitability analysis without reconciliation with inventory is very typical for OLAP tools. This makes sense because it is very easy and you don't need many details about costing. The top focus usually is the sales numbers, which are valuated by sales prices and costs. Additionally, discounts can be assigned. Sometimes statistical numbers like interest are included.

The sales prices are retrieved from a market cube:

```
['Sales']=N:DB('TC Market V2', !TC Scenarios 2, !TC Markets, 'Price',
!TC Products, '2009', 'Local')*['Volume'];
```

Actual costs can be calculated by the moving average of the stock (we will introduce the inventory calculation later):

```
['Actuals']=N:IF(!TC Calculation @= 'Volume',CONTINUE,
DB('TC Inventory V3', !TC Periods, 'Out', !TC Products, !TC Calculation,
!TC Scenarios 2)\
DB('TC Inventory V3', !TC Periods, 'Out', !TC Products, 'Volume',
!TC Scenarios 2)*['Volume']);
```

Plan costs can be derived from the plan calculation:

```
['Plan']=N:IF(!TC Calculation @= 'Amount',CONTINUE,
DB('TC Level Calculation', 'All', !TC Calculation, !TC Products,
!TC Scenarios 2)
*['Volume']);
```

This doesn't look very complicated. However, a lot of preparation work is necessary, particularly to calculate the actual. The inventory valuation, for instance, needs production orders. Production orders are valuated by using the bill of material. An order consists of material according to the BOM and the assigned routing. We show a high-level calculation.

In the actual, we take the completion messages, which are identical with the inventory access.

It is important to keep the formulas as generic as possible. Changes in the primary parts should not result in a change of the calculation rules. Even if you think about using an additional dimension, the changes should be minor.

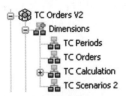

Let's take a look at the "TC Orders" definition: The orders are sequentially numbered. Each order has a product or part as output and thus can be aggregated accordingly:

With this cube we can do an order calculation. We get the planned costs simply by multiplying the planned volume (directly entered) by the valuation vector of the plan calculation per part:

TC Calculation	Plan	Actuals
Volume	40	38
-- Total	69,440.00	80,646.94
-- Fix	4,620.00	4,332.22
-- Indirect production costs	4,620.00	4,332.22
Maintenance	240.00	253.33
Production planning	2,780.00	2,878.89
Other production costs	1,600.00	1,200.00
-- Variable	64,820.00	76,314.72
Wages (var)	6,620.00	6,827.78
External work	2,200.00	2,530.00
-- Direct material costs	56,000.00	66,956.94
Material $ dependent	1,200.00	0.00
Material generic	54,800.00	66,956.94

The plan values of the order are taken from product calculation. This isn't problematic because orders are assigned to a subassembly or a final product. Actual data will be collected directly or imported from ERP or shop floor management tools.

The Orders BOM looks like this:

TC Calculation	Plan -- All	Main group	Drive unit	Brake system	Actuals -- All	Main group
-- Total	64,440.00	57,640.00	2,000.00	4,800.00	75,486.94	75,486.94
-- Fix	3,020.00	3,020.00	0.00	0.00	3,132.22	3,132.22
-- Indirect production costs	3,020.00	3,020.00	0.00	0.00	3,132.22	3,132.22
Maintenance	240.00	240.00	0.00	0.00	253.33	253.33
Production planning	2,780.00	2,780.00	0.00	0.00	2,878.89	2,878.89
-- Variable	61,420.00	54,620.00	2,000.00	4,800.00	72,354.72	72,354.72
Wages (var)	5,420.00	5,420.00	0.00	0.00	5,397.78	5,397.78
-- Direct material costs	56,000.00	49,200.00	2,000.00	4,800.00	66,956.94	66,956.94
Material $ dependent	1,200.00	0.00	1,200.00	0.00	0.00	0.00
Material generic	54,800.00	49,200.00	800.00	4,800.00	66,956.94	66,956.94

```
SKIPCHECK;
['Plan']=N:IF (!TC Calculation @= 'Volume',DB('TC Orders V2', !TC Periods,
!TC Orders,!TC Calculation, !TC Scenarios 2)*
DB('TC BOM Calculation', !TC Products Flat, ELPAR('TC Orders',
!TC Orders,1),
!TC Calculation, !TC Scenarios 2), ['Volume']*
DB('TC Level Calculation', 'All', !TC Calculation, !TC Products Flat,
!TC Scenarios 2));

['Actuals']=N:IF(!TC Calculation @= 'Volume',CONTINUE,
IF (['Amount'] <> 0,['Volume']*DB('TC Inventory V3',
!TC Periods, 'Opening + Input', !TC Products Flat, !TC Calculation,
!TC Scenarios 2)\
DB('TC Inventory V3', !TC Periods, 'Opening + Input', !TC Products Flat,
'Volume', !TC Scenarios 2), CONTINUE));

FEEDERS;
['Volume']=>['Total'];
```

This is a practical way to implement production costing. It is a lean model to implement major requirements. However, there are a lot of possibilities for enhancing the model:

- Valuation for scrap
- Direct cost tracking from order to order
- Multiperiod spanning orders with short-term valuation
- Usage order
- Work-in-progress valuation

Inventory Valuation

Cost calculations are not always limited to a certain period. A typical requirement is to use costs for inventory valuation. If you want a closed-loop costing system, it is necessary to link costing with inventory.

Again, if this is sufficiently covered by your ERP system, it is fine. There are some strengths like near-time valuation; all data is available.

However, if you need more flexible calculation and analysis, think about using Cognos TM1. You should also consider Cognos TM1 if the structures change often so that you have to adapt the primary parts. We will refer to a specific calculation for group costing in Chapter 23.

Inventory management systems are really complex systems that cover various tasks. This leads to high complexity and to limited flexibility. Thus they often have limitations when it comes to valuation. If you have to change your method of valuation, you need more flexibility.

An important aspect is how to handle transactions level. For valuation methods like LIFO, HIFO, it is sometimes necessary to look at the single transaction. With Cognos TM1 it makes sense to work on an aggregate level. This can be based on averages.

You have to decide which advances are more important. Experience shows that in most cases, averages are sufficient. And it is also possible to allocate potential variances later in the period end.

Reconciliation with a closed profit calculation is easy with the available data. Inventory values are stored for raw material, groups, and finished goods. Please be aware that we don't differentiate between these product types.

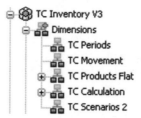

The Movement dimension is important:

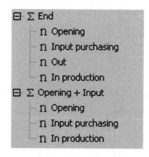

The volume elements can be imported from an inventory ledger. In our example we linked it to our production costing system:

TC Products Flat	TC Movement	Jan	Feb	Mar	Apr	May	Jun	Jul	Aug	Sep	Oct	Nov	Dec
Aluminium frame	Opening	300	10	50	50	50	50	50	50	50	50	50	50
	Input purchasing	20	40	0	0	0	0	0	0	0	0	0	0
	Out	310	0	0	0	0	0	0	0	0	0	0	0
	+ End	10	50	50	50	50	50	50	50	50	50	50	50
Handlebar	Opening	100	20	20	20	20	20	20	20	20	20	20	20
	Out	80	0	0	0	0	0	0	0	0	0	0	0
	+ End	20	20	20	20	20	20	20	20	20	20	20	20
Plates	Opening	0	750	750	750	750	750	750	750	750	750	750	750
	Input purchasing	1.000	0	0	0	0	0	0	0	0	0	0	0
	Out	250	0	0	0	0	0	0	0	0	0	0	0
	+ End	750	750	750	750	750	750	750	750	750	750	750	750
Accessories	Opening	0	20	20	20	20	20	20	20	20	20	20	20
	Input purchasing	100	0	0	0	0	0	0	0	0	0	0	0
	Out	80	0	0	0	0	0	0	0	0	0	0	0
	+ End	20	20	20	20	20	20	20	20	20	20	20	20
Rack	Opening	0	20	20	20	20	20	20	20	20	20	20	20
	Input purchasing	100	0	0	0	0	0	0	0	0	0	0	0
	Out	80	0	0	0	0	0	0	0	0	0	0	0
	+ End	20	20	20	20	20	20	20	20	20	20	20	20

Let's now discuss the inventory valuation. The objective is that all movements are valuated with a standardized granularity, which is centrally defined in the dimension "TC Calculation." This vector is identical with the calc structure of the plan calculation. You can easily change this vector by adding or removing an item.

We start with the usual carryover rule (for January, we simply imported the data):

```
['Opening','Jan']=N:STET;
['Opening']=N:DB('TC Inventory V3', DIMNM('TC Periods',
DIMIX('TC Periods',!TC Periods)-1), 'End', !TC Products Flat,
!TC Calculation, !TC Scenarios 2);
```

The inventory valuation uses two formulas. We take the completed items and the valuation vector from the order calculation.

For raw material we enter this vector manually. So we only need a rule to link production costing with inventory:

```
['In Production']=N:DB('TC Orders V2', !TC Periods,
!TC Products Flat, !TC Calculation, !TC Scenarios 2);
```

The "Out" number can be taken from sales or from order calculation. The valuation takes place in the third formula to simplify average costs. Other valuation methods are possible. We simply take the Input and the Opening stock to define the allocation base:

```
['Out']=N: IF(!TC Calculation @= 'Amount',DB('TC Orders BOM 2', 'All',
!TC Periods, !TC Products Flat, !TC Calculation, 'Actuals')+ DB('TC DB',
!TC Scenarios 2, !TC Products Flat, 'All', !TC Periods,
!TC Calculation),['Opening + Input']\['Opening + Input','Amount']*['Amount']);
```

City Bike

TC Calculation	TC Movement	Jan Actuals	per item	Feb Actuals	per item	Mar Actuals	per item	Apr Actuals	per item
Volume	Opening	36	1	46	1	15	1	(16)	1
	In production	38	1	0	0	0	0	0	0
	Out	28	1	31	1	31	1	29	1
	+ End	46	1	15	1	(16)	1	(45)	1
-- Total	Opening	72,900.00	2,025.00	95,448.10	2,074.96	31,124.38	2,074.96	(33,199.34)	2,074.96
	In production	80,646.94	2,122.29	0.00	0.00	0.00	0.00	0.00	0.00
	Out	58,098.84	2,074.96	64,323.72	2,074.96	64,323.72	2,074.96	60,173.80	2,074.96
	+ End	95,448.10	2,074.96	31,124.38	2,074.96	(33,199.34)	2,074.96	(93,373.14)	2,074.96
+ Fix	Opening	4,400.00	122.22	5,428.14	118.00	1,770.05	118.00	(1,888.05)	118.00
	In production	4,332.22	114.01	0.00	0.00	0.00	0.00	0.00	0.00
	Out	3,304.08	118.00	3,658.09	118.00	3,658.09	118.00	3,422.09	118.00
	+ End	5,428.14	118.00	1,770.05	118.00	(1,888.05)	118.00	(5,310.14)	118.00
-- Variable	Opening	68,500.00	1,902.78	90,019.96	1,956.96	29,354.34	1,956.96	(31,311.29)	1,956.96
	In production	76,314.72	2,008.28	0.00	0.00	0.00	0.00	0.00	0.00
	Out	54,794.76	1,956.96	60,665.63	1,956.96	60,665.63	1,956.96	56,751.72	1,956.96
	+ End	90,019.96	1,956.96	29,354.34	1,956.96	(31,311.29)	1,956.96	(88,063.01)	1,956.96
Wages (var)	Opening	6,000.00	166.67	7,974.02	173.35	2,600.23	173.35	(2,773.57)	173.35
	In production	6,827.78	179.68	0.00	0.00	0.00	0.00	0.00	0.00
	Out	4,853.75	173.35	5,373.80	173.35	5,373.80	173.35	5,027.10	173.35
	+ End	7,974.02	173.35	2,600.23	173.35	(2,773.57)	173.35	(7,800.68)	173.35
External work	Opening	2,500.00	69.44	3,126.76	67.97	1,019.59	67.97	(1,087.57)	67.97
	In production	2,530.00	66.58	0.00	0.00	0.00	0.00	0.00	0.00
	Out	1,903.24	67.97	2,107.16	67.97	2,107.16	67.97	1,971.22	67.97
	+ End	3,126.76	67.97	1,019.59	67.97	(1,087.57)	67.97	(3,058.78)	67.97
-- Direct material costs	Opening	60,000.00	1,666.67	78,919.18	1,715.63	25,734.52	1,715.63	(27,450.15)	1,715.63
	In production	66,956.94	1,762.02	0.00	0.00	0.00	0.00	0.00	0.00
	Out	48,037.76	1,715.63	53,184.67	1,715.63	53,184.67	1,715.63	49,753.40	1,715.63
	+ End	78,919.18	1,715.63	25,734.52	1,715.63	(27,450.15)	1,715.63	(77,203.55)	1,715.63
Material generic	Opening	60,000.00	1,666.67	78,919.18	1,715.63	25,734.52	1,715.63	(27,450.15)	1,715.63
	In production	66,956.94	1,762.02	0.00	0.00	0.00	0.00	0.00	0.00
	Out	48,037.76	1,715.63	53,184.67	1,715.63	53,184.67	1,715.63	49,753.40	1,715.63
	+ End	78,919.18	1,715.63	25,734.52	1,715.63	(27,450.15)	1,715.63	(77,203.55)	1,715.63

Top-Down-Oriented Target Costing

Target costing is a good example of the need to have more flexible cost management systems. We don't want to go too deep into the technique of target costing. The basics are simple: Instead of doing a bottom-up calculation, you start with allowed costs. These costs are based on the external market view—what the market is willing to pay for a product instead of what a product will cost.

The calculation of the allowed costs is simple—on the top level. The challenge is to disaggregate these costs to the detailed level of a product structure. Take a bicycle as an example. The possible market price can be derived from market analysis, competitor analysis, and so on. But when you break it down to subassemblies or raw material, this question is harder to answer. What is a potential customer willing to pay for the brackets, the wheels, the saddle? The purpose of target costing is to provide meaningful data for this question.

Again the question, why should we use Cognos TM1 and not ERP or specific tools? Although some ERP systems provide solutions, in most cases more flexibility is needed. That is the reason why such calculations are done externally and mostly—not really surprising—with Excel. Dedicated packaged software is rarely available. In other words, these situations are the perfect ground for Cognos TM1. We see some additional arguments:

- It is very often used parallel to construction. This means that the structure must be flexible. Simulations of structure changes should be possible.

- It is not stable from a methodical point of view. The disaggregation of customer requirements into functional groups can be done via several methods.

We created a prototype that can handle the main requirements of target costing. It is part of a complete cost calculation, which has been already explained.

The starting point is a planning model that shows a business plan for multiple years. This is the cube with the necessary dimensions:

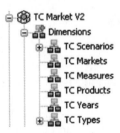

Usually the calculation starts with a targeted margin. With this a backward calculation of the so-called allowed costs is necessary:

```
['Sales']=N:['Volume']*['Price'];
['Price']=N:STET;C:['Sales']\['Volume'];
['Margin']=N: STET;c:(['Sales']-['Allowed Costs'])\['Sales']*100;
```

The allowed costs can be simply derived from sales and the requested margin:

```
['Allowed Costs']=N:['Sales']*(100-['Margin'])/100;
['Allowed Costs per Item']=['Allowed Costs']\['Volume'];
```

				Sales Planning Results			

		Deployment					

TC Scenarios							
Target							
TC Products							
City Bike							

Year	Organisation	Volume	Price	Sales	Margin	Allowed costs	Allowed costs per item
- All	- All	155,000	1,892.70	293,368,000	12.00	258,163,840	1,665.57
	- GAS	55,000	1,579.42	86,868,000	12.00	76,443,840	1,390
	Germany	37,000	1,764.00	65,268,000	12.00	57,435,840	1,552.32
	Austria	0	0.00	0	0.00	0	0.00
	Switzerland	18,000	1,200.00	21,600,000	12.00	19,008,000	1,056.00
	- Europe	100,000	2,065.00	206,500,000	12.00	181,720,000	1,817
	France	0	0.00	0	0.00	0	0.00
	Great Britain	100,000	2,065.00	206,500,000	12.00	181,720,000	1,817.20
2009	- All	76,000	1,895.24	144,038,000	12.00	126,753,440	1,667.81
	- GAS	26,000	1,568.77	40,788,000	12.00	35,893,440	1,381
	Germany	17,000	1,764.00	29,988,000	12.00	26,389,440	1,552.32
	Austria	0	0.00	0	12.00	0	0.00
	Switzerland	9,000	1,200.00	10,800,000	12.00	9,504,000	1,056.00
	- Europe	50,000	2,065.00	103,250,000	12.00	90,860,000	1,817
	France	0	0.00	0	12.00	0	0.00
	Great Britain	50,000	2,065.00	103,250,000	12.00	90,860,000	1,817.20
2010	- All	79,000	1,890.25	149,330,000	12.00	131,410,400	1,663.42
	- GAS	29,000	1,588.97	46,080,000	12.00	40,550,400	1,398
	Germany	20,000	1,764.00	35,280,000	12.00	31,046,400	1,552.32
	Austria	0	0.00	0	12.00	0	0.00
	Switzerland	9,000	1,200.00	10,800,000	12.00	9,504,000	1,056.00
	- Europe	50,000	2,065.00	103,250,000	12.00	90,860,000	1,817
	France	0	0.00	0	12.00	0	0.00

On the basis of this calculation, we must break down the costs to the components of the bill of material. But we need additional information like customer requirements. What are the specific reasons why customers will buy this product? What are the important requirements? We assume that this information is available and the importance can be weighted.

The task is to use this information to break it down to product components. This process is often called *deployment*. To fulfill this, we break it down into two steps:

- Deployment from customer requirements to product functions
- Deployment from product functions to components

For this we use a scoring method. We create two cubes (deployment 1 and deployment 2):

We define the following customer requirements (dimension TC requirements):

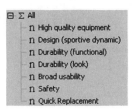

And we need an impact matrix:

City Bike ▼	Target ▼	Local	▼			
	TC Product Functions					
TC Requirements	Corrosion endurance	Smooth running	Collision stability	Fraction stability	Easy to assemble	Replacement within 48 Hrs.
High quality equipment	5.00	1.00	5.00	5.00	1.00	3.00
Design (sportive dynamic)	5.00	0.00	0.00	1.00	1.00	0.00
Durability (functional)	5.00	1.00	3.00	5.00	0.00	0.00
Durability (look)	5.00	0.00	1.00	1.00	1.00	0.00
Broad usability	0.00	3.00	3.00	3.00	3.00	0.00
Safety	5.00	1.00	5.00	3.00	3.00	0.00
Quick Replacement	0.00	0.00	0.00	0.00	0.00	5.00

A formula in Cognos TM1 could be defined as follows:

```
['Weighted'] =N:['Local']* DB('TC Assessment V2', 'Final Weighting',
!TC Products, !TC Requirements, !TC Scenarios );

['Relative Importance' ] =['Weighted']\
['Weighted','TC Product Functions':'All' ] *100;
```

To weight the allowed costs per piece, we have to get access to the market cube.

```
['Target Costs']=['Relative Importance']*DB('TC Market V2', !TC Scenarios,
'All', 'Allowed Costs per Item', !TC Products, 'All', 'Global')\100;
```

	City Bike ▾	Target ▾						
		TC Product Functions						
TC Types	**TC Requirements**	Corrosion endurance	Smooth running	Collision stability	Fraction stability	Easy to assemble	Replacement within 48 Hrs.	+ All
Relative Importance	-- All	29.17	7.02	21.43	25.00	7.62	9.76	100.00
	High quality equipment	25.00	5.00	25.00	25.00	5.00	15.00	100.00
	Design (sportive dynamic)	71.43	0.00	0.00	14.29	14.29	0.00	100.00
	Durability (functional)	35.71	7.14	21.43	35.71	0.00	0.00	100.00
	Durability (look)	62.50	0.00	12.50	12.50	12.50	0.00	100.00
	Broad usability	0.00	25.00	25.00	25.00	25.00	0.00	100.00
	Safety	29.41	5.88	29.41	17.65	17.65	0.00	100.00
	Quick Replacement	0.00	0.00	0.00	0.00	0.00	100.00	100.00
Target Costs	-- All	485.79	116.99	356.91	416.39	126.90	162.59	1,665.57
	High quality equipment	416.39	83.28	416.39	416.39	83.28	249.84	1,665.57
	Design (sportive dynamic)	1,189.70	0.00	0.00	237.94	237.94	0.00	1,665.57
	Durability (functional)	594.85	118.97	356.91	594.85	0.00	0.00	1,665.57
	Durability (look)	1,040.98	0.00	208.20	208.20	208.20	0.00	1,665.57
	Broad usability	0.00	416.39	416.39	416.39	416.39	0.00	1,665.57
	Safety	489.87	97.97	489.87	293.92	293.92	0.00	1,665.57
	Quick Replacement	0.00	0.00	0.00	0.00	0.00	1,665.57	1,665.57

In the second step, the product features are mapped to the groups. This can be a bill of material. A reduction of parts by using an ABC method (see Chapter 15) could also be helpful to avoid assessments across hundreds of positions.

	Target ▾	City Bike ▾	Local ▾			
	TC Product Functions					
TC Product Structure	Corrosion endurance	Smooth running	Collision stability	Fraction stability	Easy to assemble	Replacement within 48 Hrs.
-- City Bike	26.00	29.00	5.00	28.00	20.00	9.00
-- Main Group	24.00	22.00	5.00	21.00	15.00	4.00
-- Frame	3.00	5.00	0.00	3.00	3.00	0.00
Bottom Bracket	3.00	5.00	0.00	3.00	3.00	0.00
Aluminium Frame	5.00	0.00	2.00	2.00	0.00	0.00
Handlebar	5.00	3.00	0.00	0.00	5.00	0.00
Plates	5.00	0.00	3.00	4.00	0.00	0.00
Accessories	3.00	4.00	2.00	0.00	3.00	4.00
Rack	4.00	3.00	0.00	5.00	0.00	0.00
Fitting	1.00	3.00	0.00	5.00	0.00	0.00
Gear Shift	3.00	4.00	0.00	4.00	4.00	0.00
Drive Unit	0.00	5.00	0.00	3.00	5.00	0.00
Brake System	2.00	2.00	0.00	4.00	0.00	0.00
Spare Units	0.00	0.00	0.00	0.00	0.00	5.00

The calculation in deployment 2 is quite similar. With this weighting we can calculate the target costs.

```
SKIPCHECK;
['Target Costs']=N:['Local']*DB('TC Deployment 1', !TC Product Functions,
!TC Products, 'All', !TC Scenarios, 'Target Costs')\
['Local','TC Product Structure':'City Bike'];

FEEDERS;
['Local']=>['Target Costs'];
```

TC Product Structure	-- All	Corrosion endurance	Smooth running	Collision stability	Fraction stability	Easy to assemble	Replacement within 48 Hrs.
-- City Bike	1,665.57	485.79	116.99	356.91	416.39	126.90	162.59
-- Main Group	1,373.81	448.42	88.75	356.91	312.29	95.18	72.26
-- Frame	139.87	56.05	20.17	0.00	44.61	19.04	0.00
Bottom Bracket	139.87	56.05	20.17	0.00	44.61	19.04	0.00
Aluminium Frame	265.93	93.42	0.00	142.76	29.74	0.00	0.00
Handlebar	137.25	93.42	12.10	0.00	0.00	31.73	0.00
Plates	367.05	93.42	0.00	214.15	59.48	0.00	0.00
Accessories	306.25	56.05	16.14	142.76	0.00	19.04	72.26
Rack	161.20	74.74	12.10	0.00	74.36	0.00	0.00
Fitting	105.14	18.68	12.10	0.00	74.36	0.00	0.00
Gear Shift	157.05	56.05	16.14	0.00	59.48	25.38	0.00
Drive Unit	96.51	0.00	20.17	0.00	44.61	31.73	0.00
Brake System	104.92	37.37	8.07	0.00	59.48	0.00	0.00
Spare Units	90.33	0.00	0.00	0.00	0.00	0.00	90.33

In this cube we finally put the target costs together with the standard costs from the product calculation:

```
['Standard costs','Basis']=C:DB('TC Level Calculation', 'All',
'Total', !TC Product Structure, 'Plan');
```

This is the perfect starting point for cost reduction. Particularly interesting are the high variances between target and standard costs. There are activities to define to lower the costs.

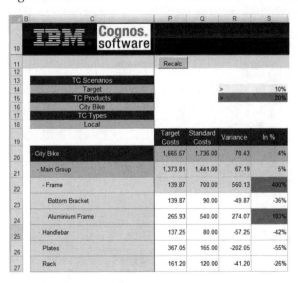

With this information we can create a typical target costing diagram: the trumpet diagram. We need also the standard costs, which can be transferred from the product calculation. A diagram could look like the following illustration:

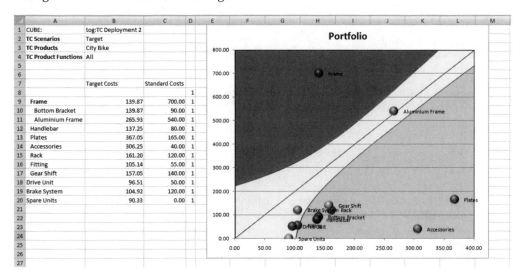

Select the bubble chart:

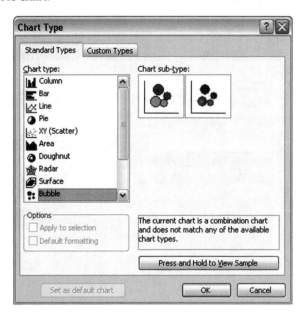

Select a picture file for the plot area.
Select the appropriate data sources.

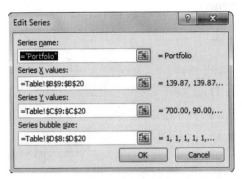

You will see some of the disadvantages of Excel:

- You can't label it automatically.
- Label overlap is not avoided.
- And the biggest issue: it is not Web-enabled. Bubble charts are not properly translated into Cognos TM1 Web forms.

At least to overcome the label problem, we wrote a small macro:

```
Sub AdjustLabel()
Dim i
ActiveSheet.ChartObjects("PortfolioDiagram").Activate
With ActiveChart.SeriesCollection("Portfolio")
For i = 1 To .Points.Count
    .Points(i).ApplyDataLabels Type:=xlShowLabel
    .Points(i).DataLabel.Text = Range("Products").Cells(i, 1)
Next i
End With
End Sub
```

The Excel name "Products" refers to A9:A20.

After finding out where imbalances are located, an important step is to define activities. It is necessary to define activities to reduce the standard costs. An unlimited number of activities can be defined. Entering comments can also be helpful.

The next picture shows the cumulative effects of the activities ("TM1 Level Calculation"). We don't want to discuss the activity management behind this, which will be (at least for the Cognos TM1 part) rather generic.

	All ▼	Total ▼						
			TC Scenarios					
TC Product Structure	Target	Plan	-- Scenario 1	Activity 1	Activity 2	Activity 3	Activity 4
-- City Bike	1,665.57	1,736.00	1,683.00	(40.00)	(10.00)	(3.00)	0.00
-- Main Group	1,373.81	1,441.00	1,388.00	(40.00)	(10.00)	(3.00)	0.00
-- Frame	139.87	700.00	647.00	(40.00)	(10.00)	(3.00)	0.00
Bottom Bracket	139.87	90.00	90.00	0.00	0.00	0.00	0.00
Aluminium Frame	265.93	540.00	487.00	(40.00)	(10.00)	(3.00)	0.00
Handlebar	137.25	80.00	80.00	0.00	0.00	0.00	0.00
Plates	367.05	165.00	165.00	0.00	0.00	0.00	0.00
Accessories	306.25	40.00	40.00	0.00	0.00	0.00	0.00
Rack	161.20	120.00	120.00	0.00	0.00	0.00	0.00
Fitting	105.14	55.00	55.00	0.00	0.00	0.00	0.00
Gear Shift	157.05	140.00	140.00	0.00	0.00	0.00	0.00
Drive Unit	96.51	50.00	50.00	0.00	0.00	0.00	0.00
Brake System	104.92	120.00	120.00	0.00	0.00	0.00	0.00
Spare Units	90.33	0.00	0.00	0.00	0.00	0.00	0.00

Summary

You see, Cognos TM1 can provide a lot more "business intelligence" than just budgeting and simple planning. In our experience it is still a white space. We know only a few projects where Cognos TM1 is used for production. We think the reason is that the calculation capabilities of Cognos TM1 are underappreciated. To change this, we wrote this chapter.

19
CHAPTER

Profit and Cash Flow Planning

In the business world, the success of a company is measured by profitability. There are different ways to measure it: In the long run, companies strive to maximize their cash flow. In the short term, they focus on profit maximization. But an old saying goes: "Profit is an opinion; cash is a fact!" In the short term, companies work with accounting rules and more or less artificial periodical assignments to get a more or less fair view of the periodical success. For example, depreciation is needed to get a realistic view of the period, but depreciation doesn't have a direct cash effect. Hence the profit view varies significantly from the cash. And what's more critical is that the cash situation is sometimes a little bit out of view, particularly when it comes to yearly planning. Needless to say, cash is important in short-term planning, too. You can argue that you can react to cash problems when they occur. However, the earlier you are able to state your cash request, the cheaper the financing will be. Thus integrated profit and cash flow planning is a key requirement for modern planning tools.

It is not surprising that TM1 is a perfect starting point to support an integrated planning model. Financial calculations can be easily implemented because most of the calculation is based on + and −, which can be performed by hierarchies. Even calculations like cash flow can be derived by +/− operations. And if it gets more complicated, you are well prepared with TM1: The rules engine supports even the most complex Key Performance Indicator (KPI) calculations. In this chapter we will show and discuss

- Cash flow and profitability planning
- Working with Days of Sales Outstanding (DSO)
- Financing
- Interest iteration

The Business Challenge

To ensure the ability to pay debts, it is important to take a look at the available cash in the near future. It is not about cash maximization, but about keeping a balance: too little liquidity is risky, and too much is expensive due to interest payments.

The problem is that profit planning and liquidity planning are sometimes not optimally integrated. Very often these processes have different responsibilities and different frequencies.

573

Profit planning is year-end focused. Liquidity planning is usually implemented as a rolling forward forecast.

To give a complete view, it is also necessary to plan the balance sheet. As you can easily see in Figure 19-1, all three pillars are integrated. Profit is part of the retained earnings. Cash out of the cash flow statement is the liquidity.

The cash flow statement is a requirement that gives insight into the financing strength of a company. The cash-related reporting should demonstrate the ability of a company to achieve cash surplus, to pay the debts in the future. In contrast to the P&L-related earnings, the cash flow is unbiased from "earning games" and other non-cash-related activities; hence it is also seen as a more objective measure for success.

An important aspect is the structure of the cash report. A detailed and well-structured report gives an excellent insight into how stable the flow is and whether cash is related to operational business or by finance activities. The following structure might be appropriate (and is part of International Financial Reporting Standards [IFRS] and other country-specific General Accepted Accounting Principles [GAAPs]):

- Cash flow from operating activities
- Cash flow from investing activities
- Cash flow from financing activities

There are several ways to create a cash flow statement (see Figure 19-2):

- The apparently most straightforward method uses cash accounts for banks accounts, funds, and so on. This can be called original cash planning. But this is not the usual way companies organize their planning process. A payment is always related to business activities like material purchase, investment, lending, and so on.

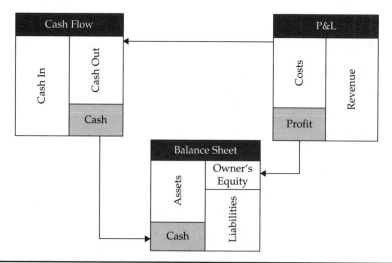

Figure 19-1   Three reporting pillars, the basis of integration

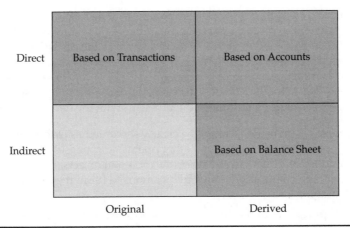

FIGURE 19-2   Alternative cash flow concepts

- It is much simpler to derive the cash movements from the profit and loss statement and the balance sheet or related accounts. This is often called the *derivative method*. It is simple because no additional information beside P&L and balance sheet is necessary. But it mostly gives only a rough overview of the real cash flow, since the sources are highly aggregated.

- Further on, it makes sense to separate the direct method and the indirect method. Indirect means that the statement starts with the net income and corrects the amount by depreciation, changes in accounts receivables, inventories, and so on, as shown in the following illustration. In many cases, the indirect method is used for the calculation of the operative cash flow. Although it can be refined by greater balance sheet granularity, it lacks insight in the profit and loss activities.

```
Profit / Loss
+ Depreciation
+ Provisions
Simple Cash Flow
```

The indirect method for operating cash flow has some severe disadvantages, so it might be better to use the so-called direct method. The direct method starts with the profit and loss positions and corrects these figures by balance deltas. For instance, the sales position has to be corrected by balance sheet positions like increase or decrease of accounts receivables, down payments, and so forth. The story is quite simple: If a company increases sales by improving the payment terms, for instance prolonging the due date, the sales would go up, but the receivables would go up as well. As a consequence, the cash effect is much lower than the effect on the profit.

We want to focus on the derivative direct method. The concept is easy and gives good insights. But the direct method involves some problems if the planning system is not correctly set up. Here are some examples of some of the problems with the derivative method:

- Some positions in the P&L cannot be clearly separated as cash-related or non-cash-related. For instance, the position "other operating expenses" could contain changes in the accruals or direct cash transactions for rental objects. However, in most cases, it is possible to define additional P&L positions to fulfill the requirements for the cash flow statement.

- Accounts payables can result from materials or investments. By using one position, it is not clear whether the amount should be assigned to cash flow from investment activities or to cash flow from operating activities.

It is not possible to state a general rule about the advantages of the derivative method. Each company must individually consider how much time they want to invest.

An important aspect of integrated planning is to derive balance sheet positions from P&L and the reverse. For instance, accounts receivables aren't planned without estimations of sales. The same occurs with account payables. Investments and financing for the balance sheet have consequences on the P&L (depreciation and interests). Hence it might be a long-term journey to come to a highly integrated plan. A compromise could be to not start on the high-level balance sheet but to steadily increase automation.

How TM1 Can Help

Although all necessary information is available in a sophisticated planning environment, we have to cope with high complexity. Modularization is usually an appropriate answer to that. We made some suggestions about modularization in Chapter 14.

There is more than one approach to modeling integrated profit and cash planning, and there is no superior one. For instance, one basic question you should ask is how many cubes are needed. In our work, we see a lot of implementations, and in many cases a cube was used for each statement. Profit and Loss, Balance Sheet, and Cash Flow were separate cubes linked together by rules (and we also saw an example where a TI script was written for each cash flow statement—please don't do this). The reason for doing this is modularization due to different calculations and complexity. This is obvious because P&L is flow, and balance sheet is about stock. And although cash is flow, the derivation uses balance sheet items.

Other P&L positions don't have a cash effect. Provisions, depreciations, and so on have no cash effect. Thus they must not be part of the cash flow statement.

However, we think that one reporting cube should be enough. There is one simple reason: The derived cash flow statement is an aggregation of P&L and the transformed balance sheet, better known as fund movement.

Integrated Profit, Asset, and Cash Planning

Let us look at the process of definition. This structure is obvious and needs no further explanation. We split the time aspects into two dimensions. Feel free to use one time dimension if rolling forward aspects are important.

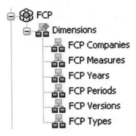

For this example we don't use a dimension for the movements. We simply assume that balance items are stock and P&L positions are flow.

Only the large measure dimension is interesting. We include all three report structures here. So we end up with a hodge-podge of information:

- Flow and Assets
- Cash Flow
- P&L to Balance, CF to Balance

You can already see the linkage of P&L and balance sheet:

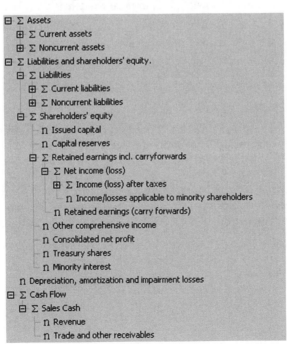

The calculation of cash is easy. You can do it in the measure dimension. For example, take the sales. Sales are not automatically cash related. Why? Here is a simple example: You sell a new machine to some customers. To force the sale, you offer a specific finance model: use the machine now, pay later. Have sales increased after selling? Yes. Do you have more cash directly after selling a machine? No.

So you need to correct the sales. You should do this by using the aggregation with the weighting. In our example, we have to correct sales cash by the accounts receivables. (But you have to consider whether there is matching or not. In the example we have to check whether receivables also include parts that are not sales related.) A first approach could look like the following illustration.

But think what we now aggregate: Sales is flow, receivables is stock. This is not allowed. What we need is the period difference. We don't have a movement dimension, so we need a calculation. This calculation must be dynamic. It should always take the current and the previous period into account.

Instead of defining this for every cash position, we prefer to define a type called "Movement." This transforms the whole balance sheet into a funds flow statement. The flow numbers don't have to be translated. Therefore we define an element in the type dimension and assign this with a rule.

```
['Movement']=N:
['Value']-IF(SCAN(ATTRS('FCP Measures',!FCP Measures,'Type'),'RC')=0,
DB('FCP', !FCP Companies, !FCP Measures, !FCP Years,
ATTRS('FCP Periods',!FCP Periods,'Prev'), !FCP Versions, 'Value'),0);
```

This rule needs some explanation. First, we always use an attribute for previous calculation. There is, of course, a dimension position counter, which could also help (using DIMIX/DIMNM). But we want this calculation on every period level. With this in mind, we would have a more complicated rule because quarters and months have to be handled differently.

Why do we need the "IF" condition? Flow positions are identical with the movement. We only need this calculation for stock. So we need an attribute in the measurement dimension to differentiate the calculation. We use the following attributes:

- R Revenues
- C Costs
- L Liabilities

- E Equities
- A Assets

To avoid long statements with complex conditional checks, we prefer the SCAN function.

The result is convincing. It is simple because a cash flow statement is an aggregation of P&L and balance sheet positions. You can see how this works in the following illustration. Receivables increases in June by 100, which means some customers have a delay in their payments (obviously in July). The cash effect can be seen directly in the Sales Cash: In June it is reduced to 900, and in July it is increased by 100.

FCP Types	FCP Measures	Jan	Feb	Mar	Apr	May	Jun	Jul	Aug	Sep	Oct	Nov	Dec
Value	-- Sales Cash	0	0	0	0	0	-100	0	0	0	0	0	0
	Revenue	1000	1000	1000	1000	1000	1000	1000	1000	1000	1000	1000	1000
	Trade and other receivable	1000	1000	1000	1000	1000	1100	1000	1000	1000	1000	1000	1000
Movement	-- Sales Cash	1000	1000	1000	1000	1000	900	1100	1000	1000	1000	1000	1000
	Revenue	1000	1000	1000	1000	1000	1000	1000	1000	1000	1000	1000	1000
	Trade and other receivable	0	0	0	0	0	100	-100	0	0	0	0	0

This approach can be used for all versions including the actual figures.

But this adjustment is more complicated. The next illustration shows a more complex derivation because you also have to consider prepayments and perhaps split up your receivables. When you include all P&L and balance sheet positions (without cash), you will come to a reconciled cash flow statement. In consequence, you don't need to plan the cash position: This is the result of carryover and the cash flow calculation.

```
Sales Cash
       + Sales
       - Delta Account Receivables (from Products & Services)
       - Delta Account Receivables Associated Companies (from products & Services)
       + Unearned Revenue (from products & services)
```

Working with Payment Terms

Our approach is to plan the P&L and the balance sheet figures. However, not all balance sheet positions must be planned. Some items can be derived from P&L with some additional assumptions. Take the sales position as an example again. Why should we plan accounts receivables at all? We shouldn't plan this directly because we cannot drive this directly. However, we can use past data to forecast, so we can plan this indirectly with our payment behavior and the behavior of our customers. So the best way is to use payment behavior in the plan.

We want to introduce two approaches. First, let's talk about payment schemes.

Payment terms might be an interesting basis. However, this can be sometimes misleading. Why? Because they are planned. But what if the customer doesn't behave in the expected way? Then statistics might be better.

You cannot use payment schemes for all positions. Typical payment schemes can be used, for example, for

- Sales
- Material
- Investments
- Other costs (but you have to split between cash relevant and non-cash-relevant positions)

Let's take a simple example. We have the following example:

- Forty percent paid in the same month
- Thirty percent paid after one month
- Twenty percent paid after two months
- Ten percent paid after three months

With this information we can calculate the payments, as shown in Figure 19-3.

You see that the payment column for January, February, and March is not completed. The best thing might be to use a rolling model. If not, we have to take an opening position (receivables) into account.

The payment schemes can be derived out from statistics or reports out of transactional systems. Many ERP systems offer standard reports for this.

This approach is easily implemented if we have functions to access previous periods. In this case, one period is not enough. We need as many periods back as we have entered percentages. We have to make a decision about how much. In most cases, three months might be enough, but the approach must be open for further enhancements.

We need a certain cube to store the payment schemes:

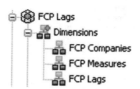

We don't have any specific elements like customers or products. Feel free to enhance the concept by adding customers, customer types, vendors, regions, and/or products.

The interesting dimension is "FCP Lags":

```
⊟ Σ 4
   ⊟ Σ 3
      ⊟ Σ 2
         ⊟ Σ 1
            ├─ n 0
            └─ n 1 E
         ─ n 2 E
      ─ n 3 E
   ─ n 4 E
```

	%	Jan	Feb	Mar	Apr	May	Jun	Jul	Aug	Sep	Oct	Nov	Dec
Sales		2000	3000	1000	4000	5000	4000	3000	2000	1000	2000	4000	1000
Direct Cash	40%	800	1200	400	1600	2000	1600	1200	800	400	800	1600	400
after 1 month	30%		600	900	300	1200	1500	1200	900	600	300	600	1200
after 2 months	20%			400	600	200	800	1000	800	600	400	200	400
after 3 months	10%				200	300	100	400	500	400	300	200	100
Payment		**800**	**1800**	**1700**	**2700**	**3700**	**4000**	**3800**	**3000**	**2000**	**1800**	**2600**	**2100**
Receivables													
Opening		0	1200	2400	1700	3000	4300	4300	3500	2500	1500	1700	3100
Sales		2000	3000	1000	4000	5000	4000	3000	2000	1000	2000	4000	1000
Payments		800	1800	1700	2700	3700	4000	3800	3000	2000	1800	2600	2100
End		1200	2400	1700	3000	4300	4300	3500	2500	1500	1700	3100	2000

FIGURE 19-3 Payables plan

The numbers with the postfix " E" stand for the time delay. It states how many months usually pass by until the payment takes place. To calculate the related stock position, we need the outstanding payments. Hence we define the accumulation. We enter the numbers shown in the following illustration for revenue:

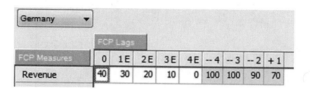

First, we need the forecast values for the previous periods:

```
[{'Sep','Oct PY','Nov PY', 'Dec PY'},'Plan']=N:DB('FCP', !FCP Companies,
!FCP Measures, STR(NUMBR(!FCP Years)-1,4,0), SUBST(!FCP Periods,1,3) ,
'Forecast', !FCP Types);
FEEDERS;
[{'Oct','Nov', 'Dec'},'Forecast']=>DB('FCP', !FCP Companies, !FCP Measures,
STR(NUMBR(!FCP Years)+1,4,0), !FCP Periods | ' PY' , 'Plan', !FCP Types);
```

Unfortunately, time distance functions don't exist in TM1, so we have to work with attributes.

Attributes Editor: tog->FCP Periods				
File Edit Help				
	Prev0 (Text)	Prev3 (Text)	Prev2 (Text)	Prev1 (Text)
OS	Dec PY	Sep PY	Oct PY	Nov PY
Dec PY				
Nov PY				
Oct PY				
Jan	Jan	Oct PY	Nov PY	Dec PY
Feb	Feb	Nov PY	Dec PY	Jan
Mar	Mar	Dec PY	Jan	Feb
Apr	Apr	Jan	Feb	Mar
May	May	Feb	Mar	Apr
Jun	Jun	Mar	Apr	May
Jul	Jul	Apr	May	Jun
Aug	Aug	May	Jun	Jul
Sep	Sep	Jun	Jul	Aug
Oct	Oct	Jul	Aug	Sep
Nov	Nov	Aug	Sep	Oct
Dec	Dec	Sep	Oct	Nov
Year				

We want to derive the accounts receivable automatically. We have the basic situation shown in the following illustration:

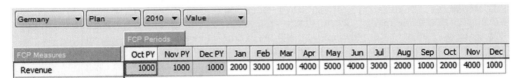

Germany ▼	Plan ▼	2010 ▼	Value ▼														
FCP Periods																	
FCP Measures	Oct PY	Nov PY	Dec PY	Jan	Feb	Mar	Apr	May	Jun	Jul	Aug	Sep	Oct	Nov	Dec		
Revenue	1000	1000	1000	2000	3000	1000	4000	5000	4000	3000	2000	1000	2000	4000	1000		

To calculate the balance sheet items, we need the reference to the P&L position. We define the attribute "Derived," as shown in the following illustration:

	Derived (Text)	Type (Text)
Assets		A
Current assets		A
Cash and cash equivalents		A
Trade and other receivables	Revenue	A
Current recoverable income taxes		A
Other current financial assets		A
Inventories		A
Other current assets		A
Noncurrent assets		A
Liabilities		L

The result should look like the following illustration:

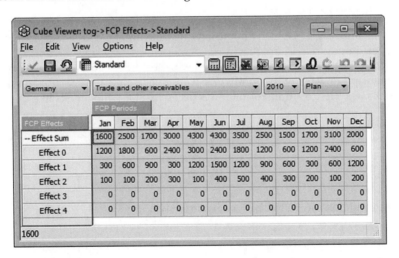

Cube Viewer: tog->FCP Effects->Standard

File   Edit   View   Options   Help

Standard

Germany ▼	Trade and other receivables ▼	2010 ▼	Plan ▼

FCP Effects	Jan	Feb	Mar	Apr	May	Jun	Jul	Aug	Sep	Oct	Nov	Dec
-- Effect Sum	1600	2500	1700	3000	4300	4300	3500	2500	1500	1700	3100	2000
Effect 0	1200	1800	600	2400	3000	2400	1800	1200	600	1200	2400	600
Effect 1	300	600	900	300	1200	1500	1200	900	600	300	600	1200
Effect 2	100	100	200	300	100	400	500	400	300	200	100	200
Effect 3	0	0	0	0	0	0	0	0	0	0	0	0
Effect 4	0	0	0	0	0	0	0	0	0	0	0	0

1600

You see the effect of the opening stock: 600 is the open amount from December (100–40), 300 from November (100–70) and 100 from October (100–90).

This is the rule:

```
[]= N:(100-DB('FCP Lags',!FCP Companies, ATTRS('FCP Measures',
!FCP Measures,'Derived'), SUBST(!FCP Effects,8,1)))\100   *
DB('FCP',!FCP Companies, ATTRS('FCP Measures',!FCP Measures,'Derived'),
!FCP Years, ATTRS('FCP Periods',!FCP Periods,'Prev' |
SUBST(!FCP Effects,8,1)), !FCP Versions,  'Value');
```

Working with DSOs and Factoring

It might be simpler to implement a method that only uses the DSO (days of sales outstanding). The DSO is simply the average time it takes until a customer pays his debts.

```
DSO = Accounts Receivables / Sales * Days of the Period
```

Example: You have accounts receivable of 1000 Euro. Your yearly sales is 4000 Euro. Thus your customers need 91.25 days to pay.

```
1000 / 4000 * 365
```

What do you have to change if you use the monthly sales instead?

```
1000 / (4000 12) * 365 / 12
```

This is simply the same. But we are now in a planning mode. We want to forecast the accounts receivables by using DSOs. With the given equation, we can transform this into

```
Accounts Receivables = Sales / DSO
```

An important question is which dimensions are relevant. Of course, this is relevant for customer or customer groups.

Usually we have payment terms negotiated with customers and vendors. In our calculation we want to work with months. We want to calculate the accounts receivables resulting from sales. Hence a transformation is necessary. Our cube looks like this:

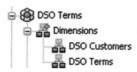

This transformation can be easily done by a rule script:

```
SKIPCHECK;
['1 M'] = IF (['Payment Terms']>30,1,['Payment Terms']\30);
['2 M'] = IF (['Payment Terms']>60,1,if (['Payment Terms']<30,0,
(['Payment Terms']-30)\30));
```

```
['3 M'] = IF (['Payment Terms']>90,1,if (['Payment Terms']<60,0,
(['Payment Terms']-60)\30));
FEEDERS;
['Payment Terms']=>['1 M'];
['Payment Terms']=>['2 M'];
['Payment Terms']=>['3 M'];
```

Now we can enter our data, as shown in the next two illustrations:

DSO Customers	DSO Terms				Payment Terms
	1M	2M	3M	4M	
-- All Customers	1	1	1	0	225
C1	1	1	0.5	0	75
C2	1	0.5	0	0	45
C3	1	1	0	0	60
C4	1	0	0	0	30
C5	0.5	0	0	0	15

- DSO Factoring
  - Dimensions
    - DSO Organisations
    - DSO Customers
    - DSO Positions
    - DSO Periods
    - DSO Scenarios
    - DSO Types

The following illustration shows the calculation.

Org 1 ▼ Plan ▼ Value ▼

DSO Customers	DSO Positions	2010.Jan	2010.Feb	2010.Mar	2010.Apr	2010.May	2010.Jun	2010.Jul	2010.Aug	2010.Sep	2010.Oct	2010.Nov	2010.Dec
-- All Customers	Revenue	0	0	2000	3000	3000	2000	4000	0	1000	0	0	1000
	AR Gross	0	0	2000	5000	6000	4000	2595	0	1000	1000	595	1000
C1	Revenue	0	0	0	0	1000	0	0	0	1000	0	0	1000
	AR Gross	0	0	0	0	1000	1000	595	0	1000	1000	595	1000
C2	Revenue	0	0	0	0	2000	0	0	0	0	0	0	0
	AR Gross	0	0	0	0	2000	1000	0	0	0	0	0	0
C3	Revenue	0	0	2000	3000	0	0	0	0	0	0	0	0
	AR Gross	0	0	2000	5000	3000	0	0	0	0	0	0	0
C4	Revenue	0	0	0	0	0	2000	0	0	0	0	0	0
	AR Gross	0	0	0	0	0	2000	0	0	0	0	0	0
C5	Revenue	0	0	0	0	0	0	4000	0	0	0	0	0
	AR Gross	0	0	0	0	0	0	2000	0	0	0	0	0

PART III

However, we also want to implement factoring:

```
DB('DSO Factoring', !DSO Organisations, !DSO Customers, !DSO Positions,
attrs('DSO Periods',!DSO Periods, 'Next'), !DSO Scenarios, !DSO Types);
```

DSO Customers	DSO Positions	2010.Jan	2010.Feb	2010.Mar	2010.Apr	2010.May	2010.Jun	2010.Jul	2010.Aug	2010.Sep	2010.Oct	2010.Nov	2010.Dec
-- All Customers	Revenue	0	0	2000	3000	3000	2000	4000	0	1000	0	0	1000
	Factoring	0	0	0	0	1500	0	0	0	500	0	0	0
	Factoring E	0	0	0	0	1500	0	0	0	500	0	0	0
	Accounts Receivables	0	0	2000	5000	4500	3000	2250	0	500	500	250	1000
	AR Gross	0	0	2000	5000	6000	4000	2595	0	1000	1000	595	1000
	AR Base	0	0	2000	3000	1500	2000	4000	0	500	0	0	1000
	Factoring Interests	0	0	0	0	40	0	0	0	10	0	0	0
C1	Revenue	0	0	0	0	1000	0	0	0	1000	0	0	1000
	Factoring	0	0	0	0	500	0	0	0	500	0	0	0
	Factoring E	0	0	0	0	500	0	0	0	500	0	0	0
	Accounts Receivables	0	0	0	0	500	500	250	0	500	500	250	1000
	AR Gross	0	0	0	0	1000	1000	595	0	1000	1000	595	1000
	AR Base	0	0	0	0	500	0	0	0	500	0	0	1000
	Factoring Interests	0	0	0	0	10	0	0	0	10	0	0	0
C2	Revenue	0	0	0	0	2000	0	0	0	0	0	0	0
	Factoring	0	0	0	0	1000	0	0	0	0	0	0	0
	Factoring E	0	0	0	0	1000	0	0	0	0	0	0	0
	Accounts Receivables	0	0	0	0	1000	500	0	0	0	0	0	0
	AR Gross	0	0	0	0	2000	1000	0	0	0	0	0	0
	AR Base	0	0	0	0	1000	0	0	0	0	0	0	0
	Factoring Interests	0	0	0	0	30	0	0	0	0	0	0	0
C3	Revenue	0	0	2000	3000	0	0	0	0	0	0	0	0
	Factoring	0	0	0	0	0	0	0	0	0	0	0	0
	Factoring E	0	0	0	0	0	0	0	0	0	0	0	0
	Accounts Receivables	0	0	2000	5000	3000	0	0	0	0	0	0	0
	AR Gross	0	0	2000	5000	3000	0	0	0	0	0	0	0
	AR Base	0	0	2000	3000	0	0	0	0	0	0	0	0
	Factoring Interests	0	0	0	0	0	0	0	0	0	0	0	0

The reporting script would read as follows:

```
SKIPCHECK;
['Value']=N:CONTINUE;C:IF(ATTRS('DSO Positions',!DSO Positions,'Type')@='B',
DB('DSO Reporting', !DSO Organisations, !DSO Positions,
ELCOMP('DSO Periods',!DSO Periods,ELCOMPN('DSO Periods',!DSO Periods)),
!DSO Scenarios, !DSO Types),CONTINUE);

['DSO']=['Accounts Payables']\['Revenue']*
IF(ELLEV('DSO Periods',!DSO Periods) = 0, 30,360);

[{'Revenue','Accounts Payables','Factoring Interests','AP Gross'}]=N:
DB('DSO Factoring', !DSO Organisations, 'All Customers',!DSO Positions,
!DSO Periods, !DSO Scenarios, !DSO Types);
```

And the result would look like the following illustration:

Org 1 ▾	Plan	▾	Value	▾											
		DSO Periods													
DSO Positions	-- 2010	2010.Jan	2010.Feb	2010.Mar	2010.Apr	2010.May	2010.Jun	2010.Jul	2010.Aug	2010.Sep	2010.Oct	2010.Nov	2010.Dec
Revenue	16000	0	0	2000	3000	3000	2000	4000	0	1000	0	0	1000
DSO	427.5	0	0	30	50	45	45	16.875	0	15	0	0	30
Factoring	0	0	0	0	0	0	0	0	0	0	0	0	0
Accounts Receivables	19000	0	0	2000	5000	4500	3000	2250	0	500	500	250	1000
Factoring Interests	50	0	0	0	0	40	0	0	0	10	0	0	

Financing

Integrated profit and cash flow planning reveals the cash situation during the planning period. Perhaps you discover a cash need because liquidity is below a certain limit or even negative (which of course can happen in the plan, but not in reality).

In this situation you have to start to think about financing. You will define a (planned) financing transaction. We will use a simple financing example to show how to integrate an operational plan with the finance transaction planning.

Modeling of the finance transaction can be of unlimited complexity. We would have to go through all the different financing methods. We limit this discussion to a very simple financing method: the bank credit. And we also assume a simple payback method: You take a fixed interest rate and a fixed payback amount for the payback period.

If we talk about financing, we need line items. The situation is that we need to fix gaps. In a year-based plan, these gaps can occur in different months where we need very short-term help. What parameters do we need?

- The contract amount
- A possible agio/disagio
- The interest rate

We create a transaction cube where we can collect the parameters for the planned contracts:

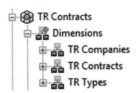

The important dimension is TR Types, which contains the following attributes:

S Description
n Amount
n Discount
n Payback Time
n Interest Rate
S Starting Period
S Account

For Account and Starting Period, we define picklists (referring to TR Measures and TR Periods).

In a second cube, we calculate the financial consequences, as shown in the following illustration.

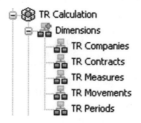

For the calculation of the cash and profit consequences, we need movement positions again:

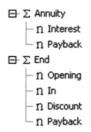

Now we can start to collect contracts:

TR Contracts	Description	Amount	Discount	Payback Time	Interest Rate	Starting Period	Account	Start/End
-- All		2000	10	24	10			
1		1000	5	12	5	2011.Apr	Short Term Liabilities	End
2		1000	6	14	5	2011.Apr	Long Term Liabilities	Start
3		0	0	0	0			
4		0	0	0	0			

(Germany / TR Types)

For our little model, we use one of the rare financial functions within TM1. PAYM calculates the amount to pay on a periodical basis.

We assume that the payment takes place at the beginning of the period:

```
['Opening']=N:
DB('TR Calculation', !TR Companies, !TR Contracts, !TR Measures,
'End',attrs('TR Periods',!TR Periods,'Prev'));

['Interest'] =N: IF(['Opening']+['In'] < 0,0, DB('TR Contracts',
!TR Companies, !TR Contracts, 'Interest Rate')
/12/100 * (['Opening']+['In']));

['Payback']=N:IF(['Opening']+['In'] <= 1,0, PAYMT(DB('TR Contracts',
!TR Companies, !TR Contracts, 'Amount'),
DB('TR Contracts', !TR Companies, !TR Contracts, 'Interest Rate')/100/12,
DB('TR Contracts', !TR Companies, !TR Contracts, 'Payback Time'))-
['Interest']);

['In'] = N:IF(!TR Periods@= DB('TR Contracts', !TR Companies,
!TR Contracts, 'Starting Period'),
DB('TR Contracts', !TR Companies, !TR Contracts, 'Amount'),0);
```

The contract cube must feeder the calculation cube:

```
FEEDERS;
['Amount']=>DB('TR Calculation', !TR Companies, !TR Contracts,
DB('TR Contracts', !TR Companies, !TR Contracts, 'Account') , 'In',
DB('TR Contracts', !TR Companies, !TR Contracts, 'Starting Period'));
```

The following illustration shows the aggregated calculation:

TR Periods	-- Annuity	Interest	Payback	-- End	Opening	In	Discount	Payback
2011.Jan	0	0	0	0	0	0	0	0
2011.Feb	0	0	0	0	0	0	0	0
2011.Mar	64.736549785	4.166666667	60.569883118	939.430116882	0	1000	0	60.569883118
2011.Apr	64.736549785	3.914292154	60.822257631	1878.607859251	939.430116882	1000	0	60.822257631
2011.May	150.344031573	7.827532747	142.516498826	1736.091360425	1878.607859251	0	0	142.516498826
2011.Jun	150.344031573	7.233714002	143.110317571	1592.981042853	1736.091360425	0	0	143.110317571
2011.Jul	150.344031573	6.637421012	143.706610561	1449.274432292	1592.981042853	0	0	143.706610561
2011.Aug	150.344031573	6.038643468	144.305388105	1304.969044187	1449.274432292	0	0	144.305388105
2011.Sep	150.344031573	5.437371017	144.906660556	1160.062383631	1304.969044187	0	0	144.906660556
2011.Oct	150.344031573	4.833593265	145.510438308	1014.551945323	1160.062383631	0	0	145.510438308
2011.Nov	150.344031573	4.227299772	146.116731801	868.435213522	1014.551945323	0	0	146.116731801
2011.Dec	150.344031573	3.618480056	146.725551517	721.709662006	868.435213522	0	0	146.725551517
2012.Jan	150.344031573	3.007123592	147.336907981	574.372754024	721.709662006	0	0	147.336907981
2012.Feb	150.344031573	2.393219808	147.950811765	426.42194226	574.372754024	0	0	147.950811765
2012.Mar	150.344031573	1.776758093	148.56727348	277.854668779	426.42194226	0	0	148.56727348
2012.Apr	150.344031573	1.157727787	149.186303787	128.668364993	277.854668779	0	0	149.186303787
2012.May	64.736549785	0.536118187	64.200431597	64.467933396	128.668364993	0	0	64.200431597
2012.Jun	64.736549785	0.268616389	64.467933396	-0	64.467933396	0	0	64.467933396
2012.Jul	0	0	0	-0	-0	0	0	0

Germany   All   Liabilities

TR Movements

A simple example shows how this works. In a planning system, the screen to create financing alternatives could look like this:

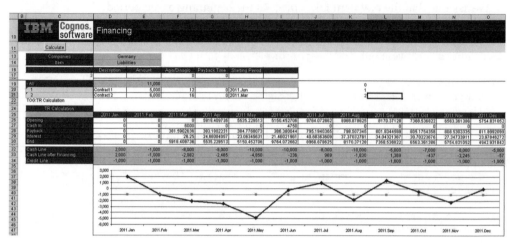

You usually have a credit line (with a safety line), which you shouldn't exceed. Liquidity is cash line + financing. You see, you have to do some homework. Particularly in May, the situation will become critical.

What do we have to do to change some assumptions? For instance, one question is when to pay:

```
['Interest'] =N: IF(['Opening']+['In'] < 0 %
(['In'] <> 0 & DB('TR Contracts', !TR Companies, !TR Contracts,
'Start/End')@='End'),0,
 DB('TR Contracts', !TR Companies, !TR Contracts, 'Interest Rate')/12/100 *
 (['Opening']+['In']));

['Payback']=N:IF(['Opening']+['In'] <= 1 %
(['In'] <> 0 & DB('TR Contracts', !TR Companies, !TR Contracts,
'Start/End')@='End'),0,
Paymt(DB('TR Contracts', !TR Companies, !TR Contracts, 'Amount'),
DB('TR Contracts', !TR Companies, !TR Contracts, 'Interest Rate')/100/12,
DB('TR Contracts', !TR Companies, !TR Contracts, 'Payback Time'))-
['Interest']);
```

Another question is disagio. What does this mean? You get a credit of 1000 but the payout is only 950 with a 5 percent disagio. On the other hand, you have an agio of 5 percent with the same amount. This means that your debt is 1050. A possible approach might be as follows:

```
['Cash']=N:IF(['Agio/Disagio'] > 0,['Amount'],['Amount']*
(100 + ['Agio/Disagio'])/100);
['Credit']=N:IF(['Agio/Disagio'] < 0,['Amount'],['Amount']*
(100 +['Agio/Disagio'])/100);
```

The contracts can be entered as follows:

Germany ▾										
TR Types										
TR Contracts	Description	Amount	Agio/Disagio	Payback Time	Interest Rate	Starting Period	Account	Start/End	Cash	Credit
-- All		2000	0	28	10				1950	2050
1		1000	-5	12	5	2011.Apr	Short Term Liabilities	End	950	1000
2		1000	5	16	5	2011.Mar	Long Term Liabilities	Start	1000	1050
3		0	0	0	0				0	0

With this information the periodic values can be calculated.

Germany ▾ 2 ▾ Liabilities ▾										
TR Movements										
TR Periods	-- End	Opening	In	Payback	+ Annuity	Interest	Payback	+ Cash	Cash In	+ Annuity
2011.Jan	0	0	0	0	0	0	0	0	0	0
2011.Feb	0	0	0	0	0	0	0	0	0	0
2011.Mar	986.401622726	0	1050	63.598377274	67.973377274	4.375	63.598377274	932.026622726	1000	67.973377274
2011.Apr	922.538252214	986.401622726	0	63.863370513	67.973377274	4.110006761	63.863370513	-67.973377274	0	67.973377274
2011.May	858.408784324	922.538252214	0	64.12946789	67.973377274	3.843909384	64.12946789	-67.973377274	0	67.973377274
2011.Jun	794.012110318	858.408784324	0	64.396674006	67.973377274	3.576703268	64.396674006	-67.973377274	0	67.973377274
2011.Jul	729.347116837	794.012110318	0	64.664993481	67.973377274	3.308383793	64.664993481	-67.973377274	0	67.973377274
2011.Aug	664.412685883	729.347116837	0	64.934430954	67.973377274	3.03894632	64.934430954	-67.973377274	0	67.973377274
2011.Sep	599.207694801	664.412685883	0	65.204991083	67.973377274	2.768386191	65.204991083	-67.973377274	0	67.973377274
2011.Oct	533.731016255	599.207694801	0	65.476678546	67.973377274	2.496698728	65.476678546	-67.973377274	0	67.973377274
2011.Nov	467.981518216	533.731016255	0	65.749498039	67.973377274	2.223879234	65.749498039	-67.973377274	0	67.973377274
2011.Dec	401.958063934	467.981518216	0	66.023454281	67.973377274	1.949922993	66.023454281	-67.973377274	0	67.973377274
2012.Jan	335.659511927	401.958063934	0	66.298552007	67.973377274	1.674825266	66.298552007	-67.973377274	0	67.973377274
2012.Feb	269.084715953	335.659511927	0	66.574795974	67.973377274	1.3985813	66.574795974	-67.973377274	0	67.973377274
2012.Mar	202.232524995	269.084715953	0	66.852190957	67.973377274	1.121186316	66.852190957	-67.973377274	0	67.973377274
2012.Apr	135.101783242	202.232524995	0	67.130741753	67.973377274	0.842635521	67.130741753	-67.973377274	0	67.973377274
2012.May	67.691330065	135.101783242	0	67.410453177	67.973377274	0.562924097	67.410453177	-67.973377274	0	67.973377274
2012.Jun	-0	67.691330065	0	67.691330065	67.973377274	0.282047209	67.691330065	-67.973377274	0	67.973377274
2012.Jul	-0	-0	0	0	0	0	0	0	0	0
2012.Aug	-0	-0	0	0	0	0	0	0	0	0
2012.Sep	-0	-0	0	0	0	0	0	0	0	0

Interest Iteration

The experts among you have already realized it: Cash generates interest. Interest generates cash. And so forth. Sounds like a cycle.

Within an integrated planning system, cash is derived from profit planning. This ends in a calculation cycle that can't be handled by TM1 rules. TurboIntegrator helps. The good thing is that TM1 iterates quite fast: due to the interest rate, the number of iterations is limited. Take the following example:

First Iteration:

Delta Cash	−1,000
Financing	+1,000
Net	0
Interests	+100

Second Iteration:

Delta Cash	−100
Financing	+100
Net	0
Interest	+10

Third Iteration:

Delta Cash	−10

and so on…

We implemented a small prototype. See the example in the following illustration:

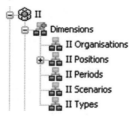

We use a simple position dimension, "II Positions." We set Cash Flow equal to profit, as shown in the following illustration. No investments are planned, no depreciation occurs, and accounts receivables and accounts payables have a constant level over the year. We already presented a more complex Cash Flow calculation in this chapter.

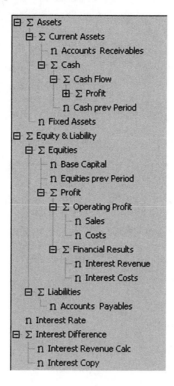

We also define statistics like Interest Rate in this dimension. See our simple data example in the next illustration.

	B	C	D	E	F	G	H	I	J
10		IBM		Cognos. software					
11								Reset	Iteration
13		ll Organisations		Org 1			Iterations	2	
14		ll Scenarios		Actuals			Residual	1	
15		ll Types		Value					
18				B	Q1	Q2	Q3	Q4	Year
19		- Assets		2,000.00	2,050.00	2,100.00	2,150.00	2,200.00	2,200.00
20		- Current Assets		1,000.00	1,050.00	1,100.00	1,150.00	1,200.00	1,200.00
21		Accounts Receivables		1,000.00	1,000.00	1,000.00	1,000.00	1,000.00	1,000.00
22		- Cash		0.00	50.00	100.00	150.00	200.00	500.00
23		+ Cash Flow		0.00	50.00	50.00	50.00	50.00	200.00
24		Cash prev Period		0.00	0.00	50.00	100.00	150.00	300.00
25		Fixed Assets		1,000.00	1,000.00	1,000.00	1,000.00	1,000.00	1,000.00
26		- Equity & Liability		2,000.00	2,050.00	2,100.00	2,150.00	2,200.00	2,200.00
27		- Equities		1,000.00	1,050.00	1,100.00	1,150.00	1,200.00	1,200.00
28		Base Capital		1,000.00	0.00	0.00	0.00	0.00	1,000.00
29		+ Profit		0.00	50.00	50.00	50.00	50.00	200.00
30		Equities prev Period		0.00	1,000.00	1,050.00	1,100.00	1,150.00	4,300.00
31		- Liabilities		1,000.00	1,000.00	1,000.00	1,000.00	1,000.00	1,000.00
32		Accounts Payables		1,000.00	1,000.00	1,000.00	1,000.00	1,000.00	1,000.00
33		Interest Rate		0.00	5.00	5.00	5.00	5.00	20.00
34		- Interest Difference		0.00	1.25	3.75	6.25	8.75	20.00
35		Interest Revenue Calc		0.00	1.25	3.75	6.25	8.75	20.00
36		Interest Copy		0.00	0.00	0.00	0.00	0.00	0.00
37		- Profit		0.00	50.00	50.00	50.00	50.00	200.00
38		- Operating Profit		0.00	50.00	50.00	50.00	50.00	200.00
39		Sales		0.00	100.00	100.00	100.00	100.00	400.00
40		Costs		0.00	-50.00	-50.00	-50.00	-50.00	-200.00
41		- Financial Results		0.00	0.00	0.00	0.00	0.00	0.00
42		Interest Revenue		0.00	0.00	0.00	0.00	0.00	0.00
43		Interest Costs		0.00	0.00	0.00	0.00	0.00	0.00

You can see the interest calculation: The cash surplus is invested and we get interest revenue, which accumulates over the year to 20. These interest amounts are payments, which changes profit and cash flow.

We define an TI process that copies data from "Interest Revenue Calc" to "Interest Copy." "Interest Revenue" and "Interest Costs" refer to this position.

After the first iteration, we see the results shown in the following illustration:

	B	C	D	E	F	G	H	I	J
10		IBM		Cognos. software					
11								Reset	Iteration
13		II Organisations		Org 1			Iterations	2	
14		II Scenarios		Actuals			Residual	1	
15		II Types		Value					
18				B	Q1	Q2	Q3	Q4	Year
19		- Assets		2,000.00	2,051.25	2,105.00	2,161.31	2,220.31	2,220.31
20		- Current Assets		1,000.00	1,051.25	1,105.00	1,161.31	1,220.31	1,220.31
21		Accounts Receivables		1,000.00	1,000.00	1,000.00	1,000.00	1,000.00	1,000.00
22		- Cash		0.00	51.25	105.00	161.31	220.31	537.88
23		+ Cash Flow		0.00	51.25	53.75	56.31	59.00	220.31
24		Cash prev Period		0.00	0.00	51.25	105.00	161.31	317.56
25		Fixed Assets		1,000.00	1,000.00	1,000.00	1,000.00	1,000.00	1,000.00
26		- Equity & Liability		2,000.00	2,051.25	2,105.00	2,161.31	2,220.31	2,220.31
27		- Equities		1,000.00	1,051.25	1,105.00	1,161.31	1,220.31	1,220.31
28		Base Capital		1,000.00	0.00	0.00	0.00	0.00	1,000.00
29		+ Profit		0.00	51.25	53.75	56.31	59.00	220.31
30		Equities prev Period		0.00	1,000.00	1,051.25	1,105.00	1,161.31	4,317.56
31		- Liabilities		1,000.00	1,000.00	1,000.00	1,000.00	1,000.00	1,000.00
32		Accounts Payables		1,000.00	1,000.00	1,000.00	1,000.00	1,000.00	1,000.00
33		Interest Rate		0.00	5.00	5.00	5.00	5.00	20.00
34		- Interest Difference		0.00	0.03	0.16	0.35	0.54	1.07
35		Interest Revenue Calc		0.00	1.28	3.91	6.66	9.54	21.39
36		Interest Copy		0.00	1.25	3.75	6.31	9.00	20.31
37		- Profit		0.00	51.25	53.75	56.31	59.00	220.31
38		- Operating Profit		0.00	50.00	50.00	50.00	50.00	200.00
39		Sales		0.00	100.00	100.00	100.00	100.00	400.00
40		Costs		0.00	-50.00	-50.00	-50.00	-50.00	-200.00
41		- Financial Results		0.00	1.25	3.75	6.31	9.00	20.31
42		Interest Revenue		0.00	1.25	3.75	6.31	9.00	20.31
43		Interest Costs		0.00	0.00	0.00	0.00	0.00	0.00

You can see that the "Interest Revenue Calc" is still bigger than "Interest Revenue." So further iterations must be executed. After the *n*th iteration, we see the results shown in the following illustration:

	B	C	D	E	F	G	H	I	J
10		IBM		**Cognos. software**					
11								Reset	Iteration
13		II Organisations		Org 1			Iterations	100	
14		II Scenarios		Actuals			Residual	1	
15		II Types		Value					
18				B	Q1	Q2	Q3	Q4	Year
19		- Assets		2,000.00	2,051.28	2,105.19	2,161.87	2,221.45	2,221.45
20		- Current Assets		1,000.00	1,051.28	1,105.19	1,161.87	1,221.45	1,221.45
21		Accounts Receivables		1,000.00	1,000.00	1,000.00	1,000.00	1,000.00	1,000.00
22		- Cash		0.00	51.28	105.19	161.87	221.45	539.80
23		+ Cash Flow		0.00	51.28	53.91	56.68	59.58	221.45
24		Cash prev Period		0.00	0.00	51.28	105.19	161.87	318.35
25		Fixed Assets		1,000.00	1,000.00	1,000.00	1,000.00	1,000.00	1,000.00
26		- Equity & Liability		2,000.00	2,051.28	2,105.19	2,161.87	2,221.45	2,221.45
27		- Equities		1,000.00	1,051.28	1,105.19	1,161.87	1,221.45	1,221.45
28		Base Capital		1,000.00	0.00	0.00	0.00	0.00	1,000.00
29		+ Profit		0.00	51.28	53.91	56.68	59.58	221.45
30		Equities prev Period		0.00	1,000.00	1,051.28	1,105.19	1,161.87	4,318.35
31		- Liabilities		1,000.00	1,000.00	1,000.00	1,000.00	1,000.00	1,000.00
32		Accounts Payables		1,000.00	1,000.00	1,000.00	1,000.00	1,000.00	1,000.00
33		Interest Rate		0.00	5.00	5.00	5.00	5.00	20.00
34		- Interest Difference		0.00	0.00	0.00	0.00	0.00	0.00
35		Interest Revenue Calc		0.00	1.28	3.91	6.68	9.58	21.45
36		Interest Copy		0.00	1.28	3.91	6.68	9.58	21.45
37		- Profit		0.00	51.28	53.91	56.68	59.58	221.45
38		- Operating Profit		0.00	50.00	50.00	50.00	50.00	200.00
39		Sales		0.00	100.00	100.00	100.00	100.00	400.00
40		Costs		0.00	-50.00	-50.00	-50.00	-50.00	-200.00
41		- Financial Results		0.00	1.28	3.91	6.68	9.58	21.45
42		Interest Revenue		0.00	1.28	3.91	6.68	9.58	21.45
43		Interest Costs		0.00	0.00	0.00	0.00	0.00	0.00

The necessary calculation is listed in the following code. We need two carry-forward rules for Cash and Equities. Furthermore, we want to check whether cash for a certain period is positive or negative. This alternatively results in interest revenue or cost.

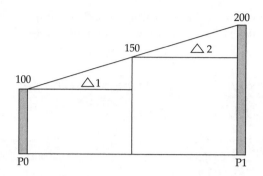

FIGURE 19-4 Average calculation

And finally, we have the interest rate calculation. We assume a steady cash change during the period. Thus we have to take the average. Figure 19-4 shows the concept.

```
SKIPCHECK;
['Year']=IF(ATTRS('II Positions',!II Positions,'Type')@='B',['Q4'],continue);
['Equities Prev Period']=N:DB('II', !II Organisations, 'Equities',
ATTRS('II Periods',!II Periods,'Prev'), !II Scenarios, !II Types);

['Cash Prev Period']=N:DB('II', !II Organisations, 'Cash',
ATTRS('II Periods',!II Periods,'Prev'), !II Scenarios, !II Types);

# Split between Costs and Revenue
['Interest Revenue']=N:IF(['Interest copy']>0,['Interest copy'],0);
['Interest Costs']=N:IF(['Interest copy']<0,['Interest copy'],0);
# Interest calculation based on average cash
['Interest Revenue Calc']=N:(['Cash']+
 DB('II', !II Organisations, 'Cash', ATTRS('II Periods',!II Periods,'Prev'),
!II Scenarios, !II Types))/2*['Interest Rate'] /100;


FEEDERS;
['Equities']=>DB('II', !II Organisations, 'Equities prev Period',
ATTRS('II Periods',!II Periods,'Next'), !II Scenarios, !II Types);
['Cash']=>DB('II', !II Organisations, 'Cash Previous Period',
ATTRS('II Periods',!II Periods,'Next'), !II Scenarios, !II Types);
['Interest Rate']=>['Interest Revenue calc'];
['Interest copy']=>['Interest Revenue'];
['Interest copy']=>['Interest Costs'];
```

However, when TM1 initially calculates the rule, script interests are not calculated because "Interest copy" equals zero. This position has to be filled by the iteration. To run the iteration, we define three TI processes, as shown in the following illustration:

"II Reset" is to set "Interest Copy" to zero.

We start with "II Iteration." Similar to cost allocation iteration (see Chapter 17), we need two stop criteria (as shown in the following illustration), which we would like to hand over by the Excel formula.

Parameters	Prolog	Metadata	Data	Epilog		

Parameter	Type	Default Value	Prompt Question
PnCount	Numeric	100.000000	
PnResidual	Numeric	1.000000	

Again the Prolog code is similar to the cost allocation iteration:

```
i=1;
Val = 9999;
WHILE (i < PnCount & ABS(Val) > ABS(PnResidual));
Val =  CELLGETN('II', 'Org','Interest Difference','Year','Actuals','Value');
EXECUTEPROCESS('II Copy');
i = i +1;
END;
```

With each iteration, the position "Interest difference" gets closer to the limit set with PnResidual.

The following procedure calls "II Copy," which simply copies the position "Interest Revenue Calc" to the position "Interest Copy," thus creating the cycle:

Data Source	Variables	Maps	Advanced	Schedule		

	Variable Name	Variable Type	Sample Value	Contents	Formula
1	vsType	String	Value	Element	
2	vsScenario	String	Actuals	Element	
3	vsOrganisation	String	Group	Element	
4	vsPosition	String	Interest Revenue Calc	Element	
5	vsPeriod	String	Year	Element	
6	vnValue	Numeric	20.000000	Data	

```
vsPosition = 'Interest Copy';
#****Begin: Generated Statements***
if (VALUE_IS_STRING=1, CellPutS(SVALUE,'II',vsOrganisation,vsPosition,vsPeriod,
vsScenario,vsType),
CellPutN(NVALUE, 'II', vsOrganisation,vsPosition,vs
Period,vsScenario,vsType));.
#****End: Generated Statements****
```

Summary

Profit and cash calculation is one of the core strengths of Cognos TM1. Although not much built-in financial intelligence is implemented in Cognos TM1, standard calculations like cash flow can be easily implemented. With a little practice, you will appreciate the flexibility to enhance standard calculations without spending much time on thinking about so-called "financial intelligence."

20
CHAPTER

Driver-Based Planning with Rolling Forecast

Forecasting is an important task within the planning process. It is a natural preparation step for all kinds of planning. Although we can't predict the future, forecasting gives us a better understanding of possible dependencies and thus helps us to be prepared for future events. You can do this intuitively by contemplating, or mathematically based on drivers, or with statistical calculations. All of these methods are used in planning processes in conjunction with other methods: You start with a statistical calculation and then do manual modification because you have additional information, for instance, about a new order within the next month.

A specific way of doing the forecast is a rolling forecast. For some industries with a dynamic environment like high tech, it can be seen as best practice. The year-end orientation in traditional financial planning processes leads to problems, particularly if you want to look beyond the year end. That is why a so-called rolling forecast is occasionally suggested. It should replace the traditional year-based budgeting. However, many companies try to combine both.

You may ask: where is the problem? And perhaps you are right: Building up a rolling forecasting model is not that complex. The challenge is to combine this rolling model with the static model. You will find more information in this chapter.

Although TM1 doesn't have a portfolio of statistical functions for prediction, it is flexible enough to support the forecasting process. You must spend a little bit more time on the rules, but the result is a flexible and powerful forecasting environment, which can be closely integrated with other management processes.

Modeling a Rolling Forecast

A rolling forecast can be easily described:

- There is a periodical, most often a monthly or quarterly, revision.
- The plan horizon, that is, the distance between plan end and the recent period, is constant.

(•) The rolling forecast contains financial and nonfinancial parts. The latter is the
foundation for the calculation of the financial consequences. To work on these
drivers is the primary focus of forecasting.

Sometimes there are different levels of granularity within a forecasting process. For
instance, the periods closer to the starting period are planned in more detail.

A rolling forecast in financial management usually spans at least five quarters or 15 months.
This is a means to link the forecast to the traditional yearly process: The forecast of the four
quarters spans the whole next year so that it can be linked to classical budgeting. Sometimes
this version is planned with more effort than the other forecast versions.

The decision about which horizon and granularity are chosen should depend on the
forecasting area. Complexity and turbulence of the environment are usually the drivers for
this decision. It is quite common that different function departments are working with
different time structures.

Figure 20-1 shows a typical forecasting scheme. Due to the rolling window, the previous
version can be used as the starting point and then be adjusted to new development.

The terms "rolling planning" and "rolling forecast" are used for dynamic planning beyond
the static timeline budget. We want to separate these terms because they mean different things.

An important difference is the orientation against targets and consequently the
responsibility of the statements. A rolling plan is usually a contract with targets between
the management levels with defined activities. The objectives are frequently discussed, and
adjusted if necessary. The rolling plan is the only target and thus is binding. It is a declaration
of commitment to reach the target.

The target adjustment aspect is usually missing when it is about forecasting. It is about
the best anticipation for future development. The target remains the same so that a specific
variance, "Target versus Expected," can be created. Targets are usually adjusted once a year.

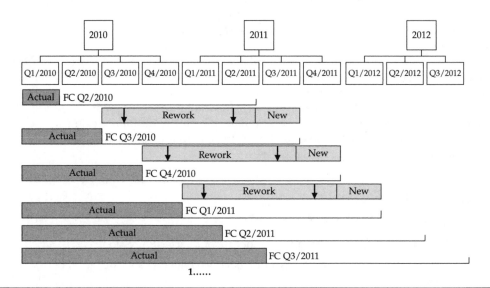

FIGURE 20-1   Rolling forecast

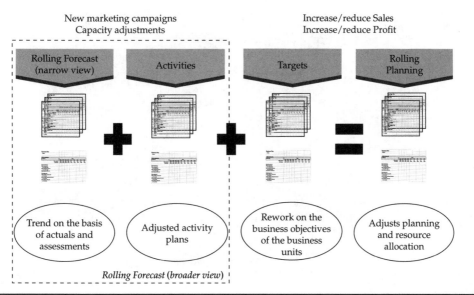

FIGURE 20-2   Process of rolling planning

If you use the term "forecasting" accurately, there is no active element. No activities are planned, but only the consequences of external effects are shown. This very passive view of a forecast is very rarely used in management. Almost always there are active components. Figure 20-2 shows the different concepts.

However, if there is a high level of delegation, the rolling forecast is only binding in a limited way. This is the case with the "Beyond Budgeting" discussion. In this case the forecast is only a frame in which the departments define their activities.

The members of the Beyond Budgeting Roundtable (www.bbrt.org/) mentioned that by a missing target and the elimination of budgeting, the quality of forecasting is increased (see *Beyond Budgeting*, by Hope and Fraser [2003], p. 168). The dysfunctional behavior is eliminated because the lack of rectification motivates people to communicate early problems. But this idea can only be successful in a changed environment. A rolling mechanism by itself can't help.

The Process of Rolling Forecasting/Planning

Usually a lot of people are involved in the rework of the rolling plan. Thus the coordination of the working steps is important. What does such a process look like? Figure 20-3 shows a rough outline of the important steps.

Crucial for the importance of process support is the number of adjustment activities. For changes, an approval process is necessary. Also the reconciliation between dependent departments is necessary when activities change the relationship.

It is recommended to use the workflow component.

The rolling planning can be described as a process, as shown in Figure 20-3.

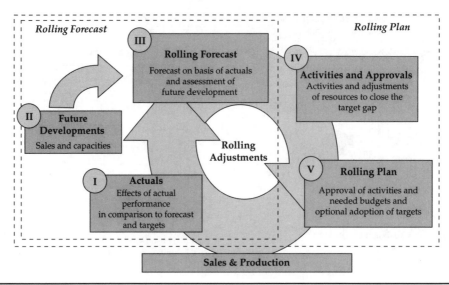

FIGURE 20-3   Closed-loop process of rolling planning

An important difference from the traditional yearly planning is the leanness of the process. The rolling planning must be updated several times a year. The traditional process usually takes three months or longer. Thus speeding up the process is of the essence. To speed up the process, it is necessary to streamline the process and make it leaner.

However, speeding up the process doesn't have to mean poorer quality. The Hackett Group, for instance, revealed that faster processes lead to higher forecast accuracy. But this is not automatic and needs to be founded on hypotheses. Perhaps companies that forecast successfully use drivers for automation and thus gain time and quality. An example for driver orientation may be to focus on material needed for a product and multiply this by a standard price instead of forecasting the accounting position "Material," which contains only the value, not the number. These companies focus on the important driver, get rid of financial details, and can use dependencies for simulations.

The number of line items is often discussed. But it is not that simple to aggregate budgeting line items and define something as miscellaneous. It is more important to focus on the driver. Here are some examples:

- Instead of sales in the order pipeline or even earlier, the leads are estimated. Sales numbers can be derived from win rates resulting from statistical analysis.

- Instead of overhead planning, only the important drivers (that is, number of employees, number of orders, and so on) are planned. The cost rates and prices remain steady unless a bigger change takes place.

It is essential to focus on the important drivers because it is also possible to overstrain the system by too many dependencies. We recommend a simple portfolio schema, as shown in Figure 20-4. You should use drivers that have a significant impact and also change a lot over time.

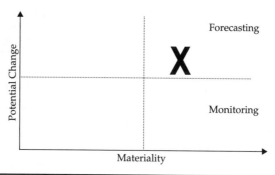

FIGURE 20-4 Selection of drivers

What should an ideal process look like? Here are some ideas:

- The administrator creates a first guess by using the previous forecast as a basis. The last period of the new forecast is empty and must be filled in. The values of the mid-term plan can be used for this. An alternative might be an automated trend calculation (for instance, exponential smoothing). Sometimes this period remains intentionally on zero because the planner should think about possible developments.

- The responsible planners get the entry forms with data to rework. Sometimes they can select statistical methods like trends. The dependencies of an integrated model must be considered. For instance, the sales numbers must be forecasted before an adjustment of inventory and production can occur.

- In the area of intercompany transactions, the receiving areas adjust the requests. The sending areas get the plan to adjust their plans. It is necessary to communicate changes early and not via communication of a central instance. If there are limits, adjustments must be discussed.

- If there are significant variances between the targets, activities must be defined.

- These activity plans must be communicated to the next management level. This can be approved or rejected if the adjusted plan doesn't meet the target.

Another important aspect is about dependencies and drivers. It is obvious that changes to the driver, for instance, changes in production, have consequences for other planning elements. As a simple example, take a sales order. This order has consequences for costs and capacities. Thus it is important to provide a flexible means to map these functional dependencies. These are often referred to as drivers. Costs and revenue are the results of price and volume planning. To focus on this driver and let the financial consequences be calculated can speed up the forecasting process. Another challenge can also be improved: the manual adjustment of dependent positions is error-prone. The driver mapping can be within an area (that is, Price * Volume = Sales) or across departments (Volume + Delta inventory = Production).

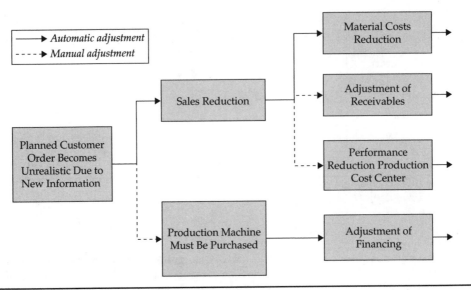

FIGURE 20-5   Possible effects on changes in forecasting

A central question is how these multiple effects can be implemented effectively. High automation is useful but could sometimes be complicated. The problems occur when separate decisions are necessary because the base parameters have changed. For instance, take capacity: The number of orders is reduced, so you have free capacity on one of your production machines. How do you use this? Can you fill up the gap with other orders? What if you don't have enough capacity? Can you use outsourcing? Is your external contractor able to support you? You see, often there is no automation possible. You have to check on a case-by-case basis what the effect on the dependencies is. Sometimes simplifications are useful, but be careful with the results.

To create a formula is important, but it is not everything. If necessary adjustments can't be automated and the responsibilities are assigned to other departments, it is necessary to inform them about the changes. They have to be informed early so that they can react in time. Additional information like comments or even probabilities is helpful. Figure 20-5 shows possible decisions based on a change in the order forecasting.

Rolling Forecast with TM1: Linking Year-Based and Dynamic Models

We will show how you can map this concept into TM1. We use a dynamic approach, which is a result of various projects. A helpful entry point might be a diagram. You can see the actuals, the planned data, and the three forecasts, as shown in Figure 20-6.

We defined two cubes to combine the old with the new dynamic world. This is not mandatory, but you have a clear separation of two different tasks. The two cubes shown in Figure 20-7 are closely connected.

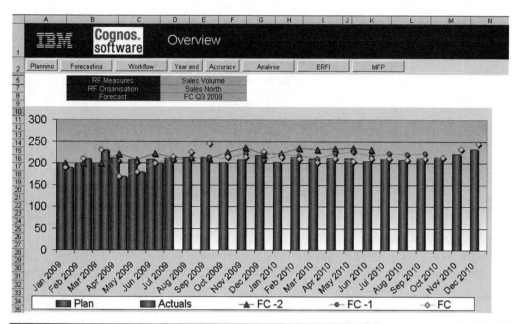

FIGURE 20-6   The entry view

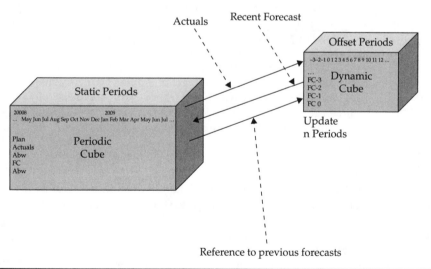

FIGURE 20-7   Two forecasting cubes

The base cube, "RF Basis," contains five "classical" dimensions, as shown in the following illustration:

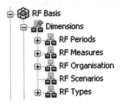

In our example, the plan is to update the forecast on a quarterly basis, hence the forecast versions (and some additional elements) shown in the next illustration exist.

Be sure that the names of the forecasting versions can be automatically transferred to periodic elements. Otherwise you will have problems with finding the starting period for the respective version. In this case we can simply use the rule

```
SUBST(!RF Scenarios,4,7)
```

to extract the starting period out of the version name. An alternative could be using attributes.

The dimension "RF Measures" contains all reporting positions (that is, sales, costs, and so on) and drivers like volumes and prices. Drivers instead of accounting positions play an important role in a rolling forecast concept. Due to the usual high time pressure in a forecasting process, account values like revenue or profit are derived from more operational terms like sales numbers, cost-to-price ratio, and more.

The scenario dimension includes the versions and actual and plan figures (and sometimes also target and other plan versions).

As we almost always do, we use the generic types dimension with value and comment for textual information. For the rolling forecast, we add the Period names.

The forecasting cube ("RF Dynamic") has a similar structure, as shown in the illustration.

But instead of a classic period dimension, it contains a dynamic structure with relative period names ("RF Dynamic Types"), as shown in the illustration at right.

This means that the last three quarters per forecast are always available. Feel free to enhance this structure.

The link between the dynamic and the static cube is an interesting challenge: To replace the offset, the names for the periods must be replaced by the real period name, as shown in the following illustration. This assignment is dynamic and changes from forecast to forecast. Thus we don't want to use aliases.

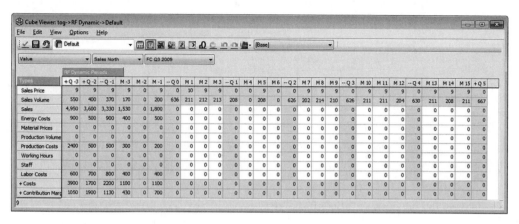

We need a rule that transfers the current period name into a text field. We suggest the following algorithm to find the period name:

- Take the first quarter with actual data (Q-3). For this we need the current forecast version (that is, "FC Q2 2009"). We have to go back three elements. Q4 2008 is the first quarter with actual data. This can be derived by a "PREV" attribute. With a string operation, the period can be derived. Unfortunately, there is no offset function.

- The following quarters can be reached by a "NEXT" attribute, as shown in the following illustration.

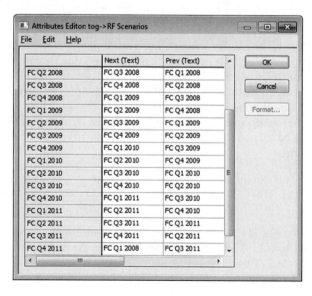

- Finally, the Months have to be found. We can do this by using the child position.

Here is the rule:

```
['PeriodName']=S: IF(!RF Dynamic Periods @= 'Q -3',
SUBSTR(ATTRS('RF Scenarios',
ATTRS('RF Scenarios', ATTRS('RF Scenarios',
!RF Scenarios,'Prev'),'Prev'),'Prev'),4,7),
# If not aggregated take the base elements (month):
IF(ELLEV('RF Dynamic Periods',!RF Dynamic Periods)=0,ELCOMP('RF Periods',
# and fetch the static periods
DB('RF Dynamic', !RF Measures, !RF Organisation, ELPAR('RF Dynamic Periods',
!RF Dynamic Periods,1),!RF Scenarios, 'PeriodName'),
ATTRN('RF Dynamic Periods',!RF Dynamic Periods,'Position')),
ATTRS('RF Periods',DB('RF Dynamic', !RF Measures,
!RF Organisation, ATTRS('RF Dynamic Periods',
!RF Dynamic Periods,'Prev'),
!RF Scenarios,'PeriodName'),'Next')));
```

The result assigns the period names dynamically to "RF Dynamic Periods":

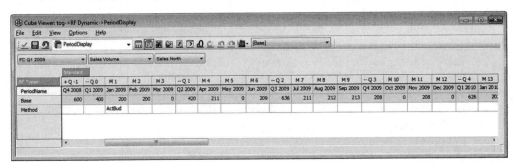

An alternative approach might be to use aliases. It can be helpful when you use other tools like Contributor and so on. For this you need a unique alias for each period, which means you must work with a prefix or postfix because the same period name will occur in the aliases of different (relative) period elements.

When you are facing performance issues, it might be helpful to make this rule static by copying this text into another S element.

With this trick the reference to the static cube is simple. By using a DB function we get actual data out of the base cube ("RF Basis"). We only have to replace the period with the calculated period name:

```
DB('RF Basis',DB('RF Dynamic', !RF Measures, !RF Organisation,
!RF Dynamic Periods, !RF Scenarios, 'PeriodName'),!RF Measures,
!RF Organisation, 'Plan', 'Base');
```

In the second step we need to forecast. And we want some automatic methods as a starting point for manual adjustments. A lot of methods are available. We describe some simple methods:

- Manual entry
- Trend
- Actual/Budget

We use one calculation rule:

- For actual periods, the data is simply copied. We have defined a flag within the dynamic period dimension to find this out.
- For forecasting periods, we ask for the method. Here we use a picklist element.
- The method "Actual/Budget" simply copies a reference version into the current forecast.
- The TREND function takes the actual variances and adjusts the forecast according to the variances.
- And finally, a manual entry is possible.

	1	2	3	4	5	6	7	8	9	10	11	12	Year
Actuals	800	800	1,200										
Budget	1,000	1,000	1,000	1,000	1,000	1,000	1,000	1,000	1,000	1,000	1,000	1,000	12,000
Manual Entry				1,200	1,100	1,100	1,100	1,100	1,100	1,100	1,100	1,100	
1: Budget/ Actuals	800	800	1,200	1,000	1,000	1,000	1,000	1,000	1,000	1,000	1,000	1,000	11,800
2: Overwrite	800	800	1,200	1,200	1,100	1,100	1,100	1,100	1,100	1,100	1,100	1,100	12,800
3: Trend	800	800	1,200	933	933	933	933	933	933	933	933	933	11,200
Variance	93%												
4: Goal	800	800	1,200	1,022	1,022	1,022	1,022	1,022	1,022	1,022	1,022	1,022	12,000
Target 12,000, we miss 200	200												
# of forecasted periods	9												
6: Linear	800	800	1,200	1,400	1,600	1,800	2,000	2,200	2,400	2,600	2,800	3,000	22,600
....													

```
['Value']=N:
IF(ATTRS('RF Dynamic Periods',!RF Dynamic Periods,'AF')@='A',DB('RF Basis',
DB('RF Dynamic',!RF Measures,!RF Organisation,
!RF Dynamic Periods, !RF Scenarios,'PeriodName'),
!RF Measures, !RF Organisation, 'Actuals', 'Base'),
IF(DB('RF Dynamic', !RF Measures,!RF Organisation,
'M 1', !RF Scenarios, 'Method')@='ActBud',['Base'],
IF(DB('RF Dynamic', !RF Measures,!RF Organisation,
'M 1', !RF Scenarios, 'Method')@='Trend',['Base'] *
['RF Dynamic Periods':'Actuals','Value']/['Base',
'RF Dynamic Periods':'Actuals'],CONTINUE)));
```

The results must be transferred back to the periodic cube. We use the same method again to reference the periods. Actual data doesn't have to be transferred back.

- The starting point of the mapping is where the period is identical with the (translated) forecast name (that is, "Q3 2009" = "FC Q3 2009").

- For all following quarters, we take the next quarter.
- The months are derived according to the previously described algorithm.

The corresponding rule for the "RF Basis" cube is

```
['PeriodName'] = S:IF(SUBST(!RF Scenarios,4,7) @=
!RF Periods, 'Q 0',IF(ELLEV('RF Periods',
!RF Periods)=0,ELCOMP('RF Dynamic Periods',
DB('RF Basis', ELPAR('RF Periods',!RF Periods,1),
!RF Measures,!RF Organisation,!RF Scenarios,!RF Types),
ATTRN('RF Periods',!RF Periods,'Position')),
ATTRS('RF Dynamic Periods', DB('RF Basis',
ATTRS('RF Periods',!RF Periods,'Prev'),!RF Measures,
!RF Organisation,!RF Scenarios,'PeriodName'),'Next')));
```

Now we can simply use a rule to calculate the reference function:

```
DB('RF Dynamic',!RF Measures, !RF Organisation,
DB('RF Basis',!RF Periods, !RF Measures,
!RF Organisation,!RF Scenarios, 'PeriodName'),
!RF Scenarios, 'Total')
```

With this rule the view shown in the following illustration can be created:

And finally we want to model driver dependencies. This is easily mapped within TM1. For instance, we plan the volume instead of the sales. Hence you need the following rule:

```
['Sales Price']=N:CONTINUE; C: ['RF Measures':'Sales']\['Sales Volume'];
['RF Measures':'Sales']=N:['Sales Price']*['Sales Volume'];
```

Now let's go over to data entry. We need actual data. And the absolute period names should be shown. A data entry screen could look like the following illustration:

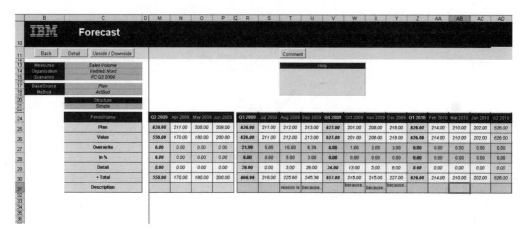

As explained previously, we calculate the driver forecast. Cost and profit figures can be derived. A side effect of using two cubes is that the cubes can contain the same driver calculation twice.

Sometimes it is necessary to have a more granular level below the forecasting calculation. An example might be to forecast different single orders as a foundation of the forecast position "Volume." We show this in Figure 20-8. From a workflow perspective, it is helpful to provide a drill-through from the forecast overview to the detail level. After the drill-through, the details are available. New elements can be entered easily. (For how to create dynamic line item forms, we refer you to Chapter 17.)

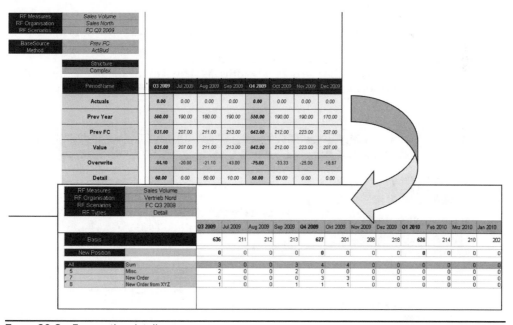

FIGURE 20-8 Forecasting details

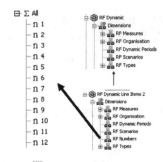

FIGURE 20-9   Line-item concept within rolling forecast

We implemented two versions:

- Simple Detail
- Upside and Downside

From a modeling perspective, this is very easy. In addition to the forecasting cube, we have a second cube with the same dimensions but an additional dimension, "RF Numbers." This includes a counter and a total element that aggregates all count elements, as shown in Figure 20-9.

And finally, the base cube must be linked to the forecasting cube. This is easy because the cubes are almost identical. The only difference is the counter dimension.

```
[{'Detail','Upside','Downside'}]=N:DB('RF Dynamic Line Items 2', !RF Measures,
!RF Organisation, !RF Dynamic Periods, !RF Scenarios, 'All', !RF Types);
```

The line-item cube is referenced by the count aggregation ("all").

Another interesting case is the use of bandwidths, as shown in the following illustration. This can help when you want to have different judgments regarding the probability of incoming orders.

		Q3 2009	Jul 2009	Aug 2009	Sep 2009	Q4 2009	Oct 2009	Nov 2009	Dec 2009	Q1 2010	Feb 2010	Mar 2010	Jan 2010	Q2 2010
Basis		687	216	226	245	657	215	215	227	626	214	210	202	626
Upside		701	219	234	248	707	218	251	238	672	254	213	205	635
New Item		0	0	0	0	0	0	0	0	0	0	0	0	0
All		14	3	8	3	50	3	36	11	46	40	3	3	9
1	Adjustment	9	3	3	3	9	3	3	3	46	40	3	3	9
2	New hope	5	0	5	0	0	0	0	0	0	0	0	0	0
3	Order X	0	0	0	0	9	0	9	0	0	0	0	0	0
4	Order Y	0	0	0	0	32	0	24	8	0	0	0	0	0
Downside		653	208	208	237	611	207	185	219	602	206	202	194	602
New Item		0	0	0	0	0	0	0	0	0	0	0	0	0
All		34	8	18	8	46	8	30	8	24	8	8	8	24
1	Adjustment	24	8	8	8	24	8	8	8	24	8	8	8	24
2	Risk	10	0	10	0	0	0	0	0	0	0	0	0	0
3	Order Z	0	0	0	0	22	0	22	0	0	0	0	0	0

IBM   Cognos. software   Upside/Downside

Back   Diagram

RF Measures — Sales Volume
RF Organisation — Sales North
RF Scenarios — FC Q3 2009
RF Types — Upside

Based on this information, reports on the bandwidths can be easily produced (as shown in the following illustration).

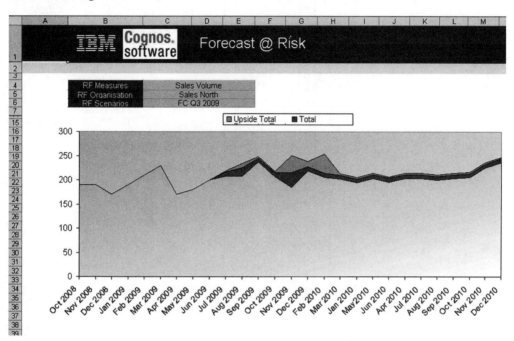

Forecasting with Dynamic Horizons

Sometimes a varying granularity for different forecast versions is helpful. This is often the case when there should be a link to the yearly plan. In Figure 20-10 we show such a structure. The total horizon is 15 months. RF3 spans the whole next year, so that integration with traditional budgeting will be easy.

Such a plan structure raises significant work for IT support because each version usually needs a specific entry form.

The perfect solution would be to have the behavior of Active Forms also available for columns. Unfortunately, this is not supported, but maybe it will be in a future enhancement. For now, we have to rely on "traditional" dynamic methods within Excel.

Let's look at how this is implemented. The approach is to use a definition cube for the columns, as shown in the following illustration.

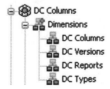

	Current Year				Year 1				Year 2				Year 3			
	Q1	Q2	Q3	Q4	Q1	Q2	Q3	Q4	Q1	Q2	Q3	Q4	Q1	Q2	Q3	Q4
	J F M	A M J	J A S	O N D	J F M	A M J	J A S	O N D	J F M	A M J	J A S	O N D	J F M	A M J	J A S	O N D
RF 1																
RF 2																
RF 3																
RF 4																

FIGURE 20-10 Variable horizon/granularity

The reports form a separate dimension:

- ∏ P&L
- ∏ WC
- ∏ FTE
- ∏ Payable
- ∏ Cash Flow
- ∏ Assets
- ∏ Bridge
- ∏ Article planning
- ∏ StraCo
- ∏ Top-Down Budget
- ∏ MEND

We store the entry period into the column:

FTE	Column									
DC Columns										
DC Versions	1	2	3	4	5	6	7	8	9	10
RF1	04.2009	05.2009	06.2009	07.2009	08.2009	09.2009	10.2009	11.2009	12.2009	
RF2	04.2009	05.2009	06.2009	Q2.2009	Q3.2009 E	Q4.2009 E	2009			
RF3										
RF4										

The "multiple" active form can be easily created. We select the Report "FTE" and the forecast RF2. The postfix "E" marks entry elements for quarters.

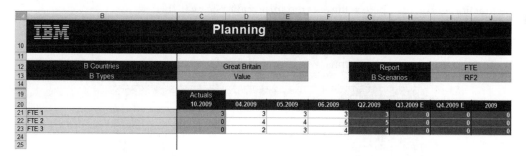

		B		C	D	E	F	G	H	I	J
	IBM				**Planning**						
10											
11											
12		B Countries			Great Britain				Report		FTE
13		B Types			Value				B Scenarios		RF2
14											
19				Actuals							
20				10.2009	04.2009	05.2009	06.2009	Q2.2009	Q3.2009 E	Q4.2009 E	2009
21	FTE 1			3	3	3	3	3	0	0	0
22	FTE 2			0	4	4	5	5	0	0	0
23	FTE 3			0	2	3	4	4	0	0	0
24											
25											

We define a second granularity for the P&L report:

P&L	Column														
DC Columns														
DC Versions	1	2	3	4	5	6	7	8	9	10	11	12	13	14	15
RF1	04.2009	05.2009	06.2009	Q2.2009	Q3.2009 E	Q4.2009 E	2009								
RF2	07.2009	08.2009	09.2009	Q3.2009	Q4.2009 E	2009	Q1.2010 E	Q2.2010 E	Q3.2010 E	Q4.2010 E	2010				
RF3	10.2009	11.2009	12.2009	Q4.2009	2009	01.2010	02.2010	03.2010	04.2010	05.2010	06.2010	07.2010	08.2010	09.2010	10.2010
RF4	12.2009	2009	01.2010	02.2010	03.2010	Q1.2010									

Changing the report parameters leads to the report shown in the following illustration:

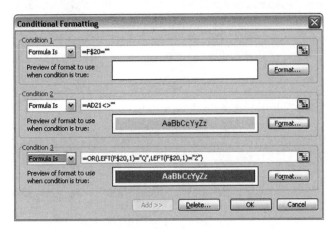

	Actuals 10.2009	07.2009	08.2009	09.2009	Q3.2009	Q4.2009 E	2009	Q1.2010 E	Q2.2010 E	Q3.2010 E
Other income and costs	400	300	400	500	1.200	0	1.600	0	0	0
+ Marginal Income III		0	0	0	0	0	0	0	0	0
Research and Development costs	0	0	0	0	0	0	0	0	0	0
General BG/SD costs, market	0	0	0	0	0	0	0	0	0	0
General BG/SD costs, headquarter	0	0	0	0	0	0	0	0	0	0
Goodwill amortization	0	0	0	0	0	0	0	0	0	0
- Marginal Income IV	400	300	400	500	1.200	0	1.600	0	0	0
Thereof	0	0	0	0	0	0	0	0	0	0
Special items	0	0	0	0	0	0	0	0	0	0
- Marginal Income V	400	300	400	500	1.200	0	1.600	0	0	0
Manufacturing overheads	0	0	0	0	0	0	0	0	0	0
R&D overheads	0	0	0	0	0	0	0	0	0	0
Marketing overheads	0	0	0	0	0	0	0	0	0	0
Administrative overheads	0	0	0	0	0	0	0	0	0	0
Other overheads	0	0	0	0	0	0	0	0	0	0
- Overheads	0	0	0	0	0	0	0	0	0	0
- EBIT	400	300	400	500	1.200	0	1.600	0	0	0
Total DA from Bayinfo	0	0	0	0	0	0	0	0	0	0
Depreciation goodwill	0	0	0	0	0	0	0	0	0	0
Amortization other intangible assets	0	0	0	0	0	0	0	0	0	0
Amortization fixed assets	0	0	0	0	0	0	0	0	0	0
- Depreciation, Amortization	0	0	0	0	0	0	0	0	0	0
- EBITDA	400	300	400	500	1.200	0	1.600	0	0	0

Row 19 contains the column number (dimension "DC Columns"):

```
D19:=1
```

Row 20 holds the DBRW function for the column definition:

```
D20:=DBRW("ToG:DC Columns",D$19,$I$13,$I$12,"Column")
```

Be sure to use the DBR function to get the values. This is necessary because otherwise the function is executed before the column information is available:

```
=DBR($B$9,PCountry,$B21,D$20,$C$19,"Value")
```

To suppress unneeded columns, we use conditional formatting:

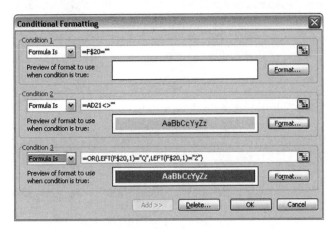

Advanced Topics: Trends and Other Statistics

Have you ever searched for statistical functions within TM1? Not successfully, we guess, unless you have found some undocumented functions. But you don't have to feel desperate. It is possible to do statistical analysis with TM1, although this can be extended by IBM SPSS. Sometimes the so-called best of breed is not the best, but the combination of features makes you successful. And assessing a complex planning environment requires not only looking at statistical functions but also looking at business modeling and so on.

However, we don't want to hide the fact that it isn't as easy as using a simple Excel function. But after you go through the development process, you will have a tool that can be easily adapted.

What is the business problem? Sometimes it might be helpful to create a trend out of actual numbers, let's say sales numbers for the rest of the year. This might be trivial when you use a simple calculation like cumulative numbers multiplied by 12 divided by the actual period number. But sometimes you want to do a more accurate estimation. You can do this when you have steady development. Also it might be helpful when you want to create a first scenario that you want to modify later.

Here's a simple example: We have sales numbers for the first nine periods. There is an obvious trend, but it isn't a constant development.

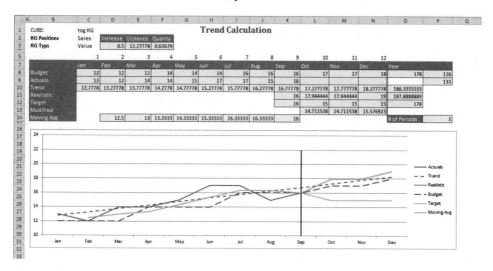

For most of us, the statistics lessons at school or university are far in the past. The key word is regression analysis. And the method is called least squares. We don't want to write a book about statistics, so you should refer to your old statistics textbook.

But it shouldn't be too hard to understand the definition of the trend formulas. To describe linear functions, you need two parameters, as shown in the following two equations:

$$m = \frac{\sum (x - \bar{x})(y - \bar{y})}{\sum (x - \bar{x})^2}$$

$$b = \bar{y} - m\bar{x}$$

We need various steps to calculate the trend:

- First, we should transfer the period names into numbers. Since the time dimension is more or less static, we can simply do this with an attribute. We should also consider that we don't know the number of actual periods in advance. So we have to find out the filled actual periods. We define a period flag:

We create the *x* elements only for actual data by using "Periods":

```
['Periods'] = N:IF(['Actuals']=0,0,1);
```

The *x* value can be easily defined:

```
['x']=n:ATTRN('RG Periods',!RG Periods,'Pos')*['Periods'];
```

- The next step is to create the averages. To calculate the trend curve, we need averages for both the *x* and *y* parameters. As mentioned, no standard function is available within TM1. We have to define it ourselves. The definition for the average is

Sum(value)/Number of Elements

With this definition we simply calculate the averages:

```
['yavg'] = N:['Actuals','Year'] \['Periods','Year'];
['xavg'] = N:['x','year'] \['Periods','year']*['Periods'];
```

Alternatively, in version 10 you can use the new consolidation functions, for example, the yavg function:

```
['yavg'] =N:ConsolidatedAvg(2,'',!RG Positions, 'Year','Actuals','Value');
```

With these definitions we are able to create the four deviations:

```
['xvar']=N:['x']-['xavg'];
['xyvar'] = N:['xvar']*['yvar'];
['xvarsquare']=N:['xvar']^2;
['yvar']=N:['Ist']-['yavg']*['Periods'];
```

The calculation is now easy:

```
['m'] =N:['xyvar','year']\['xvarsquare','year'];
['b']= N:['yavg','jan']-['m']*['xavg','jan'];
['Trend'] = N: ['b']+['m']*
ATTRN('RG Periods',!RG Periods,'Pos');
```

And don't forget the feeders:

```
['Actuals', 'year']=>['Periods'],['x'],['xyvar'],['xavg'],
['yavg'],['xvar'],['xvarsquare'],['yvar'],['m'],['b'],['Trend'];
```

So a lot of work is necessary for a simple statistical calculation, right? Doing this with Excel is easier; this is quite obvious. Of course, this is definitely true for small examples. But our model has advantages when it comes to larger models and when you work with more than a handful of numbers.

This is not the end of statistics, but just the start. More sophisticated trend analysis also includes seasonal variations. We can do this with TM1, but you should also ask whether you can use specific statistical tools like SPSS. SPSS provides a number of algorithms for data mining, segmentation, and confidence-level generated forecasts.

Measuring Forecast Accuracy

Good forecasting can generate value. How? The better you forecast, the higher the confidence of analysts in your company. You don't need to be an expert to understand that there is a certain risk-reward combination: Lower risks means lower profit expectations. So you have to pay less interest if your risk situation is improved. And you can show this by meeting your expectations, which is nothing more than your forecast results. So to measure risk is something that is really important.

This can be done very easily with TM1 if you store the different forecast versions. See the report in the following illustration:

	Q2 2008	Q3 2008	Q4 2008	Q1 2009	Q2 2009	Q3 2009	Q4 2009	Q1 2010
- All	0.00%	0.00%	-5.71%	-0.53%	-3.04%	0.00%	0.00%	0.00%
- Production	0.00%	0.00%	0.00%	0.00%	0.00%	0.00%	0.00%	0.00%
Production I	0.00%	0.00%	0.00%	0.00%	0.00%	0.00%	0.00%	0.00%
Production II	0.00%	0.00%	0.00%	0.00%	0.00%	0.00%	0.00%	0.00%
+ Misc	0.00%	0.00%	0.00%	0.00%	0.00%	0.00%	0.00%	0.00%
- Administration	0.00%	0.00%	0.00%	0.00%	0.00%	0.00%	0.00%	0.00%
Controlling	0.00%	0.00%	0.00%	0.00%	0.00%	0.00%	0.00%	0.00%
Restaurant	0.00%	0.00%	0.00%	0.00%	0.00%	0.00%	0.00%	0.00%
Accounting	0.00%	0.00%	0.00%	0.00%	0.00%	0.00%	0.00%	0.00%
Marketing	0.00%	0.00%	0.00%	0.00%	0.00%	0.00%	0.00%	0.00%
- Sales	0.00%	0.00%	-5.71%	-0.53%	-3.04%	0.00%	0.00%	0.00%
Sales North	0.00%	0.00%	-5.71%	5.00%	-8.99%	0.00%	0.00%	0.00%
Sales Central	0.00%	0.00%	-5.71%	-1.59%	0.58%	0.00%	0.00%	0.00%
Sales South	0.00%	0.00%	-5.71%	-4.55%	0.00%	0.00%	0.00%	0.00%

To create this report, you can use Active Forms with conditional formatting in Excel. You can either define the tolerance parameters in a specific cube or simply enter them within the Excel form.

Use conditional formatting and refer to the parameters shown in the following illustration:

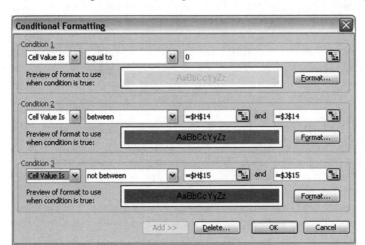

The most important thing is the calculation. It is easy because we can calculate the last RF using the current period.

```
['Var Actuals / Last RF']=IF(['RF Scenarios':'Actuals']=0,STET,
(['RF Scenarios':'Actuals'] -DB('RF Basis', !RF Periods, !RF Measures,
!RF Organisation, INSRT ('FC ',!RF Periods,1), !RF Types))\
DB('RF Basis', !RF Periods, !RF Measures, !RF Organisation,
INSRT('FC ',!RF Periods,1), !RF Types));
```

Summary

Forecasting is a very heterogeneous topic. It can vary from simple extrapolation to sophisticated statistical methods to complex cause-and-effect models. So every company-specific planning system contains a varying number of forecasting functions. This clearly shows that a toolbox is the right approach to map typical requirements.

Multiyear Scenario Planning

In this chapter we want to show how you can do quantitative long-range scenario planning with Cognos TM1. Before we dive deeper into this domain, let's discuss the challenges and possible answers more generally, from a conceptual point of view. It might be obvious to use TM1 for strategic planning. But scenario planning is more than adapting operational planning to a longer horizon.

Do you know what will happen in the next five to ten years? Clearly, the answer should be no (otherwise you don't need any planning tool). We can more or less make assumptions, but we can't be sure about developments, even in a short time frame. So why do we bother about planning and particularly long-term planning at all? The key concept is time to react. Think about it: A significant change, such as a new competitor, enters our core market. If we have thought through various possible developments and defined some appropriate activities, we can react much faster, in contrast to just being hit by surprise.

Although our forecast and plan can always change, we should have a more or less clear understanding about the important parameters that drive our business. With these parameters we can do two things:

- Create various scenarios (that is, optimistic, pessimistic, realistic)
- Define action plans according to these scenarios

This is called *scenario planning* and is intensively used in dynamic environments. However, this is different from traditional long-year planning, which is nothing new. Long-year planning usually focuses on a financially oriented extrapolation of the current status, sometimes enhanced by planned activities. Scenario planning, in contrast, concentrates on different possible developments, including coordinated activities adjusted to the needs of the respective scenarios.

Many companies have developed models for scenario planning, mostly in Excel. Usually they started with more or less simple models, which became more and more complex over time. Such a home-grown development can be error-prone, but it is better than nothing, and it might be the starting point to simulate different future developments. The drawbacks should be commonly known:

- **Links need to be complex** Scenario planning should not stop with isolated models but should integrate into a multiyear profit and loss statement, and even more important, cash flow plan with KPIs like economic value added (EVA), and shareholder value as outcome.

- **It is difficult to compare different business scenarios** We have rarely met Excel experts who use tools like the Scenario Manager or even the Solver. (These tools are provided by Microsoft as add-ins to Excel.)

- **Collaboration is needed on the scenarios** Long-year scenario planning should not be only for experts. Everybody in a management position can contribute something to scenario planning.

There are special tools available for scenario planning. But it is important that the model is closely linked to spreadsheets (for temporary calculations) and various data sources and also has a strong database. So again TM1 is the appropriate tool.

How can TM1 help? With some basic knowledge about TM1, you can already see the difference from a simple Excel simulation:

- All scenarios are in one central database, a TM1 application. Hence comparisons are easy to set up. Calculations are defined centrally within a rule script.

- Collaboration is possible. Every participant can add comments and can do local simulations via sandbox.

We will show aspects like these:

- Creating the core model
- Linking projects with the core model
- Creating a scenario manager
- Goal seeking

A Base Cube

There is a lot of potential to support this process. But first let us introduce a framework. It is important to begin with a forecasting part, which extrapolates the current development and includes known changes. It might be also helpful to work with different variations, that is, worst case, best case, or standard. This might be the most important difference from traditional long-term planning (see Figure 21-1).

The next step is to move into an active part of planning where you should consider what to do when facing the various scenarios. Usually you define projects. And hopefully you have more ideas than you can realistically implement for each scenario. For each scenario you select a portfolio of projects and activities with regard to the respective scenario parameters, as shown in Figure 21-1. With a set of calculation methods, you can check whether the projects have a positive value. You usually do this for a single project in isolation. If the project result is positive, you assign these projects to your scenarios.

With this pre-work you can do simulations, but in a different way. You can, for instance, check whether you can afford specific projects, or whether you have enough cash.

The starting point is a simple multiyear planning cube, as shown in the illustration.

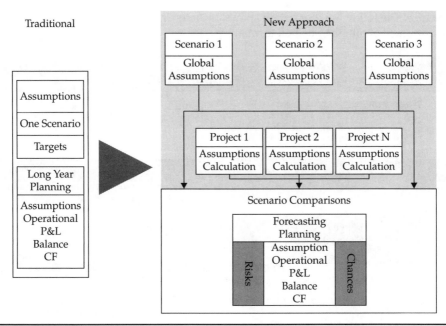

FIGURE 21-1 A modern planning approach

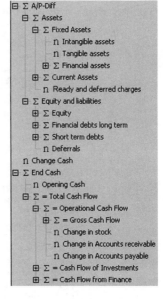

In our example we restrict the multiyear planning to a yearly granularity. Feel free to enhance it to a quarterly or monthly level. Sometimes companies work with mixed granularity: for instance, the first year is planned on quarters or months and the following years are less granular. But this increases complexity, of course.

The central dimension is again an integrated P&L statement, balance sheet, and cash flow model. We choose the same approach as used in Chapter 19: one cube and one dimension holding the report structure.

A helpful hint about formatting: You should consider using formatting statements for the measure dimension. Otherwise, your standard reporting with Active Forms will not look nice. The following illustration shows an Active Form where column A contains a DBRA formula to obtain the position format.

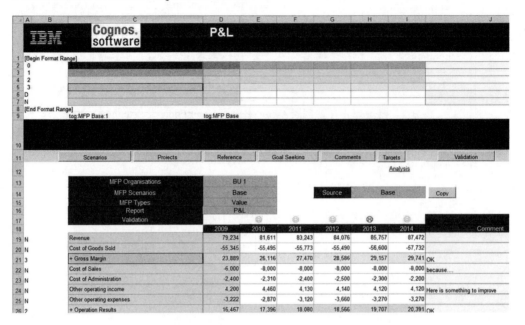

Therefore, you must define an attribute for the positions. You will incur the least effort if you choose the default characters (that is, 1,2,3,N,D) offered by the Active Form standard.

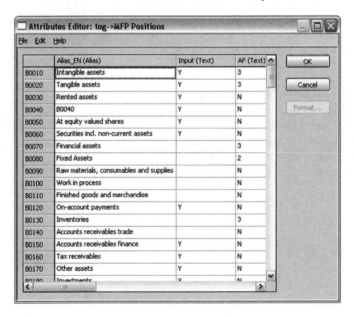

In the Excel form you have to change the default formula in row A to

```
=DBRA("TOG:MFP Positions",C19,"AF")
```

A nice effect is that you can almost do ad-hoc formatting since the DBRA function is write-back–enabled.

Value-Based Calculation

It is important to understand all ramifications of scenario planning. Particularly with a multiple-year horizon, the dynamic aspects of investments are important. It is obvious that 1000 Euros or dollars today are worth more than the same amount in 10 years due to inflation and alternatives to invest the amount and get a higher return. That is why you should set up value-based calculation.

We don't want to explain the background in detail. Value-based management is well discussed in the literature. See, for instance, the standard book, *Creating Shareholder Value* by Alfred Rappaport (1998). Simply put, it is about earning your cost of capital. From a legal point of view, you cannot include opportunity costs for your own equity in the P&L statement. To compare your investment with other alternatives, you should consider interest on your equities, although they don't have to be real cash flow. Hence you need your invested capital and an appropriate interest rate, which should reflect your individual company risk.

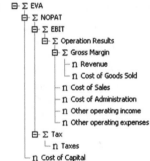

To find the right calculation method is a subject for experts. We will take a more or less generic approach, as shown in Figure 21-2.

In TM1 a value-based concept (in this case economic value added, or EVA) could look like this:

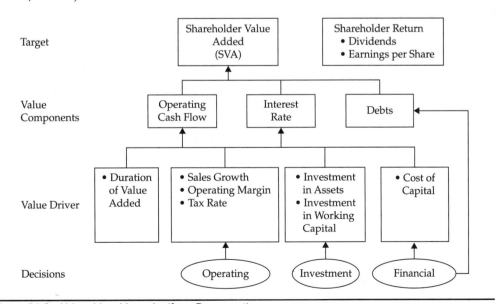

FIGURE 21-2   Value driver hierarchy (from Rappaport)

Now we are in the middle of the discussion about value-based management:

- **The first discussion point is**   What is the appropriate capital? This is, of course, owner's equity. It should not include liabilities because for this you pay your interest directly. But where do you get this value from? You can take it from the balance sheet. However, your balance sheet doesn't always contain unbiased values, so some corrections are usually necessary. You can do this by using the assets and applying appropriate valuation methods.

- **Then we need an interest rate**   This can be derived from external sources. But it should reflect your individual risk. It is obvious that to invest in a company is more risky than to put the capital in a bank account (okay, not such a good example in recent times, but at least in the past it was true in most cases). What is also driving the risk is the ratio between owner's equity and liabilities. The lower the owner's equity, the higher the risk.

So we need some simple calculation rules for the interest calculation. (We don't want to deepen the discussion about equity correction, but be prepared that this will be a longer discussion in your project.)

```
['Equity/Total Capital']=['Equity']\['Total Capital'];
['Liabilities/Total Capital']=['Liabilities']\['Total Capital'];
```

Next, we need the capital costs of equities. The external capital costs can be easily derived. That is when the beta factor comes into the discussion. This is something that is available for industries and reflects a kind of standard risk factor for your company. If you have divisions in different areas, it makes sense to use different beta factors for the business units.

You take a risk-free base rate and add a premium (the expected return rate minus the risk-free base rate). This is multiplied by the beta factor.

```
['Cost of Capital Equity']= N:['Return of investments in securities']+
(['market return']-['Return of investments in securities'])*
['beta factor'];
```

With this information, you can derive the so-called weighted average cost of capital (WACC):

```
['WACC'] = N:
['Equity/Total Capital']*['Cost of Capital Equity']+
['Liabilities/Total Capital']*['Cost of Debts'];
['Cost of Capital']=N:-['WACC']*['Net Assets'];
```

For "Net Assets" we don't need a formula. It is a simple addition/subtraction and can be achieved by using hierarchies. The following illustration shows the basis for the Net Assets calculation:

BU 1 ⌄ Base ⌄ Value ⌄					
MFP Positions / MFP Years	2010	2011	2012	2013	2014
-- Net Assets	27549.590862586	28669.436152456	29810.596420151	31133.1121332	32495.450480509
-- Working Capital	39879.333281843	40802.184152456	40697.624420151	42418.1401332	42390.478480509
+ Current Assets	53941.455692802	53672.31717547	53328.986618869	55201.529575892	54828.935712055
+ Short term debts	14062.122410959	12870.133023014	12631.362198718	12783.389442692	12438.457231546
-- Financial debts long term	44607.714419257	44162	42624	43114	41976
Amounts due to banks	33458.341668614	33302	32964	33709	32716
+ Accruals	11149.372750643	10860	9660	9405	9260
-- Fixed Assets	32277.972	32029.252	31736.972	31828.972	32080.972
Intangible assets	4256.681	4256.681	4256.681	4256.681	4256.681
Tangible assets	20517	20000	20000	20000	20000
+ Financial assets	7504.291	7772.571	7480.291	7572.291	7824.291

With this in mind we can calculate the EVA (see the following illustration). It is not surprising that WACC varies from year to year.

BU 1 ⌄ Base ⌄ Value ⌄					
MFP Positions / MFP Years	2010	2011	2012	2013	2014
-- EVA	8,830.28	9,236.64	9,414.65	9,811.39	10,124.51
-- NOPAT	10,009.61	10,482.36	10,730.32	11,195.12	11,591.34
+ EBIT	17,395.53	18,080.27	18,565.73	19,707.44	20,390.59
+ Tax	-7,385.92	-7,597.91	-7,835.41	-8,512.33	-8,799.25
Cost of Capital	-1,179.33	-1,245.72	-1,315.68	-1,383.73	-1,466.83
WACC	0.04	0.04	0.04	0.04	0.05
Cost of debts	0.03	0.03	0.03	0.03	0.03
Return of investments in securities	0.03	0.03	0.03	0.03	0.03
beta factor	0.70	0.70	0.70	0.70	0.70
market return	0.09	0.09	0.09	0.09	0.09
Cost of Capital Equity	0.07	0.07	0.07	0.07	0.07

Working with Strategic Projects across Multiple Years

Project planning should include investment planning: You collect the data for multiple years and you want to calculate a net present value or an internal rate of return in order to decide whether the individual project should be implemented or not. But whereas investment planning models are unified, project planning sheets are much more granular and differ substantially from each other.

Project types can differ significantly in structure. Hence a possible input form must be very flexible unless you want to handle and maintain a lot of different entry forms. We decide to use subsets to model planning sheets that are specific to the project type. However, more is necessary to implement a flexible data collection form:

- Which elements should be planned directly? These values should be marked in the sheet.

- Areas that are not relevant should be grayed out.

- Should we plan amount or price * number?

We are using two cubes: one for the basic scenario and the final calculation and the second one for the projects. This is more granular.

As you can see in the following two illustrations, both of the projects' forms show a different behavior. The light shaded areas are for input.

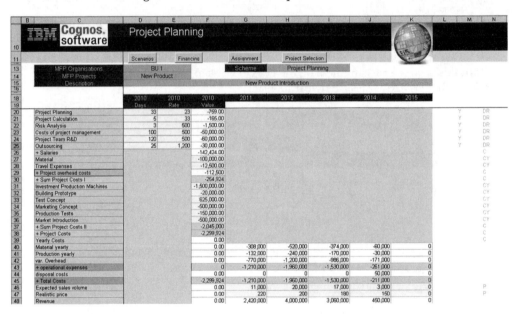

The next illustration shows an entry form for investment projects:

		2010 Days	2010 Rate	2010 Value	2011	2012	2013	2014	2015	M	N
20	Project Planning	33	23	-759.00						Y	DR
21	Project Calculation	5	33	-165.00						Y	DR
22	+ Project Costs			-2,299,924							C
23	Yearly Costs			0.00							C
24	Material yearly			0.00	-308,000	-520,000	-374,000	-60,000	0		
25	Production yearly			0.00	-132,000	-240,000	-170,000	-30,000	0		
26	var. Overhead			0.00	-770,000	-1,200,000	-986,000	-171,000	0		
27	+ operational expenses			0	-1,210,000	-1,960,000	-1,530,000	-261,000	0		
28	disposal costs			0.00	0	0	0	50,000	0		
29	+ Total Costs			-2,299,924	-1,210,000	-1,960,000	-1,530,000	-211,000	0		
30	Expected sales volume			0.00	11,000	20,000	17,000	3,000	0		P
31	Realistic price			0.00	220	200	180	150	0		P
32	Revenue			0.00	2,420,000	4,000,000	3,060,000	450,000	0		
33	Direct material costs			0.00	28	26	22	20	0		P
34	Direct production costs			0.00	12	12	10	10	0		P
35	allocated activity costs			0.00	70	60	58	57	0		P
36	+ Project Cash Flow			-2,299,924.00	1,210,000	2,040,000	1,530,000	239,000	0		
37	discounted project cash flow			-2,299,924.00	1,110,092	1,717,027	1,181,441	169,314	0		
38	Return on Inv			81.65							C

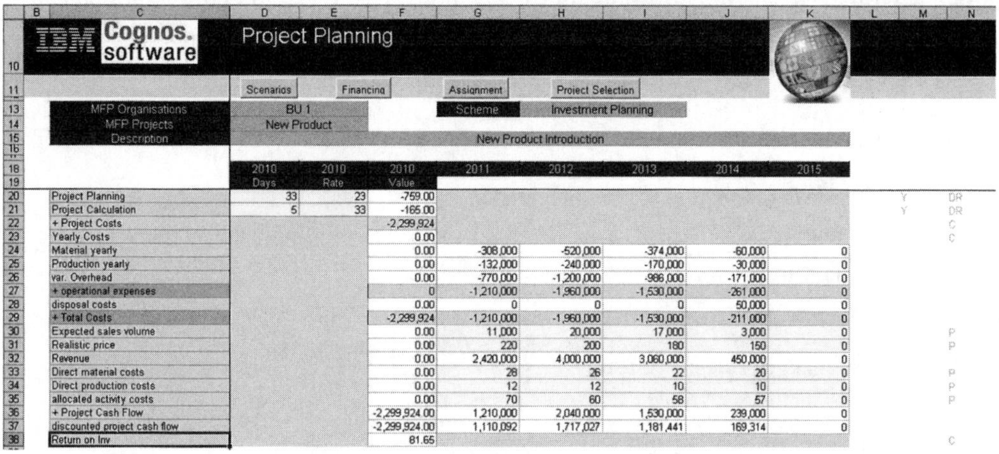

To implement the different behavior, we use conditional formatting a lot. Although Excel after 2007 is a little confusing and restrictive regarding customizing, a good thing with Excel 2007 is that conditional formatting is not limited to three conditions any more. However, before you start, you should have a clear concept, because sometimes conditional formatting can be painful, particularly when it is combined with Active Forms. Active Forms makes it even more complex because conditional formatting is copied from the formatting area to the data area when you re-create the active form. So you can only test your formatting ideas indirectly. The following illustration shows some of the "driving" attributes:

	Alias_EN (Alias)	AF (Text)	Type (Text)	Alias_DE (Alias)
P0010	Project Planning	N	DR	Projektplanung
P0020	Project Calculation	N	DR	Projektkalkulation
P0030	Risk Analysis	N	DR	Risikoanalyse
P0040	Costs of project management	N	DR	Aufwand Projektmanagements
P0050	Project Team R&D	N	DR	Projektteam F&E
P0060	Outsourcing	N	DR	Fremdleistungen
P0070	Salaries	N	C	Personalkosten
P0080	Material	N	CY	Materialaufwand
P0090	Travel Expenses	N	CY	Reiseaufwand
P0100	Project overhead costs	3	C	Projektgemeinkosten
P0110	Sum Project Costs I	2	C	Summe Projektkosten I
P0120	Investment Production Machines	N	CY	Anschaffung Fertigungsmaschinen
P0130	Building Prototype	N	CY	Prototypenbau
P0140	Test Concept	N	CY	Testkonzept
P0150	Marketing Concept	N	CY	Marketingkonzept
P0160	Production Tests	N	CY	Anlauf Produktion (Nullserie)
P0170	Market Introduction	N	CY	Markteinführung
P0180	Sum Project Costs II	2	C	Summe Projektkosten II
P0190	Project Costs	2	C	Kosten Projekt
P0200	Yearly Costs	N	C	Jährlicher Aufwand
P0210	Material yearly	N		Materialausgaben (jährlich)
P0220	Production yearly	N		Fertigungsaufwand (Jährlich)
P0230	var. Overhead	N		Verr. Gemeinkosten

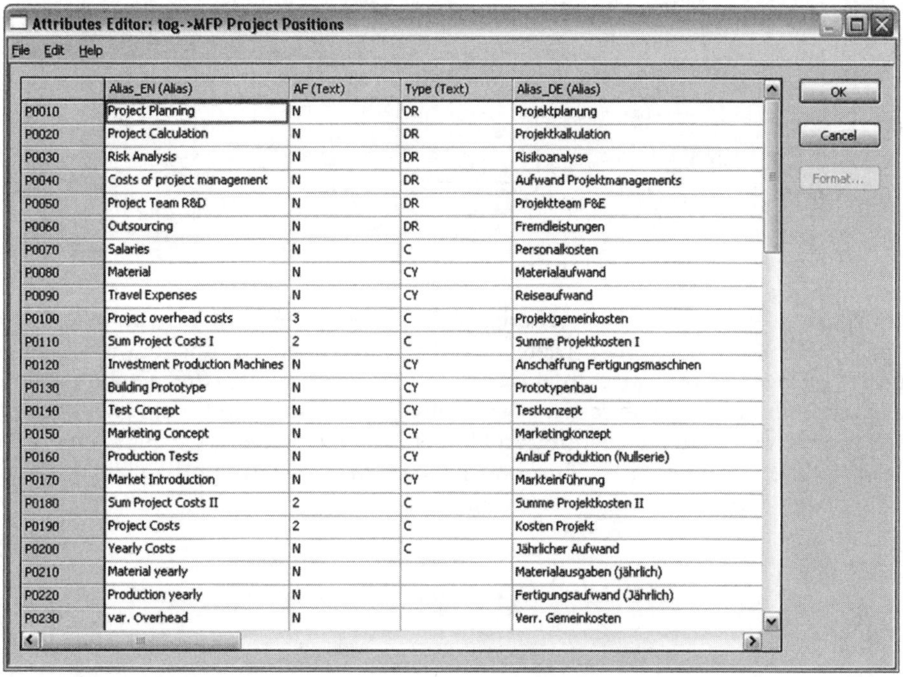

First, you need formatting criteria for the first column of an Active Form document. Again we use the formatting attribute for the positions. This shouldn't be an automatically generated rule but an attribute of the position element:

```
=DBRA("TOG:MFP Project Positions",C20,"AF")
```

The second attribute we use for formatting is the plan type:

- DR for Days * Rates
- C for Calculated
- P for Planning
- CY Current Year

This is also used in rules:

```
['Value']=N:IF(ATTRS('MFP Project Positions',!MFP Project Positions,
'Type')@='DR',-['Rate']*['Days'],CONTINUE);

N20:=DBRA("MFP:MFP Project Positions",$C20,"Type")
```

For the rows D:K we use conditional formatting. See the conditional formatting for the following five years (G:K). For the rows D:E and row F, it is slightly different:

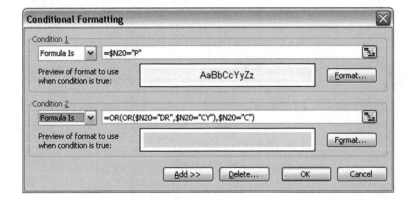

Furthermore, we need decision criteria. We implemented ROI (Return on Investment) and the NPV (Net Present Value). There are only limited financial functions available within TM1. However, this calculation is easy stuff. Please be aware that a long-term project calculation should be based on cash, not on profit. Depreciations and so on are not relevant. Depreciation is relevant for accounting and has only an indirect effect: a high depreciation rate leads to lower profit, which reduces tax payments (if you have profit at all, of course).

In the first step we calculate the interest factor. This is a recursive function because it has to take the previous years into account.

1*(1+ip1)*(1+ip2)*(1+ip3) ....

```
['discount factor']=N:
IF (ATTRS('MFP Years',!MFP Years, 'Base') @= 'P',1,
(1+['market return'])* DB('MFP Base', !MFP Organisations, !MFP Positions,
!MFP Scenarios, ATTRS('MFP Years',!MFP Years,'Prev'), !MFP Types));
```

Then you only need the overall project aggregation (after you have multiplied the cash flow).

- Calculate the cash flow:

```
['Project Cash Flow discounted']=N:['Project Cash Flow']\DB('MFP Base',
!MFP Organisations, 'Discount factor', 'Base', !MFP Years, 'Value');
['Capital Value']=['Project Cash Flow discounted','MFP Years':'Total'];
```

- An alternative calculation would be:

```
['ROI']=['Project Cash Flow discounted','MFP Years':'Total']\
-['Cost Project','MFP Years':'Total']*100;
```

On the other side, we have to think about the financing of the project. Although not all projects are financed individually, sometimes it makes sense to link specific finance decisions to the project.

	2010	2011	2012	2013	2014	
loans with installments	500,000	375,000	250,000	125,000	0	
+ borrowing (installments)	500,000					CY
- redemption (installments)	0	-125,000	-125,000	-125,000	-125,000	
- interests(installments)	0	-25,000	-18,750	-12,500	-6,250	
Runtime (installments)	4					CY
loans with final payment	500,000	500,000	500,000	0	0	
+ borrowing (final payment)	500,000					CY
- redemption (final payment)	0	0	0	-500,000	0	
- interests (final payment)	0	-25,000	-25,000	-25,000	0	
Runtime (final payment)	3					CY
loans with annuity	500,000	383,994	262,188	134,291	0	
+ borrowing (annuity)	500,000					CY
Annuity	141,006	0	0	0	0	
- redemption (annuity)	0	-116,006	-121,806	-127,897	-134,291	
- interests(annuity)	0	-25,000	-19,200	-13,109	-6,715	
Runtime (annuity)	4					CY
+ Loans total	1,500,000	1,258,994	1,012,188	259,291	0	

The following code shows some financing methods:

```
['loans with installments']=n: DB('MFP Projects', !MFP Organisations,
!MFP Project Positions, !MFP Projects, !MFP Scenarios,attrs('MFP Years',
!MFP Years,'Prev'), !MFP Types)+ ['+ borrowing (installments)']+
['- redemption (installments)'];

['loans with final payment']=n: DB('MFP Projects', !MFP Organisations,
!MFP Project Positions, !MFP Projects, !MFP Scenarios,attrs('MFP Years',
!MFP Years,'Prev'), !MFP Types)+ ['+ borrowing (final payment)']+
['- redemption (final payment)'];

['loans with annuity']=N: DB('MFP Projects', !MFP Organisations,
!MFP Project Positions, !MFP Projects, !MFP Scenarios,attrs('MFP Years',
!MFP Years,'Prev'), !MFP Types)+ ['+ borrowing (annuity)']+
['- redemption (annuity)'];

['Annuity','2010'] =PAYMT(['+ borrowing (annuity)'],
DB('MFP Base', !MFP Organisations, 'Kreditzinsen', 'Base', !MFP Years,
!MFP Types),[,Runtime (annuity)']);

['- redemption (installments)'] = n: -IF( numbr(!MFP Years) - 2010 > 0 &
numbr(!MFP years) <= 2010 + DB('MFP Projects', !MFP Organisations,
'Runtime (installments)', !MFP Projects, !MFP Scenarios, '2010', !MFP Types),

DB('MFP Projects', !MFP Organisations, '+ borrowing (installments)',
!MFP Projects, !MFP Scenarios, '2010', !MFP Types)\DB('MFP Projects',
!MFP Organisations, 'Runtime (installments)', !MFP Projects, !MFP Scenarios,
 '2010', !MFP Types),0);

['- redemption (annuity)'] = N: -IF( numbr(!MFP Years) - 2010 > 0 &
NUMBR(!MFP years) <= 2010 +DB('MFP Projects', !MFP Organisations,
'Runtime (annuity)', !MFP Projects, !MFP Scenarios, '2010', !MFP Types),
DB('MFP Projects', !MFP Organisations, 'Annuity', !MFP Projects,
!MFP Scenarios, '2010', !MFP Types),0)-['- interests(annuity)'];

['- redemption (final payment)'] = N: -IF( NUMBR(!MFP years) = 2010
+DB('MFP Projects', !MFP Organisations, ' Runtime (final payment)',
!MFP Projects, !MFP Scenarios, '2010', !MFP Types),DB('MFP Projects',
!MFP Organisations, '+ borrowing (final payment)', !MFP Projects,
!MFP Scenarios, '2010', !MFP Types),0);

['- interests(annuity)'] = N: -DB('MFP Projects', !MFP Organisations,
'loans with annuity', !MFP Projects, !MFP Scenarios, attrs('MFP Years',
!MFP Years,'Prev'), !MFP Types)*DB('MFP Base', !MFP Organisations,
'Credit interests', 'Base', !MFP Years, !MFP Types);

['- interests(installments)'] = N: -DB('MFP Projects', !MFP Organisations,
'loans with installments', !MFP Projects, !MFP Scenarios, attrs('MFP Years',
!MFP Years,'Prev'), !MFP Types)*DB('MFP Base', !MFP Organisations,
'Credit interests', 'Base', !MFP Years, !MFP Types);
```

```
['- interests (final payment)'] = N: -DB('MFP Projects', !MFP Organisations,
'loans with final payment', !MFP Projects, !MFP Scenarios, attrs('MFP Years',
!MFP Years,'Prev'), !MFP Types)*DB('MFP Base', !MFP Organisations,
'Credit interests', 'Base', !MFP Years, !MFP Types);
```

Linking Projects with the Company View

We are working with two additional dimensions: types and scenarios. This is necessary because we always have the scenario 0 (before all activities) and the scenario after projects.

As you can see in the following code, we define an attribute for each scenario, which refers to a basic scenario. So we need two rules to create the two scenarios (in the cube "MFP Base"):

```
['mfp types':'Scenario 0']=n:DB('MFP Base', !MFP Organisations,
!MFP Positions, attrs('MFP Scenarios',!MFP Scenarios,'Base'),
!MFP Years, 'Value');
```

The "After" is calculated as follows:

```
['mfp types':'Scenario']=N:['Scenario 0']+DB('MFP Projects',
!MFP Organisations, !MFP Positions, 'All', !MFP Scenarios,
!MFP Years, 'Scenario')\1000;
```

Since we show the overall planning in 1000 EUR/USD, we transfer.

Many "MFP Project Positions" elements match the "MFP Positions" elements. Hence the linking is quite intuitive.

For the project activation, we define a third cube. It simply controls the assignment. We can simply select the relevant projects:

MFP Projects	MFP Scenarios		
	Scenario 1	Scenario 2	Scenario 3
-- All			
1	Y		Y
2		Y	Y
3	Y		Y
4			
5			
6			
7			

With this approach we can define as many projects as we want independent of the scenarios. For a specific scenario, we select the appropriate projects. We transfer the numbers of the assigned projects into the Project cube with a conditional rule:

```
['Scenario'] = N:IF(DB('MFP ProjectActivation2', !MFP Scenarios,
!MFP Projects,'Select')@='Y',['Value','Projects'],0);
```

To reference the project positions to the position, we define a mapping area within the project positions:

MFP Project Positions	2010 -- All	1	2	2011 -- All	1	2	2012 -- All	1	2	2013 -- All	1	2
-- Sales	0.00	0.00	0.00	3,220,000.00	2,420,000.00	800,000.00	5,600,000.00	4,000,000.00	1,600,000.00	4,660,000.00	3,060,000.00	1,600,000.00
Revenue	0.00	0.00	0.00	3,220,000.00	2,420,000.00	800,000.00	5,600,000.00	4,000,000.00	1,600,000.00	4,660,000.00	3,060,000.00	1,600,000.00
-- cost of goods sold	0.00	0.00	0.00	-1,110,000.00	-1,710,000.00	600,000.00	-1,260,000.00	-2,460,000.00	1,200,000.00	-830,000.00	-2,030,000.00	1,200,000.00
+ operational expenses	0.00	0.00	0.00	-610,000.00	-1,210,000.00	600,000.00	-760,000.00	-1,960,000.00	1,200,000.00	-330,000.00	-1,530,000.00	1,200,000.00
Depreciation	0.00	0.00	0.00	-500,000.00	-500,000.00	0.00	-500,000.00	-500,000.00	0.00	-500,000.00	-500,000.00	0.00
-- Interest expenses	0.00	0.00	0.00	-75,000.00	-75,000.00	0.00	-62,949.70	-62,949.70	0.00	-50,609.39	-50,609.39	0.00
- interests(installments)	0.00	0.00	0.00	-25,000.00	-25,000.00	0.00	-18,750.00	-18,750.00	0.00	-12,500.00	-12,500.00	0.00
- interests (final payment)	0.00	0.00	0.00	-25,000.00	-25,000.00	0.00	-25,000.00	-25,000.00	0.00	-25,000.00	-25,000.00	0.00
- interests(annuity)	0.00	0.00	0.00	-25,000.00	-25,000.00	0.00	-19,199.70	-19,199.70	0.00	-13,109.39	-13,109.39	0.00
-- Loans total	1,500,000.00	1,500,000.00	0.00	1,258,994.08	1,258,994.08	0.00	1,012,187.87	1,012,187.87	0.00	259,291.35	259,291.35	0.00
loans with installments	500,000.00	500,000.00	0.00	375,000.00	375,000.00	0.00	250,000.00	250,000.00	0.00	125,000.00	125,000.00	0.00
loans with final payment	500,000.00	500,000.00	0.00	500,000.00	500,000.00	0.00	500,000.00	500,000.00	0.00	0.00	0.00	0.00
loans with annuity	500,000.00	500,000.00	0.00	383,994.08	383,994.08	0.00	262,187.87	262,187.87	0.00	134,291.35	134,291.35	0.00
-- Change in loans	1,500,000.00	1,500,000.00	0.00	-241,005.92	-241,005.92	0.00	-246,806.21	-246,806.21	0.00	-752,896.52	-752,896.52	0.00
- redemption (installments)	0.00	0.00	0.00	-125,000.00	-125,000.00	0.00	-125,000.00	-125,000.00	0.00	-125,000.00	-125,000.00	0.00
- redemption (final payment)	0.00	0.00	0.00	0.00	0.00	0.00	0.00	0.00	0.00	-500,000.00	-500,000.00	0.00
- redemption (annuity)	0.00	0.00	0.00	-116,005.92	-116,005.92	0.00	-121,806.21	-121,806.21	0.00	-127,896.52	-127,896.52	0.00
+ borrowing (installments)	500,000.00	500,000.00	0.00	0.00	0.00	0.00	0.00	0.00	0.00	0.00	0.00	0.00
+ borrowing (final payment)	500,000.00	500,000.00	0.00	0.00	0.00	0.00	0.00	0.00	0.00	0.00	0.00	0.00
+ borrowing (annuity)	500,000.00	500,000.00	0.00	0.00	0.00	0.00	0.00	0.00	0.00	0.00	0.00	0.00
+ Depreciation on assets	0.00	0.00	0.00	500,000.00	500,000.00	0.00	500,000.00	500,000.00	0.00	500,000.00	500,000.00	0.00
-- Tangible Assets	1,500,000.00	1,500,000.00	0.00	1,000,000.00	1,000,000.00	0.00	500,000.00	500,000.00	0.00	0.00	0.00	0.00
Assets	1,500,000.00	1,500,000.00	0.00	1,000,000.00	1,000,000.00	0.00	500,000.00	500,000.00	0.00	0.00	0.00	0.00
-- Investments in fixed assets	-1,500,000.00	-1,500,000.00	0.00	0.00	0.00	0.00	0.00	0.00	0.00	0.00	0.00	0.00
Investment Production Machines	-1,500,000.00	-1,500,000.00	0.00	0.00	0.00	0.00	0.00	0.00	0.00	0.00	0.00	0.00
+ Other expenses	-454,924.00	-254,924.00	-200,000.00	0.00	0.00	0.00	0.00	0.00	0.00	0.00	0.00	0.00

With this basic concept we can now do analysis. We have the zero alternative for each scenario and the situation after the projects, as shown in the following illustration. This could be a typical analysis starting point.

MFP Scenarios	MFP Types	+ NOPAT	Cost of Capital	-- EVA
Scenario 1	Scenario 0	10009.605312	-1179.32667355	8830.27863845
	Scenario Diff	-147.85592	7.255589822	-140.600330178
	Scenario	9861.749392	-1172.071083728	8689.678308272
Scenario 2	Scenario 0	7322.91748	-39.006584533	7283.910895467
	Scenario Diff	-116	0.442735116	-115.557264884
	Scenario	7206.91748	-38.563849417	7168.353630583
Scenario 3	Scenario 0	10009.605312	-1179.32667355	8830.27863845
	Scenario Diff	-263.85592	7.856280925	-255.999639075
	Scenario	9745.749392	-1171.470392625	8574.278999375

Copy versus Reference

We mentioned that the foundation of scenario planning is the possibility of working with different scenarios. Hence there must be a way to easily create new alternatives based on the forecasted versions with certain changes. There are many ways to create scenarios and populate them with data:

- You can use the built-in distribution functions. You collect the top element and then enter any adjustments. This works for simple scenarios but not for complex ones, for instance, when you have to copy data from more than one cube. By the way, this could be an argument for single cubing. It can also lead to the problem that you must define artificial elements. For instance, you need an element "Copy" as parent of price and numbers to copy both elements in one step.

- Or you can use the built-in sandbox function. The challenge is that in this case a scenario is a personal copy. This can be sufficient. However, if you want to work in a team on a specific scenario, you need more support. Our scenarios should be communicated.

- TI scripting is much more flexible, but you need support from a TM1 specialist. This can be a time-consuming task. We will define a small scenario manager with the possibility to create new scenarios over the web.

- The last proposal is not really copying but referencing. The advantage is that you don't need a copy script. And very important: changes in the base scenario can be automatically transferred to the derived scenario. This can reduce the maintenance effort dramatically.

But first we want to introduce the Scenario Manager. We defined a small cube for demonstration, as shown in the illustration here.

A view could look like the following:

	B	C	D	E	F	G	H	I	J
10									
11	**SM Organisations**	BU 1				Copy Scenario			New Scenario
12	**SM Types**	Value							Test2
13		Source			Target				
14		Scenario 1			Scenario 2	Delete Scenario			
15		Scenario 1	Scenario 1	Scenario 1	Scenario 2	Scenario 2	Scenario 2		
16		2010	2011	2012	2010	2011	2012		
17	Revenue	1000	1200	1300	1000	1200	1300		
18	Cost of sales	0	0	0	0	0	0		
19	- Gross profit/loss from sales	1000	1200	1300	1000	1200	1300		
20	Selling costs	0	0	0	0	0	0		
21	General administrative costs	0	0	0	0	0	0		
22	Other operating income	0	0	0	0	0	0		
23	Other operating expenses	0	0	0	0	0	0		
24	- Operating results = EBIT	1000	1200	1300	1000	1200	1300		
25	Financial income/expense, net	0	0	0	0	0	0		
26	- Income before taxes = EBT	1000	1200	1300	1000	1200	1300		
27	Income taxes	0	0	0	0	0	0		
28	- Income (loss) after taxes	1000	1200	1300	1000	1200	1300		
29	Income/losses applicable to minority shareholders	0	0	0	0	0	0		
30	- Net income (loss)	1000	1200	1300	1000	1200	1300		
31									
32									

We need the following TI processes:

- Generate a new scenario including reference for variance analysis
- Copy data from one scenario to another
- Delete a scenario

The first TI process is simple. You just add something to the scenario dimension. This works, but you should consider restricting the use by not allowing everybody to use this feature. In addition to the scenario, we also create a variance element.

```
sDimension = 'SM Scenarios';
sCompEl = 'Var ' | psNewScenario | ' to ' | psReferenceScenario;
DimensionElementInsert(sDimension, '',sCompEl ,'C');
DimensionElementComponentAdd(sDimension,sCompEl, psNewScenario, 1);
DimensionElementComponentAdd(sDimension,sCompEl, psReferenceScenario, -1);
```

In the Epilog section we enter some attributes that enable us to identify new scenarios:

```
AttrPutS('Automatic', sDimension, psNewScenario, 'Type');
AttrPutS(PUser, sDimension, psNewScenario, 'Owner');
AttrPutS(Today(1), sDimension, psNewScenario, 'Created');
```

It's also important to do some housekeeping by deleting a scenario. The only needed parameter is "psScenario." We only allow deleting scenarios with the type "Automatic." This is the relevant part of the Prolog section:

```
sDimension = 'SM Scenarios';
IF(ATTRS(sDimension,psScenario,'Type')@= 'Automatic');
  DimensionElementDelete(sDimension, elpar(sDimension,psScenario,1));
  DimensionElementDelete(sDimension, psScenario);
ENDIF;
```

A copy script (as a standard task) can be created without much thought. Here is a checklist:

- Consider which parameter should be changed by the user.

- Define a view of the copy data for reference elements. If you copy within a cube, you likely should ignore consolidated and rule-calculated values, as shown in the following illustration.

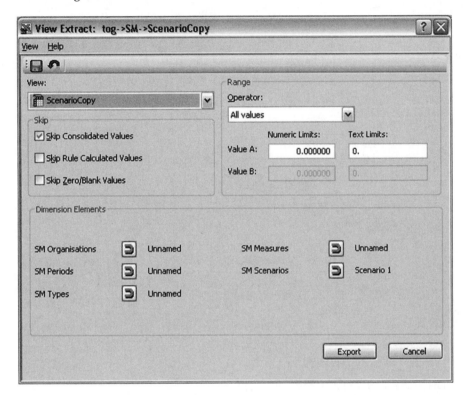

- If you use zero suppression, you can generate nonsense results: If a source cell in the first run contains a value and later it is set to zero, this leads to false data because the original value is skipped, so it is not overwritten. If you use zero suppression, you must delete the destination either by deleting the scenario element or with a zero-out file (unless you are absolutely sure that no values are generated). There is a tradeoff: Zeroing out by a view performs faster, but it requires more effort.

- Create a TI script. If you plan to copy not only values but also comments, you have to set the data field to "string"; otherwise, the copy would end with an error.

See the TI-Definitions in the following two illustrations.

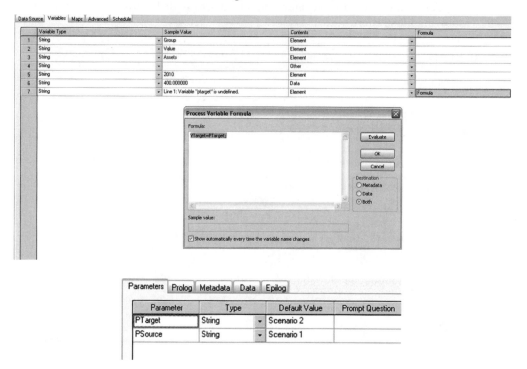

The Data section looks like this:

```
IF (VALUE_IS_STRING=1);
SVALUE = CellGetS('SM',vsOrganisation,vsMeasure,vsPeriod,vsSource,vsType);
ELSE;
NVALUE=CellGetN('SM', vsOrganisation,vsMeasure,vsPeriod,psSource,vsType);
ENDIF;
#****Begin: Generated Statements***
vsTarget=psTarget;
if (VALUE_IS_STRING=1,
CellPutS(SVALUE,'SM',vsOrganisation,vsMeasure,vsPeriod,vsTarget,vsType),
CellPutN(NVALUE, 'SM', vsOrganisation,vsMeasure,vsPeriod,vsTarget,vsType));
#****End: Generated Statements****
```

The alternative for copying the numbers is referencing and then doing adjustments. We discussed the pro and cons already. See the illustration.

		Base		Worst		
		Value	Change in %	Change	Replace	Value
19	Revenue	81,611.020	0.000	-10,000.000	0.000	71,611.020
20	Cost of Goods Sold	-55,495.494	0.000	0.000	0.000	-50,127.714
21	+ Gross Margin	26,116	0	-10,000	0	21,483
22	Cost of Sales	-8,000.000	0.000	0.000	0.000	-8,000.000
23	Cost of Administration	-2,310.000	0.000	0.000	0.000	-2,310.000
24	Other operating income	4,460.000	0.000	0.000	0.000	4,460.000
25	Other operating expenses	-2,870.000	0.000	0.000	0.000	-2,870.000
26	+ Operation Results	17,396	0	-10,000	0	12,763
27	Income from investments	300.000	0.000	0.000	0.000	300.000
28	Income from securities	160.000	0.000	0.000	0.000	160.000
29	Interest expenses	-660.000	0.000	0.000	0.000	-660.000
30	Interest income	410.000	0.000	0.000	0.000	410.000
31	+ Interest results	-90	0	0	0	-90
32	Other finance results	-20.000	0.000	0.000	0.000	-20.000
33	+ Financial results	190	0	0	0	190
34	+ EBT	17,586	0	-10,000	0	12,953
35	Taxes	-7,385.921	0.000	0.000	0.000	-5,440.389
36	+ EAT	10,200	0	-10,000	0	7,513
37	Increase reserves	-45.000	0.000	0.000	0.000	-45.000
38	Decrease reserves	0.000	0.000	0.000	0.000	0.000
39	+ Retained earnings	10,155	0	-10,000	0	7,468

Because it is that easy, we should enter a little bit more flexibility:

- Enter a change in percent
- Enter an absolute change
- Replace the value
- No changes (default)

This is the rule. We limit this to two scenarios. It would also be possible to use attributes to select the validation:

```
['Value',{'Worst','Best'}]=n:IF(['Replace'] = 0,
['Base']*(1+['Change in %'])+ ['Change'],['Replace']);
```

Goal Seeking with TM1

When we talk about simulation in the context of TM1, it is always mainly about the so-called "what if" analysis. We simply ask what will happen if we change one or more parameters. So we modify the input parameters and look at the results, usually some KPIs. And we calculate the variance between the basis and the simulation scenario to get a better understanding of the effects. This has a sophisticated name: sensitivity analysis.

But there is another way of doing simulation: It is called "how to achieve." We ask what we have to change to get a certain result. This can be quite complex if we allow modification not only of a single input, but also of more parameters. And it becomes more complicated if we have to consider constraints. This can lead to operational research models and is far beyond what we want to discuss. This is definitely not the purpose of TM1. However, sometimes a simple goal-seeking function can be helpful.

By default TM1 can't solve this. But with an interpolation process within TurboIntegrator, this can be implemented. It is not very complicated. However, the TI process needs several parameters to work in a flexible manner. And this can be error-prone, of course. We need this high number to specify input and output as granular as possible. The more parameters you use, the bigger the logical distance between source and target parameter can be. For instance, you can find out what the sales figure in 2010 in Business Unit 1 must be to have a profit of 100 M in the group in 2012. But of course, this can only work when there is a direct or indirect relation. In other cases we run into an endless loop.

In this case we assume that we use sales growth parameters, as shown in the following illustration, to calculate the sales for 2011 and 2012. Otherwise, this wouldn't work. Keep in mind that target cells are always calculated members and input cells are not.

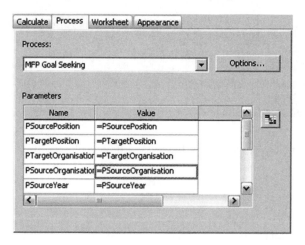

As you can see, we always use Excel names, not references. This is important. Otherwise, you will very likely run into surprises when you insert columns or rows or move the referenced cells. Here is the calculation script. We use the interpolation technique.

- We increase or decrease the input parameter.
- Then we check the result. If we have made progress towards the target, we increase the speed. If we haven't made progress, we change the direction.

```
sCube = 'MFP Base';
vnPrev = CellGetN(sCube , psTargetOrganisation, psTargetPosition,
psScenario , psTargetYear, psTargetType);
vnSource = CellGetN(sCube , psSourceOrganisation, psSourcePosition,
psScenario , psSourceYear, psSourceType);
```

```
i = 1;
vnChange = 1;
vnSource = vnSource+vnChange;
WHILE (i < 9999);
    CellPutN(vnSource, sCube , psSourceOrganisation, psSourcePosition,
psScenario ,
    psSourceYear, psSourceType);
    vnTarget = CellGetN(sCube , psTargetOrganisation, psTargetPosition,
    psScenario ,
    psTargetYear, psTargetType);
    nDiffNew = pnTargetValue - vnTarget;
    nDiffOld = pnTargetValue - vnPrev;
    IF(ROUNDP(nDiffnew,6) = 0) ;
      i = 10000;
    ELSEIF(nDiffNew*nDiffOld< 0);
      VvnChange = if(vnChange < 0, vnChange/4,-vnChange/4);
      sRule = '1';
    ELSEIF (ABS(nDiffNew) < ABS(nDiffOld));
        vnChange = vnChange * 2;
        sRule = '2';
    ELSE;
        vnChange = - vnChange;
        sRule = '3';
    ENDIF;
    vnSource = vnSource + vnChange;
    vnPrev = vnTarget;
    i =i +1;
END;
```

Here's a short example to show how this works. We select EAT as the target for 2014. What sales growth do we need in 2012 to push the target to 40,000?

We enter the parameter, as shown in the following illustration.

	2009	2010	2011	2012	2013	2014	Comment
Target							
EAT	10,698.00	26,932.85	38,765.96	33,609.77	34,930.24	36,327.45	
	2009	2010	2011	2012	2013	2014	Comment
Revenue Growth	0.00 %	1.00 %	4.00 %	4.00 %	4.00 %	4.00 %	
% Cost of Goods sold	0.00 %	30.00 %	16.00 %	30.00 %	30.00 %	30.00 %	
common inflation rate	0.00 %	0.00 %	0.00 %	0.00 %	0.00 %	0.00 %	
dividend payout (in %)	80.00 %	0.00 %	0.00 %	0.00 %	0.00 %	0.00 %	
Tax rate	40.00 %	0.00 %	0.00 %	0.00 %	0.00 %	0.00 %	
Credit interests	4.00 %	0.00 %	0.00 %	0.00 %	0.00 %	0.00 %	
Cost of debts	3.00 %	0.00 %	0.00 %	0.00 %	0.00 %	0.00 %	
Return of investments in securities	4.00 %	0.00 %	0.00 %	0.00 %	0.00 %	0.00 %	
beta factor	0.05	0.00	0.00	0.00	0.00	0.00	
market return	3.00 %	0.00 %	0.00 %	0.00 %	0.00 %	0.00 %	
DSO	0.00	0.00	0.00	0.00	0.00	0.00	
DPO	0.00	0.00	0.00	0.00	0.00	0.00	
DIO R	0.00	0.00	0.00	0.00	0.00	0.00	
DIO UE	0.00	0.00	0.00	0.00	0.00	0.00	
DIO RD	0.00	0.00	0.00	0.00	0.00	0.00	
Average depreciation time	0.00	0.00	0.00	0.00	0.00	0.00	

We run the calculation by clicking the "Goal Seeking" button. This is the result:

		Source			Target	38000		
	MFP Organisations	BU 2			Target	BU 2		
	MFP Scenarios	BaseCase1			GoalSeeking			
	MFP Types	Value						
	Report	Parameters				Year		
	Year	2011				2014		
	Input	Sales Growth						

Target	2009	2010	2011	2012	2013	2014	Comment
EAT	10,688.00	26,932.86	40,550.23	35,156.14	36,538.46	38,000.00	
	2009	2010	2011	2012	2013	2014	Comment
Revenue Growth	0.00 %	1.00 %	8.79 %	4.00 %	4.00 %	4.00 %	
% Cost of Goods sold	0.00 %	30.00 %	16.00 %	30.00 %	30.00 %	30.00 %	
common inflation rate	0.00 %	0.00 %	0.00 %	0.00 %	0.00 %	0.00 %	
dividend payout (in %)	80.00 %	0.00 %	0.00 %	0.00 %	0.00 %	0.00 %	
Tax rate	40.00 %	0.00 %	0.00 %	0.00 %	0.00 %	0.00 %	
Credit interests	4.00 %	0.00 %	0.00 %	0.00 %	0.00 %	0.00 %	
Cost of debts	3.00 %	0.00 %	0.00 %	0.00 %	0.00 %	0.00 %	
Return of investments in securities	4.00 %	0.00 %	0.00 %	0.00 %	0.00 %	0.00 %	
beta factor	0.05	0.00	0.00	0.00	0.00	0.00	
market return	3.00 %	0.00 %	0.00 %	0.00 %	0.00 %	0.00 %	
DSO	0.00	0.00	0.00	0.00	0.00	0.00	
DPO	0.00	0.00	0.00	0.00	0.00	0.00	
DIO R	0.00	0.00	0.00	0.00	0.00	0.00	
DIO UE	0.00	0.00	0.00	0.00	0.00	0.00	
DIO RD	0.00	0.00	0.00	0.00	0.00	0.00	
Average depreciation time	0.00	0.00	0.00	0.00	0.00	0.00	

It works fine in some tested situations. However, there are some limitations:

- It is more complex than Excel, where you can easily use this function on an ad-hoc basis.

- It is hard to standardize, so we can't easily adapt this to various situations.

- We assume a linear or at least a steady relation between source and target. This will be valid in many situations, but not in all. And how would we find this out?

Summary

Scenario planning is more than simple "what if" analysis on a financial multiyear planning model. Thus more sophisticated TM1 models are necessary. We provided a planning framework and some "comfort" functions like copy versions and goal seeking within a single cube. But working with estimated developments (that is, best, worst, normal) and an unlimited number of sometimes competing projects leads to a complex environment. So we split between a base and a project-specific cube. Some enhancements are common: For instance, we don't work with probabilities in this chapter. If you are inclined to enhance the model, it is crucial to have a clear concept. Otherwise, you risk achieving only little progress in comparison to the traditional spreadsheet models.

KPIs, Dashboards, and Balanced Scorecards

J ust give me a dashboard." That's what a lot of managers ask for. They ask for a couple of key measurements that help to make the right decisions. There is nothing wrong with that. However, creating a dashboard is not an easy task. The problem is not only the data provision. The typical reporting and dashboarding capabilities are also not sufficient.

- What are the objectives behind the numbers?
- How are the KPIs linked together? What is the overall (strategic) story?
- What do we have to do improve? Who should do what?

You see, there are a lot of questions to answer. We want to provide some insights into these questions, but most of all we want to show how Cognos TM1 can help. There is no doubt that almost all kinds of KPIs can be defined with rules. However, a management concept like the balanced scorecard (BSC) is more. It is a complete management system.

So we want to discuss these aspects:

- Complex KPI calculations
- Balanced scorecard with perspectives, objectives, measures, and activities
- Activity monitoring

An item to consider is: can we use Cognos TM1 stand-alone, or does it makes sense to use the Metrics Studio of Cognos 10 BI? A predefined tool, the IBM Cognos Metrics Studio, is available, which provides specific support for the balanced scorecard. This tool is also certified by the Balanced Scorecard Collaborative. This is always the same discussion: make or buy. With Cognos 10 Metrics Manager you get something out of the box. In Cognos TM1 there is much more to define. So if you have a clear understanding of your processes and this really matches with Cognos 10 BI, you can save a lot of implementation time. If you have more individual needs or you are not clear about the implementation, it might make sense to think about a Cognos TM1 implementation.

If you want to implement all aspects of a true balanced scorecard, it might be interesting to think about Cognos Metrics Manager. So why should you use Cognos TM1?

- You only need parts of the overall concept. For instance, only measurement calculation is important.

- You have a lot of specific adaptations. For instance, you defined your own assessment method.

- You want to integrate your BSC into planning and/or risk management, which you have implemented with TM1.

The Business Problem

The success story of the balanced scorecard is impressive. It was introduced by Kaplan and Norton in 1992, and almost all bigger companies have tried to implement it. What is the reason for the success of management systems like the balanced scorecard? It is not only the integration of nonfinancial KPIs. That had already been suggested several times. We think that the mixture of KPIs, strategy modeling, and initiatives is something very compelling. Usually the implementation of strategy is weak, so the balanced scorecard appeared at the right time. A logical deduction of strategy, cause-and-effect relations, and the integration of initiatives make it possible to implement a strategy. It is still a complex journey, and many companies have failed.

So the most important aspect is: the balanced scorecard is more than a simple KPI system. It spans a complete management system. Let's start with the challenges. The balanced scorecard addresses the following problems:

- Vision and strategy cannot be implemented.

- There is no link between strategy and target setting by departments and employees.

- There is no link between strategy and resource allocation.

- Feedback is tactical instead of strategic.

The professional implementation lags the business discussion. In the beginning a scorecard is, at least for implementation aspects, rather simple. There's nothing wrong with starting with an office product like Microsoft Excel. You start with a company scorecard and some crucial business units or functional areas.

But with further breakdown, a scorecard usually becomes really complex. More scorecards for departments are generated. These scorecards must be linked. The more people are involved, the more has to be coordinated. We have seen scorecard systems with 20 scorecards, which is not much, but more than 200 people were involved with tasks like providing data, assessing KPIs, and so on.

There is often a "soft start" by only reusing existing information. Many people start to look for KPIs that are already there and implement the new process around this. But a good scorecard instead follows the strategy process. New KPIs must be implemented. The discussion of how to get the relevant basis is important.

Cause-and-effect modeling is very important for the implementation. It means that the modeling of objectives is more important than the measures. With a multiple-layer process, the measures are developed out of a well-defined strategy.

A lot of scorecard implementations have a strong focus on measures. This is easier to implement but lags behind in strategy modeling. But a process might be better. Kaplan and Norton introduced a process to implement a strategy:

- Formulation and implementation of vision and strategy
- Communication and linkage
- Planning and target setting
- Strategic feedback and learning

Formulation and implementation are supported by a cascading scorecard. Strategy must be formulated in cause-and-effect chains. It must be focused on the important objectives.

The whole company must be included. All strategies must be transformed into concrete targets. The question is how detailed the strategy should be. It is time-consuming, so on a departmental level, it is seldom used.

The strategy should drive the definition of objects. Practices should be critically discussed. In contrast to concepts like downsizing or re-engineering (although often differently stated), the target is the creation of strategic potentials.

Strategic feedback is important. It is not about supervision. The strategic hypothesis must be checked in a continuous learning process. The dynamic environment requires a permanent check of the formulated hypothesis and whether the initiatives are still appropriate.

What are the building blocks of a balanced scorecard (Balanced Scorecard Functional Standards, Release 1.0)?

- A *perspective* is a part of a strategy. At least four standard perspectives (finance, customers, processes, and learning/innovation) must be supported. It should be possible to create additional perspectives. Often vendors, organization, or financing are discussed.

- A *theme* is a major component of a strategy, as articulated at the highest level in the vision. Themes represent vertically linked groupings of objectives across several scorecard perspectives.

- *Strategic initiatives* are bundles of activities to meet one or more strategic objectives. For instance, quality improvement can be reached by various means: new vendors can be selected, and quality checks can be intensified, to name a few. Sometimes bigger projects are necessary. Thus a breakdown in detailed steps is necessary. An initiative must be assigned at least to one objective.

- An *objective* is a means to operationalize the strategy. It could be an improvement of quality. It must be assigned to a perspective. An objective is a concise statement articulating a specific component of what the strategy must achieve and what is critical to its success. Each perspective usually contains three to six primary objectives that state key aspects of the strategy to be achieved over the next three to five years.

- A *measure* supports the strategy by making the target measurable. For instance, the improvement of quality itself is not measurable. A measure for quality might be the number of complaints or the percentage of scrap in production. A measure is assigned to one or more objectives.

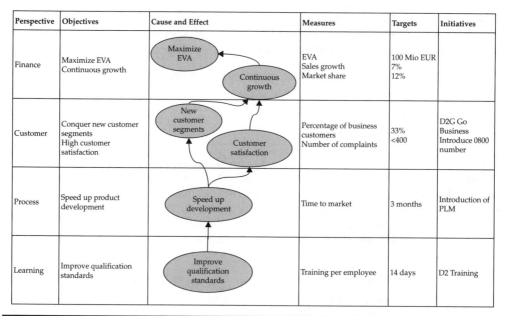

Perspective	Objectives	Cause and Effect	Measures	Targets	Initiatives
Finance	Maximize EVA Continuous growth	Maximize EVA, Continuous growth	EVA Sales growth Market share	100 Mio EUR 7% 12%	
Customer	Conquer new customer segments High customer satisfaction	New customer segments, Customer satisfaction	Percentage of business customers Number of complaints	33% <400	D2G Go Business Introduce 0800 number
Process	Speed up product development	Speed up development	Time to market	3 months	Introduction of PLM
Learning	Improve qualification standards	Improve qualification standards	Training per employee	14 days	D2 Training

Figure 22-1   Balanced scorecard

- *Targets* describe the level of performance or rate of improvement required for a particular measure. Targets are the starting point for the management process. Targets are set for a specific time frame.

- *Cause-and-effect linkages* represent the assumed dependencies between objectives. For instance, there should be a strong connection between quality improvement and customer satisfaction. This can be mapped in a cause-and-effect diagram, like the one in Figure 22-1. Objectives are linked by a directional arrow.

These aspects are more or less minimal standards a system has to support. However, a comfortable level of support goes beyond this. Some aspects are

- Additional attributes, like responsible personnel, are necessary.
- The flexible calculation of KPIs must be supported.
- Frequency of data collection can differ.
- Comments can be added.
- Milestones can be recorded.
- Delay can be calculated.

How Cognos TM1 Can Help

Many software tools compete against each other—OLAP, specific tools, office programs, and groupware, to name a few. High flexibility is crucial. This is not only about four or five perspectives; integration aspects are very important. There are also other concepts like total quality management that should be integrated. The focus on a pure BSC neglects other aspects.

Cognos TM1 and balanced scorecard have a long relationship. Although there is no specific support, a scorecard system can be easily implemented. However, we want to start a little bit earlier and discuss the need for KPI implementation. The question is: how do you calculate dynamic and/or complex measurements?

KPI Calculations

Calculating KPIs in Cognos TM1 is easy. Just create a rule and create a report with the result. Okay, we have to consider feeders, but that's it. In many cases it is that easy. But there are some more complex measures to calculate. It always gets complex when KPIs need data across several dimensions:

- Measures with a dynamic time frame
- Multiperiod measures (CFROI)
- On Top 5 selections

This is very often the case when we have to mix flow numbers with numbers from the balance sheet or other figures like inventory. Although you shouldn't add flow numbers with balance sheet numbers, you are allowed to create a relative KPI. Take a simple ROI calculation, for instance. It is calculated as follows:

```
['Profit'] / ['Equity']
```

But if you want to have the average, you need a modification. If you need more than one KPI with this average number, we recommend defining a value type "Average." With Cognos TM1 10, there is enhanced support for this.

In Cognos TM1, a time difference function is missing. What you can do instead is to work with attributes, as shown in the following code and illustration:

```
['DSO','PTD']=['AR']\['Revenue / Day'];
['YTD'] =N:['PTD']+
DB('KPIs',!KPI Organisations,ATTRS('KPI Periods',!KPI Periods,'Prev'),
!KPI Positions,!KPI Scenarios,'YTD');

['Revenue / Day','PTD']=N:(['Revenue','YTD']-
DB('KPIs',!KPI Organisations,
ATTRS('KPI Periods',!KPI Periods,'PrevYear'),'Revenue',
!KPI Scenarios,'YTD'))\360;
```

KPI Positions	-- 2011	-- Q1.2011	01.2011	02.2011	03.2011	-- Q2.2011	04.2011	05.2011	06.2011
DSO	58.26028321	59.833795014	60	59.504132231	60	58.064516129	59.016393443	57.6	57.6
AR	24000	6000	2000	2000	2000	6000	2000	2000	2000
Revenue / Day	411.944444444	100.277777778	33.333333333	33.611111111	33.333333333	103.333333333	33.888888889	34.722222222	34.722222222
Revenue	12500	3000	1000	1100	900	3500	1200	1300	1000

A very interesting aspect is ranking or sorting in rules. Sometimes we need to calculate averages on a dynamic group. For instance, what is the average sales of our top five customers last quarter? This is not easy to calculate with rules. How can I calculate the top five out of a group? You can use TI, but it is also possible to use rules.

What are the advantages of using rules?

- It is dynamic for all dimensions.
- You have the results instantaneously.

We have the following numbers for January and February. The ranking calculation might be easy in Excel. However, we want this calculation to be expressed dynamically in rules, as shown in the following illustration, so that we can use it for measures.

			Jan				Feb		
			0	2 kum	2 kum		0	2 kum	2 kum
			Revenue	Top	Rank		Revenue	Top	Rank
- A			881	283			894	338	
- A1			366	146			266	107	
1			23	0	0		23	0	0
2			33	0	0		24	0	0
3			45	0	0		25	0	0
4			24	0	0		26	0	0
5			48	48	2		27	0	0
6			34	0	0		28	28	3
7			52	52	1		45	45	1
8			43	0	0		23	0	0
9			18	0	0		34	34	2
10			46	46	3		11	0	0
- A2			515	137			628	231	
11			22	0	0		24	0	0
12			23	0	0		35	0	0
13			34	0	0		44	0	0
14			23	0	0		33	0	0
15			22	0	0		45	45	3
16			14	0	0		34	0	0
17			32	0	0		76	76	1
18			35	0	0		65	65	2
19			33	0	0		43	0	0
20			22	0	0		25	0	0
21			43	43	2		32	0	0
22			23	0	0		35	0	0
23			38	0	0		45	45	3
24			23	0	0		34	0	0
25			34	0	0		23	0	0
26			53	53	1		12	0	0
27			41	41	3		23	0	0

MAX Periods — Top: 3

What is the trick? We need several steps to calculate. We need a MAX function for a set of elements. The MAX function exists. However, only a pairwise comparison is possible.

Hence we must make Cognos TM1 work recursively. Take the cube shown in the next two illustrations:

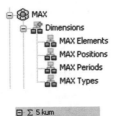

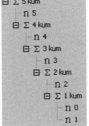

We are using the calculation elements ("MAX Types") shown in the following illustration:

We work with an elimination method:

- First we run through the group elements for revenue and identify the max element by a pairwise comparison and carry the max forward to the last element (Position element "Order").

- We can identify the highest element (Position "Top") by comparing "Revenue" with the last element of the group (Position "Last Element").

- We set this element to zero in the next round and start the process again.

- By accumulating the runs, we get the desired result, as shown in the following code.

```
['Order']=N: IF(ELLEV('MAX Elements',DIMNM('MAX Elements',
DIMIX('MAX Elements',!MAX Elements)-1))<>0,['Revenue'],
MAX(['Revenue'],DB('MAX',DIMNM('MAX Elements',DIMIX('MAX Elements',
!MAX Elements)-1),   'Order', !MAX Periods, !MAX Types)));

['Rank']=N:IF(['TopCount']=1,NUMBR(!MAX Types)+1,0);
```

```
['Last Element']=N: IF(ELCOMP('MAX Elements', ELPAR('MAX Elements',
!MAX Elements,1), ELCOMPn('MAX Elements', ELPAR('MAX Elements',
!MAX Elements,1))) @= !MAX Elements,['Order'],0);

['Revenue']=N:IF(!MAX Types @= '0',stet,IF (DB('MAX', !MAX Elements,
'Revenue', !MAX Periods, ATTRS('MAX Types',!MAX Types,'Prev')) =
DB('MAX',!Max Elements, 'Top', !MAX Periods,
ATTRS('MAX Types',!MAX Types,'Prev')),0,
DB('MAX', !MAX Elements, 'Revenue', !MAX Periods,
ATTRS('MAX Types',!MAX Types,'Prev'))));

['Top']=N:IF (['Revenue'] = DB('MAX', elpar('MAX Elements',
!MAX Elements,1), 'Last Element', !MAX Periods, !MAX Types),
['Revenue'],0);

['TopCount']=N:IF(['Top']<>0,1,0);
```

The next illustration shows how the stepwise calculation works:

MAX Elements	Revenue	Order	Last Element	Top	TopCount	Revenue	Order	Last Element	Top	TopCount	Revenue	Order	Last Element	Top	TopCount
-- A	881	1091	105	105	2	776	1055	91	91	2	685	1000	87	87	2
-- A1	366	450	52	52	1	314	434	48	48	1	266	417	46	46	1
1	23	23	0	0	0	23	23	0	0	0	23	23	0	0	0
2	33	33	0	0	0	33	33	0	0	0	33	33	0	0	0
3	45	45	0	0	0	45	45	0	0	0	45	45	0	0	0
4	24	45	0	0	0	24	45	0	0	0	24	45	0	0	0
5	48	48	0	0	0	48	48	0	48	1	0	45	0	0	0
6	34	48	0	0	0	34	48	0	0	0	34	45	0	0	0
7	52	52	0	52	1	0	48	0	0	0	0	45	0	0	0
8	43	52	0	0	0	43	48	0	0	0	43	45	0	0	0
9	18	52	0	0	0	18	48	0	0	0	18	45	0	0	0
10	46	52	52	0	0	46	48	48	0	0	46	46	46	46	1
-- A2	515	641	53	53	1	462	621	43	43	1	419	583	41	41	1
11	22	22	0	0	0	22	22	0	0	0	22	22	0	0	0
12	23	23	0	0	0	23	23	0	0	0	23	23	0	0	0
13	34	34	0	0	0	34	34	0	0	0	34	34	0	0	0
14	23	34	0	0	0	23	34	0	0	0	23	34	0	0	0
15	22	34	0	0	0	22	34	0	0	0	22	34	0	0	0
16	14	34	0	0	0	14	34	0	0	0	14	34	0	0	0
17	32	34	0	0	0	32	34	0	0	0	32	34	0	0	0
18	35	35	0	0	0	35	35	0	0	0	35	35	0	0	0
19	33	35	0	0	0	33	35	0	0	0	33	35	0	0	0
20	22	35	0	0	0	22	35	0	0	0	22	35	0	0	0
21	43	43	0	0	0	43	43	0	43	1	0	35	0	0	0
22	23	43	0	0	0	23	43	0	0	0	23	35	0	0	0
23	38	43	0	0	0	38	43	0	0	0	38	38	0	0	0
24	23	43	0	0	0	23	43	0	0	0	23	38	0	0	0
25	34	43	0	0	0	34	43	0	0	0	34	38	0	0	0
26	53	53	0	53	1	0	43	0	0	0	0	38	0	0	0
27	41	53	53	0	0	41	43	43	0	0	41	41	41	41	1

With functions like ConsolidatedMax, the script is simpler. We don't need the calculation for "Order." The calculation for "Revenue" and "Top" remains the same.

```
['Revenue']=N:IF(!MAX Types @= '0',STET,IF (DB('MAX', !MAX Elements,
'Revenue', !MAX Periods, ATTRS('MAX Types',!MAX Types,'Prev')) =
```

```
DB('MAX',!Max Elements, 'Top', !MAX Periods,
ATTRS('MAX Types',!MAX Types,'Prev')),0,DB('MAX 2', !MAX Elements,
'Revenue', !MAX Periods, ATTRS('MAX Types',!MAX Types,'Prev'))));

['Last Element']=IF(ELLEV('Max Elements', !Max Elements)>0,
ConsolidatedMax( 0, '', !Max Elements, 'Revenue',!Max Periods,
!Max Types),0 );['Top'] =N: IF(['Revenue'] =
DB('MAX',elpar('Max Elements',!MAX Elements,1),
'Last Element',!MAX Periods,!MAX Types),['Revenue'],0);
```

Objectives, Measures, and Activities

How do we model a balanced scorecard? Although the name "balanced scorecard" sounds kind of old-fashioned, it is a very compelling story. And many companies have tried it. Only a fraction of the concept has been implemented successfully. But this doesn't mean that the concept is poor. And although Kaplan and Norton stated that the concept should only be implemented as a whole, perhaps parts of this concept can be helpful.

A core BSC is not complex, and with four dimensions it is possible to create something meaningful. The illustration shows the dimensions of a basic cube.

Important objects (as standardized by the balanced scorecard collaborative functional specification) are

- Objectives
- Measures
- Activities

We put all objects into the measure dimension; thus this becomes the most important dimension, without question.

We have a single hierarchy with "All" as the top node. The next level is perspectives. Each objective is assigned to a perspective:

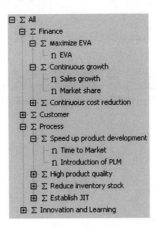

To differentiate between the object types, we define an attribute to describe the object type.

An important item to consider is the relation between KPIs and organizations. Sometimes it is stated that every organization needs its own individual balanced scorecard. However, when you model functional scorecards (for instance, for sales units), the stories of strategy including objectives and measures of the business units and departments can be quite similar. At least the financial perspective has a big overlap. Hence it is obvious that object types should be reused.

We define an assignment table to map the object types to the departments. We use 0/1 later multiplication. A further advantage is that all parents are also automatically assigned.

You can either define a separate cube or a certain type element. We prefer time-dependent assignment, as shown in the following illustration:

Assignment ▼ Jan 2009 ▼				
	BSC areas			
BSC Elements	Logistics &Transportation	D2G Headquarter	Procurement	Marketing & Promotion
-- All	7	21	0	0
-- Finance	0	4	0	0
-- maximize EVA	0	1	0	0
EVA	0	1	0	0
-- Continuous growth	0	2	0	0
Sales growth	0	1	0	0
Market share	0	1	0	0
-- Continuous cost reduction	0	1	0	0
EBIT	0	1	0	0
-- Customer	0	5	0	0
-- High customer retention	0	2	0	0
rebuy quote	0	1	0	0
Introduction of customer card	0	1	0	0
-- Conquer new customer segments	0	2	0	0
Percentage business customers	0	1	0	0
D2G Go Business	0	1	0	0
-- High customer satisfaction	0	1	0	0
Number of complaints	0	1	0	0
+ Introduce 0800 number	0	0	0	0

Another important aspect is that a scorecard should be created out of different organizations. A typical example might be the company scorecard, which often "reuses" the objectives, measures, and initiatives from the functional or business unit scorecards.

With this definition, we can already define our first report. We set up an active form, as shown in the following illustration, because we need zero suppression.

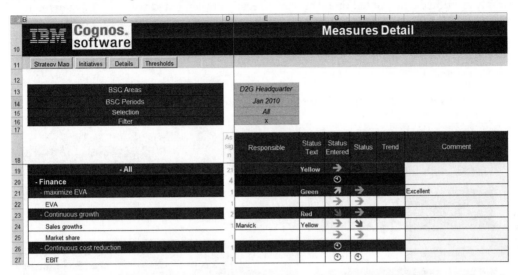

If you switch to Logistics and Transportation, you can see a completely different scorecard.

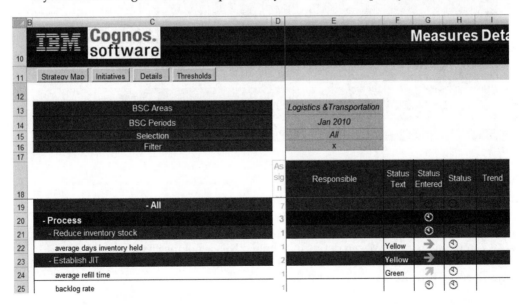

We have implemented a filter to focus on the specific object types "Measures" and "Activities." Since we always want to show the assigned perspectives and objectives, we simply exclude the unwanted one. This can be easily implemented with an MDX statement. We use the MDX filter statement to suppress either measures or activities:

```
=TM1RPTROW($C$9,"TOG:bsc elements",,,,,
"FILTER(DESCENDANTS([bsc elements].["&$E$15&"]),
[bsc elements].[type]<>'"&$E$16&"')",,)
```

With the selection "M," we only see the activities assigned to objectives and perspectives:

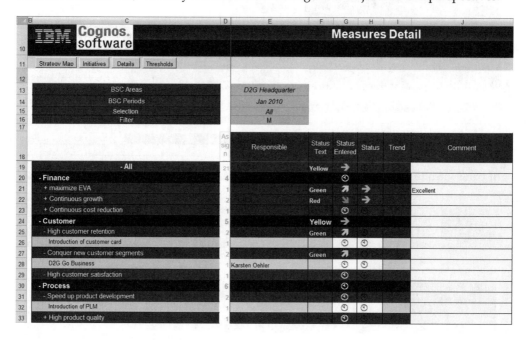

Variances and Aggregation

Aggregation is a specific topic for balanced scorecards. The good old OLAP automatic aggregation is not always helpful when it is about aggregation of weighting and so forth. How can we aggregate? We can define thresholds. This is not the challenge.

It's more important to aggregate measures into targets (of course, not the values but the assessment). There are several possibilities:

- Calculate the average
- Calculate the lowest assessment ("one measure is red -> objective is red")

In the first step we calculate the "Status value." We have six behavior types implemented:

- U   Upper is bad
- L   Lower is bad
- U%   Upper in % is bad
- L%   Upper in % is bad
- UL   Upper and Lower is bad
- UL%   Upper and lower in % is bad

This is an attribute that is assigned to the measure dimension.
The following illustration shows a definition form:

			Jan 2009	Jan 2009	Jan 2009	Jan 2010	Jan 2010	Jan 2010	Jan 2010	Jan 2010	Jan 2010
	BSC Areas	D2G Headquarter	Threshold Type	Threshold Red	Threshold Yellow	Plan	Actual	Variance	Var in %	Status	Status Value
	BSC Period	Jan 2010									
- All									0%	⊙	0
- Finance									0%	⊙	0
- maximize EVA									0%	→	-1
EVA		L%	10	5	30	27	-3	-10%	→	-1
- Continuous growth									0%	→	-1
Sales growths		L	3	1	10	6	-4	-40%	↘	-2
Market share		L	3	1	12	9	-3	-25%	→	-1
- Continuous cost reduction									0%	⊙	0
EBIT		0	0	0	0	0	0	0%	⊙	0
- Customer									0%	⊙	0
- High customer retention									0%	⊙	0
rebuy quote		0	0	0	0	0	0	0%	⊙	0
Introduction of customer card		0	0	0	0	0	0	0%	⊙	0

For the representation of the status, we use the Wingdings character set.
You can imagine that such an assessment can result in long rules. You are right; see the following example code.

```
['Status value']=N: IF(['Actual'] = 0,0,
  IF(DB('BSC', !BSC Areas, !BSC Measures, 'Basis' ,'Threshold Type')
  @='l%',
    IF(['Actual']<['Plan'] *(100-['Threshold Red','basis']) / 100,-2,
    IF(['Actual']<['Plan'] * (100-['Threshold Yellow','basis']) / 100,
    -1,1)),
  IF(DB('BSC', !BSC Areas, !BSC Measures, 'Basis', 'Threshold Type')
  @='u%',
    IF(['Actual']>['Plan'] * (100+   ['Threshold Red','basis']) / 100,-2,
    IF (['Actual']>['Plan'] * (100+ ['Threshold Yellow','basis']) / 100,
    -1,1)),
  IF(DB('BSC', !BSC Areas, !BSC Measures, 'Basis' ,'Threshold Type')
  @='ul%',
    IF (ABS(['Actual']-['Plan'])>['Plan','Jan']*
    (['Threshold Red','basis']) / 100,-2,
```

```
    IF (ABS(['Actual']-['Plan']) >['Plan','Jan'] *
      (['Threshold Yellow','basis']) / 100,-1,1)),
  IF (DB('BSC', !BSC Areas, !BSC Measures, 'Basis' ,'Threshold Type')
  @='ul',
    IF ( abs( ['Variance']) > ['Threshold Red','basis'],-2,
    IF (abs(['Variance']) >['Threshold Yellow','basis'],-1,1)),
  IF (DB('BSC', !BSC Areas, !BSC Measures, 'Basis' ,'Threshold Type')
  @='u',
    IF (['Variance']>['Threshold Red','basis'],-2,
    IF (['Variance']>['Threshold Yellow','basis'],-1,1)),
  IF (DB('BSC', !BSC Areas, !BSC Measures, 'Basis', 'Threshold Type')
  @='l',
    IF (['Variance']<-['Threshold Red','basis'],-2,
    IF (['Variance']<-['Threshold Yellow','basis'],-1,1)),0)))))));

C: DB('BSC', !BSC Areas, ELCOMP('BSC Measures', !BSC Measures,
ELCOMPN('BSC Measures', !BSC Measures)), !BSC Periods, !BSC Scenarios);
```

We do this in two steps: first we standardize. In a second step, we create the symbols used in Excel.

```
['Status'] = S:
IF (DB('BSC', !BSC Areas, !BSC Measures, !BSC Periods, 'Status Value') = -1, 'è',
IF (DB('BSC', !BSC Areas, !BSC Measures, !BSC Periods, 'Status Value') = -2, 'î',
IF (DB('BSC', !BSC Areas, !BSC Measures, !BSC Periods, 'Status Value') =
1,'ì','Ä')));
['Status Min'] = N:IF(['Status Value'] <= -1, -1, ['Status Value']) ;
```

It is also important to overwrite the status manually. Why? This is one of the core concepts of the BSC. Because we try to measure "soft facts," the chosen measure is very often not the best indicator. Thus the measure should give only an impression of change. Together with other facts, the responsible manager should state his opinion. An example: the customer satisfaction rate is green due to a given threshold. The responsible manager knows of some recent complaints that will lead to a changed index in the next interview round. So why should we suppress this information? Okay, you can argue that the measure has a lower fit, but that is reality.

It would be helpful to enter the symbols directly. This can be easily done with the drop-down capabilities of Excel. The problem is that the format is not shown in the list box:

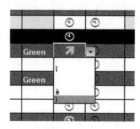

Hence we have to implement a method. We define a "BSC Types" element "Status Text." A picklist referring to the dimension BSC Status is defined. Finally, we need a rule for the transformation.

```
['Status Entered']=S: IF (DB('BSC', !BSC Areas, !BSC Measures,
!BSC Periods, 'Status Text') @= 'Yellow', 'è', IF (DB('BSC', !BSC Areas,
!BSC Measures, !BSC Periods, 'Status Text') @= 'Red', 'î',
IF (DB('BSC', !BSC Areas, !BSC Measures, !BSC Periods, 'Status Text')
@= 'Green', 'ì',DB('BSC', !BSC Areas, !BSC Measures,
!BSC Periods, 'Status') )));
```

The following illustration shows the result.

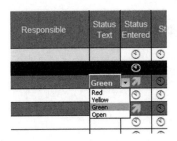

And do not forget the aggregation. We calculate the weighted variance:

```
['WeightVariance']=N:['Var in %']*
NUMBR(DB('BSC', !BSC Areas, !BSC Measures, 'Basis', 'Weight'))\100;
['Variance'] = ['Actual']-['Plan'];
['Var in %'] = N:['Variance'] \ ['Plan'];C:['WeightVariance'];
```

Model Cause-and-Effect Diagram

An important aspect of the balanced scorecard concept is the graphical representation of cause-and-effect relations. This should make the story of strategy transparent to the readers. So you understand intuitively, for instance, that customer satisfaction influences revenue.

Objective bubbles are simply linked by arrows. Please note that objectives should be connected, not measures. A cause-and-effect diagram shows the relations between the objects and explains how the objectives cause each other.

There are various variations of cause-and-effect diagrams. The modern name, by the way, is *strategy map*. It should tell a story.

Some say that this is the most important aspect of a scorecard. The map should be intensively communicated. So that is something for Cognos TM1 Web. You can transfer pictures from Excel to Web. No problem at all. But take a look to the following strategy map:

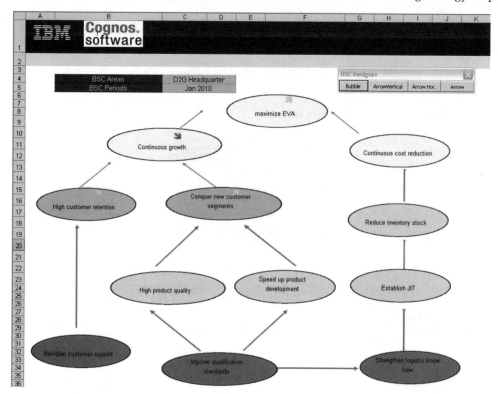

You see the colored arrows? If you change the period or area, you will get different signs and colors. This is something that can be done with Excel. And the good thing is that this is transferred to the Web.

We would like to get color coding into the Web. But our bubbles are not cells. The trick is to transfer the content of a cell into a textbox element. The good thing is that it works. The bad thing is that it takes over only the content, not the format. So you need three textboxes to do traffic lightning.

But it is more complicated. You need to do this for every text box. Create three boxes, apply formatting, and set the reference. You can do this manually, but we prefer to write an Excel macro. The illustration shows the color coding symbol together with an objective bubble.

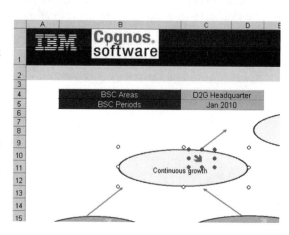

We have stored our templates in a file called "Scorecard Designer.xls."

First we need a data area. The idea is to mark the relevant area and then run a VBA macro across the selected area. Column C gets the status via a DBR function. Then we calculate the symbols:

```
D45:=IF(C45="î","î","")

E45:=IF(C45="è","è","")

F45:=IF(C45="ì","ì","")
```

The last column in the marked area is an ELPAR function:

	A	B	C	D	E	F	G	H	I
37									
38									
39									
40									
41									
42									
43									
44		Objective	status entered	Red	Yellow	Green	Perspective		
45		maximize EVA	ì				Finance		
46		Continuous growth	è				Finance		
47		Continuous cost reduction	À				Finance		
48		High customer retention	ì				Customer		
49		Conquer new customer segments	ì				Customer		
50		Speed up product development	À				Process		
51		High product quality	À				Process		
52		friendlier customer support	À				Innovation and Learning		
53		Improve qualification standards	À				Innovation and Learning		
54		Reduce inventory stock	À				Process		
55		Establish JIT	À				Process		
56		Strengthen logistic know how	À				Innovation and Learning		
57									
58									

The first procedure runs through the table and generates a bubble per item. We create a simple form in VBA:

By clicking on the Bubble button, we start a procedure. Here's the code for the procedure:

```
Private Sub CommandBubbleClick()
    Set r = Selection
    For a = 1 To Selection.Areas.Count
    For i = 1 To Selection.Areas(1).Rows.Count
      If Selection.Areas(a).Cells(i, 1) <> "" Then
      TextAdress = Selection.Areas(a).Cells(i, 1).Address
      RedAddress = Selection.Areas(a).Cells(i, 3).Address
      YellowAddress = Selection.Areas(a).Cells(i, 4).Address
```

```
        GreenAddress = Selection.Areas(a).Cells(i, 5).Address
        perspective = Selection.Areas(a).Cells(i, 6)
        CreateSingleButton perspective, TextAddress, RedAddress, _
        YellowAddress, GreenAddress, i
        r.Select
      End If
    Next
    Next
End Sub
```

The Bubble function is more interesting.

The line break is important. The transfer to Web is not perfect. So we have to do this manually, as shown in the following code:

```
Sub CreateSingleButton(perspective, TextAddress, RedAddress, _
YellowAddress, GreenAddress, counter)
Select Case perspective
  Case "Finance"
    bubble = "BubbleFinance"
  Case "Customer"
    bubble = "BubbleCustomer"
    Case "Process"
    bubble = "BubbleProcess"
Case "Innovation and Learning"
    bubble = "BubbleLearning"
End Select
With Workbooks("Scorecard Designer.xls").Sheets("Scorecard")
    .Shapes(bubble).Copy
    ActiveSheet.Paste
    ActiveSheet.Shapes(bubble).Top = 103
    ActiveSheet.Shapes(bubble).Left = 20
    ActiveSheet.Shapes(bubble).ZOrder 1

    .Shapes("YellowArrow").Copy
    ActiveSheet.Paste
    ActiveSheet.Shapes("YellowArrow").Top = 103
    ActiveSheet.Shapes("YellowArrow").Left = 110
    ActiveSheet.Shapes("YellowArrow").Select
    Selection.Formula = YellowAddress

    .Shapes("RedArrow").Copy
    ActiveSheet.Paste
    ActiveSheet.Shapes("RedArrow").ZOrder msoBringToFront
    ActiveSheet.Shapes("RedArrow").Top = 103
    ActiveSheet.Shapes("RedArrow").Left = 110
    ActiveSheet.Shapes("RedArrow").Select
    Selection.Formula = RedAddress

    .Shapes("GreenArrow").Copy
    ActiveSheet.Paste
    ActiveSheet.Shapes("GreenArrow").ZOrder msoBringToFront
    ActiveSheet.Shapes("GreenArrow").Top = 100
    ActiveSheet.Shapes("GreenArrow").Left = 110
```

```
   ActiveSheet.Shapes("GreenArrow").Select
   Selection.Formula = GreenAddress

   txt = Range(TextAddress).Text
   If Len(txt) > 27 Then
   For i = 1 To Len(txt)
    If Mid(txt, i, 1) = " " And i <= 27 Then stp1 = i
    If Len(txt) > 54 Then
       If Mid(txt, i, 1) = " " And i > 27 Then stp2 = i
    Else
       stp2 = 53
    End If
   Next

  .Shapes("TargetText1").Copy
   ActiveSheet.Paste
   ActiveSheet.Shapes("TargetText1").Top = 110
   ActiveSheet.Shapes("TargetText1").Left = 26
   ActiveSheet.Shapes("TargetText1").Select
   Selection.Text = Mid(txt, 1, stp1)

   .Shapes("TargetText2").Copy
   ActiveSheet.Paste
   ActiveSheet.Shapes("TargetText2").Top = 125
   ActiveSheet.Shapes("TargetText2").Left = 26
   ActiveSheet.Shapes("TargetText2").Select
   Selection.Text = Mid(txt, stp1 + 1, stp2 - stp1)

   .Shapes("TargetText3").Copy
   ActiveSheet.Paste
   ActiveSheet.Shapes("TargetText3").Top = 140
   ActiveSheet.Shapes("TargetText3").Left = 26
   ActiveSheet.Shapes("TargetText3").Select
   Selection.Text = Mid(txt, stp2 + 1)

Else
   .Shapes("TargetText").Copy
   ActiveSheet.Paste
   ActiveSheet.Shapes("TargetText").Top = 125
   ActiveSheet.Shapes("TargetText").Left = 26
   ActiveSheet.Shapes("TargetText").Select
   Selection.Text = Range(TextAddress).Text
End If

 If Len(txt) > 27 Then
    ActiveSheet.Shapes.Range(Array(bubble, "RedArrow", "TargetText1",
 "TargetText2", "TargetText3", "GreenArrow", "YellowArrow")).Select
 Else
    ActiveSheet.Shapes.Range(Array(bubble, "RedArrow", "TargetText",
"GreenArrow", "YellowArrow")).Select
 End If
 Selection.ShapeRange.Group.Select
End With
End Sub
```

And finally we want to use arrows. Since this should also work on the web, we can't use Office objects. Instead we use bitmaps. We need basically three bitmaps for horizontal, vertical, and 45-degree. These pictures are simply copied:

```
Private Sub CommandButton1_Click()
Workbooks("Scorecard Designer.xls").Sheets("scorecard") _
.Shapes("ArrowVertical").Copy
ActiveSheet.Paste
End Sub
```

Activity Control

The last important aspect is monitoring the initiatives or activities. Activity control can be enhanced to professional project control. But project control is excessive in most cases. Mostly initiatives are set up as small projects, which nevertheless should be traced.

We want to show a simple concept that can be easily adapted to other performance management areas where tracking of activities is important. A typical entry form for activities could look like the following illustration:

Typical information is collected with attributes:

- Responsibilities
- Status for time, costs, and quality

When we talk about activities, it is also about timing and delays. To calculate time, we collect the following attributes.

- Due dates
- Days left
- Delays

It makes sense to calculate delays within rules. So you can filter dynamically, for instance, in an active form.

We take the following rules:

```
['Days to Complete']= ['Completion Date']- NOW-    21915;
['Completion date']=N:STET;
C:DB('BSC Attributes',elcomp('BSC Elements',!BSC Elements,
ELCOMPN('BSC Elements',!BSC Elements)),!BSC Attributes);
```

The good thing is that we can use the way Excel stores data. However, Excel starts with 1.1.1900. Cognos TM1 starts with 1.1.1960. Hence we need to allow for the difference of 21915 days, to use the Excel formatting properly. For the completion date of activities with subtasks, we adopt the last child.

We define a dynamic view for the activity.

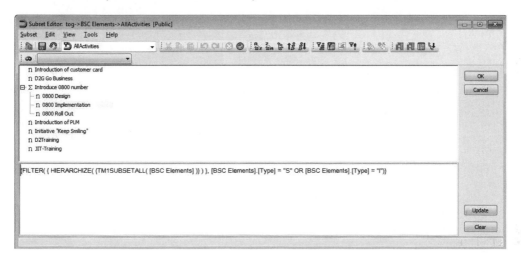

With this we can create the following filter for overdue activities:

```
C18: =TM1RPTROW($C$9,"tog:BSC Elements",,,,,IF(N14="yes",$Q$14,$Q$13))
Q13:="[BSC Elements].[AllActivities]"
Q14:="FILTER([BSC Elements].[AllActivities],
[BSC Attributes].([BSC Attributes].["&$R$16&"])<0)"
```

Summary

KPIs shouldn't be assessed in isolation. They should be part of an overall management concept. The balanced scorecard might be the most popular system. So it can be seen as a benchmark for implementation.

Cognos TM1 can play a critical role in your BSC strategy in your organization. Cognos TM1's key attributes for real-time calculations and linked metrics can help automate and transform your scorecarding solutions from isolated spreadsheets into a comprehensive network of cascading goals linked to key strategic KPIs.

Cognos TM1 implementation shouldn't be reduced to KPI modeling. The system is flexible enough to map all parts of the management system we described.

Group Performance Management

W hen we started working in performance management several years ago, IT support in group corporations was mainly focused on statutory consolidation. That statement isn't true any more. Group corporations are complex structures that must be controlled efficiently. Our goal is to provide you with some ideas on how to use TM1 in this environment—you can use these proposals stand-alone or in conjunction with IBM Cognos Controller.

To standardize the combined use of Controller and TM1, the Financial Analytics Publish (FAP) has been developed. It is a near-real-time interface that automatically creates a TM1 cube out of Controller structures and transfers data within a definable frequency to TM1. You don't have to care about time-dependent organization structures, difficult eliminations, or currency calculation. This is done within the controller. TM1 gets only the results.

However, there are group topics beyond statutory consolidation. Pure accounting data is too limited to answer various questions about effectiveness and efficiencies of strategies, products, resources, and so on across companies. Distributed processes across the group companies must be coordinated. Financial numbers give too narrow a view on this. Thus nonfinancial KPIs and qualitative information like risk assessments are necessary. This is true not only for an operationally working holding with close collaboration, which is already closely integrated and has a strong focus on operational control, but also for financial holdings.

For management in single companies, sophisticated concepts for information provision and standards exist, mainly with the support of a central data warehouse. A well-defined data cleansing process is usually the starting point for all analysis. Furthermore, transactional systems are very standardized in many companies, so that filling of this structure is not that complicated any more.

But this cannot be simply adapted to group structures. The subsidiaries often have very heterogeneous systems. Larger groups buy and sell companies very frequently. Newly acquired companies often do not have the preferred information architecture. Experienced group managers often don't want to massively change the environment of a newly acquired company in favor of an overall unified system because, in consequence, working processes that are often based on specific software might be destroyed. The reason is that the leaders in ERP software are usually excellent in functions with a high degree of standardization, like accounting, but are sometimes poor when it comes to industry-specific requirements.

Architecture for group management solutions must be somewhat specific. It is a combination of consolidation tools and—that is why we are focusing on this topic—OLAP tools. We developed several proposals to enhance IBM Cognos Controller with TM1 to support these requirements. Although IBM Cognos TM1 is already part of the analysis capabilities of IBM Cognos Controller, we focus on value-adding parts like intercompany matching and group contribution margin calculation, which you can use stand-alone or in combination with the IBM Cognos Controller.

An Overall Group Performance Management Architecture

A lot of functions spread across various group departments are necessary. Subsidiaries must be integrated in these functions. Just allowing accounting data to flow from subsidiaries to the group is not sufficient: for instance, planning information goes top down and bottom up.

But as with single companies, function integration is a key requirement: A lot of information is used by more than one group department. For instance, risk management needs information about the most recent forecast and planning details, too. The profit plan is the basis for the midterm cash planning and so forth. These dependencies must be considered even if the local and the group departments work more or less independently. The overall target is that all process participants can get their information out of the process.

IBM has been working on a complete but open architecture. The traditional statutory consolidation is solved with IBM Cognos Controller (see Figure 23-1). Tasks like elimination, currency translation, and so on are functions within the Controller. Additional functions are implemented with TM1.

There are three levels of support:

- The *information transformation level* helps with standardizing and quality assurance. This is very close to the classic extract, transform, and load (ETL). But there are also additional tasks necessary in a group that are usually not relevant or specifically considered for single companies, like account mapping or intercompany matching.

- On the *functional level*, all the data processing is organized. This includes typical management tasks like planning, treasury, and so on. A specific focus is set on the coordination between the group departments and the subsidiaries.

- The *analysis and reporting level* provides the results to the various stakeholders. This should include the group view and the local views and most important the link between both.

In addition to the three levels, a process control is necessary. A lot of activities are to be coordinated. For instance, the elimination process shouldn't start before intercompany matching is completed. Intercompany matching within bigger groups involves a lot of managers.

To provide the functions, no new software is necessary. All tasks can be implemented with either with Controller or TM1, sometimes with both. Some enhancements like group contribution margin based on supply chains or combined reporting on local and group

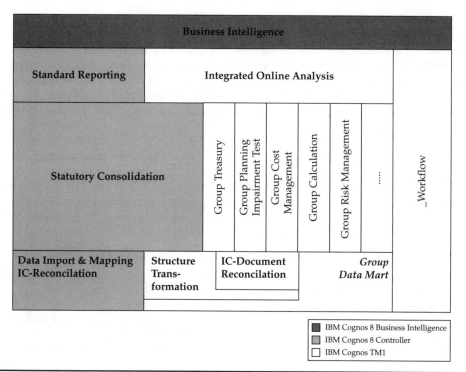

FIGURE 23-1 IBM Cognos: House of group performance management

accounts can be modeled with TM1 on top of IBM Cognos Controller. We want to introduce the following TM1 concepts:

- Currency conversion
- Harmonization between local and group structures by mapping
- Organization by period
- Eliminations
- Quotal consolidation
- Intercompany matching
- Group contribution margin

Most of these concepts are professionally implemented within the IBM Cognos Controller. However, sometimes using the Controller might be more than you need; for instance, when you only need a few elimination functions for management consolidation or group planning. Or if you need more flexibility, you are free to decide between built (TM1) or buy (Controller).

Currency Conversion

Currency conversion is quite simple—usually. You take the amount in local currency, for instance, British pounds (GBP), multiply this by a currency rate, and work with the result (in dollars and/or Euros). This should be easily implemented with the use of a TM1 rule. But if you are working as a group controller in an international group with subsidiaries around the world, you certainly disagree about ease of implementation. The discussion usually starts with the question about the right currency rate. It can be the daily rate, a budgeted rate, a forecasted rate, and other rates. Is there a right one? No, this is usually assigned to the specific reporting need. Take the account receivables as an example. You can take the single transaction times and use the respective daily rate. If you sum up all transactions and use an average rate for currency conversion, it is very likely that you will come to a different result than if you sum up the transactions and translate the sum. How should you book the differences? Currency variations are an important topic in groups.

We want to discuss some typical requirements:

- Usually reporting positions can be categorized into flow and stock. Items in the balance sheet are stock values. Most items in the P&L are flow values. That looks quite simple. You usually calculate flow positions with an average rate and stock positions with a period end rate. (In a group balance sheet, equity items are often multiplied by a historic rate.) The best thing is to assign the conversion method to the position dimension. But there are still challenges: for instance, how to handle retained earnings? Is this stock or flow? And how do you handle historical rates that are required for equity positions?

- A derived cash flow statement consists of flow elements. But because in most cases a cash flow statement is derived from the P&L statement and balanced sheet, cash positions are aggregations of P&L and balance sheet positions. For P&L we can take the usual average rate. But the end rate for balanced sheet items is not appropriate for the cash flow. We have to define a currency conversion rule for the cash flow statement. Think about possible differences. When you calculate some items with an average rate and some with an end rate, it is very likely that the asset sum doesn't equal equity and liabilities any more.

- And finally you want some insights into variance analysis. Most managers are not responsible for currency variations. So we need to split up into currency and so-called operational variance.

But what is a good starting point? There is a standard model, which is more or less described in training books (implementation shouldn't take more than 30 minutes). The simplest design decision is about the currency cube, as shown in the following illustration:

We have defined a currencies dimension ("GCT Currencies") and the Currency Translations dimension, which stores the different versions "AVG" and "END," as shown in the following illustration. Sometimes more types like historical rates or no translation for non-financial KPIs are necessary.

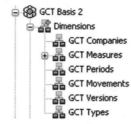

The following illustration shows our data cube for the financial statements:

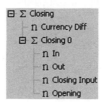

For the "GCT Basis 2" cube, we define a Movements dimension. We will need them later for the calculation of the currency variances. This is necessary to capture the different currency valuations. We will describe the difference between "Closing" and "Closing 0" later.

For a single position, we need to store stock and flow, as shown in the following illustration. This is necessary to create the change statement for the balance sheet as preparation for the cash flow statement.

We also need to define attributes:

- The dimension "GCT Companies" holds the currency information.
- The dimension "GCT Measures" has an attribute "Type" to get the currency type, as shown in the following illustration:

	CarryOver (Text)	Type (Text)
Sales		AVG
Costs		AVG
Profit		AVG
Assets		END
Fixed Assets		END
Current Assets		END
Equity		END
Capital Reserves	Y	END
Retained Earnings	Y	END
Liabilities		END
Cash Flow from operations		AVG
Cash Flow from Investments		AVG
Cash Flow from Financing		AVG
Equity and Liabilities		END
Cash	Y	END
Change in Liquidity		AVG
Receivables		END

With this definition, an easy standard rule can be set up. The two ATTRS functions fetch the relevant attributes to get the appropriate currency rate. Feeder setting is also not a challenge.

```
SKIPCHECK;
['GCT Types':'Group']=N:['local']*DB('GCT Rates', ATTRS('GCT Companies',
!GCT Companies,'Currency'), ATTRS ('GCT Measures',
!GCT Measures,'Type'), !GCT Periods, !GCT Versions);
FEEDERS;
['Local']=>['GCT Types':'Group'];
```

However, the real world is more complicated. Here are some examples:

- Sometimes you need more than one group currency.
- Currency variations must be analyzed.
- Particularly in the financial service industry, you need more than one local currency. This is very often the case when you have a lot of intercompany transactions.
- You have to include historic rates for equity transactions.

We can't provide solutions for all possibilities. However, we want to improve the model a little bit to show how complex currency calculation can be mapped in TM1. Let us do this with the cash flow calculation. We built up an integrated model where the cash flow is calculated by P&L and the statement of changes for the balance sheet. The bottom-line cash effect should be identical with the cash change in the balance sheet between opening and closing.

We use the same cash flow calculation mechanism as explained in Chapter 19: We assume that AVG is used as a synonym for flow and END as a synonym for stock:

```
['Local Flow','Closing Input']=N:['Local'] -IF(ATTRS('GCT Measures',
!GCT Measures,'Type') @='AVG',0, DB('GCT Basis 2',
!GCT Companies, !GCT Measures, ATTRS('GCT Periods',
!GCT Periods,'Prev'), !GCT Movements,!GCT Versions, 'Local'));
```

The following illustration shows the result. Since we start with 2010, "local" and "local flow" are identical for 2010.

Subsidiary 1 ▾	Actuals ▾	Closing ▾			
		GCT Periods		GCT Types	
		2010		2011	
Standard		Local	Local Flow	Local	Local Flow
-- Assets		450	450	700	250
Fixed Assets		250	250	350	100
-- Current Assets		200	200	350	150
Cash		100	100	200	100
Receivables		100	100	150	50
-- Equity and Liabilities		450	450	700	250
-- Equity		250	250	400	150
Capital Reserves		100	100	150	50
Retained Earnings		150	150	250	100
Liabilities		200	200	300	100
-- Change in Liquidity		100	100	50	100
-- Cash Flow from operations		250	250	250	150
-- Profit		150	150	100	100
Sales		400	400	300	300
Costs		-250	-250	-200	-200
Receivables		100	100	150	50
Liabilities		200	200	300	100
-- Cash Flow from Investments		-250	-250	-350	-100
Fixed Assets		250	250	350	100
-- Cash Flow from Financing		100	100	150	50
Capital Reserves		100	100	150	50

You can see further that the change in Liquidity/Local Flow (100) is identical with the change of cash between 2010 and 2011. For this we wrote a rule:

```
['Cash','In',{'Local','Local Flow'}]=N:
['Change in Liquidity','Closing','Local Flow'];
```

We also take the profit over into the retained earnings:

```
['Retained Earnings']=N:['Profit'];
```

But we also want to work with a carryover logic. That is why we have defined the Movements dimension. With this structure in mind, let us think about the behavior. Even if we handle balance sheet items with a generic end currency rate, this is not appropriate. So we have to assign a currency attribute, as shown in the following illustration:

	Type (Text)
Opening	END
Closing	END
In	AVG
Out	AVG
Closing Input	
Currency Diff	
Closing 0	

It is obvious that we don't need carryover for flow items. But we don't want to use END as a generic function for all positions with the attribute "END." There is the attribute "CarryOver" where we can flag the carryover behavior. For items that we don't want to have this behavior, we use the manual input.

To carry over, we wrote a rule line:

```
['Opening',{'Local','Group'}]=IF (ATTRS('GCT measures',!GCT Measures,'Carry
Over')@='Y',DB('GCT Basis 2',!GCT Companies, !GCT Measures,  ATTRS('GCT
Periods',!GCT Periods,'Prev'), 'Closing',!GCT Versions,!GCT Types),STET);
```

This was the basic stuff. Now we have to calculate the currency conversion. We only need the account-based rate for "Closing Input." For the rest we fetch the rate from the Movements dimension.

```
['GCT Types':'Group']=N:['local']*IF (!GCT Movements @= 'Closing Input' ,
DB('GCT Rates', ATTRS ('GCT Companies',!GCT Companies,'Currency'),
ATTRS('GCT Measures',!GCT Measures,'Type'), !GCT Periods, !GCT Versions),
DB('GCT Rates', ATTRS ('GCT Companies',!GCT Companies,'Currency'),
ATTRS('GCT Movements',!GCT Movements,'Type'), !GCT Periods, !GCT Versions));
```

Furthermore, we need a specific calculation for the group flow. Every single flow position (even the derived ones for the cash flow statement) must be converted with the average rate.

```
['Group Flow']=N:['Local Flow'] * DB('GCT Rates', ATTRS('GCT Companies',
!GCT Companies,'Currency'), 'AVG', !GCT Periods, !GCT Versions);
```

Let's see how this works in the following illustration:

	B	C	D	E	F	G	H	I	J	K
10					CUBE:	tog:GCT Rates			Actuals	
11	GCT Companies	Subsidiary 1	USD		GCT Currencies	USD	AVG		0,8	
12	GCT Versions	Actuals			GCT Periods	2011	END		0,9	
13	GCT Movements	Closing 0								
14										
15										
16		2010	2010			2011	2011	2011		2011
17		Local	Group			Local	Local Flow	Group	Rate	Group Flow
18	- Assets	450	315			700	250	600	0,857	200
19	Fixed Assets	250	175			350	100	315	0,9	80
20	- Current Assets	200	140			350	150	285	0,814	120
21	Cash	100	70			200	100	150	0,75	80
22	Receivables	100	70			150	50	135	0,9	40
23	- Equity and Liabilities	450	315			700	250	600	0,857	200
24	- Equity	250	175			400	150	330	0,825	120
25	Capital Reserves	100	70			150	50	135	0,9	40
26	Retained Earnings	150	105			250	100	195	0,78	80
27	Liabilities	200	140			300	100	270	0,9	80
28	- Change in Liquidity	100	70			50	100	35	0,7	80
29	- Cash Flow from operations	250	175			250	150	215	0,86	120
30	- Profit	150	105			100	100	80	0,8	80
31	Sales	400	280			300	300	240	0,8	240
32	Costs	-250	-175			-200	-200	-160	0,8	-160
33	Receivables	100	70			150	50	135	0,9	40
34	Liabilities	200	140			300	100	270	0,9	80
35	- Cash Flow from Investments	-250	-175			-350	-100	-315	0,9	-80
36	Fixed Assets	250	175			350	100	315	0,9	80
37	- Cash Flow from Financing	100	70			150	50	135	0,9	40
38	Capital Reserves	100	70			150	50	135	0,9	40

You see that group conversion is slightly out of balance. Cash conversion is wrong and retained earnings are wrong, too. What has happened? The group cash flow (80) is identical with the cash delta (80). But the balanced sheet cash conversion is wrong because it is a mixture of flow and stock conversion. And the capital reserves and retained earnings are incorrect too, for the same reason.

Let us investigate the movements, as shown in the following illustration:

Subsidiary 1 ▾ Actuals ▾

		GCT Periods				GCT Types			
		2010				2011			
GCT Measures	GCT Movements	Local	Local Flow	Group	Group Flow	Local	Local Flow	Group	Group Flow
Cash	-- Closing 0	100	100	70	70	200	100	150	80
	In	100	100	70	70	100	100	80	80
	Out	0	0	0	0	0	0	0	0
	Closing Input	0	0	0	0	0	0	0	0
	Opening	0	0	0	0	100		70	0
Capital Reserves	-- Closing 0	100	100	70	70	150	50	135	40
	In	0	0	0	0	0	0	0	0
	Out	0	0	0	0	0	0	0	0
	Closing Input	100	100	70	70	150	50	135	40
	Opening	0	0	0	0	0	0	0	0
Retained Earnings	-- Closing 0	150	150	105	105	250	100	195	80
	In	0	0	0	0	0	0	0	0
	Out	0	0	0	0	0	0	0	0
	Closing Input	150	150	105	105	100	100	90	80
	Opening	0	0	0	0	150	0	105	0
+ Change in Liquidity	-- Closing 0	100	100	70	70	50	100	35	80
	In	0	0	0	0	0	0	0	0
	Out	0	0	0	0	0	0	0	0
	Closing Input	100	100	70	70	50	100	35	80
	Opening	0	0	0	0	0	0	0	0

So we define a movement line, "Currency Diff." And we need a second one to calculate the variances. We can't use "Closing" because this would lead to a circular reference:

```
['Currency Diff','GCt Types':'Group']=N:['Closing 0','GCT Types':'Local'] *
DB('GCT Rates', ATTRS('GCT Companies',!GCT Companies,'Currency'),
ATTRS ('GCT Measures',!GCT Measures,'Type'), !GCT Periods, !GCT Versions)
-['Closing 0','GCT Types':'Group'];
```

What does this difference mean? It is the difference between the standard rate (from the account definition) and the movement rate. For instance, cash from the cash flow statement has taken the average rate of 0.8. To have a "balanced" balance sheet, you need to calculate with 0.9 (the end rate). Thus the difference is 0.1 * 100 + 0.2 * 100. With this definition we can provide a proper reporting, as shown in the following illustration:

	B	C	D	E	F	G	H	I	J	K
10					CUBE:	tog:GCT Rates			Actuals	
11	GCT Companies	Subsidiary 1	USD		GCT Currencies	USD		AVG	0,8	
12	GCT Versions	Actuals			GCT Periods	2011		END	0,9	
13	GCT Movements	Closing								
14										
15										
16		2010	2010				2011	2011	2011		2011
17		Local	Group				Local	Local Flow	Group	Rate	Group Flow
18	- Assets	450	315				700	250	630	0,9	200
19	Fixed Assets	250	175				350	100	315	0,9	80
20	- Current Assets	200	140				350	150	315	0,9	120
21	Cash	100	70				200	100	180	0,9	80
22	Receivables	100	70				150	50	135	0,9	40
23	- Equity and Liabilities	450	315				700	250	630	0,9	200
24	- Equity	250	175				400	150	360	0,9	120
25	Capital Reserves	100	70				150	50	135	0,9	40
26	Retained Earnings	150	105				250	100	225	0,9	80
27	Liabilities	200	140				300	100	270	0,9	80
28	- Change in Liquidity	100	70				50	100	35	0,7	80
29	- Cash Flow from operations	250	175				250	150	215	0,86	120
30	- Profit	150	105				100	100	80	0,8	80
31	Sales	400	280				300	300	240	0,8	240
32	Costs	-250	-175				-200	-200	-160	0,8	-160
33	Receivables	100	70				150	50	135	0,9	40
34	Liabilities	200	140				300	100	270	0,9	80
35	- Cash Flow from Investments	-250	-175				-350	-100	-315	0,9	-80
36	Fixed Assets	250	175				350	100	315	0,9	80
37	- Cash Flow from Financing	100	70				150	50	135	0,9	40
38	Capital Reserves	100	70				150	50	135	0,9	40

Account Mapping

Account and further structure mapping is a prerequisite for consolidation. Subsidiaries are often free to choose their own structure definitions, and thus there are challenges to bringing the data together even if the technical integration aspects are solved.

Sometimes legal requirements force companies to not use group-wide standards. And legacy systems can cause problems with adapting group standards. Even though standardization is possible from a theoretical point of view, a lot of groups acquire new companies very often. It usually takes time to adapt. Although standardization can be helpful, it should be carefully considered. In a very dynamic group this can take too long, so that in a short time frame, a solution must be provided. Perhaps the energy can be invested in more profitable areas. Hence there is a valid need for structure mapping in groups.

The main purpose of structure transformation is to provide a link between local and group views so that an audit trail is always possible. This concept isn't limited to accounts and can be adapted to almost all dimensions. Very often bridging cubes are defined to cover all dimensions. A bridging cube can be used for reporting. The structures can be maintained centrally and/or locally. With such a concept, a drill-down to the local view to the subsidiary data could be possible. The rules should be part of the group data mart and thus be transparent for all subsidiaries.

Here's a very typical situation: the group has defined a common set of structures. The local subsidiaries have to provide data to fulfill the reporting requirements. However, they have a local structure that doesn't match exactly with the global requirements. An important step in the consolidation is to bring data from different organizational units together. For this we need a structure-mapping feature.

An important question to consider is: who knows how to map between local and group structures? In our view it is mainly the local unit. This means that account mapping should be a local task. If it is performed only centrally, this could be very time-consuming because local information of all subsidiaries must be available on a group level. And it must be understood well by group managers. Realistically, we can't assume that. Hence decentralization is an important aspect in group mapping.

We will introduce two concepts:

- Simple account/structure mapping
- Complex assignments. You can also use this approach to build heterogeneous segment creation. But more on that later.

First, let's start with the "simple" account mapping. We defined the following cube ("AmGlobal") for the group reporting:

We work with a simple group structure ("AM Companies"). In our example we refer to the subsidiary "111."

We only work with a very small dimension for the positions. The positions of the global reporting are defined as follows ("AM Global Measures"):

For each local organization we have a local measure dimension. We take company 111 and their accounts ("AM 111 Local Accounts"):

With this data in mind, we can define the mapping. We will show an entry form using the Active Forms concept. We will need a separate cube per subsidiary for the mapping task. This makes sense because content including the dimensions should be maintained by the local organization. It might be possible to combine this within a single cube for all subsidiaries; however, it can happen that you have overlapping account names. Then you have to work with prefixes and postfixes.

We use the "AM 111 Mapping" cube for mapping, as shown in the following illustration:

In the first step we define a picklist for the assignment task. We refer to the global account dimension. With this definition we can map any hierarchical relationship between local and global accounts. However, it is sometimes necessary to map a local account to more than one global account. For this we define up to three assignments (which can be enhanced, of course), as shown in the following illustration:

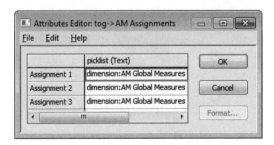

Now we can enter the local mapping. It is possible to assign many local accounts to one global account:

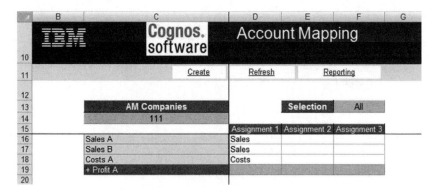

The local information can be collected within a local cube. The owner of this cube is the local organization. Here is the cube for the company 111:

However, we need the global assignments. We need to assign the global accounts "Sales" and "Costs" to the local accounts. The trick is to manipulate the dimension "AM 111 Account Structure" to include the global account assignment. The result should look like this:

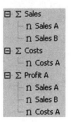

We start with the local structure (accounts with the postfix "A"). The task is to generate the bridging dimension for the mapping. We define a TI script that uses a generic mapping cube ("AMTemp") as a basis to use the standard routines of the TI.

| Data Source | Variables | Maps | Advanced | Schedule |

	Variable Name	Variable Type	Sample Value	Contents
1	VLocal	String	Sales A	Element
2	VAssignment	String	Assignment 1	Element
3	VGlobal	String		Data

The Prolog section creates the temporary cube on the base of the passed parameters (psCompany):

```
sDim = 'AM ' | psCompany | ' Account Structure';
IF (DimensionExists(sDim)=0);
DimensionCreate(sDim);
ENDIF;
IF(CubeExists('AMTemp') = 1);
 CubeDestroy('AMTemp');
ENDIF;
CUBECREATE('AMTemp', 'AM ' | psCompany | ' Local Accounts', 'AM Assignments');
VIEWCREATE('AMTemp', 'Default');
ViewExtractSkipZeroesSet ('AMTemp', 'Default', 0);
DIMENSIONDELETEALLELEMENTS(sDim);
```

In the Metadata section we create the mapping dimension:

```
vsGlobal = CELLGETS('AM ' | psCompany | ' Mapping', vsLocal,  vsAssignment);
i=1;
WHILE ( i < ELPARN('AM 111 Local Accounts', vsLocal));
DIMENSIONELEMENTCOMPONENTADD(sDim,
ELPAR('AM 111 Local Accounts',vsLocal,i) ,vsLocal,1);
i = i +1;
END;
IF (vsGlobal @<> '' & vsLocal  @<> '');
DIMENSIONELEMENTINSERT(sDim, '', vsGlobal,'C');
DIMENSIONELEMENTCOMPONENTADD(sDim, vsGlobal,vsLocal,1);
ENDIF;
```

The final task is to link the cubes. The rule is very generic: Since the cube reference is a text field itself, it can be created dynamically by a current member.

```
[] = N: DB('AM ' | !AM Companies, !AM Global Measures,!AM Periods,
!AM Versions);
```

However, there is a challenge with these generic rules. The crucial question is how to feed them efficiently. It is obvious that we have to feed from the local cubes. But we can't restrict to global accounts. This makes this approach a little bit weak.

However, let's look at the result. We created a simple reporting for the group with the possibility of drilling down to the local views, as shown in the following illustration:

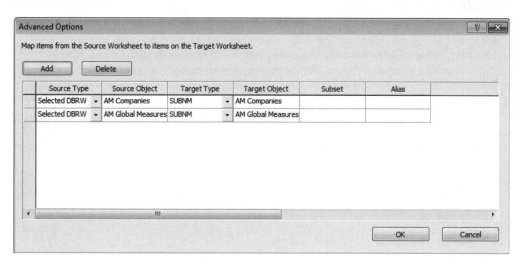

Try a drill-down. You can jump directly into the local cube. We have set up the Action button as follows:

It is interesting that the cube reference is dynamic, as you can see in the following Excel formula:

```
C9:=TM1RPTVIEW("tog:AM "&$D$13&":2", 0,
TM1RPTTITLE("tog:AM Versions";$D$14),TM1RPTFMTRNG,TM1RPTFMTIDCOL)
```

This is the local report (after drill-down from "Sales" and "111"):

	B	C	D	E	F	G	H	I
10	IBM **Cognos. software**		Local Reporting					
11						Refresh		
12								
13		Org	111					
14		AM Scenarios	Actuals					
15		Position	Sales			Selection	Account	
16								
17		Positions	2010	2011				
18		- Sales	220	140				
19		Sales A	100	110				
20		Sales B	120	30				
21								

Complex Structure Mapping

This was a simple example for linear account mapping. However, sometimes the real world is more complex. There are many typical requirements, which go far beyond simple aggregation. For example, more than one dimension can trigger the account mapping.

An accounting example: depending on your business partner, a different global account must be assigned because you want to globally separate external and internal transactions by accounts.

This is also very often the case when you have to create segments. For instance, a product in a specific region constitutes a segment. Another segment comprises another region with totally different products. From a global point of view, you want to compare these segments, doing flexible analysis on these structures.

So we have to open up this approach. We will work with a bridge cube. So we have three levels, as shown in Figure 23-2:

- Group cube
- Bridge cube
- Several local cubes

The approach is that we create a level 0 element for each existing combination of the local dimension and link it to the global account. First we must do the assignment. The bridging cube should contain all mapping dimensions, as shown in the following illustration:

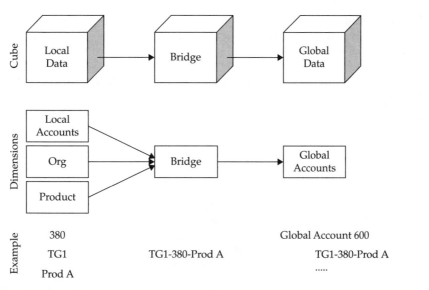

Figure 23-2 Mapping with a bridging cube

We created an entry form on the basis of the "MM Assignment" cube. The example shows that if product B is selected, then it goes to account 500. The default setting is 600, as shown in the following illustration:

112 ∨		MM Assignment		
MM Local Accounts	**MM Products**	**Assignment 1**	**Assignment 2**	**Assignment 3**
379	No Product	600		
	A			
	B	500		
	C			
380	No Product	500		
	A			
	B	600		
	C			
381	No Product	500		
	A	600		
	B	700		
	C	600 ▾		
		600		
		500		
		700		

The "No Product" element is important. We implemented a default mechanism: To avoid entering assignments for all products, we enter a default assignment on "No Product," and only if there is another assignment for a specific product, the system should overwrite the default setting.

With this definition we would like to create a bridge dimension, which should look like this:

For reporting we now need three cubes. The first cube is "MM Global Data" for group reporting:

Then we have the local data. We simply put local data for all subsidiaries in one cube, "MM Local Data":

For analysis and drill-down we define the bridging cube, "MM Bridge":

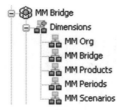

Now we come to the analysis. Let's assume the following entries for subsidiary 112:

2009 ▼	Actuals ▼	112 ▼			
		MM Products			
All		-- All	A	B	C
379		1500.00	500.00	500.00	500.00
380		600.00	200.00	0.00	400.00
381		900.00	600.00	100.00	200.00

The following illustration shows the aggregation from the group perspective:

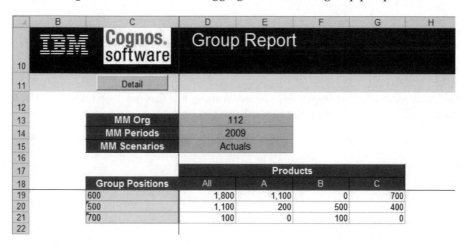

	Group Report				
MM Org	112				
MM Periods	2009				
MM Scenarios	Actuals				
			Products		
Group Positions	All	A	B	C
600	1,800	1,100	0	700
500	1,100	200	500	400
700	100	0	100	0

You can guess what the local accounts are. But remember, we chose a very simple structure. In reality you might have hundreds of accounts and thousands of products.

We see 1800 on group position 600 for all products. Let's do a drill-down. We can see the detail in the following illustration:

	Organisation	Accounts	All	A	B	C
Account			600			
MM Org			112			
MM Periods			2009			
MM Scenarios			Actuals			
			Products			
	Organisation	Accounts	All	A	B	C
600	112	600	1,800	1,100	0	700
112-381-A	112	381	600	600	0	0
112-381-C	112	381	200	0	0	200
112-379-A	112	379	500	500	0	0
112-379-C	112	379	500	0	0	500

One objective is to minimize the administrative work. We wrote a script that generates cubes for bridging. We show only the Metadata section:

```
IF( (vsGlobal @<> '' & vsLocal @<> '') & (vsProduct1 @<> 'No Product'));
DIMENSIONELEMENTINSERT('MM Bridge', '', vsGlobal,'C');
DIMENSIONELEMENTCOMPONENTADD('MM Bridge', vsGlobal, vsOrg | '-' |
vsLocal | '-' |vsProduct1,1);
ENDIF;
```

The "No Product" generation might be interesting. For this we need a loop within the Metadata section of the second-generation process:

```
IF (vsGlobalAccount @<> '' & vsLocalAccount  @<> '');
i = 1;
WHILE(i < DIMSIZ('MM Products'));
sCurrentProduct = DIMNM('MM Products' , i) ;
IF((sCurrentProduct @<> 'No Product' &
ELLEV('MM Products',sCurrentProduct) = 0) &
(ELPARN('MM Bridge', vsOrg | '-' | vsLocalAccount | '-' |
sCurrentProduct) = 0));
DimensionElementInsert('MM Bridge', '', vsGlobalAccount,'C');
DimensionElementComponentAdd('MM Bridge', vsGlobalAccount, vsOrg | '-' |
vsLocalAccount | '-' | sCurrentProduct,1);
ENDIF;
i = i + 1;
END;
ENDIF;
```

Now let's focus on the (dynamic) calculation. We need the following rules. The group cube refers to the bridging cube:

```
[]=N:DB('MM Bridge', !MM Org, !MM Global Accounts, !MM Products, !MM Periods,
!MM Scenarios);
```

The rule script of the bridging cube collects the data by dissolving the company/account/product string into the correct DB formula:

```
SKIPCHECK;
[] = N:IF ( !MM Products  @= SUBST (!MM Bridge, LONG(!MM Bridge)
- LONG (!MM Products)+1,LONG(!MM Products))
&!MM Org @= SUBST(!MM Bridge,1,3),
DB('MM Local Data', !MM Org, SUBST (!MM Bridge ,5,3), !MM Products,
!MM Periods, !MM Scenarios),  0);
FEEDERS;
[]=>DB('MM Global Data', !MM Org, !MM Bridge, !MM Products, !MM Periods,
!MM Scenarios);
```

The local cube rule file contains only a feeder:

```
SKIPCHECK;
FEEDERS;
[]=>DB('MM Bridge', !MM Org, !MM Org |'-' |!MM Local Accounts | '-' |
!MM Products , !MM Products, !MM Periods, !MM Scenarios);
```

With small dimensions, this approach works nicely. But we don't assume that this approach works in every environment. The "no element" enhancement, for example, could be critical if there are a large number of dimension elements to assign.

Organization by Period

A very common requirement is to have a dimension structure varying by period. This is often the case when you have to model organizations or companies. But also for other dimensions, it could be essential to track the changes. Data warehouse experts call it "slow changing dimensions."

But why do you need this? There are typically two different requirements:

- Sometimes high auditing requirements exist. Auditors often ask, "Show me the revenue of last year for a specific organization." If you have only the most recent version and you are just beyond the last reorganization process, hopefully you are in a lucky situation having a backup. But even so, you can't answer as you could with OLAP: in an instant without preparation.

  But also within a planning period, it could be necessary to handle different organizational structures. You plan to reorganize at the end of next year, but this should be reflected in your multiyear planning. You have to report both: the consequences of your planning activities on the next year and on the following year.

- You are looking into the future. But you want to compare existing data. When you do comparisons, it might be necessary to aggregate past data with new structures to make it compatible with your new organization. This is often necessary for forecasting.

This is much easier to handle with relational star schemes. It is easy to define two attributes, "valid from" and "valid to." An SQL query is simple, too.

It is not that easy with TM1 because TM1 needs predefined hierarchies to work efficiently and the valid from/to attribute is simple to maintain but simply overstrains TM1. But don't despair—there is hope. It's not that flexible, but it's sufficient in most cases and what is more important, it allows both old-to-new comparisons and audit.

The approach is simple: Generate a separate hierarchy for each period. We created this for our organizational structure:

This is definitely not complex. You can use the TurboIntegrator to create these hierarchies automatically from your ERP system. As always, there are good and bad things:

- A positive thing is that you can do all kinds of variance analysis. You can compare old data with old structures, new data with new structures, new data with old structures, and old data with new structures.

- However, what if you have to handle changes with periods (that is, months)? To handle hundreds of hierarchies can be painful sometimes.

- The hierarchy elements must be unique. This is also true for additional aliases. This is good and bad: You always see the time tag in standard reports and this can be annoying. However, it is not possible to refer to an outdated hierarchy element.

You see, the concept is easy. However, the reporting is somewhat tricky. For instance, sometimes people do not wish to see the hierarchy version. In Excel it is easy either to define an attribute or simply cut off the prefix or postfix with a statement like this:

```
D18:=IF(ELLEV("ToG:OBP Companies",C18)<>0,
MID(C18,1,LEN(C18)-5), C18)
```

However, we prefer the attribute version:

```
D18:=DBRA("ToG:OBP Companies",$C18,"Name")
```

We created an Active Form example that suppresses the period in the name. This report consists of two reports:

- The first one shows the historic structure (which can be selected by the period). Furthermore, it shows the period-specific aggregation values. This is possible with this formula statement:

  ```
  =DBRW(SetCube,IF($A18="N",$C18;$D18&" "&F$17),$F$13,F$17,$F$14)
  ```

- The second one shows the most recent organization structure.

To get the chosen company structure, we use MDX instead of defining static subsets:

```
=TM1RPTROW($C$9,"ToG:OBP Companies",,,,,
"TM1DRILLDOWNMEMBER( TM1FILTERBYPATTERN(TM1SUBSETALL([OBP Companies]),
""Group "&$F$15&""""), ALL , RECURSIVE ) ",,)
```

And the following illustration shows the report:

			Positions	Revenue				
			Scenarios	Actuals				
			Period	2010			Current	2011
			Hist Structure	2009	2010	2011		
18	- Group 2010		Group	20,000	26,000	24,000		
19	- Europe 2010		Europe	11,000	14,000	10,000		
20	France		France	5,000	5,000	4,000		
21	Great Britain		Great Britain	6,000	7,000	6,000		
22	Italy		Italy	1,000	2,000	1,000		
23	- GAS 2010		GAS	9,000	12,000	14,000		
24	Germany		Germany	4,000	5,000	6,000		
25	Austria		Austria	3,000	4,000	4,000		
26	Switzerland		Switzerland	2,000	3,000	3,000		
			Current Structure	2009	2010	2011		
36	- Group 2011		Group	21,000	25,000	24,000		
37	- Europe 2011		Europe	11,000	12,000	10,000		
38	France		France	5,000	5,000	4,000		
39	Great Britain		Great Britain	6,000	7,000	6,000		
40	- GAS 2011		GAS	10,000	13,000	14,000		
41	Lichtenstein		Lichtenstein	1,000	1,000	1,000		
42	Germany		Germany	4,000	5,000	6,000		
43	Austria		Austria	3,000	4,000	4,000		
44	Switzerland		Switzerland	2,000	3,000	3,000		

You can see some remarkable constellations:

- The historical view shows the aggregated value of the respective period regardless of the summation. For instance, Europe 2010 shows 10,000 in the 2011 column, which is not the sum of France, Great Britain, and Italy. The reason is obvious: Italy doesn't belong to Europe in 2011 any more.

- The "current view" recalculates the values. Thus Europe in 2010 is not 14,000 but 12,000 because we want to compare apples to apples.

This example again shows the flexibility of the combination of TM1 and Excel. Unfortunately, these ideas rarely work in other analysis tools.

Elimination

Can you use TM1 as a group management tool including elimination? Some say this is not the perfect fit; others say "no way." We strongly disagree. Although of course there are better tools, particularly for statutory consolidation, TM1 has some excellent features for elimination. And not every group needs highly sophisticated features. Let's first discuss the requirements and then judge.

The cornerstone is to look at the group and all subsidiaries as a "single company." All intercompany transactions and contracts are only internal staff and thus not part of the external representation.

- Handling of differences
- Stepwise eliminations
- Complex revaluation tasks (that is, capital consolidation)

It is important to split this challenge into separate problems. Otherwise, it is quite likely that you will be overwhelmed by complexity. In this section we want to focus on elimination.

What is the basic modeling approach? We only need a simple cube architecture. We usually work with two company or organizational dimensions that are almost identical. The first one is the "true" organizational dimension. We kept it as simple as possible:

The number of levels doesn't matter. In our cases we focus on three levels. But the concepts are set up in such a way that you can enhance it to an unlimited count of levels.

The second one is almost identical, with two additions: First we have an element called "external." This is necessary to collect external business. So a typical external transaction has the elements ['ORG':'Org xx','C_ORG': 'External']. Second, we have the "All" element. It is an aggregation on top of "extern" and the top element of the first hierarchy:

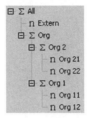

Now let's think about what elimination really means. It simply means that you don't show intercompany transactions. And this is more than easy. Simply slice the second organization dimension C_ORG to "external." Unconsolidated reports must be set to "All" and the intercompany transaction can be reported on the element "ORG." You can also drill down to see intercompany details.

The following example gives a simple demonstration of this: Elimination means only to consider the "ELIM COrg" element "External." Unconsolidated means to look at "All":

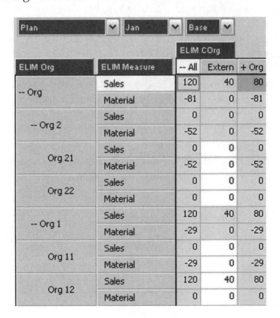

Plan ⌄	Jan ⌄	Base ⌄		
			ELIM COrg	
ELIM Org	ELIM Measure	-- All	Extern	+ Org
-- Org	Sales	120	40	80
	Material	-81	0	-81
-- Org 2	Sales	0	0	0
	Material	-52	0	-52
Org 21	Sales	0	0	0
	Material	-52	0	-52
Org 22	Sales	0	0	0
	Material	0	0	0
-- Org 1	Sales	120	40	80
	Material	-29	0	-29
Org 11	Sales	0	0	0
	Material	-29	0	-29
Org 12	Sales	120	40	80
	Material	0	0	0

Stepwise Intercompany Elimination

But—the real world isn't easy—again. The approach we've explained is simple when we cope with simple structures with two levels. But there is a specific challenge when transfers between companies or organization units take place.

Here's a rather simple scenario: We collect data from different subsidiaries, aggregate it, and need to show only the sales without intercompany transactions instead of the gross

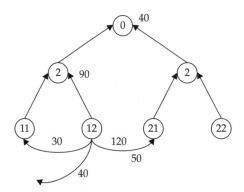

Figure 23-3   Intercompany elimination

sales, which is the simple aggregation. As already stated, just leave the intercompany numbers out. But now the complication occurs: From a conceptual point of view, it is okay just to show all items that are not assigned to intercompany or interorganizational sales. But on every level, the numbers to eliminate are different, because from the view of a subgroup, an external company means something different than from the group view. Sales to another subgroup are external for the subgroup. But they are internal for the total group.

Let us take a look at Figure 23-3. We have four organizational units, two subgroups, and a overall group. The transfer from 12 to 21 is intercompany sales but only from the point of view of the group organization. For the subgroups and the organizational units, it is external sales. Thus this amount should only be eliminated on a group level, but not on the levels below.

How can we solve this? As you can see, it is not a typical OLAP-like aggregation. The aggregation has to consider the respective level.

Before we discuss the algorithm, let us start with dimension modeling. We create the "ELIMINATION" cube, as shown in the following illustration:

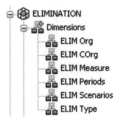

As always when we have to collect intradimensional relationships, we have to add a counter-dimension. In our example we defined the counter-organization ELIM COrg in addition to the base organization. The Type dimension contains the calculation steps:

We enter the numbers in a Cube Viewer sheet, as shown in the following illustration:

ELIM Type	ELIM Org	ELIM COrg								
		-- All	Extern	-- Org	-- Org 2	Org 21	Org 22	-- Org 1	Org 11	Org 12
Base	-- Org	120	40	80	50	50	0	30	30	0
	-- Org 2	0	0	0	0	0	0	0	0	0
	Org 21	0	0	0	0	0	0	0	0	0
	Org 22	0	0	0	0	0	0	0	0	0
	-- Org 1	120	40	80	50	50	0	30	30	0
	Org 11	0	0	0	0	0	0	0	0	0
	Org 12	120	40	80	50	50	0	30	30	0
ToElim	-- Org	1	1	1	0	0	0	0	0	0
	-- Org 2	1	1	1	1	0	0	1	1	1
	Org 21	1	1	1	1	1	1	1	1	1
	Org 22	1	1	1	1	1	1	1	1	1
	-- Org 1	1	1	1	1	1	1	1	0	0
	Org 11	1	1	1	1	1	1	1	1	1
	Org 12	1	1	1	1	1	1	1	1	1

You see an aggregation of 120, which is correct but only for nonelimination. Also the 40 on the "ELIM Corg" Element "Extern" is okay. But where do we get the 90 as shown in the example?

To solve this, a single rule is enough. But we explain the approach first. The idea is to generate 0/1 switches. Look at the following rule:

```
['ToElim'] =IF(ELISANC('ELIM ORG',!ELIM Org,!ELIM CORG)=1, 0, 1);
```

What does this rule do? It simply looks at whether the current counter organization (CORG) is a descendant of the current org (ORG). If so, it simply puts an elimination flag. We use the ELISANC function to find out whether the current Counter Organization Unit is an ancestor of the recent Organization. If this is the case, we must eliminate this position; that's why we enforce a 0.

You can see the effect. For each possible intercompany transaction, a zero is written into the cell. But you will also see a negative effect when you try to multiply the element "ToElim" by the "Base" value: no aggregation takes place because we don't use the base level specification "n:" for this rule.

So what could we do? The multiplication is okay, but we have to enforce a specific calculation behavior. Fortunately, there is a function that does exactly this. CONSOLIDATECHILDREN calculates the dimension. The only thing we need is to enforce the summing of the CORG dimension.

What does the function CONSOLIDATECHILDREN do and why do we need that? The syntax is as follows:

```
CONSOLIDATECHILDREN(DimName1, DimName2, ...)
```

This function forces consolidated values to be calculated by summing immediate children along a specified dimension. This is helpful when intermediate consolidations are calculated by rules and you want a parent consolidation to be calculated by summing the intermediate consolidations rather than by summing the underlying leaf values. The function requires at least one DimName argument, and can accept as many DimName arguments as there are dimensions in the cube for which the rule is written. The final elimination rule looks like this:

```
['Result'] =IF(ELLEV('ELIM CORG',!ELIM CORG)=0,['Base']*
(IF(ELISANC('ELIM ORG',!ELIM Org,!ELIM CORG)=1, 0, 1)),
CONSOLIDATECHILDREN('ELIM CORG'))
```

The feeder is easily set and shouldn't raise any problems.

```
['Base']=>['Result'];
```

And the result is shown in the following illustration:

ELIM Type	ELIM Org	ELIM COrg -- All	Extern	-- Org	-- Org 2	Org 21	Org 22	-- Org 1	Org 11	Org 12
Base	-- Org	120	40	80	50	50	0	30	30	0
	-- Org 2	0	0	0	0	0	0	0	0	0
	Org 21	0	0	0	0	0	0	0	0	0
	Org 22	0	0	0	0	0	0	0	0	0
	-- Org 1	120	40	80	50	50	0	30	30	0
	Org 11	0	0	0	0	0	0	0	0	0
	Org 12	120	40	80	50	50	0	30	30	0
Result	-- Org	40	40	0	0	0	0	0	0	0
	-- Org 2	0	0	0	0	0	0	0	0	0
	Org 21	0	0	0	0	0	0	0	0	0
	Org 22	0	0	0	0	0	0	0	0	0
	-- Org 1	90	40	50	50	50	0	0	0	0
	Org 11	0	0	0	0	0	0	0	0	0
	Org 12	120	40	80	50	50	0	30	30	0

Let us investigate the result, which looks fine on the "ALL" level in CORG:

- Sales Org 12 = 120
- Sales Org 1 = 70
- Sales Org = 40

But does this rule work? Take the sales from Org 12 to Org 21 (50). This is correctly eliminated on level 2. Sales from Org 12 to 11 is already eliminated on level 1.

Working with Elimination Differences

Mission one is completed. We eliminated single-sided. But to every elimination activity, there must be a second site: An outgoing invoice has an equivalent in the receiving company. An accounts receivable entry has a corresponding accounts payable entry, and so forth. The elimination is easy: apply the same algorithm to the other side.

Intercompany matching is an important and time-consuming process. First the question: how can differences occur at all? The reason is that the same information is entered twice in two systems that are not integrated. One company enters an outgoing invoice. The counterpart company enters the same invoice, now incoming. Usually the amount should be the same. During consolidation this information is brought together. And often it turns out that data is not the same:

- Currency variances
- Goods on one hand delivered but not yet arrived
- False booking
- Different valuations
- And many more

But first we have to find out whether we have intercompany variances. Let us assume we have corresponding accounts. In this case Sales is corresponding with Material. Later we will build matching groups to assign more than one account on each side.

To calculate variances, we have to turn one part of the cube by comparing the one side with the other side where CORG is exchanged with ORG, as shown in Figure 23-4.

We only want the calculation for positions flagged as intercompany. So we simply enter the counterpart information into an attribute "CounterPart."

This is the matching rule:

```
['Matching'] = N:IF (ATTRS('ELIM Measure',!ELIM Measure,'CounterPart')@<> ''
& !ELIM COrg @<>'Extern',['Base'] + DB('ELIMINATION', !ELIM COrg, !ELIM ORG,
ATTRS ('ELIM Measure',!ELIM Measure,'CounterPart'),!ELIM Periods,
!ELIM Scenarios,'Base'),0);
```

ORG	CORG	Position	Amount
ORG 11	ORG 12	Sales	1000
....	....	....	....

ORG	CORG	Position	Amount
ORG 12	ORG 11	Costs	980
ORG 12	External	Costs	100
...	...	...	...

FIGURE 23-4 Matching

We want to enhance our small example. We have two accounts: material and sales. And we have two transactions:

- Org 12 sells 30 to Org 21, Org 21 only books 29.
- Org 12 sells 50 to Org 11, Org 11 only books 52.

Now we can analyze the matching differences: On sales and on material we have –1, which nets out –2 and +1.

Only one thing is surprising: Why do we have an overall elimination of –2 for the profit? Shouldn't this net out?

ELIM Measure	ELIM Org	Base							Matching						
		-- Org	-- Org 2	Org 21	Org 22	-- Org 1	Org 11	Org 12	-- Org	-- Org 2	Org 21	Org 22	-- Org 1	Org 11	Org 12
Sales	-- Org	80	50	50	0	30	30	0	-1	-2	-2	0	1	1	0
	-- Org 2	0	0	0	0	0	0	0	0	0	0	0	0	0	0
	Org 21	0	0	0	0	0	0	0	0	0	0	0	0	0	0
	Org 22	0	0	0	0	0	0	0	0	0	0	0	0	0	0
	-- Org 1	80	50	50	0	30	30	0	-1	-2	-2	0	1	1	0
	Org 11	0	0	0	0	0	0	0	0	0	0	0	0	0	0
	Org 12	80	50	50	0	30	30	0	-1	-2	-2	0	1	1	0
Material	-- Org	-81	0	0	0	-81	0	-81	-1	0	0	0	-1	0	-1
	-- Org 2	-52	0	0	0	-52	0	-52	-2	0	0	0	-2	0	-2
	Org 21	-52	0	0	0	-52	0	-52	-2	0	0	0	-2	0	-2
	Org 22	0	0	0	0	0	0	0	0	0	0	0	0	0	0
	-- Org 1	-29	0	0	0	-29	0	-29	1	0	0	0	1	0	1
	Org 11	-29	0	0	0	-29	0	-29	1	0	0	0	1	0	1
	Org 12	0	0	0	0	0	0	0	0	0	0	0	0	0	0
+ Profit	-- Org	-1	50	50	0	-51	30	-81	-2	-2	-2	0	0	1	-1
	-- Org 2	-52	0	0	0	-52	0	-52	-2	0	0	0	-2	0	-2
	Org 21	-52	0	0	0	-52	0	-52	-2	0	0	0	-2	0	-2
	Org 22	0	0	0	0	0	0	0	0	0	0	0	0	0	0
	-- Org 1	51	50	50	0	1	30	-29	0	-2	-2	0	2	1	1
	Org 11	-29	0	0	0	-29	0	-29	1	0	0	0	1	0	1
	Org 12	80	50	50	0	30	30	0	-1	-2	-2	0	1	1	0

To have a professional solution, we need some enhancements. Here are some important additions:

- Matching groups, more than 1:1 matching
- A decision about what to do with these differences. Very often limits are defined. If a variance is below this limit, the difference is automatically posted. If it is higher, the partners have to correct this.
- This process can be linked with a workflow.

Proportional Consolidation

Proportional consolidation is another concept that might be important within a group environment. If you have acquisitions that are significant but you don't dominate, you likely need a quotal consolidation. The positions are weighted by a factor. This is often the case when you have joint ventures. The required function should work recursively, and it should also work across multiple paths.

A trivial approval might be to use the element weighting. However, this has some disadvantages:

- The weighting can't be time-based.
- It cannot be changed within an Excel formula.

The bad thing is that it must be recursive. On each level there must be a new calculation. Or we can express this more formally in an equation:

$$Quotal_{org} = Value_{org} \times \prod^{n} Percentage^{n}$$

We want to clarify this with a simple example. Take the structure shown in Figure 23-5. The reporting numbers of the subsidiaries should only be aggregated by using the percentage shown. As you can see, multiple parents also are possible (with the restriction that the percentage can't be greater). The value for O2 is shown in the following equation:

$$Quotal_{O2} = 1,000 \times 0.6 \times 0.7 + 1,000 \times 0.3 \times 0.5 = 150 + 420 \times 570$$

By the way, this is very similar to our BOM approach, so we can reuse the approach shown in Chapter 18. This time we create two cubes where QC Basis is the reporting cube

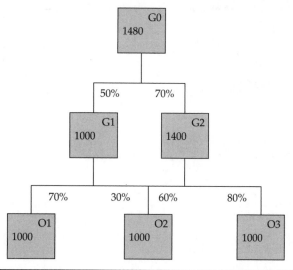

Figure 23-5 Proportional group structure

(as shown in the following illustration) and QC can be hidden. We do this to let the data user focus on reporting and not on implementation details.

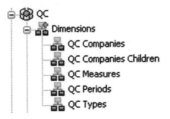

QC has an additional dimension to map the parent child structure, as shown in the following illustration:

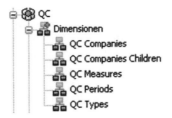

Here is the structure collection (cube "QC"). You can see that we even use the element name "BOM" to collect the structural dependencies.

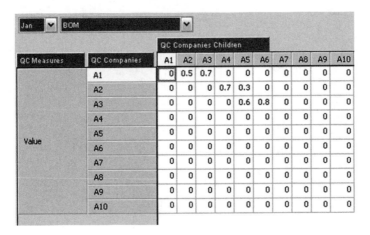

Jan ⌄	BOM	⌄									
		QC Companies Children									
QC Measures	**QC Companies**	A1	A2	A3	A4	A5	A6	A7	A8	A9	A10
	A1	0	0.5	0.7	0	0	0	0	0	0	0
	A2	0	0	0	0.7	0.3	0	0	0	0	0
	A3	0	0	0	0	0.6	0.8	0	0	0	0
	A4	0	0	0	0	0	0	0	0	0	0
	A5	0	0	0	0	0	0	0	0	0	0
Value	A6	0	0	0	0	0	0	0	0	0	0
	A7	0	0	0	0	0	0	0	0	0	0
	A8	0	0	0	0	0	0	0	0	0	0
	A9	0	0	0	0	0	0	0	0	0	0
	A10	0	0	0	0	0	0	0	0	0	0

You can see the result on the "QC Types" element "Translated" for the cube "QC Basis":

QC Types	QC Measures	QC Companies									
		A1	A2	A3	A4	A5	A6	A7	A8	A9	A10
Basis	Sales	0	0	0	1000	1000	1000	0	0	0	0
	Costs	0	0	0	-800	-800	-800	0	0	0	0
	Value	0	0	0	0	0	0	0	0	0	0
	+ Profit	0	0	0	200	200	200	0	0	0	0
Translated	Sales	1480	1000	1400	1000	1000	1000	0	0	0	0
	Costs	-1184	-800	-1120	-800	-800	-800	0	0	0	0
	Value	0	0	0	0	0	0	0	0	0	0
	+ Profit	296	200	280	200	200	200	0	0	0	0

And finally, these are the rules for the quotal consolidation:

```
SKIPCHECK;
['Basis']= N:IF( !QC Companies @= !QC Companies Children, DB('QC Basis',
!QC Companies, !QC Measures, !QC Periods, !QC Types),
DB('QC', !QC Companies, !QC Companies Children, 'Value', !QC Periods,'BOM')
* DB('QC', !QC Companies Children,'Total',
!QC Measures, !QC Periods,'Basis'));
FEEDERS;
['BOM','Value']=>['Basis','Profit','Year'];
```

The rule for the reporting cube is simple.

```
['Translated']=
DB('QC', !QC Companies, 'Total', !QC Measures, !QC Periods, 'Basis');
FEEDERS;
['Basis']=>DB('QC', !QC Companies, !QC Companies, !QC Measures,
!QC Periods, !QC Types);
['Basis']=>['Translated'];
```

Intercompany Matching on the Document Level

There is another aspect of intercompany transactions we want to discuss: intercompany matching on the document level. What is the basic challenge? A (logically single) transaction between two subsidiaries is booked independently twice by the two firms. So double booking is actually "quadruple" booking. But it is fundamentally different from double booking where we automatically have a match between credit and debit. We don't have a guarantee for this equation across firms. This imbalance is uncritical for the single firm's closing.

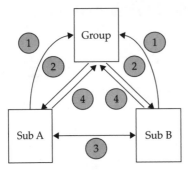

1. Subsidiaries transfer data
2. Group discovers differences and approaches subsidiaries
3. Subsidiaries check data and approach partner
4. Subsidiaries transfer corrected data (often as delta information)

FIGURE 23-6   Slow intercompany matching process

On a group level, various variances can occur, like different currency rates, items delivered but not arrived at the customer, and also errors in accounting. Intercompany matching is timely and critical and, most of all, a very time-consuming process. The higher the volume, the longer the delay.

A lot of manual tasks are necessary to reconcile the data. This is often done by the staff people of the group who have to communicate intensively with the subsidiaries. Very often, this becomes a bottleneck.

Look at a typical process: The subsidiaries report their data. The group is doing the aggregation and realizes variances. It contacts the subsidiaries for clarification. The subsidiaries do the reconciliation and (hopefully) submitted the corrected data.

So we propose a tool to collect the documents with the possibility to mutually clarify differences on a local level. We focus on transactions, which might be a little bit surprising for TM1 experts.

The results of the intercompany matching process can be processed by specific consolidation tools like IBM Cognos Controller. The adjustments that are stored in TM1 can be automatically processed.

The TM1 cube is set up as a global data collection base where all subsidiaries can have access with limitations to their data and the necessary counterpart information. For example, together with the list of all their own liabilities, the receivables of all group companies where the own company is counterpart can be seen (and of course not edited because the ownership of the latter is with the counterpart).

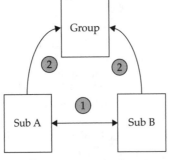

1. Subsidiary A discovers differences and approaches Subsidiary B
2. Subsidiaries do the adjustments and transfer data to the group.

FIGURE 23-7   Intercompany matching between subsidiaries

With this concept it is possible that the group can delegate the cumbersome reconciliation process to the subsidiaries. These companies can start as early as possible, perhaps directly after both transactions (for instance, the original invoice and the counterpart invoice) are entered.

The reconciliation process is very similar to what is well known with document reconciliation in accounts receivables: It is like clearing your open items in accounts receivable. And like accounts receivable, this is something that is done on a transactional level. You have a list of receivables and a list of bank transactions. The job is to bring both transaction lists together.

The concept is simple: a batch run filters matching documents and sets the status to "Reconciled." Only the nonmatching documents should be selected for rework by the respective owners. It should be also possible to define thresholds for automatic reconciliation with minor variances. It is also important to comment specific variances and mark them as ready to process. A status monitor could show the open and reconciled transactions.

Process support can also be delivered by TM1. For instance, an activity like delivering data can only be finished after all documents are reconciled. The quality is increasing because manual activities can be reduced. With local intercompany matching, the time-critical process can be relieved. To speed up the closing process, the intercompany matching starts early before the reporting process.

The reconciliation process should be auditable. The reporting should be linked to the single document so that manual reconciliation can be reduced to a minimum. A drill-through to the ERP system is not necessary.

TM1 was not built for document handling. This is no big news. But with its modern structure and its outstanding sparsity handling, it is possible to work efficiently with transactions. The advantage of this concept is that you don't need multiple databases, since consolidation tools often work with heterogeneous databases. It is always painful to synchronize different databases.

We define a single cube for all tasks:

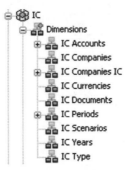

Again we have the Companies and the Counterpart dimension to store the intercompany bookings. We use a counter dimension, "IC Documents," to store the documents like invoices and so on.

Another important dimension is IC Currencies. In previous examples we used a separate currency cube. With a transaction cube for intercompany matching, it must be different. IC partners can have various transaction currencies. Even the same two partners can interact in many currencies. And furthermore, we need to store the daily rate per transaction.

An important requirement is to support many-to-many account matching. That is why we have defined matching groups. We simply defined the attribute "Matching Group" in the "IC Accounts" dimension.

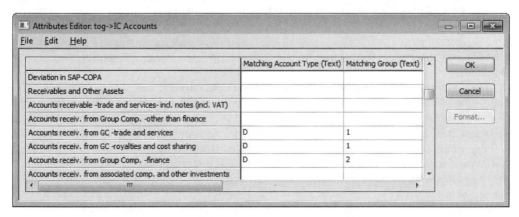

We want to describe the process, not the technological concept. Usually the starting point is a report, like the one in the following illustration:

We use a counter to show the nonreconciled documents. For this we need to count the respective states:

```
['Open and Proposed']=N:If(['Value'] <>0 & DB('IC', !IC Accounts, !IC Companies,
!IC Companies IC, !IC Currencies, !IC Documents, !IC Periods, !IC Scenarios,
!IC Years, 'Status')@<>'Closed',1,0);

['Closed']=N:IF(['Value'] <>0 & DB('IC', !IC Accounts, !IC Companies,
!IC Companies IC, !IC Currencies, !IC Documents, !IC Periods, !IC Scenarios,
!IC Years, 'Status')@='Closed',1,0);
```

```
['OnlyOpen']=N:IF(['Value'] <>0 & DB('IC', !IC Accounts, !IC Companies,
!IC Companies IC, !IC Currencies, !IC Documents, !IC Periods, !IC Scenarios,
!IC Years, 'Status')@='' % DB('IC', !IC Accounts, !IC Companies,
!IC Companies IC,
!IC Currencies, !IC Documents, !IC Periods, !IC Scenarios,
!IC Years, 'Status')@='Open' ,1,0);

['Status Count Proposal']=N:IF(['Value'] <>0 & DB('IC', !IC Accounts,
!IC Companies, !IC Companies IC, !IC Currencies, !IC Documents, !IC Periods,
!IC Scenarios, !IC Years, 'Status')@='Proposed',1,0);

['Status Count Open']=N: ['OnlyOpen'];
['Status Count Closed']=N:['Closed'];
```

Within the active form, you can select a value cell you want to investigate and click on the Action button "intercompany." A new sheet opens and you see the details. Now all counterparts are visible. We work with heterogeneous accounts where we can store external and internal transactions. Hence you also see external transactions on this account. With this report all accounts of a matching group are shown.

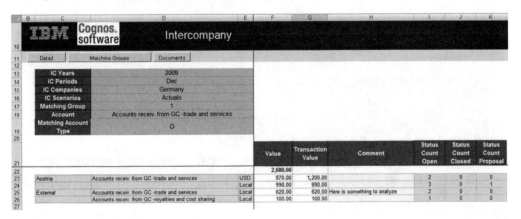

We use an MDX statement to create the subset for the active form. Since we only want to have the counterpart information, we use the account type to select the respective account. We use Excel names for reference:

```
D23:=TM1RPTROW($C$9,"ICMS:IC Accounts",,,,,$H$15)

H15:="FILTER( TM1SUBSETALL( [IC Accounts] ), [IC Accounts].[Matching Group]
= """&Matching_Group&""" AND [IC Accounts].[Matching Account Type]
= """&IF(Matching_Account_Type="C","C","D")&""")"
```

Be aware that up to now we show only our own data. To reconcile, we need information from our counterparts. We want to investigate the USD positions of Austria. With the next drill-down, we are able to match all positions per period. For this we mark the value for "USD" and "Austria" and select the Action button "Detail."

We need to hand over the necessary parameters, as shown in the next two illustrations:

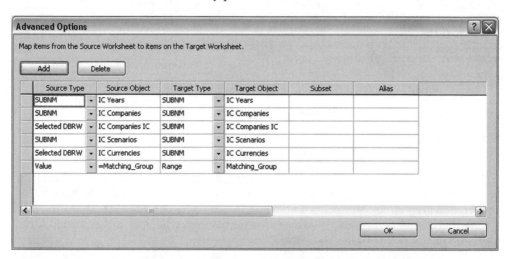

Here we can see all positions. To find the appropriate positions, we don't restrict to certain periods. Hence you can also see open items from other periods. You can change this easily; however, one of the reasons why the counterpart transactions don't match is that they are booked in different periods.

```
C38:=TM1RPTROW($C$28,"ICMS:IC Accounts",,,,,$J$16)

J16:="FILTER( TM1SUBSETALL( [IC Accounts] ), [IC Accounts].[Matching Group]
= """&Matching_Group&""" AND [IC Accounts].[Matching Account Type]
= """&IF(Matching_Account_Type="C","D","C")&""")"
```

We are still not on the deepest level because we refer to the "IC Documents" dimension element "All." Let's do a final drill-down to the document level. Mark the December value and click on "Documents." Now we see the detail (which means all individual postings of both companies are shown) in the following illustration:

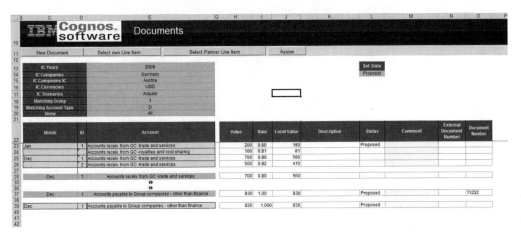

We also see the counterpart postings.

We can mark elements for potential matching. The first step is to select the two matching documents. For this we defined two buttons:

- "Select Own Line Item"
- "Select Partner Line Item"

You must select an appropriate DBRW formula and click one of the buttons. The dimension elements are copied into the matching area.

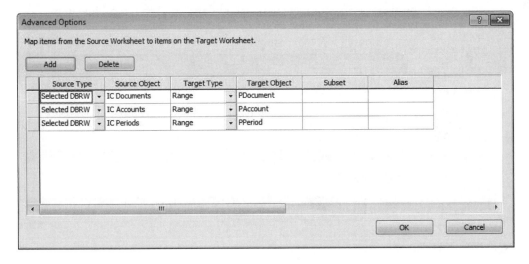

The next step is to run the matching process. Click the button "Assign." With this a TI process is started, which marks both documents as reconciled. You can imagine that a lot of parameters must be transferred to the process:

| Data Source | Variables | Maps | Advanced | Schedule |

| Parameters | Prolog | Metadata | Data | Epilog |

Parameter	Type		Default Value	Prompt Question
PCompany	String	▾	Germany	May
PCompany_IC	String	▾	Austria	
PYear	String	▾	2009	ny_IC
PScenario	String	▾	Actuals	C
PPeriod	String	▾	Jan	o
PAccount	String	▾	Accounts receiv. fror	
PCurrency	String	▾	EUR	C
PDocument	String	▾	1	C
PAction	String	▾	Closed	t
PAccount2	String	▾	Accounts payable to	C
PDocument2	String	▾	1	
PPeriod2	String	▾	May	2

This process has only two statements in the Prolog section:

```
CellPutS(psAction,'IC',psAccount,psCompany,psCompany_IC,psCurrency,
psDocument,psPeriod,
psScenario,psYear,'Status');
CellPutS(psAction,'IC',psAccount2,psCompany_IC,psCompany,psCurrency,
psDocument2,
psPeriod2,psScenario,psYear,'Status');
```

And it should be also possible to create new documents. This is a typical line item function we already discussed in Chapter 16.

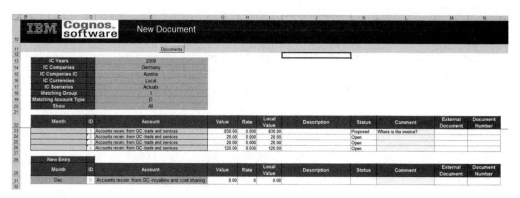

```
D31:=MAX(O23:O27)+1
```

```
O23:=VALUE(D23)
```

To create a new entry, select the account on cell E31:

```
E31: =SUBNM("ToG:IC Accounts","MatchingGroupAll",
"Accounts receiv. from GC -royalties and cost sharing")
```

Now you can enter the elements. To keep the balance, you should always enter matching credit and debit items. Up to now there is no validation included.

This is of course only an outline of a more complex process. The heart of reconciliation is an automatic process that is able to reconcile elements with some kind of fuzzy logic. If document numbers and amounts are identical, reconciliation is easy. But what if there are slight variances? To a certain degree this could be handled automatically.

Margin Calculation in Groups

A more sophisticated task is to calculate profit in a complex group structure. The challenge is that you usually have profit parts when a product is sold between two companies of a group. From a group perspective, a profit only occurs when a product is sold to an external customer.

Furthermore, it is not possible to understand the group-related costs parts for the receiving companies. The company controller only sees its own cost structure and usually the price * unit value. This could cause wrong decisions. Figure 23-8 explains this problem. This problem

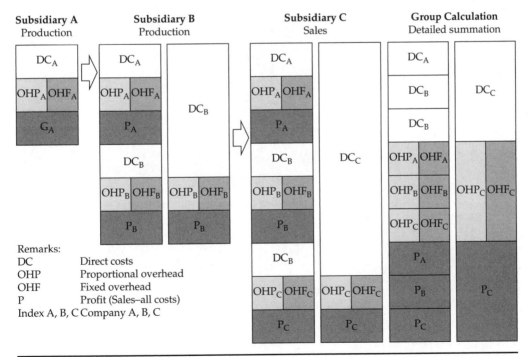

Remarks:
DC   Direct costs
OHP   Proportional overhead
OHF   Fixed overhead
P   Profit (Sales–all costs)
Index A, B, C Company A, B, C

FIGURE 23-8   The babuschka effect

is sometimes referred to as the "babuschka problem." Why? It is like the babuschka dolls: each time you look behind the figure, it contains more granular data.

TM1 is able to handle this problem. It is a little bit more work but it is possible. We created just one cube for all the calculations:

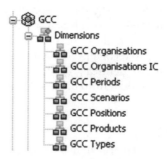

We choose the following dimension structure:

- "GCC Organisations." This contains the company structure of the group.
- "GCC Organisations IC." This dimension is necessary to map relationships between two companies. It is also important that this dimension has one element called "external" or a similar name, to map external transactions.

- "GCC Products." This contains all sales products of all companies. Sold services should also be included.

- The "GCC Positions" dimension contains the profitability calculation and also the inventory calculation. The calculation scheme implicitly contains the product structure (redundant to the product structure). This is necessary to map the bill of materials.

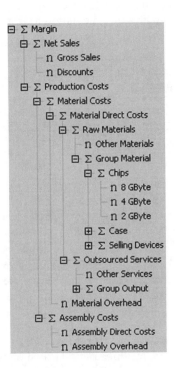

- We choose the additional dimension "GCC Types" to handle additional information like comments, currency calculation, and so on. In this case we store units, amounts, prices, and the price valuation vector we discussed in Chapter 17. This vector is used to keep the cost structure when handing over products from one company to the next company. This vector can be simply enhanced.

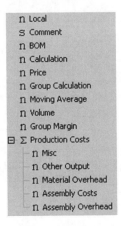

A simple example should explain how such a model could work. It is a supply chain with three elements. In the German plan, cases for electronic devices are produced. These cases are used by the Austrian plan to produce GPS devices and MP3 players. A third company, Switzerland, bundles final products to product sets.

The German plan controller creates the calculation for three periods, as shown in the following illustration:

Actual ▼	Calculation ▼	MP3 Small ▼	Germany ▼

Periods	AllExternal					
	Per 1		Per 2		Per 3	
Production Costs	-- All	External	-- All	External	-- All	External
-- Production Costs	17.00	17.00	18.00	18.00	17.00	17.00
-- Material Costs	10.00	10.00	11.00	11.00	10.00	10.00
-- Material Direct Costs	8.00	8.00	9.00	9.00	8.00	8.00
-- Raw Materials	4.00	4.00	5.00	5.00	4.00	4.00
Other Materials	4.00	4.00	5.00	5.00	4.00	4.00
-- Outsourced Services	4.00	4.00	4.00	4.00	4.00	4.00
Other Services	4.00	4.00	4.00	4.00	4.00	4.00
Material Overhead	2.00	2.00	2.00	2.00	2.00	2.00
-- Assembly Costs	7.00	7.00	7.00	7.00	7.00	7.00
Assembly Direct Costs	5.00	5.00	5.00	5.00	5.00	5.00
Assembly Overhead	2.00	2.00	2.00	2.00	2.00	2.00

The plant Austria is the sole customer. It produces GPS devices and MP3 players. The plant controller creates a calculation for three periods, as shown in the following illustration:

Actual ▼	Calculation ▼	Austria ▼

Periods	Organisations								
		Per 1			Per 2			Per 3		
Products	**Production Costs**	+ All	Germany	External	+ All	Germany	External	+ All	Germany	External
Informa GPS-1090	-- Production Costs	26.00	18.00	8.00	27.00	18.00	9.00	26.00	18.00	8.00
	-- Material Costs	22.00	18.00	4.00	23.00	18.00	5.00	22.00	18.00	4.00
	-- Material Direct Costs	22.00	18.00	4.00	23.00	18.00	5.00	22.00	18.00	4.00
	-- Raw Materials	20.00	18.00	2.00	21.00	18.00	3.00	20.00	18.00	2.00
	Other Materials	2.00	0.00	2.00	3.00	0.00	3.00	2.00	0.00	2.00
	-- Group Material	18.00	18.00	0.00	18.00	18.00	0.00	18.00	18.00	0.00
	-- Case	18.00	18.00	0.00	18.00	18.00	0.00	18.00	18.00	0.00
	MP3 Small	18.00	18.00	0.00	18.00	18.00	0.00	18.00	18.00	0.00
	-- Outsourced Services	2.00	0.00	2.00	2.00	0.00	2.00	2.00	0.00	2.00
	Other Services	2.00	0.00	2.00	2.00	0.00	2.00	2.00	0.00	2.00
	-- Assembly Costs	4.00	0.00	4.00	4.00	0.00	4.00	4.00	0.00	4.00
	Assembly Direct Costs	3.00	0.00	3.00	3.00	0.00	3.00	3.00	0.00	3.00
	Assembly Overhead	1.00	0.00	1.00	1.00	0.00	1.00	1.00	0.00	1.00
Colossal MP3 XR 128	-- Production Costs	14.00	0.00	14.00	14.00	0.00	14.00	14.00	0.00	14.00
	-- Material Costs	14.00	0.00	14.00	14.00	0.00	14.00	14.00	0.00	14.00
	-- Material Direct Costs	14.00	0.00	14.00	14.00	0.00	14.00	14.00	0.00	14.00
	-- Raw Materials	14.00	0.00	14.00	14.00	0.00	14.00	14.00	0.00	14.00
	Other Materials	14.00	0.00	14.00	14.00	0.00	14.00	14.00	0.00	14.00

The production costs for "Informa-GPS-1090" are 26 in period 1. The supply from Germany is the biggest share (18). From the Austrian point of view, these are variable costs because there is no obligation to buy the boxes.

A central question is: how much information must be provided from the subsidiaries? The data delivery can be limited to the product units and the prices.

At the next stage Austria delivers 50 "Informa GPS-1090" and 50 "Colossal MP3 XR 128" to Switzerland. Thirty units of each product are sold externally. Switzerland bundles these two products and sells them. The following illustration shows the Swiss calculation. The group part that is shown as material costs is 93 percent in Period 1 (50/54), as shown in the illustration:

Actual ▼	Calculation ▼	Switzerland ▼									
			Periods	**Organisations**							
			Per 1			Per 2			Per 3		
Basis	**Production Costs**		+ All	Austria	External	+ All	Austria	External	+ All	Austria	External
	-- Production Costs		54.00	50.00	4.00	54.00	50.00	4.00	54.00	50.00	4.00
	-- Material Costs		54.00	50.00	4.00	54.00	50.00	4.00	54.00	50.00	4.00
	-- Material Direct Costs		54.00	50.00	4.00	54.00	50.00	4.00	54.00	50.00	4.00
	-- Raw Materials		54.00	50.00	4.00	54.00	50.00	4.00	54.00	50.00	4.00
Colossal / Informa 1	Other Materials		4.00	0.00	4.00	4.00	0.00	4.00	4.00	0.00	4.00
	-- Group Material		50.00	50.00	0.00	50.00	50.00	0.00	50.00	50.00	0.00
	-- Selling Devices		50.00	50.00	0.00	50.00	50.00	0.00	50.00	50.00	0.00
	Informa GPS-1090		25.00	25.00	0.00	25.00	25.00	0.00	25.00	25.00	0.00
	Colossal MP3 XR 128		25.00	25.00	0.00	25.00	25.00	0.00	25.00	25.00	0.00

The next illustration shows the relevant prices.

Austria ▼	Actual ▼	Price ▼	Price ▼				
	Periods	**External Internal**					
		Per 1		Per 2		Per 3	
ZG Produkte		Extern	Intern	Extern	Intern	Extern	Intern
Colossal MP3 XR128		30.00	25.00	30.00	25.00	30.00	25.00
Colossal MP3 JT32		30.00	25.00	30.00	25.00	30.00	25.00
Informa GPS-4000		30.00	25.00	30.00	25.00	30.00	25.00
Informa GPS-1090		30.00	25.00	30.00	25.00	30.00	25.00

You can see the supply structure in the next illustration.

Sales Volume ▼	Actual ▼	Volume ▼				
				Periods		
Countries	**Basis**		**Basis**	Per 1	Per 2	Per 3
Germany	MP3 Small		Austria	100	90	100
Austria	Informa GPS-1090		Switzerland	50	50	50
			External	30	30	30
Switzerland	Colossal / Informa 1		External	45	54	40

The (simplified) Bill of Materials contains relations between group-related material and the product:

Actual	BOM			Periods		
Countries	Basis	Basis	AllBasis	Per 1	Per 2	Per 3
Austria	Germany	Informa GPS-1090	MP3 Small	1.00	1.00	1.00
Austria	Austria	Informa GPS-1090	MP3 Medium	1.00	1.00	1.00
Switzerland	Austria	Colossal / Informa 1	Informa GPS-1090	1.00	1.00	1.00
Switzerland	Austria	Colossal / Informa 1	Colossal MP3 XR128	1.00	1.00	1.00

With this information, it is possible to create a group profitability calculation without much effort. For the group-related calculation we can use the price vector. Per material flow, the valuation vector is used. This can be done with the following rule:

```
[]=N: IF(ELISANC('ZG Type', 'manufacturing costs', !ZG Type)=1,
['BOM']*DB('ZG Base', !ZG Organisations IC, 'All',
!ZG Periods, !ZG Scenarios, !ZG Type, !ZG Positions,
'Group Calculation'), CONTINUE);
```

This rule should only be applied to the elements of the valuation vector. Therefore we use the ELISANC function. The multiplication of BOM is reduced to the existing supply relations. This is the definition for the group calculation:

```
['Type':'Group Calculation']=N: IF(!Organisations IC @='External',
['Local Calculation'],DB('Basis', !Organisations, !Organisations IC,
!Periods, !Scenarios, 'manufacturing costs', !Products, !Positions));
```

If there is no group intern supply, the local calculation is used. Otherwise, the valuation vector will be used. With this information a group calculation can be created:

ZG Organisationen	ZG Produkte	Calculation	Per 1 +All	Germany	Austria	External	Per 2 +All	Germany	Austria	External	Per 3 +All	Germany	Austria	External
Germany	MP3 Small	--Production Costs	17.00	0.00	0.00	17.00	18.00	0.00	0.00	18.00	18.00	0.00	0.00	17.00
		-- Material Costs	10.00	0.00	0.00	10.00	11.00	0.00	0.00	11.00	11.00	0.00	0.00	10.00
		+ Material Direct Costs	8.00	0.00	0.00	8.00	9.00	0.00	0.00	9.00	9.00	0.00	0.00	8.00
		Material Overhead	2.00	0.00	0.00	2.00	2.00	0.00	0.00	2.00	2.00	0.00	0.00	2.00
		-- Assembly Costs	7.00	0.00	0.00	7.00	7.00	0.00	0.00	7.00	7.00	0.00	0.00	7.00
		Assembly Direct Costs	5.00	0.00	0.00	5.00	5.00	0.00	0.00	5.00	5.00	0.00	0.00	5.00
		Assembly Overhad	2.00	0.00	0.00	2.00	2.00	0.00	0.00	2.00	2.00	0.00	0.00	2.00
	MP3 Medium	-- Production Costs	20.00	0.00	0.00	20.00	20.00	0.00	0.00	20.00	20.00	0.00	0.00	20.00
		-- Material Costs	20.00	0.00	0.00	20.00	20.00	0.00	0.00	20.00	20.00	0.00	0.00	20.00
		+ Material Direct Costs	20.00	0.00	0.00	20.00	20.00	0.00	0.00	20.00	20.00	0.00	0.00	20.00
	MP3 Large	-- Production Costs	22.00	0.00	0.00	22.00	22.00	0.00	0.00	22.00	22.00	0.00	0.00	22.00
		-- Material Costs	22.00	0.00	0.00	22.00	22.00	0.00	0.00	22.00	22.00	0.00	0.00	22.00
		+ Material Direct Costs	22.00	0.00	0.00	22.00	22.00	0.00	0.00	22.00	22.00	0.00	0.00	22.00
Austria	Informa GPS-1090	-- Production Costs	25.00	17.00	0.00	8.00	27.00	18.00	0.00	9.00	25.00	17.00	0.00	8.00
		-- Material Costs	14.00	10.00	0.00	4.00	16.00	11.00	0.00	5.00	14.00	10.00	0.00	4.00
		+ Material Direct Costs	12.00	8.00	0.00	4.00	14.00	9.00	0.00	5.00	12.00	8.00	0.00	4.00
		Material Overhead	2.00	2.00	0.00	0.00	2.00	2.00	0.00	0.00	2.00	2.00	0.00	0.00
		-- Assembly Costs	11.00	7.00	0.00	4.00	11.00	7.00	0.00	4.00	11.00	7.00	0.00	4.00
		Assembly Direct Costs	8.00	5.00	0.00	3.00	8.00	5.00	0.00	3.00	8.00	5.00	0.00	3.00
		Assembly Overhad	3.00	2.00	0.00	1.00	3.00	2.00	0.00	1.00	3.00	2.00	0.00	1.00
	Colossal MP3 XR128	-- Production Costs	14.00	0.00	0.00	14.00	14.00	0.00	0.00	14.00	14.00	0.00	0.00	14.00
		-- Material Costs	14.00	0.00	0.00	14.00	14.00	0.00	0.00	14.00	14.00	0.00	0.00	14.00
		+ Material Direct Costs	14.00	0.00	0.00	14.00	14.00	0.00	0.00	14.00	14.00	0.00	0.00	14.00
Switzerland	Colossal / Informa 1	-- Production Costs	43.00	0.00	39.00	4.00	45.00	0.00	41.00	4.00	43.00	0.00	39.00	4.00
		-- Material Costs	32.00	0.00	28.00	4.00	34.00	0.00	30.00	4.00	32.00	0.00	28.00	4.00
		+ Material Direct Costs	30.00	0.00	26.00	4.00	32.00	0.00	28.00	4.00	30.00	0.00	26.00	4.00
		Material Overhead	2.00	0.00	2.00	0.00	2.00	0.00	2.00	0.00	2.00	0.00	2.00	0.00
		-- Assembly Costs	11.00	0.00	11.00	0.00	11.00	0.00	11.00	0.00	11.00	0.00	11.00	0.00
		Assembly Direct Costs	8.00	0.00	8.00	0.00	8.00	0.00	8.00	0.00	8.00	0.00	8.00	0.00
		Assembly Overhad	3.00	0.00	3.00	0.00	3.00	0.00	3.00	0.00	3.00	0.00	3.00	0.00

With this information an appropriate profit calculation can be created. The group profitability calculation is a simple multiplication:

```
['Group Margin']=N: ['Units','Sales']*['Group Calculation',
'ZG Organisations IC':'All'];
```

The sales can be calculated as follows:

```
['Gross Sales','Extern']=N:['Sales','Units']*['Positions':'Price','Type':
'Price'];
['Gross Sales']=N:['Sales','Units']*['Positions':'Price','Intern',
'Type':'Price'];
```

You see that the order is important. In this case, the external sales calculation is fired first. The second rule is ignored in this case and only used for internal calculation.

Let us compare the local and the group calculation. What does the contribution margin of the Switzerland product look like? Switzerland sells 50 bundles for 45. There is an interesting consequence. From a local point of view, it doesn't make sense to sell the bundle in period 1, because the transfer price is too high. But from a group point of view, the selling increases the profit (contribution margin is 100).

Actual ▾	Switzerland ▾	All ▾						
			LocalGroup		Periods			
			Local			Group Margin		
Basis	Contribution Margin		Per 1	Per 2	Per 3	Per 1	Per 2	Per 3
	Gross Sales		2,025.00	2,430.00	1,800.00	2,025.00	2,430.00	1,800.00
	+ Net Sales		2,025.00	2,430.00	1,800.00	2,025.00	2,430.00	1,800.00
	-- Raw Materials		2,430.00	2,916.00	2,160.00	1,080.00	1,404.00	960.00
	Other Materials		180.00	216.00	160.00	1,080.00	1,404.00	960.00
	-- Group Material		2,250.00	2,700.00	2,000.00	0.00	0.00	0.00
	-- Selling Devices		2,250.00	2,700.00	2,000.00	0.00	0.00	0.00
	Informa GPS-1090		1,125.00	1,350.00	1,000.00	0.00	0.00	0.00
	Colossal MP3 XR128		1,125.00	1,350.00	1,000.00	0.00	0.00	0.00
	-- Outsourced Services		0.00	0.00	0.00	270.00	324.00	240.00
	Other Services		0.00	0.00	0.00	270.00	324.00	240.00
Colossal / Informa 1	-- Material Direct Costs		2,430.00	2,916.00	2,160.00	1,350.00	1,728.00	1,200.00
	+ Raw Materials		2,430.00	2,916.00	2,160.00	1,080.00	1,404.00	960.00
	-- Outsourced Services		0.00	0.00	0.00	270.00	324.00	240.00
	Other Services		0.00	0.00	0.00	270.00	324.00	240.00
	Material Overhead		0.00	0.00	0.00	90.00	108.00	80.00
	+ Material Costs		2,430.00	2,916.00	2,160.00	1,440.00	1,836.00	1,280.00
	Assembly Direct Costs		0.00	0.00	0.00	360.00	432.00	320.00
	Assembly Overhead		0.00	0.00	0.00	135.00	162.00	120.00
	+ Assembly Costs		0.00	0.00	0.00	495.00	594.00	440.00
	+ Production Costs		2,430.00	2,916.00	2,160.00	1,935.00	2,430.00	1,720.00
	+ Margin		-405.00	-486.00	-360.00	90.00	0.00	80.00

The difference between the local and the group contribution margin can be explained as follows:

```
Sales Units * (transfer price - group costs) : 50 * (50-39) = 550
```

With this information it is possible to do a stock valuation. The new aspect is to include dependencies between periods. The important thing is that the initial stock for one period is derived from the final stock of the last period. You need a recursive behavior since the initial stock of the last period is indirectly derived from the initial stock of the first period (using all others periods in between).

We use TM1 rules:

- The initial stock is copied from the closing level of the previous period (with the exception of the first period).

- The additions to stock are valuated with the group values.

- The stock withdrawal is calculated by a moving average. The moving average is easy to calculate. We add the value of the stock addition to the total stock amount and divide the sum by the opening and addition numbers.

- The final stock is a simple aggregation of these items.

Once again, it is astonishing how easily this can be done with TM1, as shown in the following code and illustration:

```
['Initial Stock'']=N:IF(!ZG Periods @='Jan', CONTINUE,
DB('ZG Base', !ZG Organisations, !ZG Organisations IC,
ATTRS('ZG Periods',!ZG Periods,'Prev'), !ZG Scenarios,
'Final Stock', !ZG Products, !ZG Type));

['Withdrawals']=n:IF(!ZG Type @='Units', ['Sales'],
['Units'] *DB('ZG Base', !ZG Organisations, 'All',
!ZG Periods, !ZG Scenarios, !ZG Type, !ZG Products, 'Moving Average'));

['Additions']=n:IF(!ZG Type @='Units', CONTINUE,
['Units']*DB('ZG Base', !ZG Organisations,
'All', !ZG Periods, !ZG Scenarios, !ZG Type,
!ZG Products, 'Group Calculation'));
```

Countries	ZG Products	ZG Type	Per 1 In	Out	+Ending	Per 2 Opening	In	Out	+Ending	Per 3 Opening	In	Out	+Ending
Germany	MP3 Small	Volume	100	100	0	0	100	90	10	10	100	100	10
		-- Production Costs	1,700.00	1,700.00	0.00	0.00	1,800.00	1,620.00	180.00	180.00	1,700.00	1,709.09	170.91
		Misc	400.00	400.00	0.00	0.00	500.00	450.00	50.00	50.00	400.00	409.09	40.91
		Other Output	400.00	400.00	0.00	0.00	400.00	360.00	40.00	40.00	400.00	400.00	40.00
		Material Overhead	200.00	200.00	0.00	0.00	200.00	180.00	20.00	20.00	200.00	200.00	20.00
		Assembly Costs	500.00	500.00	0.00	0.00	500.00	450.00	50.00	50.00	500.00	500.00	50.00
		Assembly Overhead	200.00	200.00	0.00	0.00	200.00	180.00	20.00	20.00	200.00	200.00	20.00
Austria	Informa GPS-1090	Volume	100	80	20	20	80	80	20	20	80	80	20
		-- Production Costs	2,500.00	2,000.00	500.00	500.00	2,160.00	2,128.00	532.00	532.00	2,000.00	2,025.60	506.40
		Misc	600.00	480.00	120.00	120.00	640.00	608.00	152.00	152.00	480.00	505.60	126.40
		Other Output	600.00	480.00	120.00	120.00	480.00	480.00	120.00	120.00	480.00	480.00	120.00
		Material Overhead	200.00	160.00	40.00	40.00	160.00	160.00	40.00	40.00	160.00	160.00	40.00
		Assembly Costs	800.00	640.00	160.00	160.00	640.00	640.00	160.00	160.00	640.00	640.00	160.00
		Assembly Overhead	300.00	240.00	60.00	60.00	240.00	240.00	60.00	60.00	240.00	240.00	60.00
Switzerland	Colossal / Informa 1	Volume	50	45	5	5	50	54	1	1	50	40	11
		-- Production Costs	2,150.00	1,935.00	215.00	215.00	2,250.00	2,420.18	44.82	44.82	2,150.00	1,721.43	473.39
		Misc	1,200.00	1,080.00	120.00	120.00	1,300.00	1,394.18	25.82	25.82	1,200.00	961.43	264.39
		Other Output	300.00	270.00	30.00	30.00	300.00	324.00	6.00	6.00	300.00	240.00	66.00
		Material Overhead	100.00	90.00	10.00	10.00	100.00	108.00	2.00	2.00	100.00	80.00	22.00
		Assembly Costs	400.00	360.00	40.00	40.00	400.00	432.00	8.00	8.00	400.00	320.00	88.00
		Assembly Overhead	150.00	135.00	15.00	15.00	150.00	162.00	3.00	3.00	150.00	120.00	33.00

With this calculation it is possible to get the group journal for the legal intercompany profit elimination. This example shows a simple prototype but can be easily enhanced to a larger structure with several products. However, a complete calculation should consider additional aspects:

- Sometimes it is important to define consumption orders (that is, LIFO, CIFO).

- So-called mixed calculations when intermediate products can be delivered internally and from outside of the group.

- There should be more than one delivery per period with daily prices.

- Include work in progress.

- Sometimes cycles in the product flow can occur. This can be seen in the chemical industry, for example.

Summary

The models and methods shown in this chapter can be again seen as a toolbox to support specific group company requirements. You should always ask whether you can solve your specific problem with statutory consolidation systems or with the more flexible TM1. For this decision you should take integration aspects into account. Although IBM Cognos provides a close connection between Controller and TM1, sometimes additional exchanges are necessary. However, the use of the functions shown in this chapter can go far beyond traditional statutory consolidation.

24
CHAPTER

Risk Management

Risk and compliance management is a fast-growing topic in almost all companies. The IBM CFO study (www-05.ibm.com/innovation/de/cfostudy/) shows that trust and accountability issues receive attention similar to that for business intelligence. But requirements for risk management differ significantly from those for typical business intelligence solutions. First, the collected information must be auditable. Secondly, the process is important. And lastly, a lot of unstructured data must be collected.

Although Cognos TM1 has little out-of-the-box support for risk management, it is possible to design individual risk management systems with a lot of support for specific requirements. We will discuss some of them in detail.

Some words about positioning: Although professional tools like IBM Open Pages provide out-of-the-box support for compliance processes like risk management, there are some valid reasons to use TM1 for additional support:

- For smaller companies, a complex compliance process may be overkill. Cognos TM1 supports simple risk collection.

- Complex risk calculations might be necessary. However, if the calculations become too complex, you may consider statistical tools like IBM SPSS or ILOG.

- The most important reason might be the easy integration with planning purposes. Although this is quite a new topic, it is becoming more important to connect risk management and planning.

Governance, Risk, and Compliance (GRC) has become an immense, broad movement in recent years. We have only limited space, so we want to focus on Operational Risk Management (ORM). We will briefly articulate the requirements and then show how to implement them with Cognos TM1:

- Standard reporting
- Risk assessment
- Portfolio analysis
- Text handling
- Compliance process
- Monte Carlo simulation

With this final chapter, we leave the classical OLAP focus a little bit. Although this chapter is mainly about handling typical risk management challenges, the ideas presented can also give some ideas for other areas, whether compliance topics or topics totally outside the OLAP scope. This is typical for Cognos TM1: its flexibility and unique capabilities can be applied to areas that are out of scope for most OLAP products.

The Business Problem

The economic developments of the last few years have shown clearly that risk management is a growing market. All companies need support for this topic. In several countries, the regulatory requirements regarding risk management are increasing.

Risk management is a very heterogeneous topic, which includes typical tasks like these:

- Collecting risks
- Assessing the risks
- Defining activities to mitigate risks
- Reporting and analysis
- Simulations

These activities are part of an overall process. Let's take a look at a typical risk management process.

- The first important step is to identify and assess the important risks (this process can also be enhanced to identify opportunities). Usually there are two parameters: possible damage and probability. Although it is often criticized (how can you assess currency risk with these two parameters?), it is a natural starting point.

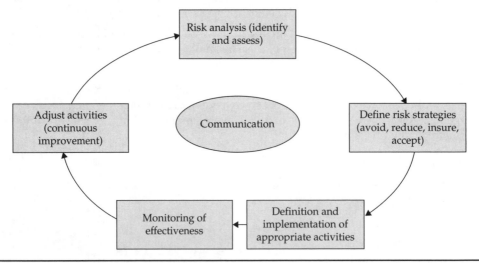

FIGURE 24-1   A closed-loop risk management system

- Often the situation turns out to be too risky after assessing all risks. Hence you have to mitigate. You can insure against risk, reduce it (for instance, search for alternative vendors if your risk of delivery stoppage is too high), or simply accept the risk.

- The activities have to be planned and budgeted and responsibilities assigned.

- Risk and mitigation activities must be monitored.

- If significant variances or new risks occur, the activities must be adjusted, or new activities must be defined.

An important aspect of risk management is integration. Often, there is an articulated need to integrate the planning process with risk management. This is quite obvious: When you plan, you automatically think about what can go wrong. On the other hand, when you assess the identified risk, you need future estimations that stem out from the planning.

So why is integration between the management accounting world, where OLAP is quite common, and the risk management world so rarely implemented? We think that communication is limited because different user groups are involved: management accounting has been working with OLAP for a long time. Auditors and risk management may not have this experience. However, with Cognos TM1 there is a realistic chance to bring these two groups together.

Cognos TM1 Can Help

How do you start with risk management? It can be quite complex, but in most cases it is a simple process of collecting risks and making small calculations. First, we need to describe and assess risks. For the assessment, we define a cube, "Risk Assessment":

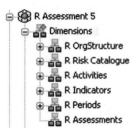

Let's discuss the dimensions briefly: The Risk Catalogue is quite obvious. The starting point is a risk catalogue, which lists risks and groups them into categories. This simply helps to structure the risks. Typically, risks are collected by business divisions. A centralized risk management unit has to bring these risks together to identify dependencies and risk heaps. Good categorization supports this process.

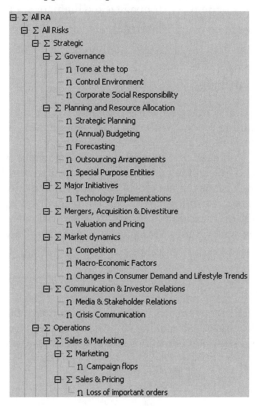

In the preceding illustration, it is not obvious what element is a risk and what is a risk category. You can define level 0 elements as risk. But what about risk categories that don't have concrete risks yet? Also, the depth of the structure can vary from branch to branch. The good thing is that Cognos TM1 doesn't need balanced trees. We suggest identifying risks and categories by an attribute.

Do we need a dimension for organization? This seems to be intuitive. However, given the specific domain, it is worthwhile to discuss it. We can argue about it, and we have seen applications where organizations are only aggregated elements within the Risk dimension. But it can also be the case that more than one organizational unit are responsible for one single risk. That is why we design it as a separate dimension.

We also included the activities as a separate dimension. Activities can influence more than one risk. But why did we include this in the assessment cube? We do this because we want to assess risks before and after one or more activities. To enter the effect of an activity on a risk, it is necessary to have separate dimensions. Furthermore, it is important to have the "NA" element ("No activity") in it because we want to collect data before any activities:

The next dimension, "R Indicators," holds the indicators and all the planning figures. We have defined a small planning model and some typical risk indicators, as shown in the following illustration. The risk indicators are part of the planning model, and some of the values of these indicators can be derived from the model rules.

Again the question, why do we need a separate dimension? We think that an indicator could be assigned to more than one risk.

To assess the risks, we need several "attributes." However, the attribute concept is not strong enough because we need to update the attributes on a periodical basis, and we also need the older versions. So we defined the following elements in "R Assessments" (selection):

- Threshold indicator
- Possible damage
- Likelihood
- Likelihood after activities
- Damage after activities
- Comment

With this setup we can collect the necessary information. A proposal for a risk report could look like the following illustration:

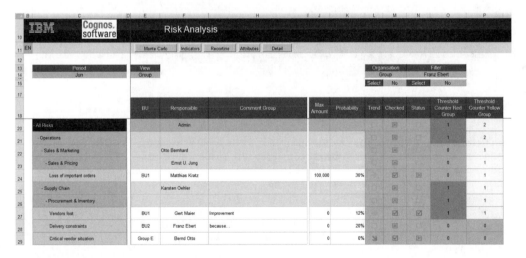

Working with Warning Indicators

It could be helpful to have early warning indicators. For instance, if the insolvency rate in your vendor's industry increases, it could be a warning signal that your own vendor could be in a critical situation. So to collect data and link it to the specific risk is helpful.

By the way, there is an ongoing discussion about bringing risk management together with management concepts like the balanced scorecard. It is very logical since a balanced scorecard focuses on leading indicators for early warnings, which are also necessary for risk management. The biggest difference is that measures in the balanced scorecard should be a measure for performance, whereas the risk indicators should give early warnings about the overall environment. From a technical point of view, there is no difference. Hence integration might not be complex.

We reuse the threshold model we developed for the balanced scorecard, with one exception—we have two limit types:

- One is for local reporting.
- The other for group assessment.

The rationale behind this is that group and business units often have a different understanding of risk situations, and consequently the assessment can vary. The next illustration shows a form where you can switch between global and local assessment (cell C16).

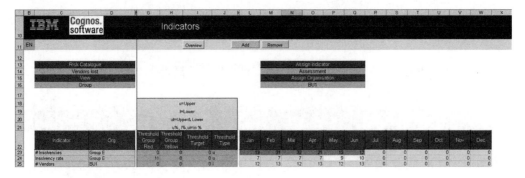

This is the calculation for the local assessment:

```
['ThresholdIndicatorLocal']=
IF(['Middle Case'] = 0,0,
IF(DB('R Assessment 5', !R OrgStructure, !R Risk Catalogue, !R Activities,
  !R Indicators,'Period0','Threshold Type') @='l%',
  IF(['Middle Case']<['Threshold Target','Period0']*
    (100-['ThresholdLocalRed','Period0'])/100,
    -2,
    IF(['Middle Case']<['Threshold Target','Period0'] * (100-
      ['ThresholdLocalYellow','Period0']) / 100,
      -1,0)),
IF(DB('R Assessment 5', !R OrgStructure, !R Risk Catalogue, !R Activities,
  !R Indicators,'Period0','Threshold Type') @='u%',
```

```
    IF(['Middle Case']>['Threshold Target','Period0'] * (100+
      ['ThresholdLocalRed','Period0']) / 100,
      -2,
      IF(['Middle Case']>['Threshold Target','Period0'] * (100+
        ['ThresholdLocalYellow','Period0']) / 100,
          -1,0)),
IF(DB('R Assessment 5', !R OrgStructure, !R Risk Catalogue,
    !R Activities, !R Indicators,'Period0','Threshold Type') @='ul%',
    IF(ABS(['Middle Case']-['Threshold Target','Period0']) >
      ['Threshold Target','Period0'] *( ['ThresholdLocalRed','Period0']) /
100,
      -2,
      IF(ABS(['Middle Case']-['Threshold Target','Period0'])
        >['Threshold Target','Period0'] *
        (['ThresholdLocalYellow','Period0']) /      100,
          -1,0)),
IF(DB('R Assessment 5', !R OrgStructure, !R Risk Catalogue, !R Activities,
    !R Indicators,'Period0','Threshold Type') @='ul',
    IF(abs(['Middle Case']-['Threshold Target','Period0'])>
      ['ThresholdLocalRed','Period0'],
      -2,
      IF(abs(['Middle Case']-['Threshold Target','Period0'])>
        ['ThresholdLocalYellow','Period0'],
          -1,0)),
IF(DB('R Assessment 5', !R OrgStructure, !R Risk Catalogue,
    !R Activities,!R Indicators,'Period0','Threshold Type') @='l',
    IF(['Middle Case']<['ThresholdLocalRed','Period0'],
      -2,
      IF(['Middle Case']<['ThresholdLocalYellow','Period0'],-1,0)),
IF(DB('R Assessment 5', !R OrgStructure,!R Risk Catalogue, !R Activities,
    !R Indicators,'Period0','Threshold Type') @='u',
    IF(['Middle Case']>['ThresholdLocalRed','Period0'],
    -2,
     IF(['Middle Case']>['ThresholdLocalYellow','Period0'],
     -1,0))
,0)))))));
```

With this definition we can include the indicator model in the risk analysis. We simply define a counter for each status so that we can aggregate per risk. We store the indicator assignment per risk within the same cube (as a 1/0 matrix).

```
['Threshold Counter Yellow Group']=N:['Assignment','Period0']
*IF(['ThresholdIndicatorGroup','Basis Risk']=-1,1,0);
['Threshold Counter Red Group']=N:['Assignment', 'Period0']
*IF(['ThresholdIndicatorGroup','Basis Risk']=-2,1,0);
['Threshold Counter Yellow Local']=N:['Assignment', 'Period0']
*IF(['ThresholdIndicatorLocal','Basis Risk']=-1,1,0);
['Threshold Counter Red Local']=N:['Assignment', 'Period0']
*IF(['ThresholdIndicatorLocal','Basis Risk']=-2,1,0);
```

With this little concept, we can show indicators in the risk report.

	BU	Responsible	Comment Group	Trend	Checked	Status	Threshold Counter Red Group	Threshold Counter Yellow Group
All Risks		Admin			☒		1	2
- Operations					☒		1	2
- Sales & Marketing		Otto Bernhard			☒		0	1
- Sales & Pricing		Ernst U. Jung			☒		0	1
Loss of important orders	BU1	Matthias Kratz			☑	☒	0	1
- Supply Chain		Karsten Oehler			☒		1	1
- Procurement & Inventory					☒		1	1
Vendors lost	BU1	Gert Maier	Improvement		☑	☑	1	1
Delivery constraints	BU2	Franz Ebert	because...		☒		0	0
Critical vendor situation	Group E	Bernd Otto		↘	☑	☒	0	0

Risk Analysis — EN — Monte Carlo | Indicators | Reporting | Attributes | Detail — Period: Jun — View: Group — Organisation: Group — Filter: Franz Ebert — Select No Select No

Mitigating Risk

An important aspect of risk management is, without any question, to work with risks (so-called *risk mitigation*). After a risk is identified and assessed, you can do the following:

- Reduce the risk
- Avoid the risk
- Transform the risk (for instance, insure against it)
- Accept the risk

Let's take a deeper look into the activities. We decided to implement activities independently of risks because an activity can have an impact on more than one risk.

To do the assignment, we again work with a risk/activity matrix that holds 0/1 values. To hide this more or less technical construct, a TI process can be started from Excel or over the web to do the assignment.

The view in the following illustration lists some assignments:

		R Assessments
R Risk Catalogue	R Activities	Assignment
Laboratory disaster	Improve Protection	1
	Training Initiatives	1
$ development	Hedge currency deposits	1
	Diversify vendors	1

The entry form, in the following illustration, shows how to select an activity and assign it to a risk:

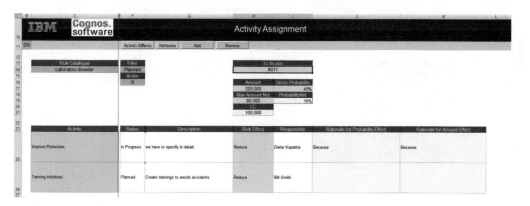

We decide to enter the effects manually and jointly for all assigned activities, for two reasons:

- In a very few cases, you can automatically calculate the direct effect of activity attributes.
- If you have more than one activity, the single effects usually can't be summed up simply.

The cube looks like the following illustration:

And we created an entry form to specify the activities, as shown in the following illustration. Since we want to have auditable activities, we implement the same concept as we used for the risk attributes. We will explain the version concept later in this chapter, in the section "Maintaining Risks with Time-Based Attributes."

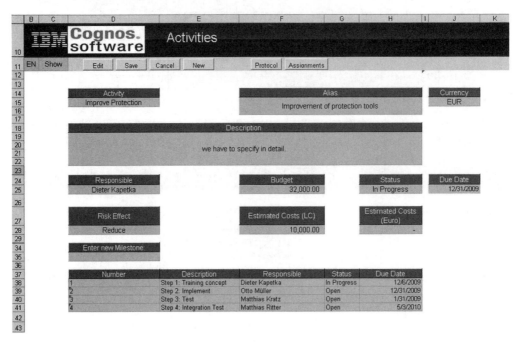

Using Risk Portfolios with TM1 Web

The portfolio with the two axes "possible damage" and "probability" is the typical risk report. It shows risks in the portfolio with the axes "damage" and "probability." The idea behind this is easy: Focus on the risks with a high probability and possible high damage. Neglect unlikely and low-damage risks.

It makes sense to build segments. The quadrant in the upper-right corner is the dangerous one: high probability and high damage. This portfolio, like all portfolios, gives a hint about what risk you should concentrate on.

And actually you need two portfolio diagrams: one before activities and one after.

Of course, you can do portfolios with Excel. But you can't show them in TM1 Web. It simply doesn't work properly. And also within Excel, it is not that easy, because Excel has limitations regarding names. So a lot of manual work is necessary.

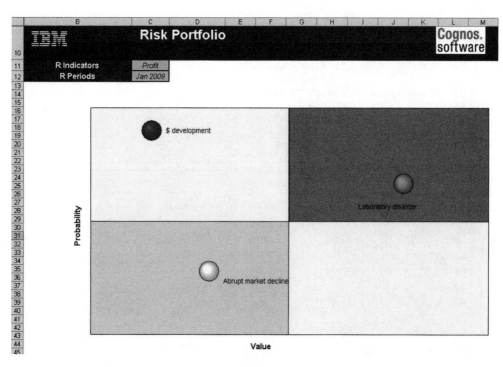

In addition to the problems we have with proper portfolio analysis, there is another challenge: Risks can overlap regarding probability and amounts of possible damage. This looks nasty in the diagram.

It is more interesting to have classes defined. We want to have these classes dynamically defined. The class members can vary from period to period. Since you don't have to sort, it is relatively easy to calculate.

We define classes. In this example we want to create a 5×5 matrix, as shown in the illustration.

We define the boundaries as attributes:

n 1
n 2
n 3
n 4
n 5
n 0

	Max (Numeric)
1	0.100000
2	0.150000
3	0.200000
4	0.400000
5	1.000000
0	0.000000

Now we can define the Risk Classes cube, as follows:

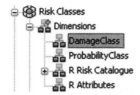

We collect data from the risk assessment on the class '0':

```
['R ProbabilityClass':'0','R DamageClass':'0']=N:
DB('R Description', '0', !R Risk Catalogue, !R Attributes);
```

So class '0' contains all necessary values in detail.

Basis risks	MaxAmountGross(LC)	MaxAmountNet(LC)	ProbabilityNet	ProbabilityGross
Campaign flops	10000	0	0	0
Loss of important orders	0	0	0	0,2
R151	1000000	500000	0,2	0,3
R196	200000	0	0	0,2
Laboratory disaster	400000	100000	0,1	0,4
$ development	250000	200000	0,1	0,3
Abrupt market decline	20000000	10000000	0	0
Market development eastern europe	500000	400000	0	0
R150	0	0	0	0,5
Vendors lost	300000	200000	0,05	0,12
Delivery constraints	40000	200000	0,1	0,12
Critical vendor situation	100000	50000	0,05	0,12

```
['MaxAmountGross']=N:
IF(['R ProbabilityClass':'0','R DamageClass':'0']>
  ATTRN('R DamageClass',STR(NUMBR(!R DamageClass)-1,2,0),'MAX') &
  ['R ProbabilityClass':'0','R DamageClass':'0']<=
  ATTRN('R DamageClass',!R DamageClass,'MAX')
  & (['R ProbabilityClass':'0','R DamageClass':'0','ProbabilityGross']>
  ATTRN ('R ProbabilityClass', STR (NUMBR (!R ProbabilityClass)-1,2,0),'MAX')
  &['R ProbabilityClass':'0','R DamageClass':'0','ProbabilityGross']<=
  ATTRN ('R ProbabilityClass',!R ProbabilityClass,'MAX')),
  1,0);
```

To calculate the number of risks for a class, you simply have to select "All Risks." Now it is easy to create a report like this:

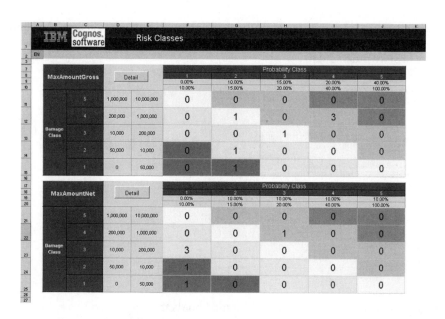

Maintaining Risks with Time-Based Attributes

To be honest, auditing and Cognos TM1 might not be the best story. And particularly when it is about text handling, Cognos TM1 has some obvious disadvantages. As we already described, there is no out-of-the-box protocol.

However, sometimes it is helpful to track changes. This is crucial for all risk management and compliance processes.

We would like to show how you can do this with Cognos TM1. Of course, there are tools that can handle this better. However, it is also possible with Cognos TM1 with a little bit of preparation.

First, we define a separate cube for the risk attributes with a specific dimension to keep the versions, as shown in the following illustration:

We have to define numbers to count the versions (within the dimension "R Versions"). Don't be too restrictive with the number of elements. Risk management systems usually don't have to store much data.

n 0
n Temp
n 1
n 2
n 3
n 4
n 5
n 6
n 7
n 8
n 9
n 10
n 11
n 12
n 13
n 14
n 15

Version 0 is the most current version. "Temp" holds the data when it is edited.

We also have a dimension for the attributes, as shown in the following illustration. This allows us to use the picklist feature.

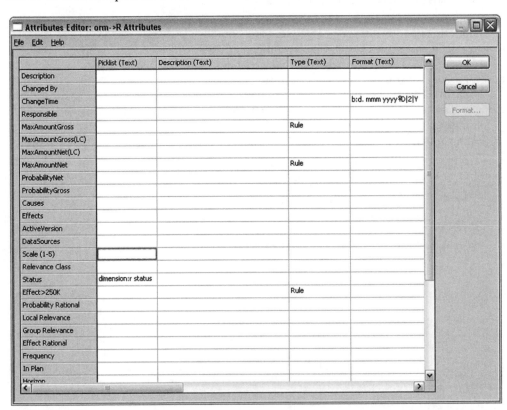

It is also possible to define calculated attributes. This could be used for currency calculation, for example:

```
['MaxAmountGross']=N:['MaxAmountGross(LC)']*
DB('Currencies', ATTRS('R OrgStructure',attrs('R Risk Catalogue',
!R Risk Catalogue,'Organisation'),'Currency'), 'Basis','Plan' );

['MaxAmountNet']=N:['MaxAmountNet(LC)']*
DB('Currencies', ATTRS('R OrgStructure',attrs('R Risk Catalogue',
!R Risk Catalogue,'Organisation'),'Currency'), 'Basis','Plan' );

['Effect>250K' ] =S:IF (['MaxAmountGross']>250000,'Yes','No');
['Risk Value Gross'] = N:['MaxAmountGross']*['ProbabilityGross' ] ;
['Risk Value Net'] = N:['MaxAmountNet']*['ProbabilityNet' ] ;
```

We defined an entry form for the attributes, as shown in the following illustration. This is a typical transactional formula. For this we implemented an entry mode and a view mode. When you open the form, you start with the view mode. To start in entry mode, the data from version 0 is copied into "Temp." When you click the Save button, the version 0 is copied to the first empty count element and the Temp data is copied into the "0" element.

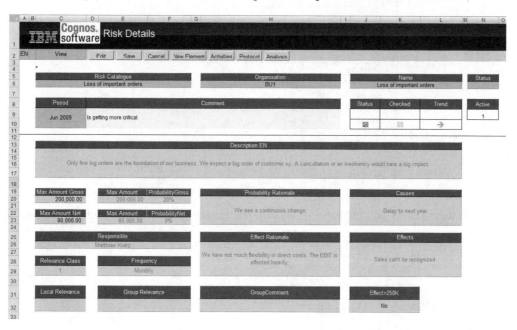

Data validation is an important concept. In our examples we simply require the user to fill mandatory fields. An aggregation of all risks gives an overall validation status. You can link the result of the validation to a workflow:

```
['VProbabililityGross'] =N: IF(['ProbabilityGross' ] <> 0,0,1);
[ 'VMaxAmountGross'] =N: IF(['MaxAmountGross' ] <> 0,0,1);
['VResponsibility' ] =N: IF(DB('R Description', !R Versions,
!R Risk Catalogue, 'Responsible') @='',1,0);
```

We want to start with the "Save" and "Edit" processes. We solve this with a generic process, "Copy Version," as shown in the following illustration:

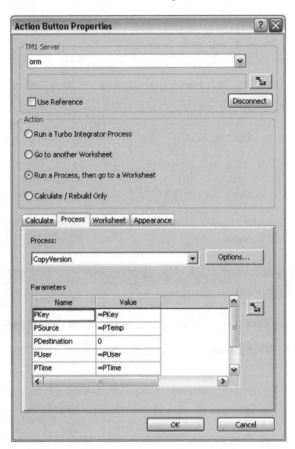

With saving or editing the process, we also change the status within Excel, as follows:

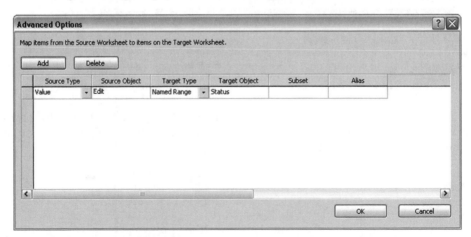

We have to define the "Save" process so flexibly that new attributes are automatically detected. Here is the Prolog section:

```
j = 1;
WHILE (j < 100);
  IF (CellGetN(PCube , STR (j,3,0),PKey,'ActiveVersion') = 1);
    ActiveVersion = j;
     j = j + 100;
  ENDIF;
   j = j +1;
END;
IF (PDestination @= '0');
  CellPutn(0, PCube , STR (ActiveVersion,3,0), PKey, 'ActiveVersion');
  ActiveVersion = ActiveVersion + 1;
  CellPutn(1, PCube ,STR(ActiveVersion,3,0), PKey, 'ActiveVersion');
ENDIF;
```

The Epilog section looks like this:

```
i = 1;
WHILE  (i <= DIMSIZ(AttrDimension));
  IF (DIMNM(AttrDimension,i) @<> 'ActiveVersion');
    #Save the last version
    IF(PDestination @= '0');
      IF (DTYPE(AttrDimension,dimnm(AttrDimension,i))@='S');
        IF(attrs(AttrDimension,dimnm(AttrDimension,i),'Type') @<> 'Rule');
        as= CellGets(Cube,'0',PKey,dimnm(AttrDimension,i));
        CellPuts(as, Cube ,str(ActiveVersion,3,0), PKey,
dimnm(AttrDimension,i));
        ENDIF;
      ELSE;
        IF(ATTRS(AttrDimension,dimnm(AttrDimension,i),'Type') @<> 'Rule');
          a= CellGetN(Cube ,'0',PKey,dimnm(AttrDimension,i));
          CellPutn(a, Cube ,str(ActiveVersion,3,0), PKey,
dimnm(AttrDimension,i));
        ENDIF;
      ENDIF;
    ENDIF;
    IF (DTYPE(AttrDimension,dimnm(AttrDimension,i))@='S');
      IF(ATTRS(AttrDimension,dimnm(AttrDimension,i),'Type') @<> 'Rule');
        as= CellGets(Cube, PSource,PKey,dimnm(AttrDimension,i));
        CellPuts(as, Cube ,PDestination, PKey, dimnm(AttrDimension,i));
      ENDIF;
    ELSE;
      IF(ATTRS(AttrDimension,dimnm(AttrDimension,i),'Type') @<> 'Rule');
        a= CellGetN(Cube ,PSource,PKey,dimnm(AttrDimension,i));
        CellPutn(a, Cube ,PDestination, PKey, dimnm(AttrDimension,i));
      ENDIF;
    ENDIF;
  ENDIF;
```

```
   i = i + 1;
END;
IF (PDestination @= '0');
  CellPuts(PUser, Cube ,pDestination, PKey, 'Changed By');
  CellPutn(PTime, Cube ,PDestination, PKey, 'ChangeTime');
ENDIF;
```

How can we control the behavior? We use conditional formatting, as shown in the following illustration:

You should also consider protecting the entry cells:

	Description	Changed By	ChangeTime	Responsible	Frequency	ProbabilityNet	MaxAmount Net	ProbabilityGross	MaxAmountGross	Causes	Effects
0	Only few big orders are the foundation of our business. We expect a big order of customer xy. A cancelation or an insolvency would have a big impact.	Admin	0/1/00 0:00	0	0	0%	80,000	20%	200,000	Delay to next year	Sales can't be recognized.
2	Only few big orders are the foundation of our business. We expect a big order of customer xy. A cancelation or an insolvency would have a big impact.	Admin	0/1/00 0:00	0	0	0%	0	0%	0	Delay to next year	Sales can't be recognized.
3	Only few big orders are the foundation of our business. We expect a big order of customer xy. A cancelation or an insolvency would have a big impact.	Admin	0/1/00 0:00	0	0	0%	0	20%	0	Cancellation	Sales can't be recognized.
4	Only few big orders are the foundation of our business. We expect a big order of customer xy. A cancelation or an insolvency would have a big impact.	Admin	0/1/00 0:00	0	0	0%	0	20%	0	etc.	Sales can't be recognized.
5	Only few big orders are the foundation of our business. We expect a big order of customer xy. A cancelation or an insolvency would have a big impact.	Admin	0/1/00 0:00	0	0	0%	0	20%	0	Delay to next year	Sales can't be recognized.
6	Only few big orders are the foundation of our business. We expect a big order of customer xy. A cancelation or an insolvency would have a big impact.	Admin	0/1/00 0:00	0	0	15%	0	20%	0	Cancellation	Sales can't be recognized.

Creating New Risks with Automatic Key Generation

Operational risk management is a distributed process. This also means that risks are identified locally. Thus there must be a possibility to create risk via TM1 Web by a local risk manager. This should be a structured process; otherwise, it might end in chaos. Hence we use a TI script to change the structure.

A user starts the page and enters the name for the new risk. Because we use the name as an alias, a check for uniqueness must take place. We generate a message in Excel if the process failed. Instead of using a generic message "failed," we think it is helpful to give more information about what exactly failed:

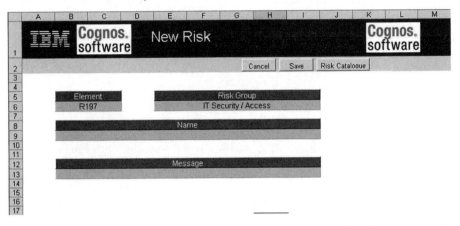

For the display of the error message, we refer to our suggested implementation in Chapter 8.

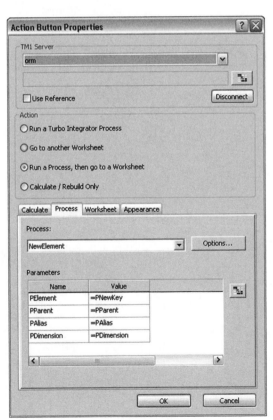

We use the same process for risks and activities. Here are the necessary prechecks:

```
sMessageCube = 'TBB TI Messages';
sStringCube = 'TBB Strings';
sParameterCube = 'TBB User Parameters';
sUser = TM1User();
sThisProcess = GETPROCESSNAME();
sLanguage = CELLGETS(sParameterCube,sUser,'TBB Language','S');
IF ( sLanguage @= '' );
  sLanguage = 'EN';
ENDIF;

IF ( TRIM(PAlias) @= '');
  sMessage = EXPAND(CELLGETS(sStringCube, 'TBB TI No Alias provided',
sLanguage));
  CELLPUTS(sMessage, sMessageCube, sUser, sThisProcess, 'Message');
  ProcessError;
ENDIF;
IF ( TRIM(PParent) @= '');
  sMessage = EXPAND(CELLGETS(sStringCube, 'TBB TI No Group provided',
sLanguage));
  CELLPUTS(sMessage, sMessageCube, sUser, sThisProcess, 'Message');
ProcessError;
ENDIF;

i = 1;
WHILE ( i < DIMSIZ(PDimension));
 IF (PAlias @= Attrs(PDimension, dimnm(PDimension, i), 'Alias'));
  sMessage = EXPAND(CELLGETS(sStringCube, 'TBB TI Element already exist',
  sLanguage));
  CELLPUTS(sMessage, sMessageCube, sUser, sThisProcess, 'Message');
   ProcessError;
 ENDIF;
 i = i + 1;
END;

DimensionElementComponentAdd(PDimension, PParent,PElement, 1);
IF (PDimension @= 'R Activities');
  PAttr = 'NewActivity';
  Prefix = 'A';
ELSE;
PAttr = 'NewRisk';
  Prefix = 'R';
ENDIF;
ExecuteProcess('GenerateNewKey', 'PAttribute', PAttr,'Prefix',Prefix);
```

Not only for risk management, it can also be helpful to have an automatic key generation. That can be done by a key generation mechanism. We simply want to generate keys like this:

- R1, R2, R3…. for risks
- A1, A2, A3… for activities

```
a = ATTRS('Parameters','Basis', PAttribute);
PnNewNumber = Prefix | str(numbr(subst(a,2,3))+1,3,0);
AttrPutS(PnNewNumber, 'Parameters','Basis', PAttribute);
```

Reporting Risk

How should you do reporting? It is very much text-based, and this is definitely not the strength of Cognos TM1. You will very soon realize disadvantages compared to relational reporting:

- The reporting is basically focused on single-cube reporting. Now a view concept exists. Excel and Active Forms are limited ways to bring in more reporting flexibility.
- The report offers dynamic sizing with text boxes.
- The window fix is problematic when the length cannot be estimated in advance.

With risk reporting you have to develop complex reports. We want to show how to do this, even if we know that this is not the best concept:

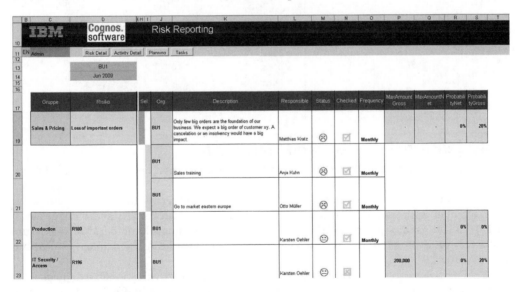

You can see the combination of activities:

```
K19:=IF(D19=D18,E19,DBRW("TOG:R Description","0",$D19,K$18))
```

You can also see grouping:

```
=ELPAR("TOG:R Risk catalogue",D19,1)
```

Since this is a combination of various Cognos TM1 functions, we recommend a drill-down position. This formula ensures that the drill-down works.

Drill-through to other forms is important. Although it is easy to use the link feature of the Action button, it can be cumbersome with complex reports. Report columns often are attribute functions where the requested DBRW parameters can't be handed over. That is why we use a specifically formatted cell to be marked before drilling. If the user wants to drill down, he will always have to select this special cell. If you use this feature, you should implement a similar function in worksheets so that the user becomes familiar with this concept.

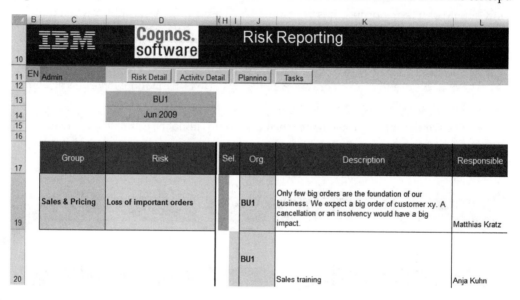

Aggregating Risk with Monte Carlo Simulation

As a result of the risk management process, we collected information about the probability and the possible damage of every risk before and after activities. With this we can calculate the maximum loss and some other KPIs. There is a slight problem with risk aggregation. You remember we talked about risk assessment, and we used probability and damage as the key indicators. But how can we aggregate them to a meaningful number? The maximum risk is very unlikely; every risk would have to occur. Simply adding the damage value can't be the solution.

A better idea might be to do this by multiplying probability by the possible damage and aggregating this number. This is very easy but also is not very meaningful. It ends in a single value that gives no real impression about possible damage or about its likelihood.

A good method might be simulation. Monte Carlo simulation can be used to aggregate risks. Let us briefly describe this method.

We create a business model, for instance, a profit calculation. It could be as simple as taking sales as first input, a cost/sales relation as second input, and the profit as output. In reality, it would be more complex:

- We define distribution functions per input parameter.

- We take a number generator and calculate the model repeatedly (>100 times).

- We show the distribution curve of one of the output parameters (the profit, for instance).

This doesn't sound like Cognos TM1, does it? But it is possible. First we need to generate distribution functions. Here we could have an endless discussion about the right statistical functions. We suggest three distribution functions (see Figure 24-2).

- Steady three-point

- Discrete three-point

- Normal curve

Furthermore, we have to define a calculation model. We take a simple model but only with non-cross-dimensional operators.

```
['Sales Tubes']=N:['Tubes Numbers']*['Tubes Price'];
['Sales']=n:['Sales Tubes']+['Sales Automobile Parts'];
['Contribution']=N:['Sales']-['Direct Costs'];
['Direct Costs']=N:['R Indicators':'Material']+['Labour'];
['Ebitda']=N:['Contribution']-['R Indicators':'Marketing']-
['Administration']-['R&D']-['Other Costs'];
['EBIT']=N:['Ebitda']-['Depreciation'];
['EBT']=N:['EBIT']-['Interests'];
['Profit']=N:['EBT']-['Taxes'];
```

You can see that we don't use aggregation. The idea is to have the simulation cube free of calculations. We use our base cube "R Assessment 5" to store the input data. We need

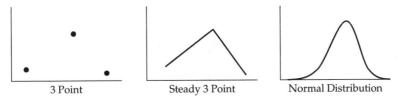

| 3 Point | Steady 3 Point | Normal Distribution |

Figure 24-2 Used distributions

a collection form. For each position, you can choose a distribution curve (see the method in column J in the following illustration).

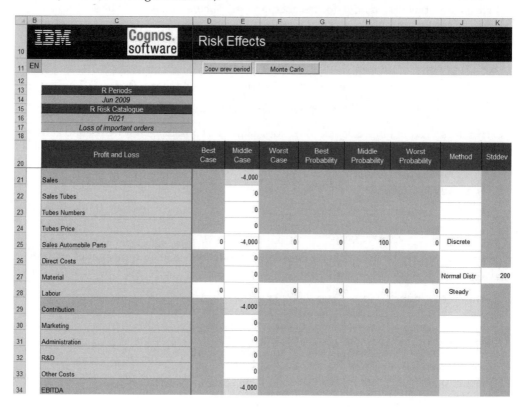

	Profit and Loss	Best Case	Middle Case	Worst Case	Best Probability	Middle Probability	Worst Probability	Method	Stddev
21	Sales		-4,000						
22	Sales Tubes		0						
23	Tubes Numbers		0						
24	Tubes Price		0						
25	Sales Automobile Parts	0	-4,000	0	0	100	0	Discrete	
26	Direct Costs		0						
27	Material		0					Normal Distr	200
28	Labour	0	0	0	0	0	0	Steady	
29	Contribution		-4,000						
30	Marketing		0						
31	Administration		0						
32	R&D		0						
33	Other Costs		0						
34	EBITDA		-4,000						

To store the simulation data, we created a cube for the result of the Monte Carlo simulation, as shown in the following illustration. It includes a counter dimension. We don't include activities in here. From a conceptual point of view it would be necessary.

The dimension "R Simulation Runs" stores the results of each simulation run. But cluster elements (to count the results per cluster) are also stored:

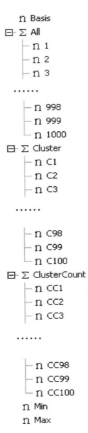

```
    n  Basis
 ⊟ Σ All
        ├ n  1
        ├ n  2
        ├ n  3
        ......
        ├ n  998
        ├ n  999
        └ n  1000
    ⊟ Σ Cluster
        ├ n  C1
        ├ n  C2
        ├ n  C3
        ......
        ├ n  C98
        ├ n  C99
        └ n  C100
    ⊟ Σ ClusterCount
        ├ n  CC1
        ├ n  CC2
        ├ n  CC3
        ......
        ├ n  CC98
        ├ n  CC99
        └ n  CC100
    n  Min
    n  Max
```

We create a reference view to "pull" data out of the risk assessment cube:

R Simulation Runs	Tubes Numbers	Tubes Price	Sales Automobile Parts	Material	Labour	Marketing	Administration	R&D	Other Costs	Depreciation	Interests	Taxes
	Plan	Plan	Plan	Plan	Plan	Plan	Plan	Plan	Plan	Plan	Plan	Plan
772	0.00	0.00	0.00	0.00	0.00	0.00	0.00	0.00	0.00	0.00	0.00	0.00
773	0.00	0.00	0.00	0.00	0.00	0.00	0.00	0.00	0.00	0.00	0.00	0.00
774	0.00	0.00	0.00	0.00	0.00	0.00	0.00	0.00	0.00	0.00	0.00	0.00
775	0.00	0.00	0.00	0.00	0.00	0.00	0.00	0.00	0.00	0.00	0.00	0.00
776	0.00	0.00	0.00	0.00	0.00	0.00	0.00	0.00	0.00	0.00	0.00	0.00
777	0.00	0.00	0.00	0.00	0.00	0.00	0.00	0.00	0.00	0.00	0.00	0.00
778	0.00	0.00	0.00	0.00	0.00	0.00	0.00	0.00	0.00	0.00	0.00	0.00
779	0.00	0.00	0.00	0.00	0.00	0.00	0.00	0.00	0.00	0.00	0.00	0.00
780	0.00	0.00	0.00	0.00	0.00	0.00	0.00	0.00	0.00	0.00	0.00	0.00
781	0.00	0.00	0.00	0.00	0.00	0.00	0.00	0.00	0.00	0.00	0.00	0.00

Jan ▾ R171

Simulations Input   R Scenarios

We simply write a TI process that runs a thousand times and generates random data.

Unfortunately, there is no function to convert a linear random function into a normal curve. We have to compute the inverse normal cumulative distribution, which we couldn't find in the rules library (don't search for that…). Fortunately, TI is very close to Basic, so we can find some code on the web (http://home.online.no/~pjacklam/notes/invnorm/index. html, and VBA implementation: www.vbarchiv.net/tipps/tipp_2111-inverse-der-kumulativen-standard-normalverteilung.html). There is always a bias but it is very small.

We need some basis parameters (within the Prolog section):

```
a1 = -39.6968302866538; a2 = 220.946098424521;
a3 = -275.928510446969; a4 = 138.357751867269;
a5 = -30.6647980661472;  a6 = 2.50662827745924;
b1 = -54.4760987982241; b2 = 161.585836858041;
b3 = -155.698979859887; b4 = 66.8013118877197;
b5 = -13.2806815528857; c1 = -0.00778489400243029;
c2 = -0.322396458041136; c3 = -2.40075827716184;
c4 = -2.54973253934373; c5 = 4.37466414146497;
c6 = 2.93816398269878; d1 = 0.00778469570904146;
d2 = 0.32246712907004; d3 = 2.445134137143;
d4 = 3.75440866190742;p_low = 0.02425; p_high = 1 - p_low;
```

With this preparation we can start the simulation run. It is executed for every cell. The most complex calculation handles the normal distribution:

```
p=rand;
vPeriod = Period;
IF(CellGetS('R Assessment 2',VRisk,VIndicator,VPeriod,'Method')
   @='Normal distributed');
  IF ( p < 0 % p > 1 ) ;
     temp=1;
  ELSEIF (p < p_low);
     q = SQRT(-2 * LOG(p));
     NormSInv2 = (((((c1 * q + c2) * q + c3) * q + c4) * q + c5) * q + c6) /
        ((((d1 * q + d2) * q + d3) * q + d4) * q + 1);
   ELSEIF (p <= p_high);
     q = p - 0.5; r = q * q;
     NormSInv2 = (((((a1 * r + a2) * r + a3) * r + a4) * r + a5) * r + a6) * q /
        (((((b1 * r + b2) * r + b3) * r + b4) * r + b5) * r + 1);
   ELSE;
     q = SQRT(-2 * LOG(1 - p));
     NormSInv2 = -(((((c1 * q + c2) * q + c3) * q + c4) * q + c5) * q + c6) /
        ((((d1 * q + d2) * q + d3) * q + d4) * q + 1);
  ENDIF;
  temp= NormSInv2*
  CellGetN('R Assessment 2',VRisk,VIndicator,VPeriod,'Stddev') +
  CellGetN('R Assessment 2',VRisk,VIndicator,VPeriod,'Middle Case');
ELSEIF (CellGetS('R Assessment 2',VRisk,VIndicator,VPeriod,'Method')@='s');
   temp = CellGetN('R Assessment 2',VRisk,VIndicator,VPeriod,'Middle Case') +
   (p-0.5)*CellGetN('R Assessment 2',VRisk,VIndicator,VPeriod,'Worst Case');
ELSEIF (CellGetS('R Assessment 2',VRisk,VIndicator,VPeriod,'Method')
   @='Discrete');
   temp =
```

```
IF (p*100<= CellGetN('R Assessment 2',VRisk,VIndicator,VPeriod,
'Best Probability'),
CellGetN('R Assessment 2',VRisk,VIndicator,VPeriod,'Best Case'),
 IF (p*100<=CellGetN('R Assessment 2',VRisk,VIndicator,VPeriod,
   'Best Probability')+
CellGetN('R Assessment 2',VRisk,VIndicator,VPeriod,'Middle Probability'),
CellGetN('R Assessment 2',VRisk,VIndicator,VPeriod,'Middle Case'),
CellGetN('R Assessment 2',VRisk,VIndicator,VPeriod,'Worst Case')));
ELSE;
    temp=CellGetN('R Assessment 2',VRisk,VIndicator,VPeriod,'Middle Case');
ENDIF;
CellPutN(Temp,'R Simulations 2',VIndicator,VPeriod,VRisk,'Simulation',V4);

IF (1<>1);
#****Begin: Generated Statements***
if (VALUE_IS_STRING=1, CellPutS(SVALUE,'R Simulations 2',
VIndicator,VPeriod,VRisk,V5,V4), CellPutN(NVALUE, 'R Simulations 2',
VIndicator,VPeriod,VRisk,V5,V4));
#****End: Generated Statements****
ENDIF;
```

An alternative to this approach is to let Excel generate the distribution curve. Let's take a look at how such a distribution function works. The function NORM.INV needs the parameter's probability, mean, and standard deviation. With these parameters, the function generates a value according to the normal distribution. NORM.INV(0.1,0,5), for instance, results in −6.40776. If you create a row of 1000 numbers by varying the first parameter probability from 0.001 to 0.999 by 0.001 steps and round the results, the numbers around zero occur more often than the numbers around 10 or −10 (according to the normal distribution). The illustration shows an Excel sheet that could be the basis for a distribution cube.

You store the results in a cube. Use a simple TI script for this. The first dimension contains a running number from 1 to 1000. The second dimension contains the element in which to store the results of the inverse distribution function. In our case we use the dimension elements NormInv and LogInv.

Now you can start using the distribution cube. For each simulation run, you let the TI process generate a value between 1 and 1000. You use this number to get the distribution value. The frequency of the numbers is similar to the result of the chosen distribution function.

	A	B	C	D
1	Element	NormInv	LogInv	
2	1	-309.023	0.045491385	
3	2	-287.816	0.056238048	
4	3	-274.778	0.06406985	
5	4	-265.207	0.07050513	
6	5	-257.583	0.076090694	
7	6	-251.214	0.08109416	
8	7	-245.726	0.085669073	
9	8	-240.892	0.089912748	
10	9	-236.562	0.093891246	
11	10	-232.635	0.097651733	
12	11	-229.037	0.101229215	
13	12	-225.713	0.10465048	
14	13	-222.621	0.107936545	
15	14	-219.729	0.111104245	
16	15	-217.009	0.114167298	
17	16	-214.441	0.117137055	
18	17	-212.007	0.120023024	
19	18	-209.693	0.122833263	
20	19	-207.485	0.125574668	
21	20	-205.375	0.128253191	
22	21	-203.352	0.130874013	
23	22	-201.409	0.133441672	
24	23	-199.539	0.135960169	
25	24	-197.737	0.138433055	
26	25	-195.996	0.140863494	
27	26	-194.313	0.143254322	
28	27	-192.684	0.145608091	
29	28	-191.104	0.147927107	
30	29	-189.57	0.150213461	
31	30	-188.079	0.152469057	
32	31	-186.63	0.154695634	
33	32	-185.218	0.156894785	
34	33	-183.842	0.159067972	
35	34	-182.501	0.161216544	
36	35	-181.191	0.163341746	
37	36	-179.912	0.165444728	
38	37	-178.661	0.167526561	

You simply get the number using the following code:

```
temp =CellGetN('R Distribution',round(rand*1000,0), 'NormInv') *
CellGetN('R Assessment 2',VRisk,VIndicator,VPeriod,'Stddev') +
    CellGetN('R Assessment 2',VRisk,VIndicator,VPeriod,'Middle Case');
```

The advantage of this approach is that you can use many more distribution functions without more extensive programming.

Next, we need to work on the results. We like to build clusters that are easier to report on. We could do this in Excel; however, we have to handle 1000 runs. This makes reporting ineffective. We defined 100 clusters.

Let's take a look into the second TI process. In the first step we have to define the min and the max values.

```
CellPutN(Temp,'R Simulations 2',VIndicator,VPeriod,VRisk,'Simulation',V4);
TRisk = 'Basis Risk';
ChildrenCont = ELCOMPN('R Simulation Runs' , VSimulationRun);
i=1;
#Step 1: Calculation of Min and Max
minValue=9999999999;
maxValue=0;
WHILE (i<=ChildrenCount);
TSimulationrun=  ELCOMP('R Simulation Runs', 'All', i);
ActNumber= CellGetN('R Simulations 2',VIndicator,PPeriod,VRisk,VScenario,
TSimulationRun);
    IF( ActNumber>maxvalue);
      maxValue=ActNumber;
    ENDIF;
    IF(ActNumber<minValue);
      minValue=ActNumber;
    ENDIF;
i=i+1;
END;
CellPutN(MinValue, 'R Simulations 2', VIndicator,PPeriod,TRisk,VScenario,'Min');
CellPutN(MaxValue, 'R Simulations 2', VIndicator,PPeriod,TRisk,VScenario,'Max');
```

In the second step we define the cluster bounds.

```
ClusterCount = ELCOMPN('R Simulation Runs' , 'Cluster');
i=1;
WHILE(i <= ClusterCount);
  TSimulationRun = ELCOMP('R Simulation Runs', 'Cluster', i);
  ClusterVal = Minvalue + (MaxValue-MinValue)/ClusterCount*i;
  CellPutN(clusterval, 'R Simulations 2', VIndicator,
  PPeriod,TRisk,VScenario,TSimulationRun);
  TTSimulationrun = INSRT('C',TSimulationrun,1);
  CellPutN(0, 'R Simulations 2',VIndicator,PPeriod,
  TRisk,VScenario,TTSimulationRun);
  i = i +1;
END;
```

And finally, we count the entries per cluster.

```
#Counting of clusters
i=1;
WHILE (i<=ChildrenCount);
  TSimulationrun=  ELCOMP('R Simulation Runs', 'All', i);
  ActNumber= CellGetN('R Simulations 2',VIndicator,PPeriod,
  VRisk,VScenario,TSimulationRun);
  Class = ROUND((ActNumber - Minvalue) / ((MaxValue-MinValue)/
  (ClusterCount-1)))+1;
  TTSimulationRun = INSRT('CC',trim(str(Class,3,0)),1);
  IF(TTsimulationRun @<> 'CC...');
    Counter = CellGetN('R Simulations 2',VIndicator,PPeriod,
    TRisk,VScenario,TTSimulationRun);
    CellPutN(Counter+1, 'R Simulations 2', VIndicator,PPeriod,
    TRisk,VScenario,TTSimulationRun);
  ENDIF;
  i=i+1;
END;
IF(1<>1);#Ignore automatic generated code
#****Begin: Generated Statements***
if (VALUE_IS_STRING=1, CellPutS(SVALUE,'R Simulations 2',VIndicator,VPeriod,
VRisk,VScenario,VSimulationRun), CellPutN(NVALUE,
'R Simulations 2', VIndicator,VPeriod,VRisk,VScenario,VSimulationRun));
#****End: Generated Statements****
ENDIF;
```

With this we get a good background for analysis. For instance, we look at the profit as the output indicator, and we can see what the possible distribution is in the following illustration:

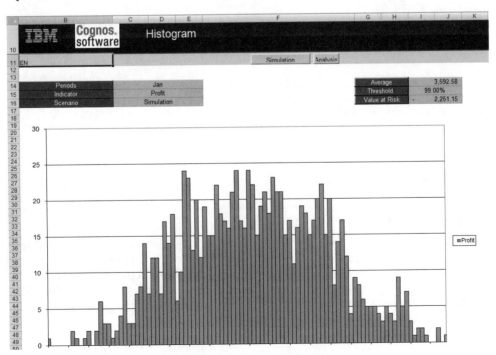

An interesting aspect might be the value at risk. This KPI is calculated in Excel.

First we query the bottom elements of the simulation, as shown in the following illustration and code:

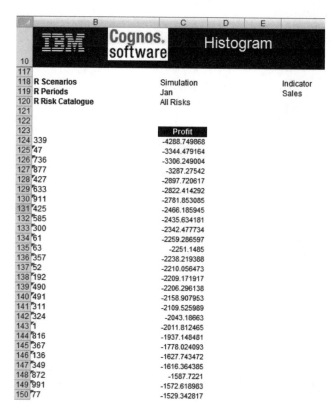

```
B124: =TM1RPTROW($B$9,"TOG:R Simulation Runs",,,,,
"BOTTOMCOUNT(DESCENDANTS([R Simulation Runs].[All]),100,
[R Simulations 2].([R Indicators].["&$C$123&"],[R Periods]."&$C$119&"],
[R Risk Catalogue].[All Risks],[R Scenarios].["&$C$118&"])))",,)
```

With this row we can calculate the value at risk:

```
I16:=INDEX(DataValues,(1-I15)*1000+2,1)
```

Working with Correlations

Our simulation concept is far from perfect. However, a professional solution is beyond the scope of this book. We have worked on the most important missing point: the correlations between risks. There is very often a stochastic dependency between parameters. For instance, if a service runs but has quality problems, the revenue is negatively affected. To model this, correlations (usually normed from −1 to 1) are necessary. To get these dependencies, statistical analysis with tools like IBM SPSS is helpful.

The challenge with Monte Carlo simulation is that each parameter has a specific distribution. If you consider the dependencies, you have to combine the correlation and the assigned distribution curve to create the values. This means that a statistical analysis of the created value must reveal the correlation and the chosen distribution curve.

If you are using normal distributions for your parameters, you can use the Cholesky decomposition to generate dependent values. For other distributions, it is not recommended. A triangle matrix is searched, which when multiplied by the transposed matrix, results in the original matrix. The requirement is that the original matrix must be symmetrical and positive-definite.

We created a simple example with three parameters. Imagine a shop that sells ice cream (A), sausages (B), and umbrellas (C). A little simulation cube is created for simulation runs, as shown in the illustration:

We generate a distribution that randomizes the sales figures for the three products, as shown in the following illustration:

- CO SIM
  - Dimensions
    - CO Elements
    - CO Elements 2
    - CO Runs
    - CO Types

CO Runs	A	B	C
1	226	878	1645
2	279	1230	1844
3	312	1054	1602
4	336	1013	2274
5	355	1407	1630
6	371	917	2033
7	384	1080	2173
8	397	1448	2024
9	407	816	2359
10	417	1645	1617
11	426	979	2104
12	435	852	1903
13	442	1302	1966
14	450	841	2483
15	456	790	1833
16	463	870	1917
17	469	913	2222
18	475	469	2645
19	480	1046	2008
20	485	820	1837
21	491	1324	1912
22	495	662	1945
23	500	823	1832
24	505	1003	1923
25	509	888	2058
26	513	726	2179
27	517	1279	2097
28	521	1042	1995
29	525	1044	1877
30	529	970	2019

We create a second cube for the correlations:

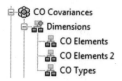

You can see the values for the element "Covariances" in the following illustration:

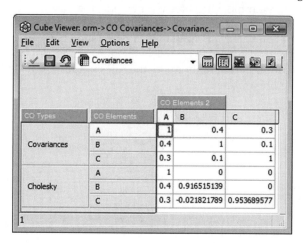

Here is a simple algorithm to calculate the Cholesky decomposition for a symmetric matrix:

```
i = 1;
WHILE (i<=DIMSIZ('CO Elements'));
  j = 1;
  WHILE (j<= DIMSIZ('CO Elements'));
    CellPutN(CellGetN('CO Covariances', DIMNM('CO Elements',i),
    DIMNM('CO Elements',j),'covariances'), 'CO Covariances',
    DIMNM ('CO Elements',i), DIMNM ('CO Elements',j),'Cholesky');
    j= j +1;
  END;
  i = i + 1;
END;

i = 1;
WHILE (i <= DIMSIZ('CO Elements'));
  j=1;
  WHILE (j<=  i -1);
```

```
      sum = CellGetN('CO Covariances', DIMNM ('CO Elements',i),
      DIMNM('CO Elements',J),'Cholesky');
      k = 1;
      WHILE (k<= J -1);
        sum = sum - CellGetN('CO Covariances', DIMNM ('CO Elements',i),
        DIMNM('CO Elements',k),'Cholesky') *
        CellGetN('CO Covariances', DIMNM ('CO Elements',J),
        DIMNM ('CO Elements',k),'Cholesky');
        k = k + 1;
      END;
      CellPutN(summe / CellGetN('CO Covariances', DIMNM ('CO Elements',j),
      DIMNM ('CO Elements',j),'Cholesky'), 'CO Covariances',
      DIMNM ('CO Elements',i), DIMNM ('CO Elements',j),'Cholesky');
      j = j + 1;
    END;
    sum =CellGetN('CO Covariances', DIMNM ('CO Elements',i),
    DIMNM ('CO Elements',i),'Cholesky');
    k=1 ;
    WHILE (k <= i -1);
      sum = sum - CellGetN('CO Covariances', DIMNM ('CO Elements',i),
      DIMNM ('CO Elements',k),'Cholesky') * CellGetN('CO Covariances',
      DIMNM ('CO Elements',i), DIMNM ('CO Elements',k),'Cholesky');
      k = k +1;
    END;
    IF (sum  <= 0);
       ProcessQuit;
    ELSE;
       CellPutN(sqrt(summe ),  'CO Covariances', DIMNM('CO Elements',i),
       DIMNM ('CO Elements',i),'Cholesky');
    ENDIF;
    j = i + 1;
    WHILE  (j <= DIMSIZ('CO Elements'));
       CellPutN(0,'CO Covariances', DIMNM ('CO Elements',i),
       DIMNM ('CO Elements',j),'Cholesky');
       j = j +1;
    END;
    i = i + 1;
END;
```

Now we can simply multiply each matrix element of the simulation runs with the Cholesky matrix:

```
SKIPCHECK;
['Cholesky']=N:DB('CO Sim',  !CO Elements 2, 'No',!CO Runs, 'Covariances')
* DB('CO Covariances', !CO Elements, !CO Elements 2, !CO Types);
FEEDERS;
['Covariances','No']=>['Cholesky','All'];
```

With a simple aggregation, we get the results (CO Elements 2: All) shown in the following illustration:

CO Runs	A --All	A	B	C	B --All	A	B	C	C --All	A	B	C
1	226	226	0	0	895	90	805	0	1618	68	-19	1569
2	279	279	0	0	1239	112	1127	0	1816	84	-27	1759
3	312	312	0	0	1091	125	966	0	1599	94	-23	1528
4	336	336	0	0	1062	134	928	0	2248	101	-22	2169
5	355	355	0	0	1432	142	1290	0	1631	107	-31	1555
6	371	371	0	0	988	148	840	0	2030	111	-20	1939
7	384	384	0	0	1144	154	990	0	2163	115	-24	2072
8	397	397	0	0	1486	159	1327	0	2017	119	-32	1930
9	407	407	0	0	911	163	748	0	2354	122	-18	2250
10	417	417	0	0	1675	167	1508	0	1631	125	-36	1542
11	426	426	0	0	1067	170	897	0	2114	128	-21	2007
12	435	435	0	0	955	174	781	0	1927	131	-19	1815
13	442	442	0	0	1370	177	1193	0	1980	133	-28	1875
14	450	450	0	0	951	180	771	0	2485	135	-18	2368
15	456	456	0	0	906	182	724	0	1868	137	-17	1748
16	463	463	0	0	982	185	797	0	1948	139	-19	1828
17	469	469	0	0	1025	188	837	0	2240	141	-20	2119
18	475	475	0	0	620	190	430	0	2656	143	-10	2523
19	480	480	0	0	1151	192	959	0	2036	144	-23	1915
20	485	485	0	0	946	194	752	0	1880	146	-18	1752
21	491	491	0	0	1409	196	1213	0	1941	147	-29	1823
22	495	495	0	0	805	198	607	0	1990	149	-14	1855
23	500	500	0	0	954	200	754	0	1879	150	-18	1747
24	505	505	0	0	1121	202	919	0	1964	152	-22	1834
25	509	509	0	0	1018	204	814	0	2097	153	-19	1963
26	513	513	0	0	870	205	665	0	2216	154	-16	2078
27	517	517	0	0	1379	207	1172	0	2127	155	-28	2000
28	521	521	0	0	1163	208	955	0	2036	156	-23	1903
29	525	525	0	0	1167	210	957	0	1925	158	-23	1790
30	529	529	0	0	1101	212	889	0	2063	159	-21	1925

With 1000 runs, we can see here that the correlation of the generated numbers is quite similar to the "planned" correlation:

1	0.381392	0.334491
0.381392	1	0.096999
0.334491	0.096999	1

Summary

You see, you can do a lot of risk management with Cognos TM1. This shows the enormous flexibility of TM1 again. However, what we showed is far from an integrated and sufficient concept. The positive thing is that this can be seen as a toolbox to support individual risk or compliance processes.

Index

G